Learning and Behavior Characteristics of Exceptional Children and Youth

A Humanistic Behavioral Approach

William I. Gardner
University of Wisconsin

Allyn and Bacon, Inc.   Boston, London, Sydney, Toronto

. . . and so there ain't nothing more to write about, and i am rotten glad of it, because if i'd 'a' knowed what a trouble it was to make a book i wouldn't 'a' tackled it and ain't agoing to no more. . . .

Mark Twain

(for awhile)

w i gardner

To Nan, Steve, and Becky, whose beings have made my search for the keys to meaningful human interaction an exciting, sometimes puzzling, but always an emotionally enhancing experience.

Second printing . . . October, 1977

Library of Congress Cataloging in Publication Data

Gardner, William I
  Learning and behavior characteristics of exceptional children and youth.

  Includes bibliographies and indexes.
  1. Exceptional children—Education. I. Title.
LC3965.G28   371.9   76-44469
ISBN 0-205-05586-9

Chapter 3 photo by F. Siteman, Stock, Boston. Chapter 12 photo by J. Berndt, Stock, Boston. Cover photo and others by Crotched Mountain Center, Greenfield, N.H.

Contents ─────────────────────────

Preface

This book is, in a sense, two books in one. It is about "exceptional" children and youth and also about an educational approach to influencing their learning and behavior characteristics. It differs from traditional introductory and methods books in that it does not follow the usual format of providing discussion of the physical and psychological characteristics of, and educational approaches to, various discrete categories of exceptional individuals. Books that provide such discussion of separate categories of children are in plentiful supply.

In replacement or, more aptly, as a contrasting alternative to this traditional approach, the present book provides discussion of factors pertinent to the unique learning conditions and characteristics of various children and the manner in which unique combinations of experiences systematically and forcefully influence their learning and behavioral characteristics. The book, in representing a broadly based sociobehavioral approach to the development, maintenance, and modification of a variety of learning and behavior characteristics of "exceptional" children and youth, provides a thorough and flexible system consistent with the complexities of the learner and with the requirements and constraints of the educational institution. This generalist view is called a *humanistic behavioral approach.*

This book is written both for students preparing to become professionals and for those presently involved in creating learning environments to foster behavior development and to facilitate behavior management of children and youth who present exceptional learning and behavior characteristics. It assumes no background in behavioral psychology or exceptional education nor in related procedures of influencing these characteristics. Although addressed primarily to regular and special educators who interact with "exceptional" children in the school setting, the book is suited for a variety of other professional areas: school and clinical psychologists, speech therapists, school nurses, child care workers, occupational therapists, psychiatrists, social workers, school counselors, and others searching for behavior principles that provide direction to and related techniques of behavior change. Such professionals are challenged (1) to pursue a functional analysis of behavior in their interaction with the problems presented to them and (2) to use a broad-spectrum humanistic behavioral approach in viewing behavior development and in devising methods of facilitating behavior change.

But the book is not just another methods book with a behavior modification flavor. In fact, it represents the views of an educator and psychologist who believes that contemporary behavior modification frequently is too narrowly defined and mechanically practiced. Traditional behavior modification undoubtedly has made its contribution in creating tremendous interest among educators, especially those responsible for the education and therapy of children with exceptional learning and behavior characteristics. Some educators are vigorous supporters; others are outspoken antagonists. The conflicting views created among educators emphasize that if methods of behavior influence become too effective—even potentially—in circumscribed areas, problems antithetical to a broad view of education are posed. Ethical issues become more pertinent as systems of education become more effective and predictable. There is no doubt that traditional behavior modification, as practiced by many educational personnel, does have some distinct limitations and does pose some potential dangers. The present book, in response to these ethical and practical concerns, not only broadens the cognitive and humanistic base of behavior modification but also presents a wide range of integrated viewpoints from which to understand what the child is and what he may become.

The book is based on the premise that the best way to influence the teaching practices of educators who deal with children and youth presenting unusual learning and behavior characteristics is (1) to introduce the educator early in his or her professional training to some of the major thorny issues that presently confront the field of special education and (2) to provide the professional with an integrated conceptual and methodological approach to dealing with these issues. Typically, the student is provided cursory exposure to basic issues and related criticisms of traditional concepts and practices but then is offered courses that tend to ignore these issues. Whether intentional or not, attitudes, values, thinking sets, and teaching practices are colored in favor of "categories" of exceptional children and related educational practices. The student soon thinks of children with difficulties as comprising different *types* of children requiring different *types* of educational approaches in different programs provided in different settings, for example, the "mentally retarded," "emotionally disturbed," "learning disabled," "auditorily impaired," "gifted," or the like. The noncategorical view of the present book offers a more generalist approach to children with exceptional characteristics.

WIG

Learning and Behavior Characteristics of Exceptional Children and Youth

PART I —————————————

Children with Exceptional Learning and Behavior Characteristics: Contrasting Views and Practices

1

1

Children with Exceptional Learning and Behavior Characteristics: Introduction

Recent reports indicate that up to 20 percent or more of school-age children and youth[1] exhibit exceptional or out-of-the-ordinary learning and behavioral characteristics which interfere significantly with their educational and personal-social development. Literally hundreds of thousands of children and youth present difficulties of behavioral development and functioning of such severity that the attention of medical, mental health, and educational specialists is required.* In some areas of large cities, it is reported that from 60 to 70 percent of children present school maladaption problems.* Many of these children present such intense, chronic, and pervasive problems that placement in total care and treatment residential programs is necessary. Such programs include both long-term residential placement for care and treatment of children with severe intellectual, emotional, and social difficulties as well as short-term placement of less severely handicapped children for intensive treatment with the expecta-

Dunn 1973; Glidewell and Swallow 1969; Kirk 1972; Swift and Spivack 1974

Glasser 1969; Kellam et al. 1972; Kellam and Schiff 1967

Asterisks have been used throughout the text as a convenience to the reader. The reference note will be found in the margin opposite the text line. Complete references are in bibliographies at the end of each chapter.

1. *Children* is used as a matter of convenience to refer to the entire range of children and youth served by the school system (chronological age from preschool through late adolescence). The terms "children and youth" and "children and adolescents" will be used on occasion to emphasize this inclusive use. At other times, when reference is made to specific subgroups within the total school-age population, more specific descriptions will be provided, e.g., the preschool child, the child in the early grades, young adolescents, or older adolescents.

3

tion that the latter will return to their natural environments within a relatively short period of time.

Report of the Joint
Commision on Mental
Health of Children 1970

The Report of the Joint Commission on Mental Health of Children* suggested that "at least 1,400,000 of our youngsters under eighteen need immediate psychiatric care" (p. 250). This number undoubtedly has increased in the years since the report was issued. Other children experiencing unusual difficulty in learning and social adaptation have sensory, neurological, or physical characteristics which render the educational process a more difficult endeavor.

But why should it be any more difficult under appropriate learning conditions for children and youth to acquire socially appropriate means of interacting with their social and physical environment than to acquire maladaptive means of interaction? It should be, under appropriate learning conditions, no more or less difficult for most children to acquire an extensive range of behaviors that result in ease of social interaction, achievement, and self-satisfaction than for them under less favorable conditions to learn to be anxious, grouchy, loud, overbearing, disinterested, or aggressive. *There is sufficient reason to believe that the same principles of learning are involved in each.* Cohen and Filipczak,* Hamblin et al.,* Hewett and Forness,* Lovaas and Bucher,* Ross,* and scores of others have presented data in support of this in their reports of research and clinical programs with children and adolescents who present a wide range of developmental, cognitive, and social difficulties. Children with highly inappropriate learning and behavior characteristics have acquired more appropriate patterns when exposed to well-designed and stimulating learning environments.

Cohen and Filipczak
1971; Hamblin et al.
1971
Hewett and Forness
1974; Lovaas and
Bucher 1974; Ross 1974

Baer and Wolf 1968

Baer and Wolf* present data from a number of different studies which suggest that in many instances inappropriate behavior patterns in young children can be replaced by socially desirable ones merely by initiating rather minor changes in the manner in which classroom teachers respond to the child following his behavior. In a similar vein, Thomas et al.* provide data to demonstrate that teacher behavior in the classroom can produce either bothersome, disruptive behavior or appropriate behavior in his pupils. In some instances, only minor changes in the nature of teacher behavior may result in rather dramatic changes in the child's behavior. Gardner,* Patterson,* Quay and Werry,* and Staats* all describe the manner in which social learning experiences can produce both appropriate and inappropriate modes of behavior.

Thomas et al. 1968

Gardner 1974; Patterson
1971; Quay and Werry
1972; Staats 1971, 1975

Likewise, it should be no more difficult *under appropriate learning conditions* for most children to acquire adequate reading, language, and arithmetic skills than it is under inappropriate conditions for them to become problem readers or failures in arithmetic computation. Demonstration that many children and adolescents with difficult problems of learning and social adaptation can become successful learners, and the approaches used to insure these changes, have been the topic of numerous recent reports.*

Haring 1974; Haring
1975; Haring and
Phillips 1972; Kauffman
1975; Lovaas and
Bucher 1974; O'Leary
and O'Leary 1972

PROBLEMS ARE PREVALENT

But, as noted, it remains true that literally hundreds of thousands of children and adolescents present chronic patterns of difficulty in development, learning, and social adaptation.

In many school systems, management problems are prevalent. Children and adolescents are uninterested in the academic curriculum, skip school excessively, fight with teachers, steal, fail to adhere to rules, and fail to develop desired academic skills. Many display hyperactivity, inattention, disinterest, and other behavior patterns which interfere with effective acquisition of skills, knowledge, and appropriate modes of emotional expression. Other children are characterized by poor social skills, poor interpersonal skills, excessive shyness, withdrawal patterns, or inappropriate emotional behavior. A large number of children attempt to learn, and initially are quite interested in learning, but soon get "turned off" after excessive failure with the educational program provided them. Still other children with accelerated learning and creative possibilities are stifled in their development by an inappropriate educational environment. In short, too many children and youth experience excessive failure and do not realize their potential during the developmental years.

Even in seemingly adequate school environments, many children fail to acquire academics at the rate and level expected. Coleman et al.,* *Coleman et al. 1966* after a comprehensive study of a large number of schools throughout the United States, concluded that school physical facility, school curriculum, level of educational expenditure, and various teacher variables bore little relationship to children's academic achievement measures. Stephens's* *Stephens 1967* review of hundreds of studies resulted in the same general conclusion— that a wide range of learning environments, which presently characterizes the American educational scene, exerts little differential effect on the educational achievement of children. A recent report by Fox* on an exper- *Fox 1967* iment in New York City also suggests that some critical elements are missing even in greatly enriched educational programs. In this study emphasizing small classes, team teaching, diagnostic testing and counseling, and specialized and remedial teaching, there was no consistent improvement in the children's performance in the classroom or on standardized tests of mathematics and reading. *Again, some critical and basic program components appear to be lacking in far too many educational programs, even so-called "enriched ones."*

POOR LEARNING NEITHER INHERENT NOR PLANNED

Although children and youth differ widely in the rate of learning and in the level at which various skills can be developed, few children are poor learners in any inherent and absolute sense. Some of the individual differences present among children may indeed be related to genetic and other congenital factors reflected in neurophysiological, sensory, and muscular-mobility differences. Other differences apparently are related to underdevelopment of and/or damage to some aspect of the central nervous system, the sensory system, or the neuromuscular system. Some children with auditory and visual impairments, for example, do experience difficulty in attending to and discriminating among various types of stimulation present in informal and in formally structured environments. Other children have difficulty in acquiring and using various aspects of language and speech. It is reasonable to assume that there is a maximum ceiling on what any given child can learn or can perform. In most cases the specifics of what a child can or cannot learn or do at some future time cannot be determined on an a priori basis. Present evaluation procedures lack the validity required for such predictions. Such test procedures mostly reflect what a child is presently doing and are not sufficiently predictive of the specifics of what he may be able to acquire under more *favorable* conditions of learning and performance. These can only be determined by exposing the child to that favorable learning environment.

It is also true that children do not intend to fail, to be miserable, to become obnoxious, anxious, or withdrawn from social contact with others. No child has ever decided that he will fail to learn to read, or become autistic, emotionally disturbed, learning disabled, socially inept, delinquent, or functionally retarded. It is true, however, that all too frequently insensitive and poorly designed learning environments force children into inappropriate modes of learning and behaving which only serve to further confound their ability to adapt. Hamblin et al.,* after study of problem learners from inner-city schools, concluded, "The data suggest that the defects which result in the cumulative deficit typical of many children in inner city schools lie not with the children but with their educational environment" (p. 62). Gardner,* in discussion of problem behavioral characteristics of cognitively limited adolescents noted:

Hamblin et al. 1971

Gardner 1971

> Low frustration tolerance, excessive emotional outburst, limited self-confidence and self-control, hesitancy over becoming involved in new or competitive experiences, and refusal to continue problem-solving effort in the face of difficulty all appear to have evolved out of a poor learning environment which either has failed to match behavior requirements to present behavioral characteristics or to provide adequate reinforcing consequences for appropriate behavior. [p. 257]

The child or adolescent with exceptional learning and behavior characteristics arising out of a history of excessive failure and related unpleasant emotional reactions has little opportunity to become an active participating learner unless his experiences undergo drastic and consistent changes. Exploration, curiosity, self-direction skills, enthusiasm, and the like either have never been encouraged by his environment or else emerging patterns have been inhibited or even extinguished by excessive failure.

CHILDREN CAN LEARN

Numerous studies suggest that consistent experiences in appropriate learning environments may produce rather dramatic differences in what a child learns and how he behaves even in the presence of adverse genetic, neurological, sensory, or general environmental conditions. As an example, studies suggest that children called mentally retarded, under appropriate conditions, can become enthusiastic, effective, active, and competent learners who can utilize their skills in a manner which contributes to a satisfying adaptation to self and environment.*

For example, Bijou et al. 1966; Birnbrauer et al. 1965; Brown 1973; Gardner 1971

Heber et al. 1972

The recent work of Heber et al.* with a group of inner-city children who represented very high risk of manifesting serious cognitive and emotional difficulties further illustrates this point, as do works of Hamblin et al.,* Staats,* and many others. Heber et al. report encouraging data that an adequate early education experience provided high-risk children can result in highly verbal, spontaneous, emotionally expressive, and cognitively sensitive children. Hamblin et al. report significant behavior changes in young, language handicapped inner-city children and in children who displayed hyperactive behavior patterns. Language skills within the normal range and desirable prosocial behavior patterns were acquired in programs structured specifically to facilitate these patterns. Staats presents a wealth of data and an impressive theoretical system which provide convincing support of the position that just as handicapping cognitive, social, and emotional patterns of children may result from faulty learning environments, these can be modified by exposure to a more appropriately designed and presented set of experiences.

Hamblin et al. 1971; Staats 1971, 1975

THE DEVIANCY MODEL IN THE SCHOOL SETTING

In spite of the obviousness of this position of environmental causation and of data supporting the efficacy of a variety of intervention programs, the major assumption which provides structure and organization to many educational, mental health, and social welfare institutions in our culture is that something is *wrong with or within the child* when he presents unusual developmental, behavioral, learning, emotional, or social adaptation problems. Unacceptable learning and behavioral patterns are assumed to be surface symptoms or manifestations of some presumed internal psychological disabilities or other psychic factors. This general position represents the central assumption of an *internal deviancy model*.[2]

Glasser 1969   Glasser,* for example, has noted: "The schools assume built-in motivation, but when it does not occur, they attempt to motivate children with methods analogous to using a gun. . . . The schools, struggling to solve their problems, resort to using bigger and bigger guns—more restrictions and rules, more threats and punishments" (p. 19).

The child thus frequently is viewed as the deviant component in the system. His inadequate motivation, his communication disorders, his poor attitude, his neurological impairment, his sensory limitations, his disturbance, or his inadequacy is implicated. The school program, for example, is structured to teach various predetermined behavioral skills at specific times. Simplified and sometimes naive criteria are used to determine both *what* the child should learn and *when* he should learn these skills. To illustrate, at chronological age six it is assumed that all children should begin to acquire, within circumscribed limits, the curriculum set for the

Ames 1968   first grade. Ames,* of the Gesell Institute of Child Development, has commented in respect to this practice:

> Current findings at the Gesell Institute suggest that from one-third to one-half of the children in our public schools today may lack the maturity required for the work of the grade in which they have been placed. This occurs because children are entered in school on the basis of their birthday or calendar age. The assumption is that the mere attainment of one's fifth, or sixth birthday guarantees the maturity of a five-, or six-year-old, as the case may be. [p. 208]

Quite obviously, all children do not successfully acquire even the minimally acceptable educational objectives of the first-grade curriculum. It is quite unrealistic to expect young children from twelve to eighteen months below the developmental level of their classmates to be successful

Koppitz 1971   in catching up within a year or so. Koppitz* suggests: "School beginners vary enormously in their degree of maturity and mental ability. Even if the kindergarten curriculum is aimed somewhat below the average mental age level, a sizeable number of pupils will fall below the expected level of functioning from the very outset and will begin their school career with

Ilg, Ames, and Apell   frustration and failure" (p. 183).
1965

Ilg, Ames, and Apell* report that up to 33 percent of the children

Glasser 1969   they studied were not successful with the school curriculum. Glasser* reports that "experience in the central city of Los Angeles reveals that 75 percent of the children do not achieve a satisfactory elementary education"

Kellam et al. 1972;   (p. 9). Data from the Chicago-Woodlawn ghetto area indicate that school
Kellam and Schiff 1967;   maladaptation characterizes nearly 70 percent of the school enrollment.*
Schiff 1972

---

2. Various labels, including *internal psychic pathology, internal causation, psychological illness, psychological disease, pathology-symptom, disability,* and *internal deficit,* have been applied to this position. These terms will be used interchangeably in this book.

Sabatino* notes: "Traditional education, whatever it is, may be fine for the   *Sabatino 1971*
child who learns, but it should be obvious that a fairly high percentage
(about 20 percent of school age children) initiate a career of chronic failure
by mid-year of first grade" (p. 15).

Many children, after considerable and chronic failure and the resulting negative effects on their cognitive, social, and emotional characteristics
are transferred out of the mainstream into special classes organized for
such categories of children as the mentally retarded, emotionally disturbed, learning disabled, or socially maladjusted.

INDIVIDUAL DIFFERENCES NOT SUFFICIENTLY RESPECTED

It is true that individual differences are recognized by most school
programs and program allowances are made, but only within narrow limits
in too many instances and for the wrong purposes in others. Harshmann,*   *Harshmann 1969*
in commenting on the use of special class arrangements as a means of
providing for individual differences among children, suggested: "One
would hope that the purpose of any special grouping or class arrangement
would be to provide a differential treatment of curriculum materials. But
alas, in the past as too often in the present, educators have tried various
administrative devices to get rid of individual differences in children" (p.
386).

Rubin and Balow* reported that, when educational handicaps were   *Rubin and Balow 1971*
defined in terms of a child's inability to meet the requirements of the
educational system, over 40 percent of a large group of children served
were identified as exhibiting significant problems. These data emphasize,
as noted earlier, the narrow range of individual differences among children, especially boys, which the regular educational system does accommodate.

Under this approach, many children do fail. *They do learn,* but in
too many instances not the academic, emotional, and social skills deemed
desirable for them. Instead, many of these children learn that they cannot
do what other of their peers can do, with the result that a wide range of
negative emotional and avoidance behaviors are developed around school,
teacher, peers, and self. Such practices not only "result in poor grades and
failure to work up to one's supposed 'potential,' but in many instances
immaturity can produce school failures and personality problems so extreme that they require special psychological help" (p. 208).*   *Ames 1968*
Such a state of affairs led Harshmann* to plead: *Harshmann 1969*

When will we start working with these individual differences as we find them
in our classrooms? When will we start to tailor an educational program to the

needs of each child? If we are to give more than just lip service to the sacred dictum of the teaching profession, i.e., that we are to "teach children," then surely we will take our cues from the children we have and move in the direction of changing classroom management techniques and altering methods for building effective levels of performance. [p. 386]

THE CHILD IS BLAMED FOR DEVIANCY

But if the child does not learn academic skills at the rate or level expected, or if he does not behave emotionally and socially as expected, too frequently it is assumed categorically that the fault lies within the child. *Gnagey 1965* Misbehavior frequently is viewed as deviancy.* Retardation in development and effective use of cognitive skills is viewed as a manifestation of some within-the-child pathological influence such as limited intelligence, psycholinguistic disabilities, or poor innate abilities. In a similar manner, inappropriate behaviors with disruptive emotional components are assumed to be a surface manifestation of an internal emotional disorder, *Tift 1968* disturbance, or dysfunction. Tift* provides a good example of this in an article addressed to classroom teachers concerning children whose disruptive behavior patterns upset classroom routine. The writer declared: "You will become increasingly aware that the behavior which angers you is a signal of an illness, just as red spots are a signal of measles. You will understand that a disturbed child does not have a disease of destroying property or hurting people; these are but symptoms of his emotional disorder" (p. 12).

A wide array of specialists has been employed by educational, mental health, and social welfare agencies to examine children (who do in fact present learning and behavior difficulties) and to identify and analyze the presumed internal factors which might account for these difficulties. Social workers, psychiatrists, psychologists, counselors, diagnostic teachers, special educational personnel, pediatricians, neurologists, and others may become involved in one aspect or another of this examination. As illustrated in the previous example, an "illness or internal pathology model" of learning and behavior functioning and deviation typically provides major direction to the evaluation process. That is, an attempt is made during the examination process to identify the presumed internal, underlying, "within-the-child" variables that interfere with, disrupt, or block the acquisition of the teachings of the school program. The individuality of the child and the complex reciprocal relationship between the child and his social and school environments are too frequently ignored or minimized in attempts to find the "real internal" causes of his problems. This was illustrated in a recent teacher conference attended by the writer. Five classroom teachers and a counselor were discussing a thirteen-year-old boy who was creating disturbances in his classrooms. The discussion was focused on answering the question raised by several of the teachers, "What is *wrong* with *him?*" No time was spent on the more pertinent questions of "What is wrong with the school experiences being provided this boy?" and "How do these experiences interact with the child's characteristics to produce the problems?" This attitude has prompted Bartel and Guskin* to suggest: "The assumption is that some individuals *are* mentally ill, mentally retarded, physically disabled, or delinquent and that a society is simply acknowledging the presence of pre-existing, objective characteristics when it labels them as such and groups them according to their own kind" (p. 76).

Bartel and Guskin 1971

    The frequent effect of such practices, thus, is to shift the blame *from* the child's environments (the home, the general school environment, the specific instructional program) *to* the child. Kauppi* noted that if a "student does not learn what he is supposed to, it is because he is retarded [or deaf, or blind, or crippled], not because the educational system has failed to measure and meet his needs" (p. 395).

Kauppi 1969

CATEGORIES OF "EXCEPTIONAL CHILDREN"

    A wide array of constructs and diagnostic labels have been created to assist the school system specialists in their attempt to diagnose these presumed within-the-child wrongs or causes of his problems and in the process to classify him into the appropriate category.* Sabatino* has noted: "And if a child failed to adjust to the academic learning situation, he was given a medically adapted label which frequently became the vehicle through which he was removed to a 'special setting' defined as special education" (p. 15).

Hobbs 1975a, 1975b; Sabatino 1971

    The generic concept of *exceptional children* has been devised to refer to a wide range of sensory, physical, learning, and behavior characteristics of children which create difficulty for the regular class school setting. Representative of this usage is the definition by Kirk:*

Kirk 1972

> The exceptional child is defined as the child who deviates from the average or normal child (1) in mental characteristics, (2) in sensory abilities, (3) in neuromuscular or physical characteristics, (4) in social or emotional behavior, (5) in communication abilities, or (6) in multiple handicaps to such an extent that he requires a modification of school practices, or special educational services, in order to develop to his maximum capacity. [p. 4]

    Such "exceptional children," on the basis of various definitional criteria and diagnostic practices, may be classified into one of many categories used by the educational system in one way or another to make decisions about the educational placement and program experiences provided the child. These include:

emotionally disturbed (Morse 1967)
learning disabilities (Kirk and Bateman 1962; Kirk 1972)
learning dysfunctions and learning disorders (Ross 1967)
brain damage (Haywood 1968)
slow learner (Johnson 1963; Kephart 1960)
mentally handicapped (Kirk and Johnson 1951)
behavioral disability (Dunn 1973)
oral communication disabilities (Hull and Hull 1973)
visual disabilities (Harley 1973)
auditory disability (McConnell 1973)
superior cognitive abilities (Martinson 1973)
minimal brain dysfunction (Clements 1966)
crippling and health disabilities (Wilson 1973)

Many other children present more circumscribed and less chronic exceptional learning and behavior characteristics. Examples of these would include school phobias, various sexual problems, mild generalized learning difficulties, reading problems, generalized and specific anxiety reactions, hyperactivity, dependency, shyness, and various habit difficulties such as enuresis, encopresis, thumbsucking and mild speech problems. These and numerous other problem characteristics are well known to the classroom teacher, counselor, and school psychologist. Although children, as a result of any single or small number of these or similar problematic characteristics, are not diagnosed as "exceptional children" and provided alternative special educational experiences, the presence of an excessive number of these may well result in such a classification.

RATIONALE FOR "EXCEPTIONAL CHILD" CLASSIFICATION

Some children have been labeled as exceptional on the basis of sensory, neuromuscular, and special health differences. These children present educational problems due to the restrictions in the type of instruction that can be presented and to the physical requirements placed on the educational environment by their particular physical characteristics. In illustration, the blind child requires educational experiences that focus on auditory and tactual stimulation instead of on visual presentation, which would be needed by the deaf child. Behavioral characteristics may contribute to the educational problems of these children but do not represent the primary factors involved in their classification as exceptional.

There is a major difference, however, between those children labeled exceptional on the basis of sensory, physical, and neuromuscular factors and other children classified primarily on the basis of psychometric, psychiatric, or psychological characteristics. The visual-perceptual differences between the child who has 20/20 vision and the one who has only light perception can be related primarily to differences in sensory equipment. The physical limitations of the cerebral palsied or the otherwise orthopedically handicapped child can be related to demonstrated central nervous system damage or an atrophied leg or arm muscle. The limitations or differences in sensory or muscular functioning result from and are a manifestation of the sensory and physical apparatus as it exists. In each of these instances, educational experiences are needed which accommodate to the sensory and response characteristics of these children.

In contrast, children identified as exceptional on the basis of behavioral or psychological characteristics frequently present no specifically identifiable cause or basis for their learning or behavioral characteristics. A specific, readily identifiable physical basis, as an example, has not been found for all children whose language development (or any other behavioral dimension) differs significantly from that of other children of similar chronological ages. A neurological-damage base may be assumed* for children with specific learning difficulties, but this remains an assumption in the great majority of cases.

See Clements 1966; Johnson and Myklebust 1967

Even for the vast majority of children labeled as cognitively impaired, no measurable or identifiable physical basis has been identified for the differences in the rate of learning which characterize these children. However, the use of the same "pathology-symptom" model used with children characterized by physical, sensory, or neurological difficulties is reflected in much of the psychological and educational practices in the school setting. That is, just as the physician examines a child and declares that the visual acuity of the child of 10/400 is the result of a damaged retina, the school or clinical psychologist examines a child who presents a range of learning and behavioral characteristics which disturbs the school environment and awards, for example, the child with a diagnosis of "emotionally disturbed." Further, the assumption is made that this diagnostic "insight" explains the child's poor progress in his academic subjects or accounts for his interpersonal difficulties. Or the child may be viewed as having a "learning disability" and as not really being "mentally retarded," "culturally deprived," or "emotionally disturbed."*

*Friedland and Shilkret 1973; Herrick 1973; Wagonseller 1973
Kirk and Bateman 1962*

Kirk and Bateman's* definition of learning disability is an illustration of the symptom-internal pathology assumption:

A *learning disability* refers to a retardation, disorder, or delayed development in one or more of the processes of speech, language, reading, writing, arithmetic, or other school subjects resulting from a psychological handicap caused by a possible cerebral dysfunction and/or emotional or behavioral disturbances. It is not the result of mental retardation, sensory deprivation, or cultural or instructional factors. [p. 73][3]

In this definition, the learning difficulties which the child may exhibit are said to be a result of an undefined and unmeasurable internal factor called *psychological handicap,* which is further hypothesized as resulting from a possible cerebral dysfunction and/or emotional disturbance. Never articulated are the definitions of these latter two variables and the measurement procedures for establishing their presence nor the manner in which either of these may result in a psychological handicap, which in turn may result in learning difficulties.

RESULTS OF "EXCEPTIONAL CHILD" DIAGNOSIS

The school system has adopted the practice of grouping children for educational purposes on the basis of assigned diagnostic exceptional child categories. Children with similarities along a few medical, psychometric, psychological, and psychiatric dimensions frequently are grouped together. Administrative program decisions are made which assume commonality among many other behavioral or physical dimensions which relate to or interact with instructional factors. This is done under the assumption of providing the child more appropriate specialized group instruction. Such diagnostic and classification practices and the subsequent assignment to educational programs designed for the various categories of children appear to be prerequisite to attempts at developing a match between the personal characteristics of a unique child and the specific educational experiences which should be provided him. The assumption that the child is the inadequate component of the educational enterprise thus results in his removal, either totally or on a part-time basis, from the mainstream program and into special programs designed for his special features.

This alternative special program is provided with the justification that it is "for his own good," and, furthermore, it is to the benefit of all, as such action reduces the disruption to those other children who under regular classroom conditions do maximize their potential without unusual difficulties. Such alternative programs range from *partial separation* from the regular class mainstream (such as seeing a psychiatrist, psychologist,

---

3. Although changes are reflected in later definitions of learning disability by Kirk and Kirk (1971) and Bateman (1965), their modifications as well as definitions offered by other leaders in the field (Johnson and Myklebust 1967; Kass and Myklebust 1969) and as included in federal legislation (National Advisory Committee on Handicapped Children 1968) all reflect an internal deficit, dysfunction, or disorder position.

speech therapist, counselor, or social worker for special therapy) to *more complete separation* involved in variously arranged special class placements and finally to the *complete separation* of residential placement. It is assumed that after appropriate diagnosis and specialized treatment the child may return to the normal mainstream educational program if his "exceptionality" has changed sufficiently to permit satisfactory adaptation to the requirements of that environment.

Telford and Sawry* provide an illustration of the justification for special programs in their statement:

Telford and Sawry 1972

> A part of the segregation imposed on the handicapped is for the purpose of best providing for their education and training and for their protection. . . . The segregation of the handicapped into special classes, schools, and institutions is seldom for the purpose of limiting their contacts with other people. . . . Handicapped people are segregated because this is perceived as the most effective way of providing for their special needs. [p. 49]

Baker,* Cruickshank and Johnson,* Dunn,* Jordan,* and Kirk* all have agreed that the purpose of special programs is that of meeting the needs of exceptional children more adequately than could be met in mainstream or regular classroom programs. As examples of factors considered in arriving at this position, Bruininks and Rynders,* in reviewing the presumed justifications for special class placement of those children classified as mildly retarded, list among others the following:

Baker 1959; Cruickshank and Johnson 1958; Dunn 1963, 1973; Jordan 1962; Kirk 1962, 1972

Bruininks and Rynders 1971

1. Research evidence indicates that mentally retarded children in regular classrooms are usually rejected by more able classroom peers.
2. Mentally retarded children in regular classrooms experience loss of self-esteem because of their inability to compete with more able classroom peers.
3. It is logically absurd to assign children to instruction without considering differences in ability of achievement level.

    •

    •

    •

6. The alternatives to present practices are less desirable and would lead to social promotion as an approach to dealing with mildly retarded children.
7. Properly implemented special classes are optimally suited to deal with the major learning problems of retarded children.
8. A democratic philosophy of education does not dictate that all children have the same educational experiences, but that all children receive an equal opportunity to learn according to their individual needs and abilities. [p. 3]

Although having specific reference to the mentally retarded, the stated justifications are equally as applicable to other groups of exceptional

Dunn 1968; Hammons 1972; Johnson 1963; Lilly 1970; Christoplos and Renz 1969

children. Dunn,* Hammons,* Johnson,* Lilly,* and Christoplos and Renz* provide detailed discussion of these and related positions.

Different programs have been organized under the assumption of providing differential educational experiences for different categories of exceptional children. Since considerable resources frequently are expended to make the "correct" diagnosis, it is assumed essential that the child be placed in the "correct" special remediation, therapy, education, or

Herrick 1973; Kirk and Kirk 1971; Redelheim 1973

treatment program.* The diagnostic procedure attempts to determine, for example, if the child is really "emotionally disturbed" and not "mentally retarded" or that he is "functionally retarded due to his disadvantaged home life" instead of being "truly" mentally retarded. For another child with learning and behavior problems, it must be determined whether his learning difficulties are a result of his "cultural deprivation" or a reflection

Hartman 1973; Moss 1973

of a "learning disability."* Still another child may receive the diagnosis of minimal brain damage, if his academic retardation is sufficiently severe, and be placed in the special education category of "learning disability."[4]

This is undertaken under the assumption that these categories of disabilities represent major etiologic or other pertinent factors which can be dealt with best by providing special educational programs designed to deal differentially with each disability. This is done even though "in many cases once the 'correct' label is applied, the prescriptive program for a child with one label is no different than that for a child tagged with another

Redelheim 1973

label" (p. 401).* Nevertheless, these children then become "special or exceptional" children who are provided with "special" programs designed to accommodate to the basic disability.

MAJOR ISSUES RELATING TO CATEGORY APPROACH

School systems across the country provide categorical special education programs for such groups as the mentally retarded, the emotionally disturbed, the learning disabled, and the visually impaired. Further, university and college teacher training programs are designed to train educators in this categorical manner. The student is prepared to teach the mentally retarded, or the emotionally disturbed, or the learning disabled, or the visually impaired, or the gifted.

There are two major issues associated with such diagnostic and classification procedures and associated special education practices. *First is the issue of assigning category labels to children.* There is increasing concern that such a practice has considerable negative consequences for the child so labeled. The very nature of most of the labels carries negative

---

4. Although such traditional diagnostic practices warrant considerable criticism, the possible usefulness of more empirically focused "diagnostic" procedures are described in Chapters 5 and 14.

connotation—the *retarded, disabled, disordered, damaged, disturbed, handicapped, impaired.*

   The second major issue relates to the predictive relationship which is assumed to exist between the diagnostic—classification systems used to place children in categories and the resulting educational decisions and practices. As noted, the assumption is made that there exists a distinct and useful relationship between (1) the categories of exceptional children and (2) the educational programs which have been designed for each of the separate categories. This is known as the aptitude treatment interaction (ATI) assumption. If a child is really mentally retarded, the assumption states, then this child must be correctly diagnosed and classified and then placed in the program designed for the mentally retarded. To leave him in regular education or to place him in educational programs designed for other categories of exceptional children would not meet the educational needs created by his "mental retardation." In like manner, if the child is really emotionally disturbed, has specific learning disabilities, is visually impaired, or perceptually handicapped, it is essential that a correct classification be effected to insure correct placement in the category special class environment in which the content, teaching methodology, and materials are designed to be provided by a teacher especially trained for this type of child.

   Prior to a more detailed discussion of these issues in Chapter 3, description will be provided in Chapter 2 of each of the major categories of children and youth which presently comprise special education. The criteria used in diagnosis and classification are described, along with a delineation of physical, psychological, and social characteristics of children assigned to each category. With this background, the reader will be in a better position to assimilate and evaluate contrasting concepts and practices of the humanistic behavioral approach.

SUMMARY

A "special" education structure, both in organization and practice, has been devised to handle categories of "exceptional children." The disabilities, differences, or shortcomings involved in the diagnosis and labeling of the children become the major focus of such special programs. In illustration, programs are designed to deal with the mental *retardation*, the perceptual *handicap*, intellectual *acceleration*, the emotional *disturbance*, the visual *impairment*, the social *deviation*, or the learning *disability*. Children are removed from the natural environment of the regular classroom, either on a part-time or full-time basis, because they are unable to adapt appropriately to various requirements of the rather narrowly structured mainstream or regular education program provided. Special classes, remedial programs, schools, and residential centers have all been devised as a means of segregation and specialized education and therapy. This three-step process may be summarized as follows: (1) A child does not adapt to the instructional arrangements of the regular school program. (2) In terms of labels of a medical nature (cerebral palsy, visual impairment, auditory impairment, epilepsy), psychiatric nature (emotional disturbance), or psychometric nature (mentally retarded, gifted), he is assigned to a *disability* or *difference* category. (3) On the basis of this diagnosis he is assigned to alternative instructional programs such as a program for the emotionally disturbed, class for the mentally retarded, or diagnostic center for the learning disabled.

Dunn (1973) reports that over three million children were receiving special education services in the early 1970s. Federal, state, and local administrative structure and funding patterns are inextricably interwoven with diagnostic groupings of children (Hobbs 1975a). In fact, in numerous school systems throughout the country various needed services for children with exceptional learning and behavior characteristics simply are not available unless the child fits into one of the categories of disabilities that have been created.

Obviously, children and youth do have problems relating to their education. The central issue posed repeatedly throughout this book is: "What educational practices can best meet these educational needs? What combination of assumptions and practices will prove most productive?"

REFERENCES

Ames, L. B. Learning disabilities often result from sheer immaturity. *Journal of Learning Disabilities,* 1968, 1, 207–212.

Baer, D. M., and Wolf, M. M. The reinforcement contingency in preschool and remedial education. In R. D. Hess and R. M. Bear (Eds.) *Early Education: Current Theory, Research, and Action.* Chicago: Aldine, 1968. Pp. 119–129.

Baker, H. J. *Introduction to Exceptional Children.* New York: Macmillan, 1959.

Bartel, N. R., and Guskin, S. L. A handicap as a social phenomenon. In W. M. Cruickshank (Ed.) *Psychology of Exceptional Children and Youth.* Englewood Cliffs, N. J.: Prentice-Hall, 1971. Pp. 75–114.

Bateman, B. An educator's view of a diagnostic approach to learning disorders. In J. Hellmuth (Ed.) *Learning Disorders.* Vol. 1. Seattle: Special Child Publications, 1965. Pp. 219–238.

Bijou, S. W., Birnbrauer, J. S., Kidder, J. D., and Tague, C. Programmed instruction as an approach to teaching of reading, writing, and arithmetic to retarded children. *The Psychological Record,* 1966, 16, 505–522.

Birnbrauer, J. S., Wolf, M. M., Kidder, J. D., and Tague, C. E. Classroom behavior of retarded pupils with token reinforcement. *Journal Experimental Child Psychology,* 1965, 2, 219–235.

Brown, L. Instructional programs for trainable level retarded students. In L. Mann and D. Sabatino (Eds.) *The First Review of Special Education.* Philadelphia: Buttonwood Farms, 1973. Pp. 103–136.

Bruininks, R. H., and Rynders, J. E. Alternatives to

special class placement for educable mentally retarded children. *Focus on Exceptional Children*, 1971, 3, 1–12.

Christoplos, F., and Renz, P. A critical examination of special education programs. *Journal of Special Education*, 1969, 3, 371–379.

Clements, S. D. *Minimal Brain Dysfunction in Children*. Public Health Service Publications. No. 415. Washington, D.C.: U.S. Department of Health, Education, and Welfare, 1966.

Cohen, H. L., and Filipczak, J. A. *A New Learning Environment*. San Francisco: Jossey-Bass, 1971.

Coleman, J. S., *et al. Equality of Educational Opportunity*. Washington, D.C.: U.S. Government Printing Office, O.E. 38001, 1966.

Cruickshank, W., and Johnson, G. O. *Education of Exceptional Children and Youth*. Englewood Cliffs, N.J.: Prentice-Hall, 1958.

Dunn, L. M. (Ed.) *Exceptional Children in the Schools*. New York: Holt, Rinehart & Winston, 1963.

Dunn, L. M. Special education for the mildly retarded: Is much of it justified? *Exceptional Children*, 1968, 35, 5–22.

Dunn, L. M. (Ed.) *Exceptional Children in the Schools: Special Education in Transition*. (2nd Ed.) New York: Holt, Rinehart & Winston, 1973.

Fox, D. J. *Expansion of the More Effective Schools Program*. New York: Center for Urban Education, 1967.

Friedland, S. J., and Shilkret, R. B. Alternative explanations of learning disabilities: Defensive hyperactivity. *Exceptional Children*, 1973, 40, 213–215.

Gardner, W. I. *Behavior Modification in Mental Retardation*. Chicago: Aldine-Atherton, 1971.

Gardner, W. I. *Children with Learning and Behavior Problems: A Behavior Management Approach*. Boston: Allyn and Bacon, 1974.

Glasser, W. *Schools without Failure*. New York: Harper, 1969.

Glidewell, J. C., and Swallow, C. S. *The Prevalence of Maladjustment in Elementary Schools: A Report Prepared for the Joint Commission on the Mental Health of Children*. Chicago: University of Chicago Press, 1969.

Gnagey, W. J. *Controlling Classroom Misbehavior*. Washington, D.C.: NEA, 1965.

Hamblin, R. L., Buckholdt, D., Ferritor, D., Kozloff, M., and Blackwell, L. *The Humanization Processes: A Social, Behavioral Analysis of Childrens' Problems*. New York: Wiley-Interscience, 1971.

Hammons, G. W. Educating the mildly retarded: A review. *Exceptional Children*, 1972, 38, 565–570.

Haring, N. G. Application of behavior modification techniques to the learning situation. In W. M. Cruickshank and D. P. Hallahan (Eds.) *Perceptual and Learning Disabilities in Children*. Vol. 1. Syracuse: Syracuse University Press, 1975. Pp. 197–226.

Haring, N. G. (Ed.) *Behavior of Exceptional Children: An Introduction to Special Education*. Columbus, Ohio: Charles E. Merrill, 1974.

Haring, N. G., and Phillips, E. L. *Analysis and Modification of Classroom Behavior*. Englewood Cliffs, N. J.: Prentice-Hall, 1972.

Harley, R. K., Jr. Children with visual disabilities. In L. M. Dunn (Ed.) *Exceptional Children in the Schools: Special Education in Transition*. (2nd Ed.) New York: Holt, Rinehart & Winston, 1973. Pp. 413–466.

Harshman, H. W. Toward a differential treatment of curriculum. *Journal of Special Education*, 1969, 3, 385–387.

Hartman, R. K. Differential diagnosis: assets and liabilities. *Journal of Special Education*, 1973, 7, 393–397.

Haywood, H. C. (Ed.) *Brain Damage in School Age Children*. Washington, D.C.: Council for Exceptional Children, 1968.

Heber, R., Garber, H., Harrington, S., Hoffman, C., and Falender, C. *Rehabilitation of Families at Risk for Mental Retardation*. Madison, Wisc.: Rehabilitation Research and Training Center in Mental Retardation Progress Report, 1972.

Herrick, M. J. Disabled or disadvantaged: What's the difference? *Journal of Special Education*. 1973, 7, 381–386.

Hewett, F. M., and Forness, S. R. *Education of Exceptional Learners*. Boston: Allyn and Bacon, 1974.

Hobbs, N. *The Futures of Children*. San Francisco: Jossey-Bass, 1975a.

Hobbs, N. (Ed.) *Issues in the Classification of Children*. Vol. I, II. San Francisco: Jossey-Bass, 1975b.

Hull, F. M., and Hull, M.E. Children with oral communication disabilities. In L. M. Dunn (Ed.) *Exceptional Children in the Schools: Special Education in Transition*. (2nd Ed.) New York: Holt, Rinehart & Winston, 1973. Pp. 299–350.

Ilg, F. L., Ames, L. B., and Apell, R. J. School readiness as evaluated by Gesell developmental, visual, and projective tests. *Genetic Psychology Monographs*, 1965, 71, 61–91.

Johnson, D. J., and Myklebust, H. R. *Learning Disabilities: Educational Principles and Practices*. New York: Grune and Stratton, 1967.

Johnson, G. O. *Education for the Slow Learners*. Englewood Cliffs, N. J.: Prentice-Hall, 1963.

Jordan, T. E. *The Exceptional Child*. Columbus, Ohio: Charles E. Merrill, 1962.

Kass, C., and Myklebust, H. Learning disabilities: An educational definition. *Journal of Learning Disabilities*. 1969, 2, 377–379.

Kauffman, J. M. Behavior modification. In W. M. Cruickshank and H. P. Hallahan (Eds.) *Perceptual and Learning Disabilities in Children*. Vol. 2. Syracuse: Syracuse University Press, 1975. Pp. 395–446.

Kauppi, D. R. The emperor has no clothes: Comments on Christoplos and Renz. *Journal of Special Education*, 1969, 3, 393–396.

Kellam, S. G., Branch, J. D., Agrawal, L. C., and Grabill, M. E. Woodlawn Mental Health Center: An evolving strategy for planning in community mental health. In S. E. Golann and C. Eisdorfer (Eds.) *Handbook of Community Mental Health*. New York: Appleton-Century-Crofts, 1972.

Kellam, S. G., and Schiff, S. K. Adaptation and mental illness in the first-grade classrooms of an urban community. *Psychiatric Research Reports*, 1967, 21, 79–91.

Kephart, N. C. *The Slow Learner in the Classroom*. Columbus, Ohio: Charles E. Merrill, 1960.

Kirk, S. A. *Educating Exceptional Children*. Boston: Houghton Mifflin, 1962.

Kirk, S. A. *Educating Exceptional Children*. (2nd Ed.) Boston: Houghton Mifflin, 1972.

Kirk, S. A., and Bateman, B. Diagnosis and remediation of learning disabilities. *Exceptional Children*, 1962, 29, 73–78.

Kirk, S. A. and Johnson, O. *Educating the Retarded Child*. Boston: Houghton Mifflin, 1951.

Kirk. S. A., and Kirk, W. D. *Psycholinguistic Learning Disabilities: Diagnosis and Remediation*. Chicago: University of Illinois Press, 1971.

Koppitz, E. M. *Children with Learning Disabilities: A Five Year Follow-up Study*. New York: Grune and Stratton, 1971.

Lilly, M. S. Special education: A teapot in a tempest. *Exceptional Children*, 1970, 37, 43–59.

Lovaas, O. I., and Bucher, B. D. (Eds.) *Perspectives in Behavior Modification with Deviant Children*. Englewood Cliffs, N.J.: Prentice-Hall, 1974.

McConnell, F. Children with hearing disabilities. In L. M. Dunn (Ed.) *Exceptional Children in the Schools: Special Education in Transition*. (2nd Ed.) New York: Holt, Rinehart & Winston, 1973. Pp. 351–413.

Martinson, R. A. Children with superior cognitive abilities. In L. M. Dunn (Ed.) *Exceptional Children in the Schools: Special Education in Transition*. (2nd Ed.) New York: Holt, Rinehart & Winston, 1973. Pp. 191–244.

Morse, W. C. The education of socially maladjusted and emotionally disturbed children. In W. M. Cruickshank and G. O. Johnson (Eds.) *Education of Exceptional Children and Youth*. (2nd Ed.) Englewood Cliffs, N.J.: Prentice-Hall, 1967. Pp. 569–627.

Moss, J. W. Disabled or disadvantaged: There is a difference. *Journal of Special Education*, 1973, 7, 387–391.

National Advisory Committee on Handicapped Children. *Special Education for Handicapped Children*, First Annual Report. Washington, D.C.: U.S. Department of Health, Education, and Welfare, January 31, 1968.

O'Leary, K. D., and O'Leary, S. G. *Classroom Management: The Successful Use of Behavior Modification*. New York: Pergamon, 1972.

Patterson, G. R. *Families*. Champaign, Ill.: Research Press, 1971.

Quay, H. C., and Werry, J. S. (Eds.) *Psychopathological Disorders of Childhood.* New York: John Wiley, 1972.

Redelheim, P. S. Learning disabled or culturally disadvantaged: A separate piece? *Journal of Special Education,* 1973, 7, 399–408.

Report of the Joint Commission on Mental Health of Children. *Crisis in Child Mental Health: Challenge for the 1970's.* New York: Harper, 1970.

Ross, A. O. Learning difficulties of children: Dysfunctions, disorders, disabilities. *Journal of School Psychology,* 1967, 5, 82–92.

Ross, A. O. *Psychological Disorders of Children.* New York: McGraw-Hill, 1974.

Rubin, R., and Balow, B. Learning and behavior disorders: A longitudinal study. *Exceptional Children,* 1971, 38, 293–299.

Sabatino, D. A. A scientific approach toward a discipline of special education. *Journal of Special Education,* 1971, 5, 15–22.

Schiff, S. K. Free inquiry and the enduring commitment: The Woodland Mental Health Center, 1963–1970. In S. E Golann and C. Eisdorfer (Eds.) *Handbook of Community Mental Health.* New York: Appleton-Century-Crofts, 1972.

Staats, A. W. *Child Learning, Intelligence, and Personality.* New York: Harper, 1971.

Staats, A. W. *Social Behaviorism.* Homewood, Ill.: Dorsey, 1975.

Stephens, J. M. *The Process of Schooling.* New York: Holt, Rinehart & Winston, 1967.

Swift, M. S., and Spivack, G. Therapeutic teaching: A review of teaching methods for behaviorally troubled children. *Journal of Special Education,* 1974, 8, 259–289.

Telford, C. W., and Sawrey, J. M. *The Exceptional Individual.* (2nd Ed.) Englewood Cliffs, N.J.: Prentice-Hall, 1972.

Thomas, D. R., Becker, W. C., and Armstrong, M. Production and elimination of disruptive classroom behavior by systematically varying teacher's behavior. *Journal of Applied Behavior Analysis,* 1968, 1, 35–45.

Tift, K. F. The disturbed child in the classroom. *NEA Journal,* 1968, 57, 12–14.

Wagonseller, B. R. Learning disability and emotional disturbance: Factors relating to differential diagnosis. *Exceptional Children,* 1973, 40, 205–206.

Wilson, M. I. Children with crippling and health disabilities. In L. M. Dunn (Ed.) *Exceptional Children in the Schools: Special Education in Transition.* (2nd Ed.) New York: Holt, Rinehart & Winston, 1973. Pp. 467–532.

2

Children with Exceptional Learning and Behavior Characteristics: Current Categories and Educational Practices

Children differ along numerous physically, psychologically, and socially defined dimensions. As noted previously, if these differences are of sufficient magnitude to create unusual and consistent problems to the regular education program, children are diagnosed and classified in categories based on medical, psychiatric, psychological, and psychometric criteria. The traditional approach to providing for the educational needs of these children has been assignment to the appropriate category of special education program. These educational experiences have been provided most frequently in self-contained classroom or school arrangement, although presently a wide variety of other delivery systems is being utilized.

HOW MANY CATEGORIES?

Table 2.1 presents the categories of "exceptional" children that are provided separate chapter discussions in the five most currently popular basic survey or introductory texts in exceptional education. The Telford and Sawrey* and the Hewett and Forness* books include separate discussions of the culturally, socially, and economically disadvantaged. These

Telford and Sawrey 1972; Hewett and Forness 1974

Dunn 1973

topics are assimilated by the other three books into the discussions of mental retardation and communication difficulties. The Dunn* text, a book with multiple authors, uses the concept of disability and ability as a central theme in its presentation. The remaining books use in a nonsystematic manner such concepts as disorder, deviance, disturbance, handicapped, impaired, disadvantaged, retarded, superior, and gifted to describe the various categories of exceptional children.

The present discussion uses the terms suggested by the Dunn text with the exception of the general learning disabilities concept. The traditional term *mental retardation* is used to reflect its widespread current use. Description of each of the categories (see table 2.1) of exceptional children is organized around the following areas:

1. How is the category disability (or ability) defined and classified?
2. How many children and youth meet the defining criteria?
3. What more specific disability or unusual ability characteristics are descriptive of each category? These characteristics are abstracted from the five texts listed in table 2.1.
4. What special education arrangements are used to deal with these "exceptional" characteristics?

BEHAVIORAL DISABILITIES

How Defined and Classified?

Graubard 1973

Graubard* favors the term *behavioral disabilities* as an inclusive category for the traditional special education categories of "emotionally disturbed" and "socially maladjusted" and the legally defined category "juvenile delinquent." Behavioral disabilities is defined "as a variety of excessive, chronic deviant behaviors ranging from impulsive and aggressive to depressive and withdrawal acts (1) which violate the perceiver's expectations of appropriateness, and (2) which the perceiver wishes to see stopped" (p. 246).

Although recognizing the need for some type of classification or subgrouping system for educational management purposes, Graubard concludes that there presently are insufficient research data to lend direction to a useful scheme.

Bower 1969, 1970

Bower* recommends the term *emotionally handicapped* to replace such terms as "emotionally disturbed" or "socially maladjusted." He suggests that the term *handicap* implies a more lasting and persistent quality and is less suggestive of a type of behavior pattern of aggressive disturbed emotional expression frequently associated with formal psychological or psychiatric appraisal. Bower* defines emotionally handicapped children as characterized by one or more of the following (to a marked extent and present over a period of time):

Bower 1969

TABLE 2.1   *Comparison of Terms Used in Introductory Texts to Denote Categories of Exceptional Children*

Dunn (1973)	Haring (1974)	Hewett and Forness (1974)	Kirk (1972)	Telford and Sawrey (1972)
behavioral disabilities	severely emotionally disturbed; social and emotional behavior disorders	emotionally disturbed	behavior disorders	social deviance
major specific learning disabilities	learning disabilities	learning disabilities	specific learning disabilities	learning disabilities
		socially and economically disadvantaged		culturally disadvantaged
visual disabilities	visually impaired	visually handicapped	visually handicapped	visually handicapped
hearing disabilities	hearing impaired	hearing handicapped	auditory handicapped	aurally handicapped
oral communication disabilities	communication disorders	speech handicapped	speech handicapped	speech handicaps
crippling and health disabilities		physically handicapped	neurologic, orthopedic, and other health impairments	orthopedically handicapped and the epileptic
superior cognitive abilities	gifted	gifted	intellectually gifted	intellectually superior
mild general learning disabilities	educable mentally retarded	mentally retarded	educable mentally retarded	mild mental retardation
moderate and severe general learning disabilities	trainable mentally retarded		trainable mentally retarded	severe mental retardation

1. An inability to learn, which cannot be explained by intellectual, sensory, or health factors.
2. An inability to build or maintain satisfactory interpersonal relationships with peers and teachers.

3. Inappropriate types of behavior or feelings under normal conditions.
4. A general pervasive mood of unhappiness or depression.
5. A tendency to develop physical symptoms, pain, or fears associated with personal or school problems.

Bower 1970

Bower* offers a five-level classification scheme for mental health problems of childhood. The Bower system emphasizes the relative inability of the child in the school setting to handle or cope with his psychological difficulties. The five categories in the classification system are defined as those children who manifest:

1. Ordinary, everyday problems.
2. Minor problems in learning and behavior.
3. Marked and recurrent learning and behavior problems.
4. Severe learning and behavior problems.
5. Problems of such severity that the child cannot be maintained in the public school setting.

Kirk 1972

Kirk* defines a *behavior disorder* as "a deviation from age-appropriate behavior which significantly interferes with (1) the child's own growth and development and/or (2) the lives of others" (p. 389). In this definition Kirk assumes a broad-spectrum approach and avoids traditional definitions and classification schemes which make use of such categories as "emotional disturbance," "socially maladjusted," "conduct problem," "delinquent."

Kirk emphasizes the relationship between the labels used to classify children and the orientation, training, and/or setting of the person assigning the label in his comments:[1]

A child who is extremely withdrawn and does not relate to other people, who does not seem to respond to his environment (even though he is average in intelligence) is one whose behavior is interfering with his own growth process. Such children have been termed "withdrawn," "neurotic," "autistic," or "schizophrenic." A child who behaves in such a way that he has repeated conflict with his siblings, parents, classmates, teachers, and community is interfering with the lives of other people. Parents call him a "bad boy." Teachers call him a "conduct problem." Social workers say he is "socially maladjusted." Psychiatrists and psychologists may say he is "emotionally disturbed." And if he comes in conflict with the law, the judge calls him "delinquent." [p. 389]

1. From S. A. Kirk, *Educating Exceptional Children*, 2nd ed. (Boston: Houghton Mifflin, 1972). Copyright © 1972 by Houghton Mifflin Co. Reprinted by permission of Houghton Mifflin and George G. Harrap & Company, Ltd., London.

Finally, while not providing a formal definition of behavioral disabilities, Quay* offers a behavioral-cluster classification system for use by educators. The Quay classification system is comprised of patterns of (1) *aggression* (conduct disorder), (2) *withdrawal* (personality disorder), (3) *immaturity*, and (4) *socialized delinquency*. These four major behavior patterns or clusters of "childhood psychopathology" have resulted from a large number of multivariate statistical studies of problem behaviors in children and adolescents (see Quay* for a description of these studies). The studies, conducted by different investigators studying children in a variety of settings, included children in public schools, child guidance clinics, institutions for delinquents, and hospitals and institutions for the mentally ill and mentally retarded. The method used in these studies involves isolating statistically interrelated patterns of behaviors and life history characteristics. In this approach, individual children are rated on a series of descriptive statements. The behavioral data obtained are based on direct observations, analysis of data from case records, analysis of life histories, and by responses of children and adolescents to questionnaires. Parents, teachers, child guidance clinic staff, and correctional workers have served as raters in various studies. Intercorrelations among all items are obtained and this matrix is further analyzed by means of factor analysis. This analysis results in a small number of factors, patterns, or clusters, which are then provided labels consistent with the descriptive items that comprise the separate patterns. Each factor is comprised of highly interrelated items that hold low relationships with items of other factors.

Quay 1972

Quay 1972

The four patterns of the Quay system are described as:

Conduct disorder. This pattern involves active aggressive behavior of an antisocial nature, both verbal and physical, and poor interpersonal relationships with both adults and peers. Other descriptions which define the pattern include conscienceless, impulsive behavior, disobedience, disruptiveness, quarrelsome, defies authority. and irresponsibility.

Personality disorder. This pattern is defined by behaviors, attitudes, and feelings as reflected in such descriptions as expressed unhappiness, physical complaint, feelings of distress, and anxiety. Fears of a general and specific nature are central features of personality disorders. In general the child is characterized by withdrawal behavior which removes him from active social interaction.

Immaturity. This third pattern, while not as distinct or as widespread in its prevalence, is found in children and adolescents seen in a range of different settings. Such behavioral traits and life history characteristics as the following are descriptive of this pattern: preoccupation, passivity, prefers younger playmates, clumsiness, incompetent, unable to cope with a complex world, and short attention span.

Socialized delinquency.   The final pattern "represents behavior which is neither generally a source of personal distress nor clearly maladaptive when one considers social conditions under which it seems to

Quay 1972

arise" (p. 14).* It reflects behavioral patterns acquired as the adolescent learns to adapt to his peer group and adults who engage in such behavior. Life history characteristics include: engages in gang activities, engages in cooperative stealing, habitually truant from school, accepted by delinquent subgroups, and strong allegiance to selected peers.

How Many Meet the Criteria?

Estimates of prevalence of children and youth with behavioral disabilities vary considerably due to the nebulousness of the criteria used by

U.S. Office of Education 1971

Schultz et al. 1971

various definitions. The U.S. Office of Education* presents an estimate of 2 percent of school-age children in need of special education services as a result of behavioral disabilities. Schultz et al.* report that prevalence figures used by various states for special education purposes vary from .05 percent to 15 percent. Data suggest that behavioral disabilities are not evenly distributed throughout the population, with a higher prevalence

Pate 1963

being present in lower sociocultural classes.*

Characteristics

Extreme withdrawal (low rate of social interaction)
Does not seem to respond to his environment
Repeated conflict with siblings, parents, classmates, teachers, and
    community
Timid, shy, withdrawn, sensitive, submissive
Defies authority, hostile toward authority figures
Displays antisocial behavior which interferes with the lives of others,
    delinquent
Characterized by inner tensions and anxieties
Neurotic and psychotic behavior
Immature, daydreaming, lack of interest
Academic achievement retardation
Hyperaggressive (high rate of hitting, spitting, pushing, profanity, kicking)
Hyperactive (high rate of getting out of seat, moving about, touching)
Autistic
Nonattending to class instruction, short attention span
Chronic violation of broad cultural mores and social values
Phobic reactions, feelings of inferiority
Excessive attention seeking, boisterousness
Severe learning deficiencies
Little motivation for academic learning

Educational Provisions

Part- or full-time education classes. Typically the classes are comprised of children with a wide range of characteristics which necessitate their removal from the regular class setting.

Resource rooms, used for children enrolled in the regular class part of the day and in which special instructional assistance is provided.

Regular class attendance with consultative and/or itinerant teacher assistance provided the regular class teachers.

Special day schools.

Residential schools and hospital programs for the more severely disabled.

MAJOR SPECIFIC LEARNING DISABILITIES

How Defined and Classified?

The concept of learning disabilities evolved as a classification category in special education to encompass a rather heterogeneous group of children who did not fit neatly into traditional categories of handicapped children. Kirk* offered the category *specific learning disability* for this group, but cautioned: *Kirk 1972*

"Because of the heterogeneous nature of the group of children, the concept of specific learning disability has been hard to define. Numerous definitive labels have been used, employing such terms as 'minimal brain dysfunction,' or 'central processing dysfunction,' or 'perceptually handicapped children.' Specific disabilities have been labeled 'dyslexia' for severe reading disabilities, or 'aphasia' for children who are delayed in learning to talk. Because the field of learning disabilities is of interest to psychiatrists, neurophysiologists, psychologists, speech pathologists, and educators, the problem has been viewed from these various perspectives" (p. 42).

Current definitions reflect two categories of learning disabilities: those that focus on a neurological etiology of learning difficulties and those with an educational focus that emphasize the learning difficulties without reference to an underlying neurological disorder. The definition of Myklebust* illustrates the first category: "We use the term 'psychoneurological learning disorders' to include deficits in learning, at any age, which are caused by deviations in the central nervous system and which are not due to mental deficiency, sensory impairment, or psychogenicity. The etiology might be disease and accident, or it might be developmental" (p. 27).   *Myklebust 1963*

As representative of the latter category, Kirk* offered the following: "A learning disability refers to a specific retardation or disorder in one or more of the processes of speech, language, perception, behavior, reading, spelling, writing, or arithmetic" (p. 398).   *Kirk 1968*

Kirk in 1972 added the word "specific" to the term (thus, *specific learning disabilities*) to emphasize the focus on a specific developmental problem instead of on general problems of learning. He commented, "Hence, the term 'specific learning disabilities' refers to severe handicap in central processes, which inhibit the child's normal development in such specific areas as talking, thinking, perceiving, reading, writing, and spelling" (p.44).

In 1968 a National Advisory Committee on Handicapped Children, of the U.S. Office of Education, proposed the following definition, which was included in Public Law 91-320, "The Learning Disabilities Act of 1969":

> Children with special (specific) learning disabilities exhibit a disorder in one or more of the basic psychological processes involved in understanding or in using spoken or written language. These may be manifested in disorders of listening, thinking, talking, reading, writing, spelling, or arithmetic. They include conditions which have been referred to as perceptual handicaps, brain injury, minimal brain dysfunction, dyslexia, developmental aphasia, etc. They not include learning problems which are due primarily to visual, hearing, or motor handicaps, or mental retardation, emotional disturbance, or to enviromnental disadvantage. [p. 14]

Dunn 1973   Dunn,* in response to what he identified as a number of inherent problems in the Kirk and USOE definitions, offered the category label *major specific learning disabilities* (MSLDs) and defined it as those 1 to 2 percent of the school population:

> (1) who display one primary severe or moderately severe discrepancy between capacity and performance in a specific basic learning process involving perception, conception, or expression associated with the areas of oral and written language or mathematics; (2) yet whose MSLDs are neither mental retardation nor any of the other traditional handicapping conditions; (3) but who may have one or more additional, secondary traditional or specific learning disabilities to a milder degree; (4) none of whom have MSLDs that can be adequately treated in the regular school program when only remedial education is provided as an ancillary service; (5) not more than one half of whom have MSLDs that can be adequately treated in the regular school program even when special education consultant-helping teacher services are extensively provided; (6) half or more of whom, therefore, will require more intensive special education instruction under such administrative plans as the resource room, the combined resource room and special class, the special class, and the special day and boarding school; and (7) yet any of whom may also require other remedial and special education services to deal with their secondary traditional or specific learning disabilities. [p. 542]

In emphasizing the wide variation in classification practices of children with learning difficulties among state educational agencies, *Wepman et al. 1975*   Wepman et al.* reported the following:

Term	State Statute
educational handicap	California
specific learning disabilities	Florida
extreme learning problems	Oregon
communicative and intellectual deviations	West Virginia
neurologically handicapped or impaired	Connecticut Nevada Oklahoma
perceptually handicapped	Colorado Indiana New Jersey Washington
brain damaged	Pennsylvania
learning disability	Delaware

These writers, accepting the need for some means of classifying children with learning problems for the purpose of facilitating individualized intervention, offer the following definition: "*Specific learning disability* refers to those children of any age who demonstrate a substantial deficiency in a particular aspect of academic achievement because of perceptual or perceptual-motor handicaps, regardless of etiology or other contributing factors" (p. 306).

They add as further clarification:

> From this definition it follows that perceptual or perceptual-motor inadequacies produce specific learning disabilities. Learning problems due to emotional, socioeconomic, or peripheral sensory or motor impairment are excluded. Behavior disturbances, severe mental retardation, poverty, lessened educational opportunity, visual impairment, hearing loss, or muscular paralysis all may produce educational problems but do not fall into the classification of specific learning disabilities. [p. 306]

Finally, Gleason and Haring* provide a general behavioral definition of learning disabilities in their statement: "We define a learning disability as a behavioral deficit almost always associated with academic performance and that can be remediated by precise, individualized instructional programming" (p. 226). *Gleason and Haring 1974*

How Many Meet the Criteria?

The U.S. Office of Education* suggests a prevalence estimate of 1 percent of the school-age population. Dunn* includes a prevalence estimate of 1 to 2 percent of the school population in his definition of major *U.S. Office of Education 1971; Dunn 1973*

Kirk 1972 specific learning disabilities. Kirk* suggests that the best "guessimate" is that from 1 to 3 percent at the least and possibly 7 percent at the most of the school population may be classified as requiring special remedial education as a result of specific learning disabilities.

Characteristics

Hyperactivity

Perceptual-motor impairment, neuromuscular or motor coordination difficulties

Disorders of attention (short attention span, distractibility)

Impulsiveness

Specific learning difficulties in reading, writing, arithmetic, and spelling which cannot be accounted for by other major disabilities

Disorders of listening, memory, thinking, conceptualization, and oral language

Visual and auditory perceptual difficulties

Developmental discrepancies in abilities

Presumed central nervous system deviations

Differential between capacity and achievement

Educational Provisions

Self-contained classroom comprised of a small number of children who receive individual instruction for a part of the day.

Resource-room plan in which the child, enrolled in regular class, spends part of his day for individualized instruction in his areas of difficulty. Resource room teacher also may provide consultation to regular teacher.

Itinerant diagnostic remedial specialist (helping-teacher plan) provides specific consultative assistant to regular classroom teacher in devising and monitoring an individualized academic program.

VISUAL DISABILITIES

How Defined and Classified?

Traditionally, visually handicapped children were classified into two categories on the basis of legal and medical criteria: (1) *partially sighted*—visual acuity greater than 20/200 but not greater than 20/70 in the better eye with correction, and (2) *legally blind*—visual acuity for distance vision of 20/200 or less in the better eye, with best correction; or visual acuity of more than 20/200 if the widest diameter of field of vision subtends an angle no greater than 20 degrees.*

National Society for the
Prevention of Blindness
Fact Book 1966

However, as these definitions carry no direct implications for educational needs or services,* the following terms and related definitions used by special educators and based on the reading medium of the child were developed: (1) *visually impaired; partially sighted*—children who can use sight for purposes of reading but who primarily read large print or regular print under special conditions; (2) *blind; braille reader*—children who principally read braille as the reading medium. Harley* suggested the term "braille reader" be used in preference to the term "blind," as it is more descriptive of the media of instruction required by some children.

Bateman 1967

Harley 1973

How Many Meet the Criteria?

The U.S. Office of Education estimates that approximately 0.1 percent of the school population require special education services as a result of visual impairment. Thus, one out of every 1,000 children will require adaptation in the mode of instruction provided in the school setting.

Characteristics

Visual impairments requiring a media of instruction different from that provided the child with normal visual features—braille, audio presentation, tactual aids, and large print

Mobility and orientation difficulties

Basic educational needs generally similar to those of normally seeing children

Variance in abilities comparable to that of normally seeing children

Possible cognitive development difficulties if the visually impaired child is highly restricted in exposure to sensory stimulation

Space perception difficulties

Academic retardation related to underachievement

Requires concreteness in instructional procedures prior to emphasis on abstractness

Minor social adjustment problems of children with moderate visual impairments

Educational Provisions

Teacher-consultant plan in which child is enrolled in regular classes with direct or indirect services provided as needed by a teacher consultant.

Itinerant-teacher plan which provides more individual instruction to the child.

Resource-room or resource-teacher plan in which children do the majority of their work within the regular classroom but go as the need arises to a special room for help and special materials from the resource teacher.

Cooperative class in which children enroll in a special class but spend the majority of their time integrated into the regular classes.

Special class provides entire day instruction by the special teacher in a self-contained room.

Residential school provides a total educational program within a residential facility for children.

HEARING DISABILITIES

How Defined and Classified?

In defining hearing disabilities from an educational needs viewpoint, consideration is given both to the *age of onset* of the hearing loss and to the *degree of hearing loss*. Degree of hearing impairment is based on hearing loss in decibels. For example, a child will have frequent difficulty with speech at normal loudness if his hearing level in his better ear reflects a loss of more than 40 decibels. A child with a loss of more than 55 decibels will understand conversation only if it is loud and is likely to have speech difficulties and to be deficient in language usage and comprehension.

Age of onset of hearing loss is of importance due to its relationship to language and speech acquisition. If the loss is prelingual, that is, occurring before the child has begun to acquire oral language, the effect of the loss is more damaging than would be noted if the loss was postlingual. The later in life hearing impairment occurs, the more vocabulary and related linguistic concepts the child will have acquired.

The following definitions, reflecting degree of loss and age of onset, represent the most commonly used for educational purposes:

1. *The deaf*—those whose hearing loss is so severe that it precludes the normal development of speech. This loss is present at birth or prior to two or three years of age.
2. *Partially hearing; hard of hearing*—those whose hearing is not of sufficient severity to preclude development of some spoken language. This includes those who had acquired speech before the loss of hearing (described by the term "deafened").

How Many Meet the Criteria?

U.S. Office of Education 1971

Silverman 1957

The U.S. Office of Education* reports a prevalence estimate of 0.58 percent of school-age children as having an educationally handicapping hearing loss. Of this percentage, 0.50 represent the partially hearing and 0.08 the deaf. This is consistent with Silverman's* estimate that about 5 in 1,000 children will require special educational attention due to a hearing difficulty.

Characteristics

Auditory impairment requiring possible modifications in the manner in which instruction and/or communication is provided

Severe auditory impairment results in difficulty in development of abstract language skills

Mild to severe retardation in academic achievement depending upon the degree of disability

Mild to moderate personal-social difficulties more likely due to loss of normal channels of communication

Educational Provisions

Regular class with the assistance of an itinerant teacher helping the hard-of-hearing child in (1) use of hearing aid, (2) auditory training, (3) speechreading, and (4) speech training.

Special class or school for deaf children. The curriculum for deaf children includes an emphasis on development of speech, speechreading, reading, and language, in addition to the regular school curriculum.

ORAL COMMUNICATION DISABILITIES

How Defined and Classified?

Present views of oral communication disabilities include both *language* and *speech* disorders or impairments. Hull and Hull* describe categories of language expression disabilities as (1) those language problems associated with some form of central nervous system malfunction and (2) those related to lack of experience because of environmental factors that provide inadequate linguistic models. Disabilities associated with central nervous system impairment are called *childhood aphasia* (deficiencies in the ability to use linguistic symbols—spoken words—for oral communication) if the damage occurred after language had begun to develop. Central nervous system impairment prior to the development of language is referred to as *developmental or congenital aphasia.*

Hull and Hull 1973

Language disorders associated with lack of appropriate experience are described as deficits in the linguistic structure of the language system, that is, at the phonological, morphological, and/or syntactic level.* Many such language disorders occur among economically disadvantaged and minority group children. Although there is considerable disagreement with the position, many educators and language developmentalists hold that the oral language of disadvantaged children is substandard and, further, that such language deficits interfere with learning and academic achievement.

McLean 1974

Van Riper 1972

Speech disabilities is defined by Van Riper* as follows: "Speech is defective when it deviates so far from the speech of other people that it calls attention to itself, interferes with communication, or causes its possessor to be maladjusted." Hull and Hull,* emphasizing the interrelation of language and speech offer the following: "A speech deviation may be considered a disability when there is an interference in the production of audible utterances of such proportion that it does not serve satisfactorily as the basic tool for oral expression" (p. 308).

Hull and Hull 1973

Speech disabilities are classified as involving (1) *articulation*—substitutions, omission, distortion, and/or addition of consonant and/or vowel sounds; (2) *voice problems*—quality, flexibility, duration, pitch, or loudness; and (3) *stuttering*. These speech disabilities are found among children with no other disabilities, as well as among those with such conditions as mental retardation, cerebral palsy, cleft palate, and impaired hearing.

How Many Meet the Criteria?

U.S. Office of Education 1971

Kirk 1972

Hull and Hull 1973

The U.S. office of Education* reported an estimated prevalence of 3.5 percent of school-age children as presenting oral communication disabilities. Kirk* favors a 3 to 5 percent estimate. As many as 80 percent of children with speech disabilites display articulation difficulties. Hull and Hull* report the following estimated prevalence of oral communication disorders accompanying other types of handicapping conditions: partially hearing—9.49 percent; cerebral palsy—50 percent; cleft palate—25 percent; mild mental retardation—8 to 37 percent; moderate and severe mental retardation—94 percent.

Characteristics

Seriously speech-handicapped children exhibit language defects.

Oral communication disabilities may occur independently of or may coexist with any area of exceptionality.

Speech disability is frequently correlated with reading disability.

Specific behavioral, learning, and personal-social characteristics of children with oral communication disabilities are dependent upon the type and severity of the disability, as well as on the presence of coexisting disabilities.

Educational Provisions

Direct remediation services to the disabled child by a speech clinician.

Consultative services by a speech clinician to the classroom teacher in developing speech and language experiences for children with oral communication disabilities.

CRIPPLING AND HEALTH DISABILITIES

How Defined and Classified?

Children with crippling and health disabilities represent the most medically oriented and the most heterogeneous of the various categories of exceptional children. Kirk* defines this category as comprising those chil- *Kirk 1972* dren "who are crippled, deformed, or otherwise physically handicapped (exclusive of the visually and auditorily handicapped) and those who have health problems which interfere with normal functioning in a regular classroom" (p. 349). Most of these children, however, are able to learn as other children learn and do not experience educational difficulties in a classroom in which adjustments have been made as needed in facilities, equipment, and materials.

Wilson* uses the following classification scheme in describing *Wilson 1973* children with crippling and health disabilities:

Children with disorders of the nervous system
    cerebral palsy
    convulsive disorders (epilepsy)
    multiple sclerosis
Children with musculoskeletal conditions
    clubfoot
    scoliosis
    Legg-Perthe's
    rheumatoid arthritis
    osteomyelitis
    progressive muscular dystrophy
Children with congenital malformations
    malformations of the heart
    dislocation of the hip
    limb deficiencies
    spina befida
    hydrocephalus
Children with other crippling and health conditions
    miscellaneous crippling conditions (e.g., poliomyelitis,
        tuberculosis of bones and joints, birth injuries)
    miscellaneous health conditions (e.g., cystic fibrosis,
        pulmonary tuberculosis, hemophilia, asthma, diabetes)

How Many Meet the Criteria?

Dunn* suggests a prevalence of 0.36 percent with approximately *Dunn 1973* half of these children having cerebral palsy and other crippling conditions and the other half chronic health problems. The U.S. Office of Education* *U.S. Office of Education* suggested a prevalence estimate of 0.5 percent of school-age children with *1971* crippling and health disabilities who require special education services.

Characteristics

Children with crippling and health disabilities are more likely to exhibit behavior and emotional difficulties than their unimpaired peers. The more severe and debilitating the disabilities, the greater the possibility of behavioral-emotional problems. More specific learning, motivational, and personal-social characteristics are functions of the type, severity, age of onset, and psychological experiences of each child.

Educational Provisions

Regular class enrollment with adjustments in the physical conditions to accommodate the disabilities of the specific child.

Itinerant or remedial teacher program to assist with specific learning or language difficulties.

Special schools or classes in regular schools represent the most common plan for physically handicapped children.

Home instruction when the child is severely disabled or when a suitable school placement is unavailable.

SUPERIOR COGNITIVE ABILITIES

How Defined and Classified?

Historically, definitions of the gifted, talented, or creative child were in terms of precocious accomplishment. With the principal criterion being that of actual achievement, there was greater possibility of agreement as to who should be so described. Present views, however, expand this achievement criterion to children who display *unusual promise* of accomplishment and greatly compound the problem of definition.

A variety of terms and associated defining criteria are available— superior cognitive abilities, the gifted, the academically talented, the superior, the able and ambitious, the creative, the socially, mechanically, musically, physically, or linguistically talented.

Representative of definitions reflecting varying viewpoints are as follows:

1. "A talented or gifted child is one who shows consistently remarkable performance in any worthwhile line of endeavor. Thus, we shall include not only the intellectually gifted but also those who show promise in music, the graphic arts, creative writing, dramatics, mechanical skills, and social leadership" (p. 19).*

Education of the Gifted 1958

2. "Those who possess a superior central nervous system characterized by the potential to perform tasks requiring a comparatively high degree of intellectual abstraction or creative imagination or both" (p. 4).*

Sumption and Luecking 1960

3. "The term *gifted* encompasses those children who possess a superior

intellectual potential and functional ability to achieve academically in the top 15 to 20 percent of the school population; and/or talent of a high order in such special areas as mathematics, mechanics, science, expressive arts, creative writing, music, and social leadership; and a unique creative ability to deal with their environment" (p. 409).*

Fliegler and Bish 1959

4. "Students with superior cognitive abilities include approximately the top 3 percent of the general school population in measured general intelligence and/or in creative abilities or other talents that promise to make lasting contributions of merit to society. These students are so able that they require special provisions if appropriate educational opportunities are to be provided for them" (p. 193).*

Martinson 1973

How Many Meet the Criteria?

The prevalence figure for children with superior cognitive abilities obviously depends upon the particular definition followed and the specific criteria used in identification. The Fliegler and Bish* definition includes the top 15 to 20 percent of the school population. The Martinson* definition includes approximately the top 3 percent of the general school population. Marland* in his recent report to the United States Congress entitled *Education of the Gifted and Talented,* restricted the gifted to 3 to 5 percent of the general population. Using the 3 percent prevalence estimate, Martinson* estimated that in the early 1970s there were 510,000 preschool, 960,000 elementary school, and 465,000 high school students in United States public schools who could be considered as gifted.

Fliegler and Bish 1959
Martinson 1973

Marland 1972

Martinson 1973

Characteristics

Displays originality and/or artistry

Learns rapidly and easily, displays active curiosity

Displays talent that gives evidence or promise of contribution of lasting merit

Above average in height, weight, general body development, strength, energy, and in general health

Uses large number of words early and accurately

Retains easily what has been heard or read

Is alert, keenly observant, responds quickly

Displays capacity to solve important problems at high level of abstraction

Tends to develop reading skills easily

Excellent scholastic attainment in areas requiring verbal comprehension and usage

As a group makes superior social and emotional adjustment, more self-sufficient, more dominant

Highly gifted, prone to develop personal-social problems due to isolation from contemporaries, frustration of learning needs, boredom, and concern for ethical and moral problems

Displays talent so unusually advanced that special arrangements are
needed for its fullest development
Displays wider range of interests than normal peers

Educational Provisions

Enrichment in the form of providing educational experiences over and
above those in the regular program, including grouping a few gifted in
same class, offering additional courses, use of a special teacher consultant to regular teacher, providing seminars, special interest groups,
and the like.
Ability grouping in special classes and/or schools, including provision of
special sections in subject matter areas; offering advanced courses for
superior students in secondary schools; modified special class in
which child attends regular class part of the day and ability-defined
class part of the day; self-contained special classes; special schools
which admit only superior students.
Acceleration in the form of early school admission, grade skipping, tele-
scoping grades, early college admission.

MENTAL RETARDATION

How Defined and Classified?

Mental retardation may be defined from a psychological or from an
educational viewpoint. The following definition of the American Association on Mental Deficiency (AAMD) and the description in the *Manual on*
Grossman 1973   *Terminology and Classification of Mental Retardation** are the most relevant to the educator of the presently used psychological definitions:
"Mental retardation refers to significantly subaverage general intellectual
functioning existing concurrently with deficits in adaptive behavior, and
manifested during the developmental period" (p. 11).

As noted, this definition requires deficits in both general intellectual
functioning and in adaptive behavior skills. Table 2.2 represents the intelligence quotients associated with four levels of mental retardation. Adaptive behavior is defined by the AAMD system as "the effectiveness or
degree with which the individual meets the standards of personal independence and social responsibility expected of his age and cultural group"
Sloan and Birch 1955   (p. 11). Table 2.3, adapted from Sloan and Birch,* illustrates various adaptive behavior characteristics associated with the mild, moderate, severe,
and profound levels of retardation. The *Manual* recommends that "mild
retardation is highly equivalent to the educational term 'educable,' moderate retardation includes those individuals who are likely to fall into the
educational category of 'trainable,' the severe group includes individuals

TABLE 2.2   *IQs Associated with Levels of Mental Retardation (AAMD)*

Levels	IQ Range	
	Stanford-Binet	**Wechsler Scales**
Mild	68–52	69–55
Moderate	51–36	54–40
Severe	35–20	39–25
Profound	19 and below	24 and below

sometimes known as 'dependent retarded'; individuals in the profound retardation level are among those sometimes called 'life support' level" (p. 18).

Kirk* suggests that children with limited cognitive skills are "classified educationally into four groups: (1) the slow learner (IQ 80–90); (2) the educable mentally retarded (IQ 50–55 to 75–79); (3) the trainable mentally retarded (IQ 30–35 to 50–55); and (4) the totally dependent or profoundly mentally retarded (IQ below 25–30)" (p. 164).   *Kirk 1972*

Dunn* proposes that the term "mental retardation" no longer be applied to pupils for special education purposes. He suggests that it is not educationally relevant and is associated with the stigmatizing condition of social incompetence. Dunn offers the concept of *general learning disabilities* as being a more appropriate one to indicate marginal social competence, educational retardation, or limitations in adult life. Children with general learning disabilities require special education because they score within the second percentile on verbal and performance tests of intellectual functioning. Dunn requires that the tests be administered in the child's most facile language and that the child be judged in relation to his ethnic or racial subgroup. He further calls for the abandonment of the terms "educable," "trainable," and "custodial" due to their derogatory and defeatist implications. Dunn supports a "mild," "moderate," "severe," and "profound" classification scheme.   *Dunn 1973*

Peterson,* also preferring the term "general learning disability," provides an even more educationally relevant definition: "A general learning disability refers to school-age children manifesting a significant degree of substandard achievement in a wide array of developmental and/or academic skills which may be associated with low measured intelligence" (p. 315). This definition represents a dramatic departure from the usual educational view of "mental retardation"; it would include some underachieving children who demonstrate average mental abilities.   *Peterson 1974*

How Many Meet the Criteria?

The number of children identified as mentally retarded obviously would depend upon the criteria used in defining the category. Traditional prevalence figures identify from 2 to 3 percent of school children as men-

TABLE 2.3   *Adaptive Behavior Characteristics of the Mentally Retarded*

Degrees of Mental Retardation	Preschool Age 0–5: Maturation and Development	School Age 6–20: Training and Education	Adult 21 And Over: Social and Vocational Adequacy
Mild	Can develop social and communication skills; minimal retardation in sensorimotor areas; often not distinguished from normal until later age.	Can learn academic skills up to approximately sixth grade level by late teens. Can be guided toward social conformity. ("Educable")	Can usually achieve social and vocational skills adequate to minimum self-support but may need guidance and assistance when under unusual social or economic stress.
Moderate	Can talk or learn to communicate; poor social awareness; fair motor development; profits from training in self-help; can be managed with moderate supervision.	Can profit from training in social and occupational skills; unlikely to progress beyond second grade level in academic subjects; may learn to travel alone in familiar places. ("Trainable")	May achieve self-maintenance in unskilled work under sheltered conditions; needs supervision and guidance when under mild social or economic stress.
Severe	Poor motor development; speech is minimal; generally unable to profit from training in self-help; little or no communication skills.	Can talk or learn to communicate; can be trained in elemental health habits; profits from systematic habit training.	May contribute partially to self-maintenance under complete supervision; can develop self-protection skills to a minimal useful level in controlled environment.
Profound	Gross retardation; minimal capacity for functioning in sensorimotor areas; needs nursing care.	Some motor development present; may respond to minimum or limited training in self-help.	Some motor and speech development; may achieve very limited self-care; needs nursing care.

Adapted from W. Sloan and H. Birch, "A rationale for degree of retardation," *American Journal of Mental Deficiency* 60 (1955), pp. 258–264. Used with permission of the publisher and authors.

Farber 1968; U.S. Office of Education 1971; Dunn 1973

tally retarded.* The U.S. Office of Education* offers a 2.3 percent estimate, with 0.3 percent viewed as trainable and 2 percent as educable. Dunn* suggests a maximum prevalence rate of 2 percent of the school population.

Kirk 1972

Kirk* suggests that in an average community for each 1,000 school-age children approximately 25 will be educable mentally retarded, four will be trainable, and one will be a totally dependent child. The actual number of children identified as mildly (educable) mentally retarded will vary considerably across communities which differ in socioeconomic conditions.

Dunn 1973; Heber 1970

As socioeconomic conditions become worse, the number of children identified as mildly retarded increases sharply.*

Characteristics: Mildly Retarded

Performance on appropriate intelligence tests yields IQ score between 50–55 and 75–80 (precise range dependent upon specific definition followed).

Academic progress expected to be between one-half and four-fifths of that made by the average child during an academic year; does not begin to acquire basic skills in reading, writing, spelling, and arithmetic until he is from eight to eleven years of age.

Optimum academic achievement level ranges from third to seventh grade.

The child, significantly behind others in his grade level (based on the chronological age placement) in reading, writing, arithmetic, and other subjects, will fall further behind his classmates each successive year.

Of children classified as mildly retarded for special education purposes, (1) about 10 percent either will have neurological impairment and/or be multiply handicapped and represent families from all strata of society, (2) about 90 percent will come from poverty backgrounds characterized by an intellectually nonstimulating environment and representing Anglo, black, and bilingual slum subgroups.

Speech defects are more prevalent than in general school population.

Retarded oral language development will become increasingly serious as the child grows older.

Mildly retarded children placed in the regular grades will have difficulty with social acceptance.

The child is likely to develop characteristics of short attention span, low frustration tolerance, disinterest in academic subjects, and the like if exposed to an academic program which results in excessive failure.

The child is likely to exhibit motivational characteristics which, unless individually programmed, interfere with successful school progress.

Educational Provisions

Mainstreaming in the regular class with assistance by an itinerant or resource teacher

Self-contained special classes in which the child (1) spends the entire day or (2) is integrated with regular students in some nonacademic areas for part of the day

Residential schools for severely disturbed, delinquent, or multihandicapped.

Characteristics: Moderately and Severely Retarded

Performance on intelligence tests yields IQ scores in the 20 to 25 percent range

Develops at a rate of one-fifth to one-half that of the normal child

Will be semidependent throughout life

Can learn basic self-care skills and to adjust socially to family and neighborhood

Sensory defects and physical-motor impairments common

May learn basic functional skills in reading and arithmetic

Mental retardation associated with a wide range of medical conditions

May become economically useful in the home or sheltered environment

Educational Provisions

Self-contained classes and schools in which the child remains for the entire day, including public and private preschools

Residential schools in which the child lives

Sheltered workshops for the older adolescent and adult

Comprehensive community centers which provide a full range of diagnostic, day-care, residential care, and sheltered work services.

SUMMARY

This chapter has provided a brief description of the categories of exceptional children for which special education services are provided. As noted, the most prevalent educational provision is the self-contained special class organized around various types or categories of children.

Although systems that provide services to children on the basis of gross categories of differences or disabilities obviously have some merit, these have severe limitations when viewed from the individual child's perspective. Most categories are described by negative labels. Such systems are relatively insensitive to the rapid changes that take place in children. They represents "types" of children. Even the quantitative system represented by Quay (1972) results in placement of the child in one major category of disorder.

Children are assigned to a major or dominant category of pathology. A child who does not fit one of the categories may experience difficulty in obtaining adequate educational services. The writer recently witnessed such a consequence. A seven-year-old child with severe learning difficulties was denied specialized educational services because he was too bright to qualify for services for the "mentally retarded," too emotionally and behaviorally stable to qualify for individualized assistance provided for the "emotionally disturbed," and too young to meet the criterion of "two years delayed in academic achievement" to qualify as a "learning disabilities" child. The North Carolina Study Commission for Emotionally Disturbed Children ("Who Speaks for Children" 1971), as another example, reports an incident in which a child was denied services for the retarded because he demonstrated hearing loss, was turned away from classes for the deaf because he had emotional difficulties, and from classes for the emotionally disturbed because he had cognitive deficits.

Although assignment to some categories does provide general predictive information (e.g., a child classified as "mental retardation—severe" would not be expected to learn as rapidly as a child of typical cognitive skills), the negative aspects of such classification far outweigh the possible value.

The writer is in complete agreement with Hobbs (1975) that, for the purpose of effective individualized educational programming, conventional "categories, and labels and procedures for arriving at them, are inadequate. They are imprecise: they say too little, and they say too much. They suggest only vaguely the kind of help a child may need, and they tend to describe conditions in negative terms" (p. 102). Other problems inherent in the category approach are discussed in the following chapter.

REFERENCES

Bateman, B. D. Visually handicapped children. In N. G. Haring and R. L. Schiefelbusch (Eds.) *Methods in Special Education.* New York: McGraw-Hill, 1967.

Bower, E. *Early Identification of Emotionally Handicapped Children in School.* (2nd Ed.) Springfield: Charles C. Thomas, 1969.

Bower, E. M. Mental health. In R. Ebel (Ed.) *Encyclopedia of Educational Research.* (4th Ed.) New York: Macmillan, 1970. Pp. 811–828.

Dunn, L. M. (Ed.) *Exceptional Children in the Schools: Special Education in Transition.* (2nd Ed.) New York: Holt, Rinehart & Winston, 1973.

Education of the Gifted. *Fifty-seventh Yearbook of the National Society for the Study of Education,* Part 2. Chicago: University of Chicago Press, 1958.

Farber, B. *Mental Retardation.* Boston: Houghton Mifflin, 1968.

Fliegler, L. A., and Bish, C. E. Summary of research on the academically talented student. *Review of Educational Research,* 1959, 29, 408–450.

Gleason, G., and Haring, N. Learning disabilities. In N. G. Haring (Ed.) *Behavior of Exceptional Children.* Columbus, Ohio: Charles E. Merrill, 1974. Pp. 217–252.

Graubard, P. S. Children with behavioral disabilities. In L. M. Dunn (Ed.) *Exceptional Children in the Schools: Special Education in Transition.* (2nd Ed.) New York: Holt, Rinehart & Winston, 1973. Pp. 245–295.

Grossman, H. J. (Ed.) *Manual on Terminology and Classification in Mental Retardation.* Baltimore: Garamond-Pridemark, 1973.

Haring, N. G. (Ed.) *Behavior of Exceptional Children: An Introduction to Special Education.* Columbus, Ohio: Charles E. Merrill, 1974.

Harley, R. K., Jr. Children with visual disabilities. In L. M. Dunn (Ed.) *Exceptional Children in the Schools: Special Education in Transition.* (2nd Ed.) New York: Holt, Rinehart & Winston, 1973. Pp. 413–466.

Heber, R. *Epidemiology of Mental Retardation.* Springfield, Ill.: Charles C. Thomas, 1970.

Hewett, F. M., and Forness, S. R. *Education of Exceptional Learners.* Boston: Allyn and Bacon, 1974.

Hobbs, N. *The Futures of Children.* San Francisco: Jossey-Bass, 1975.

Hull, F. M., and Hull, M. E. Children with oral communication disabilities. In L. M. Dunn (Ed.) *Exceptional Children in the Schools: Special Education in Transition.* (2nd Ed.) New York: Holt, Rinehart & Winston, 1973. Pp. 299–350.

Kirk, S. A. The Illinois Test of Psycholinguistic Abilities: Its origin and implications. In J. Hellmuth (Ed.) *Learning Disorders.* Vol. 3. Seattle: Special Child Publications, 1968.

Kirk, S. A. *Educating Exceptional Children.* (2nd Ed.) Boston: Houghton Mifflin, 1972.

McLean, J. Language development and communication. In N. G. Haring (Ed.) *Behavior of Exceptional Children.* Columbus, Ohio: Charles E. Merrill, 1974. Pp. 449–492.

Marland, S. P. *Education of the Gifted and Talented.* Washington, D.C.: U.S. Office of Education, 1972.

Martinson, R. A. Children with superior cognitive abilities. In L. M. Dunn (Ed.) *Exceptional Children in the Schools: Special Education in Transition.* (2nd Ed.) New York: Holt, Rinehart & Winston, 1973. Pp. 191–244.

Myklebust, H. R. Psychoneurological learning disorders in children. In S. A. Kirk and W. Becker (Eds.) *Conference on Children with Minimal Brain Impairment.* Urbana, Ill.: University of Illinois, 1963.

National Advisory Committee on Handicapped Children. *Special Education for Handicapped Children.* First Annual Report. Washington, D.C.: U.S. Department of Health, Education, and Welfare, January 31, 1968.

National Society for the Prevention of Blindness. *NSPB Fact Book: Estimated Statistics on Blindness and Visual Problems.* New York: NSPB, 1966.

Pate, J. E. Emotionally disturbed and socially maladapted children. In L. M. Dunn (Ed.) *Exceptional Children in the Schools.* New York: Holt, Rinehart & Winston, 1963.

Peterson, D. Educable mentally retarded. In N. G. Haring (Ed.) *Behavior of Exceptional Children.* Columbus, Ohio: Charles E. Merrill, 1974. Pp. 295–374.

Quay, H. C. Patterns of aggression, withdrawal, and immaturity. In H. C. Quay and J. S. Werry (Eds.) *Psychopathological Disorders of Childhood.* New York: John Wiley & Sons, 1972. Pp. 1–29.

Schultz, E. W., Hirsharen, A., Manton, A., and Henderson, R. Special education for the emotionally disturbed. *Exceptional Children,* 1971, 38, 313–320.

Silverman, R. Education of the deaf. In L. E. Travis (Ed.) *Handbook of Speech Pathology.* New York: Appleton-Century-Crofts, 1957.

Sloan, W., and Birch, H. A rationale for degree of retardation. *American Journal of Mental Deficiency,* 1955, 60, 258–264.

Sumption, M. R., and Luecking, E. M. *Education of the Gifted.* New York: Ronald Press, 1960.

Telford, C. W., and Sawrey, J. M. *The Exceptional Individual.* (2nd Ed.) Englewood Cliffs, N.J.: Prentice-Hall, 1972.

U.S. Office of Education. Estimated number of handicapped children in the United States, 1971–72. Washington D.C.: U.S. Office of Education, 1971.

Van Riper, C. *Speech Correction: Principles and Methods.* (5th Ed.) Englewood Cliffs, N.J.: Prentice-Hall, 1972.

Wepman, J.M., Cruickshank, W.M., Deutsch, C.P., Morency, A. and Strother, C. P. Learning disabilities. In. N. Hobbs (Ed.) *Issues in the Classification of Children.* Vol. 1. San Francisco: Jossey-Bass, 1975.

Who Speaks for Children? The Prime Recommendations of the North Carolina Study Commission for Emotionally Disturbed Children—An Advocacy Commission for Children. *Popular Government,* 1971, 37, 12–19.

Wilson, M. I. Children with crippling and health disabilities. In L. M. Dunn (Ed.) *Exceptional Children in the Schools: Special education in Transition.* (2nd Ed.) New York: Holt, Rinehart & Winston, 1973. Pp. 467–532.

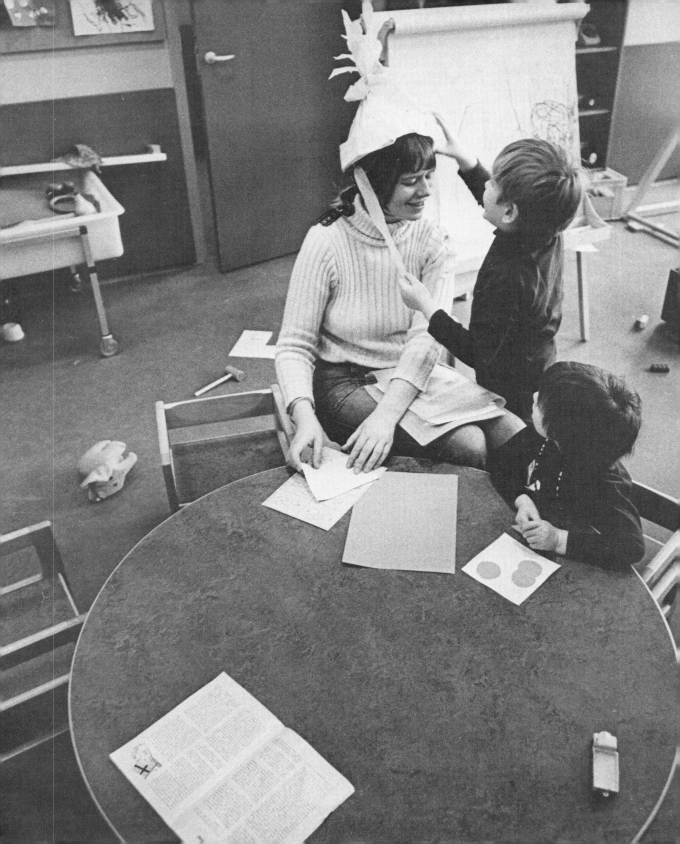

3

Evaluation of the Category Approach

The category approach to classification and special education placement, as noted in Chapter 1, raises some critical issues relative to its effects and effectiveness. These issues revolve around (1) the effects of classification with disability labels derived from an internal-deviancy model, (2) the subsequent practices associated with the labels provided children, and (3) the adequacy of the ATI (aptitude treatment interaction) assumption which underlies category-defined special education programs.

As noted earlier, the internal-deviancy attitude places the blame on the child for any unusual learning and/or behavior difficulties which he may experience in the school environment. The child has difficulty because *he is* mentally retarded, or *has* a language disorder, or *is* emotionally disturbed, or *is* blind. The regular educational environment is seldom implicated. If the child cannot adapt to the regular education requirements, he then is deviant, and the source of his difficulty must be diagnosed in order to correctly place him in a special program designed to meet his disability needs.

This type of attitude led Knoblock,* a leader in education of children who demonstrate behavior difficulties, to state, "School agents frequently believe that the child is doing things to the environment rather than acknowledging the reciprocal impact of school practices on the child" (p. 567), and to raise the provocative question, "Have we redefined emotional disturbance in terms of what the school can and cannot tolerate without looking inward to examine the abrasive characteristics of our schools" (p. 567)? Adelman,* in offering an alternative to the "disordered child" model of learning disabilities, stresses "that a given youngster's success or failure in school is a function of the interaction between his strengths, weaknesses, and limitations and the specific classroom situational factors he encoun-

Knoblock 1971

Adelman 1971

49

ters, including individual differences among teachers and differing approaches to instruction" (p. 529).

Rubin and Balow 1971

Rubin and Balow* suggest that there is "a need for diagnostic and remedial procedures directed toward school systems at least equivalent to those directed toward school children" (p. 299). However, the methods of providing school experiences and the content of the educational experiences to which the child has been exposed and in which his difficulties become apparent are seldom evaluated, dissected, assessed, or reviewed in an effort to determine the relevance of various components to the difficulties presented by a specific child or group of children. This is true even though there is strong support for the statement by Glasser* that "there are factors inherent within the education system itself that not only cause many school problems but that accentuate the problems a child may bring to school" (p. 8). Holt,* Illich,* Karier et al.,* and Silberman,* all active critics of general education in this country, heartily agree with Glasser.

Glasser 1969

Holt 1969, 1972; Illich 1970; Karier et al. 1973; Silberman 1970

EFFECTS OF LABELING AND SPECIAL CLASS PLACEMENT

There is considerable and increasing disagreement over the merits of category-based special education practices as well as concern about the underlying purposes of such a separated approach to education of children who pose problems for the regular education program. Although minor dissatisfaction had been raised previously, this has become more frequent and widespread since the now classic Dunn* position paper in which he questioned the justification of special education for the "mildly retarded" child.*

Dunn 1968; Bartel and Guskin 1971; Christoplos and Renz 1969; Glasser 1969; Quay 1968; Reynolds and Balow 1972

Objections to Category-based Special Education

The following are some of the major objections raised over categorical placement in self-contained special classes of children labeled as mentally retarded. These objections, many of which were discussed by Bruininks and Rynders,* are representative of the objections voiced against segregated placement of other children with other category labels.

Bruininks and Rynders 1971

Special class placement isolates exceptional children from normal classroom peers.

Special class placement results in stigmatizing the exceptional child, resulting in a loss of self-esteem and lowered acceptance by other children.   Bloom et al.* have suggested:

Bloom et al. 1971

The result of this method of categorizing individuals is to convince some
... that they are deficient, bad, and undesirable. It is not likely that this
continued labeling has beneficial consequences for the individual's educational development, and it is likely that it has an unfavorable influence on
many a student's self-concept. To be physically (and legally) imprisoned in a
school system for ten or twelve years and to receive negative classifications
repeatedly for this period of time must have a detrimental effect on personality and character development. [p. 7]

**There is little evidence to support the practice of ability grouping of
children.**   Dunn* notes: "From more recent U.S. studies, it would appear
that *homogeneous grouping works to the disadvantage of slower children
in most of today's schools*" (p. 45).

Dunn 1973

**Mildly retarded children make as much or more academic progress
in regular classrooms as they do in special classrooms.**   Bartel and Guskin* indicate that "attaching the label of mental retardation to an individual and segregating him in a special class with other individuals of
similar evaluation has yet to be shown to result in unique social, educational, or vocational advantage for that individual" (p. 104).

Bartel and Guskin 1971

**There are few if any reliable and educationally relevant differences
between different categories of children nor commonalities within children comprising specific categories.**   In illustration, Haring and Ridgeway* found few common deficits in children showing learning difficulties
at the kindergarten level. They favored "individual assessment, individual
programming, and individual teaching of individual behaviors" (p. 393).
O'Grady* found that elementary-age children assigned to different classes
for the "learning disabled" and for the "emotionally disturbed" demonstrated comparable deficits in overall psycholinguistic abilities but
no common deficits associated with the different educational placements.
He found that psycholinguistic abilities were more related to intelligence
test scores and socioeconomic status than to educational placement
or diagnosis.

*Haring and Ridgeway
1967*

O'Grady 1974

**There is little point in investing further energy in improving segre-
gated special classes, since this arrangement poorly serves the social and
educational needs of children.**   Vacc* and McKinnon,* as examples,
report that children who spent time in special programs for the emotionally
disturbed were no different on follow-up on measures of academic and
social skills from children with similar difficulties who had remained in
the regular classes. Sabatino* states: "There is no instructional homo-
geneity in most classes of EMRs, emotionally disturbed, and brain-
damaged children. There are few instructional similarities in classes for the

*Vacc 1972; McKinnon
1969*

Sabatino 1972

visually or hearing impaired, and it is ludicrous to create a special class for these or any other categorical type of handicapped children and view it as an all-encompassing learning center" (p. 337).

Special class arrangements inappropriately place the responsibility for academic failure on children rather than upon schools and teachers.

The very existence of special classes encourages the misplacement of many children, particularly children from minority groups.   Rivers et al.* speak of the "six-hour mentally retarded black child" created by inappropriate testing practices which result in the child's placement in "special classes" from 9:00 to 3:00 daily.

Rivers et al. 1975

Special class placement is inconsistent with the tenets of a democratic philosophy of education because it isolates exceptional from normal children and vice versa.   Categorical removal of the child from the educational mainstream may not only produce significant damage to the child but also usually represents an active infringement on his constitutional rights of equal and appropriate educational opportunity.*

Abeson et al. 1975; Hall 1970; Kirp et al. 1975; Ross et al. 1971; Weintraub 1972

Such diagnostic and related program placement practices may contribute to and perhaps even create many of the problems these practices were designed to alleviate.   Ullman and Krasner* have noted, "Once the diagnosis has been arrived at there is a presumption that all people so classified share basic common traits in terms of underlying illness, treatment of choice and prognosis" (p. 9). Reynolds and Balow* similarly suggest: "There is a tendency to stereotype or to ascribe characteristics of the group to individuals. The practice, crude at best, is frequently in error and prejudicial to the interests of the individuals" (p. 357). There is real danger of overgeneralization—of assuming that the person so labeled has characteristics other than those involved in arriving at the diagnosis. In this vein, Stuart* commented: "Once a negative label has been applied, there is a clear and present danger that the person so identified will be the victim of additional negative inference solely on the basis of his having been designated as a deviant, without reference either to the behavior which culminated in his having been labeled or to any subsequent actions on his part" (p. 104).

Ullman and Krasner 1965

Reynolds and Balow 1972

Stuart 1970

As an illustration, children with scores on intelligence tests below a designated level are viewed as slow learners or mentally handicapped. Characteristics other than those measured by the intelligence tests are commonly ascribed to such children. This is evident in the statement presented in a recent book written for school psychologists,* that "mentally retarded children, for example, have short attention spans, low frustration tolerance, and limited motivation" (p. 39). There is no question that

Herron et al. 1970

some children classified as mentally retarded do have the characteristics noted, just as do many other children not so classified. At the same time, there are many children labeled as mentally retarded who *do not* exhibit short attention spans, low frustration tolerance, and limited motivation.

Once a child is labeled and segregated in one manner or another, it is difficult for him to regain his original status of being "normal" like everyone else.   "The category labels tend to become stigmatic and to be attached indelibly to the individual, often resulting in scapegoating" (p. 357).* Rivers et al.* have commented, "Labels are not merely psychologically harmful badges which are attached to an individual at one point in time and later removed; for black children they are highly functional in every sense. They often determine an individual's destiny" (p. 215). Empey,* in discussing the functional value of labeling an adolescent as delinquent, suggested that "the labeling process is often a means of isolating offenders from rather than integrating them in, effective participation in such major societal institutions as schools, businesses, unions, churches, and political organizations" (pp. 4–5).

Reynolds and Balow 1972; Rivers et al. 1975

Empey 1967

The internal-deviancy connotation of category labels sets into action a self-fulfilling prophecy.   Most labels and descriptive terms associated with models of human functioning which focus on positive or competency features (open education, child-centered, or humanistic behavioral model, for instance) are satisfying and enhancing both to the child so described and to others who respond socially to this child. Such terms could include: pretty, friendly, intelligent, athletic, smart, musical, helpful, good student, or artistic. Compare these with the labels associated with the deviancy model. Try to imagine a child being proud of such labels as slow learner, mentally retarded, emotionally disturbed, language disordered, or learning disabled. These labels are nothing short of derogatory. Reynolds and Balow* have commented: "The field of special education . . . has tended not only to list various categories of exceptional children but to use negatively loaded terminology to do so: the mentally *retarded*, the visually *handicapped*, the hearing *impaired*, the emotionally *disturbed*, and the socially *maladjusted*" (p. 357).

Reynolds and Balow 1972

Children frequently become what they are called. Rivers et al.* have emphasized the effects of such labels on the lives of children in their statement: "Any attempt to convey in words the brutal impact that unfair and unfortunate labeling practices have had on the lives of black children is a depressing but necessary venture. The deleterious effects of traditional labeling practices on the progress through life of black children have been manifested socially, economically, educationally, politically, and, most important, within the emotional and cognitive systems of our children" (pp. 213–214).

Rivers et al. 1975

Such negative labels seemingly influence the social feedback that others provide children so labeled. This social feedback by peers and adults is frequently of a sort that has few positive features and consists of pity, ridicule, low expectations, isolation, rejection, and overpoliteness. "People who work with exceptional children may associate the categories with negative expectations and then carry them into their relationship with the children and into curriculum planning. A degree of diagnosogenic or prophecy fulfilling inadequacy in the child's development may result" (p. 357).*

Reynolds and Balow 1972; Meacham and Wiesen 1969

Meacham and Wiesen* suggested: "The diagnosis of 'mental retardation' frequently sets into action a self-fulfilling prophecy in which the individual so labeled is excluded from an opportunity to remedy his educational deficits" (p. 167). Dunn* noted: "We must expect that labeling a child 'handicapped' reduces the teacher's expectancy for him to succeed" (p. 9). Beez* and Haskett,* as examples, provide data in support of this prophecy fulfillment notion. Beez reported that children attending a Head Start program learned a cognitive task with significantly greater ease when teachers were led to expect good learning than when teachers had been given unfavorable expectation about their pupils. Haskett reports that groups of children attending classes for the mentally retarded made different performance gains, even though matched on initial ability and performance level, as a result of different information provided teachers about the potential of each child. Children represented as having more potential made greater gains than others who were labeled as having less potential for performance gains.

Dunn 1968

Beez 1968; Haskett 1968

Brophy and Good* noted that teachers were more likely to socially reinforce more correct responses and less likely to criticize incorrect responses of high achieving children than was true of low achieving children. It was also noted that in relating to incorrect responses of children identified as "high achievers," teachers were more likely to repeat or rephrase the problem and less likely to supply answers or to ask another child to answer in comparison to her reactions to "low achievers." Kester and Letchworth* and Rothbart et al.* also noted that more positive attention was provided to high- than to low-expectation students.

Brophy and Good 1970

Kester and Letchworth 1972; Rothbart et al. 1971

Foster et al. 1975

Foster et al.* demonstrated that the negative expectations held by teachers may be formed early in their college training experience. These educators found that undergraduate students (enrolled in an introductory course in education of the emotionally disturbed) have preconceived stereotypical expectancies of children labeled as emotionally disturbed. Groups of students viewed the same child engaging in a variety of academic and related activities. Students in one group had been informed that they were observing an emotionally disturbed child, while the other group was informed that the child was considered normal. The child was provided more negative ratings on a behavior rating scale by the group viewing him as emotionally disturbed. The writers suggested "I wouldn't have seen it if I hadn't believed it."

These studies support the notion that teachers do have different expectations for children (based on a variety of factors) and that these expectations are reflected in their teaching styles. Children respond differentially to differences in teacher behavior in a manner that is consistent with this teacher behavior. As a result, the academic, motivational, emotional, attitudinal, and other personal-social characteristics of some children are enhanced and in other children are depressed.

When children with differences are labeled and segregated from the regular classes, the children left in the mainstream have little opportunity to form desirable attitudes toward them. Unfamiliarity with the more appropriate characteristics of children with exceptional learning and behavioral characteristics and the absence of an opportunity for frequent social contact and interaction can only result in biased responding toward the child with exceptional characteristics. This is supported by Allport's* theory that separateness among groups leads to exaggeration of differences.

Allport 1961

Hobbs* emphasized, "We strongly believe that normal children of all ages should have an opportunity to know handicapped children sufficiently well to appreciate them as people. If such experiences were started early enough and continued under sensitive guidance, the handicapped would no longer be alienated and the lives of the nonhandicapped would be enriched" (p. 197).

Hobbs 1975

Total or partial segregation of children may greatly reduce the likelihood that they will attain those normal social experiences critical to the development of appropriate social and emotional skills. Christoplos and Renz* have argued that "the adjustment of the exceptional child to the normal world is unlikely to occur unless he has frequent and familiar interaction with it" (p. 376).

Christoplos and Renz 1969

Additional Effects of Labeling and Homogeneous Groupings

In spite of the theoretic and philosophic desirability of various types of heterogeneous group experiences, it is not unusual for disruptive children to be placed together with other children who display disruptive behaviors. Children with socially inadequate behaviors are placed with other children with socially inadequate behaviors. The problems of learning and expressing appropriate emotional and social behaviors are greatly increased in such settings. Intellectually limited children with poor study skills are placed with other children with similar characteristics. Thus, unless highly individualized learning experiences are provided, the child is quite likely to learn additional inappropriate ways of behaving. The perceptually handicapped, hyperactive, and highly distractible child is placed with peers with similar learning and behavior difficulties. In such settings, peers frequently exert powerful social reinforcement influence

Bandura 1969

Gampel et al. 1974

Gardner 1971

Bartel and Guskin 1971

Sutherland and Cressey 1960

Dunn 1968

over the behavior of their fellow students. Additionally, principles of observational learning* suggest that homogeneous groups of children with inadequate or inappropriate modes of behavior significantly compound the child's difficulty since he is likely to imitate the inappropriate behavior patterns of peers. Gampel et al.* reported that "mildly retarded" children in segregated special classes in middle-class suburban schools exhibit a higher incidence of hostile and aggressive behavior and more restlessness than do comparable children who either had been reintegrated into regular classes or who were never labeled nor removed from the mainstream educational setting. These writers suggested that these "mildly retarded" children were more apt to view their normal class peers as more competent and thus were more likely to imitate their appropriate modeled behaviors.

Gardner* has noted: "The practice of placing a group of highly inadequate retarded clients together in a program could not be recommended as there would be no suitable behavior models . . . Such a procedure merely produces the strengthening through various modeling effects of the very ineffective behaviors which are in need of change" (p. 135).

Further, Bartel and Guskin* have suggested: "This treatment appears self-defeating when one considers that their problem might in fact derive from having lived in an emotionally, socially, or intellectually inadequate enivronment . . . If children learn from their peers—and most persons agree that they do—then placing deviant children with others of their own kind is disastrous for they will learn more delinquent, disturbing, or retarded behavior" (p. 83).

In the same vein, Sutherland and Cressey* hypothesize that much delinquent behavior is the result of excessive association with persons exhibiting such behavior patterns. Dunn* also agrees that if homogeneous groups of children are formed on the basis of learning and behavior difficulties, this actually tend to work to the disadvantage of those children who are slow learners and who live in underprivileged homes. In commenting about the effects on children of disability labels and the subsequent program placements, he suggests:

> Certainly none of these labels are badges of distinction. Separating a child from other children in his neighborhood—or removing him from the regular classroom for therapy or special class placement—probably has a serious debilitating effect upon his self-image. . . . While much more research is needed, we cannot ignore the evidence that removing a handicapped child from the regular grades for special education probably contributes significantly to his feelings of inferiority and problems of acceptance. [p. 9]

Meyerowitz 1965

Meyerowitz 1967

Meyerowitz* has presented data which suggest that after one year in special classes, feelings of self-derogation increased in a group of educable mentally retarded pupils. More recently, Meyerowitz* suggested that special class placement hindered, rather than assisted, such a child to adjust to his neighborhood peers.

Bartel and Guskin* further support the disturbing possiblity that the special treatment itself, along with the segregation and isolation that is involved, may contribute significantly to the difficulties which some children experience. They indicate that handicapping could be reduced (1) by minimizing the segregation of the disabled child and (2) by avoiding those treatment procedures which have not been demonstrated to be effective.

Bartel and Guskin 1971

Christoplos and Renz* are even more inclusive in their statement: "Amorphous good intentions have often substituted for lack of more objective accomplishments. Throughout the substantial number of years special education programs have been in operation, research findings have consistently indicated no differences in performance between those placed in special classes and those placed in regular classes" (p. 371).

Christoplos and Renz 1969

In view of these and similar data concerning the possible damaging effects of labeling and segregation, Bartel and Guskin* raise the most provocative and disquieting possibility: "Society, of course, may be forced to recognize (or admit) that its goal is not individual benefit of the handicapped but comfort or protection of others" (p. 104). In a similar vein, Christoplos and Renz* comment more pointedly: "That segregation is for the good of the exceptional, rather than for the comfort of the normal population, may be a deluding rationalization" (p. 376).

Bartel and Guskin 1971

Christoplos and Renz 1969

Concluding Remarks Concerning
Labeling and Homogeneous Groupings

It is not being suggested that the label itself, nor the process of arriving at the label, in isolation represents major critical factors underlying the difficulties of children with exceptional learning and behavior characteristics. Obviously the child's learning and behavior characteristics and the environments in which these developed (which in turn resulted in the labeling) had created the chronic failure and resulting negative emotional impact long before the label was finally awarded. The effects of a diagnostic label per se cannot be isolated from the child's history of experiences and the effects which these have on the present reactions of children at the time the label is awarded. These characteristics interact with whatever effects the label may have, and both in turn interact with the reactions of others to the behavior of the child and his label.

It is being suggested, however, even though Guskin et al.* and MacMillan et al.* note the extreme difficulty in isolating the precise negative effects of diagnostic labeling, that the label, and practices resulting from the label, are *possible additional negative factors in the child's experience that he could well live without.* The writer is in agreement with Guskin's* statement that "the labeling controversy is in actuality a political argument between those who support the current system of special educa-

Guskin et al. 1975
MacMillan et al. 1974

Guskin 1974

tion and psychological diagnosis as a constructive and altruistic arrangement and those who wish to break up that system because they see it as oppressive and destructive" (p. 263). The interested reader should consult Davis,* Mercer,* and Rowitz* for additional viewpoints concerning labeling of deviancy.

Davis 1972; Mercer 1973; Rowitz 1974

Neither is it being suggested that mere attendance in any specific type of classroom arrangement is the primary cause of personal or social difficulties nor that attendance in any contrasting specific arrangement would ipso facto avoid problems of the kind described by Meyerowitz.* Remaining in the regular classes, for example, would not categorically prevent such difficulties. Martin* has noted that attempts at providing an adequate education

Meyerowitz 1967

Martin 1972

> for handicapped children by integrating them into regular education programs will not succeed without modification in the system. Millions of handicapped children are now in regular classrooms, and too frequently their fate is failure, frustration, and social isolation . . . . Our societal mechanisms for excluding handicapped children from schools, from transportation, from public parks, playgrounds, and buildings, from jobs, and from social contacts have worked all too well. This lack of familiarity and confidence in human relations with handicapped persons means that many teachers will need special assistance if they are to interact successfully to help handicapped children learn. [p. 520]

Bruininks et al. 1974; Gottlieb 1974; Gottlieb and Budoff 1973; Gottlieb and Davis 1973; Peterson 1974; Sheare 1974; Strichart 1974; Strichart and Gottlieb 1975

Thus, unless the social and educational structures of school programs are adapted to the individual characteristics, placement in any particular types of classroom may well *contribute to* the child's difficulties. A series of studies by Gottlieb and others on the social relationships between the "mentally retarded" and nonretarded peers in the regular classroom has emphasized this.*

Summary

Mere placement in any type of class arrangement, including the mainstream class, will not ipso facto alleviate problems. Nor will the placement or removal of deviancy labels in isolation create or alleviate negative consequences of the characteristics which resulted in the label. But consistent with the philosophic and theoretical position of the humanistic behavioral approach, and in view of some compelling empirical data relative to social learning factors involved in the acquisition and maintenance of behavioral, attitudinal, and emotional characteristics, it is concluded: (1) Deviancy labels contribute nothing of positive value to the child, (2) The child cannot learn the competencies needed to adapt to a "normalized" environment without experiencing it, and (3) The normalized environment cannot adapt to the characteristics of children with exceptional learning and behavior characteristics without direct exposure to these.

The child with exceptional learning and behavior characteristics not only must learn to adopt those behavioral characteristics which others will find valuable, but others also must learn to accept and interact with, in a positive manner, behavioral and physical characteristics noticeably different from their own. This can be accomplished only in educational environment designed to support these new modes of social acceptance and interaction. The educational philosophy of the school program, the attitudes and competencies of individual teachers, and the attitudes of all children in the school/social environments must be positive for the optimal acceptance and development of all children to become a reality.*

Hobbs 1975; MacMillan et al. 1976; Martin 1972

APTITUDE TREATMENT INTERACTION ASSUMPTION REMAINS AN ISSUE

To summarize the previous discussion, there presently is little support for the assumption that there is a relationship between the global child features used to diagnose and classify children into categories and the effectiveness of the various category-based special education programs which have been devised. Thus, in terms of differential effectiveness, there is minimal if any interaction between category of child and category of program. Additional developments within special education, which represent variations of an ability-training model, however, continue to highlight the aptitude treatment interaction assumption. Instead of assuming an interaction between gross categories of exceptionality and related programs, the new variation assumes an interaction between various perceptual and psycholinguistic disabilities and specific individualized educational programs designed to accommodate or to remediate these.

Diagnostic-Prescriptive Teaching

After the relative ineffectiveness of the category approach to education of children with learning and behavior differences became apparent, a new approach called *diagnostic-prescriptive teaching* began to evolve. Focusing on and prescriptively dealing with individual child characteristics were concepts well known to remedial education and medical practice.* Ysseldyke and Salvia* describe diagnostic-prescriptive teaching as "an attempt to identify the most effective instructional strategies for children who differ on any number of variables believed to be related to academic learning. Educators and psychologists believe that some children learn best under one instructional strategy (particular materials, teaching techniques, methods of content presentation, and reinforcers) while other children learn best when another instructional strategy is employed" (p. 181). This diagnostic-prescriptive teaching movement gained tremendous momentum with the development of the youngest area

Peter 1965; Ysseldyke and Salvia 1974

Bannatyne 1968;
Bateman 1967; Frostig
1967; Johnson and
Myklebust 1967; Kirk
and Kirk 1971

Kirk 1966
Frostig et al. 1964

Ysseldyke and Salvia
1974

of special education, that of "learning disabilities." Educators with a variety of theoretical concepts about underlying disabilities and process dysfunctions all call for specific diagnosis of a child's strengths and weaknesses and translation of these into teaching prescriptions for remediating the weaknesses and developing the strengths.* A number of diagnostic tests and related teaching programs have appeared within the last decade. The Illinois Test of Psycholinguistic Abilities (ITPA)* and the Frostig Developmental Test of Visual Perception (DTVP)* represent the most widely used of these.

As noted, *the diagnostic-prescriptive teaching approach, just as was true of the more general category approach, is based on an aptitude treatment interaction assumption.* In fact, due to the emphasis on identification of a child's numerous strengths and weaknesses, a number of other assumptions become apparent. These, enumerated by Ysseldyke and Salvia* are as follows:

Assumption 1   Children with learning difficulties are characterized by learning-related strengths and weaknesses.

Assumption 2   These identified strengths and weaknesses are functionally related to the child's aquisition of academic skills.

Assumption 3   There are assessment procedures available which result in reliable and valid measures of these strengths and weaknesses.

Assumption 4   There is a relationship between these strengths and weaknesses and the relative effectiveness of various instructional programs (materials, procedures). This represents the ATI assumption and is crucial to the entire diagnostic-prescriptive teaching approach.

There are two theoretical models which guide the educator in his approach to diagnostic-prescriptive teaching: the *ability-training* model representing the internal-deviancy approach and the *task-analysis* model representing the behavioral approach. Each of these is examined.

Internal-Deviancy Ability-Training Model

The purpose of diagnostic activities in the ability-training model is, first, to identify psycholinguistic, perceptual, cognitive, and/or psychomotor ability (process) strengths and weaknesses and, second, to develop prescriptively-based educational experiences designed to remediate the presumed internal disabilities or dysfunctions. The focus is on *identification* of these internal process variables because the assumption is made that weaknesses in these cause observed difficulties in academic skill development.

The assumption is made that strengths in internal processes or abilities (e.g., perceptual, psycholinguistic) are necessary prerequisites to the effective learning of academic skills. *Yet there is no suitable empirical support for the assumption that training or remediation of presumed perceptual, psycholinguistic, or motoric weaknesses is a necessary prerequisite to academic skill attainment.**

Ysseldyke 1973

Further, recent critical evaluation of psychoeducational assessment procedures associated with the ability-training model *has led to the conclusion that problems of reliability and validity are sufficiently serious to warrant a cautious attitude in making prescriptive decisions about a child's strengths and weaknesses.**

Hammill and Larsen 1974; Hammill and Wiederholt 1973; Sedlak and Weener 1973; Ysseldyke 1973

The ATI assumption associated with the ability-training model—that educational programs prescriptively differentiated on the basis of differential performance on diagnostic measures produce different results—finds little empirical support. *That is, children who earn high scores on certain diagnostic devices do not profit more from one type of instruction in comparison with a child who scores low and who is provided the same type or a different type of instructional program.**

Ysseldyke and Salvia 1974

A recent study illustrates the lack of support for the ATI assumption of the ability-training model to diagnostic-prescriptive teaching. Sabatino and Dorfman* identified two groups of children who differed in terms of perceptual modality strengths and weaknesses. One group of children was characterized by visual strengths and auditory weaknesses and the other by auditory perceptual strengths and visual weaknesses. Children with each combination of strengths and weaknesses were provided reading and arithmetic instructional programs which emphasized the visual perceptual modality or the auditory perceptual modality. No ATI effects were noted. The authors concluded:

Sabatino and Dorfman 1974

> Diagnostic-prescriptive teaching based on measurement of the perceptual modality strengths of educable mentally retarded children may well be a premature endeavor until further observations relating the importance of perceptual modalities to academic learning is better understood for handicapped children. The absence of significant aptitude by treatment interaction in this study suggests that the two curricula approaches used are not superior, one to the other, for educable retarded children with relative measured perceptual strengths or weaknesses. [p. 89]

Task-Analysis Model

The task-analysis model to diagnostic-prescriptive teaching represents the central tactic of the humanistic behavioral approach. The child's behaviors are evaluated along various skill dimensions. These behaviors are viewed as component parts of more complex skills to be acquired. No assumption is made about internal abilities or processes as is done in the ability-training model. The training program provided is designed to improve specific academic skills of the child by directly teaching to the component skills and moving the child along a skill sequence in the direction of the terminal behavior objective. This approach is described in detail in future chapters.

SHORTAGE OF PROGRAM RESOURCES

Kirk 1972

Joint Commission on Mental Health of Children 1970; Cowen and Lorion 1974

Even assuming that category-trained special educators had the necessary critical skills to remediate or otherwise deal successfully with the educational needs of exceptional children and youth, studies have emphasized the tremendous shortage of special personnel to handle learning and adjustment problems of children in the intensive manner called for by these specialized approaches. Kirk* reported that less that 40 percent of children identified as handicapped receive special education services. The Report of the Joint Commission on Mental Health of Children* detailed similar personnel and related program shortages. Cowen and Lorion* emphasize "school mental-health professionals are in short supply everywhere. Thus, identified school maladaptation problems far exceed the professional's ability to deal with them. The serious imbalance between known problems and available resources dictates that conceptual alternatives to traditional school mental-health practices be considered" (p. 187).

AN ALTERNATIVE MODEL

The shortage of personnel coupled with the apparent ineffectiveness of traditionally structured special therapy or education approaches emphasize that alternative means of dealing with the learning and behavior problems of children and youth must be explored. Ideally, these alternative approaches would utilize procedures of early identification of learning and behavior difficulties, both primary and secondary prevention, effective behavior change procedures, as well as the maximum and effective utilization of personnel resources available in the natural environments of the child.

The remainder of this book is devoted to a description of a behavioral approach alternative to the internal deviancy model (1) that has provided impetus to traditional special education practices and (2) that continues to influence the new face of special education, that of ability-training diagnostic-prescriptive teaching.

REFERENCES

Abeson, A., Bolick, N., and Hass, J. A primer on due process: Education decisions for handicapped children. *Exceptional Children,* 1975, 42, 68–75.

Adelman, H. S. The not so specific learning disability population. *Exceptional Children,* 1971, 37, 528–533.

Allport, G. W. *Patterns and Growth in Personality.* New York: Holt, Rinehart & Winston, 1961.

Bandura, A. *Principles of Behavior Modification.* New York: Holt, Rinehart & Winston, 1969.

Bannatyne, A. Diagnosing learning disabilities and writing remedial prescriptions. *Journal of Learning Disabilities,* 1968, 1, 242–249.

Bartel, N. R., and Guskin, S. L. A handicap as a social phenomenon. In W. M. Cruickshank (Ed.) *Psychology of Exceptional Children and Youth.* Englewood Cliffs, N.J.: Prentice-Hall, 1971. Pp. 75–114.

Bateman, B. Three approaches to diagnosis and educational planning for children with learning disabilities. *Academic Therapy Quarterly,* 1967, 3, 11–16.

Beez, W. V. Influence of biased psychological reports on teacher behavior and pupil performance. *Proceedings of the 76th Annual Convention of the American Psychological Association,* 1968. Pp. 605–606.

Bloom, B. S., Hasting, J. T., and Madaus, G. F. *Handbook on Formative and Summative Evaluation of Student Learning.* New York: McGraw-Hill, 1971.

Brophy, J. E., and Good, T. L. Teacher communications of differential expectations for children's classroom performance: Some behavioral data. *Journal of Educational Psychology,* 1970, 61, 365–374.

Bruininks, R. H., and Rynders, J. E. Alternatives to special class placement for educable mentally retarded children. *Focus on Exceptional Children,* 1971, 3, 1–12.

Bruininks, R. H., Rynders, J. E., and Gross, J. C. Social acceptance of mildly retarded pupils in resource rooms and regular classes. *American Journal of Mental Deficiency,* 1974, 78, 377–383.

Christoplos, F., and Renz, P. A critical examination of special education programs. *Journal of Special Education,* 1969, 3, 371–379.

Cowen, E. L., and Lorion, R. P. Which kids are helped? *Journal of Special Education,* 1974, 8, 187–192.

Davis, N. J. Labeling theory in deviance research: A critique and reconsideration. *Sociological Quarterly,* 1972, 13, 447–474.

Dunn, L. M. Special education for the mildly retarded: Is much of it justified? *Exceptional Children,* 1968, 35, 5–22.

Dunn, L. M. (Ed.) *Exceptional Children in the Schools: Special Education in Transition.* (2nd Ed.) New York: Holt, Rinehart & Winston, 1973.

Empey, L. T. *Alternative to Incarceration.* Washington, D.C.: Department of Health, Education and Welfare, Office of Juvenile Delinquency and Youth Development, 1967.

Foster, G. G., Ysseldyke, J. E., and Reese, J. H. "I wouldn't have seen it if I hadn't believed it." *Exceptional Children,* 1975, 41, 469–473.

Frostig, M., Lefever, D. W., and Whittlesey, J. R. B. *The Marianne Frostig Developmental Test of Visual Perception.* Palo Alto, Calif.: Consulting Psychologist Press, 1964.

Gampel, D. H., Gottlieb, J., and Harrison, R. H. Comparison of classroom behavior of special class EMR, integrated EMR, low IQ, and nonretarded children. *American Journal of Mental Deficiency,* 1974, 79, 16–21.

Gardner, W. I. *Behavior Modification in Mental Retardation.* Chicago: Aldine-Atherton, 1971.

Glasser, W. *Schools without Failure.* New York: Harper, 1969.

Gottlieb, J. Attitudes toward retarded children: Effects of labeling and academic performance. *American Journal of Mental Deficiency,* 1974, 79, 268–273.

Gottlieb, J., and Budoff, M. Social acceptability of retarded children in nongraded schools differing in architecture. *American Journal of Mental Deficiency,* 1973, 78, 15–19.

Gottlieb, J., and Davis, J. E. Social acceptance of EMR children during overt behavioral interactions. *American Journal of Mental Deficiency,* 1973, 78, 141–143.

Guskin, S. L. Research on labeling retarded persons: Where do we go from here? *American Journal of Mental Deficiency*, 1974, 79, 263–264.

Guskin, S. L., Bartel, N. R., and MacMillan, D. L. Perspective of the labeled child. In N. Hobbs (Ed.) *Issues in the Classification of Children*. Vol. 2. San Francisco: Jossey-Bass, 1975. Pp. 189–212.

Hall, E. The politics of special education. In *Inequality in Education*. Nos. 3 and 4. Cambridge, Mass.: Harvard Center for Law and Education, 1970. Pp. 17–22.

Hammill, D. D., and Larsen, S. C. The effectiveness of psycholinguistic training. *Exceptional Children*, 1974, 41, 5–15.

Hammill, D. D., and Wiederholt, J. L. Review of the Frostig Visual Perceptual Test and the related training program. In L. Mann and D. A. Sabatino (Eds.) *The First Review of Special Education*. Philadelphia: Journal of Special Education Press, 1973. Pp. 33–48.

Haring, N. G., and Ridgeway, R. W. Early identification of children with learning disabilities. *Exceptional Children*, 1967, 2, 387–395.

Haskett, M.S. An investigation of the relationship between teacher expectancy and pupil achievement in the special education class. Unpublished dissertation, University of Wisconsin, 1968.

Herron, W. G., Green, M., Guild, M., Smith, A., and Kantor, R. E. *Contemporary School Psychology*. Scranton: Intext Educational Publishers, 1970.

Hobbs, N. *The Futures of Children*. San Francisco: Jossey-Bass, 1975.

Holt, J. *The Underachieving School*. New York: Dell Publishing, Co., 1969.

Holt, J. *Freedom and Beyond*. New York: E. P. Dutton, 1972.

Illich, I. *Deschooling Society*. New York: Harper & Row, 1970.

Johnson, D. J., and Myklebust, H. R. *Learning Disabilities: Educational Principles and Practices*. New York: Grune and Stratton, 1967.

Karier, C. J. Violas, P., and Spring, J. *Roots of Crisis: American Education in the Twentieth Century*. Chicago: Rand McNally, 1973.

Kester, S. W., and Letchworth, G. A. Communication of teacher expectations and their effects on achievement and attitudes of secondary school students. *Journal of Educational Research*, 1972, 66, 51–54.

Kirk, S. A. *The Diagnosis and Remediation of Psycholinguistic Disabilities*. Urbana: University of Illinois Press, 1966.

Kirk, S. A. *Educating Exceptional Children*. (2nd Ed.) Boston: Houghton Mifflin, 1972.

Kirk, S. A., and Kirk, W. D. *Psycholinguistic Learning Disabilities: Diagnosis and Remediation*. Chicago: University of Illinois Press, 1971.

Kirp, D. L. Kuriloff, P. J., and Buss, W. G. Legal mandates and organizational change. In N. Hobbs (Ed.) *Issues in the Classification of Children*. Vol. 2. San Francisco: Jossey-Bass, 1975. Pp. 319–382.

Knoblock, P. Psychological considerations of emotionally disturbed children. In W. M. Cruickshank (Ed.) *Psychology of Exceptional Children and Youth*. (3rd Ed.) Englewood Cliffs, N. J.: Prentice-Hall, 1971. Pp. 565–599.

McKinnon, A. A. A follow-up and analysis of the effects of placement in classes for emotionally disturbed children in elementary school. *Dissertation Abstracts*, 1969 (5-A), 1872.

MacMillan, D. L., Jones, R. L., and Aloia G. F. The mentally retarded label: A theoretical analysis and review of reserarch. *American Journal of Mental Deficiency*, 1974, 79, 241–261.

MacMillan, D. L., Jones, R. L., and Meyers, C. E. Mainstreaming the mildly retarded. *Mental Retardation*, 1976, 14, 3–10.

Martin, E. W. Individualism and behaviorism as future trends in educating handicapped children. *Exceptional Children*, 1972, 38, 517–525.

Meacham, M. L., and Wiesen, A. E. *Changing Classroom Behavior: A Manual for Precision Teaching*. Scranton: International Textbook, 1969.

Mercer, J. R. *Labeling the Mentally Retarded*. Berkeley: University of California Press, 1973.

Meyerowitz, J. H. Family background of educable mentally retarded children. In H. Goldstein, J. W. Moss, and L. J. Jordan. *The Efficacy of Special Education Training on the Development of Mentally Retarded Children*. Urbana: University of Illinois Institute for Research and Exceptional Children, 1965. Pp. 152–182.

Meyerowitz, J. H. Peer groups and special classes. *Mental Retardation*, 1967, 5, 5, 23–26.

O'Grady, D. J. Psycholinguistic abilities in learning-disabled, emotionally disturbed, and normal children. *Journal of Special Education,* 1974, 8(2), 157–165.

Peter, L. J. *Prescriptive Teaching.* New York: McGraw-Hill, 1965.

Peterson, G. F. Factors related to the attitudes of nonretarded children toward their EMR peers. *American Journal of Mental Deficiency,* 1974, 79, 412–416.

Quay, H. C. The facets of educational exceptionality: A conceptual framework for assessment, grouping, and instruction. *Exceptional Children,* 1968, 35, 25–32.

Report of the Joint Commission on Mental Health of Children. *Crisis in Child Mental Health: Challenge for the 1970's.* New York: Harper & Row, 1970.

Reynolds, M. C., and Balow, B. Categories and variables in special education. *Exceptional Children,* 1972, 38, 357–366.

Rivers, L. W., Henderson, D. M., Jones, R. L., Lodner, J. A., and Williams, R. L. Mosaic of labels for black children. In N. Hobbs (Ed.) *Issues in the Classification of Children.* Vol. 1. San Francisco: Jossey-Bass, 1975. Pp. 213–245.

Ross, S. L., DeYoung, H. G., and Cohen, J. S. Confrontation: Special education placement and the law. *Exceptional Children,* 1971, 38, 5–12.

Rothbart, M., Dalfen, S., and Barrett, R. Effects of teacher's expectancy on child-teacher interactions. *Journal of Educational Research,* 1971, 62, 49–54.

Rowitz, L. Sociological perspective on labeling. *American Journal of Mental Deficiency,* 1974, 79, 265–267.

Rubin, R., and Balow, B. Learning and behavior disorders: A longitudinal study. *Exceptional Children,* 1971, 38, 293–299.

Sabatino, D. A. Resource rooms: The renaissance in special education. *Journal of Special Education,* 1972, 6, 335–347.

Sabatino, D. A., and Dorfman, N. Matching learner aptitude to two commercial reading programs. *Exceptional Children,* 1974, 41, 85–91.

Sedlak, R. A., and Weener, P. Review of research on the Illinois Test of Psycholinguistic Abilities. In L. Mann and D. A. Sabatino (Eds.) *The First Review of Special Education.* Vol. 1. Philadelphia: Journal of Special Education Press, 1973. Pp. 113–164.

Sheare, J. B. Social acceptance of EMR adolescents in integrated programs. *American Journal of Mental Deficiency,* 1974, 78, 678–682.

Silberman, C. *Crisis in the Classroom.* New York: Random House, 1970.

Strichart, S. S. Effects of competence and nurturance on imitation of nonretarded peers by retarded adolescents. *American Journal of Mental Deficiency,* 1974, 78, 665–673.

Strichart, S. S., and Gottlieb, J. Imitation of retarded children by their nonretarded peers. *American Journal of Mental Deficiency,* 1975, 79, 506–512.

Stuart, R. B. *Trick or Treatment: How and When Psychotherapy Fails.* Champaign, Ill.: Research Press, 1970.

Sutherland, E. H., and Cressey, D. R. *Principles of Criminology.* (6th Ed.) Chicago: Lippincott, 1960.

Ullman, L. P., and Krasner, L. (Eds.) *Case Studies in Behavior Modification.* New York: Holt, Rinehart & Winston, 1965.

Vacc, N. A. Long term effects of special class intervention for emotionally disturbed children. *Exceptional Children,* 1972, 39, 15–22.

Weintraub, F. J. Recent influences of law regarding the identification and educational placement of children. *Focus on Exceptional Children,* 1972, 4 (2), 1–11.

Ysseldyke, J. E. Diagnostic-prescriptive teaching: The search for aptitude-treatment interaction. In L. Mann and D. A. Sabatino (Eds.) *The First Review of Special Education.* Philadelphia: Journal of Special Education Press, 1973. Pp. 5–33.

Ysseldyke, J. E., and Salvia, J. Diagnostic-prescriptive teaching: two models. *Exceptional Children,* 1974, 41, 181–185.

4

Humanistic Behavioral Approach: Introduction

The problems confronting the educational system obviously cannot be solved merely by a discontinuation of the practices of diagnosing, labeling, and grouping children into special education and treatment programs. Children do differ along many physical and psychological dimensions relevant to development of appropriate educational, social, and emotional characteristics. These differences range from (1) relatively simple patterns—being mildly disruptive, experiencing mild learning difficulties, stubborn, lazy, or quarrelsome—which tend to disappear over time or at least to remain mild, to (2) major patterns of differences, which produce widespread and long-term problems. Thus many children do not meet many of the learning and behavioral expectations set by family and school or by other more general social environments. Not all children acquire new modes of behavior at the rate and level expected. Even children with adequate prerequisite skills may experience difficulty acquiring more complex skills. Some children do learn a wide range of behavior patterns unacceptable to aspects of environments in which they reside or are placed. Again, the problem obviously is not solved by ignoring these individual differences.

SPECIAL EDUCATION OR MAINSTREAM EDUCATION

The behavior position minimizes the widely accepted distinction between mainstream education and "special" education or "therapy." Learning takes place in many settings. Those settings differ in many respects. However, to resort to the practice of calling one learning experience "education" and another "therapy" or one "normal" education and the other "special" education only serves to perpetuate an artificial and somewhat dangerous concept. This concept, regardless of its various articulations, basically assumes that the child who learns well in the mainstream education environment is *normal* and that the child who does not is *abnormal* and must be provided "special" or "therapy" experiences. Labels denoting abnormality traditionally associated with special education, such as "retarded," "disabled," "disturbed," and "handicapped," emphasize the cleavage between the normal and the exceptional.

Assumptions of this *special vs. normal* dichotomy are frequently accompanied by those of "internal pathology and causation"[1] and the related position that only specially trained experts can deal successfully with internal pathology. The "special teacher" and the "therapist" of one kind or another have been created to deal with the child mostly *out of the mainstream* since the regular education program is not presently designed to accommodate the wide range of individual differences found within the typical school population. This was most vividly illustrated in a

Rubin and Balow 1971　longitudinal study by Rubin and Balow.* In a large group of "normal population" children, 41 percent were classified by teachers and other school personnel as exhibiting learning and behavior difficulties. Special class placements or special services had been instituted for 24.3 percent of the group. The writers indicate: "The findings suggest that schools and teachers are oriented to a narrow band of expected pupil behaviors which are not consonant with typical behavior patterns of young boys; any pupil outside of that narrow range is treated as needing special attention" (p. 298).

Children with exceptional learning and behavioral characteristics differ from other children *not in kind but only in degree* along various behavioral and physical dimensions. Children differ in terms of the frequency, generality, and intensity of problems. The child may differ in terms of the types and arrangements of incentive conditions needed for effective learning and performance. Also, some children have developed clusters of learning and behavior problems that interact with and thus mutually influence and intensify each other. A child with one exceptional learning and/or behavior characteristic is likely to develop others, i.e., a chronic learning problem is likely to result in emotional, motivational, and social problems.

The behavior position recognizes that there are *no known principles* of behavior influence available for use by the "special" teacher or the "therapist"—whether speech therapist, psychotherapist, occupational therapist, recreation therapist, play therapist—that are not equally availa-

---

1. This assumption that the observed learning or behavioral retardation, disturbance, or deviation is a surface symptom of some internal pathology is discussed in detail in later chapters.

ble to and used by the mainstream educator and others in their interaction with the "normal" child. The manner in which the education environment is arranged and the specific instructional techniques used to influence behavior development and maintenance may be different. The child's prerequisite motivational and behavioral characteristics on which an instructional program is based may be more varied and erratic. The specific experiences provided children may be individualized to varying degrees. But the *basic principles of behavior influence which underlie their effectiveness are not different.* The behavioral position thus calls for a flexible and natural approach to the wide range of individual differences characteristic of children and adolescents and poses the questions empirically: *"How can the individual differences among children be viewed and dealt with in order to promote the best behavior development and functioning of all children?" "How can learning experiences be organized and administered so that children differing from other children along various physical and psychological dimensions do not suffer unnecessary and damaging adverse effects?"*

Special Program for All Children

The humanistic behavior approach suggests that *every* child in the school system should be offered a special program—special in the sense that it represents the best match between a child and a learning program which will promote development and functioning along all behavior dimensions deemed relevant by the school program. This educational experience may be through group instruction, through highly individualized experiences within the boundaries of the regular classes, or, in highly selective cases, through some additional arrangements designed to facilitate the general competency of the individual child. Although there presently is insufficient experimentally derived evidence to detail the variety of "best-fit" arrangements which would be most enhancing to children with various exceptional learning and behavior characteristics, there is sufficient evidence, as detailed, to change the present widespread practice of *categorical* placement in isolated, self-contained special education classes. The child characterized by various exceptional learning and behavior patterns will require a more individualized and carefully designed arrangement of his educational experiences, which may be provided in any of a variety of settings.

Children should not be treated as a commodity to be shuffled around into rigid and narrowly conceived experiences which are predesigned to insure that a certain percentage of children will fail. Rather, school programs must be designed to accommodate a wider band of individual differences as a natural course of events. At the same time, it is obvious that presently structured regular classroom arrangements cannot accommodate the full range of individual differences found in children. Although mainstreaming has become the present vogue in special education circles, such a practice may create more problems than it solves unless accommodations are made to meet the individual needs of the children so served. Moderate and severe degrees of emotional, learning, and behavior problems may well require other combinations of classroom arrangements. But as noted by Reynolds* and Hobbs,* the *learning requirements* of children with exceptional learning and behavior difficulties, and not their discrete-group labels, should determine the organization and administration of appropriate educational experiences. Hobbs summarizes this position:

Reynolds 1971; Hobbs 1975

> In schools that are most responsive to individual differences in abilities, interests, and learning styles of children, the mainstream is actually many streams, sometimes as many streams as there are individual children, sometimes several streams as groups are formed for special purpose, sometimes one stream only as concerns of all converge. We see no advantage in dumping exceptional children into an undifferentiated mainstream; but we see great advantage to all children, exceptional children included, in an educational program modulated to the needs of individual children, singly, in small groups, or all together. Such a flexible arrangement may well result in functional separations of exceptional children from time to time, but the governing principle would apply to all children: school programs should be responsive to the learning requirements of individual children, and groupings should serve this end. [p. 197]

The behavioral approach suggests that children can be provided appropriate educational experiences without the questionable practice of labeling and categorical placement into separate groups and program environments on the basis of similarities along single or a small number of psychological or physical dimensions. If the child is either partially or completely removed from the usual classroom arrangements for individualized educational experiences, this should be based upon those specific program-relevant variables empirically related to the child's learning or behavior characteristics.[2]

Some children, as a consequence of certain sensory characteristics, require reading materials with large print. Other children are able to make adequate visual discriminations with much smaller print. Why is one any more or less special, disordered, or deviant than the other? Some children differ from others in that more immediate, tangible, and frequent reinforcing consequences are required for the most effective learning to occur. Why should these children be labeled as special, deviant, or exceptional and awarded negative disability labels? Some children acquire new behavior patterns at a slower rate than others. Why should they be viewed as

---

2. Bruininks and Rynders (1971), Deno (1970; 1973), Dunn (1973), Hobbs (1975), and Reynolds and Balow (1972) describe a variety of instructional arrangements which could accommodate a wide band of learning requirements of children and adolescents.

retarded or *deviant?* Other children require specific training in auditory memory. Why are they called *learning disabled?* All are merely children with some exceptional learning and/or behavior characteristics requiring more individualized and intensive learning experiences than that required by some other children. Some children are able to work at a task for sixty minutes at a time; others for only fifteen minutes at a time. Why should the latter child be labeled special any more than the former? Surely the educational environment should make use of such individual and educationally relevant data. As noted, there appears to be only flimsy justification for categorical segregation into self-contained and frequently isolated programs or in removing the child from his home and community in any but the more severe cases.

Glasser,* in addressing the problem of providing appropriate school experiences for children who present severe educational problems, suggests: *Glasser 1969*

> We must and we can find ways to help them gain enough from regular schools and regular classes so that they need not be removed from them for individual and group treatment by specialists. The specialists in the schools— counselors, psychologists, remedial instructors—should help the teacher in the classroom cope with the problems she has, both disciplinary and educational. They should examine in what ways classroom education can be improved and they should implement their ideas in the regular classes *in cooperation* with the classroom teachers. [p. 9]

In a similar vein, Cohen* indicates: *Cohen 1973*

> It is my conviction that it is undesirable to remove a juvenile, for rehabilitative purposes, from the community in which he lives. He needs help in adjusting his behavior to this environment, not to that of a correctional institution. I believe that all rehabilitative programs for juveniles should be carried out in the community, where situations requiring decisions and appropriate behavior abound. Only in the "real world" of the community can young people be given guidance and practice in making sound decisions and establishing viable relationships with other people. [p. 307]

EXCEPTIONAL LEARNING AND BEHAVIOR CHARACTERISTICS

The concept of children with "exceptional learning and behavior characteristics" is suggested as an alternative to the concept of "exceptional children." The "exceptional child," as a concept, is too all encompassing and carries with it the dangers of stereotyping, overgeneralization, and a range of other implications which potentially are derogatory. Children identified as "exceptional" too often are exposed to drastic curtailment of normal life experiences due to an unwarranted assumption that behavioral differences along a limited number of dimensions require (1) a different type of educational experience, (2) which is provided in different and sometimes isolated environments, and (3) which is provided by different "special" personnel.

The concept "children with exceptional learning and behavior characteristics" as used here is no more than a description of what has been observed, and it implies nothing beyond the observation that many children do present, for a variety of reasons, learning and behavioral characteristics that are problematic and/or out of the ordinary. Such characteristics may produce chronic and unusual or excessive difficulties for the child as well as for the ordinary educational environment. The factors related to the development and present occurrence of these learning and behavior difficulties are numerous and varied. For all but the more severely and profoundly involved child, many other of his learning and behavior characteristics may not be exceptional and may well complement the usual educational experiences provided. *The recognition that children do present various exceptional learning and behavior characteristics alerts the educational environment to the fact that educational experiences should be more individualized in these exceptional areas.* The concept that some, but not necessarily all, of a child's learning and behavior characteristics may be of an exceptional, different, or out-of-the-ordinary nature emphasizes and protects the uniqueness of individual children.

BEHAVIOR THEORY AND EDUCATION TACTICS

The behavioral approach represents a set of assumptions and related behavior principles and procedures relevent to the development, management, and modification of both normal behavior as well as various exceptional learning and behavior difficulties of children and youth who presently, in educational and psychological circles, are labeled "exceptional" children. The behavior principles presented have been evaluated in laboratory settings and have been demonstrated by clinical and applied studies to have applicability to the classroom, the home, and to many other settings in which children learn and behave.[3]

Focus on Promoting Prosocial Behavior

The behavioral position represents concepts and techniques of increasing the learning efficiency of children and thus of influencing

3. This statement is documented throughout the book.

prosocial adaptive behaviors. It does not focus, as is true of many contemporary systems of special education and therapy, on remediation and treatment of presumed internal deviations and related learning and behavior difficulties. Concepts of *social learning* derived from various learning theories, as well as principles of behavior change from social and developmental psychology, form the basis for influencing prosocial behavior development. In addition, the *humanistic behavioral approach*[4] described incorporates an ecological-interactional stance as it focuses on present behavior patterns observed as the child interacts with a social/physical environment. Both the presence and seriousness of most exceptional learning and behavior problems are quite relative to the requirements imposed on the child by the environment.* A child's behavioral capabilities at any moment represent the end result of a most complex learning history which has accumulated to provide both the form of the behaviors as well as the "meanings" or influences which certain environmental events have on the child. No learning or behavior occurs in isolation or in a vacuum. Behavior occurs in a complex environment. Learning and behaving not only result in feedback from the external world, these activities also may influence other behavioral repertoires which characterize the child at the moment.

Knoblock 1971; Rhodes 1967

Empiricism Emphasized

The objectivity of the approach represented provides a basis for evaluating its educational or therapeutic effectiveness. Its focus is on the child as he functions in his present environment, a focus derived from the assumption that the significant variables which influence the child's present behavior are found in this environment. This focus provides a basis for optimism that something can be done within the child's natural surroundings to facilitate effective behavior change. In a sense it represents a flexible position from which to view the development and change of a wide range of educational, social, affective, verbal, and related behaviors of children and youth. The positive approach engendered by the assumption that behavior changes can be facilitated by a variety of persons through systematic arrangement of the social and physical environments is in marked contrast to the "reserved for sacred hands only" orientation that characterizes many other systems of therapy, specialized education, or training. It is too early to determine empirically whether the humanistic behavioral alternative described in this book is generally more valuable than the "internal deviation" model that presently gives major direction to special education practices. Perhaps the future will realize a viable functional integration of the two models, representing the best theoretical, methodological, and empirical features of each. The present alternative, in a

4. Humanistic aspects of the approach are detailed in Chapters 6 and 7.

sense, represents an initial step in that direction as an effort is made to emphasize the empirical contributions of other approaches, while describing a procedure for evaluating the usefulness of a number of contrary assumptions, theoretical notions, and related practices.

Emphasizes Common Set of Principles

Although the discussion is focused on children with exceptional learning and behavior characteristics, no assumption is made that there are any unique or separate psychological or educational principles which distinguish "exceptional" children from "normal" children. The author is

Kaplan and Lotsof 1968

in agreement with Kaplan and Lotsof* "that behavioral differences in groups of 'exceptional' children do not imply different principles of behavior are applicable to each group, as is often suggested, but instead are consequents of differences in learning capacity and modified environmental conditions associated with the exceptionality" (p. 1207). In the same vein, there are no unique strategies for use with "exceptional" children which differ in kind from those used with "normal" children.

The behavioral position assumes that the vast majority of learning and behavior characteristics labeled as abnormal, problematic, maladaptive, bizarre, undesirable, unexpected, unhealthy, and the like do not differ in kind from any other learned behavior: Both normal behavior and most exceptional learning and behavior characteristics are the end products of unique individuals and their unique social learning histories. Although the types of learning experiences may differ dramatically among children, the same basic principles are assumed to be involved in the development and continuation of varying learning and behavior characteristics.

The implication of this position is clear. Many learning and behavior problems could be minimized, and some prevented altogether, by more discerning attention to the total learning experiences to which children are exposed, and by dealing *promptly and thoroughly with problems as these become apparent.* If, for example, pervasive and chronic problems are outgrowths of small problems, just as complex positive behavior patterns represent an accumulative integration of numerous less complex behaviors, these serious problems may be avoided or minimized by dealing with the small ones in a routine fashion as these occur in the child's home and school environments.

The following recent experience illustrates this supposition. An eleven-year-old boy attending fourth grade was referred at the end of the school year for assistance in devising a reading program. The boy was reading at a beginning second-grade level. He had been moved along from grade to grade, apparently under the supposition that his difficulties in reading would somehow disappear. Finally, after four years of failure and all the accompanying frustration and negative emotional impact, the boy was provided an individualized reading program with which he was successful. However, during the course of the four years of failure, he had developed generalized behavior patterns described as "shyness, not sure of himself, poor self-concept, limited persistence, low frustration tolerance, and becomes over-emotional when he fails." It does not take much imagination to speculate that most, if not all, these undesirable behavior patterns may have been minimized or avoided altogether if the child's early difficulty in reading had resulted promptly in a specially designed program. The problem was not great, initially. It became so over the years as the deficit reading skills and the resulting effect on a range of other behavioral characteristics became more chronic and pervasive.

Cowen and Lorion* and Koppitz* lament the all too frequent practice followed in the public schools of waiting until problems become chronic and pervasive prior to intervention efforts. In reporting a longitudinal study of children identified as learning disabled, Koppitz wrote, "Youngsters were usually tolerated in regular classes as long as they were not *too* disruptive. Only after they had failed repeatedly and had become quite frustrated and disturbed, were the more intelligent pupils finally sent to the LD classes. It would have been far more efficient and effective, in the long run, to give these children extra help before the secondary emotional problems developed" (p. 183). Cowen and Lorion's* data indicate that younger children with fewer and less chronic failure experiences benefit more from specialized intervention efforts than do older children.

Cowen and Lorion 1974; Koppitz 1971

Cowen and Lorion 1974

Behavior Modification and Beyond

The basic behavior intervention/educational system described has its roots in what presently is known as *behavior modification*. This name, however, has acquired a range of different meanings. To many, it has reference to providing M&Ms and other tangible rewards to insure that a child will perform single or highly circumscribed behaviors. This is a grossly oversimplified view of the system. To others, behavior modification represents a broader view but remains a set of procedures based on strict adherence to operant learning concepts and a related methodology of behavior analysis. Such a strict and limiting position has been labelled as *radical behaviorism.**

Skinner 1974

Others, including the present author, take a more flexible position and go beyond these traditional and rather restrictive views of behavior modification. Intervention procedures derived from various learning theories, although of considerable usefulness, do not represent answers to all problems faced by the classroom teacher and other professionals in the school setting. The humanistic behavioral approach represents a flexible integration of concepts from a variety of empirical and theoretical positions. It emphasizes that the educator remain open to any principles, theories, or practices that result in more effective and efficient procedures of promoting desired behavior development and performance in children with exceptional learning and behavior characteristics. The teacher is guided by the question "How can I best organize a wide array of learning experiences in which children will learn and maintain desirable behavioral qualities?" In seriously addressing this question, the educator assumes major responsibility (1) for insuring that highly appropriate educational goals have been set, (2) for providing the structure in which children interact with educational experiences, and (3) for evaluating the effectiveness of these experiences in attainment of these goals. If a child does not benefit, or if he is actively resistant to the educational efforts, no attempt is made to blame the difficulty on the child. Rather, the teacher views the components of the experiences as being inadequate for that child. The content, manner of presentation, or the relationships between the child and the educational environment are examined in an effort to devise more appropriate learning experiences.

The humanistic behavioral approach is chiefly a *delivery system*. It provides general guidelines as well as more specific direction to designing and delivering learning experiences and insuring that these will have more than a momentary influence on the behavioral repertoires of children and youth. It is concerned with cognitive, academic, and other "school-defined" learning and performance, as well as with broader social, emotional, interpersonal, self-awareness, and self-management behavioral characteristics. The behavioral approach makes use of any rules or constructs which:

1. *Denote the conditions which result in increase in strength of behavior and best insure retention or maintenance of the behavior* (e.g., reinforcing events that are provided after a child behaves in a certain manner increase the strength of that behavior).
2. *Denote the manner in which instructional materials should be presented, sequenced, and repeated to best facilitate acquisition and/or retention* (e.g., labeling a visual symbol facilitates the acquisition of a discrimination involving the symbol).
3. *Denote the learning histories which result in a likelihood that a child will exhibit certain behavior characteristics or will have a high probability of being influenced in a given manner by certain experiences or stimulus conditions* (e.g., a child who has been punished frequently for his failure in school will be prone to excessive emotionality when presented with academic materials).
4. *Denote the conditions under which given types of behaviors are likely to occur* (e.g., a child is likely to explore or express curiosity when provided novel situations if he is relatively free of threat of punishment; when placed in a conflict situation, a child is likely to engage in behavior that reduces or resolves the conflict).
5. *Denote the prerequisite behavioral skills or capabilities for effective learning of other, usually more complex, behavior patterns* (e.g., visual discrimination skills precede the development of effective reading skills).

The empirical attitude which describes the humanistic behavioral approach is thus sufficiently flexible to utilize constructs from nonbehavioral models which suggest possible relationships between stimulus conditions (external and internal) and behavioral effects. This is done without the necessity of accepting various of the theoretical explanatory constructs used to account for these relationships. As examples, the behavioral approach would make use of the observation that "there is high likelihood that young children will exhibit spontaneous exploration of their environment" without the necessity of accepting the theoretical proposition that "children have an innate need to explore." The behavioral approach would not categorically reject a philosophic concept such as "self-actualization" but would not depend upon the presence of such an internal driving force. Rather, it would attempt to provide the many day-by-day experiences that would result in a "self-actualized" child.

As other examples, Gagné* enumerates the conditions most favorable to effective acquisition and memory of various types of learning tasks. Although disagreement may be voiced about Gagné's "eight types of learning," his enumeration of prerequisite skills and the conditions of learning situations provide considerable direction to the teacher's task of organizing an instructional program.

Gagné 1970

Piaget* suggests that learning of new materials may be facilitated by processes which he defines as assimilation and accommodation. Although one may reject these and other of Piaget's constructs, such as his stages of cognitive operation, the educator may well find useful many of his suggestions concerning the manner in which learning experiences should be structured and sequenced. Normative data from developmental psychology,* as well as knowledge of the hierarchical nature of various learning tasks,* are useful in deciding upon the behavioral objectives set for specific children and the types of sequential steps or stages that a child's behavior will follow in some areas.

Flavell 1963

Mussen 1970
Gagné 1970

Many child developmentalists report that children are characterized by a high likelihood of engaging in play activities and that such play activities are reinforcing to children independent of prior or present learning or incentive conditions. A basic drive or motive is suggested by some as underlying this behavior.* Some psychologists* feel that a child is likely to attempt to develop competency (i.e., mastery of his environment). Others suggest that in a conflict situation, a person is likely to engage in behaviors which will reduce cognitive dissonance.* Although the explanatory constructs may be viewed as adding little to an understanding of the child, the teacher may find the observational data (which these constructs attempt to explain) to be of value in structuring the learning experiences provided children.

Cofer 1972; for example, White 1965

Festinger 1957

Again, any concepts and related procedures may be evaluated for possible use in designing appropriate learning experiences. The behavioral position requires, however, the following criterion of selection: Are there reliable empirical data to support a relationship between en-

Nawas 1970

vironmental conditions or events and behavioral influence? Thus the approach, although appearing to be quite eclectic on the surface, remains behavioral in its insistence on "identifiable referents, empirical testing, and internal consistency" (p. 364).*

SETTING EDUCATIONAL GOALS

A variety of philosophic concepts is most useful in setting both broad behavioral goals and more specific educational objectives, but may offer little direction in arranging the day-by-day experiences of a child to insure that the human characteristics reflected in these objectives will be acquired and utilized. As the procedures which comprise the humanistic behavioral approach are applicable to the "how" of influencing children with exceptional learning and behavior characteristics, the practitioner must use constructs from developmental psychology, educational philosophy, and from other empirical and subjective positions as a basis for deciding "what" the child should be taught or encouraged to develop. The behavioral characteristics deemed desirable for a child must be decided upon prior to the organization and implementation of programs of behavior change. Once these behavioral objectives have been agreed upon, principles and practices of the humanistic behavioral approach may then be used to design learning programs to assist the child in reaching these goals. "Should a child be polite?" "Should a child be happy?" "Should a child learn to read and enjoy a variety of materials reflecting different value positions?" "Should a child be responsible for selecting his educational goals?" "Should a child remain quiet while an adult is talking?" "Should a child learn to share possessions with others or to comply without objection to adult requests?" These and thousands of similar questions must be decided upon by those involved in influencing children in their development.

Goals and Procedures Carefully Selected

In selecting educational program goals, regardless of the methodology used by the educator in facilitating goal attainment—that is, whether it is based on procedures derived from the humanistic behavioral approach, an open classroom model, a cognitive model, a self-concept model, a developmental model, or a combination of these or other approaches—the educator must be most sensitive both to the goals selected and to the potential influence which he may have on children and adolescents with whom he interacts in the instructional environment. This becomes especially significant both in view of the potential efficacy of the humanistic behavioral approach in facilitating behavior change in children and youth and the concern which various writers have about the power of control which educators potentially can hold over students.*

Eddy 1967; MacMillan 1973; Moore 1967; Wood 1968

The goals set and procedures used in facilitating attainment of these goals should be those which *serve the child*. Whenever a teacher walks into the classroom, he or she is potentially influencing the child's learning and behavior characteristics. This is true regardless of the teacher's awareness or intent. Whether or not his behavior is carefully practiced in relation to predefined educational objectives, whether or not he has some articulated empirical or theoretic basis for assuming that what he does will facilitate positive growth in his students, *the fact remains* that potentially the educator will influence children in some manner. The educator makes a value decision about how he intends to influence his students—as examples, whenever he chides a child for expressing an unpopular decision or insults another child because his assignment time requirements were not met.

The Educator and Accountability

The humanistic behavior approach emphasizes that the educator is *accountable* for what he or she does, and that it is his responsibility to recognize the potential influence (positive, neutral, or negative) that he or she may have. The behavioral approach emphasizes to the educator: "As there are behavioral principles and related educational procedures which potentially can exert an obvious effect on the behavioral development and functioning of your students, you have the personal responsibility both to decide carefully on what your educational objectives are and also to monitor your behavior and the related educational experiences to insure that these, instead of less favorable ones, are being attained." Even though, as Wood* suggested, "Like many 'tools,' behavior modification techniques are morally blind," the teacher cannot escape his responsibility in setting those educational goals and in selecting for use those educational procedures that hold best promise of being most enhancing to his students. An educator who is sarcastic or demeaning is, in fact, influencing the emotional and attitudinal characteristics of his students, regardless of his intent or of his knowledge of the rules by which such characteristics are influenced. A teacher whose views are quite discrepant from those of his colleagues, whether he accepts or rejects the tenets of a broad spectrum humanistic behavioral approach, is, in fact, influencing a variety of student behaviors. Particular attention given to those students who find him refreshing and interesting will be especially influential. Behavioral effects consistent with rules of positive reinforcement and those of emotional and attitudinal learning do result, whether or not the teacher recognizes these or is in agreement with these.

Wood 1968

Again, the humanistic behavioral approach confronts the educator with concepts and procedures which require him or her to look carefully at what he or she is doing and at what he or she is attempting to accomplish. The behavioral approach has no preconceived notions about what a child should learn or what the educational environment should attempt to teach. It does provide various general and specific rules of learning, and emphasizes that the teacher be aware of these as attempts are made to influence the student's academic, social, attitudinal, and emotional behaviors. It represents a facilitative, and not a value-based approach.

Goals Are Individually Determined

Some goals are viewed by almost everyone as being desirable for all children. Almost everyone would agree that children should develop an adequate verbal language system, or should learn basic skills of self-care and self-management. But the universal desirability of many other behavioral characteristics is open to varied opinions. Should all children dress neatly, respect authority, learn grammatically correct English, and strive for economic independence? Parents, teachers, and children alike, on the basis of legal, ethical, philosophic, religious, cultural, economic, and other conceptual and emotional considerations, may respond negatively to these and similar questions. Differences in any of these areas may form the basis for quite different behavioral goals. Again, the behavioral approach is useful in the *how* of influencing behavior development, maintenance, and modification after a decision has been made about *what* behavior should be influenced.

As noted earlier, a variety of developmental data and related curriculum guides will provide direction to sequencing or arranging the goals into meaningful educational programs. Certain skills must be obtained prior to achieving more difficult or complex skills and knowledge. However, the goals, and the basis for these, must be decided upon prior to initiating an educational experience.

Definition of Desirable and Undesirable

In view of this relative view of what a child should learn or be, the terms *desirable behavior, appropriate behavior,* and *acceptable behavior* are used in future discussion to refer to those specific and general learning and behavioral characteristics which are so defined by the child and adolescent and by those who comprise the student's environments. *Undesirable, inappropriate,* and *unacceptable* will be used to refer to those specific and general learning and behavioral characteristics which are objectionable to or which cause negative reactions in the child and in those of his social environments. Ideally, children will be involved in decisions which denote behavioral characteristics as acceptable or unacceptable. In any event, the specific behavioral characteristics viewed as desirable or as undesirable will vary across different social environments.

CONSTRUCTS, THEORIES, AND EXPLANATIONS

As a basis for the discussion to follow, it should prove helpful at this point to comment briefly on the nature of the concepts held by educators concerning child and adolescent behavior. Whether articulated or not, everyone has a set of notions or "theories" about the factors involved in the development, maintenance, and modification of behavior and these form the basis for many of the practices seen in contemporary "special education." These range from loosely elaborated concepts such as "a person does what he really puts his mind to," to highly structured theoretical systems of learning and personality.* The "theories" of child learning and behavior held by educational personnel vary both in completeness and in validity. Many teachers, psychologists, other school personnel, and parents alike, even in the absence of reliable data supporting various notions, adhere to many of their concepts of child and adolescent behavior as if these were true. Theories, constructs, and hypotheses not infrequently are confused with facts.

Hall and Lindzey 1970; Rhodes and Tracy 1974; Wiggins et al. 1971

Regardless of the particular theoretical orientation held by psychological and educational staff members as they view children and youth with exceptional learning and behavior characteristics, *the common point of departure available to all is the observable behaviors, both historical and contemporary, which characterize individual children.* Beyond this common observation point, however, tremendous differences exist among people.

AREAS OF DIFFERENCES	EXAMPLES OF DIFFERENCES
Theoretical Models The theories and related ideas held about the past and present factors which underlie, cause, control, or influence the behavior patterns which a child exhibits. These concepts may be related to such systems as self-concept (Rogers 1951), psychoanalytic (Hall 1954), learning (Bandura 1969), need theory (Murray 1938), or ability training (Frostig 1967).	*Internal deviancy models.* The child cannot read because of an emotional block related to castration anxiety (psychoanalytic model); the child cannot read because of perceptual-linguistic disabilities (psycholinguistic disability model). *Behavioral model.* He does not read because of reinforcement deficits in the school environment.
Procedures of Evaluation The procedures selected by persons differing in theoretical orientations as means of evaluating etiology or causes of present behavior patterns.	*Internal deviancy models.* A battery of projective procedures will be administered (psychoanalytic and need models); the ITPA will be administered (psycholinguistic disability model).

Behavioral model. Behavioral observations will be made of the child in the classroom setting.

Interpretations Provided
Evaluation Data
The interpretations made of the evaluation data obtained.

Internal deviancy models. The presence of aggressive content on projective evaluation represents pent up hostility based on unconscious conflicts between love and hate of mother (psychoanalytic model); the ITPA profile reveals an auditory decoding deficit (psycholinguistic disability model).

Behavioral model. His high rate of aggressive behavior is the result of excessive negative reinforcement.

Methods of Devising
Intervention Programs
The procedures for translating "etiology or cause" inferences into intervention procedures designed to change the problematic behavior.

Internal deviancy models. The poor self-concept should be dealt with in play therapy (self-concept model); the child should be provided auditory decoding training (ability-training model).

Behavioral model. Specific discrimination training and reinforcement of self-management skills should be initiated to deal with the behavioral deficits noted.

Intervention Program
Objectives
The specific objectives of a program designed to influence the problem area.

Internal deviancy models. The goal of play therapy is that of strengthening his self-concept (self-concept model); the goal of training is to strengthen the child's psycholinguistic abilities (ability-training model).

Behavioral model. The objectives of the behavior therapy program are to increase the frequency and duration of positive social interaction with peers.

Methods and Criteria for
Evaluating Effects of
Intervention Program
The criteria of success and the methods used to determine program effects.

Internal deviancy models. The adolescents will complete a Q-sort prior to and following client-centered therapy. A change in the direction of the ideal self is expected (self-concept model); the child's performance on the ITPA should reflect the ability-training program (ability-training model).

Behavioral model. Frequency and duration data will be obtained prior to and throughout the program. A 75 percent reduction in self-derogatory comments will be expected.

No single theory, or specific combination of them, is right or wrong. These constructs and related practices either prove useful, or they do not, in accounting for present exceptional learning and behavior characteristics and in providing direction to effective programs of behavior change.

BEHAVIORAL VS. INTERNAL DEVIANCY MODELS

Even though there is great variation among educational and psychological personnel in the specifics of their assumptions and practices relative to exceptional learning and behavior characteristics of children, the general constructs and related practices used can be grouped into two general positions: the *internal deviancy* and the *behavioral. Internal deviancy* is the position that best describes most of the practices and assumptions of the vast majority of persons in the educational and mental health enterprises in their consideration of problematic or exceptional learning and behavior patterns. As noted, its chief characteristic is its focus on presumed internal factors as major sources of symptomatic behavioral or learning deviancy. The *behavioral* approach, in contrast, focuses on present environmental events and the effects which these events have on the child's learning and behavior characteristics. While based on principles which have been known to educators and psychologists for some years, this latter position has only recently been articulated as representing a viable system for application to the educational endeavor.*

The remaining chapters, while examining the developmental, learning, and behavior adjustment difficulties of children and adolescents from a humanistic behavioral approach, provide further comparison of the two models. This comparison is presented not to suggest the superiority of the behavioral approach (although the author's bias in this respect will consistently show itself) but rather to provide the reader with an exposure to contrasting concepts and practices. Too frequently, students are presented components of one system or the other without adequate opportunity to compare and contrast, to understand assumptions which underlie practices, or to recognize the implications for practice of contrasting basic

Gardner 1974; Haring and Phillips 1972; Lovitt 1970; O'Leary and O'Leary 1972; Skinner 1968; Thoresen 1972

assumptions. As a choice illustration of this, teachers and school psychologists are taught to use "disability" evaluation procedures such as the Frostig Developmental Test of Visual Perception (DTVP) and the Illinois Test of Psycholinguistic Abilities (ITPA) and to prescribe related perceptual and psycholinguistic training or remediation programs. Far too few, however, have a keen appreciation of the theoretical models on which these tests and training programs are based and the present scarcity of empirical data supportive of the associated assumptions and practices.

The student should recognize that no two persons following either the internal deviancy or the behavioral position are precisely alike in their assumptions, assessment procedures, or intervention practices. There are sufficient similarities within positions and sufficient striking differences across approaches, however, to warrant examination of major characteristics of the positions.

SUMMARY

The humanistic behavioral approach represents a set of assumptions and practices concerned with development and maintenance of various desired learning and behavior characteristics. It presents the concepts of exceptional learning and behavior characteristics of children and youth and delineates the manner by which these may be acquired and maintained. It is not a substitute for nor does it preclude the use of knowledge from a variety of other positions concerned with the way a child learns and behaves. Obviously, considerably more data are needed to design best a total educational program most appropriate for children with exceptional learning and behavior characteristics.

REFERENCES

Bandura, A. *Principles of Behavior Modification.* New York: Holt, Rinehart & Winston, 1969.

Berry, K. E. Mainstreaming: A problem and an opportunity for general education. *Focus on Exceptional Children,* 1974, 6, 1–7.

Bruininks, R. H., and Rynders, J. E. Alternatives to special class placement for educable mentally retarded children. *Focus on Exceptional Children,* 1971, 3, 1–12.

Chaffin, J. D. Will the real "mainstreaming" program please stand up! (or . . . should Dunn have done it?) *Focus on Exceptional Children,* 1974, 6, 1–18.

Cofer, C. N. *Motivation and Emotion.* Glenview, Ill.: Scott, Foresman, 1972.

Cohen, H. L. Behavior modification and socially deviant youth. In C. E. Thoresen (Ed.) *Behavior Modification in Education.* The 72nd Yearbook of the National Society for the Study of Education. Chicago: University of Chicago Press, 1973. Pp. 291–314.

Cowen, E. L., and Lorion, R. P. Which kids are helped? *Journal of Special Education,* 1974, 8, 187–192.

Deno, E. Special education as developmental capital. *Exceptional Children,* 1970, 37, 229–237.

Deno, E. N. (Ed.) *Instructional Alternatives for Exceptional Children.* Arlington, Va.: Council for Exceptional Children, 1973.

Dunn, L. M. (Ed.) *Exceptional Children in the Schools: Special Education in Transition.* (2nd Ed.) New York: Holt, Rinehart & Winston, 1973.

Eddy, E. M. *Walk the White Line: A Profile of Urban Education.* New York: Doubleday Anchor, 1967.

Festinger, L. *A Theory of Cognitive Dissonance.* Evanston, Ill.: Row, Peterson, 1957.

Flavell, J. H. *The Developmental Psychology of Jean Piaget.* Princeton, N. J.: Van Nostrand, 1963.

Frostig, M. Testing as a basis for educational therapy. *Journal of Special Education,* 1967, 2, 15–34.

Gagné, R. M. *The Conditions of Learning.* (2nd Ed.) New York: Holt, Rinehart & Winston, 1970.

Gardner, W. I. *Children with Learning and Behavior Problems: A Behavior Management Approach.* Boston: Allyn and Bacon, 1974.

Glasser, W. *Schools without Failure.* New York: Harper, 1969.

Grosenick, J. Assessing the reintegration of exceptional children into regular classes. *Teaching Exceptional Children,* 1970, 2, 113–119.

Grosenick, J. Integration of exceptional children into regular classes: Research and procedures. *Focus on Exceptional Children,* 1971, 3, 1–8.

Hall, C. S. *A Primer of Freudian Psychology.* Cleveland: World, 1954.

Hall, C. S., and Lindzey, G. *Theories of Personality.* (2nd Ed.) New York: John Wiley, 1970.

Haring, N. G., and Phillips, E. L. *Analysis and Modification of Classroom Behavior.* Englewood Cliffs, N.J.: Prentice-Hall, 1972.

Hobbs, N. *The Futures of Children.* San Francisco: Jossey-Bass, 1975.

Kaplan, M. F., and Lotsof, E. J. Are the principles

of behavior of "exceptional children" exceptional? *Psychological Reports*, 1968, 23, 1207–1213.

Knoblock, P. Psychological considerations of emotionally disturbed children. In W. M. Cruickshank (Ed.) *Psychology of Exceptional Children and Youth.* (3rd Ed.) Englewood Cliffs, N.J.: Prentice-Hall, 1971. Pp. 565–599.

Koppitz, E. M. *Children with Learning Disabilities: A Five Year Follow-up Study.* New York: Grune and Stratton, 1971.

Lovitt, T. Behavior modification: The current scene. *Exceptional Children*, 1970, 37, 85–91.

MacMillan, D. L. *Behavior Modification in Education.* New York: MacMillan, 1973.

Moore, G. A. *Realities of the Urban Classroom: Observations in Elementary Schools.* New York: Doubleday Anchor, 1967.

Murray, H. A. *Explorations in Personality.* New York: Oxford, 1938.

Mussen, P. H. (Ed.) *Carmichael's Manual of Child Psychology.* (3rd Ed.) Vols. 1 and 2. New York: John Wiley, 1970.

Nawas, M. M. Wherefore cognitive therapy?: A critical scrutiny of three papers by Beck, Bergin, and Ullman. *Behavior Therapy*, 1970, 1, 359–370.

O'Leary, K. D., and O'Leary, S. G. *Classroom Management: The Successful Use of Behavior Modification.* New York: Pergamon, 1972.

Reynolds, M. C. Policy statements: Call for response. *Exceptional Children*, 1971, 37, 421–433.

Reynolds, M. C., and Balow, B. Categories and variables in special education. *Exceptional Children*, 1972, 38, 357–366.

Rhodes, W. The disturbing child: A problem of ecological management. *Exceptional Children*, 1967, 33, 449–455.

Rhodes, W. C., and Tracy, M. L. (Eds.) *A Study of Child Variance.* Vol. 2. *Interventions.* Ann Arbor: University of Michigan Press, 1974.

Rogers, C. R. *Client-centered Therapy: Its Current Practice, Implications, and Theory.* Boston: Houghton Mifflin, 1951.

Rubin, R., and Balow, B. Learning and behavior disorders: A longitudinal study. *Exceptional Children*, 1971, 38, 293–299.

Skinner, B. F. *The Technology of Teaching.* New York: Appleton-Century-Crofts, 1968.

Skinner, B. F. *About Behaviorism.* New York: A. A. Knopf, 1974.

Thoresen, C. E. (Ed.) *Behavior Modification in Education.* The Seventy-second Yearbook of the National Society for the Study of Education. Chicago: University of Chicago Press, 1972.

White, R. W. Motivation reconsidered: The concept of competence. In I. J. Gorden (Ed.) *Human Development: Readings in Research.* Glenview, Ill.: Scott, Foresman, 1965.

Wiggins, J. S., Renner, K. E., Clore, G. L., and Rose, R. J. *The Psychology of Personality.* Menlo Park, Calif.: Addison-Wesley, 1971.

Wood, F. H. Behavior modification techniques in context. *Newsletter of the Council for Children with Behavior Disorders*, 1968, 5, 12–15.

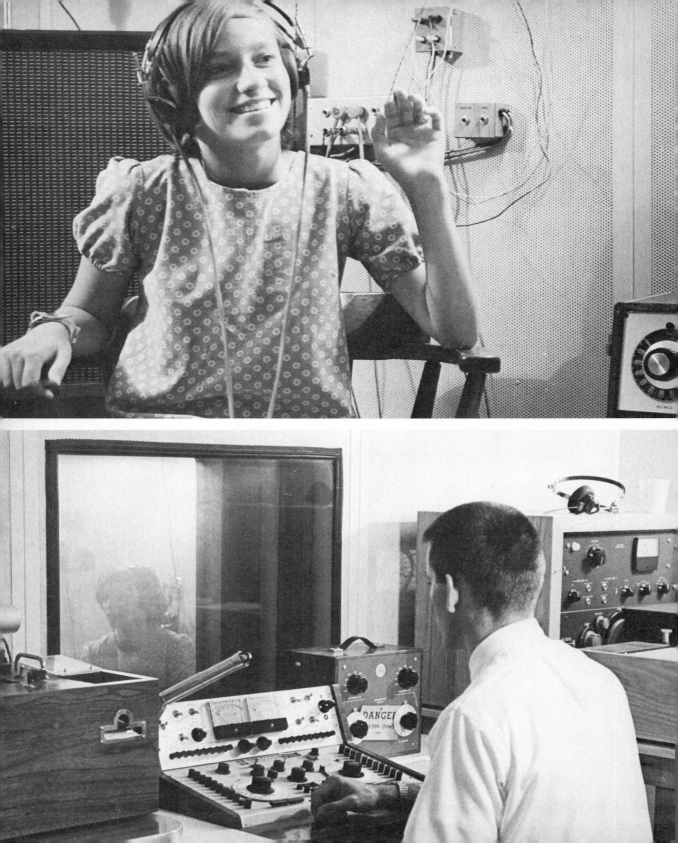

5

A Behavioral Scheme for Classification of Exceptional Characteristics

Even though present medical, psychological, psychiatric, and psychometric diagnostic and classification schemes for children with exceptional characteristics are inadequate from an educational program viewpoint, there obviously remains a need for a functional classification format. A system of describing the exceptional characteristics is needed, as these characteristics form the basis for specialized educational services. Dunn* *Dunn 1973* has noted that the *special* aspects of special education reside in the curricular content, method of instruction, instructional materials, and in the specialized skills of the special educator. But the nature of each of these components rests upon an initial detailed identification of the exceptional features of the exceptional learner. What characteristics does the learner have that require specially trained educators who provide special curricular content, instructional methodologies, and instructional materials? If gross category features such as mental retardation, emotional disturbance, learning disabilities, communication disorders, sensory disabilities, or crippling conditions are not suitable program variables, what alternative scheme might be available? The present chapter describes one such scheme which reflects the conceptual and methodological features of the humanistic behavioral view of exceptional characteristics. The classification scheme is individualized program oriented. In light of the lack of present research support for any specific administrative arrangements, such as mainstreaming, self-contained special classes, resource room, or for such groupings as conduct problems, perceptually impaired, blind, or behaviorally disordered, the classification system provides no specific direction as to how children should be grouped for instructional purposes. Other aspects of the humanistic behavioral approach, to be described throughout the book, however, do provide suggestions about features of the learning environment most supportive of development of competency characteristics.

INTERRELATIONSHIPS OF EXCEPTIONAL CHARACTERISTICS

Exceptional learning and behavior characteristics are not infrequently observed to cluster together. For example, an adolescent who generally is negativistic may be likely to engage in violent temper tantrums on occasion. A child with limited sensory discrimination skills due to a severe hearing loss may be excessively shy and anxious around peers with normal hearing functions. A child with general or specific learning difficulties is likely to demonstrate "emotional" problems. In viewing these correlations, the following should be considered:

Although the exceptional learning and behavior characteristics which different children exhibit may appear to be highly similar, and although various characteristics of a specific child may appear to be related, both the historical factors involved in the development of these characteristics and the present factors which exert influence over these may be quite different.

One child's aggressive behavior may be a result of a rich history of positive social reinforcement for such behavior from parents, siblings, or peers, while a similar pattern of behavior in another child may have been strengthened because it removed a source of unpleasantness—for example, siblings and peers stopped aggravating him about his physical features whenever he yelled at or physically attacked them. Hyperactivity, distractibility, and short attention span may reflect central nervous system pathology in one instance and be a result of learning in another.

Highly similar reading difficulties may be a result of such different factors as poor instruction, linguistic and/or perceptual difficulties, limited capacity, sensory/motor difficulties, or emotional/motivational characteristics which interfere with acquisition and performance of reading skills.

Children with different clusters of exceptional learning and behavior characteristics may have many characteristics in common.

These common characteristics may or may not be a result of common etiologies. O'Grady* found that children labeled as "learning disabled" and others labeled as "emotionally disturbed" exhibited similar patterns of language difficulties. Bryan and Bryan* describe the "emotional distur-

O'Grady 1974

Bryan and Bryan 1975

bance" features of "learning disabled" children, while Neisworth and Greer* describe the functional similarities of "learning disability" and "educable mental retardation."

Neisworth and Greer 1975

Factors involved in the initial development of a pattern of behavior may or may not be those factors which presently influence the behavior.

Thus, present exceptional characteristics may be changed even though they may be due in part to constitutional-biological factors. Sensory, neurological, physical, or motoric factors may have influenced the child's exceptional characteristics and the manner in which the child presently responds to and thus is influenced by various experiences. At the same time, it is recognized that the learner may acquire quite different characteristics within the limits imposed by physical factors if exposed to different learning experiences. In the same manner, successful application of specific learning parameters to modify exceptional characteristics does not demonstrate that these same principles were involved in the initial learning or even in the present maintenance of these characteristics.

Describing the child as being aggressive, shy, language impaired, negativistic, excessively emotional, learning disabled, or hyperactive does not imply that the child has some behavior traits or is of a personality type which reflects some internal basic features.

No characteristics or combination of characteristics represent all-or-nothing features of a child. The basic consideration is not whether the child is, for instance, shy or not shy, does or does not have cognitive limitations, or has or does not have communication difficulties. Shyness is merely a descriptive name for what the child does in various situations, which creates certain reactions from those in his social environment. Describing Jim as aggressive, or noting that an adolescent is gifted or creative, does not tell us much about what the person actually does. To be most useful, a description of the specifics of what Jim does, the strength of these behaviors, and the conditions under which these are likely to occur would be necessary.

No exceptional learning or behavior characteristic is categorically or inherently inappropriate or inadequate.

Aggressiveness, giftedness, impulsiveness, or shyness reside partially in the view of the observer and are not absolute characteristics. The same child may be labeled aggressive by one observer and delightfully assertive by another. A child may be deemed "hyperactive" by some who control certain environments and who do not accept behaviors they themselves view as hyperactive. In this environment the child is likely to be responded to in a manner designed to eliminate or discourage the "hyperactive" behavior. Thus, "inappropriateness" is not an all-or-none characteristic of a child's behavior. The acceptability of behavior is obviously related to the requirements or expectations held by the child or adolescent for himself or to those held by others in specific environments.

> **Some exceptional learning and/or behavior characteristics are highly restrictive and occur only in specific situations; others are more general and may occur in many different types of situations.**

One child may be hyperactive, detached, and nonattentive only in group settings where he receives little individual attention. He may be quite attentive, cooperative, and enthusiastic in small groups or in one-to-one relationships where he is provided considerable amounts of support and reinforcement. This is reflected in the following descriptions of a six-year-old boy. The first report was written by the teacher and by an independent observer and describes the boy's behaviors in a large kindergarten class setting. "Hyperactive, disruptive, doesn't follow teacher instructions, seldom sticks to a task until finished, aggressive toward peers, seldom expresses positive emotions." The second represents the boy's behavior in a one-to-one situation in which his academic readiness skills were being evaluated. "Cooperative, attentive, persistent, expressed pleasure over task accomplishments, responded well to the close personal attention provided, enjoyed approval, would attempt difficult tasks when encouraged to do so." The psychologist completing the evaluation in the clinic commented, "I thought there had been a mistake. The boy was not at all as the school report described him to be."

Other behavior patterns may be quite pervasive and remain relatively the same across numerous different settings. Thus a child may be negativistic, nonattentive, fearful, shy, or hyperactive whether at home, school, playgound, or at grandmother's house.

FEATURES OF A CLASSIFICATION SYSTEM

A classification system of exceptional characteristics should:

1. Focus on measurable child characteristics and not on hypothetical variables.
2. Provide descriptive *categories of behaviors* instead of categories of children.
3. Be an empirical system and make no a priori assumptions about common causation (etiology), common maintaining conditions, or common intervention approaches.

Further, the measurable child characteristics should be viewed as subject to change and as reflecting active or dynamic aspects of the child as these interact with and are influenced by other learner characteristics (physical and behavioral) and environmental conditions. The characteristic included may be both a focus of an educational program designed to change the characteristic *and* a learner-characteristic variable in programs designed to change other exceptional characteristics. In illustration, a program of teaching implicit rehearsal strategies may be designed to improve the deficit memory skills of a child. During the course of this program, the memory difficulties of the child may influence the procedures used in teaching specific curricular content in areas of academic deficiency. Procedures of overlearning and frequent practice of information acquired may be used. As the child learns more effective verbal rehearsal strategies, the procedures of overlearning and frequent practice may be deleted as the memory deficit no longer is regarded as an exceptional characteristic.

RATIONALE FOR A CLASSIFICATION SYSTEM

The classification system described is based on the rationale that classes of exceptional characteristics are related to various limitations and/or distortions in the learning history and present environment of the child as these have and do interact with the physical features and/or the psychological repertoires of that child. Present behavioral and learning characteristics reflect both a complex present external and internal stimulus environment as well as the cumulative effects of a complex learning history. Any child may be characterized by one or by any combination of the behavioral classes suggested. Thus, by describing the child along a number of different exceptional characteristic dimensions, the educator is directed toward providing differential programs for the different characteristics. This procedure replaces that of programming for a central diagnostic feature such as mental retardation, learning disabilities, giftedness, or deafness. Thus, the multiple-characteristics classification system emphasizes the uniqueness of each child and avoids the dangers of stereotyping and overgeneralization associated with the classification of *children* into discrete categories.

IDENTIFICATION OF EXCEPTIONAL CHARACTERISTICS

Exceptional learning and behavior characteristics are identified in the following manner:

step 1 | Initially, the child is *exposed* to situations that require, expect, or accept a certain type or range of learning and behaving. These requirements may be highly specific such as, "John, turn to page three and read for all to hear. I'll tell you when to stop," "Learn the math rules in section 2." Or these may involve a broader range of possibilities such as that associated with the request, "You should be good while I am out of the room." The expectations may refer to even broader categories such as "positive interpersonal skills," "positive contact with authority figures," "learning the fifth-grade curriculum at the pace presented," or "develop reading skills."

step 2   *A present standard norm or expectation* is delineated which forms the basis for assuming that a child should exhibit specific or general learning or behavior characteristics under specified conditions. For example, "John is nine years old," "regular education curriculum," "Susan attends the first grade," "Nan has a Stanford-Binet mental age of ten years," "Sue is an adolescent," "Calvin comes from a creative family," "member of a middle-class family."

Norms that define expected learning in the educational environment consist of the following instructional parameters:

1. *Type of instructional presentation.* The regular education classroom program is predicated on normal sensory-perceptual functions of the children served.
2. *Methods of instructional presentation.* The regular education classroom program is organized to be presented at a certain rate, in a certain sequence, and has an evaluation procedure to facilitate retention and generalization of learning.
3. *Content of instruction.* The regular education program is a curriculum designed around grade levels or content areas.
4. *Types of responses required.* The regular classroom program requires verbal and written communication, general mobility, and general attentional skills.
5. *Types and patterns of motivational conditions.* The regular classroom program requires the child to learn effectively under social, goal-attainment, and intrisic conditions.

step 3   Observation is made of *present learning and behavior characteristics* which differ from the amount or type of learning or behavioral characteristics required—sensory, motor, perceptual, linguistic, and motivational differences requiring more specialized and/or individualized educational accommodations. For example, "John sits and stares at the ceiling and finally bursts into tears instead of reading aloud to the class," "Ellen, with a severe hearing loss, has numerous disruptive outbursts in the regular class," "Katherine, who is twelve and attends the sixth grade, is able to read with understanding at a ninth grade level," "Tom requires frequent tangible consequences for adequate learning and behavior control," "Stephen learns only 10 percent of the academic material."

step 4   Assuming the reliability of observations that in defined situations the child or adolescent consistently demonstrates learning and/or behavior characteristics other than those expected, this discrepancy between (1) how and what the child learns or how he behaves and (2) that which the situation expects or is designed to accommodate defines the exceptional learning and/or behavior characteristics. The discrepancy may reflect rather specific differences—Jill is frequently late for class—or more general ones as implied in "eight-year-old John earned a mental age of 5.0," or "Anthony requires auditory or tactile instructional presentation."

GENERAL CLASSES OF EXCEPTIONAL CHARACTERISTICS

Exceptional learning and behavior characteristics may be broadly viewed as reflecting a combination of (1) *learning difficulties and behavioral deficits*, (2) *behavioral excesses*, and (3) *learning acceleration and creative activities*.

Exceptional charactistics may range from mild to profound discrepancies. Numerous extreme patterns of learning and behavior discrepancies in the cognitive and adaptive behavior areas are seen in children traditionally categorized as highly gifted or as severly and profoundly retarded or those traditionally provided the label of infantile autism. Less discrepant patterns of generalized and/or specific learning or behavior characteristics result in children being provided such categorized labels as mildly retarded, emotionally disturbed, learning disabled, or academically accelerated. The present scheme, by focusing on a variety of possible exceptional learning and behavior characteristics, provides direction to more differentiated and individualized educational programs.

LEARNING DIFFICULTIES AND BEHAVIOR DEFICITS

The educational environment does expect children and youth to learn and behave within general limits both in structured situations such as the classroom and in unstructured settings such as the home, the playground, the coffee house, and the peer groups. Children are shown pictures of various geometric forms and asked to identify the squares. Some do not do so. Others are provided a list of twenty-five words and asked to read them. Some are able to recognize only two of the words, although most of their classmates can read twenty or more of the words. Ethel does not learn the spelling words that her peers learn, even though she attends the same spelling classes and attempts to learn them. Jonathan sits and stares in a blank fashion at a cartoon movie while his peers respond with laughter and animated pleasure. Tom, a sixteen-year-old, fails most of his high school courses. Each child in these examples exhibits exceptional learning and behavior characteristics. This conclusion stems from the observation that behaviors in the form and strength expected and programmed for by the educational environment did not occur. A discrepancy existed *between what the child did and what various situations required or expected. This discrepancy represents the major focus of an intervention program.* The deficit represents a relative inferential construct, not a characteristic of the child. The child does not have a deficit in any absolute sense. He merely exhibits learning and behavioral characteristics that differ from those expected under the conditions of a specified instructional program.

Characteristics of Learning Difficulties

Prior to discussion of various classes or degrees of behavior deficits, clarification should be made of the difference between *learning difficulties* and *behavior deficits.* The term learning difficulties is a descriptive one and implies nothing more than the observation that a child so described does consistently demonstrate problems in the acquisition, short- and long-term retention, and performance of various academic and related tasks under specific types of instructional/learning conditions. Observation of the child's behavior in other types of situations (as examples, braille reader, amplified auditory signals, or frequent tangible reinforcers), along with information relative to his psychological/sensory characteristics, may result in the identification of factors which correlate with, contribute to, or produce these learning difficulties. For example, general intelligence test data may suggest that the learning difficulties on academic tasks are consistent with other types of behavioral/cognitive limitations. Data concerning visual and auditory functioning may suggest that the learning difficulties are related, at least partially, to sensory difficulties.

Thus, a distinction is made between learning difficulties and behavioral deficits. Learning is inferred from reliable changes in a child's behavior following exposure to a training, teaching, or educational experience. If a child consistently fails to exhibit the *expected* amount of behavior change—fails to learn after being provided structured and/or unstructured educational experiences—*learning difficulties* have been demonstrated. In this analysis the expected amount of learning or behavior change is based on a variety of child variables such as chronological age, mental age or other indices of cognitive characteristics, previous learning progress, level of skill development relative to specific learning tasks, and the conditions under which other types and levels of learning tasks were previously attained. Again, *learning difficulties* is an inference or, more appropriately, a conclusion drawn after reliable observations of a performance deficit. The critical factor in arriving at this conclusion is that a child does not acquire (learn) or retain (memory) expected behaviors after being exposed to a defined instructional program. This does not imply an absolute learner characteristic. Under other instructional conditions, the child may well demonstrate more effective learning and adaptive behavior.

This view of learning difficulties recognizes that a child who has been highly restricted in his contact with teaching experiences may demonstrate specific and even generalized behavior (achievement or skill) deficits, *but no learning difficulties*. He may learn quite satisfactorily, employing his present learning characteristics, after being provided educational experiences designed to teach specific behavioral skills. Many children and adolescents from inner-city neighborhoods or isolated rural areas may exhibit behavioral deficits due to lack of exposure to experiences designed to teach the skills on which the middle-class school curriculum and instructional method is based. They should not be viewed, however, as exhibiting generalized learning difficulties.[1]

Characteristics of Behavioral Deficits

The behavioral deficits of a given child may reflect one or a combination of the following:

The desired behavior may be completely absent or only poorly developed.   Laurie may be unable to read a single word in the primer used in her remedial reading program. Barbara may be able to recognize concepts of gender but only in an inconsistent and laborious manner. Susan may never have been able to reproduce geometric figures or to recognize the difference between *b* and *d*. The deficient behavior may be a result of *lack of opportunity to learn the desired behavior*. She may be unable to cut with scissors, to blend sounds, or to read a story because she has never been exposed to a learning environment designed to facilitate development of these behaviors. There has been no instruction. In other instances, *the child may have been provided inadequate or inappropriate learning experiences*. She may have been exposed to a learning program which made major use of auditory stimulation when she learns mostly by visual means. She may have grown up in a poverty environment which provided only limited stimulation or poor early education. Another child may have been exposed to standard teaching methods and materials but was unable to learn.

The desired behavior may be in the child's repertoire but may not occur on a consistent basis.   The child may be able to engage in the desired behavior but does so only infrequently. He knows how to be polite, but seldom is polite. He knows how to solve math problems, to write, or to stick to a difficult task until completed. Yet he seldom engages in these behaviors in situations which require them.

1. There obviously is an interaction between learning facility and the degree and length of time spent in a restricted or deprived environment. If previous restrictions have been lengthy and severe, a generalized reduction in learning facility may result. A more highly individualized remedial, compensatory, as well as developmental, educational program may be required to offset or lessen the adverse effects of such restrictions.

The desired behavior may occur but only under restricted cue and reinforcement conditions.   The child will talk with mother but is mute in the classroom. The adolescent is able to read third-grade-level materials but does so only when encouraged to do so by his football coach. Desired behavior may be in the child's repertoire but occurs only under conditions of frequent tangible reinforcement. Under less favorable conditions, the behavior becomes erratic or does not occur at all. Jim will complete his table work when the teacher sits next to him and provides frequent praise; he seldom completes a task when left alone.

The desired behavior may be present but not in the correct form. John may misarticulate or present a number of words in a dysrhymic manner even though he can be understood.

Bijou 1971; Clements 1966; Rimland 1964

Behavior deficits may reflect neurologic or other physical conditions which may restrict or greatly impede the learning or performance of the desired behavior.* Care must be exercised, however, in assuming that these deficits are, in fact, totally a result of physical limitations. The child with obvious neurological, sensory, or muscular impairment may well be able to acquire new behavior patterns and to engage in these under normal conditions if provided carefully designed learning experiences which reflect his learning and performance requirements. Such requirements would include the child's present behavioral repertoires, the learning style as reflected in the types, intensities, and mode of stimulus (instructional) presentation, as well as reinforcement variables. As an example of the learning style, Ross* suggests in light of research reported by Dykman et al.* that it might be valuable for teachers of some children with learning difficulties to "speak more slowly and repeat their messages so as to accommodate to the slower 'thinking time' of their students" (p. 110).

Ross 1974
Dykman et al. 1970

In describing certain of the child's difficulties as representing behavior deficits, it is not being suggested that the child does nothing. When we report, "Ted never completes his class assignment," we are not reporting what he *does do* when presented an assignment. The child does do something in a situation that requires him to exhibit some other desired behavior. When we report that a child "does not name the primary colors correctly," we are not reporting what he in fact does when requested to name the colors. He may sit, stare, cry, fidget, say "I don't know," become overly emotional, or the like. We are merely reporting that under certain conditions, appropriate color-naming behavior does not occur. We also may know from previous exposure that color-naming behavior has *never* been observed in the child. Thus we may conclude that color-naming behavior is missing from his repertoire and label this as a *deficit behavior area.* The behaviors which *do* occur under conditions in which color-naming behavior or completion of a class assignment was required may be of two types. First, behaviors may be ones which actively interfere with the child's learning the names of the colors—high-rate stereotype behavior, short attention-span behaviors, or intense anxiety behaviors. Thus, these competing, disruptive behaviors are viewed as *excessive behavior patterns* because they actively interfere with the occurrence and/or acquisition of more desired behavior.

Or the behaviors which do occur in situations in which "missing" or deficit behaviors are inferred may be of a type which would not interfere or impede the acquisition and/or performance of the desired color-naming behavior. For example, the child may look at the colors and label them incorrectly or may engage in a wide range of other behaviors which denote that the desired behavior is not in the child's repertoire. These behaviors, however, might be easily displaced as the child acquires the appropriate color-naming responses.

One additional point needs emphasis. In designing a program to facilitate the development of desired behavior which will eliminate the deficit, the program must begin with what the child *does* do. A program cannot be based on "deficit," "absent," or what-the-child-does-not-do behavior. These do not exist. The starting point must be with what the child does do. Additionally, the primary program focus is on the development of competency—not the remediation of deficits or prevention of problems.

EXCESSIVE BEHAVIOR PATTERNS

Excessive behavior refers to that inappropriate behavior which actively interferes either with the performance of other desired behaviors or with the acquisition of new, appropriate modes of responding, and which is viewed as undesirable by others in the child's environment. The form of the behavior may be highly undesirable, e.g., stereotyped behavior or echolalia. In other instances the child may engage in behavior, which is typically viewed as appropriate, but in an excessive manner in terms of the requirements of a specific situation. For example, seeking approval is a natural and desirable social behavior, but a child who seemingly is constantly engaged in attention seeking to the detriment of his class assignments is demonstrating excessiveness. This behavior may be predominately of a social nature (as examples, talks too much or too loudly, hyperactive, too much withdrawal or avoidance, too aggressive) or of an emotional nature, such as excessive fearfulness. As noted, these behaviors usually result in adverse reactions from others due to their excessive frequency, intensity, or duration of occurrence.

Some behaviors, such as violent temper tantrums, may be excessive regardless of where or when they occur. Other behavior, such as "clowning," while being appropriate for some situations, is viewed as excessive if the place or frequency of its occurrence is not appropriate. Still other behavior, such as making apologies for wrongdoing, may be quite adaptive but could be viewed as inappropriate if a child spent excessive time and effort apologizing for every minor mistake.

It is also true that in some cases behavior appears to be excessive merely because a child or adolescent may have so many general behavior deficits in relation to the requirements for various situations. The obvious limitations of appropriate behavior overemphasize the few acceptable ones which may be present and, thus, render these excessive and inappropriate. A child with limited cognitive skills who tells the same few jokes over and over again illustrates this. If the child had a wider range of socially appropriate behaviors, the "excessiveness" quality of his telling jokes would be diminished. In this case, the child may not know what to do in various situations; therefore he engages excessively in what he does know.

Provoking Qualities of Excessive Behavior Patterns

Excessive behavior patterns are quite likely to be labeled as exceptional by the social environment. Because of the apparent visibility of such behaviors, it is easy to notice conflict with or deviation from general standards of conduct. Excessive behavior patterns also may create concern due to the fear that the child does not have control of his behavior and it thus might get out of hand. Such behaviors are most likely to be considered bothersome if they interfere with the rights and privacy of others.

One additional factor that renders excessive behavior patterns of particular concern is their apparent self-defeating character. Why, for example, does a child continue to engage in high-rate sterotyped behavior, or avoid contact with peers, or be excessively quarrelsome with his friends? It is difficult to understand what is accomplished by such behaviors. There is a tendency to view such behaviors as a result of some pathology or sickness.

Factors Maintaining Excessive Characteristics

In some instances, the factors which maintain excessive behavioral characteristics are easily identified. Even though such characteristics are constantly rejected by the teacher, peer attention may serve to provoke and maintain the problem behaviors. In other instances, excessive behavior patterns appear to persist in the absence of any discernable reinforcing conditions. These patterns become even more puzzling when they persist in the face of obvious punishment, as is evident in some instances. This persistence of excessive behavior patterns, even though punished and in spite of no obvious reinforcing conditions, has been labeled the *neurotic*

Mowrer 1948   *paradox.* *

Under such conditions it may be that the child has no alternative behavior available. While the reinforcement associated with the excessive behavior patterns may be minimal, the child simply has no other suitable behavior to exhibit. In contrast, most children will attempt various alternative behaviors when a particular behavior pattern does not result in desired consequences.

It is also true that much excessive behavior, such as temper tantrums, fighting, or stealing, may reflect the absence or low strength of other behavioral skills subsumed under the concept of self-control. That is, the observed problematic behaviors may be a reflection of behavioral deficits in aspects of self-control which, if present, might actively inhibit or control the excessive behaviors.

Viewing behavior characteristics as excessive serves a useful function in that it pinpoints response features inconsistent or perhaps even physically incompatible with desired behavior. Not only must the strength of excessive behavior be reduced but, in most instances, the child must acquire some other behavior to replace the undesired one.

In summary, a major class of behaviors which interfere with the adaptation of the child and adolescent to their social, interpersonal, and academic environments includes those which occur excessively, either generally or in relation to specific situations. Some behavior, such as interrupting others, may be inappropriate due to the high frequency of the behavior. Other behaviors such as violent temper tantrums, even if occurring at a lower rate or in isolation, may not be appropriate. The major maladaptive component is thus the frequency or the magnitude of the behavior.

Excessive patterns of behavior may interfere with the acquisition of competency behavior patterns and/or may compete with the occurrence of appropriate behavior which is in the child's repertoire. Such behaviors also increase the possiblity of confrontation with others, which in turn increases the likelihood of aversive experiences and decreases the likelihood of positive consequences. The focus of an education program thus becomes that of eliminating or decreasing the frequency or magnitude of problem behaviors while *prosocial competency behaviors are strengthened to replace these.*

INTERRELATIONSHIP OF DEFICIT AND EXCESSIVE BEHAVIOR CHARACTERISTICS

In relation to the requirements of a specific situation, it may be found that closely related patterns of excessive and deficit behaviors are present. Some may even appear to be the counterpart of the other. In illustration, a child may demonstrate learning difficulties in a school program. It may be found that the child has an obvious attentional problem and is rather hyperactive and distractible. Should the teaching strategy be directed toward reducing the child's hyperactivity (excessive behavior) or increasing his attending skills (behavioral deficit)? In this instance it would be useful to describe both the deficit and excessive behavior areas related to the learning difficulties. Reduction in activity level will not categorically insure improvement in attending skills. A child may even be hyperactive and still have good attending skills. Of central importance is describing what the child does do in situations that require (expect) some other behaviors. Labeling a problem as reflecting a deficit merely emphasizes the missing skills. A missing skill is not the counterpart of an excessive behavior pattern. Behavior that does occur may be physically incompatible with the learning and performance of more useful behaviors. But the reduction in strength or elimination of excessive behavior does not insure the appearance of the desired behavior. It just renders it more likely under appropriate learning or performance conditions.

As another example of the reciprocal relationship of excessive and deficit characteristics, an adolescent may be quite disruptive in his academic classes. In assessing this problem, the teacher was initially unable to identify events accounting for the disruptive behavior. Further assessment, however, revealed that the verbal skills and subject matter content which the adolescent did not have were required in his academic program. The situation was rather unpleasant as he was called upon frequently to perform at a level beyond his skill development at that time. The excessive disruptive behavior served to remove the unpleasant performance requirement temporarily, although such behavior merely served to increase further his general behavior deficits.

In the above example, the requirement to perform served to train the adolescent in acquisition of excessive behavior patterns. Exposure to frequent conflict or frustration experiences resulted in producing excessive negative emotionality and associated avoidance, or defensive, behavior. Excessive time and energy was thus expended in defensive behavior instead of in attending to and interacting with an instructional program in which he potentially could acquire appropriate academic, emotional, and interpersonal behavior characteristics.

ACCELERATED LEARNING AND CREATIVE ACTIVITIES

A third class of exceptional characteristics, that of accelerated learning and creative activities, is viewed as exceptional as there is a discrepancy between the regular classroom program and the learning and behavioral characteristics of the child. As a result, additional and specialized instructional systems must be provided if the child is to utilize his characteristics fully.

RELATIVE NATURE OF EXCEPTIONAL CHARACTERISTICS

In viewing behavioral patterns from the discrepancy viewpoint, it is important to remember the previous discussion that learning and behavior characteristics are not categorically or inherently inappropriate, inadeqate, or exceptional. As noted, these characteristics are defined, simply, as what a child does do under specific learning or performance conditions. They must be viewed as exceptional only in relation to the expectations of specified environments. Ethel's creative musical characteristics are exceptional when compared with those of her regular class peers. In her musically inclined family, however, she is viewed as below expectations. John, a twelve-year-old child with general cognitive behavior deficits, may read successfully at a third-grade level. He may exhibit no reading behavior deficits when reading a primer-level book to his younger sibling. On the other hand, when attending his sixth-grade class, John needs a higher level of reading skills than is required in the former situation. He exhibits deficit behavior characteristics in the reading area in relation to the requirements of the class situation or in relation to that expected of a twelve-year-old child.

Similarly, one behavior pattern may be viewed as excessive in one situation and acceptable in another. A child may be described as "too aggressive" in a situation where the person in control of that particular environment judges such behavior as "too aggressive" and will not accept it. In this environment the behavior is likely to be responded to in a manner designed to eliminate or discourage the aggressive behavior. The same behavior, viewed as aggressive in this situation, may not be viewed as such in others.

The consequences of these differences in learning and behavioral requirements can be most significant for specific children. A child may adjust in one situation but not in another even though he learns or behaves in a highly similar manner in both. A child may not be viewed by his inner-city neighborhood culture as having generalized cognitive behavior deficits but may be labeled "mentally retarded" when placed in a middle-class school system. Educational program objectives based on observed deficit and excessive behavioral areas of specific children thus must be viewed in terms of specific environmental requirements, as these define the excessiveness and deficitness.

OBJECTIVE DESCRIPTION OF EXCEPTIONAL CHARACTERISTICS

Program planning for educational activities must evidently begin with a description and reliable measure of what the child does do in the situations that define the exceptional characteristics. In many instances this assessment procedure presents no problems. A child reads five pages per class period and must produce eight in order to meet minimal teacher standards. Another reads at the second-grade level and must read at the fourth-grade level to be eligible for placement in a work-study program. Perhaps a child is unable to remember the numbers of the two different buses that he must take in order to travel from home to his special school. Or another is provided regular class instruction although able to handle two grade levels higher. The above are quite straightforward; they are easily definable, identifiable, and measurable. Exceptional characteristics can be stated in precise quantitative terms that are readily understandable.

In most other instances, however, the requirements of definition and reliable measure of exceptional characteristics are not so easily fulfilled. Learner characteristics may frequently be described in terms of typology, abilities, traits, dynamics, and the like. Such general descriptions as the following are inappropriate: "unable to assume responsibility," "socially insensitive," "can't get along with peers," "doesn't follow through," "poor cognitive skills," "blows up," "insufficient motivation," "creative," or "gets angry too frequently." These are general, somewhat vague descriptions. It becomes necessary to reduce the general description to more precise learning and behavior characteristics definable in terms of what the person actually *does*. Additionally, the characteristics must be lodged in situations where certain behaviors are *required*. The behavior description "can't get along with teachers" is defined in terms of what the child does *not* do in relation to given environmental requirements. As "getting along with teachers" may well entail a variety of behaviors, especially as teachers vary greatly in terms of the behavior they require of children, one is in a position to develop a meaningful behavior-change program only after a detailed analysis of what the child actually does in relation to what is required.

THE CLASSIFICATION SYSTEM

The following classification scheme is based on an educative model and is descriptive of the exceptional learning and behavior characteristics presented by children and adolescents. The classes are defined in terms of *relative deviation* from various environmental requirements. It recognizes that any exceptional learning or behavior characteristics are defined in a context of program or person expectations of what and how the child should learn or what he should do. In recognition of the developmental, and thus transitory, nature of many exceptional learning and behavior characteristics, the educator in using the classification scheme may expect that many problems are age, stage, or situation specific and thus may be self-correcting with the passage of time. For example, absence of toileting skills is viewed as a deficit behavior discrepancy in a four-year-old but not in an eight-month-old child.

The learning and behavior classes proposed are quite arbitrarily defined in terms of observable characteristics relative to various behaviorally defined learning and performance expectations. Again, the scheme represents a classification of behaviors (aggressive behavior) rather than of children (aggressive child). This is consistent with the position of Phillips et al.* that there is "need for a classification of behaviors and not of personality, of disorders and of individuals" (p. 43). This scheme is preferred over those discussed previously as it avoids, as noted, any preconceived or stated assumptions or implications *of specific causation or etiology, present controlling variables, prognosis, or treatment limitations.* There is insufficient knowledge at present to assume otherwise. The scheme mimimizes the dangers of overgeneralization and stereotyping which frequently accompany diagnostic and related classification schemes.

Phillips et al. 1975

The major purpose of the functional classification scheme is to facilitate the assessment procedure of pinpointing exceptional learning and behavior characteristics of children and adolescents. Each child's unique combination of difficulties must be viewed in the context of (1) his total behavioral repertoires (that is, his resources as well as his difficulties), (2) a present social environment, and (3) a history. If a child has had exceptional learning and behavior characteristics for a lengthy period of time, his total "personality" has been influenced, as have those persons who comprised his social enviornments. His present learning and behavior characteristics are not static ones. A child lives in a social environment, influences it, and is influenced by it. The classification scheme will not render more *simple* what obviously is a *complex* result of numerous historical and contemporary variables. In fact, it emphasizes, by providing a variety of exceptional learning and behavior categories, the complexity of a child's characteristics. Instead of focusing on a child's "mental retardation" or "emotional disturbance," the educator focuses on educational programming for a multitude of behavioral dimensions.

As suggested, an intervention program does not "treat" mental retardation, provide "therapy" for emotional disturbance, nor "educate" a learning disability. Rather, the intervention effort focuses on the various specific characteristics of a child. If he is hyperactive, displays a short attention span, has various other attentional difficulties relating to discrimination learning, is one year delayed in reading skills, and alienates his peers by his frequent whining and temper tantrum behavior, *these are the characteristics* which are provided attention. As described in later chapters on evaluation and program development, an analysis is made of possible factors contributing to exceptional characteristics, their possible interactions, and the possible interactions among the child's various learning and behavioral characteristics (assets and exceptional).

The scheme does not assume that the categories are totally mutually exclusive. It is recognized that various patterns frequently do cluster together.* However, unless empirical data denote etiologic or treatment significance, such co-appearance is viewed merely as correlational and not causative. Similar behavior patterns in different children may result from either similar or different factors. Even the same behavior of a child occurring in different settings may be influenced by different factors. The burden is placed on the educator to determine the functional interrelationships of various characteristics (if there are any) and the possible functional relationships between these and other situational, physiological, and personality variables.

Lovaas 1967; Quay 1972

CLASSIFICATION OF EXCEPTIONAL CHARACTERISTICS

I. Learning and behavioral deficits

A. *General and specific knowledge, ability, and skill deficits*
    A.1. *Self-help and self-care behavior deficits.* This category includes deficits in such areas as toileting (enuresis and encopresis), feeding, dressing, grooming, and independent traveling.
    A.2. *Language and cognitive behavior deficits.* This category includes difficulties in both receptive and expressive speech and language areas as well as behavioral skills subsumed under the general areas of "cognitive abilities and skills," for example, problem solving, concept formation, abstracting, generalizing, and other complex verbal behavior.[2] This category would include (1) such mediational skills as rehearsal and memory search and scanning involved in the acquisition, retention, and retrieval of information, and (2) speech production difficulties—articulation, phonation—reflecting deficit skills.
    A.3. *Academic behavior deficits.* This category includes school-related general and specific deficits in such areas as reading, spelling, and mathematics skills.
    A.4. *Sensory and perceptual discrimination deficits.* This category includes many of the difficulty areas associated with the visually and auditorially impaired, the "perceptually handicapped," and "learning disabled" child. Included would be such skills as those associated with (1) auditory, visual, and kinesthetic discriminations related to sounds, numbers, letters, words, spatial location, laterality, and directionality and

---

2. The writer follows the definition of cognitive behavior presented by Skinner (1968) and Bijou (1971) as "knowing how to do things and knowing about things." As a detailed discussion of this position is beyond the scope of this book, the interested reader is encouraged to consult these two references as well as Skinner's 1953 and 1957 books for elaboration.

(2) figure-ground discrimination, spatial and temporal orientations, integration of intersensory information and obtaining closure of discriminations.

A.5. *Locomotion and manual skills deficits.* In addition to mobility deficits associated with skeletal and muscular difficulties, this category includes those areas associated with difficulty with sensory-motor integration such as gross and fine eye-hand coordination, writing, or copying visual patterns.

A.6. *Self-management skills deficits.* This category includes those implicit verbal skills involved in self-direction, self-management, or self-control.

B. *Task-related behavior deficits*

B.1. *Deficits in prerequisite skills.* Included in this category are those weak or absent skills prerequisite to effective learning—attention span, attending to relevant aspects of learning tasks, a reflective cognitive style, persistence, concentration, and so on.

B.2. *Deficits in output skills.* This includes poor quality output, poor quantity output, and erratic output, for instance, a child requiring 50 percent more time to complete an assignment than do his classmates.

C. *Interpersonal (social) behavior deficits*

C.1. *Deficits in sex-role behaviors.* This category would include the excessively effeminate male and the excessively masculine female.

C.2. *Deficits in play and/or social interaction skills.* This category would include the child who may be labeled as shy or as being a "loner." (It would not include the child who actively withdraws from social interaction in an effort to avoid aversive experiences. This avoidance behavior reaction is included in II. D.2 as an excessive reaction.)

D. *Affective behavior deficits*

D.1. *Deficits in the types of emotional behavior expressed.* This category includes the child who has difficulty in expression of such emotional reactions as "glee," "happy," "laughing," "affection," "sad," "guilt," "shame," "apprehension," "love," or "anger."

D.2. *Deficits in the intensity of emotional behaviors.* Included in this category would be the child who has difficulty in expressing, in a free, spontaneous, intense manner, the variety of emotions described above. Such a child is frequently described as being overly inhibited, excessively shy, or "too guarded."

D.3. *Deficits in the appropriateness of emotional behaviors.* This category describes the child who expresses various positive or negative emotional reactions under inappropriate stimulus situations (e.g., laughs when a peer gets hurt, becomes highly jealous when others are praised, is apathetic under happiness-provoking conditions).

E. *Deficits in level of motivational development*
  E.1. *Deficits in the types and amounts of incentive conditions required for learning and performance.* This category is illustrated by the child who is not influenced consistently by the types and amounts of incentive conditions provided in a specific learning or performance situation. A classroom situation may depend upon such motivational features as task completion, parental approval, self-reinforcement, grades, and occasional teacher praise to insure learning and performance. A child who requires large amounts of contrived teacher-provided consequences would not be successful in this environment.
  E.2. *Deficits in the reinforcement schedule required for learning and performance.* The child who consistently requires excessive teacher approval or frequent peer attention would demonstrate a deficit in reinforcement schedule in an environment which provided these consequences only on an infrequent basis.
  E.3. *Deficits in self-managed motivational skills.* This category is illustrated by the child who is excessively dependent upon externally managed incentive and reinforcement events due to poorly developed skills of self-arousal, self-reinforcement, and self-punishment.

F. *Deficits in age-relevant personal and social responsibility behaviors.* This category includes the overly dependent child who lacks the skills to react in the absence of excessive support or direction from others.

G. *Others.* (Specify.)

II. Excessive behaviors
  A. *Excessive disruptive and nonfunctional competing behavior*
    A.1. *Excessive disruptive interpersonal behavior.* This includes such behaviors as aggression, threatening others, noncompliance, defiance, negativism, and other excessive behavior involving direct social interaction, which is of a disrupting nature.
    A.2. *Excessive disruptive socially inappropriate behavior.* This includes the variety of behaviors which are called "delinquent" in which the defining characteristic is that of being illegal. Such behaviors as truancy, stealing, fire setting, property damage or destruction, and the like are included here. It also would include socially rejected sexual differences such as homosexuality.
    A.3. *Excessive nonfunctional competing behaviors.* This category includes such behaviors as stereotyped responses, self-mutilation, compulsive rituals, excessive eating, excessive

fantasy, daydreaming, excessive masturbation, impulsivity, antilearning attitudes, and bizarre speech (both production and content). These behaviors are nonfunctional in that they do not contribute to the personal, social, or physical adaptation or well-being of the child.

B. *Excessive affective reactions*

B.1. *Excessive emotional reactions resulting from presentation of external events.* This category includes a variety of phobias, generalized anxieties, or oversensitivity to reprimand or other cues of rejection.

B.2. *Excessive emotional reactions resulting from removal of events.* The "separation anxiety" reaction illustrates this category.

B.3. *Excessive emotional reactions resulting from various frustration conditions.* This category includes excessive reactions resulting from conflict, delay of reward, or thwarting of ongoing or anticipated activity; temper tantrum behaviors as well as those described as low-frustration and tolerance-related; overreaction to failure.

B.4. *Excessive emotional reactions resulting from self-generated cognitive behaviors.* This includes states of misery, depression, specific fears, anxiety, and related emotional behaviors created by self-generated verbal behaviors. The child or adolescent who excessively labels himself as inadequate, worthless, sinful, or unacceptable represents an example.

C. *Excessive motor behaviors*

C.1. *Excessive speech-related reactions.* This category includes such speech features as stuttering and vocal intensity.

C.2. *Excessive activity level.* This category includes hyperactivity and distractibility.

D. *Excessive avoidance behaviors*

D.1. *Excessive avoidance of tasks and activities.* This includes mobility avoidance of aversive features of various academic endeavors, competitive activities, or situations such as the classroom.

D.2. *Excessive avoidance of interpersonal and social contact and/or interaction.* This category would include the child who actively avoids or withdraws from interpersonal contact and/or interaction in an effort to avoid aversive experiences. The category also includes active nonresponsiveness when confronted with social stimulation.

E. *Others.* (Specify.)

III. Acceleration in learning and creative activities
This category includes accelerated learning and creative activities defined in terms of rate of acquisition of academic and related content, level of artistic development, and uniqueness of creative output.

CORRELATES OF EXCEPTIONAL CHARACTERISTICS

Although factors involved in the development and maintenance of various of these exceptional characteristics were discussed in Chapter 2 and are provided additional consideration in future chapters, these are enumerated briefly to emphasize the rather complex interrelation of contributing factors.

Some of the exceptional characteristics may reflect the effects of sensory, neurological, and other physical conditions such as skeletal and muscular mobility and strength or general and specific health aspects. A child's motor behavior deficits may be related to cerebral palsy, or such speech production features as articulation difficulties may reflect the effects of a cleft palate or a severe hearing loss. These may create difficulties in academic learning which in turn may produce excessive emotionality and social interaction problems.

Various combinations of present exceptional characteristics may interact with various environmental variables to produce learning difficulties. In illustration, deficits in generalized cognitive skills or perceptual discrimination deficits may interact with improperly organized and presented instructional experiences to produce extreme reading and math skill deficits and/or inadequate transfer of training and memory difficulties.

Some of the exceptional characteristics—generalized restrictions in cognitive skills, for example—may result from a lengthy restriction of varied experiences, as in cultural deprivation, and others from extensive culturally different learning experiences (e.g., "socialized delinquent" or "socially maladjusted" behavior). The exceptional characteristics may reflect a mismatch between the motivational characteristics of the child and the incentive conditions in the child's environments. Too few aspects of the instructional program, for example, may have positive reinforcing characteristics; too many aspects may have aversive qualities. Selected aspects of the adolescent's environment, including alcohol, drugs, food, homosexual activities, or inactivity, may be more influential than available, socially sanctioned events. Such a motivational mismatch may result in poor development of school-related skills due to the excessive influence of incentives for the competing inappropriate activities.

CLASSIFICATION AND PROGRAM DEVELOPMENT

As noted, if there is anything special about the exceptional learner, it is the necessity to provide more individualized educational experiences for maximum learning and adaptation. A suitable case has been made for the position that this cannot be done merely by providing programs based on gross category features such as mental retardation, learning disabilities, or behavioral disorders. If one child has fifteen exceptional characteristics, each of these should be considered in his educational programming. If another child has ten exceptional characteristics, each should be provided individualized attention. As an initial step in this programming process, the educator must assess the child's exceptional characteristics, identify or speculate about functional correlates of these, identify learner assets, and develop a detailed set of program implications. Table 5.1 gives a brief illustration of this assessment process. The educator is then in a position to select an instructional system(s) to devise and deliver the educational experiences required to meet the child's competency needs. Further detailed illustration of the assessment and program development process is provided in Part IV.

TABLE 5.1   Guide to Learner Assessment

Exceptional Characteristic	What Does Child Do	What Is Child Expected to Do	Possible Correlates	Learner Assets	Program Implications
I A.3. Academic behavior deficits.	When reads aloud in grade-level reading materials, exhibits omissions, sound-blending errors, hesitations, substitutions, and poor use of context cues. Comprehends only 25% of reading material.	Read with fluency and 85% comprehension.	Inadequate instruction, inadequate incentive conditions, excessive negative emotionality, hearing loss.	Normal-range cognitive skills, relates well to adults, likes school.	Task analysis of reading materials, training in sound blending, use token reinforcement procedure, use easier materials, provide frequent reinforcement and social approval. Model a relaxed pleasant manner of reading.
I B.1. Deficits in prerequisite skills.	Attends to reading instruction for 2-3 minutes.	Attend to reading instruction for 10-15 minutes.	Excessive failure in attending to reading tasks viewed as avoidance behavior.	Attends for long period when presented easy materials.	Gradually shape attending skills by providing easy and structured performance tasks, use high-value reinforcers initially, label and praise increase in attending skills.
II A.1. Excessive disruptive interpersonal behavior.	Fights with peers 3-4 times weekly, disruptive comments during class study period on average of 4-5 times daily.	No fighting, no disruptive comments.	Isolated by peer group, teased by peer group over being fat, poor self-concept behaviors.	States desire to have friends, responsive to tangible reinforcers, likes male student teacher.	Develop contingency program for appropriate classroom behavior, encourage peer group activities, use male instructor.

REFERENCES

Bijou, S. W. Environment and intelligence: A behavioral analysis. In R. Cancro (Ed.) *Intelligence: Genetic and Environmental Influences.* New York: Grune and Stratton, 1971. Pp. 221–239.

Bryan, T. H., and Bryan, J. H. *Understanding Learning Disabilities.* Port Washington, N.Y.: Alfred Publishing, 1975.

Clements, S. D. *Minimal Brain Dysfunction in Children.* Public Health Service Publications, No. 415. Washington, D.C.: U.S. Department of Health, Education and Welfare, 1966.

Dunn, L. M. (Ed.) *Exceptional Children in the Schools: Special Education in Transition.* (2nd Ed.) New York: Holt, Rinehart & Winston, 1973.

Dykman, R. A., Walls, R. C., Suzuki, T., Ackerman, P. T., and Peters, J. E. Children with learning disabilities: Conditioning, differentiation, and the effect of distraction. *American Journal of Orthopsychiatry,* 1970, 40, 766–782.

Lovaas, O. I. A behavior therapy approach to the treatment of childhood schizophrenia. *Symposium on Child Development.* Vol. I. Minneapolis: University of Minnesota Press, 1967. Pp. 108–159.

Mowrer, O. H. Learning theory and the neurotic paradox. *American Journal of Orthopsychiatry,* 1948, 18, 571–610.

Neisworth, J. T., and Greer, J. G. Functional similarities of learning disability and mild retardation. *Exceptional Children,* 1975, 42, 17–24.

O'Grady, D. J. Psycholinguistic abilities in learning-disabled, emotionally disturbed, and normal children. *Journal of Special Education,* 1974, 8(2), 157–165.

Phillips, L., Dragun, J. G., and Bartlett, D. P. Classification of behavior disorders. In N. Hobbs (Ed.) *Issues in the Classification of Children.* Vol. 1. San Francisco: Jossey-Bass, 1975. Pp. 26–55.

Quay, H. C. Patterns of aggression, withdrawal, and immaturity. In H. C. Quay and J. S. Werry (Eds.) *Psychopathological Disorders of Childhood.* New York: John Wiley, 1972. Pp. 1–29.

Rimland, B. *Infantile Autism.* New York: Appleton-Century-Crofts, 1964.

Ross, A. O. *Psychological Disorders of Children.* New York: McGraw-Hill, 1974.

Skinner, B. F. *Science and Human Behavior.* New York: MacMillan, 1953.

Skinner, B. F. *Verbal Behavior.* New York: Appleton-Century-Crofts, 1957.

Skinner, B. F. *The Technology of Teaching.* New York: Appleton-Century-Crofts, 1968.

PART II

Humanistic Behavioral Approach

6

Humanistic Behavioral Approach: Basic Viewpoints

The humanistic behavioral approach represents an alternative to the assumptions and practices of the internal deviancy approach introduced in the previous chapters. As emphasized, this alternative has a primary behavior focus. Figure 6.1 illustrates how the behavioral approach focuses on what a child *does*—how he relates to others, what he accomplishes, what he reports about his emotional experiences, how he approaches a learning task, how he performs in a competitive situation. The approach is basically empirical, observational, and pragmatic. In recognizing the essential humanness of covert verbal and emotional behaviors, it follows a strategy that attempts to describe overt manifestations of behavior in data language and to identify functional relationships that may exist between these and other stimulus and behavioral events.*

Kanfer and Phillips 1969; Thoresen and Mahoney 1974

This approach studies the child as he behaves under defined environmental conditions. If a child has difficulties adapting to classroom requirements, he is studied in the classroom environment as he actively relates to those requirements. The approach is concerned with facilitating the development of more appropriate ways of behaving in those instances where the child's behaviors do not fulfill the major requirements for success in his relevant environments. Attention focuses both on the development of new characteristics as well as on changing present characteristics to insure more competency. Any behavior patterns, including the usual academic ones such as word recognition, speed of reading, and concept formation, as well as such personal characteristics as social graces, reflectiveness, friendliness, positive emotionality, and self-confidence are of interest. It is in agreement with the position of Tharp and Wetzel* that the

Tharp and Wetzel 1969

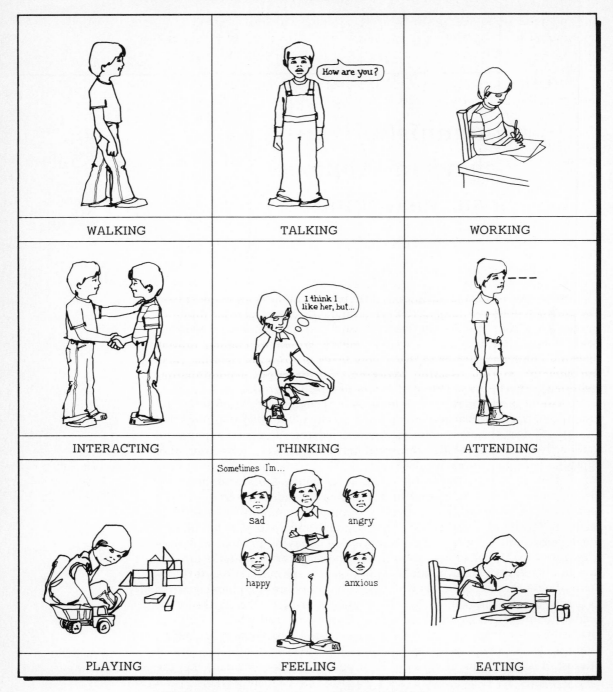

FIGURE 6.1.   Behavior Is . . . What the Child Does

most effective point of educational intervention with a child who displays exceptional learning and behavior characteristics is most likely the disturbing present environments in which the child resides, rather than an inferred disturbing set of internal conditions.

This chapter and the one following describe a series of viewpoints reflecting the major assumptions and characteristics of the humanistic behavioral approach. These viewpoints, along with the content of the six chapters of Part III on various learning theories and principles, provide the conceptual, principle, and methodological base for behavior change techniques available to those working with exceptional characteristics of children and youth.

✳ Viewpoint 1   Behavior is caused.

No behavior "just happens." The humanistic behavioral system makes use of various learning theories and principles and other related relationships in specifying (or in speculating about) the factors which cause—produce, strengthen, and maintain—learning and behavioral characteristics. It accepts the position that if a particular bothersome learning and/or behavior characteristic is viewed as resulting from previous experiences, the principles and/or constructs used to account for that previous development also can be used in efforts to change present learning characteristics or to teach new ways of thinking, feeling, relating socially, talking, reading, working, self-directing, accomplishing, planning, reflecting cognitively, and so on.

Although the major conceptual systems for viewing behavior development and change are those of learning theories, other principles and constructs of behavior development and change derived from the behavioral and social sciences are utilized. Aspects of conflict theory* and constructs describing the role of anxiety in excessive avoidance behaviors,* as discussed in Chapter 13, are examples of these.

Maher 1966

Martin 1971

✗ Behavior Strength Influenced by Consequences

The major concepts are based on empirical relationships which indicate that much behavior is influenced by changes which this behavior produces in the environment. Behavior is strengthened if it results in positive consequences or removes or decreases the intensity of unpleasant ones. To illustrate, if appropriate reading responses are followed by desired effects, such skill behaviors will be strengthened.

The same is true of a wide range of other behaviors. A child's self-management behaviors will be strengthened if these produce positive consequences or remove present or impending negative events, and such self-management behaviors are more likely to occur under future similar circumstances. A child's reflective cognitive style will be influenced by positive effects produced by certain forms of this characteristic. If a child's temper tantrums or his aggressive behaviors produce positive consequences or remove unpleasant conditions, these behavior patterns are likely to be repeated under future similar circumstances.

As the relationship between specific behavior and given consequences becomes a reliable one, the consequences begin to influence the occurrence or nonoccurrence of the related behavior in a given environment or situation. A disruptive adolescent will soon learn to complete his reading assignment if the result is additional time to participate in desired recreational activities in the gymnasium. An assignment not completed means he remains in the classroom during this free period. Completing assignments becomes a stronger behavior for the adolescent when it produces a positive consequence. It may also become enjoyable because it is associated with teacher praise, peer approval, and possible self-satisfaction for completing assignments.

On the other hand, behaviors that result in failure to complete an assignment, which is then followed by unpleasant or aversive consequences, are less likely, under usual circumstances, to reoccur for a period of time. A frown from the teacher, threats from peers, loss of recess privileges, feelings of anxiety, or a reprimand from the school principal will typically render behaviors that precede these unpleasant events less likely to occur under similar circumstances in the future. Such consequences usually produce some negative emotional reactions in the child, and these may become associated both with the preceding behavior and with the person and situations providing the negative consequences. The relationship, as the examples suggest, includes presentation of unpleasant events—a frown, for example—as well as removal of desirable events, such as loss of recess privileges, for failure to complete an assignment. Both represent punishment and exert a similar effect—that of decreasing the likelihood of future occurrence of the behavior producing the unpleasant events.

⅄Management of Contingency Relationships

Behavioral contingencies, thus, refer to relationships between behaviors and their consequences, both positive and negative. The discerning educator becomes sensitive to the various contingencies involved in a child's behaviors and arranges for those consequences which result in the more desired child reaction. *Contingency management* refers to influencing the type and time of occurrence of various positive and negative consequences. The teacher who is unwilling or unable to engage in contingency management will be haphazard in influencing how and what a child learns and how and under what circumstances the child behaves. Additionally, under such conditions, the child will experience difficulty developing sensitivity to various task requirements and the expectations of persons involved in various situations. He will also find it difficult to develop a sense of responsibility and other self-directed behaviors in dealing with his environment.

Related principles also provide some basis for estimating the amount of behavior change that can be expected within a given period of time. A behavior pattern, for example, that has been followed by desirable consequences on numerous occasions will typically be more difficult to eliminate than behavior that has only just begun to produce a favorable consequence. At the same time, behavior that has resulted in highly pre-ferred consequences on only a few recent occasions may be more likely to occur or more difficult to eliminate than behavior that has resulted in low-preference consequences on a good many previous occasions. An adolescent who is exposed to numerous reinforcing events will have an easier time learning a range of new behaviors than will the adolescent who experiences only a few reinforcing events. These examples of a few of the relationships of the behavioral approach (described in greater detail in ensuing chapters) illustrate both the simplicity and the complexity of the behavior principles and related concepts that are involved.

Approach Based on Variety of Behavioral Concepts

In addition to these and similar principles associated with such learning models as *reinforcement, emotional, social modeling (imitation)*, and *self-regulation,** the behavioral approach represented in this book emphasizes the interactional dimension articulated by Mischel* and Staats.* Present classes of behavior, or repertoires, are viewed as interact-ing with each other and with present environmental events, which results in their influencing the acquisition and performance of new behaviors. The approach, as noted, is also consistent with ecological concepts* which emphasize this reciprocal relationship between a child's behavior and his natural environments.

Bandura 1969; Kanfer and Phillips 1970; Thoresen and Mahoney 1974; Mischel 1968; Staats 1975
Barker 1968; Rhodes 1970

The relationships between behavioral characteristics and internal and external environmental events, as suggested by learning models, form the basis for a set of procedures useful in effecting behavior development and change. *These behavior principles and related concepts suggest what should be done if learning and behavior characteristics are to be influ-enced in a certain manner,* whether the program objective is one of teach-ing a child to attend to teacher instruction, to read a book, enjoy a peer, strengthen positive self-regard, make auditory discriminations, to become involved in a cooperative endeavor, improve memory skills, persist at a difficult task, learn with greater facility, decrease his feelings of inferiority, acquire self-direction skills, or assist a peer who seeks his help.

The learning and related models are useful both in developing hunches about how a present behavior pattern has been acquired and is presently being maintained and how a child may learn, maintain, and

Eysenck 1970

generalize a new or modified way of behaving. Although the principles and related procedures are emergent ones and, thus, far from being complete,* the humanistic behavioral approach does have sufficient substance for effective use by the behaviorally oriented educator, parent, or therapist.

The assumption that behavior is caused and that most behavior is learned does not imply that all children learn best under the same set of conditions. *The behavioral approach places major focus on assessing and programming for individual differences.* The approach recognizes, for example, that the same arithmetic lesson presented to a group of children will have different effects on different children as a result of numerous factors, including the present repertoires of each child, each's "motivational" states, and each's present physical and sensory characteristics.

*Viewpoint 2   Behavior principles are descriptions of relationships which exist as natural phenomena.

Although knowledge of many of these principles has evolved from basic experimental laboratory research, these principles are not mechanistic, animalistic, coersive, or fatalistic. They are merely statements of relationships between behavioral and environmental events which exist as natural phenomena. *These principles were not invented; they were discovered.* To illustrate, the law of effect is a statement of a *discovery* that human behavior is influenced in a lawful manner by events which follow the occurrence of the behavior. The manner in which relationships are put to use in influencing child learning and behavior may be coersive or self-serving, but the relationship itself is nothing more than a description of a natural phenomenon.

Behavior Principles vs. Hypothetical Constructs

These behavioral principles and related ideas should be distinguished from hypothetical constructs associated with various other motivational and personality systems which have been devised to account for exceptional learning and behavior characteristics. Theoretical constructs, and related hypothetical relationships between these constructs and various aspects of learning and behaving, may be useful in some instances, but not when used in a manner which presumes these relationships were *empirically established.* Numerous of the constructs used by educational, psychological, social work, and psychiatric personnel are confusing, and even potentially dangerous, as they frequently have minimal if any objective referents or associated means of obtaining reliable observations. This is illustrated in the statement by Morse* that "a recent study of the adolescent self-concept demonstrates how much this is the core of adjustment" (p. 576). The inference from such a statement is that the construct "self-concept" determines adjustment patterns. The overt behavior patterns, it is

Morse 1967

assumed, are mere manifestations of this more basic determinant. The implication of this inference is that maladjustments may be eliminated by changes in the hypothetical "self-concept." There is insufficient evidence to assume that such is the case. The behavioral position does recognize that self-concept behaviors may well be *one* of the multitude of interacting variables which influence the occurrence of other "adjustive" behavioral characteristics. As discussed later, it is just as likely, however, that direct change in "adjustment" characteristics may have a facilitative and reciprocal effect on changes in self-concept behaviors.

* **Viewpoint 3**   Each child's personality is unique.

The uniqueness of a child's personality, defined as enduring overt and covert behavioral characteristics and their interrelationships, is quite understandable, even though a *common* set of principles of learning and behaving is assumed to underlie such behavior development, maintenance, and modification in all children, both typical and exceptional. As each child develops under different sets of environmental conditions which interact both with different biological characteristics and with different experiential histories, each child acquires a unique set or combination of behavioral characteristics. Many exceptional learning and behavior characteristics of children are products of this complex interaction.* The totality of these, and the manner in which these interact and thus mutually influence, make up the child's personality. Since each child with exceptional learning and behavior characteristics is unique, educational experiences must be individualized to maximize this uniqueness and to respect and enhance individual development.*

Ross 1974

Haring 1973

Viewpoint 4   The behavioral approach to problems of child development and functioning is humanistic in its focus on the individual and his uniqueness.

The positivistic nature of the approach engenders a philosophy which focuses on that which is good for children and adolescents with exceptional learning and behavior characteristics. It should prove useful to pause a moment prior to an elaboration of this and comment on a controversy which has arisen between "humanism" and "behaviorism." For many persons, the concepts of "humanism" and the concepts and practices of "behavior modification" are incompatible.* Many professional persons involved in education hold strong opposition to a behavioral approach in dealing with exceptional characteristics of children and youth.* The opposition is most frequently based on a rather narrow view of behavior modification and on philosophic proclamations and not on any empirical data indicating that a sensitive use of behavioral procedures *does* produce adverse effects which conflict with tenets of humanism. On the contrary, as will be documented through the book, there is considerable opinion that

For example, Bühler and Allen 1972; Matson 1973

Carrison 1973; Lindsey and Cunningham 1973

Mahoney and Thoresen
1974

Thoresen 1972

just the opposite is true. For instance, Mahoney and Thoresen* indi-cate that "the major goals of humanists—such as heightening awareness, fostering compassion, developing a sense of unity (mind and body), and transcending the immediate environment—may be achieved by using behavioral techniques" (p. 309). Thoresen* argues cogently that abstract and subjectively based humanistic interests and goals can be translated into what children and adolescents would do.

Mechanistic Label Is Inappropriate

Black 1973; Matson
1973; Perelman 1973

Thoresen 1974
Avila 1972

Nevertheless, those who follow the behavioral approach not in-frequently are labeled as mechanistic, nonhumanistic, and concerned about only the "outside" dimension of human experience.* In contrast, humanists are depicted as expressing warm concern for the whole child, the "inside" aspects of his experiences, and his unique personality.* As Avila* noted, "Use of the term [humanism] immediately develops a good-guy/bad-guy categorization. The humanist, the one who cares, is the good guy and everyone else is a bad guy. A behaviorist, then, is automatically a bad guy" (p. 579).

Behavioral Approach Represents a Methodology

Thoresen 1974

But as Avila points out, humanism basically refers to a philosophic position, and behaviorism has reference to a methodology.[1] *As such, these are not incompatible.* Thoresen* noted:

> Educators and behavioral scientists can act to help the individual act in positive, meaningful ways with himself and with others. There are many ways to take such actions. One way offers considerable promise: the syn-thesizing of social-learning principles and techniques with the goals and concerns of "humanistic" psychologists and educators. This effort to syn-thesize is referred to as *behavioral humanism*. We can benefit from the work of both behaviorists and humanists if we reduce the confusion, ambiguity, and misunderstanding about contemporary behaviorism and humanism and if we develop and use new scientific methods tailored to the study of human phenomena. [p. 309]

Staats 1975

In a similar vein, Staats* concludes a discussion of what he terms *social behavioral humanism* with the following comments on the issues between the subjective (humanistic) and objective (behavioral) approaches:

1. Although Skinner's (1974) recent book *About Behaviorism* describes a philosophy of behaviorism, and writers in humanism such as Wilson (1970) advocate a blending of psychology as a discipline with ethical forms of humanism, this distinction remains a meaningful one.

There are no insuperable differences in the basics of the two approaches. There are essential aspects of both that can be combined to yield a framework for studying human behavior, for treating problems of human behavior, and for making social and personal decisions with respect to ourselves and others. Such a philosophy of human science, it is suggested, is more complete, less erroneous, and more productive than either approach alone. [p. 490]

Humanistic Features of Behavioral Approach

Numerous features of the behavioral approach to exceptional learning and behavior characteristics as described in this book are quite humanistic. The approach does not impose any preconceived judgments or overgeneralizations about what a child is or should be. Its keen sensitivity to the potential influence which various external and internal experiences may have on a child alerts the behaviorally oriented educator to monitor his or her program and to provide those experiences which do enhance the child's development and functioning. A major focus of social-behavior theory* as reflected in the humanistic behaviorism of this book is on the child's covert symbolic and emotional processes. As Thoresen* noted, such a position "views the individual person as a dynamically changing organism rather than a passive receptacle of enduring responses" (p. 315).

Bandura 1969; Staats 1971, 1975; Thoresen 1974

Thus, a behavioral position with its objective methodology and related behavior principles and concepts can be quite humanistic in its application to child and adolescent behavior. In fact, many contemporary behavioral educators, counselors, and psychologists view themselves as humanists.* Avila* has suggested:

For example, Day 1971; Hosford and Zimmer 1972; Lazarus 1971; Skinner 1974; Ullman and Krasner 1969; Avila 1972

Behaviorists are quite concerned with the human condition and how to improve it. They have developed some of the most effective techniques available for making people more successful and healthier. For example, some of their approaches to learning have set up classroom conditions that can really for the first time guarantee that each individual in them will be successful. [p. 579]

Emphasizes Uniqueness of Every Child

The behavioral approach articulated in this book is *humanistic* in that it recognizes and develops programs consistent with the uniqueness of each child. Every child is different to the extent that his physical characteristics, e.g., sensory, neurological, activation level, or temperament, and his previous and present experiences are different. The approach is based on various assumptions and principles which focus on the unique child as he functions in various social learning environments. The approach provides direction in designing a variety of experiences which help children to behave in more humanistic ways. As elaborated upon below, learning and behavioral inadequacies or difficulties are viewed as resulting at least partially from inadequate learning experiences. The child with difficulties has not been successful. He has not learned how to learn nor to enjoy learning. In fact, a child who is unsuccessful has been punished excessively and has thus acquired a variety of antilearning attitudinal and related escape and avoidance behaviors which further impede learning of new competencies. These difficulties are not blamed on the child or on some alien internal deviations unless these internal variables can be measured objectively and shown empirically to result in the learning and behavioral inadequacies.

Focus on Influencing Prosocial Characteristics

Ayllon et al. 1975; Ayllon and Roberts 1974; Galvin and Annesley 1971

The approach focuses on means of influencing prosocial behavior development, including positive emotional and attitudinal aspects, as the major strategy for dealing with problematic or exceptional characteristics. Ayllon et al.,* Ayllon and Roberts,* and Glavin and Annesley* all provide illustration of this approach. By emphasizing reinforcement of academic achievement in "emotionally disturbed," "learning disabled," and hyperactive children, all noted improvement in academic learning as well as in emotional and behavioral problems areas. The approach also emphasizes the prevention of problem areas through design of learning environments which match the instructional programs to learner requirements, thus insuring successful development of prosocial competency behaviors. This something-can-be-done-now position is followed, even though it is recognized that many individual differences among children may have a genetic component.*

For example, Jensen 1969, 1973; Ross 1974

The behavioral approach is humanistic in its recognition of unique "personality" characteristics of each child and in its emphasis on the development and utilization of behavioral skills of self-management and self-direction.*

Thoresen 1972; Thoresen and Mahoney 1974

Personality characteristics reflecting numerous previous learning experiences serve to influence at any given time the acquisition and performance of other characteristics. And through the acquisition of certain language and affective behavior patterns, the child can become quite actively involved in influencing and directing other of his own behaviors. Socialization and related educational experiences are viewed as being critical to the development of independence and self-direction.

Patterns of humane emotional, reasoning, self-concept, and similar behaviors are not only recognized and fostered but, further, the humanistic behavioral approach emphasizes the critical role of these and related repertoires in the development and occurrence of those prosocial behavior patterns which comprise personal competency and freedom. Problems develop frequently when aspects of these are missing. A specific child may be viewed as "emotionally disturbed," for example, when he is unable to control his fighting, his explosive emotionality, or his excessive eating and soiling. The humanistic behavioral approach, rather than focusing on the presumed "internal emotional disturbance," would provide learning experiences designed (1) to reduce or extinguish the intense disruptive emotional reaction and to foster development of more postive emotionality, (2) to provide the child with verbal behaviors which effectively serve to direct or cue other prosocial behaviors incompatible with fighting, and (3) to insure that eating the proper amount and types of foods, as well as proper toileting behavior, would be personallly reinforcing—meaningful, self-enhancing—to the child. Verbal behaviors such as "I can eat properly," and "I am strong," "I can do," "I can solve problems" may be encouraged because they could then be used by the child to direct, reinforce, and maintain his own proper eating and toileting behaviors. Such self-directing and self-reinforcing skills, however, represent the end results of numerous learning experiences and entail imitation of behaviors observed in others as well as frequent reinforcement by others of approximations of the behaviors as these evolve.

> **Viewpoint 5**   Children learn to behave in a humane manner—that is, to be emotionally warm, enthusiastic, self-reflective, concerned, sensitive, involved —by living in an environment which provides a preponderance of positive reinforcement provided by a variety of social models.

The home and school environment must arrange for the systematic development of these complex, humane behavior patterns in children and adolescents. Social models, as one example, must actively encourage and systematically reinforce approximations of complex socialization skills. The development of these characteristics is not left to chance or to some mysterious unfolding or actualization process. Mere exposure to various "actualizing" environments, such as the open classroom,* without consideration of the child's developmental facility to assimilate such experiences, can have a most devastating effect. It is recognized that the positive features of the humanistic behavioral approach can have a sufficient impact on children and adolescents to the extent that teachers, parents, and others in the child's life *live* the assumptions and utilize the principles of the approach as they interact with the child. Children cannot acquire behavior patterns of happiness, self-assurance, or social sensitivity if placed in an educational environment with peers whose major patterns of behavior are those of anxiety, hyperactivity, social isolation, low achievement, and unpredictable explosive emotional expression. Nor can these positive patterns develop fully if children interact frequently with adults who are too demanding or punitive. A serious strategic error is committed by isolating children with exceptional learning and behavior characteristics from appropriate patterns of prosocial behavior and by placing them together in a segregated and isolated manner.

Knoblock 1973; Kohl 1969; Rogers 1969; Weber 1971

To reiterate: *The humanistic behavioral approach emphasizes the individuality and integrity of every child. It does not desecrate the child by* imposing concepts of internal deviation or pathology. It enhances the child by respecting his uniqueness and by attempting to individualize an educational and humane environment in order to promote success. A child cannot learn "happy" behavior patterns unless others in his environment display such complex patterns. In like manner, a child cannot develop patterns of anxiety and defensive behaviors unless the social environment imposes these on him by modeling these or by providing him with excessive failure and other aversive experiences.

The behavioral approach emphasizes that excessive failure is highly inconsistent with the development of humanistic characteristics. An "emotionally disturbed," "mentally retarded," or "learning disabled" child cannot learn an achievement orientation, to be relaxed, satisfied, friendly, or to be free of anxiety, and related defensive behavior patterns in an environment that promotes excessive failure. A child with severe visual or auditory problems cannot learn to like himself, to relate warmly to others, or to accept his own sensory limitations realistically if he experiences a preponderance of failure.

Frequent failure seldom contributes to positive behavior development. It is probably true that a modicum of failure is valuable to children with exceptional characteristics in promoting various desirable skills of adaptation such as (1) those involved in the analysis of a problem situation in order to identify the faulty components or (2) those involved in acceptance of failure without undue emotionality or the elicitation of other disruptive and nonadaptive behaviors such as depression or withdrawal. However, education is ineffective when *excessive* failure occurs. Excessive failure, additionally, can impede learning, inhibit problem-solving behavior, or result in the development of unpleasant conditions which result in active avoidance of meaningful problem solution. An environment which produces excessive failure is thus highly inconsistent with a humanistic approach to behavior development and modification.

Viewpoint 6   It is useful to view general and complex behavioral characteristics as representing various repertoires or classes of behavior.

The total behavioral characteristics of a child may be described in terms of such classes or repertoires as verbal behaviors, cognitive behaviors, academic behaviors, motor behaviors, emotional behaviors, social behaviors, perceptual behaviors, and self-care behaviors. Or it may be useful to describe the child in terms of more circumscribed behavior patterns such as his self-concept behaviors, independence behaviors, patience behaviors, self-control behaviors, and affectionate behaviors. Behavioral descriptions reflected in adjectives (he is a *patient* child), adverbs (he behaves *patiently*), and nouns (his *patience* is) are viewed as having reference to classes or types of behaviors which the child demonstrates with some consistency. Instead of speaking of a child's self-concept, reference is made to his self-concept behaviors. In describing the child in terms of such observable behavior patterns, the teacher, parent, or therapist is in an ideal position to raise such relevant questions as: How can I influence the child's behaviors of interacting with others, his self-concept behaviors, his self-control behaviors?

These *arbitrarily defined* groups of behaviors are based on similar descriptive characteristics. It should be emphasized, however, that no assumption is made that these repertoires represent basic behavioral traits or that the same factors influence the occurrence of all behaviors within a specific repertoire. Lovaas and Koegel* suggest that various behaviors may cluster together but be functionally independent. In working with individual behaviors which frequently cluster together in autistic children, these writers report that changes in one behavior of the cluster may have little effect on other behaviors.

Lovaas and Koegel 1972

Describing a child as being shy or honest, for example, does not imply that his observed behavior reflects a basic trait of shyness or honesty. The consistency of a particular behavior pattern may vary considerably from time to time and from situation to situation.* Some behaviors may be highly consistent across many settings, others highly variable. A child may be excessively shy around strange adults but outgoing and spontaneous with familiar peers. He may be honest at home but dishonest in school. He may cheat but never steal. He may be compliant around male adults but noncompliant around female adults. He may be aggressive in school but not in other settings.* Thus, certain clusters of behaviors may appear consistently in some settings but not in others.

Mischel 1968

Hartshorne and May 1928; Patterson 1972; Sears et al. 1965; Wahler 1975

We can see, therefore, that the behavioral viewpoint accounts for behavioral consistency in terms of the consistency of specific external and internal stimulus events; it rejects the use of constructs such as traits or personality types which suggest central "cores" or layers of influence.

Viewpoint 7   Behavior is viewed as a result of a biologically and experientially unique child and his present environment.

The behavior of a child at any one time "represents the end point of the interaction of genetic-constitutional factors, the current physiological state of the individual, his current environmental conditions, and past learning which, in turn, was a function of a similar interaction"* (p. 6).

Ross 1974

In this relationship, *behavior* refers to everything that a child does. The basic units of behavior responses build up through learning into more complex behavior patterns or characteristics and into even broader behavior classes or repertoires.* The humanistic behavioral approach deals both with *overt* (publicly observable) and *covert* (private) behaviors. Private events* such as thoughts, feelings, ideas, or images, observable only to the child who is engaging in them, are recognized as assuming a vital role

Kanfer 1972; Reynolds 1968; Ross 1974

Skinner 1953

Homme 1965 in much of a child's observable behavior. Homme* suggests that these be viewed as *coverants* or covert operants. There are sufficient data available to indicate that these internal responses are influenced in their development and occurrence in the same manner as are overt behaviors (see Chapter 12).

The *biological component* refers to the child's total physical charac- Bijou 1972 teristics. As noted by Bijou,* abnormal biological factors may limit a child's response equipment—his sensory, motor, and/or neurological connecting systems—and thus interfere with or reduce his normal response potential, or they may provide an abnormal internal environment such that stimuli usually present are either absent or else occur with higher than usual intensity or duration. Under these conditions abnormal reactions may occur, as when a child is overreactive to minor distractions. Additionally, temporary current physiological states, such as fatigue, hunger, or a brief low blood sugar level, may influence how a child will behave. Any of these states may exert significant influence on the manner in which the child will respond to various external events. In the case of the latter, however, the child's responses may change noticeably under different internal conditions associated with sufficient rest and food. Other physical factors represent influences which are more consistent and lasting, as with hormonal or enzyme deficiency, a muscular injury, or a sensory irregularity such as a visual or hearing loss. In the case of sensory and muscular handicaps, the child may be limited in the types and intensities of stimuli to which he may be receptive and to the types of responses which he can make. Again, the child's current behavior will reflect the influence of these individually unique physical states or conditions.

The *environment* refers to both external and internal stimulus events. Moods, anxiety states, the stimulus components of various verbal and motor responses, as well as external events such as the teacher's instructions or the sarcastic implication of a peer's comments, all may influence behavior at any given time. These environmental events (external and internal) may exert a momentary influence, an inconsistent but yet frequent influence, a consistent but minor influence, or a consistent and strong influence.

Viewpoint 8   The child is viewed as an active, changing learner in his interactions with his environment. Behavioral characteristics which describe a child at a specific time interact with environmental events to determine the specific behavioral influence which these events will exert on the child.

The child is viewed as having the potential for acquiring skills of self-management, self-responsibility, problem solving, decision making, reality testing, and the like. Children can learn under appropriate conditions to evaluate problem situations and, on the basis of their histories of experience, to select or choose those behavioral alternatives which offer them the best possibilities of being successful. A child does not automatically develop these skills of self-control, self-direction, or independence. A child does not in some mysterious fashion become skillful in making choices and in tolerating the effects of poor choices without excessive disruptive emotionality. A behavioral system, contrary to critics who label it mechanistic, is in fact quite humanistic as it seeks to promote these skills of self-independence and self-responsibility through application of principles of behavior development and change.

A child can learn to manage himself, to make choices, and to assume responsibility for appropriate as well as inappropriate choices when in a social environment which on a daily basis and in numerous interactions respects his individuality and which provides systematic and continuous exposure to experiences designed to facilitate these characteristics. Children learn to be responsible for their own behavior as they are exposed to situations which demonstrate frequently and clearly that their own behavior does produce various positive or negative consequences. In such a setting, the child does not develop a range of defensive behavior patterns of blaming others for his own inadequacies. The child is taught to analyze failure situations and to identify the exact source of difficulty. At the same time the educational environment is so arranged that the child has a vast preponderance of success experiences. He is reinforced for maximum effort with maximum realistic consequences. He is taught that his own hard work, his own problem-solving skills, his own self-analysis, his own creative endeavors produce positive results.

In such an environment, the child also is taught to accept his limitations. He is taught to be realistic, to invest maximum organized effort but also to expect failure on occasion if his goals are set too high. He is taught to accept failure in a discriminating manner and without excessive personal disruption.

Child Both Influences and Is Influenced

At any moment in a child's life, there is constant interplay between the child's current repertoires and stimulation (external and internal) to learn and to behave. This interaction results in gradual changes in various behavior characteristics. This individual interaction between the child's behavior characteristics (personality, learning, motivation) and stimulation is viewed by some writers as reflecting the child's perceptions or his phenomenological view or interpretation of his world.* The humanistic behavioral position emphasizes this individualistic or subjective feature of the child's personality and views it as a result of the child's unique history of experiences.

For example, Patterson 1973; Rogers 1961

The child thus is not blindly at the mercy of specific rewards or punishment or of external or internal cues to respond in a designated manner. A specific consequence will have quite varied effects on different children depending upon each child's specific behavior makeup. This emphasizes the inefficiency of assuming that a common instructional program or a common set of consequences (grades, teacher praise, parent approval) will produce optimal learning and behaving in all students.

Freedom Is . . .

Much of the child's active participation with external stimulation or his freedom to make choices concerning what he is to do or what effects various external events will have on him is related generally to the variety and complexity of his behavioral repertoires, and specifically to his verbal and related emotional repertoires. As the child acquires a larger language repertoire, he develops the possibility of more self-management. He can begin to *cue himself,* to *admonish himself,* to *arouse himself,* to *reinforce himself,* or to *"turn off" the effects of external stimulus events* by engaging in a range of competing behaviors. He may be able to "talk himself into certain emotional states" such as anxiety, fear, or anger. Or he may be able to remain calm and relaxed under situations which typically produce disruptive emotional reactions. In some instances the child may have an increased readiness to respond to certain external events in one manner which may be quite different from his response to this same external event when in a different emotional state. By providing a label of "he is safe" or "she is nice," a child may respond to a person in one manner which would be quite different from his response if he labeled the person "selfish" or "dangerous." *These examples emphasize that a child is not passively at the mercy of external stimulus events.*

Staats 1971

Behavior is thus viewed both as an *effect* and as a *cause.* Behavior that a child acquires through learning is a result both of events in the child's environment as well as serving as cues for other responses. As Staats* has suggested, the "individual causes his own behavior" (p. 254). Thus, to the extent that he is characterized by a range of behaviors, he may well relate to external stimulus events in a highly active and individual manner.*

Baer 1972; Gottman and Leiblum 1974; Thoresen and Mahoney 1974

To elaborate, as a child develops a variety of behavioral possibilities he is in a position to make choices among these. A child cannot choose between reading for pleasure and watching TV as a leisure-time activity unless he can read and enjoy it. If he cannot read, he *has* no choice. Freedom of choice, then, is dependent initially on the presence of behaviors which have somewhat equal likelihood of occurrence under defined conditions. A child must first have behaviors in his repertoires before he can use these to interact with his external environment. To be free to engage in assertive behavior in a discerning fashion, a child must have assertive behaviors in his repertoire which he has learned to use in any situation in which he is being imposed upon. Such situations would include those which involve younger peers as well as those in which same-age peers, parents, teachers, and other "authority" adults are viewed as imposing themselves on the child.

Use of Counter-Influence Tactics

A self-directing child may use "counter-influence" procedures as he interacts with an environment that attempts to influence him. He may challenge, refute, refuse to accept or comply, or actively reject the influence of others. He may negate the possible effects of positive reinforcing events, for example, by labeling them in a contrary fashion: "That's childish," "He's trying to soften me up," "What a bore!" A child may be characterized by a complex set of attitudinal behaviors toward authority figures. Various verbal, emotional, and related social behavior may be of a negative sort. Praise from a teacher may actually result in negative effects rather than reinforcing ones. *Thus, an event is not defined in terms of its apparent qualities but rather in terms of the effects it has on a child's repertoires.*

Exceptional Characteristics and Freedom

Even though every child has the *potential* for some degree of active participation both in making choices about what he is to do and in influencing the effects of certain experiences on his behavior, it is recognized that a combination of inappropriate learning experiences and physical limitations can result in a child who may behave in a seemingly blind, irrational, and self-defeating manner. A child may well be so restricted or different in his behavioral repertoires, due to inadequate experiences or to physical limitations, that he appears to merely react instead of acting with any independence or self-direction. Children labeled as "emotionally disturbed" frequently react to frustrating conditions in an emotionally disruptive manner. The child appears to have little control over his behavior; when frustration occurs, he responds blindly, instantly, and intensely. Another child may be a conformist to the extent that he reacts consistently to whatever is required by the external environment. He may have little choice over what he does.

The humanistic behavioral approach views this "lack of self-direction" as most undesirable and advocates learning experiences which provide the child with more adequate self-management skills. General and specific suggestions for facilitating the development and use of self-management behaviors are presented in Chapter 12.

> **Viewpoint 9**   Present behavior is influenced by present events. These events may be of an external or internal nature.

Present environmental events, not historical ones, exert direct influence over present behavior. Some present events mark the time and place of behavior. Other events strengthen behavior due to their reinforcing qualities. Some present events discourage or suppress behavior due to their aversive qualities. Some present events trigger positive or negative emotional behaviors. Thus, behavior as it occurs in the present is a result of external and internal events that occur in the present. This position is elaborated upon in the following sections.

Learning and Behaving Influenced by Internal Events

Although a major emphasis of the behavioral approach is on the delineation of external environmental events which may be involved in the initiation, strengthening, and maintenance and persistence of behavior patterns, major consideration is also given to possible influential internal events. As noted, a child's verbal behaviors may influence other classes of behavior in numerous ways. The "emotionally disturbed" child may be preoccupied with his own thoughts—be involved in his fantasies and daydreams. He may be thinking about previous unpleasant experiences with adults, peers, classrooms, and the like at the time the teacher attempts to get his undivided attention. Emotional moods and other reactions such as anxieties, fears, excitement, sadness, and elation may be present and thus serve to facilitate, or to interfere with, a range of other emotional or nonemotional behaviors. Although these events cannot be observed directly, recognition that such internal factors may be operative emphasizes the complexity of factors which may in fact influence behavior at any given time. It also emphasizes that a suitable behavioral education program should attempt to influence appropriate verbal and related emotional and other behaviors which may successfully compete with distracting patterns of internal behavior.

Focus on Present Events

In devising an educational program to modify present behavior patterns, characteristics of the present experiences of the child should be evaluated in order to develop hunches about how the behavior is being initiated and maintained in the present. These hunches will then give direction to a program which restructures the present experiences. The relevant questions from an educative viewpoint thus become: "What *present* events (internal and external) precipitate and maintain a given inappropriate behavior pattern in the present?" "What *present* learning and behavioral characteristics and environmental conditions interfere with the development of more appropriate learning and performance?" "What present physical characteristics impede, or contribute to, various learning and behavior possibilities?" The educative implication of this position is that most behavior patterns can be changed in most instances if, and only if, aspects of present external and internal environmental conditions change.

> **Viewpoint 10**   Present events which influence behavior have acquired their influence because of previous experiences.

The vast majority of events which influence present behavior have acquired their influence over various components of a child's behavior by way of previous learning experiences of that child. Historical experiences influence the child's interpretations or perceptions of present stimulus events and thus the effects which these events have on various of the child's behaviors. The principles or rules of learning and behavior influence discussed in the following chapters denote both the manner in which behaviors may be acquired as well as how various environmental events gain certain functions and resulting influence over behaviors of the child.

> **Viewpoint 11**   Present behavior patterns, while being influenced by present events, represent the culmination of numerous previous learning experiences.

Consistently occurring behavior patterns, whether appropriate or inappropriate, are frequently the end result of literally hundreds of previous experiences. At any given time, any new experience may exert only a minute influence on the development, maintenance, modification, or elimination of various complex behavior patterns. But 25, 100, 200, 500, or even 1,000 such experiences could, on the one hand, gradually result in an obnoxious, argumentative, highly anxious, aggressive child, while more appropriate experiences could result in a cooperative, attentive, enthusiastic child.

As a child enters into new situations he brings with him those repertoires he previously acquired and maintained in other environments. Thus, experiences gained in previous settings may account for learning and behavior characteristics which occur in a present setting. In illustration:

> Jill may demonstrate temper tantrum behavior under slight provocation after entering a developmental education program. This behavior may persist, much to the puzzlement of the teacher, even though she consistently ignores it and lets it run its course. An examination of the learning history in the home may reveal that the temper tantrum behavior has on occasion produced reinforcing consequences. The mother, on an irregular basis, had given in to the child following such behavior and permitted the child to have her way. This infrequent and intermittent success has resulted in a highly persistent and difficult-to-eliminate behavior pattern. Knowledge of

*previous learning conditions under which the behavior pattern
developed removed the mystique from the behavior and provided
support for the teacher in her strategy of eliminating the behavior
through ignoring it and of teaching more appropriate
frustration-related behavior.*

This position is contrary to the popular belief that persisting learning difficulties and bothersome behaviors result from some inferred internal pathology or some single or small number of past traumatic experiences such as reflected in the statement by Palmer* that "learning through one single traumatic condition is so often reported in emotional disturbances that the clinician often looks for such an incident" (p. 15).

Palmer 1970

Except in rare instances, an analysis of a child's history will not reveal single or even a limited number of specific traumatic or other critical experiences which would account for present recurring behavior patterns. As noted, these patterns usually represent an accumulation over time of numerous specific learning experiences which gradually and insidiously produce behavioral reactions that become problematic and alarming to the teacher or parent. It may appear in some instances that a single incident was the critical event in the occurrence of a child's alarming behavior. However, in most instances this experience was only the "straw that broke the camel's back." A closer look may well reveal the gradual, although subtle, development of problematic learning and behavior patterns. The child is less and less able to concentrate for long periods of time, or to be as productive as he was at an earlier time, or to work as independently of teacher support as he had been able to do. A single or small number of final dramatic incidents may result in the "big explosion," e.g., the obvious failure, the breakdown of many of his skills of cooperation, and so forth. This breakdown experience can have rather extensive and intensive negative repercussions. The child may be highly embarrassed by his temper tantrum, for example, and the entire school environment may become "fear provoking." Thus, in analyzing the history of the child for events which may explain present behavior patterns, focus must be toward delineating the day-by-day experiences the child has had instead of seeking some exotic, crucial, or traumatic-type experiences.

In summary, although the behavioral approach focuses on exceptional learning and behavior characteristics as these occur in a present social and physical environment, the position does recognize that these behaviors are rooted in earlier experiences of the child. In fact, to the extent that present exceptional characteristics can be viewed as learned behavior, *prior* learning is a *given*. All prior experiences are viewed as possible influential factors in the creation of present behavioral repertoires. The family's role is viewed as of utmost importance in attempts to understand and delineate the *development* of present behavior in young children, since most experiences of early childhood are provided by family members.

A child who is highly aggressive, argumentative, disruptive, or difficult to manage, for example, does not behave in this manner as a result of some "emotional disturbance" or of some few past experiences. Rather, components of these complex behavior patterns have been acquired over a lengthy period as a result of literally hundreds or even thousands of social experiences with adults, siblings, and peers. Likewise, a child who is attentive, highly interested, and easily stimulated to engage in new behaviors does not exhibit these characteristics because he is "normal" or "good" or "talented." These behaviors have evolved out of numerous previous learning experiences.

>**Viewpoint 12**   Explanation of behavior may be of a contemporary or of a historical nature.

The behavioral model approaches the question of explanation (e.g., "Why can't John read?" "Why does Susan behave as she does?") from both a functional (*contemporary*) and a developmental (*historical*) viewpoint. This represents an elaboration of the previously presented viewpoints that present behavior is a result of present events which gain their meaning or influence from past experiences. From a functional viewpoint, as emphasized, present behavior is viewed as being caused or influenced by present external and internal stimulus conditions. The child's present covert behaviors—his emotional reactions, his thinking, his perceptions or interpretations of various external or internal events—may be the source of present internal stimulation that influences the likelihood of occurrence or nonoccurrence of other specific behavior patterns. As Reynolds* has noted: "An adequate explanation of behavior is one that specifies the actual conditions which reliably produce the behavior to be explained. Statements about the causes of behavior are accepted as valid only when they specify what can actually be done under given circumstances to produce that behavior" (p. 2).

Reynolds 1968

Functional Explanation

A child's fearful behavior toward dogs may be said to be caused by the presence of a dog. The dog, when present, causes or produces a fear response in the boy. A functional relationship has been established and may be depicted as follows: the fear behavior is a function of (caused by) the stimulus event, dog. Or the causes may be more complex and include, for example, the dog at night when the child is alone. Appropriate contemporary explanation, therefore, is viewed as demonstration of a functional relationship between present behavior and present precipitating events. The procedure of demonstrating a functional relationship between behavior and events is called a *functional analysis*.

Developmental Explanation

Although behavior is influenced by present covert and overt events, it is evident that these events have acquired certain behavior influence features through previous exposure. The manner in which, in the previous example, the dog acquired its fear-provoking qualities for the boy requires an analysis which differs from that undertaken in understanding the conditions which presently influence the fear behavior. If ones wishes to understand the *origin* or *development* of the fear reaction, one is engaged in establishing a *historical explanation* of the behavior pattern.

In such an attempt, an effort is made to reconstruct the previous learning experiences which have resulted in the present fear-provoking components. The behavioral approach would supplement the description of "what happened to the child" with a logical exposition of the learning principles which would account for or explain the manner in which the previous experiences resulted in the present relationship between the stimulus events of the dog and the child's reactions.

A recent experience of the author will illustrate this explanatory process. Susanne, a young child, was seen in a child development clinic as a result of the parents' concern over her extreme fearfulness of dogs:

> In addition to becoming highly upset at the sight of a dog, she objects strenuously whenever the parents mention the possibility of visiting the nearby zoo, will not ride in an automobile with her grandparents, and will leave the den whenever pictures of dogs or of zoos are presented on television.
> An interview with the grandparents revealed that the child had been frightened by a large dog some twelve months earlier when they had taken her to the zoo. They had not reported this incident to the parents because they were afraid the parents would not permit them to take the child out again. Thus, from a learning viewpoint, the historical explanation of the present puzzling behavior patterns would involve concepts of emotional learning and related generalization as well as concepts of negative reinforcement and avoidance training.[2]

It should be recognized that some functional relationships are quite strong, that is, a designated behavior may have a high likelihood of occurring on each occasion when specific conditions are present. The child, for example, may exhibit intense fearfulness every time a dog is present. Few behavior patterns, however, have a 100 percent occurrence rate. It is unusual to observe behavior patterns which always occur as specific events are presented. In most cases, the functional relationship is not so simple or reliable. Sometimes the behavior occurs under defined conditions and at other times it does not. It is thus useful to refer to behavior as having a higher or lower likelihood of occurence under varying conditions. A

2. An elaboration of these concepts is presented in later chapters.

"hyperkinetic" child may be more likely to become distractible under conditions of excessive noise or when exposed to difficult tasks than when provided simple ones. In these instances, it is assumed that events other than those identified and observed are influencing the manner in which the child is behaving. "He is quite cooperative on most occasions, but at unpredictable times, for no apparent reason, he is quite obstreperous" represents another example. An effort would be made to identify events influencing the obstreperous behavior in order to improve the predictability and possible reliable influence of it.

> Viewpoint 13   Explanations of behavior typically make use of measurable events rather than those of a hypothetical nature.

It is easy to impose on a child all kinds of inferred internal states such as major drives, intentions, purposes (as self-actualization or death wish), abilities, traits, complexes, and the like, but these lend little assistance in detailing what a child is likely to do or why one child differs from another. These are mostly philosophic constructs; these are not statements of functional relationships which would be useful in answering such questions as "I wonder, how might I specifically influence John's mode of behaving as he is interacting with his peers?" or "I wonder, how has John developed his present characteristics?"

Distinguishing Naming from Explanation

If we report that a child likes to play, we are referring to the likelihood that play behavior will occur. But it becomes circular and meaningless to report "he plays because he likes to play" unless the manner is explicated by which play behavior became a high preference or likeable activity. Similarly, such explanatory statements as "he is constantly making disruptive comments because he has such a strong need for attention" is rejected because the construct "strong need for attention" is not measurable independent of the behavior it is presented to explain. Nor does the behavioral position resort to such explanations as "he steals because of unconscious conflicts" or "he fights because he has aggressive tendencies." These types of explanations are viewed as inadequate because they do not provide information about the conditions which will reliably produce or inhibit the specific behavior.

Skinner* has noted: "When we say that a man eats *because* he is   *Skinner 1953* hungry, smokes a great deal *because* he has the tobacco habit, fights *because* of the instinct of pugnacity, behaves brilliantly *because* of his intelligence, or plays the piano well *because* of his musical ability, we seem to be referring to causes. But on analysis these phrases prove to be merely redundant descriptions" (p. 31).

A child may be angry and fight under certain conditions and angry but not fight under other conditions. If one is interested in the fighting behavior, it would be sufficient to identify those conditions under which fighting is likely to occur, including the contingent consequences of such behavior. Being angry may be one of the conditions which *increases the likelihood that fighting will occur,* but anger is not viewed as a meaningful explanation for the fighting behavior. The child may fight when angry in the presence of his peers, but he may become angry and not fight when adults are present or when father is home on furlough.

As another example, an adolescent attending a social adjustment class engages in frequent screaming temper tantrum episodes when confronted with conflict. However, he does not scream *because* he is angry. Being angry may be one of the conditions which increases the likelihood of the screaming behavior. A functional (contemporary) explanation would provide a more detailed delineation of the external and internal conditions under which he is likely to scream. A historical explanation may suggest "he engages in screaming behavior as such screaming previously has produced certain changes in his environment, e.g., attention from adults, removal of punishment, being provided permission to leave the room, or to engage in behavior which he prefers." As noted earlier, knowledge of these historical events is helpful in describing how present stimulus conditions have come to exert influence over the screaming behavior.

Functional Analysis

Contemporaneous explanation of present behavior, as noted, specifies the conditions under which certain behavior patterns are likely to occur. The focus is on the child in an environment. Our knowledge of the "child-conditions-behavior" relationships is gained from observation of the child under similar conditions—that is, through a knowledge of the recent history of the child and of the conditions which, when present, will result in given behavior.

Skinner 1953   Skinner* summarizes this position quite succinctly in his statement:

> The external variables of which behavior is a function provide for what may be called a causal or functional analysis. We undertake to predict and control the behavior of the individual organism. This is our "dependent variable"—the effect for which we are to find the cause. Our "independent variables"—the causes of behavior—are the external conditions of which behavior is a function. Relations between the two—the "cause and effect relationship" in behavior—are the laws of science. [p. 35]

Inferred versus Descriptive Explanation

It is not infrequent for a child with exceptional learning and behavior characteristics to be removed from an educational program for such reasons as "he is not sufficiently motivated" or "he exhibits no interest in the regular classroom program." Lack of motivation and poor interest, both inferred internal deficiencies, are used to explain the child's poor judgement to the program.

When we speak descriptively of someone as being indifferent, unmotivated, interested, highly involved, with high needs, timid, or minimally involved, we have reference to the general probability of occurrence of various classes of behaviors. The factors involved in the development of this behavior probability reside in the history of the individual. The behavioral probabilities may vary widely from one setting or situation to another or these may be quite similar across a number of different settings. An adolescent may, for example, be socially responsive at home but not at school, or he may be equally responsive in home, school, and other similar settings. When we speak of a deaf child as being highly motivated in art class, for example, we have reference to a high probability that various art and related behaviors will occur in certain settings. This same child may be viewed as "lazy" in other settings, for example, as he is highly unlikely to assist with household chores.

We cannot account for a child's spending a great deal of his free time in reading classics by simply stating that "he reads because he likes it" even though reading may be an enjoyable activity for him. Rather, such behavior is best understood by describing the conditions under which it developed as well as those consequences which presently maintain it. An activity such as reading may be maintained in some children partially by consequences "intrinsic" to the activity itself. As noted, the task becomes one of identifying the procedure by which such activity becomes an enjoyable, likeable, or intrinsically interesting one. The retarded adolescent makes disruptive comments in social adjustment class, not because he is delinquent or naughty, but rather as a result of certain consequences which this behavior has produced under similar circumstances in the past. The behavior will continue to occur if these or similar reinforcing consequences continue to be produced by the endeavor.

As another example, if a child is described as being disinterested in social interaction, we have reference to a low likelihood that such social behaviors will occur. But our observation that he is disinterested does not explain his lack of social interaction. It merely represents another way of reporting his lack of social interaction. We may well influence his "interest" in a situation, activity, or person by insuring that these events produce or are associated with reinforcing consequences.

In a similar manner, such pseudoexplanations as "he works well when he *wants* to" or "he can get along fine if he is in the *mood* for it" are viewed as nonfunctional. These and similar statements imply that a child behaves appropriately as he wishes or wants to and controls such behaviors at will. As a result it is easy to assume that it is the child's fault that more appropriate behavior does not occur. The responsibility for inappropriate or inconsistent behavior is placed within the child and thus removed from the educational environment. The behavioral approach, in contrast, places the blame for "poor motivation," "poor mood," or "lack of interest," for example, in the hands of those who structure the environments in which a child resides. The cause of the lack of behaviors implied by the term "poor motivation" resides in the lack of success of the educational program to provide a variety of positively reinforcing events in the school environment, or to remove or de-emphasize the aversive aspects of the program. The program goals for "unmotivated" children and adolescents become those of "how can the environment be designed to increase frequency and durability of various appropriate patterns of behaviors? Further, how can prosocial behaviors acquire intrinsic incentive properties and thus become self-maintaining?" Satisfactory attainment of these goals solves the problem of getting the child to "want to" or to "be motivated."[3]

Thus, the behavioral approach views the topic of motivation and its explanation from a descriptive empirical viewpoint. Environmental events which have the effects of increasing or decreasing the occurrence of behavior when presented contingent upon that behavior are identified. These reinforcing events will vary considerably from child to child and even from time to time for any given child. Certain classes of environmental events, such as social attention or praise, may be quite effective in influencing the probability of a wide range of behaviors. Social attention is thus identified as a reinforcing event of high value to this individual. It also may be true that such a reinforcing event shows little satiation effect under normal use. That is, it may be found that social attention can be used effectively as a reinforcing event on a number of different occasions without temporary or permanent loss of its reinforcing properties. In short, instead of inferring an internal state as implied in the statement, "He has a high need for attention," attention from peers is viewed as an effective reinforcer if it can be determined empirically that it strengthens those behaviors which precede its presentation or suppresses behaviors which result in its removal. Knowledge of such a relationship between social attention and its influence on behavior is quite helpful in planning and implementing an educational program. The manner in which social attention had acquired such powerful reinforcement value for any specific child, however, is another matter. Being accepted by others may be a cue for anxiety reduction, the removal of threat of punishment, the promise of future positive reinforcement, and the like. These effects have evolved out of a complex history of interaction with others.

Explanation of Learning Difficulties

Providing explanation for various learning difficulties resulting in behavioral deficits may involve additional considerations. In illustration,

---

3. The topics of emotional, attitudinal, and motivational learning will be discussed in later chapters.

an analysis of the concern "why doesn't John know how to read" may reveal that "John's reading difficulties are related to his poor visual-discrimination skills and his inadequate sound-blending skills." *In this contemporary explanation, present behavior deficits are accounted for by the absence of other essential prerequisite behavioral skills which may inpede effective learning.* One may go an additional step and ask the question: "Why does John have poor visual-discrimination and inadequate sound-blending skills?" One may attempt to account for these in terms of sensory-physical correlates (such as brain injury or sensory deficits) or in terms of such previous inappropriate learning conditions as poor instruction.

Both historical and contemporary explanation may provide valuable information to the educator, but these two sets of factors should be clearly delineated.* In considering historical events or conditions which may have been involved in the origin and development of present learning and behavior characteristics, caution must be exercised, however, to avoid the conclusion that these historical events or conditions also provide a contemporary explanation of the behavior. *Present events which maintain such behaviors may be quite different from those conditions associated with the initial development of the behavior.* As an example, a child may have developed a habit of crying or even of responding aggressively when confronted with aversive situations because at the time these behaviors served to remove the aversiveness. These behaviors may no longer serve this function but now may be maintained by the consistent social attention which such behavior produces.

Kauffman and Hallahan 1974

Distinguishing Behavior Strength from Explanation

As implied, the behavioral position does not use a description of the strength or generality of a behavior pattern as an explanation of that behavior. A child may be observed engaging in a variety of aggressive behaviors in structured and unstructured situations. It is tempting to explain these as resulting from "strong aggressive tendencies or impulses." In so doing, a descriptive label is used to explain the same behavior which formed the basis for the descriptive label.

> **Viewpoint 14** The child's behavior in one setting may reflect contemporary effects of numerous other present environments.

The manner in which a child responds to and behaves in the school environment is influenced not only by what goes on within this environment but also by his current experiences in environments outside the school, notably the home environment. Care must be exercised, however, in dismissing a child's difficulty in the school setting by the position, "He behaves this way [lazy, disruptive, excessively fearful, nonattentive, disinterested, or whatever] because of his poor home environment," though a child may indeed benefit from a well-designed learning environment created in the school even though present home experiences may be quite inappropriate.

The writer has been informed on numerous occasions by a distraught teacher, "Well, what difference does it make if we can teach the child adequate behavior during the few hours we have him in school. He still returns to his depressing home life at night. How can we possibly offset the bad effects of inadequate parents?"

In analyzing this very legitimate concern, a distinction should be made between previous home experiences and present ones. The child's present behavior is being influenced by present experiences. The child's present behavior is a function of the present home and school environments. Knowledge of previous experiences, to reiterate a point made earlier, can be useful only in providing some speculations about the development of present behavior patterns and the events which influence these.

As the child's behavior can be changed only by rearranging present events, the teacher's major effort must be directed toward understanding the behavior as it is occurring under present conditions. These present conditions do include those both within and outside of the school environment. A child may be punished frequently by his parents and older siblings at home. He may bring into the classroom disruptive emotional states created earlier in the day at home. These events obviously will influence the manner in which the child will respond to the school program. Additionally, the child may bring with him, due to these current experiences, various avoidance and aggressive behavior patterns.

In like manner, a child may exhibit behavior in the home that is puzzling to the parents. This is illustrated by Mindy, a healthy, socially responsive ten-year-old who began to complain of stomachaches and headaches upon arising on school days. These disappeared on the weekends. Mindy also became moody and less socially outgoing. These were behavior characteristics which Mindy had acquired from numerous previous experiences with aversive conflict situations. The parents, however, could not identify any such conflict situations in the present home environment.

Upon discussion of these reactions with the classroom teacher, it was revealed that Mindy had had a rather serious confrontation with the teacher over completion of some of her homework. The child responded fearfully to the teacher, due to previous experiences in similar situations, and dreaded going to school in anticipation of being reprimanded again. After a parent-teacher-child conference, Mindy was assured that she was liked and that no further difficulty would be experienced. The puzzling behavior seen in the home

*cleared up immediately, which emphasizes that the child's covert
behaviors may be most influential in producing overt behavior
patterns. This is especially true as the child grows older and acquires
a wider range of verbal cues and related images which may represent
disruptive emotionally provoking experiences.*

The experiences which the present home conditions are likely to
provide could be of the sort which perpetuate present exceptional learning
and behavior characteristics, and it might be highly unlikely that different
prosocial behaviors acquired in school would be tolerated and reinforced
in the home environment. To be most effective, the school program must be
cognizant of these home and other environment-related behavior reactions.
Ideally, the educational program for the child should include *both* home
and school components. However, even when this is not possible, the child
may indeed learn appropriate adaptive behaviors in the school program. It
is not, therefore, a legitimate or functionally useful position to blame the
home for the child's failure in school, but the home experiences obviously
may make it more difficult to attain the educational objectives of the school
program. Only in extreme cases, however, will the home experiences be so
negative and pervasive that the positive effects of a well-designed educational program are offset.

> **Viewpoint 15** Behaviors which cluster together in patterns
> may or may not be produced or maintained by a
> common set of controlling events.

It has been demonstrated that behavior characteristics of various
repertoires tend to coexist.* Quay, in a series of multivariate statistical   *Lovaas and Koegel
studies, describes clusters of problem behaviors which he labels Conduct   1972; Quay 1972*
Disorder, Personality Disorder, Immaturity, and Socialized Delinquency.
As detailed in Chapter 2, each cluster label represents a number of behavior
characteristics which occur in children. The Conduct Disorder cluster, for
example, includes such characteristics as disobedience, disruptiveness,
temper tantrums, attention seeking, and acting bossy. In contrast, the
Personality Disorder cluster includes such characteristics as shyness, self-
consciousness, social withdrawal, and anxiety.

The behavioral veiwpoint recognizes the possibility of response
classes—physically different behaviors under the influence of a common
contingent event—but does not assume (in the absence of confirming data)
that correlated behavior characteristics are the result of the same acquisi-
tion factors or that these are presently maintained by common events.* For   *Bijou and Baer 1961;
instance, Wahler* found highly reliable and persisting clusters of deviant   Lovaas 1961; Wahler
behavior in problem children but after careful study was unable to identify   1975; Wahler 1975*
the environmental determinants of the behavior clusters. On the other
hand, it is not unusual to find that changes in one behavior characteristic

result in spontaneous changes in others. (This finding is discussed in Chapter 9 under Concurrent Behavior Change.)

> **Viewpoint 16**   Behaviors within a specific repertoire, as well as behaviors comprising different repertoires, may have different levels of strength and be controlled by different events.

A child's thinking processes, for example, predominately may be quite logical and relevant to certain reality events of his environment. The same child, at other times and under other conditions, may be quite irrational in his covert verbal behaviors and thus engage in poor self-management. He may be characterized by adequate emotional control in the presence of most people and under most conditions of frustration but quite explosive and uncontrolled in interaction with certain other people or situations. These inconsistencies in behaviors within and across various repertoires reflect learning experiences in these or similar situations and are not viewed as signs of some internal deviancy.

> **Viewpoint 17**   Behaviors of one class or repertoire may or may not influence the behaviors of other repertoires.

Behaviors comprising a given repertoire, or the total repertoires which constitute the personality of a child, are not isolated responses controlled by isolated events. The behavior patterns, and the events which exert influence over them, become complexly interwoven as the child develops. The stimulus components of some *emotional* behaviors, for example, may serve as discriminative events for a variety of other behaviors—social, verbal, academic, or other emotional varieties. A high anxiety state may result in curt social behavior or in the loss of concentration needed for completion of a math assignment.

The occurrence of certain behaviors may greatly increase the likelihood that other behaviors will surface, just as the absence of specific behaviors may greatly decrease the occurrence of certain other behaviors. To illustrate, the occurrence of the verbal statement "I can do that and I will stick with it until it's finished" may well exert influence over a variety of other motor, verbal, cognitive, and emotional behaviors. Likewise, a behavioral reaction of anger will render less likely such behaviors as cooperation, concentration, persistence, and the like. If anxious, a child is less likely to engage in positive emotional and related behaviors.

This relationship emphasizes that behaviors which comprise various repertoires are complexly interrelated, such that:

1. *Presence of one behavior may facilitate, or may interfere with, the acquisition or occurrence of other behaviors.* Decrease in hyperactivity

or other disruptive behavior patterns occurring in the classroom may result in improved academic performance in some children or adolescents but will have no facilitative effects in other students.*

2. *Behavior of one repertoire class can serve either to facilitate or to inhibit the occurrence of behaviors of other classes.* Covert verbal behavior may increase or decrease aggressive behavior in a conflict situation.

3. *A program designed to develop, strengthen, differentially influence, or extinguish one behavior will frequently influence other behavior patterns.* In illustration, a program to decrease the physically aggressive motor behaviors of a child, such as biting, hitting, scratching, and pinching may well influence his emotional, social, and verbal behaviors even though no specific effort was directed toward influencing these latter repertoires.

Ferritor et al. 1972; Glavin and Annesley 1971

As other illustrations, it is a common observation* that after stereotyped behavior in children or adolescents is extinguished, other more socially appropriate behaviors begin to appear. Increase in the strength of study behavior frequently results in improvement in academic achievement,* and increase in academic achievement in the classroom results in a decrease in disruptive behaviors.* It is thus unusual to change a specific complex behavior pattern without concurrently influencing other patterns. Spontaneous change in some behaviors following change in another, however, does not imply categorically that both are influenced by a single or common set of controlling events.

Gardner 1969; Foxx and Azrin 1973

O'Leary et al. 1969; Schmidt and Ulrich 1969

Ayllon and Roberts 1974

Potential Interrelation of Behaviors

This observation suggests that behaviors within a child's total repertoire *potentially* are integrated, coordinated, interrelated, and interdependent. High strengths of various behavior patterns can effectively block or otherwise interfere with the occurrence of other behaviors as well as the acquisition of new behaviors or the elaboration of those presently in the child's repertoires. These high strength behaviors not infrequently are of a "negative attitude" nature or represent strong destructive behavior patterns.

There is constant interaction among behaviors of various repertoires. Verbal behaviors may come to be influenced by, and to influence, a wide range of other behaviors. Self-concept behaviors may be influenced by emotional behaviors which may in turn influence other emotional or social behaviors. When avoidance motor behaviors occur, emotional behaviors may result, which in turn may influence other classes of behavior. This interdependence and constant interaction emphasizes the interrelationship that exists within a child's total repertoire.

In children with exceptional learning and behavior characteristics, it is not unusual to find that too many different behaviors are excessively influenced by the occurrence of a few inappropriate behaviors. For example, an adolescent may think that he is being rejected, or that he is inadequate in academic and social settings. These internal behaviors may produce cues that create high levels of negative emotionality in various academic and social situations for the youth, which in turn may result in a wide range of avoidance behaviors. Such antilearning behaviors further restrict the development of competency skills.

Assumption of Rational Control

A popular assumption suggests that a child or adolescent will behave in a specific manner if he knows what is best. Also, it is commonly assumed that a high relationship exists between what a child says he will do and what he will actually do. As a consequence of these assumptions, substantial effort is expended in many therapeutic education programs to insure that a child or adolescent understands or gains insight into any misbehavior that may be present. These assumptions are based on a philosophy that a person is rationally controlled and does what is best for himself.

The behavioral viewpoint differs somewhat from these assumptions. It recognizes that the child's verbal behaviors, including those involved in reflective contemplation of alternative outcomes, may well become strong events which influence other of his behaviors. However, the mere presence of verbal behaviors which, symbolically, represent realistic outcomes of alternative ways of responding does not, ipso facto, indicate that these will exert reliable influence over behaviors in other repertoires.*
Vernon 1972 An adolescent who finds school generally unpleasant may know that it is in his best interest to attend English class, and may commit himself to do so, but when the time comes he may be unable to bring himself to attend.

One major goal of an educational program is to provide a child with a verbal repertoire which influences a wide range of other "appropriate" behaviors. Verbal behaviors may come to represent cues for a wide range of operant and emotional behaviors as well as to serve as reinforcing or as aversive events. A child may become anxious when he thinks about the consequences of not completing his assignment. Another child may, by talking to himself, insure that he does comply with parental requirements. An adolescent may reinforce his newly emerging assertive behavior by congratulating himself for his personal strength and at the same time punish his rudeness by reprimanding himself after he yells at his mother. Verbal behaviors may also be quite neutral in their influence over other behaviors. In fact, the behavioral viewpoint recognizes that one of the major troublesome characteristics of children with exceptional learning and behavior patterns is the faulty relationship between the self-control aspects of verbal behaviors and behaviors of other repertoires. The child may behave too impulsively. He may strike out physically without regard for consequences. He may withdraw physically and emotionally, seemingly without logic. He may engage in physically disorganized emotional outbursts without reason. He has too few self-directing and self-reinforcing skills.

Assumption of Inferred Internal Traits

A second popular assumption inherent in various psychodynamic systems of child or adolescent behavior is that certain hypothesized internal factors hold a basic and frequently pervasive influence over a wide range of externally observable behavior patterns. As an example, it is assumed by various self-concept and expectancy theories that such factors as feelings of competency, positive self-concept, and positive self-evaluations are critical underlying variables in the academic performance of children.* If a child is performing poorly, it is assumed that improvement would result if the child could be influenced to improve his self-evaluation regarding academic performance. The poor academic performance is viewed as a symptom or behavior manifestation of the presumed or hypothesized internal factor of poor self-evaluation.

For example, Rogers 1961

The behavior approach would, in contrast, define self-evaluation as a class of behaviors that *may* or *may not* reliably influence other classes of behavior—academic performance for one—for any particular child. In fact, it would appear that verbal statements of positive self-evaluation—"I can do well," "I am good at arithmetic," "I can learn to read better"—would be most likely to result if these represented realistic description of doing well, being good at arithmetic, or reading better. Thus, an appropriate educational strategy would be one of arranging the program so that the academic performance is improved. Along with this, the child would be encouraged to make positive self-evaluative statements which would be realistic in terms of his present success. These would be strengthened through immediate meaningful reinforcement provided by the teacher.

Bartel and Guskin,* in viewing available research related to influencing positive self-evaluative behavior, concluded: "It appears, then, that the most effective way to modify children's self-evaluation is to improve their performance, but the reverse effect, getting self-evaluation to improve performance, is more difficult to institute" (p. 91). They further stated: "The most likely way to increase a person's feeling of potency is probably to demonstrate that one can have some impact in obtaining rewards from the environment" (p. 92).

Bartel and Guskin 1971

In summary, the behavioral viewpoint makes no a priori assumption that for any child one class of behaviors (such as a child's verbal report) adequately represents internal stimulus events or that there is a functional relationship between verbal or emotional behaviors and other behavior classes. A child may report that he does not feel like working but may nevertheless perform quite satisfactorily in social and academic situations. Secondly, in the absence of reliable correlational and/or functional relationships between various behavioral events, the best tactic for influencing the strength of a given behavior class is to deal directly with that behavior class. Ferritor et al.* found that reduction in distractability and disruptive behaviors in a class of low-achieving children did not result in improved academic achievement. A successful program for improving academic achievement resulted in disruptive and nonattending behaviors. Both academic and classroom behavior improved only after both classes of behavior were dealt with directly.

Ferritor et al. 1972

It is recognized that verbal behavior may be predictive of other behaviors (i.e., "What he says, he does") but this is not necessarily true. It also is recognized that various patterns of verbal and emotional behaviors which some may choose to call self-concept behaviors may be related to the presence of other classes of behaviors. A child may be described as having high self-regard or as having positive self-concept behaviors and may also be highly successful in academic matters. This coexistence should not, however, be assumed to represent a functional relationship. The presence of one may, or may not, facilitate the occurrence of the other.

> **Viewpoint 18**   Behaviors of one class may exert influence over
> behaviors of another even though the child may
> be unable to verbalize this relationship.

Certain behavioral inconsistencies or inexplicable behavioral reactions contribute to the myth that inferred, unconscious, pathological internal factors underlie these "abnormal" behaviors. If a child behaves appropriately the popular tendency is to assume that he is in control. If misbehavior occurs and the child is unable to explain why he so behaves, the tendency is to resort to an internal deviancy explanation. This was illustrated in a recent experience with a young adolescent who would frequently lose his temper, scream, refuse to comply or cooperate, would upturn desks, and shout obscenities. Afterward he would apologize and report that he felt quite bad about his behavior but that he lost control.[4] "I couldn't help what I did," was a frequent comment. The teacher, in reporting these episodes to the writer, suggested, "There must be some emotional disturbance inside him to make him behave like that."

Other children give the impression of being in an intense struggle. "I feel so sorry for him. I know he wants to behave but he just doesn't seem to be able to. It's as if something within him forces him to be uncooperative and aggressive. He's such a good child at times." After being asked, "Why did you do that?" following his striking another child, he replies, "I don't know."

---

4. See discussion in Chapter 11 of the manner in which a specific behavioral reaction can become a cue for such emotional responses as shame or guilt.

Each of these observations leaves the impression of something inside the child that is beyond his control and that directs or forces his misbehavior.

A behavioral viewpoint would account for such occurrences in less mystical terms. Behavior reactions of various repertoires are influenced by numerous external and internal stimulus events. A child may, or may not, at any time be able to label these events. In illustration, generalized emotional reactions such as anxiety may influence the occurrence of compulsive behavior or of sudden aggressive episodes. The child may be quite unable to identify the specific events which resulted in these behaviors. However, as noted, it is assumed that the child's exceptional characteristics are understandable in terms of the same principles which underlie appropriate behavior. As suggested, one of the goals of an educational program based on the humanistic behavioral approach is that of teaching the child self-understanding (appropriate awareness or verbal identification of events influencing behavior) and associated self-direction. The specifics of this topic are discussed in Chapter 12.

REFERENCES

Avila, D. L. On killing humanism and uniting humaneness and behaviorism. *American Psychologist,* 1972, 27, 579.

Ayllon, T., and Roberts, M. D. Eliminating discipline problems by strengthening academic performance. *Journal of Applied Behavior Analysis,* 1974, 7, 71–76.

Ayllon, T., Layman, D., and Kandel, H. A behavioral-educational alternative to drug control of hyperactive children. *Journal of Applied Behavior Analysis,* 1975, 8, 137–146.

Baer, D. M. Foreword. In B. Sulzer and G. R. Mayer, *Behavior Modification Procedures for School Personnel.* Hinsdale, Ill.: Dryden, 1972. Pp. v–ix.

Bandura, A. *Principles of Behavior Modification.* New York: Holt, Rinehart & Winston, 1969.

Barker, R. G. *Ecological Psychology: Concepts and Methods for Studying the Environment of Human Behavior.* Stanford: Stanford University Press, 1968.

Bartel, N. R., and Guskin, S. L. A handicap as a social phenomenon. In W. M. Cruickshank (Ed.) *Psychology of Exceptional Children and Youth.* Englewood Cliffs, N. J.: Prentice-Hall, 1971. Pp. 75–114.

Bijou, S. W. Behavior modification in teaching the retarded child. In C. E. Thoresen (Ed.) *Behavior Modification in Education.* The Seventy-second Yearbook of the National Society for the Study of Education. Chicago: University of Chicago Press, 1972. Pp. 259–290.

Bijou, S. W., and Baer, D. M. *Child Development. I. A Systematic and Empirical Theory.* New York: Appleton-Century-Crofts, 1961.

Black, M. Some aversive responses to a would-be reinforcer. In H. Wheeler (Ed.) *Beyond the Punitive Society.* San Francisco: W. H. Freeman, 1973. Pp. 125–134.

Bühler, C., and Allen, M. *Introduction to Humanistic Psychology.* Monterey, Calif.: Brooks/Cole, 1972.

Carrison, M. P. The perils of behavior mod. *Phi Delta Kappan,* 1973, 593–595.

Day, W. F. Humanistic psychology and contemporary humanism. *The Humanist,* 1971, 31, 13–16.

Eysenck, H. J. Behavior therapy and its critics. *Journal of Behavior Therapy and Experimental Psychiatry,* 1970, 1, 5–15.

Ferritor, D. E., Buckholdt, D., Hamblin, R. L., and Smith, L. The non-effects of contingent reinforcement for attending behavior on work accomplished. *Journal of Applied Behavior Analysis,* 1972, 5, 7–17.

Foxx, R. M., and Azrin, N. H. The elimination of autistic self-stimulatory behavior by overcorrection. *Journal of Applied Behavior Analysis,* 1973, 6, 1–14.

Gardner, W. I. Use of punishment procedures with the severely retarded: A review. *American Journal of Mental Deficiency,* 1969, 74, 86–103.

Glavin, J. P., and Annesley, F. R. Reading and arithmetic correlates of conduct-problem and withdrawn children. *Journal of Special Education,* 1971, 5, 213–219.

Gottman, J. M., and Leiblum, S. R. *How to do Psychotherapy and How to Evaluate It.* New York: Holt, Rinehart & Winston, 1974.

Haring, N. G. Improved learning conditions for handicapped children in regular classrooms. In E. N. Deno (Ed.) *Instructional Alternatives for Exceptional Children.* Arlington, Va.: Council for Exceptional Children, 1973. Pp. 71–82.

Hartshorne, H. and May, M. A. *Studies in the Nature of Character.* Vol. 1. *Studies in Deceit.* New York: MacMillan, 1928.

Homme, L. E. Perspectives in psychology—XXIV—Control of coverants: The operants of the mind. *Psychological Record,* 1965, 5, 501–511.

Hosford, R. E., and Zimmer, J. Humanism through behaviorism. *Counseling and Values,* 1972, 16, 1–7.

Jensen, A. R. Intelligence, learning ability and socioeconomic status. *Journal of Special Education,* 1969, 3, 23–35.

Jensen, A. R. Skinner and human differences. In H. Wheeler (Ed.) *Beyond the Punitive Society.* San Francisco: W. H. Freeman, 1973. Pp. 177–198.

Kanfer, E. H. Behavior modification: An overview. In C. E. Thoresen (Ed.) *Behavior Modification in Education.* The 72nd Yearbook of the National Society for the Study of Education. Chicago: University of Chicago Press, 1972. Pp. 3–40.

Kanfer, F. H., and Phillips, J. S. A survey of current behavior therapies and a proposal for classification. In C. M. Franks (Ed.) *Behavior Therapy: Appraisal and Status.* New York: McGraw-Hill, 1969. Pp. 445–475.

Kanfer, F. H., and Phillips. J. S. *Learning Foundations of Behavior Therapy.* New York: John Wiley, 1970.

Kauffman, J. M., and Hallahan, D. P. The medical model and the science of special education. *Exceptional Children,* 1974, 41, 97–102.

Kohl, H. R. *The Open Classroom.* New York: Random House, 1969.

Knoblock, P. Open education for emotionally disturbed children. *Exceptional Children,* 1973, 39, 358–365.

Lazarus, A. A. *Behavior Therapy and Beyond.* New York: McGraw-Hill, 1971.

Lindsey, B. L., and Cunningham, J. W. Behavior modification: Some doubts and dangers. *Phi Delta Kappan,* 1973, 596–597.

Lovaas, O. I. Interaction between verbal and nonverbal behavior. *Child Development,* 1961, 32, 329–336.

Lovaas, O. I., and Koegel, R. L. Behavior therapy with autistic children. In C. E. Thoresen (Ed.) *Behavior Modification in Education.* Chicago: The University of Chicago Press, 1972. Pp. 230–258.

Maher, B. A. *Principles of Psychopathology: An Experimental Approach.* New York: McGraw-Hill, 1966.

Mahoney, M. J., and Thoresen, C. E. *Self-Control: Power to the Person.* Monterey, Calif.: Brooks/Cole, 1974.

Martin, B. *Anxiety and Neurotic Disorders.* New York: John Wiley, 1971.

Matson, F. (Ed.) *Without/Within: Behaviorism and Humanism.* Monterey, Calif.: Brooks/Cole, 1973.

Mischel, W. *Personality and Assessment.* New York: John Wiley, 1968.

Morse, W. C. The education of socially maladjusted and emotionally disturbed children. In W. M. Cruickshank and G. O. Johnson (Eds.) *Education of Exceptional Children and Youth.* (2nd Ed.) Englewood Cliffs, N. J.: Prentice-Hall, 1967. Pp. 569–627.

O'Leary, K. D., Becker, W. C., Evans, M. B., and

Saudargas, R. A. A token reinforcement program in a public school: A replication and systematic analysis. *Journal of Applied Behavior Analysis,* 1969, 2, 3–13.

Palmer, J. O. *The Psychological Assessment of Children.* New York: John Wiley, 1970.

Patterson, C. R. *Humanistic Education.* Englewood Cliffs, N.J.: Prentice-Hall, 1973.

Patterson, G. R. Reprogramming the families of aggressive boys. In C. E. Thoresen (Ed.) *Behavior Modification in Education.* Chicago: University of Chicago Press, 1972. Pp. 154–194.

Perelman, C. Behaviorism's enlightened despotism. In H. Wheeler (Ed.) *Beyond the Punitive Society.* San Francisco: W. H. Freeman, 1973. Pp. 121–124.

Quay, H. C. Patterns of aggression, withdrawal, and immaturity. In H. C. Quay and J. S. Werry (Eds.) *Psychopathological Disorders of Childhood.* New York: John Wiley, 1972. Pp. 1–29.

Reynolds, G. S. *A Primer of Operant Conditioning.* Glenview, Ill.: Scott, Foresman, 1968.

Rhodes, W. C. A community participation analysis of emotional disturbance. *Exceptional Children,* 1970, 36, 309–314.

Rogers, C. R. *Freedom to Learn.* Columbus, Ohio: Charles E. Merrill, 1969.

Rogers, C. R. *On Becoming a Person.* Boston: Houghton Mifflin, 1961.

Ross, A. O. *Psychological Disorders of Children.* New York: McGraw-Hill, 1974.

Schmidt, G. W., and Ulrich, R. E. Effects of group contingent events upon classroom noise. *Journal of Applied Behavior Analysis,* 1969, 2, 171–179.

Sears, R. R., Rau, L., and Alpert, R. *Identification and Child Training.* Stanford: Stanford University Press, 1965.

Skinner, B. F. *Science and Human Behavior.* New York: MacMillan, 1953.

Skinner, B. F. *About Behaviorism.* New York: A. A. Knopf, 1974.

Staats, A. W. *Child Learning, Intelligence, and Personality.* New York: Harper, 1971.

Staats, A. W. *Social Behaviorism.* Homewood, Ill.: Dorsey, 1975.

Tharp, R. G., and Wetzel, R. J. *Behavior Mod-*

ification in the Natural Environment. New York: Academic, 1969.

Thoresen, C. E. (Ed.) *Behavior Modification in Education.* The Seventy-second Yearbook of the National Society for the Study of Education. Chicago: University of Chicago Press, 1972.

Thoresen, C. E. Behavioral means and humanistic ends. In M. J. Mahoney and C. E. Thoresen. *Self-Control: Power to the Person.* Monterey, Calif.: Brooks/Cole, 1974. Pp. 308–322.

Thoresen, C. E., and Mahoney, M. J. *Behavioral Self-Control.* New York: Holt, Rinehart & Winston, 1974.

Ullman, L. P., and Krasner, L. *A Psychological Approach to Abnormal Behavior.* Englewood Cliffs, N.J.: Prentice-Hall, 1969.

Vernon, W. M. *Motivating Children.* New York: Holt, Rinehart & Winston, 1972.

Wahler, R. G. Some structural aspects of deviant child behavior. *Journal of Applied Behavior Analysis,* 1975, 8, 27–42.

Weber, L. *The English Infant School and Informal Education.* Englewood Cliffs, N.J.: Prentice-Hall, 1971.

Wilson, H. E. Humanism's many dimensions. *The Humanist,* 1970, 30, 35–36.

7

Humanistic Behavioral Approach: Additional Considerations

The basic features of the humanistic behavioral approach were introduced in the previous chapters. The present chapter extends the discussion into the definition and assessment of, and individualized educational programming for, exceptional learning and behavior characteristics of children and youth. Emphasis is placed on the relationship between the views of causation and remediation held by the educator and the manner in which these views relate to the problems of children.

> **Viewpoint 19** Exceptional learning and behavior characteristics are defined in a relative manner and in terms of multiple criteria.

Learning and behavior characteristics are viewed from the humanistic behavioral approach as bizarre, problematic, abnormal, maladaptive, or exceptional only in relation to various ethical or philosophical positions or in terms of statistical, legal, or otherwise defined norms or expectations which indicate by proclamation (rules) that certain categories of characteristics are unacceptable.* *Thus no learning or behavior characteristic is intrinsically good or bad, right or wrong, normal or abnormal, appropriate or inappropriate, deficit or excessive, acceptable or unacceptable except as it is judged and designated to be so within a given social context.* As a result, characteristics judged to be exceptional will vary considerably from place to place and even from one time to another. The same characteristics may be totally unacceptable by some and socially desirable by others. Differences in modes of dress, speech patterns, learning styles, general attitudes, and sexual practices illustrate this point.

Ross 1974; Ullman and Krasner 1969

Environmental Context and Exceptional Characteristics

Any learning or behavior characteristic becomes inappropriate or exceptional only when viewed in a situation that requires a designated range of learning or behavior such as a classroom reading period. In illustration, the teacher expects a child to read materials presented to him within a certain time period, at a certain rate, with a certain amount of voice volume, inflection, and expression, with a certain degree of correctness, and with a certain degree of understanding. If the child deviates too much in any of these areas, his behavior may be viewed as problematic. If there is deviation in too many of these reading areas, as well as in other areas of functioning, the child's behavior may be viewed as exceptional and as requiring some different program to replace or to complement that being provided.

The Observer and Exceptional Behavior

In addition to the behavior and the context in which it occurs, consideration must be given to the observer in any attempt to define problematic or exceptional characteristics. The same behavior occurring in the same social context may be labeled as inadequate, improper, or unacceptable by one observer and as appropriate, proper, and acceptable by another. A six-year-old child who engages in overt sexual play with another six-year-old child may disturb the prudish teacher to the point that she refuses to allow the "sex deviant" to remain in her class. The same behavior may be viewed by another teacher as typical curiosity behavior which is ignored at the time but which will be followed by the teacher providing sex education for the class as a whole at a later time. One teacher may become highly upset at seven-year-old Jim's temper outbursts, while another teacher may view this as a valuable experience for growing boys and further may use these instances as a natural basis for teaching self-control or the verbalizing of one's feelings.

A teacher in an upper middle-class neighborhood may view a child with a two-year delay in reading achievement as "learning disabled," while a second teacher in the inner city may view the same amount of delay as routine and expected even though both children may have the same basic cognitive skills.

Again, a child's behavior occurring in a given environmental situation produces reactions from those who are present in that particular social environment. The behavior may disrupt, upset, be obnoxious to, or otherwise disturb the social environment to the extent that something different is initiated in an attempt to influence the future occurrence of the behavior. Depending upon the attitudes held by the observer, the child may be removed, dismissed, sent to the expert who places labels on him, punished, restrained, ignored, may receive some other type of restriction or retaliation or, in contrast, may be viewed merely as a child with differences. He may be labeled as abnormal, exceptional, emotionally disturbed, mentally retarded, disordered, or minimally brain damaged or, in contrast, as a child with exceptional learning and behavior characteristics who should be provided for in an individual manner.

Behavior Can Be Judged in Many Ways

Some children have more persistent behavior patterns than others. These may or may not be socially acceptable. A child may tell more lies than is typical of his age group. However, this does not render him pathological, disordered, or as exhibiting a symptom of disturbance, *except by definition.* That is, one can choose to label such a child as abnormal if one wishes. One can also proclaim that such behavior is a manifestation of some inferred pathology; *this, however, does not make it so.* The relationship between such behavior and causative factors, as well as its relationship to other behavior characteristics, is an empirical matter and not one established on an a priori definition or proclamation basis. Such may, or may not, be a correlate of other adaptive or maladaptive patterns or of inferred (hypothesized or proclaimed) events.

The example of "telling lies" illustrates the behavior model position that no behavior is categorically, intrinsically, or inherently abnormal. It is only behavior. It may be bothersome, undesirable, indicative of other difficulties, or not understood by those in the child's environment. It may infuriate, aggravate, disturb, or frighten others.

The same behavior occurring in two different children may produce quite different reactions from others depending upon the behavioral repertoires of the two children. A child with generalized deficits in various of his behavioral repertoires may engage in certain eccentric behaviors and be responded to with social rejection by his peers. Another child who has much to contribute to his peers may engage in the same eccentric behavior and be responded to in an accepting manner. This emphasizes that "deviancy" is judged in terms of multiple criteria and is quite relative to the other characteristics of the child and of his social group peers. But nothing is accomplished either by defining children as abnormal, deviant, or pathological or by labeling their behavior as symptomatic of internal psychic difficulties. The task rather becomes that of identifying functions of, and strategies for, coping with and modifying exceptional learning and behavior characteristics.

Criteria of Exceptional Learning and Behavior Characteristics

A learning or behavior characteristic which disrupts, disturbs, or creates concern in the child or in others in the educational environment is usually viewed as exceptional and as requiring special attention or modified educational arrangements and/or procedures when:

1. *It occurs too frequently.* A child who rarely displays temper tantrum behavior or seldom cries without identifiable provocation would evoke empathy whenever a temper tantrum occurs. If such behaviors occur too frequently, on the other hand, the educational environment may view the behavior with some alarm and attempt to rectify the precipitating condition or teach different coping skills.

2. *It is too intense in magnitude and duration in relation to the precipitating event.* As examples, a child becomes highly disorganized when provided minor criticism or rejection by his peers; an adolescent remains angry and sullen for days after being required to meet an obligation which he finds distasteful; or a child becomes excessively hyperactive and distractible in unstructured situations.

3. *It represents some unusual deviation from expectations.*[1] This would involve accelerated learning rates as well as both excessive and deficit learning and behavior differences, e.g., choking kittens, exposing oneself in public, unusually poor self-concept behaviors in a thirteen-year-old adolescent, being seven years of age and being unable to articulate sufficiently to be understood, having difficulty in understanding and learning from visually presented materials, wetting the bed or soiling in a ten-year-old girl, poor reading skills in a nine-year-old boy with normal IQ, fifth-grade academic achievement level in a seven-year-old child, a mental age of five in a ten-year-old child.

4. *It is quite unpredictable,* as when a teacher says of a child, "I just never know what he will do next. You just can't trust him out of your sight." This unpredictability frequently creates the impression that the child loses control of his behavior.

5. *It is produced by events which are unusual,* as when becoming sexually aroused by objects such as shoes or hair or by members of the same sex, being fearful of crowds or of riding in an elevator.

6. *It represents an obvious change from a previous level of acceptable behavior,* for instance, an active, outgoing, friendly child becomes withdrawn and relatively lethargic.

7. *Its relationship to other behavior characteristics and/or stimulus events is unusual,* e.g., a child reports that he will engage in some future behavior but seldom does so or when social attention and affection do not function as positive consequences in influencing the child's behavior.

8. *Unusual types and intensities of stimulus presentation and physical arrangements are required.* This criterion is illustrated by the use of large size print and braille materials for the visually impaired, sound amplification equipment and sign language instruction for the auditorially impaired, ramps, open spaces, and home-bound instruction for the physically impaired and the child with chronic health problems.

---

1. The expectations may be based on chronological age, mental age, perceptual age, neurological age, psycholinguistic skill level, grade level, school rules, state laws, philosophic proclamations, curriculum, or the like.

Summary

The behavior approach views any child as a unique individual with a complex set of learning and behavior characteristics. Some behaviors have a low probability of occurrence under any conditions; others have a high probability of occurrence under specific conditions. The frequent occurrence of certain behaviors, for example, intense emotionality, may compete with and reduce the probability of occurrence of other behaviors of a child's repertoire such as interacting socially with peers of the opposite sex. The child may be in a situation requiring complex behavioral skills which he either does not have in his repertoire or which are of low strength and easily superceded by other patterns. Thus, if a child does not engage in expected social, cognitive, emotional, or motor behavior, as example, or if he engages in highly inappropriate behaviors, these characteristics are viewed as resulting from faulty learning conditions or other measurable physical or environmental factors.

The child behaves as he does as a result of a unique set of environmental events acting upon him as a physical being characterized by a complex set of behavioral repertoires. As a result of physical or experiential factors, he may not have developed adequate discrimination skills, language skills, or emotional control skills for one typical of his age or family background. Due to excessive aversive experiences, he may perhaps respond with excessive emotionality—anxiety or fearfulness—in a given setting, and this behavioral reaction may disrupt appropriate attentional skills or thinking skills.

Problematic or exceptional learning and behavior characteristics are viewed within the humanistic behavioral model as those which do not meet the expectations of the normal instructional and management arrangements of the environments in which the child and adolescent reside. These different environments—home, school, playground, day camp, grandmother's house, social studies room, music room, psychologist's office—may differ considerably from each other in their expectations of how a child should learn or behave. As a result the child's characteristics may be problematic in one setting and not in others depending upon the particular social context-observer in operation. His aggressive, loud manner may be quite adaptive in his ghetto peer group but quite unacceptable as he enters the school environment controlled by middle-class behavior standards. On the other hand, the expectations may be highly similar across environments and a general pattern of acceptable or unacceptable behavior may exist. To illustrate, a child may not exhibit the reading behavior expected of him by the teacher and the parents; thus, he would be viewed as a reading problem at school and home. Another child does not use the range and level of vocabulary that is expected of him by parents and teachers; he is viewed as having a language problem in both environments. A third child may isolate himself from peer contact to the disappointment and concern of parent and teacher; he has a social interaction problem in both contexts. Some behavior problems are more serious than others as these interfere with the acquisition and/or performance of other important behaviors. A child, for example, may be so hyperactive, regardless of the reason, that he does not attend to the instruction provided in the classroom.

> **Viewpoint 20** The same principles of behavior account for the development and occurrence of both normal and exceptional learning and behavior characteristics.

This viewpoint reiterates and expands an assumption noted earlier: Inappropriate, unwanted, or undesirable learning and behavior characteristics are not exceptional in the sense that these result from unique principles of "abnormal development" or that these represent symptoms of some inferred internal pathological perceptual, psycholinguistic, or psychic conditions. These are characteristics influenced by various environmental events in interaction with a biologically and experientially unique child. It should prove instructive to comment briefly on the internal-deviancy view of abnormality prior to a discussion of the humanistic behavior position.

Internal-Deviancy View of Exceptional Learning and Behavior Characteristics

A basic distinguishing characteristic of the internal-deviancy model is the assumption that learning and behavior difficulties in children *are symptoms of internal abnormality*. An example of this position is contained in a recent book addressed to the psychoeducational audience:

> The symptoms of problem behaviors may stem from . . . psychological sources (which would include social and emotional disturbances). . . . Social and emotional disturbances may develop from a number of possible situations; these include traumatic incidents, feelings of insecurity or inadequacy fostered within the family, cultural deprivation, unresolved conflicts, uncontrolled anxiety, and detrimental social learning experiences or lack of beneficial social learning experiences.* [p. 8]

Woody 1969

The writer is suggesting that certain behaviors which he labels as symptoms may be caused by an undefined factor called emotional disturbances which in turn may result from (1) such *contemporary* internal hypothetical factors as unresolved conflict, uncontrolled anxiety, and feelings of insecurity or inadequacy and/or from (2) such *historical* events as traumatic incidents, cultural deprivation, detrimental learning experiences, or lack of beneficial social learning experiences. The procedure is not described by which a teacher or psychologist may determine the presence or absence, or the relative or absolute strength, of feelings of insecurity or inadequacy, unresolved conflicts, or uncontrolled anxiety. Further, neither the mechanisms by which these result in "emotional disturbance" nor the process by which an "emotional disturbance" operates to produce symptomatic or problem learning or behavior is mentioned. Nor is the process included by which such general historical variables as cultural deprivation or such specific experiential parameters as traumatic experiences can produce an emotional disturbance which in turn produces the observable symptomatic behaviors. Such omissions create tremendous problems for educators who have the basic responsibilities, and opportunities, for providing those everyday experiences which will either support or detract from appropriate learning and resulting behavior development. These presumed explanatory constructs are too vague and ill-defined to provide substance upon which programs of prevention or intervention can be developed.

A whole series of related questions can be raised by such explanatory constructs. As examples:

Do all children who grow up in "cultural deprivation" develop emotional disturbance?

If not, what other children variables interact with "cultural deprivation" to produce, or not produce, an emotionally disturbed child?

What magnitude of feelings of insecurity, how many, and what types of unresolved conflicts, or how much uncontrolled anxiety must a child have prior to the development of emotional disturbance?

How can something that does not exist (i.e., lack of beneficial social learning experiences) produce emotional disturbance?

Do all children who have a deficiency of beneficial social learning experiences develop emotional disturbance? If not, why not?

These are only a few of the questions which must be answered if the symptom-underlying pathology system suggested by Woody is to have any meaningful utility for psychoeducational personnel.

The only observable and measurable events in the rather complex presumed chain of cause and effect suggested in this example are the behavior patterns which the child exhibits. One set of ill-defined and unobservable explanatory constructs (e.g., unresolved conflicts, feelings of inadequacy) is said to cause another ill-defined and equally unobservable explanatory construct (emotional disturbance) which in turn is said to produce the observed behavior.

Morse* provides a second example of such questionable reasoning   *Morse 1967*
concerning presumed internal pathological factors. After presenting brief descriptions of behavior patterns of various adolescents labeled as "showing hostility to the teacher," he concludes:

In each case the symptomatic behavior—here, the example of hostility—was and is a clue, but only a clue, to the underlying disturbance pattern. To assist children, educators need to know both what youngsters do and their motivation for doing it. The significance is a matter of the relationship of the behavior to the self-concept of the individual child. [p. 581]

This analysis appears to imply that the unacceptable "hostility" behavior is merely a surface sign or symptom of a presumed underlying disturbance pattern. Further, constructs of "motivation" and "self-concept" are suggested as relating *in some undefined manner* to the disturbance pattern and presumably to the "clue" behavior.

An additional interesting example of the difficulties created by a position which depends upon concepts of internal pathology as the underlying basis for observable behavior patterns is that provided by Clarizio and McCoy* in their statement: "We often cannot state with any degree of certitude that a child's hyperactivity, distractibility, and extreme overresponsiveness stem from a brain injury or from an emotional disturbance" (p. 64).

Clarizio and McCoy 1970

Clarizio and McCoy are implying that the behavior characteristics of hyperactivity, distractibility, and extreme overresponsiveness are in fact results of brain injury *or* emotional disturbance. In postulating a single-factor causative model—a physical base (brain injury) or a hypothetical construct base (emotional disturbance)—they leave no place for other variables, or interactions among variables, which may account for the behavior pattern although others have been suggested.* A number of questions can be raised over such conceptualization: What evidence is there that such behaviors as hyperactivity and distractibility do coexist with brain injury? If so, is the coexistence invariant? Does coexistence imply causation? Kaspar and Schulman* suggest otherwise in their statement: "The scientific literature to date does not support the contention of a convergent syndrome including hyperactivity, distractibility, performative lability, autonomic lability, and inconsistency as inevitable consequences of brain injury" (p. 223).

Friedland and Shilkret 1973; Keogh 1971

Kaspar and Schulman 1972

Could the behavior characteristics coexist with brain injury and at the same time be related to or determined by still other factors? What is implied by the explanatory construct "emotional disturbance"? How is it defined and measured independently of the behaviors from which it is inferred? How does emotional disturbance result in hyperactivity, distractibility, and overresponsiveness? And—a most critical question from an educational viewpoint—are *different* procedures of education implied by a differential diagnosis? That is, does a diagnosis of organicity necessitate a different type of treatment or render more likely a different type of response to a particular treatment as suggested by some writers such as Keogh?* If so, what evidence is there that differential results do occur upon proper identification of the correct underlying causes of the exceptional behavior

Keogh 1971

patterns and subsequent exposure to the educational program relevant to that condition? If different treatments are not implied, of what significance to the educator is it to state with "any degree of certitude" that the behavior patterns are the result of either a brain injury or an emotional disturbance? Werry and Sprague,* in addressing this question, concluded: "Although diagnosis of minimal brain dysfunction does seem to alert clinicians to the possibility of coexisting educational and perceptual-motor deficits . . . assumptions about the state of the central nervous system do not contribute in any direct way to the assessment or remediation of these deficits" (p. 399).

Werry and Sprague 1970

The Learning Disability Model.

An additional example of the internal-deviancy model is that associated with the most recent area of special education, that of learning disabilities. This position hypothesizes various internal, central, and intervening *perceptual, psycholinguistic, and/or psychomotor* capacities, abilities, processes, or functions as critical components of the psychological structure of the child.* The position in its various articulations views academic learning difficulties as symptoms or manifestations of some dysfunction, impairment, or disruption of these hypothesized internal abilities and processes (perceptual, psycholinguistic, and/or psychomotor) assumed to be critical to learning. This pathology or dysfunction typically is assumed or at least implied to be caused by some neurophysiological deficit, lack of organization, or damage. Thus the term "minimal brain dysfunction"* is frequently used to emphasize that the problem arises from within the child and is associated in some manner with central nervous system impairment. A hypothetical explanatory chain speculates that various neurophysiological variables produce or result in perceptual, psychomotor, and/or psycholinguistic dysfunctions, disabilities, or disrupted processes, which in turn create the child's difficulties in acquisition, retention, integration, and/or performance of academic and related skills.[2]

Barsh 1965; Hallahan and Cruickshank 1973; Kephart 1960; Kirk 1966; Frostig and Horne 1964; and Myklebust 1968

Hallahan and Cruickshank 1973

Problem Associated with Identifying Symptomatic Characteristics.

How can one decide if any particular learning or behavior difficulty is or is not symptomatic of some more basic internal variable? What are the rules or guidelines that can be followed? If learning or behavior problems are labeled as symptomatic, the task becomes one of looking for underlying

---

2. A distinction should be made between, *on the one hand*, the possible empirically demonstrable relationship between specific measurable physical conditions and resulting learning and behavior characteristics or deficiencies and, *on the other*, a presumed relationship between a presumed underlying physical or psychic phenomenon and a behavioral reaction. For example, certain measurable neurological, sensory, or other physically defined variables may produce or be highly involved in the development and maintenance of certain learning and behavioral characteristics. Such empirical relationships are clearly different from presumed relationships between learning and behavior characteristics and unmeasurable hypothetical psychic or physically referenced constructs.

pathology to account for the difficulties. If not symptomatic, no assumptions would be made concerning *underlying* causative factors.

This exercise of labeling some learning and behavior problems as symptomatic and others as not symptomatic is confusing because it is done so infrequently on the basis of knowledge of etiology and rather frequently in the manner suggested by Kanfer and Saslow,* that behavior patterns viewed as symptoms are defined basically by their nuisance value to the child's social environment or to himself as a social being. These writers conclude that such symptoms are quite unreliable in predicting either the person's history or his response to various procedures designed to modify the symptom behaviors.

Kaufer and Saslow 1965

Learning problems frequently are not viewed as reflecting "internal disabilities" until the child's achievement discrepancy has reached a specific point such as two grade levels delayed. Until that discrepancy level has been reached, other types of variables such as poor instruction or lack of interest are implicated.

Restated, it appears that the practice of labeling some learning and behavior difficulties as symptoms involves the assumptions that there are two processes of behavior development and functioning in operation: (1) If learning and behavior difficulties become a social nuisance or meet some predetermined criteria of difference (e.g., two grade levels below expectation), such are labeled symptomatic and as resulting from factors of an internal-deviancy nature. (2) However, if learning and behavioral differences are not of such kind or magnitude to be deemed a nuisance, these are accepted as resulting from experience, learning, and the like. Further, if one wishes to modify these difficulties, this could be accomplished directly by influencing learning variables. Labeling some learning problems as reflecting "disabilities" and others merely as learning "difficulties" illustrates this two-process position.

Humanistic Behavioral View of Exceptional Learning and Behavior Characteristics

An orientation of separate processes for "normal" and "abnormal" behaviors is difficult to accept because there is no evidence that two different sets of factors account for "symptomatic" and "nonsymptomatic" behaviors. A possible alternative solution to the problem is contained in a simple but inclusive statement presented by Ullman and Krasner:*

Ullman and Krasner 1965

Maladaptive behaviors are learned behaviors and the development and maintenance of a maladaptive behavior is no different from the development and maintenance of any other behavior. There is no discontinuity between desirable and undesirable modes of adjustment or between "healthy" or "sick" behavior.... Because there are no disease entities involved in the majority of subjects displaying maladaptive behavior, the designation of a

behavior as pathological or not is dependent upon the individual's society . . . . Maladaptive behavior is behavior that is considered inappropriate by
those key people in a person's life who control reinforcers. [p. 20]

No learning or behavior characteristic from this viewpoint is
categorically or intrinsically symptomatic or abnormal. Behavior characteristics may be viewed as problematic or exceptional to the extent that
these create difficulties for the person or for others; but the behavioral
approach makes no assumption that a problematic characteristic is
symptomatic of inferred internal psychic ability, trait, or intellect pathology. A child who is overly aggressive, nonattentive to classroom routine,
learns poorly under visual stimulation conditions, and has difficulty form-
ing friendships is viewed as exhibiting exceptional or problematic characteristics. These are viewed by the behavioral position, not as symptons of
inferred psychic, perceptual, or ability deviations, but as characteristics
acquired by a physical being in his numerous and complex interactions
with a social environment.

The relationship between environmental events and unwanted behaviors may be unusual in that these same events for most other children do
not result in similar disruptive or unusual learning and behavior characteristics. These characteristics represent the cumulative effect of "abnormal" learning experiences—that is, experiences which have strengthened
and supported the wrong learning and behavior characteristics. *These
peculiar learning experiences, resulting from peculiar types and arrangements of environmental events rather than from peculiar or abnormal
internal characteristics, in most instances produce the exceptional learning and behavior patterns.* The child is what his peculiar combination of
experiences have made him. As noted, a child's deficits have a spiraling
effect. If certain skills or discriminations are not acquired, others which
require these as prerequisites cannot be developed. Thus his learning and
behavior inadequacies are intensified.

Similar Rules Account for Varying Characteristics

It is assumed that the rules underlying the development of contrasting behavior patterns (desirable vs. undesirable) are the same. All children's experiences differ and these account for differences in behavioral
reactions (emotional, social, verbal, motor, and so on) to present specific
situations. The same stimulation, a lesson presented by a teacher, for
example, experienced by two children at the same time can evoke quite
different reactions and can have quite different learning effects on each
because both children are potentially quite different. One of the children
may be fearful of adult females; the other child may be quite attentive to and
affectionate toward female teachers. One may process visual stimulation
effectively while another cannot. One may generally acquire new patterns

much more rapidly than another. Thus, even if different children were exposed to the same experience at the same time, the behavioral effects will usually be different as a result of physical (sensory, motor, neurological) and experiential history differences. The behavioral repertoires resulting from this history and characterizing a given child at any moment will influence the effect a given experience will have on the child.

Environmental Experiences May Be Abnormal

In light of this, no constructive purpose is served by viewing a child's excessive aggressive behavior, nor the child himself, as abnormal. His behavior merely represents patterns which the social environment has created. The environments in which the behavior patterns developed have provided abnormal or inappropriate experiences for the child—experiences which have resulted in the undesired learning and behavior characteristics. These characteristics frequently represent the normal outcome of the effects of an abnormal environment. If a child is provided auditory stimulation in the classroom which assumes prerequistie auditory discrimination and auditory memory skills which he does not have, he may not learn what the teacher expects of him. The learning difficulties reflect a mismatch between the child's characteristics and the instructional program. If a child is exposed to frequent and intense abusive outbursts from an ill-tempered adult, he will develop intense and pervasive emotional reactions. *The child is not abnormal. The negative emotionality is not abnormal. It merely reflects normal results of abnormal experiences. The learning principles which account for his acquiring the pervasive negative affect are not abnormal. The environmental experiences to which the child has been exposed, however, do represent the abnormal variable in the development of the undesired behavior.*

The major implication of this viewpoint is both obvious and of considerable significance. Efforts to understand or to change the undesired learning or behavior patterns should focus on the abnormal experiences instead of on any assumed abnormality residing in the child or on a search for unique principles of learning to account for the behavior.

An example of this approach is provided by a report by Wiesen and *Wiesen and Watson 1967*   Watson:*

> *They report on the behavior change procedure used with a boy who exhibited excessive attention-getting behavior. This behavior, directed toward adult attendants in a residential living unit, was described as "almost unbearable" and consisted of constant grabbing, pulling, hitting, untying shoelaces, and the like. Unlike a psychodynamic model which would view the behaviors, for example, as symptoms of an inferred emotional disturbance or of an excessive need for attention and affection, the behaviors were hypothesized as being maintained by the adult attention which such behaviors*

brought. *It was hypothesized that the excessive high rate (over six responses per minute during the baseline or pretreatment observations) was being maintained by "an inadvertently established partial reinforcement schedule carried out unwittingly by harried attendant counselors who periodically reinforced Paul with prolonged attention" (p. 50).*

This hypothesis was translated into a behavior management program designed both for the elimination of the bothersome behaviors and for the development of more appropriate means of interacting socially with both adults and peers.

As a second example:

An adolescent described as mildly retarded in a work-study program interrupts her task assignment by frequent trips to the counselor's office to seek assurance that her completed items are satisfactory. Whenever the supervisor attempts to ignore or to reprimand her quest for assurance, Mary becomes sullen and will not return to her work table for a period of time. It could be said that Mary is emotionally disturbed, over-dependent, negativistic, has a high need for attention, or has poor achievement motivation and, further, that the excessive assurance-seeking behavior is merely a surface symptom of any one or a combination of these hypothetical conditions.

The humanistic learning approach, in contrast, may view the excessive trips to the counselor's office as the end result of a complex set of previous experiences which provided various present environmental events with certain influence over the adolescent's behavior. An examination of the environment in which this behavior occurred may reveal that the work environment was aversive and the work stoppages were strengthened as this behavior removed her temporarily from the aversiveness of the work environment. It may also be true that the counselor provided her with a type of social experience which she found enjoyable (reinforcing). A complete historical and contemporary understanding of the behavior could require such data as (1) a designation of the manner in which the work environment acquired aversive properties, (2) a description of the manner in which the person developed the behavior pattern of leaving the work bench to obtain supervisor approval, (3) the types of responses which the counselor made to the adolescent, and the like.

> **Viewpoint 21**   The views followed in accounting for exceptional learning and behavior characteristics influence the experiences provided a child.

The views held by psychoeducational personnel in accounting for exceptional learning and behavior characteristics greatly influence the educational or therapeutic objectives set and experiences provided. Hewett* has noted: "The pinning of a given label on a child with a behavior   *Hewett 1972* disorder *carries with it a bias with respect* to causal factors considered crucial and explanations of why the behavior is occurring in the classroom. *These biases have also determined the nature of educational programs provided for these children"* (p. 392) (italics mine).

The Internal Deviancy and Disciplinary Positions

If a child's deviancy is viewed as a sympton or manifestation of something beyond his control—some internal disorder, disturbance, or pathology—it is likely that an attempt will be made to provide a restorative, treatment, or therapeutic experience aimed at changing the presumed disruptive internal factors. Others who follow a contrasting *disciplinary model* may attribute the child's behavior to such internal factors as poor motivation, lack of interest, laziness, or hostility, and the child is likely to be viewed as irresponsible and as intentionally engaging in inappropriate behavior. In this latter instance, the "educational" approach would border on the following: "He is ungrateful; he will just have to suffer the consequences of his inappropriate behavior." Not unusually, he is punished, dismissed, or otherwise treated in a punitive manner.

As more concrete examples of the relationship between assumptions held concerning personal accountability and resulting child management practices, a child labeled as "minimally brain damaged" or as "emotionally disturbed" may have difficulty focusing attention on a task and in maintaining task-oriented behavior. He further may engage in emotional outbursts toward the teacher when required to complete a difficult assignment. The teacher, assuming that the behavior is caused by factors beyond the child's control—the "minimal brain damage" or the "emotional disturbance"—either may tolerate the behavior as being an inevitable symptom of the internal pathology or may attempt to deal with it in some supportive manner.

Another child, not so diagnosed, may engage in the precise same behaviors and may be sent to the principal's office or otherwise punished and labeled a disturbing influence and as a disciplinary management problem. In this case, the teacher may view the behavior as resulting from "hostility," "meanness," "poor attitude," or some other personal characteristics of the child over which it is assumed he should have control. It is implied, if not stated, that the child could do better if he wanted to.

As a result of these different views of causality, different educational management and modification procedures are used. One child is held accountable for his inadequate behavior and either punished or talked to in a stern manner in an effort to get him to exercise more control over his behavior. The other child is not held accountable due to a different view of causality held by the teacher and thus is treated in a distinctly different manner.

Groups of children labeled in the school setting as "socially maladjusted or delinquent" frequently are viewed in a disciplinary "account-ability" manner and distinguished from those labeled as "emotionally disturbed." It is implied that the socially maladjusted and the delinquent behave as they do because they choose to do so. The term "socialized delinquency" has been devised to emphasize this assumption.* Such children are viewed as having rational or volitional control over their behavior and therefore as choosing to behave in a socially inappropriate manner.

Quay, Morse, and Cutter 1966; Quay and Quay 1965; Quay 1969

In contrast, the emotionally disturbed child or youth is viewed as having minimal or insufficient personal control over his behavior. Some-thing within him is sick, deviant, ill, pathological, weak, or inadequate and, thus, it is assumed he cannot help what he is doing. He has little or no rational control; he has no choice; he does not decide to behave inappro-priately. Some "inside force" is assumed to be the culprit and thus the source of the difficulty. Such concepts as "poor ego control" or "limited impulse control" are used to account for his behavior. Again, the labels and related concepts of causation influence the manner in which the child so labeled is treated.

Educational Practices and Social Class

As illustration of more subtle influences which views of causation exert on the manner in which a child is treated, let us look briefly at the relationship between diagnostic and related educational practices and so-cial class.

McDermott et al.* report that the poorest prognosis and least favora-ble diagnoses are provided children from lower social class groups. These children typically are not referred for psychological or educational treat-ment. Children from the middle and upper social classes are provided more favorable diagnoses and are frequently referred for special intervention services. White and Charry* report similar practices: Psychological treat-ment services are provided upper class children but not lower class groups. Hollingshead and Redlich's* description of the differential treatment of two females with highly similar problem sexual behavior is most provoca-tive in its vivid documentation of these differential treatment practices. A girl from an upper-class family was treated by a psychiatrist while the adolescent from the lower-class family was sent to a woman's reformatory.

McDermott et al. 1965

White and Charry 1966

Hollingshead and Red-lich 1953

Jones* and Rivers et al.* have written pointedly about the dis-criminatory practices involving black children. Rivers et al. state: "Tradi-tional ability tests, we believe, systematically lead to the assumption of improper and false labels to black children by which racist practices are spread throughout the educational lives of black children" (p. 214).

Jones 1972; Rivers et al. 1975

As a final example, Burke* studied the placement of black and white children and youth in classes for the "educable mentally handicapped" and those for children with "learning disabilities." In elementary through

Burke 1975

high-school levels, black children received more than their share of "educable mentally handicapped" placements while white children received
more than their share of "learning disabilities" placements.

The Humanistic Behavioral Position of Accountability

The behavioral position differs from both the deviancy and the
disciplinary positions concerning causality, responsibility, and subsequent behavior change endeavors. As noted, the behavioral approach
assumes that the present behavior of any child is a reflection of his unique
history of experiences as he interacts with a present complex social environment. The "emotionally disturbed" child is *no more or no less* free of his
history than is the "socially inadequate" or "delinquent." Both behave as
they do as a result of present environmental conditions which have gained
meaning through the accumulated and differential effects of the history of
these particular individuals. Cohen,* in commenting on teen-age delinquents, suggests: "My experience with troubled young people, both in and
out of institutions, has convinced me that most of the youths who exhibit
'deviant' behaviors are neither evil nor sick . . . . The young people are
simply incompetent to obtain their share of the good things of life through
socially acceptable means" (p. 307).

Cohen 1973

Thus, rather than blaming adolescents for their misbehavior, the
educational environment should be designed to insure that they will acquire those behavioral skills needed to function in a more acceptable and
self-enhancing manner.

The behavior of the child labeled "emotionally disturbed" may be
less obviously—rationally, visibly, apparently, observably—influenced by
the past and the present social environment than may appear to be true of
the child viewed as "socially maladjusted." *But in most cases this is only
an illusion.* Both are influenced by the same general set of factors. Differences among children may be evident in the specific variables present or in
the relative importance of any given variable, but there is no evidence that
different principles or processes underlie and control varied behavior
patterns. For example, the "emotionally disturbed" child may have more
frequent and more intense emotional reactions which serve to disrupt or
interfere with his being able to process adequately the critical variables
involved in a choice or decision situation. His behavior may be more
erratic, less predictable, and more variable in extremes of behavior expressed than is typical of most children. *But these behaviors differ only in
degree, not in kind, from characteristics of other children.* And these
reflect, just as does the "delinquent" behavior of a "socially inadequate"
adolescent, the present impact of a learning history.

Thus, within the behavioral orientation, the present exceptional
learning and behavior characteristics of "emotionally disturbed" and "socially maladjusted" children and youth are viewed as reflecting inappro-

priate learning experiences. Instead of treating the characteristics in a punitive manner or of shifting the blame to some ill-defined hypothetical internal factors, attempts would be made to rearrange the learning experiences for each child to assist him in developing those features which would be most beneficial to him. If the child fights with the teacher, for example, the behavioral approach would attempt to identify aspects of the present school experiences as these interact with the child's characteristics to produce the fighting behavior. It would be assumed that some aspects of the school experiences need modification as these are evoking and maintaining the wrong types of behavior. Such changes would potentially influence various types of child behaviors (positive attitudes, cooperation, coping skills, and so forth), which in turn would result in modification in the school experiences provided. As another example, if a child refuses to comply with teacher requests or will not complete his homework assignments, the behavioral approach would suggest that the teacher examine her assumptions about why such behaviors are occurring and her methods of dealing with the problems. To dismiss the child's difficulty with such statements as "he'll do it when he's ready for it or when it becomes important to him" or "he is just naughty" contributes nothing but confusion. A child should be taught that certain behaviors produce certain consequences. At the same time, the school experience must provide the child with behavioral alternatives arranged so that he does in fact have a choice between consequences that are valuable to him and those that are not to his benefit.

> **Viewpoint 22**   As the same principles are viewed as underlying all of a child's learning and behavior characteristics, problems of differential diagnosis are minimized.

As a basis for presenting the behavioral position concerning "differential diagnosis," it is instructive to comment briefly on an assumption of the internal-deviancy model that some learning and behavior characteristics represent *real* problems and others do not. This is illustrated in the following statement by Woody:* "Teachers can identify real problem patterns" (p. 9).   *Woody 1969*

The implication of this position is that some observable problematic learning and behavior characteristics are real (reliable? valid?) signs or symptoms of presumed internal pathology or disability and others are not. The rules or guidelines by which the psychologist, teacher, parent, counselor, psychiatrist, social worker, or school administrator would separate the *real* problems from the *unreal* ones are not presented by Woody, nor by any other source which could be found.

A similar attempt to distinguish real problems is suggested by Bower* in his discussion of children in the school setting who present exceptional behavior patterns: "A major caution in the use of descriptive   *Bower 1969* definitions of the behavior of children to infer causation is the problem of differentiating incipient pathology from normal behavior deviations" (p. 24).

Underlying Pathology Implied

This position implies that there is an existing pathology, an illness, or some discrete conditions and, further, that some observable behavior patterns represent early signs of, and thus forecast later pathological manifestations. Presumably both Woody and Bower are implying that differential diagnosis must be made to insure that the child be placed in the "correct" treatment program.

A model which attempts to separate "real" learning and behavior problems or "incipient pathology" from other problems under the supposition that the real ones are symptomatic of internal disability or pathology and the "unreal" ones are just a result of the usual mundane factors involved in normal human learning and functioning has minimal utility; in fact, the possible inherent dangers are numerous. Such a position creates unnecessary difficulty for the teacher, parents, and members of the psychoeducational service staff. It creates the question: "When is a difficulty of development, learning, or functioning a problem?" When and how does a teacher or psychologist decide, "Now I have identified a *real* learning or behavior problem and should do something about it?" And after a distinction has been made: "What should be done?" Should the "real" problem be given special attention and those problems which do not qualify be ignored? What special attention should be provided? What is the relationship between diagnosis of real problems and specific intervention programs?

Mimic of Physical Illness Model

Such an orientation obviously is a mimic of the pathology model used to deal with physical illness. Just as a parent after discovering her son with a temperature of 102°, sore glands, and a rash would decide, "My son is ill and needs medical attention," Woody and Bower are suggesting that certain problem behaviors are similarly symptomatic of some inferred internal pathology which should be attended to. Such a position assumes, as is true in physical medicine, that a correct and early diagnosis is a vital prerequisite to appropriate treatment. It implies that a correct diagnosis provides knowledge of the cause of the symptom, the probable future course of the disorder, and the appropriate treatment to pursue. Thus, etiologies which result in various patterns or combination of real symptoms are assumed, and they are to be distinguished from other behavior patterns not indicative of internal difficulty. The validity of such assumptions is highly suspect. Glavin,* for example, found that only 30 percent of

Glavin 1972

children identified as "real" cases of emotional disturbance were still so characterized after a period of time during which no specific treatment was provided.

It is not being suggested that children with exception learning and behavior characteristics should be ignored. Focusing on "internal-deviancy" diagnosis without resulting implications for educationally meaningful practices, however, seems to be an exercise in futility.* Keogh and Becker,* in illustration, warn against making a differential diagnosis of "learning disability" for young children exhibiting learning difficulties. They suggest that highly individualized educational programs should be provided children, and they indicate that screening procedures which identify problems but which provide no differential educational direction not only are useless but are potentially harmful.

Sabatino 1972
Keogh and Becker 1973

Additionally, in relation to the "real" problem concept, no purpose is served by attempting to specify a certain kind, degree, or magnitude of deviation of behavior from expectations before labeling or classifying it as a "real" behavior problem. Woody* provides an example of this type of reasoning. *He defined the behavioral problem child* as "the child who cannot or will not adjust to the socially acceptable norms for behavior and consequently disrupts his own academic progress, the learning efforts of his classroom, and interpersonal relations" (p. 7).

Woody 1969

Such a definition has significant negative consequences. First, the statement that the child "will not adjust" implies that some children intentionally do not behave as is expected. While such a position may have some meaning, it is a dangerous one because it is easy to categorically blame every child for all of his wrongdoings. The frequent result of such a position is the assumption of a punitive attitude toward the child. As suggested earlier, this disciplinary view all too frequently results in the child being blamed for his behavior. The blame is conveniently shifted from the educational environment. Retaliation techniques ranging from ridicule, rejection, and physical punishment through total dismissal from the school have resulted from such a view. Such punishment hardly accomplishes a goal of promoting positive behavior development.

Further, such a definition implies that learning or behavior difficulties should not be viewed as problems until such time as these get out of hand. Many current legal definitions of learning disabilities specify a certain number of months discrepancy between expectation and achievement as denoting a "true disability." Children with less deviation do not qualify for specialized education services, presumably because less discrepancy does not reflect a "real" learning disability.

Behavioral-Approach View of Difficulties

The behavioral approach suggests that the teaching environment should be attentive to any consistent deviation between environmental requirements or expectations and the performance of the child. There should be a constant monitoring of the relationship between the child's learning and performance and the educational program objectives. If there is any stable (more than momentary) discrepancy between what is expected and what the child accomplishes at any time, then the educational staff should be immediately responsive to the discrepancy. Under no circumstances should the environment wait until the child's "academic performance . . . etc.," is disrupted prior to acting. Attending to learning and behavior difficulties as they arise can be accomplished quite easily without the necessity of a diagnosis of internal deviancy or disability.

Morse 1964
Feldhusen et al. 1967

The effects of continued failure on the child have been emphasized by Morse* in his finding that the child's concept of himself and of school becomes more negative the longer he remains in school. Feldhusen et al.* noted that by third grade, children identified by teachers as manifesting socially disapproved behavior (aggression, disruption, and the like) had already fallen far behind in both reading and arithmetic achievement. The value of earlier recognition of behavior and learning difficulties and of sucessful remediation of the academic subjects is too obvious to require further comment. Waiting until the child's difficulties are critical prior to "diagnosis" and resulting intervention is obviously quite damaging to the child.

Every Learning and Behavior Problem is Real

Again, every failure demonstrated by a child is an indication that something is wrong. It would thus appear reasonable to assume that every problem of development, learning, or functioning *is* real and *does* deserve the attention of the school program. All behavior is important as it reflects the organization of the child at the moment. If the behavior is inappropriate in relation to environmental requirements—the child's learning rate is slow, the child is not attentive, or the child cries without suitable provocation—the environment should take note. If the child does not make satisfactory progress (defined in terms of a constellation of dynamic child characteristics), some components of the program are inadequate for that child at that specific time. These might include insufficient incentive components, an instructional program which assumes prerequisite skills which are not present, insufficient opportunity provided the child to use what he has learned, requirements that are too stringent, distractions which are too great, and the like. If the child fails, someone has made a mistake.

It is thus of highly questionable utility to speak of "real" learning or behavior problems or to engage in diagnostic practices that imply that a dichotomy exists between real problem characteristics and other patterns. Behavior and behavior change (resulting from learning) is present or absent, frequent or infrequent, strong or weak. Again, *all behaviors are real.* Some behaviors are problematic; others are not.

Interrelations among Characteristics Important

It is true that some exceptional learning and behavior characteristics are momentary and others last longer, some are more predictive of future behaviors than others, some coexist at one degree or another with other exceptional characteristics, some are more difficult to modify, some are more disruptive, some involve a wider range of behaviors, some are more puzzling due to their rarity or uniqueness, and some are situationally related to highly specific combinations of controlling factors. Others are more stable and frequent. Some are controlled by minor changes in external events, while the controlling factors of others are complex and difficult to identify or control. Some learning and behavior characteristics may hold a high correlation with other behaviors or may be known to be functionally related to certain environmental events. But these and other possible relationships are *empirical* matters, and they must be determined by controlled observation and not decided upon by proclamation.

Events of which the teacher is unaware and over which she has little or no control can influence the manner in which a child learns or behaves in the classroom. These may come and go in an irregular fashion and thus influence behaviors which occur erratically. When such a possibility is accepted, the need is recognized for examining the social learning experiences provided the child both within and outside of the school environment. To illustrate, the child may come to school in a state of heightened emotionality due to the bickering which occurs in the car whenever his older brother chauffers him to school. These previous or setting events can have a distinct effect on the manner by which the child is able to concentrate or to tolerate criticism or reprimand in the school environment.

Meaningful Assessment Concerns

If the learning or behavior problem persists or if it increases in frequency, rate, or intensity, a problem does exist and steps should be taken to deal with it. Such questions as the following become meaningful:

Is too much persistence and concentration required?
Is the contingency between the child's behavior and its consequences adequate in obviousness or kind?
Does the child attend to the essential components of the learning task?
Does the learning or behavior problem occur in isolation or is it merely one of an increasing number of problem characteristics?
Does the problem behavior—for example, excessive daydreaming, hyper-

activity, apathy—interfere with the development or occurrence of other more desirable learning and behavior characteristics?
Does the behavior produce excessive immediate or delayed aversive consequences?

Supplementary Resources May Be Helpful

The teacher in the classroom may or may not be able to cope with the child's difficulties. She may seek the assistance of other psychoeducational personnel, not because she has identified a "real behavioral problem" child, but rather because she is being unsuccessful in promoting that behavior development and functioning in the child which she expects or deems desirable. As a result, other resources are sought.

It is not being suggested that the teacher should become alarmed or should seek the assistance of the psychologist, diagnostic teacher, or counselor on every occurrence of some learning or behavior difficulties. Rather, as a first step in the analysis and modification of the problem, the educator should evaluate what she is doing in relation to the child's difficulties. If unsuccessful in alleviating the difficulties, she then should seek the assistance of others in providing more appropriate educational experiences in the child's natural environments.

In summary, what the child can in fact learn or the manner in which he can behave in a specific or in a wide range of situations is not dependent upon an etiologic construct such as "learning disability" or "emotional disturbance" or some diagnostic insight which declares that the child has a "real" problem. The specifics of what the child can learn is obviously dependent upon an array of psychological and physical variables. (These are discussed throughout the book.)

Viewpoint 23   The behavioral approach is applicable to a variety of learning and behavior characteristics of both a simple and complex nature.

Applicability to a Variety of Problem Areas

Since the major task of educational programs is to create an effective learning environment, the most defensible program approach makes use of established behavior principles. Although the practice of utilizing learning and other behavior principles as a basis for deriving procedures for influencing behavior is by no means new, the systematic application to a wide range of problem behaviors is of recent origin. Some of the most exciting work has been that involving children and adolescents.

Recent results of the application of behavioral education techniques provide illustration of behavior change of a range, degree, and rate that most educational, psychological, and psychiatric personnel had not thought possible due to limitations assumed to be inherent in various conditions described as mental retardation, autism, childhood schizophrenia, severe language impairment, brain damage, and severe learning disabilities. It has been discovered that a significant degree of the behavioral limitations and difficulties of many children reside in an inappropriate or limited learning and social environment rather than being, as has been assumed, an unalterable manifestation of the individual's retardation, deficit, disability, or psychic disturbance. Severely and profoundly cognitively limited children, for example, who for years were beyond help or hope, have, as a result of treatment programs utilizing the systematic application of behavior modification procedures, developed language, motor, perceptual, cognitive, affective, social, and self-help skills which have rendered them more independent and more able to experience a meaningful personal and social existence.* Table 7.1 provides a sampling *Gardner 1971* of other types of problems responsive to a behavioral approach. Since these early application demonstrations, there have been literally thousands of more recent reports which attest to the generalized value of the behavioral education approach.

The evaluation of these and similar reports emphasizes the particular applicability of behavior change procedures even to the more severely impaired, as no particular characteristic, such as speech or a certain level of cognitive development, is a necessary requisite to behavior change. Additionally, there is ample evidence that behavioral education procedures can be utilized by a wide range of personnel in the setting in which the child resides. This is of special significance in view of the limited number of highly trained personnel who are presently available to provide specialized services to children presenting exceptional learning and behavior characteristics.

TABLE 7.1   *Examples of Application to Exceptional Characteristics*

Child Characteristic	Reference
Culturally deprived	Reynolds and Risley 1968
School phobic	Lazarus et al. 1965
Emotionally disturbed	Bernal et al. 1968
Psychotic-autistic	Lovaas 1967
Brain injured	Hall and Broden 1967
Learning disabled	Nolen et al. 1967
Disruptive	Barrish et al. 1969
Hyperactive	Patterson 1965b
Delinquent	Burchard and Tyler 1965
Visually impaired	Stolz and Wolf 1969
Auditorily impaired	Osborne 1969
Habit disturbance	Browning 1967
Physically impaired	Horner 1971
Speech and language difficulties	Sloane and MacAulay 1968

Illustration of Analytic and Operational Features

McKenzie et al. 1968;
Bijou et al. 1966; Lazarus
et al. 1965
Studies by McKenzie et al.,* Bijou et al.,* and Lazarus et al.* illustrate the operational and analytic characteristics of the behavioral approach to influencing exceptional learning and behavior patterns of children. These studies, which represent approaches to modifying various problem areas of children who are described as distractible, disruptive, learning disabled, mentally retarded, and neurotic, also illustrate that there are no essential differences in these procedures and other related learning concepts used in dealing with a wide range of problem areas.

In the McKenzie et al. study:

> *Eight highly distractible and disruptive children ranging from ten to thirteen years of age and attending a learning disabilities class were provided a number of different reinforcing events for appropriate classroom behavior. Such events as free-time activities, recess time, special privileges, weekly grades, and teacher attention were provided on a contingent basis for adequate study activities. Following a baseline period under these conditions, weekly grades were exchanged at home by parents for the child's weekly allowance. The amount of allowance earned was dependent upon the grades earned during the week. Under this additional contingency condition, academic performance increased significantly. In fact, six of the children were returned to regular classes.*

Bijou et. al. 1966
Bijou et al.* describe the classroom program which was used to develop a motivational system for strengthening academic and appropriate social behaviors in a group of "mildly retarded" students:

> *Initially, the teacher approval which was provided for desirable classroom behaviors was found to be ineffective in strengthening these classes of behaviors. Following the introduction of a token reinforcement system, higher rates of effective study and cooperation behaviors became evident. Various study habits, including such behaviors as sitting quietly, paying attention to and complying with instructions, and working productively for sustained periods, were strengthened and a range of disruptive behaviors was eliminated. Techinques involving frequent token and social reinforcement for appropriate social and study behaviors, and those using extinction and mild punishment operations such as time-out from positive reinforcement, were used by the teacher personnel. The results of these behavior modification procedures along with the use of programmed materials can best be depicted by describing the study behaviors developed by one of the students. It should be noted that initially the students were poorly motivated for academic achievement. That is, they engaged in "academic behaviors" for only short and inconsistent periods of time. The authors report:*
> *Instead of being given his assignment by the teacher, he obtained*

his own "work folder," set his own watch, and entered the data
and starting time on his daily record sheet. He chose his first task,
completed it, and went on to the next. Starting and finishing times
entered for each item. When all the work was completed, he
called a teacher and together they checked his work. Marks [token
reinforcement] were given at this time. [p. 512]

These authors provide an excellent discussion of the basic principles which guided the development of the procedures and materials used.
Specific techniques for the development of the motivation system and
prerequisite academic behaviors are discussed and should be consulted by
those interested in developing a behavioral education program for use with
children with exceptional cognitive behavior characteristics in a classroom
environment.

Lazarus et al.* describe the behavior intervention program used   *Lazarus et al. 1965*
with a nine-year-old boy with school phobia. The writers report:

"On entering the fourth grade, Paul avoided the classroom situation.
He was often found hiding in the cloakroom, and subsequently began
spending less time at school each day. Thereafter neither threats,
bribes, nor punishment could induce him to re-enter school" (p. 225).
The boy had experienced similar episodes of school phobia in
earlier grades. Behavior education procedures were used by a
psychologist who interacted with the boy in the natural environments
of the school and home. These procedures were directed toward
reducing the fear reaction which was displayed toward the school
environment and of strengthening the frequency of school attendance.
Within a week of initiating the program, the boy spent the entire
morning in school. The length of time was gradually increased until
the boy was able to attend throughout the day. In fact, it was reported
that the child showed improved behavior in areas other than those
dealt with in the program. A ten-month follow-up after termination of
the program revealed that Paul had experienced no difficulty with
school attendance. The technical aspects of the procedures used are
discussed in later chapters.

These three studies illustrate various characteristics of the humanistic behavioral approach. In each, the major emphasis was on the development of effective behavior and on the objective evaluation of the
effectiveness of the behavior change program in meeting the program
objectives. As problematic behaviors were not assumed to be symptomatic
of some internal psychological disturbance, no related diagnostic exercises
were undertaken. Further, it was not deemed necessary to delve exten-
sively into the history of the behavior patterns to identify factors associated
with initial development. This strategy was based on the behavioral approach assumption that the conditions involved in initial development of a
behavior pattern need not be the same conditions which currently maintain

the behavior. Nor was it assumed that the conditions which maintained maladaptive behavior in one setting were necessarily the same as those which maintained it in another. Additionally, in some instances behaviors other than those chosen as the focus of treatment showed change in a desirable manner. The behavioral education programs were designed not only to eliminate maladaptive behavior but also to provide more suitable behavior as a replacement.

Finally, the focus of the programs of behavior change was on modification of specific behaviors as these occurred in the natural environment of classroom and home setting. Persons in the natural setting functioned as the treatment agent in two of the studies. In the third, parents were enlisted to implement some aspects of the program. The teacher and parent arranged the environment in terms of the designated program and, in the usual course of interacting with the children involved, followed the behavior modification plan.

Applicability to Simple and Complex Problems

The behavioral approach has proved useful in dealing with exceptional learning and behavioral characteristics ranging from (a) *simple behavior patterns* such as increase in time spent in attending to a task* or improvement in reading or arithmetic skills* to (b) *broader behavioral skills* such as those comprising the learning styles and social behaviors of children* through (c) *more general and complex repertoires* which are described as childhood schizophrenia and autism,* and to (d) other *more specific but distressing behavior patterns* such as encopresis.

Ferritor et al. 1972
Lovitt and Curtiss 1968

Minuchin et al. 1967
Lovaas 1967

Conger 1970

Conger,* as an example of the latter, reports successful modification of encopresis in a nine-year-old boy who soiled himself from one to four times daily.

> The problem had existed for four years in the child, who had experienced gastrointestinal problems since birth. Repeated medical evaluation and treatment had produced no improvement. The boy also complained of physical ailments such as stomachaches and headaches. The complaining occurred whenever the boy soiled himself. An internal deviancy or psychodynamic approach to such problems would involve an attempt to uncover internal disturbance as the basis for these. A highly trained expert would then treat the "real" internal difficulties under the supposition that the symptomatic behaviors would disappear. A statement by Ginott and Harms* represents this approach: "Therapeutic approach to encopresis must deal with the child's inner conflicts as well as with the relationship between parents and children" (p. 1101).

Ginott and Harms 1965

Conger 1970

> Conger,* observed this exceptional behavior pattern as it occurred in the social context of school and home and noted that the boy soiled himself only on the way home from school or at home after

*school hours. After each occurrence, the boy would inform his mother
who then would clean and change him. It was also established that
being soiled was somewhat aversive to the boy, for he would require
that his mother change him immediately.*

*These observations, along with medical data indicating no
physical basis for the encopresis, led to the hypothesis that the
mother's attention was maintaining both the soiling and the
complaining. During a fourteen-day observation period, soiling
occurred on an average in excess of twice daily. On the fifteenth day,
the mother, upon being informed by her son that he had soiled, merely
stated that he was a "big boy" and could take care of himself. No other
form of verbal interchange or social attention occurred in relation to
the soiling. The boy soiled only once on the first day of the mother's
new approach and only once more during a ninety-day follow-up
period. The stomachaches and other physcial complaints decreased
to zero on day 1 and never reoccurred.*

This study illustrates that an extensive case history is not a necessary
prerequisite to effective intervention programs. As noted, the factors involved in the initial acquisition of behavior patterns may or may not be
those present factors influencing the behavior. There is no need for extensive examination of the "personality structure and dynamics" of the child.
Conger's relatively simple and uncomplicated behavioral analysis uncov-
ered a possible functional relationship between the problematic behaviors
and present social consequences. This hypothesis was then translated into
a behavioral change plan which was implemented by the mother in the
home setting.

It is not being suggested that every, or even most, exceptional learning or behavior characteristic is so easily understood or modified. *Obviously, many are much more complex and require more detailed
behavioral analyses.* The behavioral model, nonetheless, approaches the
tasks of evaluation and modification in a manner distinctly different from
that characteristic of the internal-pathology model.

As a second example of the learning basis for exceptional behavior
characteristics, one child may view classroom participation with fear,
while another approaches such activity with anticipation and enthusiasm.
The behavior of the first is no more, or no less, categorically related to
internal pathological factors than is that of the second. The learning histories of both have resulted in the development of the present behavioral
patterns which interact with the conditions associated with classroom
participation. One child may be unable to explain why he is fearful just as
the other child may be unable to explain why he is enthusiastic. Both fear
and enthusiasm obviously are complex behavior patterns which have developed out of past experiences. Both are present behavior patterns, however, which are influenced and determined by present covert and external
events.

Summary

As a model of development, maintenance, and modification of human behavior, the humanistic behavior approach has equal relevance to the typical as well as the atypical, to the child who presents only occasional behavior problems as well as to the child with chronic and intense problems of adaptation. It is theoretically just as applicable to the development of simple behavioral patterns as it is to more complex and general ones such as positive self-regard, self-regulation, achievement motivation, and creativity. It is just as concerned with these "essentially human" aspects of behavior as is true of any other approach.*

Bradfield 1970

Viewpoint 24   Programs of behavior development and change should be provided in the child's naturalistic settings.

The focus of the humanistic behavioral approach is on learning and behavior difficulties as these occur in the everyday environments of the child. The naturalistic environments of the child and adolescent include the classroom, the home, the playground, gym, art studio, and the like; the psychologist's testing room, the psychiatrist's play room, and social worker's and counselor's offices are all relatively alien and unnatural. Intervention programs, in most instances, should be designed for the child's naturalistic environmental settings. Providing new experiences in the naturalistic settings will maximize the likelihood that appropriate behaviors will be learned, whether these behaviors be affective, cognitive, academic, social, study, or verbal. As the major educative focus is on providing meaningful social experiences instead of on treating hypothetical, unobservable, and unmeasurable internal factors, persons in the child's naturalistic environments can provide meaningful program experiences if the external variables influencing the child's behavior can be identified and changed. To the extent that the critical environmental elements can be arranged, behavior can be influenced in a systematic and desired manner.

This approach is in marked contrast to traditional forms of child and adolescent therapy, special education, and rehabilitation which attempt, as the sole or major strategy in dealing with learning and behavior difficulties, to place the child or adolescent in an artificial environment such as a therapist's office or a residential facility where the specialists provide treatment. In these settings, the therapists are at a distinct disadvantage in most instances as they do not have control over the multitude of potentially effective day-by-day behavior change experiences.

Wahler 1969, 1975

It is also important to note that children with problem behaviors commonly engage in such behaviors in multiple settings.* Change in behaviors in one setting does not insure that the behaviors will also change in another setting. Wahler reported data which demonstrated that classes of problematic behaviors modified successfully in the home setting still occurred at pretreatment levels in the school setting. O'Leary et al.,* as another example, reported that even within the same classroom and with the same teacher, positive behavior change which followed initiation of a token reinforcement program did not generalize from the afternoon session, during which the contingency management program was in effect, to the morning session which was managed in the pretreatment manner. *O'Leary et al. 1969*

Thus, if a child is to benefit from experiences in a specialized therapy setting, there must be a high degree of similarity between its components and those of other settings in which the child moves. The types of social relations, the types of behaviors required, and the schedules of behavioral requirements and reinforcement all are critical in consideration of adjustment to different settings. The temporary environment (e.g., therapeutic, supportive, rehabilitative, and so on) must teach and maintain those habits or modes of behavior which will be adaptive at a future time in a different environment. These behaviors frequently are not those required in the therapy environment. Behavioral characteristics such as independence, self-sufficiency, individuality, and freedom of choice are all needed for independence in a child's naturalistic settings of school and home. These are hardly the behavior patterns fostered, for example, in many residential programs. In other programs which provide a therapeutic milieu, the child is provided new skills in arts and crafts, music, recreation, and even "verbal insight." However, many of these skills will not be maintained after return to the naturalistic environments as too few opportunities are available for using them. Further, even if used, the social agents in the naturalistic environments fail to provide consistent reinforcement for these behaviors. (The question of generalization and maintenance of behavior change is discussed more fully in Chapter 9).

> **Viewpoint 25**   The humanistic behavioral model recognizes that educational environments and programs vary tremendously in their impact on different children.

Some educational environments support the development of prosocial behavior patterns. Others are supportive of inappropriate patterns of emotional and motor behavior. The experiences of Hamblin et al.* with young children with severe learning and behavior difficulties led to a similar impression: *Hamblin et al. 1971*

> Learning environments can vary tremendously in value and in potency. Some are orthogenic, that is they help the child acquire pro-normal patterns; others are pathogenic, they cause the child to lose pro-normal patterns and they foster withdrawal or the development of bizarre, disruptive patterns. Furthermore, the various orthogenic and pathogenic environments apparently vary in potency. Some foster a higher rate of learning than others. [p. 67]

As environments can be relatively neutral or can be most powerful in either positive or negative influence, no single or rigidly conceived educational programs should be provided children grouped on the basis of irrelevant criteria such as brain injury or emotional disturbance. The powerfulness of an environment will depend to a great extent on the knowledge which the program designers have of the unique characteristics of each child being served and to the extent to which systematic use is made of known principles of behavior influence. As emphasized earlier, the interactions between child characteristics and specific educational intervention tactics are varied and complex. This necessitates an empirical and flexible attitude as the educator attempts to match ever-changing learner characteristics to educational procedures.

> **Viewpoint 26**   The behavior approach to modifying behavior is an educational one; it does not attempt to "cure" the child.

As implied earlier, the behavioral approach does not attempt to "cure" the child since no assumption is made that there are some "central" or "core" etiologic factors which, if changed or eliminated, would reciprocally alleviate a range of symptomatic learning and behavior difficulties. Rather, a direct attempt is made to change those learning, behavioral, and environmental features involved in, and which comprise, the child's difficulties. The behavioral position, as noted, assumes that all consistent learning and behavior characteristics of children, appropriate and inappropriate, are the end results (symptoms, if you wish) of a history of experiences and of a contemporary set of conditions as these have and do interact with specific physical and psychological characteristics.

This position does not preclude the possibility that deficit or excessive behavior patterns of various classes may be the chief or central source of difficulty. In such cases, modification of these problem areas would have initial consideration. For instance, a child may become highly emotional in a range of situations in which he does not "have his way." This behavior pattern in turn may disrupt the occurrence of appropriate prosocial behaviors which are in the child's repertoire but which are of less strength. Such disruptive emotional behaviors, by interfering with involvement in classroom instructional experiences, may impede the acquisition of new or more complex and appropriate modes of behavior. Behavior change programs would thus focus on the reduction of the high rate of disruptive emotional behaviors. At the same time, prosocial behaviors would be encouraged by a complementary program approach.

In other instances, the major focus of an educational program may be one of insuring that various environmental events are sufficient to exert a certain influence on the child's behavior. If events reinforcing to a specific

child are quite limited, the child experiences considerable difficulty learning new behavior patterns. Lovaas* has suggested that such reduction in   *Lovaas 1967*
the number of events which are reinforcing represents one of the major
deficits in children labeled as autistic. Thus, instead of attempting to cure
autism, the behavioral approach would attempt, as one tactic, to increase
the number of different events which would be reinforcing to a child. In
this manner, the likelihood is greatly increased that the child will learn
with greater facility and thus be more likely to develop competency skills.

> **Viewpoint 27**   An educational approach which focuses on di-
> rect remediation of inappropriate behavior typ-
> ically will not result in symptom substitution.

Symptom substitution, as the concept is used in the internal-
deviancy approach to psychological functioning, is not a consideration in a
behavioral education program because problem behaviors are not viewed
as symptomatic of some more basic or central underlying psychological
difficulty. As noted earlier, the behavioral position is quite a departure
from that of the general internal-deviancy model, which focuses intervention efforts on what is assumed to be the internal causes of the symptomatic
problem behavior. By treating the internal or central causes, it is assumed
by the internal-deviancy position that the danger of "symptom substitution"—one inappropriate behavior symptom substituting for or
appearing after treatment of another one—is averted. If treatment is directed only toward removing the symptom, it is assumed, the basic cause
remains and will manifest itself in other symptomatic behavior. Commenting on this difference, Skinner* noted: "Where, in the Freudian scheme,   *Skinner 1953*
behavior is merely the symptom of a neurosis, in the present formulation it
is the direct object of inquiry" (p. 376).

Phillips et al.* suggest that behaviors   *Phillips et al. 1975*

> come to be called symptoms by qualified professional observers, by strategi-
> cally placed and powerful persons whose decisions may affect the individ-
> ual's life, by peers, or by the person exhibiting the symptom. In the behavior
> modification scheme, the term symptom has no objective status; rather it is a
> shorthand designation of a social judgment that a particular category of
> behavior needs to be eliminated, reshaped, or corrected. [pp. 33–34]

The behavioral approach to symptom substitution offers the following additional considerations:

*In most cases, reduction in strength of problem learning and be-
havior characteristics should actually increase the occurrence of appropriate learning and behaving. As an example, the reduction of fear of*

authority or dislike for competition may increase the likelihood that a range of desired behavior will occur.

Other aspects of the child's environment may change in a positive direction as his problems are decreased. A child who becomes less defensive, or distractible, should be able to learn more effectively. When he acquires more competency in dealing with conflict or in paying attention to instructional components, he is more likely to receive positive reinforcement from others. These events, in turn, will increase the likelihood of a range of appropriate behaviors. (A more detailed rationale and related supporting data for this position are included in Chapter 9 under Concurrent Behavior Change.)

No psychological or educational procedure actually removes or eliminates behavior. Behavioral education or any other form of behavior influence can only change the functions of the environmental conditions which influence the behavior. Thus, even though behavior patterns may be reduced to zero frequency of occurrence in one or a dozen situations, it cannot be said that the behavior has been eliminated completely. It can only be said that the behavior is no longer under the influence of present environmental conditions or, conversely, that other behaviors have a higher likelihood of occurrence in these situations. This same "extinguished" behavior may well appear at high strength in other situations, although, as new behaviors are developed and gain in strength, this behavior pattern may become increasingly unlikely to ever occur again. Also, old behaviors may become a cue for negative emotionality which would be aversive to a child. The behavior, thus, would be even less likely to reoccur.

Following the reduction in strength of a specified behavior pattern, whether appropriate or inappropriate, it is quite possible that the behavior pattern may reappear if the initial or similar environmental conditions reappear. Additionally, new patterns of unadaptive behavior may be developed or other patterns which had not been highly functional may gain prominence.

Bandura 1969   Bandura* has suggested that:

> according to the social-learning point of view, in the course of social development a person acquires different modes of coping with environmental stresses and demands. These various response strategies form a hierarchy ordered by their probability of effecting favorable outcomes in certain situations. A particular mode of responding may occupy a dominant position in various hierarchies; subordinate strategies may differ from one situation to another and may vary widely in their frequency of occurrence relative both to the dominant response tendencies and among themselves. Consequently, the effects of removing a dominant response pattern will depend upon the number of different areas of functioning in which it is characteristically activated, and the nature and relative strength of the initially weaker response disposition. [p. 50]

The weaker response dispositions may well be behavior patterns viewed as maladaptive by the dominant social environment. In this case, what appears to be symptom substitution may be explained easily by rather simple principles of learning.

As emphasized in later chapters, behavior change programs designed only to eliminate behavior are quite apt to result in the display of other unadaptive behaviors. Such a strategy, which focuses only on the elimination of behavior, provides no guarantee that appropriate ways of performing will occur. Cahoon* has suggested that if deviant behavior is eliminated or reduced, a child may have no other appropriate behavior in his repertoire.

Cahoon 1968

A maladaptive behavior may produce a reinforcer appropriate to a specific state of deprivation. This behavior may not occur except under extreme states of deprivation. This state may, for example, be social deprivation in general or even more specific social events such as peer attention, adult affection, or the like. A program which attempts to eliminate problem behavior without providing for other means of obtaining those meaningful social consequences which reduce the deprivation state may well result in the development of other maladaptive behaviors.

Inappropriate behavior may be related to emotional states resulting from frustration, rejection, or fear of failure. Attempts at eliminating or suppressing the inappropriate behavior without concurrently reducing the frustration, rejection, or fear may well result in appearance of other behaviors which function to remove or reduce these unpleasant conditions.

Reynolds* has suggested that, depending upon previous learning conditions, attempts to eliminate behavior under one set of conditions through suppression (punishment) may actually facilitate that behavior under other conditions. Controlling a child's aggressive behavior by means of threat of punishment may be effective as long as the person who can provide the aversive consequences is present. However, in the absence of the controlling person, the aggressive behavior may actually become more frequent than before the punishment procedure was initiated.

Reynolds 1968

Programs reflecting only minor changes in environmental conditions can produce only temporary changes in behavior. An individual usually has a number of alternative patterns of behavior which will produce reinforcing consequences. Failure of one mode of problem solving will frequently result in other patterns being attempted. It is not unusual for these alternative means of behaving to be equally as unacceptable as the initial unadaptive behavior pattern.

Viewpoint 28   The behavior approach emphasizes the development of individualized learning programs, especially for children with exceptional learning and behavior characteristics.

A learning program refers to a plan for the arrangement of educational experiences to promote appropriate learning and functioning for a specific child. Learning and performing arithmetic skills, auditory discriminations, interpersonal skills, emotional skills, and self-direction skills, for example, are all important. The school environment, whether planned or not or whether systematic or not, is in fact influencing the manner in which the child thinks of himself, feels toward others, is self-controlled, is dependent, or is free in evaluating, in controlling, and in experiencing his feelings. The role of the school is not just that of teaching arithmetic skills or, for example, facts about historical events. Even more important are the influences which the educational environment can exert on characteristics of self-confidence, self-assurance, self-expression, acceptance of individual differences, tolerance of one's own differences, self-control, and the like. An educator who accepts no deviation from his or her rigid requirements may do well in teaching mathematical concepts but may rate poorly in teaching the child to respect authority and like himself at the same time.

If, from an educational viewpoint, there is anything exceptional about children so labeled, it is merely the fact that most require more individualized arrangements of their educational program than is true of *Adelman 1972;* most other children.* Most children are labeled as normal because of the *Sabatino 1972* nature and rate of behavior development in group educational programs. The child with exceptional learning and behavior characteristics does not benefit adequately from such learning programs and thus must be provided a more prescriptive, individualized one. In illustration, some children are overresponsive to irrelevant stimuli, some have extreme difficulty distinguishing among critical social cues in interpersonal relationships, some have poor concept-formation skills, and some require rather immediate and tangible consequences for appropriate behavior to occur when confronted with difficult tasks. These and a multitude of other individual learner characteristics must be utilized in arranging the learning environment for those children if adequate educational gains are to be obtained.

Learning Environment May Be Disabled

An educational evaluation of a child's difficulties may suggest that the current learning environment is "disabled," "disorganized," or "fragmented" because it assumes certain learning or behavior characteristics on *Lovaas et al. 1971* the child's part which do not exist. Lovaas et al.,* as one example, report that some children defined as autistic respond primarily to only one cue in situations which provide multiple sensory output. The child tends to be overselective and thus at a distinct disadvantage in an environment that assumes attentiveness to multiple sensory stimulation. The purpose of an educational evaluation, in such instances, would attempt to identify what a child *does do* in various behavioral dimensions *under various* environ-

mental conditions. Then the learning program could be rearranged to meet the specifications of the individual child.*

Hammill 1971

Specification of Educational Objectives

In devising individualized learning programs, it will be necessary to identify and define the *specific* learning and behavior characteristics which require special attention. Such statements as "develop a more positive attitude toward school," "create social sensitivity," "decrease his dependency," or "change his cognitive tempo" are acceptable as statements of broad educational goals but are too general to provide direction to specific educational programs. These statements must be translated into more precise behavioral objectives and into related daily experiences.

An additional aspect of this program planning activity is that of describing the *direction* of change as well as the *extent* of change necessary for attainment of a given educational goal. It is one thing to identify such goals as "to attain competence in self-help skills" or "social adequacy," but quite another to translate a general goal into specific behavioral objectives and relate it to day-by-day program experiences.

Specification of Educational Procedures

The behavioral approach requires educational personnel to step out of the realm of general, and frequently vague, behavior change methodology and into the arena of specificity. Beyond the task of specifying the behavior goals comes the problem of translating these into effective educational procedures. What procedures will be used to bring about the desired learning and behaving? If procedures to be used include verbal counseling, creation of a therapeutic milieu, information giving, classroom instruction, perceptual-motor activity therapy, psycholinguistic ability training, or relaxation training, for example, the educator not only must describe the experiences but must also justify, in terms of behavior principle or hypothesis, why these procedures of behavior change are selected for particular problems of particular children.

All too frequently, in educational and psychological practices involving children with exceptional learning and behavior characteristics, program placements are made (for example, special class placement, social adjustment training) and specific treatment procedures used (for example, verbal counseling, teaching to perceptual strengths, recreation therapy) without any clear conceptual or empirical indication of how such experiences will result in better learning or "adjustment" of the child. Some children, without question, do change during such experiences. The inefficiency and unpredictability of such practices, however, become real issues in numerous difficult problem cases.

The behavioral approach thus requires *individualized and prescrip-*

tive programming. Every educational experience provided is viewed as one of a series of steps in the direction of attaining specified educational objectives.[3] The child is provided a set of experiences designed to develop functional academic skills, for example, only if it is agreed that additional academic skills will increase his likelihood of adapting to the requirements of given situations. He is placed in a special reading program in order to develop designated reading and related behavioral patterns. These may range from learning to read under the guidance of a helpful teacher to the development of independent reading skills reflecting adequate speed and comprehension. Such an individualized and prescriptive educational attitude precludes educational placement of children on the basis of characteristics—i.e., children placed together who demonstrate hard and soft neurological signs denoting brain injury*—which do not interact with specific educational procedures.

Bortner et al. 1972

Recognition of the Changing Nature of Learner Characteristics

The implementation of the individualized learning program approach *emphasizes that a child's learning or behavior characteristics are not static.* It is recognized that some characteristics are more stable, durable, and have more pervasive effects than others. But most learner characteristics are open to change. For example, a child's learning characteristics may include those of hyperactivity, distractibility, impulsivity, and short attention span. At any specific time in the child's development, the educational program may adapt to these as new academic skills and behavior patterns are being taught. At the same time, these learner characteristics may be modified by teaching the child to become less distractible, less active, more deliberate, more attending, and more persistent which, in turn, will result in a concomitant change in the manner in which the educational program is designed. Thus, the learner's characteristics at any specific time may—or may not—be the learner's characteristics at another time. An individualized educational program is designed to modify a child's bothersome learning characteristics as well as to teach a variety of academic curricular topics. Some learner characteristics which relate to the learning process (such as neurological, muscular, or sensory features) may not be modifiable, but others which may well be changed include the cognitive, perceptual, memory, attending, and motivational ones.

Summary

Children and adolescents with learning and behavior difficulties are not inadequate in any absolute or intrinsic sense. Many act the way they do

---

3. A task analysis model of diagnostic-prescriptive teaching, as emphasized, is favored over the ability-training model of diagnostic-prescriptive teaching (Bateman 1967; Quay 1973; Ysseldyke and Salvia 1974).

only because their environments—content and arrangement—are insensitive to them as potential active and enthusiastic learners. The limitations or difficulties of many children and adolescents do not reflect inherent characteristics, but they may reflect deficits within the prevailing practices of management and education. *The humanistic behavioral model assumes that everyone can learn if provided an appropriate learning environment.* There will obviously be differences in the rate of learning and in the complexity and types of behaviors acquired. In recognition of individual differences, the elements which make up the "appropriate learning environment" will not be the same for all. This humanistic behavioral approach recognizes individual differences as a fact of human existence and provides a sensible approach to dealing with these differences. Both program content and program method are individualized to contribute to the uniqueness of each child and adolescent.

> **Viewpoint 29**   The humanistic behavioral approach focuses primarily on the development of appropriate behaviors and not on behavioral deficits, inadequacies, disabilities, shortcomings, or difficulties.

Educational programs should be directed toward the development of effective learning and behavior characteristics and not primarily toward the elimination or control of undesirable ones. Additionally, an educational program cannot be based on what a child does not do. It is useless to emphasize that "she can't do this," "she should be able to do that but she can't." The behavioral approach assumes a more positive attitude of "she is able to do such and such." The educational program will be structured to expand upon and enhance what the child can do in the direction of greater competency. The program begins with what a child can do and progresses from that point.

Once new behaviors are developed and the child is able to obtain more frequent and varied favorable consequences through her own efforts, inappropriate, disruptive, bothersome behaviors tend either to disappear or at least to decrease in visibility. As suggested, in some cases it may be necessary to focus the learning program on the reduction in strength or the elimination of some frequently occurring inappropriate behaviors (e.g., high rate of aggressive behavior, hyperactivity, excessive crying) prior to the development of desirable ways of behaving. Even this may be done, in many instances, by emphasizing the development of constructive behaviors which will compete successfully and thus replace the inappropriate ones.

Hall et al.* illustrated this strategy with first- and third-grade pupils who had high rates of disruptive or dawdling behavior. Patterson et al.* illustrated the strategy with a hyperactive brain-injured ten-year-old boy. Hall et al.:

Hall et al. 1968
Patterson et al. 1965

> reinforced study behavior with teacher attention, ignored nonstudy
> behavior, and found sharply increased study rates. A reversal of the
> contingency (attention occurring only after periods of disruptive or
> dawdling behavior) produced low rates of study. Reinstatement of
> teacher attention following study behavior produced high rates of
> study behavior and low occurrence of disruptive behavior.

The Patterson et al. study:

> arranged an environment which systematically reinforced
> "attending" and "sitting at desk" behavior in a hyperactive boy.
> These behaviors were incompatible with "constant looking around"
> and "out of seat" behaviors and, as the former were strengthened, the
> latter ones dropped in magnitude and frequency. The child then was
> in a more desirable position to attend to aspects of the instructional
> program and to choose those which most appealed to him.

Swift and Spivack 1974   Swift and Spivack* present a review and description of numerous other studies which follow the strategy of focusing on the development of appropriate behaviors in groups of children with behavior difficulties.

The humanistic behavioral approach thus is based on the recognition that success breeds success. Once a child has acquired some prosocial behaviors, he is in a better position to acquire others. Once he has had the experience of achieving a goal, he is more likely to become involved in further attempts at goal achievement. The approach emphasizes positive reinforcement for what a child does do instead of punishment for failure to attain predetermined performance standards. This difference in focus was illustrated vividly in a recent experience of the writer:

> A teacher reported that the child had been given ten consecutive
> marks of F for failure to complete at 70 percent criterion his arithmetic
> assignments. On urging from the writer, the teacher agreed to provide
> positive reinforcement for the problems which were correct, and
> matter-of-fact feedback for his errors. She reported that he was
> correctly completing only about 10 percent of his daily assignment.
> She initially set criterion for pass at 10 percent. After a few days of
> being successful (i.e., reaching pass criterion and receiving positive
> feedback from teacher and parents), the boy began completing an
> increasingly higher percentage of the problems. Within three weeks,
> the initial performance criterion of 70 percent was being surpassed.
> After a month, the teacher reported that the child seldom missed a
> problem and gave considerable evidence of enjoying his new level of
> achievement.

Focus on Development of Competency

In a vital sense the approach represents, as suggested earlier, a *competency model*. It is based on the observation that failure and the

resulting aversive consequences are generally detrimental to positive behavior development. It recognizes that many learning and behavior difficulties are created by an insensitive learning program which seems to
assume that all children are created equal and thereby should respond in
the same manner to a set educational environment. This attitude obviously
produces failure and incompetency in many children. Children soon learn
to avoid, or at least minimize involvement in, such educational experiences.

The approach is based on the assumption that a contingency environment which emphasizes positive consequences encourages creativity,
initiative, independence, success, confidence, and a positive attitude toward the educational endeavor. Success experiences result in "I like myself" behavior. Competency, confidence, a happiness state, involvement,
exploration, individual expression, and positive interpersonal relationships, as complex behavioral characteristics, are all more likely to develop
in an environment which systematically attempts to facilitate their development than in an environment which becomes concerned about these
only when there is significant difficulty in these areas. Children learn
better, assimilate more, and make better discriminations when they are
happy, achieving, free from boredom, and have friends and adequate relationships with teachers. A contingency environment based on positive
reinforcement encourages and is highly consistent with the development
of such behavior patterns.

Focus on Prevention and Remediation

The humanistic behavioral approach represents a *preventive* and
developmental orientation as well as a *remedial* one. Its focus on positive
reinforcement and successful development of a wide array of behavioral
repertoires results in the prevention of numerous problems of learning and
behavior development. At the same time, the approach provides pointed
direction to arranging developmental, remedial, and restorative experiences for children who have acquired various exceptional learning and
behavior characteristics.

Laziness and Disinterest Not Inherent Characteristics

Children do not avoid learning experiences primarily because these
are difficult; rather, children frequently do not become involved in specific
learning tasks because of (1) deficits in their own behavioral repertoires, (2)
the presence of a variety of antilearning (emotional, attitudinal, avoidance)
behavioral characteristics, and (3) due to reinforcement deficiencies or
excessive aversive elements in the learning environment. Children are not
inherently lazy. They do not object to expending energy or persisting at

activities. Look at the group on the playground, in the gym, in the TV room, and on the athletic field. Children persist at TV watching or at play activities for extended periods of time. Children perform in these settings until they are ready to drop from exhaustion. Why the difference between these behaviors and those observed in the educational setting? Could it not be that one contains numerous reinforcing events and the other does not? Also, consider the observation that while some children consistently avoid most school activities, some children do find school activities quite enjoyable as evidenced by their verbal and emotional reactions, their high level of achievement, and their persistence. Why the difference? Could it not be that the achieving children have experienced frequent success and positive consequences and the others have not?

Learning and performance of certain classes of behavior are not exciting for many children because their past experience predominately has been either neutral or negative. In many instances the present environment is not arranged to insure goal attainment and resulting contingent positive reinforcement for many types of behavior. Too many educational environments are based on the proposition that a child will enter into a learning experience when he is "ready" to do so. The behavioral approach actively assists the child in becoming ready.

> **Viewpoint 30** Knowledge of the learning history of a child, while not essential, may be helpful in designing a program for influencing his exceptional learning and behavior characteristics.

Ross 1967, 1974   Knowledge of the types of previous educational experiences provided a child with learning difficulties may be valuable in structuring a present education program. Ross* emphasizes such knowledge will be useful in distinguishing among different types of learning difficulties and in selecting the most appropriate approach to handling the difficulties. (Other factors in the learning history of a child which contribute to exceptional learning and behavior characteristics are discussed in Chapter 13.)

The behavioral approach does not assume, however, that an understanding of the historical factors contributing to the development of present learning and behavior characteristics is an essential prerequisite to the development and/or initiation of an educational program. It is not essential that a clear delineation be made of how present learning and/or behavior patterns develop out of numerous experiences of the past in order to be successful in changing these in the present. It becomes appropriate to ask "even if one could identify many of the significant historical events, what purpose would be served?" These historical events cannot be "educated," "treated," or changed. Only present events can be dealt with and *these function to influence present learning and behaving.* Thus, much of the child's behavior may be understood in terms of what is happening to him in the present, even though these behaviors typically represent the end product of a large number of previous experiences.

> **Viewpoint 31** The specific procedures used to influence exceptional learning and behavior characteristics of children are related to the factors identified as influencing these problems.

There is no predetermined relationship between the type of difficulty which a child presents and specific educational procedures. The specific program devised to influence exceptional learning and behavior characteristics is related to the total complex of factors assumed to be involved. To illustrate:

1. *Specific difficulties may be influenced simply by direct intervention.* Disruptive behavior, for example, may be inhibited by social punishment from peers.

2. *They may be influenced by changing the relative strength of other behaviors.* An adolescent may report that he is bored. Previous experience with the adolescent has suggested that when bored he is more likely to be excessively and unreasonably argumentative. Instead of dealing directly with the argumentative behavior, the parent or teacher may teach him new, exciting skills to occupy his time whenever he finds himself becoming bored. Thus, events which cued his argumentative behavior (the result of his being bored) are eliminated along with the problem behavior. As another example, a child may be rather disruptive in class. Instead of attempting to inhibit this disruption, the child is taught better skills of attending to, persisting at, and completion of class assignments.

3. *Specific difficulties may also be dealt with by identifying and changing the environmental events which influence the behavior.* A task assignment may be too difficult and thus becomes rather aversive. The child may become uncooperative if this behavior serves to get the teacher to remove the task assignment. The uncooperativeness may disappear if the task is reduced in difficulty to a level consistent with the child's skills.

4. *Specific difficulties are more likely to occur under specific setting event conditions.* Various patterns of emotional reactions, which some writers define as *setting events,** increase the likelihood of occurrence of certain subsequent responsiveness. A child who is angry is less likely to engage in cooperative and productive classroom behaviors than would be true at other times when he is not so aroused. In contrast, a child who is smiling, relaxed, or otherwise in a positive emotional state is more likely to engage in behaviors of cooperation, concentration, or even persistence in the face of difficulty.

Bijou and Baer 1961; Kantor 1958

It is not unusual for children with exceptional learning and behavior difficulties to be described as "being in a bad mood," "being grouchy," or "feeling down in the dumps." These descriptions imply that the child's emotional states influence his responsiveness to a variety of aspects of his environment. Control of those experiences which produce these emotional states may in turn influence other problem behaviors. If these cannot be avoided, an attempt is made to compete with these setting events by producing more appropriate emotional states. Verbal instructions, encouragement, "turning on a pleasing personality," and reminding the child of future positive consequences may be used to create more enhancing emotional moods. These setting events will be turn increase the likelihood of occurrence of of a range of other appropriate behaviors.

REFERENCES

Adelman, H. S. The resource concept: Bigger than a room. *Journal of Special Education,* 1972, 6, 361–367.

Baer, D. Laboratory control of thumbsucking by withdrawal and representation of reinforcement. *Journal of Experimental Analysis of Behavior,* 1962, 5, 525–528.

Bandura, A. *Principles of Behavior Modification.* New York: Holt, Rinehart & Winston, 1969.

Barrish, H., Saunders, M., and Wolf, M. M. Good behavior game: Effects of individual contingencies for group consequences on disruptive behavior in a classroom. *Journal of Applied Behavior Analysis,* 1969, 2, 119–124.

Barsh, R. *A Movigenic Curriculum.* Madison, Wisc.: State Department of Public Instruction, 1965.

Bateman, B. Three approaches to diagnosis and educational planning for children with learning disabilities. *Academic Therapy Quarterly,* 1967, 3, 11–16.

Bernal, N. E., Duryee, J. S., Pruett, H. L., and Burns, B. Behavior modification and the brat syndrome. *Journal of Consulting and Clinical Psychology,* 1968, 32, 447–455.

Bijou, S. W., and Baer, D. M. *Child Development.* Vol. I. *A Systematic and Empirical Theory.* New York: Appleton-Century-Crofts, 1961.

Bijou, S. W., Birnbrauer, J. S., Kidder, J. D., and Tague, C. Programmed instruction as an approach to teaching of reading, writing, and arithmetic to retarded children. *The Psychological Record,* 1966, 16, 505–522.

Bortner, M., Hertzig, M. A., and Birch, H. G. Neurological signs and intelligence of brain-damaged children. *Journal of Special Education,* 1972, 6, 325–333.

Bower, E. *Early Identification of Emotionally Handicapped Children in School.* (2nd Ed.) Springfield, Ill.: Charles C. Thomas, 1969.

Bradfield, R. H. Behavior modification: A most human endeavor. In R. H. Bradfield (Ed.) *Behavior Modification: The Human Effort.* San Rafael, Calif.: Dimensions, 1970. Pp. 211–218.

Browning, R. M. Operant strengthening UCR (awakening) as a prerequisite to treatment of persistent enuresis. *Behavior Research and Therapy,* 1967, 5, 371–372.

Browning, R. M., and Stover, D. O. *Behavior Modification in Child Treatment.* Chicago: Aldine-Atherton, 1971.

Burchard, J., and Tyler, V. The modification of delinquent behavior through operant conditioning. *Behavior Research and Therapy,* 1965, 2, 245–250.

Burke, A. A. Placement of black and white children in educable mentally handicapped classes and learning disability classes. *Exceptional Children,* 1975, 41, 438–439.

Cahoon, D. D. Issues and implications of operant conditioning: Balancing procedures against outcomes. *Hospital and Community Psychiatry,* 1968, 19, 228–229.

Clarizio, H. F., and McCoy, G. F. *Behavior Disorders in School-Age Children.* Scranton: Chandler, 1970.

Cohen, H. L. Behavior modification and socially deviant youth. In C. E. Thoresen (Ed.) *Behavior Modification in Education.* The 72nd Yearbook of the National Society for the Study of Education. Chicago: University of Chicago Press, 1973. Pp. 291–314.

Conger, J. C. The treatment of encopresis by the management of social consequences. *Behavior Therapy,* 1970, 1, 386–390.

Craig, H. B., and Holland, A. L. Reinforcement of visual attending in classrooms for deaf children. *Journal of Applied Behavior Analysis,* 1970, 3, 97–109.

Feldhusen, J., Thurston, J., and Beaning, J. Classroom behavior, intelligence, and achievement. *Journal of Experimental Education,* 1967, 36, 82–87.

Ferritor, D. E., Buckholdt, D., Hamblin, R. L., and Smith, L. The noneffects of contingent reinforcement for attending behavior on work accomplished. *Journal of Applied Behavior Analysis,* 1972, 5, 7–17.

Friedland, S. J., and Skilkret, R. B. Alternative explanations of learning disabilities: Defensive hyperactivity. *Exceptional Children,* 1973, 40, 213–215.

Frostig, M., and Horne, D. *The Frostig Program for the Development of Visual Perception: Teacher's Guide.* Chicago: Follett, 1964.

Gardner, W. I. *Behavior Modification in Mental Retardation.* Chicago: Aldine-Atherton, 1971.

Ginott, H. G., and Harms, E. Mental disorders in childhood. In B. J. Wolman (Ed.) *Handbook of Clinical Psychology.* New York: McGraw-Hill, 1965. Pp. 1094–1118.

Glavin, J. P. Persistence of behavior disorders in children. *Exceptional Children,* 1972, 38, 367–376.

Graubard, P. S., Rosenberg, H., and Miller, M. Ecological approaches to social deviancy. In T. Hopkins and E. Ramp (Eds.) *A New Direction for Education: Behavior Analysis 1971.* Lawrence, Kansas: Department of Human Development, University of Kansas, 1971.

Hall, R. V., and Broden, M. Behavior changes in brain-injured children through social reinforcement. *Journal of Experimental Child Psychology,* 1967, 5, 463–479.

Hall, R. V., Lund, D., and Jackson, D. Effects of teacher attention on study behavior. *Journal of Applied Behavior Analysis,* 1968, 1, 1–12.

Hallahan, D. P., and Cruickshank, W. M. *Psychoeducational Foundations of Learning Disabilities.* Englewood Cliffs, N. J.: Prentice-Hall, 1973.

Hamblin, R. L., et al. *The Humanization Processes: A Social, Behavioral Analysis of Children's Problems.* New York: Wiley, 1971.

Hammill, D. D. Evaluating children for instructional purposes. *Academic Therapy,* 1971, 6, 341–353.

Haring, N. G., and Hauck, M. A. Improved learning conditions in establishment of reading skills with disabled readers. *Exceptional Children,* 1969, 35, 341–352.

Hewett, F. M. Educational programs for children with behavior disorders. In H. C. Quay and J. S. Werry (Eds.) *Psychopathological Disorders of Childhood.* New York: John Wiley, 1972. Pp. 388–413.

Hollingshead, A. B., and Redlich, J. C. Social stratification and psychiatric disorders. *American Sociological Review,* 1953, 18, 163–169.

Horner, R. D. Establishing use of crutches by a mentally retarded spina bifida child. *Journal of Applied Behavior Analysis,* 1971, 4, 183–189.

Jones, R. L. Labels and stigma in special education. *Exceptional Children,* 1972, 38, 553–564.

Kanfer, F. H., and Saslow, G. Behavioral analysis: An alternative to diagnostic classification. *Archives of General Psychiatry,* 1965, 12, 529–538.

Kantor, J. R. *Interbehavioral Psychology.* Bloomington, Ind.: Principia, 1958.

Kaspar, J. C., and Schulman, J. L. Organic mental disorders: Brain damages. In B. J. Wolman (Ed.) *Manual of Child Psychopathology.* New York: McGraw-Hill, 1972. Pp. 207–229.

Keogh, B. K. Hyperactivity and learning disorders: Review and speculation. *Exceptional Children,* 1971, 38, 101–109.

Keogh, B. K., and Becker, L. D. Early detection of learning problems: Questions, cautions, and guidelines. *Exceptional Children,* 1973, 40, 5–11.

Kephart, N. C. *The Slow Learner in the Classroom.* Columbus, Ohio: Charles E. Merrill, 1960.

Kirk, S. A. *The Diagnosis and Remediation of Psycholinguistic Disabilities.* Urbana: University of Illinois Press, 1966.

Lal, H., and Lindsley, O. R. Therapy of chronic constipation in a young child by rearranging social contingencies. *Behavior Research and Therapy,* 1968, 6, 484–485.

Lazarus, A. A., Davidson, G. C., and Polefka, D. A. Classical and operant factors in the treatment of a school phobia. *Journal of Abnormal Psychology,* 1965, 70, 225–229.

Lovaas, O. I. A behavior therapy approach to the treatment of childhood schizophrenia. *Symposium on Child Development* (Vol. 1.) Minneapolis: University of Minnesota Press, 1967. Pp. 108–159.

Lovaas, O. I., Schreibman, L., Koegel, R., and Rehm, R. Selective responding by autistic children to multiple sensory input. *Journal of Abnormal Psychology,* 1971, 77, 211–222.

Lovitt, T. C., and Curtiss, K. A. Effects of manipulating an antecedent event on mathematics response rate. *Journal of Applied Behavior Analysis,* 1968, 1, 329–333.

Lovitt, T. C., and Esveldt, K. A. The relative effects on math performance of single versus multiple-ratio schedules: A case-study. *Journal of Applied Behavior Analysis.* 1970, 3, pp. 261–270.

McDermott, J. F., Harrison, S. I., Schrager, J., and Wilson, P. Social class and mental illness in children: Observations of blue collar families. *American Journal of Orthopsychiatry,* 1965, 35, 500–508.

McKenzie, H. S., Clark, M., Wolf, M. M., Kothera, R., and Benson, C. Behavior modification of children with learning disabilities using grades as tokens and allowances as back-up reinforcers. *Exceptional Children,* 1968, 34, 745–752.

Minuchin, S. H., Chamberlain, P., and Graubard, P. S. A project to teach learning skills to disturbed delinquent children. *American Journal of Orthopsychiatry,* 1967, 37, 558–567.

Morse, W. C. Self-concept in the school setting. *Childhood Education,* 1964, 41, 195–201.

Morse, W. C. The education of socially maladjusted and emotionally disturbed children. In W. M. Cruickshank and G. O. Johnson (Eds.) *Education of Exceptional Children and Youth.* (2nd Ed.) Englewood Cliffs, N. J.: Prentice-Hall, 1967. Pp. 569–627.

Myklebust, H. R. Learning disabilities: Definition and overview. In H. R. Myklebust (ed.) *Progress in Learning Disabilities.* New York: Grune and Stratton, 1968.

Neale, D. H. Behavior therapy and encopresis in children. *Behavior Research and Therapy,* 1968, 1, 139–149.

Nolen, P. A., Kunzelmann, H. P., and Haring, N. G. Behavior modification in a junior high learning disabilities classroom. *Exceptional Child,* 1967, 34, 163–168.

Obler, M., and Terwilliger, R. F. Pilot study on the effectiveness of systematic desensitization with neurologically impaired children with phobic disorders. *Journal of Consulting and Clinical Psychology,* 1970, 34, 314–318.

O'Leary, K. D., Becker, W. C., Evans, M. B., and Saudargas, R. A. A token reinforcement program in a public school: A replication and systematic analysis. *Journal of Applied Behavior Analysis,* 1969, 2, 3–13.

Osbourne, J. G. Free-time as a reinforcer in the management of classroom behavior. *Journal of Applied Behavior Analysis,* 1969, 2, 113–118.

Packard, R. G. The control of "classroom attention": A group contingency for complex behavior. *Journal of Applied Behavior Analysis,* 1970, 3, pp. 13–28.

Patterson, G. R. A learning theory approach to the treatment of the school phobic child. In L. P. Ullman and L. Krasner (Eds.) *Case Studies in Behavior Modification.* New York: Holt, Rinehart & Winston, 1965. Pp. 279–285. (a)

Patterson, G. R. An application of conditioning techniques to the control of a hyperactive child. In L. Ullman and L. Krasner (Eds.) *Case Studies in Behavior Modification.* New York: Holt, Rinehart & Winston, 1965. Pp. 370–375. (b)

Patterson, G. R., Jones, R., Whittier, J., and Wright, M. A. A behavior modification technique for the hyperactive child. *Behavior Research and Therapy,* 1965, 2, 217–226.

Phillips, E. L., Phillips, E. A., Fixsen, D. L., and Wolf, M. M. Achievement Place: Modification of the behaviors of pre-delinquent boys within a token economy. *Journal of Applied Behavior Analysis,* 1971, 4, 45–59.

Phillips, L., Draguns, J. G., and Bartlett, D. P. Classification of behavior disorders. In N. Hobbs (Ed.) *Issues in the Classification of Children.* (Vol. 1.) San Francisco: Jossey-Bass, 1975. Pp. 26–55.

Quay, H. C. Dimensions of problem behavior and educational programming. In P. S. Graubard (Ed.) *Children Against Schools.* Chicago: Follett, 1969.

Quay, H. C. Special education: Assumptions, techniques, and evaluative criteria. *Exceptional Children,* 1973, 40, 165–170.

Quay, H. C. and Quay, L. C. Behavior problems in early adolescence. *Child Development,* 1965, 36, 215–220.

Quay, H. C., Morse, W. C., and Cutter, R. L. Personality patterns of pupils in special classes for the emotionally disturbed. *Exceptional Children,* 1966, 32, 297–301.

Reynolds, G. S. *A Primer of Operant Conditioning.* Glenview, Ill.: Scott, Foresman, 1968.

Reynolds, N. J., and Risley, T. R. The role of social and material reinforcers in increasing talking of a disadvantaged preschool child. *Journal of Applied Behavior Analysis,* 1968, 1, 253–262.

Rivers, L. W., Henderson, D. M., Jones, R. L., Lodner, J. A., and Williams, R. L. Mosaic of labels for black children. In N. Hobbs (Ed.) *Issues in the Classification of Children.* (Vol. 1.) San Francisco: Jossey-Bass, 1975. Pp. 213–245.

Ross, A. O. Learning difficulties of children: Dysfunctions, disorders, disabilities. *Journal of School Psychology*, 1967, 5, 82–92.

Ross, A. O. *Psychological Disorders of Children.* New York: McGraw-Hill, 1974.

Sabatino, D. A. Resource Rooms: The renaissance in special education. *Journal of Special Education*, 1972, 6, 335–347.

Skinner, B. F. *Science and Human Behavior.* New York: Macmillan, 1953.

Sloane, H., and MacAulay, B. (Eds.) *Operant Procedures in Remedial Speech and Language Training.* Boston: Houghton Mifflin, 1968.

Stolz, S. B., and Wolf, M. M. Visually discriminated behavior in a "blind" adolescent retardate. *Journal of Applied Behavior Analysis*, 1969, 2, 65–77.

Sulzbacher, S. I., and Houser, J. E. A tactic to eliminate disruptive behaviors in the classroom: Group contingent. *American Journal of Mental Deficiency*, 1968, 73, 88–90.

Swift, M. S., and Spivack, G. Therapeutic teaching: A review of teaching methods for behaviorally troubled children. *Journal of Special Education*, 1974, 8, 259–289.

Ullman, L. P., and Krasner, L. (Eds.) *Case Studies in Behavior Modification.* New York: Holt, Rinehart & Winston, 1965.

Ullman, L. P., and Krasner, L. *A Psychological Approach to Abnormal Behavior.* Englewood Cliffs, N. J.: Prentice-Hall, 1969.

Wahler, R. G. Setting generality: Some specific and general effects of child behavior therapy. *Journal of Applied Behavior Analysis*, 1969, 2, 239–246.

Wahler, R. G. Some structural aspects of deviant child behavior. *Journal of Applied Behavior Analysis*, 1975, 8, 27–42.

Wasik, B., Senn, K., Welch, R. H., and Cooper, B. K. Behavior modification with culturally deprived school children: Two case studies. *Journal of Applied Behavior Analysis*, 1969, 2, 181–194.

Werry, J. S., and Sprague, R. L. Hyperactivity. In C. G. Costello (Ed.) *Symptoms of Psychopathology: A Handbook.* New York: John Wiley, 1970. Pp. 397–417.

White, M., and Charry, J. (Eds.) *School Disorders, Intelligence, and Social Class.* New York: Teachers College Press, 1966.

Wiesen, A. E., and Watson, E. Elimination of attention seeking behavior in a retarded child. *American Journal of Mental Deficiency*, 1967, 72, 50–52.

Wolf, M., Risley, T., Johnston, M., Harris, R., and Allen, E. Application of operant conditioning procedures to the behavioral problems of an autistic child: A follow-up and extension. *Behavior Research and Therapy*, 1967, 5, pp. 103–111.

Woody, R. H. *Behavioral Problem Children in the Schools.* New York: Appleton-Century-Crofts, 1969.

Ysseldyke, J. E., and Salvia, J. Diagnostic-prescriptive teaching: Two models. *Exceptional Children*, 1974, 41, 181–185.

PART III

Concepts and Methods of Influencing Behavior Change

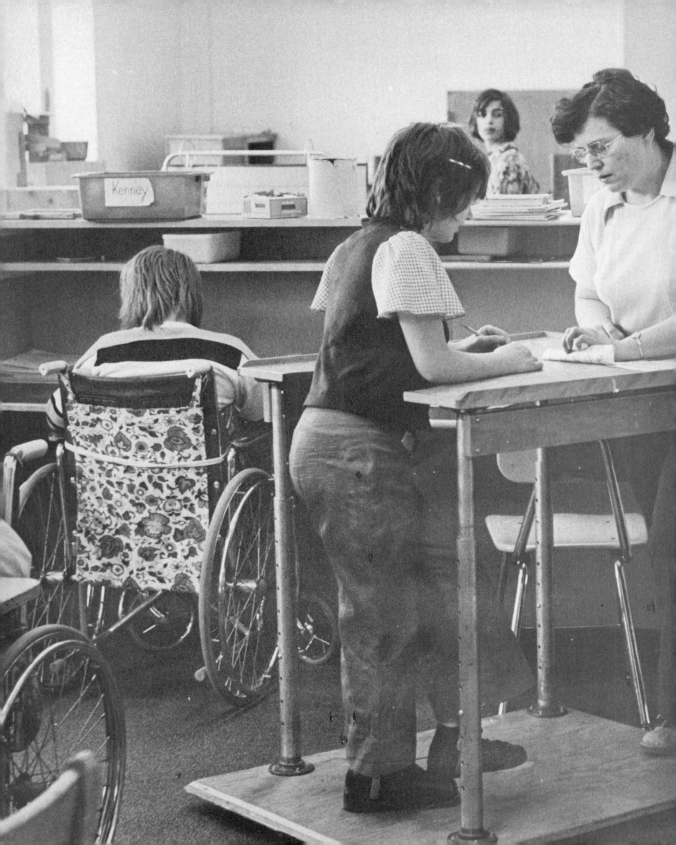

8

Concepts of Reinforcement

Consistent with the environmental bias of the humanistic behavioral approach, the discussion in this and the following chapters on learning concepts focuses primarily on a description of (1) the various classes of environmental (stimulus) events which serve certain functions in influencing behavior and (2) the manner in which these functions may be developed, modified, or eliminated.

A child's environment contains a variety of events which influence the *what, when,* and *where* of behavior. For any specific child, some of these events facilitate learning and behaving; others represent conditions which actively interfere both with learning and engaging in specific behaviors. Some events will influence the time and place of behavior. Other events may strengthen behaviors and insure that they will be maintained. Still others may discourage the occurrence of certain behaviors. Disruptive and highly unpleasant emotional reactions may result when certain events are present, while numerous aspects of a child's environment may be neutral in that, at any particular time, they may have no systematic influence on the child.

The functions of any stimulus event can be determined by observing its effect on the behavior of a child. Is specific behavior more likely to occur in the presence of certain stimulus conditions? If so, these events have a discriminative function. Does an event such as a teacher's smile following a behavior pattern strengthen or maintain that behavior? If so, it serves a reinforcing function for that particular behavior. It may or may not serve this function at another time for other behaviors or for other children. The numerous factors which may influence the various functions of stimulus events are described in the sections to follow.

Numerous stimulus events potentially may be used in a consistent manner to influence behavior in one way or another. These events may be used by the child himself as he influences his own behavior or by others as they seek to influence the child. To the extent that functional relationships between certain stimulus events and behaviors can be identified, the means of influencing behaviors are available. As Bijou and Baer* have emphasized, a study of "stimulus functions concentrate simply and objectively upon the ways in which stimuli control behavior: produce it, strengthen or weaken it, signal occasions for its occurrence or nonoccurrence, generalize it to new situations and problems, etc." (p. 19).

Bijou and Baer 1961

As noted, at any given time numerous events in the life of a child will have no systematic effect on his behavior. Most of education involves attempts at changing the "meanings" or influences of various internal and external stimulus events to insure that the child's behavioral repertoires will become more discriminating, complex, and self-enhancing. Thus, many of the multitude of neutral events—those stimulus events which have no reliable influence on or meaning to a specific child—in a child's surroundings can acquire any of a wide range of meanings or influences. A neutral event potentially can become aversive or reinforcing, may come to serve as a cue for a multitude of behaviors, or may come to produce either positive or negative emotional reactions. To complicate matters, components of the same event may acquire multiple and frequently incompatible functions. The stimulus components associated with school attendance or with heterosexual interaction, as examples, may come to influence both positive and negative emotionality and both approach and avoidance behavioral tendencies. These conflicting functions can produce a range of negative behavioral consequences, as described in Chapter 13.

As learning principles are statements of relationships between classes of stimulus events and various behavioral effects, the major concern of this book is with procedures of influencing behavior change in children with exceptional characteristics. The following discussion of learning will focus on a description of the procedures to follow in making use of the learning relationships. With this orientation, it is recognized that some of the finer technical aspects of the learning relationships discussed may be treated lightly and, at times, perhaps even oversimplified. The interested reader should refer to Bandura,* Kanfer and Phillips,* Skinner,* and Staats* for a more detailed and technical presentation of these.

Bandura 1969; Kanfer and Phillips 1970; Skinner 1953, 1969; Staats 1971, 1975

To emphasize the applicability of the learning principles, numerous examples are provided for translating these into procedures for influencing children and youth with exceptional learning and behavior characteristics. The focus of the presentation is on the following questions: *What can be done to facilitate the development of new behaviors? How can behaviors which a child has in his repertoire be strengthened, weakened, or eliminated? How can behaviors be brought under reliable influence of appropriate aspects of a child's environment? How can the child learn skills of self-control and self-direction?*

There are two different ways in which behaviors are related to environmental (stimulus) events. First are those behaviors called *operants* that are influenced by stimulus *consequences*. Such behaviors alter or "operate upon" the environment, thus producing a following consequence which comes to influence the strength of that behavior. A child who is rude to a peer may produce an angry reaction from the peer. The adolescent who completes his assignment satisfactorily produces a passing grade and praise from the teacher and interested parent. These consequences influence the future likelihood of the child's rude behavior and the adolescent's behavior of completing his assignments. Procedures of influencing operant behavior are discussed in the present and following two chapters.

Respondent or emotional behavior, in contrast, is that class of behavior which is influenced by *preceding* stimulus events.[1] The teacher smiles in an accepting manner and this produces positive emotional reactions in the child. A threatening comment from an adolescent results in a fear reaction in a younger peer. The rules denoting the manner in which a wide range of preceding stimulus events may influence emotional behavior are discussed in Chapter 11.

INFLUENCING THE STRENGTH OF OPERANT BEHAVIOR

Table 8.1 presents an overview of procedures, behavioral effects, and related learning principles involved in influencing the strength of behavior. As depicted in the table, there are two major principles and related procedures for strengthening behavior (positive reinforcement and negative reinforcement) as well as another two for decreasing the likelihood that given behaviors will occur (extinction and punishment). In brief illustration, if it is desired to increase the strength of a behavior pattern, the environment should be arranged to insure that (1) reinforcing events occur as a consequence of the behavior (positive reinforcement) or else that (2) aversive conditions are reduced or removed on the occurrence of the behavior (negative reinforcement). If, on the other hand, it is desirable to decrease the strength of a given behavior pattern, the environment should be arranged to insure that the reinforcing conditions which maintain the behavior are not provided. In other instances it may be necessary to follow the behavior with an aversive condition or else to remove positive reinforcers generally available to the child, either through a time-out or a response cost procedure. The usefulness of both of these general strategies of

1. The writer recognizes that some learning theorists view this distinction as an artificial one. However, as the present discussion is concerned with a description of those environmental arrangements which most easily and reliably result in various behavioral effects, the traditional distinction between operant and respondent behavior is maintained. The reader interested in this theoretical issue is invited to refer to Marx (1970) for elaboration.

TABLE 8.1.   *Influencing the Strength of Behavior*

Learning Concepts	Educational Procedures	Effects on Behavior	Examples of Positive or Aversive Events Presented or Removed
Positive reinforcement	Behavior is followed by positive event	Increase in strength of behavior	Smile, approval, affection, task completion, money, special privileges, recognition, passing grade
Negative reinforcement	Behavior is followed by removal of aversive event	Increase in strength of behavior	Frown, criticism, poor grade, threat of restriction of use of car, rejection, nonattention
Extinction (of behavior previously strengthened by positive reinforcement)	Behavior is not followed by positive event associated with previous occurrence	Decrease in strength of behavior	Smile, approval, affection, peer attention, bonus, special privilege
Extinction (of behavior previously strengthened by negative reinforcement)	Behavior is not followed by removal of aversive event associated with previous occurrence	Decrease in strength of behavior	Criticism, rejection, threat of loss of privileges, poor grade
Punishment: Presentation of aversive events	Behavior is followed by aversive event	Decrease in strength of behavior which results in the aversive event	Criticism, poor grade, rejection by peers, threat of dismissal from club
Punishment: Removal of positive events through time-out or response cost	Behavior is followed by temporary or permanent loss of positive events	Decrease in strength of behavior which results in loss of positive events	Smile, approval, affection, money, privilege, group membership

eliminating behavior patterns can be enhanced by a concomitant procedure of reinforcing behavior patterns to replace the extinguished ones.
Each of these procedures is discussed in this and the following chapters.

BASIC RULE OF POSITIVE REINFORCEMENT

Operant behavior is that class of behavior which is influenced in
strength by those events which follow it. Such behavior is viewed as vol-

untary behavior in the sense that it does not have an invariant relation to preceding stimulus events. Reading, dressing, reciting a poem, solving a math problem, hitting a sibling, correctly labeling a geometric figure, smiling at a peer, criticizing a friend, and driving a car are all examples of operant behaviors. *Positive reinforcement* refers to the procedure of influencing the strength of such behaviors by following the occurence of these with consequences called positive *reinforcers* or *reinforcing events*. Children will learn those behaviors which result in and enhance the availability of these positive events. If a child enjoys the praise of adults, he will learn those ways of behaving which result in adult praise. If a child enjoys the knowledge of being correct, he will pursue those activities which provide this feedback. Children seek to approach and to experience over and over again these positive reinforcing events.

A child shows interest in or is "motivated" to become involved in various activities to the extent that these or similar situations have resulted previously in positive consequences. As described in a later section, a child may even be likely to engage in behaviors observed in others which have resulted in positive consequences.

This reinforcement procedure by which the strength of behavior is influenced represents the central principal of operant learning. As such it provides educational and psychological personnel with a most valuable technique for influencing children and adolescents with exceptional learning and behavior difficulties. The major techniques of humanistic education are based on this basic positive reinforcement concept. If the teacher wishes to strengthen some behavior such as persisting at a difficulty task, improved auditory discrimination, being sensitive to the rights of others, sharing possessions with others, complying with reasonable requests, or recognizing the difference between "bat" and "bad," she must insure that these behaviors or approximations of these are followed by some reinforcing consequences.[2]

The procedure of positive reinforcement has applicability in instances of:

1. Teaching a new behavior which a child presently does not have in his repertoire
2. Increasing the strength of existing behaviors to insure consistency of occurrence under appropriate circumstances
3. Insuring the maintenance or permanency of behavior in the child's repertoire after it has gained some reliable strength

2. As described later, reinforcers are not restricted to externally delivered events. The child himself may strengthen his own behavior through a variety of self-reinforcement procedures. Additionally, an activity itself, goal attainment, informational feedback, and the like may acquire "intrinsic" reinforcing qualities which serve to maintain such activities.

RATE OF LEARNING

The rate with which children learn various types of skills is dependent on numerous variables. Obviously children exhibit considerable individual differences in the ease of, or difficulty in, learning. A child may not learn because prerequisite behaviors are absent or weak, for example, the "culturally disadvantaged" child may not have the pre-academic skills needed for successful acquisition of reading skills. He may be "unmotivated," that is, neither the task or activity nor the teaching environment may contain incentive or reinforcing events. He may have physical, sensory, or neurological characteristics which preclude or actively interfere with efficient learning and/or performance. The child with cerebral palsy, the adolescent with severe auditory or visual limitations, or the brain-damaged youngster all require specialized arrangements of the school program for effective learning to occur. Even under the most specialized environments, many experience consistent difficulty. Others may have behavioral characteristics incompatible with or otherwise disruptive of learning, such as hyperactivity, distractibility, short attention span, or disruptive negative emotionality and related avoidance behavior patterns. The special educational programs for the "emotionally disturbed," the "delinquent," and the "learning disabled" represent attempts to deal with these types of disruptive behavioral characteristics.

Children with exceptional learning and behavior characteristics thus frequently have difficulty in acquiring new ways of behaving. Even under optimal learning conditions, learning may be slow. Children with difficulties do not learn overnight to attend to and be influenced by adult requests or to recognize and label colors and forms any more than they suddenly learn to be too demanding or to fight with peers. These and similar behavior patterns may evolve slowly over numerous learning experiences in which these behaviors, or their approximations, have resulted in reinforcement. Also the more failures a child has experienced in an instructional environment, the greater the difficulty he will have in becoming a successful learner in that environment. He may lack the prerequisite skills and/or may acquire more complex and intensive anti-learning characteristics. Data reported by Cowen and Lorion* and Koppitz,* as examples, support this latter thesis. These writers found that older "learning disabled" children benefited less from specialized educational programs than did younger children.

*Cowen and Lorion 1974;
Koppitz 1971*

Thus, in the early stages of learning, the desired behaviors such as recognizing a word, learning abstract concepts, or solving quadratic equations may occur only infrequently and even then in an inconsistent manner. Frequent and consistent reinforcement of the behavior, or approximations of it, will facilitate its becoming a reliable aspect of the child's repertoire. Improvement, i.e., learning, may become evident only after a number of behavior-reinforcement experiences. This emphasizes the need for a well-designed instructional program which plans for consistent reinforcement of emerging skills over an extended period of time. Although learning will take place under less desirable conditions, the learning will be slower, inconsistent, and a more arduous and less enjoyable task for the child.

REINFORCEMENT SHOULD BE PROVIDED ON A CONTINGENT BASIS

The most effective and efficient learning occurs when reinforcing events are provided in direct relationship to the desired behavior. Just being nice or kind or affectionate to a child as he is provided an instructional program is facilitative but *not* sufficient for learning to occur in numerous children with learning and behavior difficulties. It is not sufficient, for example, merely to provide a child with reinforcing events such as acceptance, approval, or praise in a manner unrelated to the desired behavior if the goal is that of strengthening some specific behavior. This is illustrated by an experience with a five-year-old girl who engaged in a number of disturbing social behaviors while attending a preschool program.

The child was described as balky, verbally insulting, occasionally foul-mouthed, and prone to tell disjointed stories about violent accidents. Although she frequently approached other children, these contacts tended to be brief. She engaged in cooperative interaction with her peers less than 5 percent of the time available in the preschool session, even though she was in close physical proximity to children about 50 percent of the time. During the initial observation period, the teachers spent slightly in excess of 20 percent of the school day interacting with the girl.

As an initial approach to increasing the amount of time spent in cooperative play with peers, the child's teachers increased their time spent with her to 80 percent of each session. During this time the teachers talked to her, attended to her activities, gave her materials and toys, and generally "made a fuss over her." The increased social attention did not follow any particular kind of behavior but was presented randomly. Other children were attracted to the teacher's activities and thus increased the amount of time spent in proximity to the girl. The rate of cooperative play between the girl and her peers, nonetheless, remained unchanged.

The teachers then switched to socially reinforcing the child only for approximations to cooperative interactions with the other children. Cooperative play behavior increased within twelve days

Hart et al. 1968

from the original 5 percent to 40 percent of the time available in each session.*

This experience demonstrated that approval, praise, and other forms of social attention became most influential in increasing cooperative peer interaction when these reinforcing events were provided in a systematic manner following the occurrence of the behaviors which the teachers wished to influence. It supports the statement of Bettelheim* that "love is not enough." Even love in the form of attention, approval, or affection, when provided continuously regardless of the child's behavior, can interfere with normal development.

Bettelheim 1950

It is not being suggested that children and adolescents should be given personal attention in its various forms of praise, approval, affection, and the like only whenever the parent and teacher are attempting to influence some specific behavioral characteristic. Social and emotional interactions should be natural and spontaneous whenever possible. Obviously, children need to experience and will benefit from the affectionate behavior of significant adults and peers. It is desirable to indicate to a child and an adolescent on numerous occasions and in multiple ways that she is adequate, that she is liked, that she is worthwhile, that others can enjoy her and can demonstrate their interest by emotional expressions of interest, affection, love, enthusiasm, and concern. A child with learning and behavior difficulties needs the adults in her life to express to her, independently of any specific task completion or goal attainment, such feelings as "I love you," "Say, I really like you," "You are my favorite person," "I'm glad you are my friend." It is true also that a child or adolescent who has experienced personally meaningful reinforcing events, whether or not these are related contingently to some behavioral/educational objectives, will be more likely to engage in a range of prosocial behavior, even under "trying" or difficult conditions. That is, if he "feels good" he is more likely to engage cooperatively in requested or appropriate behavior and to be able to tolerate greater frustration conditions without being disruptive or disorganized. (This relationship is discussed more fully in Chapter 11.)

At the same time it is not being suggested that unconditional and nonjudgmental warmth and acceptance should be provided regardless of what the child or adolescent does. The adult must recognize that to the extent such personal attention is reinforcing to the child, behavior which immediately precedes this reinforcement will be influenced. Truax and Carkhuff* indicate that certain classes of behavior may be strengthened rather subtly by mere attention to such behaviors as these occur. Lovaas et al.* present data which demonstrate that understanding comments presented by a therapist following self-destructive behaviors in young "schizophrenic" children actually increased the rate of occurrence of these self-destructive behaviors. As another example, if the affection or other

Truax and Carkhuff
1967
Lovaas et al. 1965

forms of attention are provided most frequently when the child is engaged in various "dependency behavior," such behaviors will be strengthened. It is easy for an adult to show sympathy and concern to the child who is experiencing difficulty in completing various learning tasks or performance requirements, but if too much empathy is shown and too much assistance is offered whenever the child experiences difficulty, the child may be taught to depend on the adult to do things for him whenever faced with a difficult task. In this manner excessive dependency behavior can be developed.

A recent experience with an "emotionally disturbed" boy provides further illustration of the undesirable consequences of offering too much reinforcing attention to a child at the wrong time.

> Jim, attending a class of six boys in a day school program for children with excessive behavior management problems, had considerable difficulty remaining at any activity for more than a few seconds at a time. The teacher felt that all "emotionally disturbed" children need considerable expressions of affection and genuine concern from adults. In this class, the teacher approached Jim whenever he got out of his chair during periods in which he was instructed to complete various tasks at his desk. She would provide him with some soothing comment and gently move him back to his desk. Such social interaction apparently was quite reinforcing to him.
>
> During a ten-day observation period, Jim was out of his seat most of the time receiving "warm concern" from the teacher. "He's emotionally disturbed. He needs to know that I care for him and that I will not reject him even if he is unable to control his impulses." Under these conditions the teacher was providing the boy no opportunity to learn to control his impulses. In fact, she was inadvertently facilitating the very behaviors that interfered with his development of any self-control. The teacher, after suspecting the futility of her approach, agreed to provide just as much attention in the form of acceptance and concern as ever, but mostly after appropriate cooperative behavior. Within a few days Jim was spending an increasing amount of time at his desk engaging in his assigned academic tasks. The teacher was now able to express her acceptance in a realistic manner following competency behavior. Jim was also able to develop more competency behavior which was a source of pride to him.

A study by Osborne* is presented as a final example of the value of providing reinforcing events in direct relationship to the desired behavior. In an attempt to strengthen classroom behavior compatible with learning (remaining at the desk during academic classes), Osborne evaluated the relative effects of free time as a reinforcing event when presented in a contingent and then in a noncontingent manner.   *Osborne 1969*

Eleven- to thirteen-year-old children with severe to profound hearing losses were provided free time from class routine at the end of periods ranging from fifteen to twenty-five minutes during which they had remained seated. In comparing the occurrence of desired behavior on days when free time was provided contingently with days in which free time was provided independently of desired behaviors, the teacher noted a significantly higher rate of desired behavior whenever the reinforcing event was related specifically to it. Thus, even though the number of reinforcing events remained the same, desired behavior occurred with greater frequency when contingently reinforced.

REINFORCING EVENTS MAY EXERT AN IMMEDIATE AND AUTOMATIC EFFECT

Jim's experience illustrates another important learning concept. It is not necessary for a child to understand or even be aware of the positive effects of consequences for these consequences to influence the strength of associated behaviors. Jim did not "know" that his behavior of getting out of his seat was becoming stronger and more likely to reoccur because such behavior resulted in teacher attention. The strengthening effect of these consequences was *automatic.*

It is just as true that teachers and parents may be influenced rather automatically by consequences which follow various of their behaviors, and without being aware of the influence. Children and adults learn many unplanned behaviors, both appropriate and inappropriate, as a result of this automatic effect on behavior strength of various consequences.

This observation emphasizes the need for designing and implementing a structured learning environment for children and adolescents with learning and behavior difficulties, and for consistently analyzing the effects which various consequences do in fact have on specific of their behavior patterns. Recent studies suggest, for example, that children with learning and behavior difficulties may become more effective learners if they are encouraged to assume responsibility for aspects of their academic program. *Lovitt and Curtiss 1968* Lovitt and Curtiss* demonstrated that such children, if they themselves self-managed contingency requirements in an academic program, had higher rates of academic behavior than when the teacher controlled the contingencies. This and numerous similar studies suggest that, even though reinforcing events may exert an automatic effect without child awareness, more effective learning will occur when the child himself is made an active participant in the learning process and develops skills of identifying and managing reinforcement contingencies.

The potential automatic effect of reinforcing events emphasizes the applicability of the rule of positive reinforcement to the young, the severely retarded, and the nonverbal child as well as to the child who has limited language and related intellectual skills. It is not necessary that the nonverbal child "know" that certain of his behaviors result in various positive consequences. The educational program does not have to wait until speech develops prior to the initiation of a program of teaching basic competency behaviors. The child with severe learning and behavior difficulties— "autistic," "schizophrenic," "mentally retarded"—may be taught to attend to verbal requests, to dress and feed himself, to use speech in communicating with others, and a range of other, more complex behaviors, if these behaviors are followed consistently with reinforcing events. The reports of Kozloff,* Lovaas,* Watson,* and Wolf et al.* illustrate this application.

Kozloff 1973; Lovaas 1967; Watson 1972; Wolf et al. 1967

WHAT BEHAVIORS MAY BE INFLUENCED BY POSITIVE REINFORCEMENT?

Any behavior or combination of behaviors may be influenced by positive reinforcement. The types of consequences used in the reinforcement process may range from primary ones through contrived extrinsic events to highly personal and individualistic intrinsic and self-delivered events. Behavior patterns which may be strengthened range from simple behaviors such as completion of task assignments, recognizing and using letters of the alphabet, or feeding and grooming oneself to more complex patterns such as learning foreign language vocabulary, cooperative play, persistence at a difficult task, or reading difficult stories to a group of peers. The more difficult and complex the behavioral characteristic being taught, the greater the need for carefully designed teaching programs and related effective reinforcing consequences.

This emphasizes the general applicability of the rule of positive reinforcement. Behavioral procedures are not basically restricted to shaping behaviors of limited topography such as sitting or talking, as suggested by MacMillan.* Such simple behavior patterns are easier to influence but by no means should be viewed as the only types of behavioral characteristics that are influenced by positive reinforcement. It is also true, as described in Chapter 11, that a child's emotional and attitudinal characteristics are influenced by positive reinforcement.

MacMillan 1973

WHAT EVENTS ARE POSITIVELY REINFORCING?

A wide range of tangible, social, and activity events may serve a reinforcing function for children and adolescents. The school environment is rich with potential reinforcers—play materials, snack time, games, activities, peers, the child's accomplishments, social approval, special events, or the satisfaction of solving a challenging problem, to name a few. Additionally, the child and adolescent may be taught to self-reinforce his own behavior. It may be necessary in working with children characterized by more serious learning and behavior problems for the teacher to create new reinforcing events. The major problem facing the teacher is not one of finding reinforcing events in the school environment; these are plentiful. The major task, rather, is to successfully integrate these reinforcing events into an effective learning experience for each child or adolescent.

The teacher cannot rely on any highly effective common reinforcing event for use with all children. A child may respond well to one type of consequence at one time and poorly to it at another. Thus, the teacher should have available a wide range of events which can be arranged as consequences of desired behavior. If some events are not effective with a given child at a given time, or if an event loses its effectiveness, others should be available for immediate use.

Children and adolescents are more likely to learn in an environment which utilizes a wide range of tangible, activity, social, and "intrinsic" reinforcing events. In such an environment, satiation and adaptation to any specific event are less likely to occur. Behavior patterns of enthusiasm, cooperativeness, and persistence appear to be engendered in an environment which provides the novelty of a variety of effective reinforcers. Reinforcing events, it should be remembered, are those events which do in fact influence the behavior of a specific child or adolescent. It may seem reasonable to the educator that events such as task completion, approval, creative accomplishment, or extra leisure time would be highly reinforcing to an adolescent, but experiences in using these reinforcers with the individual may demonstrate that these have little effect on his behavior. Thus, the teacher should never assume that any event is reinforcing to a particular student until she uses it and evaluates its effectiveness.

TYPES OF REINFORCING EVENTS

Primary Reinforcers

Some events used to strengthen and maintain behavior are naturally rewarding to a child and are called *primary reinforcers*. These serve as reinforcers as a result of a basic relationship with certain physiological characeristics of the child. Food and liquid items such as candy, cookies, cereal, bread, soda pop, and milk may have primary reinforcing properties without the influence of prior learning. These and other primary types of events such as physical stimulation are quite valuable in influencing the behavior development of the younger child and of the child with the more severe learning and behavior difficulties.

TABLE 8.2. *Examples of Use of Primary Reinforcing Events*

Child Characteristics	Behavior Reinforced	Reinforcing Event	Reference
CA* =7 yrs. Autistic	Imitative behavior	Luncheon foods	Metz 1965
CA = 9.5 yrs. Mentally retarded	Verbal behavior	Ice cream, dry cereal, Kool-Aid	Sailor et al. 1968
CA = 8 yrs. Severely retarded with high-rate self-injurious behaviors	A variety of behaviors which competed with self-injurious responses	Food	Peterson and Peterson 1968
CA range from 4.5 to 13 yrs. Autistic	Attending to teacher, imitation, speech	Food	Koegel and Rincover 1974
CA range 4 to 5 yrs. Minor behavior problems	Sitting in seat during prescribed periods	Candy, raisins, nuts, marsh-mallows	Christy 1975

*Chronological age

As examples of the use of primary reinforcers, Wolf et al.* and Risley and Wolf* used a variety of food items as reinforcers in a behavior management program designed to strengthen a variety of speech and social behaviors in a young child described as autistic. These teachers identified food items for which the child showed a particular preference and presented these in small bites following desired behaviors. Ideally, food items used should be those which the child cannot play with and which the child can eat rapidly. Ice cream and sherbet are ideal food reinforcers for many young and more severely disabled children. Table 8.2 provides additional examples of the types of primary reinforcers used to influence a variety of behaviors in young and/or severely handicapped children.

Wolf et al. 1964
Risley and Wolf 1967

Secondary Reinforcers

Other events may have little or no reinforcing effect when initially presented to a child—for example, a smile, approval, acceptance, a gold star, money, educational toys, music, or the opportunity to engage in various play activities. These events may become effective reinforcers for a child if associated frequently with consequences which already are reinforcing to the child. A smile or praise may become reinforcing if paired frequently with the presentation, consumption, or manipulation of such tangible events as food, drink, toys, or play activity which already are reinforcing to a child. These *secondary, learned,* or *acquired reinforcers* assume a most important role in teaching and maintaining new behavior patterns as these events are readily available and can be provided immediately and frequently without undue difficulty. Once these events have acquired reinforcing properties, a wide range of new behavior can be strengthened and maintained by their use. This principle of generality of function is of considerable importance in the development of most of a child's behavior. Of equal importance to the teacher is the observation that, unless such secondary events are on occasion associated temporally with other reinforcing events, the reinforcing properties of these secondary events will diminish and eventually disappear entirely.

A learned reinforcer also may be generalized to the extent that it is associated with more than one reinforcing event. Such *generalized reinforcers* as attention, affection, and tokens (money) are most valuable because they can influence behavior somewhat independent of specific "needs, wishes, or desires," that is, specific deprivation states of the moment. These represent a variety of other reinforcers which can mark the occasion for, signal the future occurrence of, or be exchanged for, other reinforcing events. A smile, for instance, may suggest to the adolescent that other reinforcing events are likely to occur or to be available. A token or a good grade may represent a wide range of forthcoming reinforcing events such as parental approval, continued availability of privileges, and removal of unpleasant study requirements.

Although many educators are most reluctant to use extrinsic rewards of a tangible nature, it may be necessary to do so to insure initial successful learning. Only after considerable success and positive experiences does the child become susceptible to higher level reinforcing events. If the child's behavior is not strengthened by the usual educational incentive conditions of grades, task completion, teacher approval, or peer attention, more concrete and basic incentive conditions may be most useful in initiating learning and performance. Hewett,* in a discussion of the hierarchical nature of reinforcing events, suggests that tangible rewards "often serve as ideal 'launching fuel' for children who have come to know little joy in learning, acquired only limited knowledge and skill, received poor grades, experienced more social disapproval than approval in school, and who found classrooms generally nonstimulating and unrewarding" (p. 237). After successful experiences, events other than the tangible ones will gradually acquire influence over the child's learning and performance.

Hewett 1974

Social Reinforcers

A highly important class of secondary reinforcers of a generalized nature includes such events as smiling, providing approval, acceptance, affection, attention, submissiveness of others, praise, recognition, calling a person by his name, asking the adolescent to participate in an activity, talking with a child, being in close physical proximity to a child, looking at a child, and more subtle forms of attention such as winking, tone of voice, head nods, and gestures. Specific behavioral examples would include comments such as "Good work," "I like that," "Great thinking," "Nice going," "Thank you," "I'm impressed by what you did," "Well done," and "Great!" The central importance of the teacher's reactions in influencing child behavior is emphasized in Becker's* statement: "In the author's experience with all kinds of classroom behavior problems, it seems that 80 to 90 percent of such problems can be handled by little more than a change in the teacher's verbal behaviors, e.g., when she says what to whom" (pp. 79–80).

Becker 1971

As an example of this position, Hall et al.* studied the effects of teacher attention on various inappropriate study behaviors of elementary-age children. With one particularly disruptive boy who spent approximately 75 percent of his time during spelling class in nonstudy behavior, it was noted that 55 percent of the teacher attention he received followed such behavior. After a period of time in which teacher attention was provided only following study behavior, the desired classroom behavior occurred between 70 percent and 80 percent of time spent in class. Not only did the disruptive behavior, which no longer attracted teacher attention, reduce significantly, but also achievement level increased significantly. In a similar vein, Mordock* suggested: "Approximately 80 percent of the typical teacher's behavior toward her children is negatively oriented (e.g., giving after-the-fact reprimands, commands, threats) and only about 20% positively oriented (e.g., giving approval, expressing sympathy, asking questions)" (p. 673).

Hall et al. 1968

Mordock 1975

Thus, the degree to which educators use positive as compared to negative reactions to student behavior influences the types of classroom interactions* as well as the student's accomplishments. This observation becomes particularly pertinent to educators serving children and adolescents with exceptional learning and behavior characteristics. The very characteristics which define the "exceptionality" are those which are most likely to provoke negative reactions from the educator—the hyperactivity, distractibility, disruptive social behavior, poor achievement, learning difficulty, and poor motivation.

Becker et al. 1967;
Grieger et al. 1970

As suggested, social events such as attention and approval become generalized reinforcers when these have been a frequent condition preceding other reinforcers. Attending to a child is the first step in providing him with a wide range of positively reinforcing events. Approval in the form of verbal responses and various gestures—being recognized as "right" or "good" and being praised or provided some other social honor—comes to be reinforcing because such responses and gestures signal the subsequent appearance of other reinforcing events.

Advantages of Social Reinforcers

Social consequences as reinforcing events have a number of advantages. First, these may be used in a natural manner in a variety of situations with a variety of behaviors. Because social events such as approval, praise, and attention are *generalized* reinforcers, they are less likely to lose their effectiveness through satiation. Further, social consequences can be provided without disrupting the behavior being reinforced. A teacher may praise a child for his persistence at a difficult assignment without disrupting his activity. Finally, social events represent those natural events which socially appropriate behaviors produce.

Madsen et al. 1968   Madsen et al.* found that inappropriate behavior in an elementary classroom was best managed by praising the children for appropriate behavior. Use of social approval resulted in a lower rate of inappropriate behavior, while providing the children with rules of acceptable classroom behavior and ignoring misbehavior had little effect on improving their classroom behavior.

Teachers will find it best to be most expressive in providing various forms of social reinforcement to some children and much more subdued and subtle with others. Some children or adolescents will benefit from a healthy display of pleasure and enthusiasm following appropriate behavior. Others "can't believe" that they could please others because theirs is a history of failure, limited success, and resulting poor self-concept behaviors. Thus it is valuable to display enthusiasm following success to enhance the child's positive feelings and thoughts about himself. Other children become agitated easily. Too much enthusiastic display will elicit overactivity and subsequent distracting emotional and motor behaviors. These children require a calm and reassuring mode of special attention.

Effectiveness of Types of Social Attention

The type of social attention which is reinforcing and the frequency of reinforcement required to strengthen and maintain various skills and characteristics will vary from child to child. Some children are highly influenced by any form of attention. Other children may be influenced positively by one class of social agents—peers, for example—and not by other classes, e.g., school authorities. An adolescent may be influenced by male physical education teachers but not nearly to such an extent by female teachers of academic subjects. This was illustrated by Jack who was seldom influenced in a positive manner by his forty-year-old female homeroom teacher. This adolescent, however, was highly gratified by social attention from a male graduate student who had a full beard. Jack would spend hours involved in academic work in order to gain access to short conversation periods with the graduate student. Each child or adolescent has a different history of experience with social reinforcers and will thus respond differently to such events.

It is not unusual to find that types of social attention used by adults, such as threat or punishment, may in fact be positively reinforcing. The secondary reinforcing aspects of the attention provided in these instances add more strength to the preceding child behavior than is subtracted by the unpleasant aspects of the punishment. Thus, reprimands, ridicule, criticism, and other forms of social attention used by a teacher in an effort to reduce the occurrence of various behaviors may in fact serve to maintain the very behavior which the teacher is attempting to eliminate. O'Leary et al.,* as an example, presented data which suggested that teachers' loud reprimands, presented to reduce high rates of disruptive behavior in elementary classrooms, may actually result in even more disruptive behavior. In view of this possible effect, the teacher must distinguish between the intended effects in using various forms of social responsiveness and the effect which these consequences actually have on a child's behavior.

O'Leary et al. 1970

Attention from adults and peers in its many varieties is potentially a very powerful reinforcer for children and adolescents. There are few events in the child's life that can rival the constant availability of such social events.

Some children become so highly dependent upon adult attention that they isolate themselves from their peers. Allen et al.* describe an interesting example of this danger and demonstrate skillful use of adult attention in facilitating increased peer interaction.

Allen et al. 1964

> Ann, a four-year-old girl attending a preschool program, was described as isolating herself from her peers and engaging in many attempts to gain and prolong the attention of the teacher and other adults in the preschool environment. Frequently she would play alone and engage in various make-believe activities. Mild tic-like behaviors were present. She was described as often speaking in breathy tones at levels so low that it was difficult to understand what she said. She complained at length about minute or invisible bumps and abrasions.
>
> As most of the adult attention was provided Ann for behaviors incompatible with play behavior with peers, a plan was initiated to give her adult attention as she approached or played with another child. At the initiation of this plan, Ann spent about 10 percent of her time interacting with children and 40 percent with adults. After some three weeks during which the teachers reinforced her socially for peer interaction, Ann was spending some 55 to 60 percent of her time with children and considerably less time interacting with adults. During this time her speech rose in tempo, pitch, and volume. Complaints about abrasions and bumps disappeared entirely. She appeared to enjoy her increased peer interaction.

Social reinforcement of children by an emotionally expressive teacher may well have a most positive effect on the entire class. A recent observation of a class of "mildly retarded" and behavior problem children attending a primary special education program provides illustration of this.

> The teacher had given each child seated around a table a matching task involving geometric forms. The children were experiencing some

difficulty getting started. They were talking to each other and engaging in other behaviors which interfered with the visual attending and concentration needed for successful task completion. The teacher, noting that Bill did complete his task successfully, ignored the disruptive behaviors of other members of the class. She immediately moved close to Bill and patted him on the arm as she exclaimed in a warm, expressive manner, "Bill, look at what you did. I'm so proud of you. You really got to work and finished yours. Now do another one for me," and she placed a more difficult task on the desk for him. Other children observing this display, immediately went to work. The teacher was quite attentive to each child's effort or task completion and just as quickly and affectionately provided approval and praise. For fifteen minutes the children worked attentively and enjoyably, bursting into a smile upon task completion and looking at the teacher for the forthcoming praise.

Social reinforcement in the form of praise, approval, and positive statements may have an effect on the child's development beyond that of strengthening the specific associated behaviors. Such social events also provide the child with models of verbal statements which he may apply to himself. He may begin to label himself as "I can do," "That's great," "Good job," or "I am smart," following activity involvement or completion. These positive self-referents can become quite valuable to the child in his approach to an activity and in his involvement.

Even though many children are highly influenced by adult attention, it is essential that the educator identify and utilize only those events which do influence a specific child's behavior. Children with learning and behavior difficulties may require frequent tangible and activity reinforcers combined skillfully with adult attention for optimal behavior development. However, some children may find adult attention to be unpleasant. Such attention may disrupt or even suppress rather than reinforce preceding behavior. Levin and Simmons,* in their work with boys described as emotionally disturbed, unusually hyperactive, and aggressive, provide support for this possibility. Providing indiscriminate social attention in these instances may actually disrupt rather than facilitate the way the child learns or behaves.

Levin and Simmons 1962

The younger and more severely handicapped child or adolescent will generally require more immediate and tangible reinforcing events for effective learning than will be required by the older and more successful learner. The teacher who attempts to use social reinforcement exclusively or even as the major strategy for promoting and strengthening behavior patterns of children with learning and behavior problems will be relatively ineffective. Social reinforcement in all its many variations should be used frequently but not exclusively unless such consequences produce more effective results than other events. As noted, if social consequences are not effective reinforcers, such events should be paired frequently with other events which are reinforcing. In this manner, social attention in its many forms may become reinforcing.

Peers as Reinforcers

Other children may serve as a source of reinforcement for the behavior of a peer. Inappropriate as well as appropriate behavior patterns can be strengthened and maintained by the peer attention which follows such behaviors. Buehler et. al.* described the manner in which peers tend to reinforce delinquent behaviors—rule breaking, aggressiveness, or criticism of adults and adult rules, for example—and to punish socially conforming activities in groups of institutionalized delinquents. More than 75 percent of the adolescent's delinquent behavior was followed by attention and approval from peers. Most of the approval was of a nonverbal nature. As additional illustrations of peer influence, Evans and Oswalt* described the successful use of peer approval to accelerate academic progress of selected underachieving elementary students. Lovitt et al.* demonstrated the effects of peer influence in reducing a high rate of "nasty comments" in an elementary-age boy. After such comments, the boy was ignored by a classmate. This removal of attention resulted in a reduction in the inappropriate social behavior.

Buehler et al. 1966

Evans and Oswalt 1968

Lovitt et al. 1973

Peers with limited social reinforcement value to others will most likely be avoided by them. Additionally, the child or adolescent who does not find peers to be socially reinforcing will isolate himself or herself from them. In this instance, the educator may wish to develop or enhance the social reinforcement value of the child by insuring that he or she is associated with the delivery of reinforcing events which peers find enjoyable. In this manner the reinforcement value of the isolated child as well as the peers may be enhanced. Wiesen and Watson,* in a successful program to increase the cooperative social interaction between an isolated "severely retarded" boy and his peers, had his peers reinforce the boy with tangible events whenever he engaged in cooperative social behavior. The interaction between the boy and his peers increased considerably. Kirby and Toler* reinforced an isolated boy for passing out reinforcers to his peers. Social interaction increased considerably; apparently, the child had become an effective social reinforcer through being associated with delivery of the tangible reinforcers.

Wiesen and Watson 1967

Kirby and Toler 1970

Peers as Teachers

Peers also may be used as "teachers" in programs structured to provide various reinforcing events contingent upon occurrence of various academic and related behaviors. Peers were successful in reducing the articulation errors of two "predelinquent" boys in a study reported by Bailey et al.* The peers were reinforced with tokens for modeling, peer

Bailey et al. 1971

Surratt et al. 1969 approval, contingent points, and feedback. Surratt et al.* successfully trained an elementary student to monitor the study behavior of four younger children and to award reinforcers contingent upon desired performance. Study behavior increased in all children.

Activity Reinforcers

The opportunity to engage in various activities, for example, reading to the class and assisting the teacher, or the possibility of gaining access to certain events or stimulus environments, i.e., taking a break or watching a ball game, can also become quite reinforcing. Behaviors may be strengthened if followed by these or other activities such as listening to music, looking at books, watching TV, playing games, being first in line, being a member of a group or club, being read to, running errands, resting, talking, reading, or playing ten minutes longer.

This can be translated into a rule of behavior: *Activities which the child enjoys (behaviors which would have high preference in those situations in which the child could choose his activities) may be used to reinforce other behaviors which the child would choose less frequently.*

Premack 1959 This general principle has been described by Premack* and has sufficient experimental and clinical support to recommend its use.
Homme et al. 1963 Homme et al.* illustrated this procedure:

> In observing children in a preschool program these educators noted that the most preferred activities included running around the classroom, screaming, pushing chairs across the floor, and playing with jigsaw puzzles. Among the least likely behaviors were those of complying with the teacher's request to "sit down" or to attend to the teacher's instruction. The teacher then arranged for the children to engage in their high-preference behaviors of running and screaming following small amounts of the teacher-requested behaviors of sitting and attending. After some experience with this procedure of low-preference behavior leading to high-preference behavior, the children quickly acquired a range of appropriate behaviors.

Every child and adolescent has some preferred activities which could be used to reinforce other less-preferred activities. The highly probable behaviors can be easily identified through observation of what the child or adolescent does when provided an opportunity. The use of the Premack principle thus allows the educator to select those reinforcers most appropriate for each individual. Sitting idly, looking at magazines, being included in a peer group, shooting basketball, listening to jazz records, drawing, eating, and talking with the teacher are examples of possible high-preference activities. "As soon as we clean up the mess, we'll listen to your favorite record" represents an application of this rule for children who have a high preference for music and a low preference for cleaning up.

"Those of you who finish your geometry problems may spend your break time with the headsets listening to the new records" proved a valuable contingency in a class of "emotionally disturbed" adolescents. If a child enjoys finger painting, but is slow and uninvolved in other perceptual-motor tasks, finger painting for a longer period than usual could be provided after he finishes the perceptual-motor activities. If this were done consistently, the perceptual-motor activities should increase in strength. Being permitted to play table games following completion of a low-preference academic task should reinforce (strengthen) the academic task behavior. The important consideration is that the high-probability behavior follow the less frequent one on a contingent basis.

The educator can best make use of this rule of influencing behavior by developing a list of activities which each child or adolescent prefers and enjoys. The list may include such entries as play period, extra photo lab time, recess period, nap time, lunch period, talking loudly, clowning, looking at film strips, running around, playing with toy dump truck, listening to specific records, and painting. With this information, the teacher is in a position to precede these high-preference activities with any low-preference activities which require strengthening.

Addison and Homme* describe an interesting procedure—*a reinforcement event menu*—displaying a variety of high-preference actitives which would be available to children following desired behaviors. The reinforcement menu may consists of pictures of stick figures engaged in various activities such as playing with dolls, coloring, playing with water, painting, or climbing a rope. The activities displayed would be drawn from observation of the child or group of children for which the menu is devised. After an assignment is completed, the child would be permitted to select one of the activities and engage in it for a designated period of time. Figure 8.1 illustrates such a menu.   *Addison and Homme 1966*

Daley* used the reinforcing event menu with a group of "mentally retarded" children: *Daley 1969*

> Observation of the class produced twenty-two items which represented high-preference behaviors of various members of the group. These included such activities as talking, coloring, drawing, listening to a record, dancing, walking, drawing on the chalk board, working with jigsaw puzzles, singing, moving chairs, and looking out the window. Each activity was depicted in color and enclosed in a single book with one activity per page. The children were shown the pictures and informed that when their work was finished they could select the activity of their choice. Significant improvement in low-preference behaviors was noted.

Other illustrations of the Premack principle include Lattal's* use of swimming as a high-preference behavior with boys in a summer camp to increase the frequency of toothbrushing, Ross and O'Driscoll's* use of   *Lattal 1969*

Ross and O'Driscoll 1972

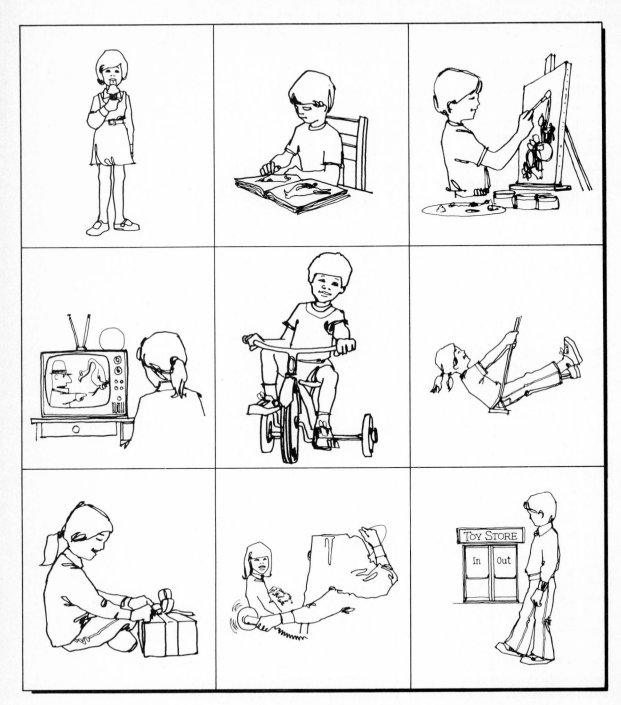

Figure 8.1   Depicting a Reinforcement Event Menu

contingent access to free time to improve spelling in the classroom, and
Hart and Risley's* success by providing access to recreational materials *Hart and Risley 1968*
following use of adjectives in spontaneous speech among children from
lower socioeconomic families.

In using a reinforcement menu, it is desirable to change the activities
routinely to avoid a child's possible disinterest. Also, it would be helpful to
include a special event on occasion to enhance the reinforcement value of
the procedure. For young children, these may include such activities as
playing "dress-up," viewing cartoons, having a party, and blowing noisy
horns. These events may be placed in the menu on an irregular basis so as to
increase their surprise value. The teacher may also find that the effectiveness of the menu may be enhanced by colored Polaroid pictures of the
children engaging in various activities which could be valuable to them.
This procedure would increase the meaningfulness of the menu to the
younger and the most severely handicapped child.

Token Reinforcers

An additional class of generalized secondary reinforcing events
available to strengthen and maintain behavior patterns consists of *token
reinforcers*. These are objects, as depicted in Figure 8.2, that have no
particular initial value of their own: grades, marks, stamps, tokens, cer-
tificates, diplomas, money, and chips.

In one way or another these items *represent other reinforcing events
which the child or adolescent will experience at a later time.* A token, for
example, may be exchanged for other objects or activities; good grades may
produce reinforcing events like praise from parents, self-satisfaction, or an
increase in allowance. These token events serve to bridge the time delay
between the behavior to be strengthened and the later presentation of other
reinforcing events. For many children and adolescents with exceptional
learning and behavior characteristics, the more tangible and physically
durable these events are that bridge the gap between behavior and the
subsequent final reinforcing event, the more effective these token events
become in strengthening and maintaining behavior. Grades have traditionally been the major token reinforcement system used in the educational
setting. But, as emphasized by McKenzie et al.,* grades for many have *McKenzie et al. 1968*
minimal effectiveness in promoting desired learning because of the
lengthy time lag between specific learning and performance activities and
the awarding of the grade. Additionally, children with exceptional learning and behavior characteristics typically earn poor grades. Thus, such
generalized events have only minimal if any positive reinforcement value.

Token events become reinforcing through previous association with
reinforcing events for which they can be exchanged. Such tokens would
soon lose any reinforcing functions, however, if they no longer resulted in
or could be exchanged for objects or privileges or no longer provided social
reinforcement such as praise or other forms of attention from others.

FIGURE 8.2.   Depicting a Variety of Token Reinforcers

In some instances it may not be feasible to provide social and certain types of tangible reinforcing consequences following behavior. Frequent social reinforcement may disturb the child or her peers. With some children social reinforcement may be ineffective in influencing desired academic and social behaviors. Broden et al.,* in illustration, reported that junior high special education youth described as exhibiting such problems as severe reading difficulties, speech difficulties, emotional instability, and acts of delinquency were only moderately influenced by teacher-provided social reinforcement. The initiation of a token system resulted in a dramatic increase in appropriate classroom behavior. In such instances, tokens could be earned by a child and used later to purchase a variety of objects, activities, or privileges. Birnbrauer and Lawler* report the development of numerous appropriate social and study behaviors when using token reinforcers with a highly disruptive "severely retarded" boy. These newly acquired behaviors were soon lost when only social approval was provided. For children who require tangible reinforcers for effective learning, it may not be possible to provide these supports immediately following the desired behavior. In such cases, use of a token reinforcement system may prove valuable. The child would be provided a small token or a check on a grid card taped to his desk. This tangible token would serve to bridge the time gap between the occurrence of the desired behavior and its later exchange for some backup tangible or activity events.

Broden et al. 1970

Birnbrauer and Lawler 1964

Such a token reinforcement system is relatively simple to administer. The tokens or marks are easily handled by the child and are a reminder of the reinforcer to be provided later. Behavior can be reinforced as it occurs. Tokens can frequently be provided without disrupting the task behavior. Clark et al.* successfully used token reinforcers to teach "delinquent" and "mildly retarded" youths (aged fourteen through sixteen years) to complete job application forms. The teacher reinforced the youths with plastic strips, both for working quietly and for completing various phases of the training program. Backup reinforcers included a variety of food, activity, and other generalized events. Birnbrauer and Lawler* provided "mentally retarded" children with aprons with front pockets into which the teacher could drop the token as specific behaviors were being reinforced. The child could easily keep his tokens without dropping them and without other children taking them.

Clark et al. 1975

Birnbrauer and Lawler 1964

Twardosz and Sajwaj* used X-marks that the teacher placed on a card which children with learning and behavior problems wore around their necks. Other teachers have provided each child with a small plastic cup in which they place a token as the child earns it. Heitzman* used red, transparent bingo markers in working with primary-level children in reading and arithmetic instruction. These were deposited in individual jar banks and exchanged at a later time for a variety of reinforcers. As suggested, a grid card taped in front of each child as he sits at the work table, or a small booklet on the child's desk, have been used successfully.*

Twardosz and Sajwaj 1972

Heitzman 1970

Ayllon et al. 1975; O'Leary and Becker 1967

The teacher marks the child's card following occurrence of the desired behavior. Phillips et al.* and Liberman et al.* awarded points to predelinquent youths and recorded these on point cards which each boy carried with him. The points were counted at the end of the day and could be used to purchase a variety of tangible events, activities, and privileges. Other possible tokens suggested by Becker et al.* include tickets, punches on a card, a counter with a light flash or buzzer, numbers on a page, marks on the blackboard, gold stars, marbles in a jar, and marks on a drawing of a ladder with fifty steps on it. These and similar experiences support the usefulness and the feasibility of using a token system of reinforcement with children and adolescents. The actual token procedure selected should be easily handled and should cause a minimum of interference with what the child is doing when the token is provided.

The tangible nature of the token is quite valuable to many children. Social praise or approval is too momentary. Once presented, there is nothing tangible to represent the approval. The concept of pleasant consequences at the end of the period or the day is too abstract to influence some children. The token, in contrast, does assist the child in making the connection between appropriate behavior at one moment and resulting pleasant consequences available later.

Steps in Implementing a Token Program

In initiating a token program, the following should be clearly delineated:

The specific behavior or accomplishment to be reinforced by tokens should be clearly described and/or demonstrated to the children. These behaviors should be of such a nature that the teacher and child can easily recognize their occurrence. Liberman et al.,* as an example, provided a written list of behaviors which would result in reinforcement for youths living in a family-style treatment center. The listing included such activities as "doing dishes, greeting a visitor, completing homework, performing maintenance tasks."

The contingency should be stated. Initially it is best to require only short behavioral segments or sequences and to permit exchange of tokens after a limited interval of time. After some success, the amount of behavior required prior to token reinforcement and the delay between receiving the token and exchanging it can be increased. After behavior has been learned and performed with acceptable accuracy, it can be maintained with a decreasing amount and frequency of reinforcement. The specific schedule of reinforcement and the value of the token reinforcer required for effective acquisition and maintenance will depend upon the child's reinforcement requirements. A token system permits maximum flexibility in adapting individual learner requirements to educational objectives.

Additional considerations include the type of token, the backup reinforcers, the method of presenting the token following desired behavior, the rate of exchange, and the method of exchange. The token selected must be appropriate to the characteristics of the child. Its value must be readily understood. It must be easy to present and easily managed by the child. Backup reinforcers should be those which have obvious reinforcement value to the child and should match the difficulty level of the behaviors required. The child must clearly understand the exchange rate and procedure. The number or value of tokens associated with each desired behavior and the cost of various backup reinforcers should be specified. As examples, Breyer and Allen* used points which the teacher wrote on a tally sheet placed on the child's desk. At the end of the day, points were exchanged in the "Good-Study Store" for a variety of prizes ranging in cash value from 5 cents to $1.50. Liberman et al.* permitted youths in his program to exchange points for a wide range of privileges and activities. For example:

Breyer and Allen 1975

Liberman et al. 1975

Privilege	Costs per Week
Visit to natural home	6,000 points
No work on Saturday	6,000 points
$2.00 allowance	6,000 points
No work during week	12,000 points

It is obvious that the specifics of any token program will depend upon the characteristics of the children or adolescents served. The younger and more immature the child, the greater the necessity of clearly defined concrete and durable tokens. Older children of greater maturity can adapt to a more abstract token program.

Introducing a Token Procedure

When introducing the use of tokens, it is useful initially with the younger and more severely disabled child to provide tangible reinforcers such as food or trinkets immediately following desired behavior. The token is next introduced as a temporary substitute for the tangible reinforcer. The child exchanges the tokens immediately for the reinforcer. Gradually, the time is extended between the presentation of the token and the exchange for the backup consequences. Baker et al.* successfully used a token system with a group of four-to seven-year-old "moderately retarded" children attending a preschool program. The children were provided

Baker et al. 1972

tokens contingent upon appropriate behavior. The procedure of establishing and maintaining the reinforcing value of the token was as follows:

> As soon as the child was given a token, another member of the program staff exchanged it for a candy or other "goody." This pattern was maintained for the first day of token introduction. On the following day the children were required to hold the token momentarily before the exchange for primary reward took place. On each successive day the length of time the child was required to hold the token before exchanging it was increased until at the end of five days the children were retaining the token for ten minutes before "cashing in." At this point small cloth pockets were tied around each child's waist and the children were instructed to save their tokens in these pockets. Over the following five days the delays between receiving tokens and their exchange was increased until all the children were able to save their tokens until the end of the morning when they would exchange them for toys, candy, and other "goodies" at a "store." The "store" consisted of a large wooden chest in which a variety of primary rewards were kept and attractively displayed during the exchange period. [pp. 17–18]

Birnbrauer and Lawler
1964

Birnbrauer and Lawler* used tokens in classes for children described as "severely retarded." Initially, the classroom teacher used a candy reinforcer for a variety of desirable social and study behaviors. These tokens were presented when a child exhibited approximations of desired behavior. Each presentation was accompanied by social approval. Within a short period of time, the children were occasionally given a poker chip following correct behavior. After the child had saved two or three chips, he exchanged these on a one-to-one basis for candy. Gradually the teacher gave more and more tokens and less and less candy reinforcers until the child earned only tokens. These could be exchanged at the end of a class period for a variety of tangible objects such as trinkets, balloons, or candy and other edibles. During the transition phase from candy to tokens, some children received tokens and others received candy. It is interesting to note that children who had learned the value of tokens were not upset that other children were receiving immediate candy reinforcers. Children were encouraged to save the tokens for longer periods of time prior to exchange. It was not long before some children were able to work throughout the school day prior to exchange. Some were able to save from one day to the next. After a few months' experience with the token system, most children were able to place their coats on hangers upon entering the classroom, sit quietly in their seats, and wait for their assignments with only an occasional reminder.

Bushell et al. 1968

The experiences of Bushell et al.* provide an additional illustration of the effective use of tokens with young children:

These children, ranging in age from three to six, attended a three-hour daily preschool program. Following the first seventy-five minutes of classroom work, a special event (such as a short movie, trip to a nearby park, an art project, a story, or a gym class) was made available to the children. After this, additional preschool activity was followed by a thirty-minute snack period. The special event and snack periods were available only to those children who had earned tokens during the preceding classroom activity periods.

The tokens—colored plastic washers about 1.5 inches in diameter—were provided by the teachers to children as they were engaging in appropriate classroom behavior. The teachers moved about the classroom and gave the tokens whenver they observed children attending to instruction, working independently or in cooperation with others, remaining with and attending to assigned tasks, and reciting after completion of assignments.

Children who had earned a sufficient number of tokens were permitted to exchange them for participation in the special event and for snack items (ice cream, cookies, milk, lemonade). Children who had an insufficient number did not participate in these special events. The teachers reported a 20 to 25 percent increase in appropriate study behavior following use of the token-reinforcement procedure.

This study illustrates the practical value of a token system in developing and maintaining higher levels of study behavior. Further, while a teacher may encounter difficulty in relying solely on verbal praise and attention as reinforcers, a token program offers a range of backup reinforcers to match the individual incentive characteristics of each child.

The following procedure has been found helpful in enhancing the effective use of a token system with young and/or severely handicapped children. An individual reinforcement menu is developed which is composed of colored Polaroid pictures of each child engaging in various reinforcing activities such as eating candy, drinking soda, listening to music, playing, painting, and playing "dress-up." In addition, a group menu is prepared which depicts special, surprise, and unusual events. At the beginning of the school day, each child selects from his individual book the activity which he wishes to earn. The picture is removed from the menu and mounted on a token card. A number of blank squares are drawn at the bottom of the card and represent the number of tokens which must be earned prior to reception of the selected reinforcer. This token card is placed on the child's table and as he engages in various appropriate behaviors the teacher places her initials in one of the squares. The card may follow the child from activity to activity and even from teacher to teacher. The child may exchange the card for the activity immediately upon filling all the squares or at specific times designated by the teacher. The number of squares required for each item may be the same for each class member or may vary from child to child. On occasion, each child is permitted to select from the special group menu. The use of a special menu adds interest and enthusiasm to the token system. Examples of cards depicting different activities and requiring different numbers of tokens are illustrated in Figure 8.3.

When Should a Token Program Be Used?

A token program may be used with an individual child, a small number of children within a class or, with all children in a class. In every instance, a token program is initiated only after other more naturally available events are insufficiently reinforcing to insure acquisition and

FIGURE 8.3   Token Cards Depicting Cost of Pictured Activity

performance of the desired educational objectives. It is especially useful with children and adolescents who are characterized by a number of persistent behavioral characteristics which actively interfere with learning and prosocial behavior—hyperactivity, disruptive social behaviors, negative emotionality. Additionally, whenever there is a relative paucity of effective generalized secondary reinforcers and whenever there are obvious behavioral deficits which preclude much success in a particular environment, tokens may be required to create an effective and efficient educational environment in which appropriate learning and behaving is likely to occur. If, for example, a child finds various activities and situations such as arithmetic lessons, competition, classroom, and so on quite uncomfortable, and the typical reinforcing events natural to the situation such as social approval, encouragement, grades, intrinsic incentives, and self-reinforcement are relatively ineffectual, it would be necessary to arrange for other reinforcing events if more appropriate behavioral, emotional, and attitudinal characteristics are to develop. Under these and similar conditions, a token program may be most desirable.

Advantages of Using Tokens

The use of a token-reinforcement system potentially has a number of positive effects on the total classroom program:

Teachers are likely to become more aware of individual student behavior and to engage in more positive interaction. They focus on the repertoires of individual children and identify those components which need specific reinforcement. Individualized instruction is a natural result. If tasks presented to a child are too difficult, he receives too few tokens or perhaps none at all. If the tasks are too easy, the child will receive too many tokens. The teacher is able to make the necessary instructional adjustments. Breyer and Allen* also noted that following implementation of a token program in a class of youngsters exhibiting academic and social deficiencies, the teacher increased her positive comments and decreased the number of negative comments made to her students.

Breyer and Allen 1975

The use of a token procedure also emphasizes the relationship between behavior and consequences. This is extremely helpful to many children with severe learning and behavior difficulties since they are relatively insensitive to behavior-reinforcement relationships. Their own behavior has not resulted in obvious accomplishments with sufficient frequency. Exposure to a token-reinforcement program which pairs appropriate behavior with tangible positive consequences provides the child with experiences which contribute to the development of self-responsibility. The child is provided tangible evidence that certain behaviors provide positive consequences. In this manner, as emphasized by

Hewett 1974

Hewett,* the child learns to enjoy accomplishments. He learns to select those behaviors which result in the positive events and to avoid those which do not contribute to the achievement of those consequences.

Token programs have been successfully used with a variety of learning and behavior difficulties of children and adolescents and in a variety of

Brigham et al. 1972; Chadwick and Day 1971 or Wolf et al. 1968; Phillips 1968; Ayllon et al. 1975; Christopherson et al. 1972

settings. To illustrate, token programs have been used successfully to influence academic performance,* standardized achievement test scores,* predelinquent boys,* hyperactive learning disabled children,* and children's disruptive behavior in a home setting.*

The token serves to overcome the delay between behaviors and the later delivery of backup reinforcers. As the token is not used immediately after awarded, more stable behavior is likely.

A token program is relatively simple to administer. Tokens are easily presented, easily handled by children, and are available to remind the child of the ultimate reinforcer. Behavior can be reinforced as it occurs. Tokens can be provided without disrupting ongoing behavior or distracting other children as may be done, for example, in using social reinforcement. Tokens can acquire rather strong secondary reinforcement value and can be used to maintain behavior for extended periods of time in the absence of backup reinforcers. When used with a suitable range of backup reinforcers, the token is less susceptible to satiation effects than are other primary and secondary events. Finally, the token optimizes individual learner susceptibility because a single event—the token—represents a

Kazdin and Boatzin 1972; MacMillan 1973; O'Leary and Drabman 1971; Walker and Buckley 1974

variety of backup reinforcers selected to meet the reinforcement characteristics of each child. (The reader should consult Kazdin and Boatzin,* MacMillan,* O'Leary and Drabman,* and Walker and Buckley* for a more detailed discussion of token programs.)

Informational Feedback

If a child is given information concerning the appropriateness of his or her performance, this may serve a facilitating function. Giving such information may serve as a discriminative event resulting in modification of some of the child's behavior. If, for example, he (or she) is informed, "You have used half of the allotted time," the adolescent may begin to work faster, noting that less than half of the test has been completed. Feedback that suggests that the child's behavior is satisfactory, in terms of his own expectations, also may serve a reinforcing function. For some children such information on performance may have acquired secondary reinforcing qualities due to the previous association of performance with subsequent reinforcing events such as praise, passing grade, prize, completion of task, and the like.

As examples of the possible positive effects of feedback, Drabman and Lahey* reported its effects on a ten-year-old girl described as having no friends, being the most disruptive child in her class, and as being either teased or ignored by her classmates. A significant decrease in the child's disruptive behaviors was noted following a period of time in which her teacher provided consistent nonemotional feedback relative to the appropriateness of her behavior. Van Houten et al.* and Fink and Carnine* provided additional data supporting the facilitative effect of informational feedback combined with graphing and public posting of academic performance. Arithmetic and writing performance improved noticeably in elementary classes under these contingency conditions. As emphasized by Kazdin,* however, the discriminative and/or reinforcing effects of feedback information does vary considerably among children and adolescents and should be viewed as only one aspect of a more comprehensive program of behavior management.

Drabman and Lahey 1974

Van Houten et al. 1975; Fink and Carnine 1975

Kazdin 1975

Self-reinforcement

A child may learn to reinforce some of his own behaviors by "patting himself on the back" while engaging in or immediately upon completion of these behaviors. In fact, such self-management is one of the ultimate goals of an educational program. The child or adolescent can learn to say to himself, "That's good work," "I'm smart," "I deserve to be proud," "Good job," "I'm proud of myself," after certain of his or her behaviors. To facilitate the development of such self-reinforcement behaviors, the teacher should encourage the student to compliment himself after appropriate behavior. If such verbal statements are associated on numerous occasions with reinforcing events presented by others, these self-delivered compliments will become reinforcing. The child becomes more independent of external reinforcers and is able to maintain present behaviors and to acquire new behaviors on his own. (See Chapter 12 for further discussion.)

Summary

The educator has available a wide range of events which have potential reinforcing value for children and adolescents. These include *consumable* items which the child may eat or drink; *durable* items such as toys, trinkets, or hobby items which may be kept by the child or which may be used by the child for a specific period of time; *activities* such as listening to music, completing art forms, and being class monitor; and *social* events such as praise, approval, attention, or acceptance. Generalized reinforcers in the form of tokens, points, grades, or informational feedback may be used effectively. The educator also may utilize those *inherent in the activity itself,* such as task accomplishment and acquisition of new skills, as well as aspects of a child's self-reinforcement system. The specific combination of

Becker et al. 1971; Bijou and Sturges 1959; Blackman and Silberman 1971, 1975; Clarizio 1971; Rosenberg 1971; Spradlin and Girardeau 1966; Sulzer and Mayer 1972

reinforcing events used at any time obviously *will be selected to coincide with the individual child's characteristics.* Reference should be made to the following for listings of a variety of specific events used successfully with differing groups of children: Becker et al.,* Bijou and Sturges,* Blackham and Silberman,* Clarizio,* Rosenberg,* Spradlin and Girardeau,* and Sulzer and Mayer.*

CONTINGENCY CONTRACTING

Homme 1970

Stuart 1971; Weathers and Liberman 1975

Some educators have found it valuable to formalize the contingency arrangements which exist between behavior and consequences. Homme* has described the basic elements for use of contingency contracting in the classroom, and Stuart* and Weathers and Liberman,* have illustrated its use with families of delinquent adolescents.

In a formal contingency contract, the parties involved develop a written agreement which specifies the relationship between certain behaviors and related positive or negative consequences. All members of the agreement sign it in recognition of their commitment to meeting the terms of the contract. The basic features of such a contingency contract include:

Stuart 1971

1. *A precise statement of the behaviors, responsibilities, or accomplishments which will be attained prior to reinforcement.* These should involve behaviors which can be observed by all parties. As an example of an unacceptable contract behavior, the child may agree to be polite to adults, but the parent could not monitor this behavior when the parents were not present. Examples of acceptable contract behaviors include school attendance, completion of homework assignments, compliance with agreed-upon curfew hours, completion of designated household chores. Stuart,* as an example of contracted behaviors for a sixteen-year-old girl, included the following responsibilities: "Candy must maintain a weekly grade average of B in the academic ratings of all her classes and must return home by 11:30 P.M." This responsibility was in exchange for the privilege of going out at 7 o'clock on one weekend evening without having to account for her whereabouts.

Stuart 1971

2. *A clear statement is made of the reinforcing consequences of meeting the designated behavioral requirements.* These reinforcing events must be those selected by the child as being valuable to him. Stuart* suggested such consequences for adolescent "delinquents" as free time with friends, spending money, choice of hair and dress style, and use of the family car.

3. *The behavioral requirements and the positive consequences should be equitable.* This equitability obviously is an individual matter and must be determined in relation to the specific child characteristics in relation to the difficulty level of the behavioral requirements. It may be

relatively easy for one adolescent to meet a specific behavioral expectation but quite difficult for another adolescent to do so. Thus, the consequences would reflect these individual differences.

4. *The contract should be stated in a positive manner.* Although penalties may be included for nonattainment of the agreed-upon behavioral objectives, such cost procedures should be a minor aspect of the contract. Emphasis should be placed on attainment and positive consequences. The less the aversive aspects of the contract, the greater likelihood the child will remain actively involved in honoring the contract. When a penalty clause is included, it should be stated in objective terms. For example, if an adolescent returns home thirty minutes late, she will be required to return thirty minutes early the following day.

5. *The contract should be arranged through mutual negotiation and*

Contract

I, *Rebecca Lyn*, agree to fulfill the following responsibilities beginning Semester 1, 1977:

   1. Attend every scheduled class.
   2. Arrive on time for each class and remain in class throughout the scheduled period.
   3. Complete all assignments in each class and turn each in on time.

In exchange, *my teachers* in each class agree to the following:

   1. To provide frequent (daily if feasible) feedback to me concerning my progress.
   2. If time permits, to provide individual assistance when homework or tests performance reflects a need or when I request assistance.
   3. To provide positive support and encouragement when appropriate.

In exchange, *my parents* agree to the following:

   1. Provide dating privileges on Friday (curfew 12:00 p.m.) and Saturday (curfew 11:45 p.m.).
   2. For each week of fulfilling these responsibilities, my parents will, in addition to my weekly allowance, provide me with a certificate for a new record or a $5 clothing certificate.
   3. For each month of attainment, my parents will provide (a) a bonus of $20 for unrestricted spending and (b) dating privileges during the week with a curfew of 10:45 p.m.

Penalty: For each violation of any of the three responsibilities, a penalty of 10 points will be assessed. An accumulation of each 30 points will result in the loss of dating privileges for one night during the following weekend.

January 15, 1977 Date	Rebecca Lyn Rebecca Lyn
Bobbie Godwin Mother	Carl L. Burst Math Teacher
Willard Godwin Father	Shandlin Nyanger History Teacher
	Science Teacher
	English Teacher
	Mark Kalan Physical Education Teacher

FIGURE 8.4   *Example of a Written Contract*

not imposed by the adult in charge. If the child or adolescent is involved in developing the contract, he is more likely to honor it.

6. *An objective record should be kept of goal attainment and subsequent reinforcement awards.* Both parties will be able to observe progress.

7. *Once desired behavioral objectives are being fulfilled, a bonus for maintenance of these behaviors over a longer period of time should be included.* In this manner, the desired behaviors are more likely to persist and to come under the influence of more naturally occurring reinforcing events. These may include such privileges as a later than usual curfew hour, extra spending money, a new record album, opportunity to have a party, tickets to a concert.

8. *The adult must be very careful to fulfill his aspects of the contract.* Any inconsistency on the part of the adult will jeopardize the specific behavioral contract and also teach the child that others are not to be trusted.

Figure 8.4 is an example of a contract for sixteen-year-old Rebecca Lyn who had experienced difficulty in class attendance and in completing homework assignments. Note that the contract was signed by the adolescent, her teachers, and her parents. It was negotiated in conference with all parties present. A weekly record card was completed by each teacher and delivered to the parents on Friday afternoon (see Figure 8.5).

AVERSIVE EVENTS

As a basis for the following discussion of negative reinforcement and the discussion in the following chapter of punishment procedures, the types of events which are aversive or unpleasant and the manner in which events may acquire aversive characteristics is described.

Some events are naturally unpleasant to the child at birth. These include, for example, extreme states of deprivation of food, water, or air, painful stimulation such as a slap on the hand, loud noises, and extremes in temperature. These are *primary* aversive events in the sense that the child without benefit of prior learning naturally seeks to *terminate or to avoid* these unpleasant conditions.

A wide range of neutral events may acquire some of the aversive qualities of these primary events. Neutral events such as a frown, threat, gesture, presence of an authority figure, elevators, darkness, or a furry animal may have little or no unpleasantness associated with them initially. *However, for any individual these once neutral events may become unpleasant events if frequently associated with the occurrence of other events which already are aversive to the child.*

These events may become aversive to the child as they signal reduction in frequency or amount of positive reinforcers. Others become aversive as they coincide with or precede and signal the occurrence of other unpleasant events. Scolding, yelling, threatening or warning, criticizing, poor grades, and disapproval and reprimanding by teacher or peer may become aversive events as they mark the occasion for a reduction in positive reinforcement. The teacher is much less likely after reprimanding a child to provide positive social comments or to grant privileges such as free play or hearing a favorite story. A threat by the teacher may become aversive; it has been associated with various aversive consequences such as being spanked or of being denied access to a TV show or to the music room. A peer's scream and angry face may become quite aversive; in the past these have coincided with painful physical attacks or by the absence for a period of time of acceptance and interaction. The child learns to avoid, dislike, or to terminate these unpleasant events as soon as possible.

Although every person's experiences contain *secondary* or *learned* aversive events, these become especially significant in the lives of children and adolescents with exceptional learning and behavior characteristics. It is not unusual for an excessively large number of events in the child's environment to acquire aversive qualities. His difficulties in learning, along with other behavioral characteristics such as hyperactivity, frequently result in failure to meet the expectations of family members and later of the educational staff. Except in a carefully designed educational environment, the child's failures result in numerous unpleasant consequences which gradually become attached to many aspects of his life. As with positive reinforcers, there is considerable variation in the types of

Subject	Monday			Tuesday			Wednesday			Thursday			Friday			Teacher Comment
	P*	OT	HW	P	OT	HW	P	OT	HW	P	OT	HW	P	OT	HW	
Math	✓	✓	✓	✓	✓	✓	✓	✓	✓	✓	0	✓	✓	✓	✓	Much improved
History	✓	✓	✓	✓	✓	✓	✓	✓	✓	✓	✓	✓	✓	✓	✓	I am Pleased
Science	✓	✓	✓	✓	✓	✓	✓	0	✓	✓	✓	✓	✓	✓	✓	Great
English	✓	✓	✓	0	0	✓	✓	✓	✓	✓	✓	✓	✓	✓	✓	Good Work
Phy. Ed.	✓	✓	✓	✓	✓	✓	✓	✓	✓	✓	✓	✓	✓	✓	✓	

Please insert check mark if responsibility was fulfilled and zero if violated.

*P = present
OT = on time
HW = homework

FIGURE 8.5   *Weekly Record of Responsibilities*

events which are aversive for children and adolescents. Being isolated may be aversive to one and neutral or positive to another. Being reprimanded or criticized by the teacher may be neutral to one child and highly aversive to another. Being given attention in a group may be quite reinforcing to one and aversive to another.

As the aversive qualities of most events have been acquired through association with other aversive events, most such events may lose their aversive qualities if not occasionally associated again with the occurrence of other unpleasant experiences. A threat or warning may be aversive to a child and effectively influence his behavior when it has been associated previously with the presentation of an unpleasant consequence or the *Phillips 1968* removal of positive reinforcers. However, as illustrated by Phillips,* continued use of warnings or threats lose their aversiveness unless on occasion the threat is fulfilled when the child or adolescent engages in inappropriate behavior.

BASIC RULE OF NEGATIVE REINFORCEMENT

As noted earlier in Table 8.1, the termination, reduction, or removal of unpleasant or aversive events has the effect of making stronger those behaviors which produced the removal or reduction. The strengthening and maintenance of behavior through removal of umpleasant events is called *negative reinforcement.*[3]

A child may report a headache when asked to perform for the class. The teacher may send him to the nurse's room where he is given medication and permitted to lie down and rest. Assuming that the activity of performing for the class is unpleasant for the child, his behavior of reporting a headache to the teacher would be strengthened under these conditions. His somatic complaints resulted in his *escaping* from an unpleasant or aversive situation. Under similar conditions in the future the same or similar behavior is likely to be repeated.

Development of Avoidance Behavior

After some experience with escaping from various unpleasant situations, a child may begin to do those things that result in his altogether *avoiding* these unpleasant situations. He learns those behaviors that prevent the occurrence of the aversive experience. Some preaversive *cue* triggers the avoidance behavior. As an example, the child may think about

---

3. The reader should make a distinction between the procedure and effects of *negative reinforcement* and those related to *punishment*. While negative reinforcement results in an increase in behavior strength, punishment (a procedure of following behavior with an aversive consequence) produces a reduction in the likelihood that the punished behavior will reoccur. Punishment in its various forms is discussed in the following chapter.

the unpleasantness of class attendance which in turn results in his finding ways to remain at home. He thus avoids the unpleasant classroom environment. His avoidance behavior—remaining at home—is strengthened by the termination of the contemplated unpleasantness of school attendance. *Thus, both escape and avoidance behaviors are strengthened by negative reinforcement.*

Some avoidance behavior is acquired without direct experience with the contemplated aversive experiences being avoided. A child learns from others a large number of verbal labels which to those others have aversive qualities, such as "bad," "harmful," "mean," "dangerous," "sinful," and "threatening." These function as preaversive cues when applied to various situations, persons, or activities. The child may thus tend to avoid those experiences which are so labeled.

A frown, anger, or verbal threat from a teacher or peer, in illustration, may be involved in reinforcing adaptive behavior if the child finds that positive behavior results in the removal of frowns, anger, or verbal threats. Returning to an unfinished task, replying "I apologize," or initiation of social interaction may all be strengthened if followed by removal of the frown, anger, or threat. As noted, the frown, anger, or threat has acquired negative reinforcing properties through previous association with other unpleasant events.

Behavior thus may become stronger both through positive and negative reinforcement procedures. Positive reinforcement works through *presentation* of a pleasant event following the desired behavior, and negative reinforcement strengthens a behavior through *removal* or reduction in intensity of an unpleasant condition. Negative reinforcement thus depends upon the presence of some unpleasant condition which the behavior may reduce or terminate.

Social Behavior Influenced by Negative Reinforcement

Both desired and undesired behavior patterns may be strengthened and maintained by negative reinforcement. Much behavior strengthened by removal or reduction of aversive or preaversive events is viewed as "good adjustment" or adaptive in nature. A significant segment of those behaviors which conform to societal rules and regulations are maintained by means of the negative consequences which are associated with their violation. Academic and social behaviors may be partially maintained at appropriate levels as a result of the aversiveness associated with being deprived of a passing grade, not graduating from driver's education, or of being accepted in a social group. Traffic regulations and many other legal and social rules or conventions are followed as a result of the threat of loss of positive events such as money, acceptance by group, privileges, freedom, after-school job, reputation, and the like. Negative consequences are avoided through use of a range of acceptable behaviors. If a child or adolescent did not "care about" such consequences (if loss of these was not aversive), much of this type of behavior would not be learned or maintained. This is evidenced in much of the "counter culture" social behavior of many adolescents.

As a specific example, an adolescent who dislikes school returns promptly to his classroom from his high-preference physical education activities in order to avoid the loss of his privilege card. Such aversive influence is easily upset, however, if the privilege card lost its positive reinforcing value. This example illustrates the necessity of using a variety of positive consequences to strengthen appropriate behavior patterns which initially may have been under the influence of aversive conditions of threat.

Thus, an event must have positive value to a child or adolescent before a threat of loss of this event will influence him. Attainment of high-quality performance or even task completion may be of minimal reinforcement value to a child. Making a mistake or producing an inferior paper or object may not be an aversive event as, for a particular adolescent, it does not postpone or result in the loss of a positive consequence. Thus, the reminder "you should work hard and do a good job or else you will not finish" or "you will get a poor grade" will not be aversive to the adolescent and thus will have little influence on his school behavior.

A teacher may inform a child that he may join his peers on the playground after he stops crying and cleans off his desk. The teacher imposed an unpleasant condition which she will promptly remove when the desired behavior occurs. Other behaviors than crying, in combination with cleaning-up behavior, are strengthened if they remove the unpleasantness of confinement to the classroom. Other examples include: "You may play the music as soon as you stop being noisy." Less noisy behaviors, because they resulted in the removal of the unpleasant restrictions, would be strengthened.[4] In these instances the teacher is focusing on the relationship between the desired behaviors and a positive consequence. The child is placed in a choice situation. He gains experience in terminating undesired behavior. He learns to control himself. He decides that he can remove the unpleasant conditions by engaging in appropriate behavior. He later decides to avoid the unpleasant conditions altogether by behaving appropriately.

Inappropriate Behavior Influenced by Negative Reinforcement

One child may learn to say, "I can't do that," or "I don't feel good, my stomach hurts," if these behavior patterns remove him from task require-

---

4. In these examples, the teacher is using a *punishment procedure* when she imposes unpleasant conditions following the child's undesired behavior. She does this to discourage the preceding undesired behavior and to create the conditions for using a procedure of negative reinforcement to strengthen more appropriate behaviors.

ments or social relationships which are unpleasant. In a similar manner, an adolescent may acquire a pattern of disruptive behavior if it removes him from a social group of a classroom experience which he finds unpleasant, for example, one concerned with teaching quantitative concepts. The adolescent's high-strength disruptive behaviors such as talking out of turn, laughing, poking peers, or getting out of his desk at inappropriate times may be reinforced if he is, on occasion, dismissed from the classroom. His being dismissed from class removes him from the unpleasant task of working arithmetic problems, being criticized by the teacher for poor performance, and the like, thus strengthening the disruptive behaviors which terminated the unplesant conditions. These disruptive behaviors are more likely to occur on future occasions of the unpleasant events. Still another child may learn to be physically aggressive if such behavior results in the termination of unpleasant teasing or ridicule on the part of other children.

The child's avoidance behaviors, influenced by negative reinforcement, may contribute to his learning difficulties. When behaviors incompatible with effective learning (e.g., hyperactivity, distractibility, limited persistence) serve to remove a child from an unpleasant learning task, these are strengthened by such negative reinforcement. As these become stronger, the child is even less able to meet the educational objectives and thus the classroom and associated events become even more aversive. The more aversive these become, the greater the likelihood of behavior occurring which will remove this unpleasantness. In this manner, the child develops ever stronger behaviors which render effective learning ever less likely.

By the same principle of negative reinforcement, a teacher may learn to yell or to threaten children in a harsh manner or to chastise adolescents in a sarcastic, demeaning manner if that behavior produces a temporary reduction in disruptive, noisy, and other unpleasant behaviors on the part of the adolescents in his class. A teacher sends a disruptive child out of the classroom. Because she has removed a source of irritation, she is more likely to repeat this tactic in the future whenever a child becomes disruptive. In this manner the teacher may slowly acquire poor educational practices.

Negative Aspects of Aversive Control

The use of aversive events to control or reduce inappropriate behavior is a self-defeating tactic in that: (1) The aversiveness associated with criticism or threat may generalize to other aspects of the class environment. The teacher may lose whatever positive reinforcement features he may have, with the result that the child will not only attempt to avoid future criticism but the teacher as well. (2) No new appropriate behaviors are being acquired, just temporary aversive control of inappropriate ones. (3) The discriminative and reinforcing control of the teacher's criticism and threats resides in the child's behavior. (4) The continued effectiveness of criticism and threats as conditioned aversive events depends upon occasional temporal association with other aversive events which these represent. Thus, such aversive control procedures have little of a positive nature to offer and should be assigned low priority as a productive educational approach.

Behavioral characteristics such as excessive shyness may result from negative reinforcement. Attention from, or interacting with, others may acquire secondary aversive qualities if attention from others previously has been the initial event in a sequence of experiences which ended in a variety of unpleasant consequences. Thus, initiation of attention may come to serve as a cue for escape behavior. The escape behavior is thus strengthened by the termination of attention. In extreme cases the child will learn to avoid situations (times, places, activities) which offer the likelihood of social attention or interaction. He may thus protect himself from the possibility of occurrence of unpleasant experiences. Such isolation may not be pleasant to a child, but it might represent the "lesser of two evils."

Because negative reinforcement depends upon the presence of some aversive conditions, the procedure has limited usefulness for the teacher in increasing the development of prosocial behaviors. However, the teacher must be sensitive to the rule of negative reinforcement since it is involved in strengthening and in maintaining considerable inappropriate behaviors among children with exceptional learning and behavior characteristics. As the process of learning new behaviors and of engaging in appropriate behaviors under desired conditions is a difficult one, many situations represent unpleasantness to these children. Any behaviors that remove this unpleasantness are strengthened. As noted, poor teacher behavior also may be influenced by negative reinforcement.

ASPECTS OF A CHILD'S MOTIVATIONAL SYSTEM

The behavioral approach views a child's motivational system as comprising those varieties of events which have either reinforcing or aversive characteristics. Although there are a few primary reinforcing and aversive events common to all children, a given child's motivational system is highly individualistic due to his unique learning history. Differences in what is rewarding to children, in what will initiate and sustain their behaviors, in what they will strive to attain or to avoid—*their motivational systems*—account for many of their differences in learning and behavior.

Most events serve a neutral function for the infant, being neither reinforcing nor aversive. Rapid changes in the child's motivational system occur as he is exposed to a variety of neutral events when experiencing primary reinforcing or aversive events. Gradually, through a process of emotional learning, a wide range of events acquires reinforcing or aversive properties. These learned events will, as suggested, serve two major roles in a child's behavior. First, as reinforcing or aversive events, they will influence the strength of behaviors which produce or remove them. Secondly, these events serve as cues which influence either approach or avoidance behavior. Thus children who find different things rewarding and unpleasant will behave quite differently. If a child has learned that academic achievement is reinforcing, situations in which the child can demonstrate achievement behavior will serve as cues for a variety of behaviors which potentially will result in satisfying academic achievement. The situation evokes "striving" behavior, that is, these situations activate and sustain behavior consistent with reinforcement attainment. In contrast, if a child has had frequent unpleasant experiences in academic activities, such activities and situations in which these occur will be aversive to him. The child will engage in a variety of behaviors which interfere with academic achievement. In a passive or active manner, he will strive to get away from or to avoid such situations. He will impress the educator as being uninterested, unmotivated, and as spending an excessive amount of his time "fooling around" and in engaging in considerable nonproductive behavior.

As emphasized, the child with exceptional learning and behavior characteristics is at a distinct disadvantage in the academic environment as typically organized since there are few events in this setting which are reinforcing and too many which are aversive. Such children have not acquired a highly functional motivational system consistent with the learning-for-learning's-sake philosophy which many educators hold. The child's learning history has not permitted him to gain much joy or satisfaction out of academic pursuits; therefore, there is a mismatch between the types of motivational characteristics required of the child and the kinds and patterns of consequences which are in fact reinforcing to him.

HOW DOES A CHILD'S MOTIVATIONAL SYSTEM DEVELOP?

Typically, as a child becomes older, an increasing number and type of events acquire reinforcing and aversive characteristics. As noted, although some events do have primary, natural, or intrinsic reinforcement or aversive qualities, most events and activities become reinforcing or aversive to a child through a process of learning.[5] The principle of learning which

---

5. The manner in which aversive components of the child's motivational system are acquired was described in an earlier section. Thus the discussion to follow is limited to the positively reinforcing aspects of the child's motivational system.

underlies the development of *secondary* reinforcing events is as follows: *A neutral event or activity will acquire reinforcing qualities if presented to a child as he is experiencing an event or activity that is reinforcing.* After a few such pairings or associations, the previously neutral event or activity will become reinforcing to the child. The child will then learn and engage in those behaviors which result in the newly acquired reinforcing event. Again, in increasing the scope of the child's motivational system, the educator will take the following steps:

step 1 | Identify events which are reinforcing for the child.

step 2 | When these are presented to the child, an event which is neutral in terms of its reinforcing effect is presented simultaneously. If the teacher wishes to increase the reward value of teacher approval, for example, she would smile and say "very good" as the child is provided a reinforcing event (e.g., a favorite toy) after some desired behavior. If a teacher wishes to increase the reinforcement value of task completion, she will say, "I'm proud of your hard work and the way you finished that," as the child completes the task.

step 3 | After a number of such associations, the smile and statement of approval and the behavior involved in task completion may acquire reinforcing characteristics. Such events could then be used independently as a rewarding event to strengthen various of the child's behaviors. The critical factor in this learning process is the close and frequent association of the neutral and reinforcing events.

The development of a child's motivational system thus depends upon the specific experiences of that child. The strength of a newly acquired reinforcer depends upon (1) the recency of its association with other reinforcers, (2) the number of times it has been paired in the acquisition process, and (3) the amount or magnitude of the reinforcer paired with it.

A child with limited experience in associating reinforcing events with neutral ones will acquire fewer secondary reinforcers. Learning new behaviors thus will be a more difficult undertaking as fewer reinforcing events are available to initiate, strengthen, and maintain new behaviors. As a result, the learning difficulties of the child are intensified.

Such events as completing a task, being successful, or even that of reaching a previously set behavior goal may become reinforcing events. In fact, a child can gain increasing independence and self-responsibility only as events natural to various behaviors become secondary reinforcers. Task involvement, task completion, creating an art form, or any other type of accomplishment can become a reinforcing event (satisfying or pleasurable to a child and therefore self-maintaining) only after being associated on numerous occasions with other reinforcing consequences provides for these or similar activities. Thus, achievement and accomplishment such as dressing without assistance, completing a project, or involvement in various motor and social activities or relationships not infrequently hold only minimal if any reinforcement value for many children with chronic learning and behavior difficulties due to their excessive failure experiences in these endeavors.

With such children, the teacher must begin with those events that are reinforcing to each child and use them to insure that the child will be successful. As these events are paired over and over again with various aspects of task involvement and completion, with social interaction, or with any other types of behavior patterns, these activities will become reinforcing and therefore self-maintaining independent of the previous reinforcing consequences.

In summary, the teacher of children with learning and behavior difficulties must pay careful attention to the process by which neutral or even unpleasant events and activities can become reinforcing. Activities and accomplishments which appear to be intrinsically motivating or reinforcing to other children cannot be depended upon for facilitating learning and thus influencing prosocial behavior of the child with chronic learning and behavior problems. The reinforcing characteristics of these events must be developed through careful arrangement of the learning environment. The goals of an educational program thus involve not only the strengthening of new academic and social behavior characteristics but also insurance that a range of naturally available events such as involvement in activities, accomplishments, and social interaction become highly reinforcing.

WHAT REINFORCING EVENTS SHOULD BE USED?

The obvious answer to this question is: "Use those consequences which result in best learning, performance, and maintenance of the academic and social behaviors being taught." If a child finds satisfaction in the acquisition and performance of various desired academic skills, the educator should by all means make use of these learner characteristics in encouraging academic and social competency. If a child gets excited by the challenge of a difficult math assignment, this motivational component should be utilized. However, if a child finds little "intrinsic" incentive value in such endeavors, and if it is deemed desirable that the child learn these academic skills, it would be foolish to dismiss the problem by blaming the child for his "lack of appropriate motivation." The educator should organize that incentive environment which will motivate and strengthen learning.

MacMillan 1973; Bijou
1970
The educator, as emphasized by MacMillan* and Bijou,* however, must guard against the tendency to use contrived or arbitrary events and should choose those events which are representative of a higher level of motivational maturity and are more natural to the learner, the situation, and the educational activities engaged in by the learner. MacMillan suggested that for some teachers, with limited exposure to the behavior modification field, events such as tokens, check marks, and M&M's are synonymous with behavior modification and further that they observe programs designed for children who deviate *markedly* from the norm (wherein low-level reinforcers were necessary) "and adopt them lock, stock, and barrel to use with children who do not begin to resemble the original class on which such procedures were used" (p.221).

Bijou writes:

> The fact that academic and social behaviors are operants, and hence sensitive to consequent stimulation, has led many teachers and researchers to use, indiscriminately, contrived contingencies such as tokens, candies, points, stars, etc. Such artificial reinforcers are not always necessary, and in many instances in which they have been used, they have not been functional. . . . Contrived reinforcers are appropriate only when the usual reinforcers applied in the classroom (confirmation, indications of progress, privileges, preferred work, approval, and the like) are not meaningful to the child. If, at times, contrived reinforcers are considered necessary in order to initiate learning, they can be scheduled so that they are gradually replaced by the reinforcers indigenous to the situation and the activity being learned. . . . The critical task in most teaching is not the incorporation of more and more new reinforcers but the effective utilization of those currently available to the teacher. [p. 68]

Hewett 1974
Thus, the particular consequences selected for use with any child or adolescent will depend upon (1) the nature and developmental maturity of the child's motivational characteristics, that is, the *learner susceptibility;** (2) the *difficulty level* of the learning or performance endeavor; and (3) whether the educational objective is that of influencing the *acquisition* of new behavioral characteristics or the *maintenance* of those already learned. Each of these will be discussed.

Learner Susceptibility

As described in the previous section, children and adolescents with exceptional learning and behavior characteristics differ markedly both among themselves and in comparison with children with more typical learning histories. Events which are reinforcing for one child may not be reinforcing for another. This principle of reinforcer effectiveness cannot be emphasized too strongly, as one of the most apparent deficits in many educational programs for children and adolescents with learning and behavior difficulties is that the same reinforcers (e.g., grades, teacher approval, parental praise) are provided for all. Little consideration is given to the possibility of individual differences. The types of consequences which are of primary importance for one child may be insignificant for another. There does not appear to be any highly effective common reinforcing event that can be used with most efficiency with all. Social reinforcement in such forms as attention, praise or approval, for example, may be neutral or even negative or aversive to some. The range of positive reinforcing events is greatly limited for many children and at times can be quite idiosyncratic. This emphasizes the critical necessity for the educator to explore what each child does relate to as incentive or reinforcing events.

If the child is motivated by curiosity, this should be utilized. If exploration represents a high-preference activity, this should be used in exposing the child to a variety of events and activities and in strengthening other behaviors by making use of the Premack relationship. If a child gets a thrill out of developing new skills, being correct, solving problems (and thereby reducing uncertainty), developing influence over others,* being autonomous,* being independent, accomplishing task solution on his own, or contributing to others, the educator should capitalize on these. If a child is challenged by contradictory or discrepant viewpoints or by inconsistencies in his own behavior,* this source of activation and potential reinforcement may be utilized to teach the child a variety of educational objectives.

Skinner 1953
White 1965

Festinger 1957

Failure itself can have an activating effect for some children. Gardner* and Maehr* have suggested that failure as an aversive event may be a challenge which produces more vigorous and persistent problem-solving behavior. If such problem-solving behavior is successful, it is reinforced both positively (task completion) and negatively (removal of aversiveness associated with failure) and thus may become quite strong. For other children, as suggested by Gardner,* failure may result in the child's avoiding the learning task and environment. Maehr* also has noted that some children learn best under conditions where there is some challenge— where there is some risk of being wrong in some of his problem-solving behaviors. A child with a rich history of success may soon be satiated when he is correct all of the time. He will lose interest and begin to seek other activities. In contrast the child with limited success will best maintain his behavior under a high reinforcement schedule. Thus, the effects of various schedules of reinforcement on learning and maintenance interact with the child's previous experience to determine the precise effect for each child.

Gardner 1966; Maehr 1968

Gardner 1966
Maehr 1968

In view of the variety of possible events and activities that can motivate the child and serve to strengthen behavior, the educator should have no preconceptions about what events will in fact be effective with an individual child or a group of children. If tasks are too easy, some children will find these unpleasant. With other children, frequent success on relatively easy assignments will be most effective. Respect for individual difference in learner susceptibility to reinforcement conditions will make a significant difference in the success of educational programs.

In summary, the particular reinforcing consequence utilized must in fact be valuable to the learner, whether this be a primary event such as candy or food, an activity such as goal attainment, or a self-delivered one of congratulating oneself for completing an unpleasant but necessary task. Grades should be used—if they are effective. Approval should be provided—if it is effective. The "desire to succeed" is an admirable quality and one that the educational environment should utilize to the maximum—if the individual learner does in fact have such a quality or if it is of sufficient strength to motivate and reinforce a wide range of learning.

Hierarchy of Reinforcing Consequences

MacMillan 1973

It should prove helpful to consider the question of a *continuum* or *hierarchy* of reinforcing consequences. MacMillan* reported the following continuum, from most basic to the most mature:

1. Primary rewards—food and water.
2. Toys and trinkets.
3. Tokens or checks—with backup reinforcers (toys, food, etc.).
4. Visual evidence of progress—graphs, letter grades.
5. Social approval.
6. Sense of mastery—"learning for the love of it."

Hewett 1974

Hewett* suggests the following seven types of reinforcing consequences, ranging from "tangible rewards" as the most basic to "joy of learning" as the "Mount Everest level of positive reinforcement in education." The types include:

1. Tangible rewards—candy, food, trinkets.
2. Task completion—"The child who completes a story-writing assignment or a page of arithmetic problems may experience real satisfaction from the simple act of completion" (p. 236).
3. Multisensory stimulation and activity—e.g., model building, playing with a caged rabbit.
4. Social approval—Hewett reports a study involving several hundred upper elementary-age children in which teacher approval was chosen as the most preferred positive consequence from among such choices as peer approval, competition, independence, or such tangible objects as candy.
5. Knowledge of results—knowing how you stand in relation to some criterion.

6. Acquisition of knowledge and skill—"The child who finds himself able to read the labels on the boxes in mother's pantry or the brand names in commercials on television is being positively reinforced for his reading efforts" (p. 235).
7. Joy of learning—"truly intrinsic satisfaction from involvement in a task" (p. 235).

Garris* suggests a developmental reinforcement hierarchy consisting of four levels: primary, social, symbolic, and abstract. The writer emphasizes that many of the learning and behavior difficulties of children and adolescents are a result of a mismatch between the child's motivational characteristics and the reinforcement characteristics assumed by the educational program. Reinforcing events that are above the child's developmental level are frequently utilized, with the result that the child is unable to succeed. He also is unable, under such conditions, to learn more adequate motivational characteristics.

Garris 1975

Difficulty Level

The type and magnitude of reinforcing consequences required by a child for effective learning and performance relates to the difficulty level of the target behavior. A difficult learning task for a child with learning and behavior difficulties will typically require a lower level (more tangible and extrinsic) consequence than is required for an easier task. The educator may find that a child who learns and performs well under social and task-accomplishment consequences on most occasions may require more tangible consequences when confronted with unusually difficult learning or behavior requirements. The difficulty level of any learning or performance pattern, of course, is quite relative to the individual learner. One child who has good skills of attending and persistence, and well-practiced skills considered prerequisite to a given task, will have a much easier time with the task than would a child who has rather strong patterns of hyperactivity, distractibility, and poor prerequisite skills. The first may learn effectively with an occasional smile of approval from the teacher while the other child may require frequent tangible consequences supported by teacher approval.

Acquisition versus Maintenance

It may be necessary during the acquisition of new skills of competency to use arbitrary or contrived reinforcing events and to make these available to the child in an immediate and frequent manner. However, as emphasized by MacMillan and Forness,* reinforcing events more natural to the behavior and to the environment must replace these consequences if the behavior is to be maintained.

MacMillan and Forness 1970

Summary

The educator must be sensitive to those consequences which do in fact strengthen and maintain behavior for any given child. In the selection of consequences and the procedures for providing these, he should be guided by the concept, "Does it represent the most natural, intrinsic, child-centered and child-managed event that would be effective with the specific learner and the behavior being taught or expected?" For some children, effective learning will occur only under conditions of frequent presentation of tangible events which can be consumed or manipulated. Such events for a child with a history of excessive failure provide him with enduring concrete evidence that he has accomplished something and that he can be successful. In such instances, the educator should be prepared to use these reinforcers. *Additionally, the educator should initiate a systematic program of moving the child from contrived reinforcing events to those that are natural, intrinsic, or self-delivered.*

As has been suggested, a verbal child had the potential for utilizing his own covert behaviors to direct and reinforce various of his activities. If, however, a child is provided contrived and externally managed reinforcers excessively and is not taught to self-manage, he will be less able to develop *Jensen 1968* into an independent learner. Jensen* emphasizes the role of what he calls the child-delivered "verbal confirming response" in reinforcing and maintaining behaviors. This is similar to the role assigned to language by the *Luria 1961* Russian psychologist, Luria,* and by such American social learning *Bandura 1969* theorists as Bandura.* The humanistic behavioral approach incorporates this emphasis on cognitive mediational processes and considers these processes of regulation of behavior as most essential to independence. Children with learning and behavior difficulties must be taught to utilize symbolic activities in developing self-prompting and self-reinforcement skills.

HOW SHOULD REINFORCING EVENTS BE ARRANGED?

The educator should be aware of the relationship between the manner in which reinforcement techniques are used and the possible differential effects which various approaches will have on the child. Misuses of reinforcement procedures have justifiably resulted in such criticisms as "mechanistic," "outer-directed," and "manipulative and coersive." An educator, as he or she is frequently in a position of power and can control many events which are reinforcing to children, can in fact use reinforcement procedures to serve his or her own purpose. It is probably true that numerous "token programs" in classrooms across the country are being used to keep children quiet, nondisruptive, and inactive. The objectives of such programs, as well as the possible long-range effects on the children served, obviously merit careful examination. *"Is the teacher being served or is the program for the benefit of each child?"* is a critical and most legitimate question.

Consequences for "desired" behavior should not be provided in an authoritarian or arbitrary manner. Such an approach would suggest to the child: "If you do what I ask, I shall give you something." In this type of arrangement, the child is taught to exchange his behavior for a reward: "Pick up your toys and I shall give you some candy!" This type of arrangement or bribery usually comes after the child has refused to pick up the toys and is highly undesirable, representing as it does an obvious poor use of the rules of reinforcement. It teaches the child to barter with those who control reinforcers. The reinforcers represent something given arbitrarily by an authority agent.

Using reinforcing events in a bribing fashion can result in some highly bothersome and undesirable behavior patterns. Such misuse of positive reinforcement can teach a child that he can "get his way" if he engages in certain inappropriate behaviors. He may learn: "In order to get teacher to give me what I want, I must begin to misbehave." The adult will then respond, "Children, if you stop that noise and play quietly until the visitors leave, I will give you a treat." In this manner a chain of events is strengthened: The child finds the adult in a vulnerable situation.   →   He begins to misbehave.   →   The adult bribes him to stop his misbehavior with a promise of a reward for good behavior.   →   The child engages in appropriate behavior.   →   The reward is given.   →   The final reinforcer strengthens the entire chain of events.

Such misuse of reinforcement produces what has been labeled the "spoiled" or "self-centered" and outer-controlled child. The child has learned: "Regardless of what I do, I will get reinforced. If I do not get my way, all I have to do is to become demanding and disruptive and the social environment will provide what I want."

A variation of this inappropriate use of reinforcement procedures involves structuring the environment so that highly prized reinforcers are provided for behaviors that are beneficial to the teacher but not necessarily to the child. The teacher who "runs a tight ship" at all cost and provides prized tangible, social, and activity reinforcers only to those children who "work quietly, independently, and finish all their work within the allotted time" may be serving her own need for things to run quietly and smoothly. She may, at the same time, be inhibiting a variety of more spontaneous, curious, active, and creative child characteristics. Also, in her disregard for individual differences, she may be creating significant difficulties for those children who either do not have the required behaviors in their repertoires or else have strong competing behaviors. These children have a high risk of being unsuccessful because they are unable to meet the inflexible and unrealistic expectations of the teacher.

A more appropriate arrangement between behavior and consequences would be one in which the consequences are provided in as logical and natural a manner as possible. An arrangement which suggests, "After we finish cleaning, we shall listen to our favorite music," or one in which a social consequence is naturally and spontaneously provided, teaches the child that certain of his behaviors produce desirable consequences. A nod of approval from an admired teacher as the adolescent finishes a difficult task will serve to strengthen a lengthy sequence of behaviors which resulted in task completion and the approval. The child's "thank you" after the teacher helps the child with his coat results in a warm smile from the teacher. Both the teacher and the child are reinforced in this interchange. The teacher does not present the smile in an arbitrary or authoritarian manner nor does she give it to the child per se; the smile represents a natural social consequence of a social behavior. The more natural and socially relevant the manner in which reinforcing consequences occur, the more such consequences will contribute to positive behavior development. Under these socially relevant conditions the child is not "forced," "pressured," "prodded," or "bribed" into desired behaviors. The child's experience suggests to him those behaviors which result in consequences of value to him; he learns to choose such behaviors and to refrain from others which result in unpleasant consequences.

EFFECTIVENESS OF REINFORCING EVENTS

The reinforcing influence of any event on a child's behavior at any specific time is related to a number of factors. In addition to those previously discussed, other important considerations include:

Kind of Reinforcer

Events reinforcing to one child may not be reinforcing to another. The implication of this is simple: The same events cannot be provided every child if maximum program effects are to be realized. These reinforcing events must be individualized. The range of events reinforcing for some children is quite varied and for others quite limited. Consideration for individual differences in relation to reinforcing events is of utmost importance in development of educational programs for children with exceptional learning and behavior characteristics. General and specific reinforcement differences are described in the final section.

New events may become reinforcing to a child as he gains familiarity with them. Various toys, novel foods, new activities, and other events may be of minimal reinforcement value initially if the child has had only limited exposure to them. The value of these novelties may be enhanced by expos ing the children to them and insuring that they sample or otherwise experience the new events. It would be best to introduce them at times when the child is enjoying something familiar to him. In a popular sense, such exposure creates a "need" for the event. After pleasant association, the event becomes reinforcing in its own right and thus can be depended upon to reinforce behavior which produces it.

Amount and Relative Value of a Reinforcer

Generally, the greater the amount of the reinforcing events provided after any specific behavior, the more it contributes to the strength and maintenance of the behavior. Providing thirty minutes of free time following task completion should be more reinforcing than providing only five minutes. Praise, while representing a single kind of event, may be more influential if provided by a highly admired teacher than if provided by a stranger. The differential value of social reinforcement is illustrated in a frequently observed occurrence. A group of children may demonstrate excellent progress in one classroom taught by a warm, expressive, and empathetic teacher who praises frequently. In another classroom in which praise is also provided, the children are noted to make much less systematic progress in acquiring new behavioral skills. The same kind of social events provided at relatively comparable frequency but by different persons may influence children differently.

The amount of reinforcement required to maintain behavior after it becomes a stable part of the child's repertoire frequently may be reduced below that level needed during the initial teaching of the behavior. Also, the child will learn to engage in more complex and lengthy behavior patterns for the same reinforcing events. Initially, the child may be reinforced with a specific event such as a token at the completion of a specified behavior. He is given a token when he completes his five-problem math assignment. Next, he may be required to complete the entire twenty-problem assignment prior to being reinforced with the token.

Hamblin et al.* demonstrated this procedure of requiring an increasingly large amount of behavior prior to reinforcement in the teaching of verbal expression skills to an extremely inhibited child in a primary classroom. The teacher initially provided M&M's if the boy would correctly label the colors of each. After a few experiences, the same method was used to reinforce prompt naming of familiar objects which the teacher would then present to the child. The teacher next required the boy to tell a story about a picture which she provided. Initially he would talk for only fifteen to thirty seconds; after two weeks he was able to continue telling a story for up to six minutes. The same reinforcing event was now maintaining behavior that was over twelve times that which initially occurred. The experiences of Staats and Butterfield* and Staats et al.* provide further illustration of this procedure of increasing the relative value of reinforcing

Hamblin et al. 1971

Staats and Butterfield 1965; Staats et al. 1967

events by progressively requiring more reading behavior from "delin-quent," "mentally retarded," and "culturally deprived" adolescents per reinforcing event provided.

The Timing of Reinforcement

In the early stages of teaching a new behavior pattern, learning will be most effective if reinforcing consequences are presented *immediately* following either the desired behavior or some acceptable approximations of this behavior. The behavior that immediately precedes the occurrence of the reinforcing event will be strengthened the most. Other behaviors, more temporally separated, will be strengthened but not to the extent as will the immediately preceding behavior. When the child who is without speech attempts to use sound in a meaningful manner, reinforcement must be provided at that moment. If a shy, isolated child approaches another child in an apparent attempt at social interaction, the teacher should reinforce that behavior when it occurs. If an adolescent makes an attempt to listen to the teacher's position on class responsibility, the teacher should reinforce this immediately. This rule of immediate reinforcement following the desired behavior is especially important in teaching children with excep-tional learning and behavior characteristics. As noted, events such as being correct, completing a task, or being promised a later reinforcement fre-quently cannot be depended upon to strengthen behavior. If it is not possible to provide immediate reinforcement, the behavior that is being reinforced should be described to the child as the consequences are pro-vided. "Susan, you finished your assignment and then helped John. I am pleased that you decided to do that. Thank You." "Stephen, I know you tried hard to be good to your sister while we were away. I won't forget your good efforts and maturity. You can have the car one night next week."

Smeets and Striefel 1975

Smeets and Striefel[*] provide an example of the value of immediate reinforcement to children with exceptional characteristics. They reported that a group of eleven- to eighteen-year-old multihandicapped deaf and hard-of-hearing children attending a special program designed to remedy their academic and behavior deficits significantly increased performance on the Raven Progressive Matrices (a nonverbal intelligence measure) following immediate reinforcement of correct responses. Performance under immediate reforcement was higher than under other conditions of end-of-session reinforcement, noncontingent reinforcement, and delayed reinforcement. In this group of subjects the immediate reinforcement, and the informational feedback which it provided, were more effective in influencing task performance than were the other contingencies evaluated.

The consistent implementation of this immediate reinforcement rule presents some obvious practical problems. In working with groups of children, for example, the teacher will find it impossible to reinforce immediately every behavior which she is attempting to influence. It may be helpful if she provides tangible events which represent later positive consequences to bridge the time delay between behavior and reinforcer. The teacher may plan to use the activity of listening to records as a reinforcing event for the children in her class for completing individually designed table work. As some children will complete their work sooner than others, there will be a delay between task completion and the availability of the reinforcing activity. The teacher may use one or both of the following procedures to bridge the time delay between behavior and reinforcement. She may indicate, as each child finishes, "Oh, I see you're finished. You may go to the music corner in just a minute or two." Or she may use a token reinforcement procedure such as a small key representing a key to the music room, or she could use a small black cardboard disk to represent a record, the disk to be exchanged later for a record which the child can play. The tangible objects could possibly serve as secondary reinforcers for the behavior of sitting quietly while the other children were finishing their table assignments.

Other more generalized events previously associated with the later availability of other reinforcers may be used. Visual and auditory signals, tokens, grades, points, stamps, and similar events may all be effective secondary reinforcers if these have been associated previously, after varying time delays, with other reinforcers. As emphasized, the *timing* requirement can be optimized under those conditions in which reinforcing events are natural to the activity itself or in which the child can self-manage his own behavior.

The Frequency of Reinforcement

In addition to the requirement of immediate reinforcement, most rapid learning will occur initially if the desired behavior is reinforced *on every occasion*. In the initial stages of teaching a child a new behavior, the teacher must be prepared to reinforce the behavior immediately each time it or an acceptable approximation occurs. Fulfilling these two requirements is essential for the child with learning difficulties. As such children typically acquire new behaviors at a slow rate, success can best be achieved by a consistent use of these two procedures. Recall that informational feedback concerning progress and success can be reinforcing. To maximize this source of reinforcement, the teacher will find it valuable to organize instructional units into a number of small segments which provide frequent opportunity for specific task accomplishments. Programmed instructional packages can be used for this purpose.

It is true that children do learn many behavior patterns even though reinforcement is infrequent, delayed, or is presented in a haphazard manner. However, such learning will be inefficient and will require considerably more time than would be necessary under more appropriate learning conditions. The child with learning and behavior difficulties can ill afford an inefficient learning environment.

The relationship between the time of a behavioral consequence and the effects which the consequence exerts on behavior provides an explanation for the development of behavior patterns which frequently are puzzling to teachers and parents: "He takes things from the dime store even though he knows he will be caught and punished." "He insists on looking at pictures during naptime even though he loses part of his play period later in the day." In these instances, it appears that having the stolen object or looking at the pictures—the immediate consequences—is quite reinforcing and serves to maintain such behaviors. If negative consequences are quite delayed, it can be assumed that they are too far removed in time to offset the immediate reinforcement effects of the behaviors which the adult views as puzzling. In some instances, though the delayed punishment may be quite severe relative to the apparent value of the positive reinforcer, the critical factor is the time interval between behavior and consequence. Behavior which produces an immediate consequence, especially in children with poorly developed self-management skills, will be more influenced by that consequence than by a delayed consequence. The immediacy factor, especially with children who receive infrequent and inconsistent positive consequences, may become a more critical variable than the magnitude of consequence if delay is long.

Variation in Reinforcer Effects

The reinforcing effect of some events may diminish or disappear following frequent use. Praise may be effective the first few times it is provided in the morning but may gradually diminish with additional use during the day. Playtime and other activities and events may be highly reinforcing if used sparingly but lose their effect if used too often. Task accomplishment or creative contributions may lose some of their positive features if tasks are too simple, if accomplishments are too frequent or too assured, or if creative activities are restricted in scope or by excessive environmental constraints.

The state of *deprivation or satiation* thus will influence the reinforcer effectiveness of numerous events. If a child has not experienced specific reinforcing events for a period of time, these events will become more valuable to the child. Food, social interaction, the opportunity to play with a highly valued toy, and completion of challenging activities represent examples. At the same time, following periods of play, social interaction, frequent task accomplishment, watching TV, or listening to music, the child may become satiated, with the result that these activities may temporarily lose some of their reinforcing value. The teacher must be sensitive to satiation effects and change to alternate reinforcing events when these are noted.

For those reinforcers which do show a satiation effect, it may be possible to re-establish the reinforcing qualities by depriving the child of the events for a period of time. If playtime, looking at a particular book, using a specific box of building blocks, meeting requirements, artistic endeavors, praise, or other forms of social attention show satiation effects, the teacher should withdraw these reinforcers for a period of time. In this manner, these events may be used again with increased effectiveness for limited periods of time.

Token reinforcers are less likely to be influenced by satiation effects as a result of the generalized nature of the token. This is especially true in those instances in which the tokens can be exchanged for a wide variety of other reinforcing events. This feature recommends the use of tokens when tangible events are required to produce best learning.

Type of Responses

A specific reinforcer will be generally more effective in strengthening simple responses than in influencing more complex behavior patterns. The kind and amount of a reinforcing event must be appropriate to the difficulty level of a behavior pattern for optimal learning to occur. There must be a reasonable match between the degree of difficulty of a given task and the type and amount of the contingent consequences. Social approval, for example, may be a valuable event for use in strengthening an attending response but be of insufficient value for use in strengthening more complex behavior such as completion of a series of math problems. Again, the simple and complex nature of behavioral requirements will vary greatly from child to child and, even for any given child, from time to time. A behavior pattern such as sitting for ten minutes and coloring and cutting may be quite simple for one child to learn and will require only brief and infrequent social praise to maintain it. For another child the same behavior pattern may be most difficult and may require much more frequent reinforcers as well as events of a different kind and amount.

As implied earlier, high-value reinforcers arranged by the educator may be needed in the early stages of teaching a child a new behavior pattern. However, as this behavior is developed, other sources of reinforcement more natural to the behavior may serve to maintain it. As this occurs, the teacher-provided reinforcing events can be removed. A child may learn new ways of playing and sharing possessions with other children under a behavior management program in which both tangible and social reinforcement are provided by the teacher. As the child develops these behavior patterns, the consequences provided by the other children may become quite sufficient in maintaining these newly acquired social interaction skills. The tangible and teacher social reinforcement can then be phased out.

Reinforcer Sampling and Exposure

There are numerous events available to the child in the school environment which could potentially serve as reinforcers but which the child has seldom if ever experienced. The child may appear to be disinterested in many aspects of his environment which are reinforcing to many children. The reinforcing qualities of these events, as noted, may be enhanced by insuring that the child observes others enjoying these events. Additionally, the child could be more actively exposed to these events and encouraged to sample or participate in them. For example, a child with little or no experience with finger painting may not want to engage in this activity. After observing others having fun using the paints and being reinforced himself by praise for initial exploration, the child may come to enjoy the activity. Finger painting, in turn, may then be used as a reinforcing event to strengthen other behaviors which the teacher wishes to encourage. Shooting pool, making a voice recording, taking snapshots with a Polaroid camera, developing and printing pictures, and spending time in the library may initially all be low-preference activities with limited interest to the child or youth, yet all may become increasingly interesting to the participants after their exposure to the activities.

After providing just a sample of these activities, the teacher may use them as "opportunities" at a later time. Again, an attempt is made to create a "need" for the activity.

Summary

Generally, the greater the number of times a behavior pattern has resulted in reinforcing consequences, the stronger the behavior. Of course, there is a practical limit beyond which response strength would not be increased. The relationship between the number of reinforced responses and the strength of the response is influenced by the interacting effects of all previously mentioned factors: temporal relationship between response and reinforcer, magnitude and kind of reinforcer, state of deprivation, and the type of response being considered. A reinforcer of high magnitude may be of limited value if delivered a number of times when the individual is satiated in reference to the reinforcing event. Or a behavior pattern may be noticeably strengthened when followed a number of times by a generally uninfluential reinforcer if the individual is in a high state of deprivation in relation to that reinforcer. The practical implication of these multifactor interrelationships is apparent. Optimal learning will generally occur in those situations where all of the factors are maximized, i.e., short time delay, high-preference reinforcer, high-magnitude reinforcer, high state of deprivation. At the same time, these same factors which maximize learning can interfere with continued or persistent high-rate performance of these same response patterns. These factors may become highly specific discriminative cues for subsequent responding and if these change significantly, performance may weaken quickly. In illustration, during teaching a new behavior, it may be reinforced immediately with a high-preference and high-magnitude reinforcer under conditions of deprivation. The behavior continues to occur at a high rate of correctness as long as the setting and reinforcing stimulus components are present. A significant change in any of these, for example, delay in reinforcement following performance or decrease in the magnitude of reinforcer, may result in a rapid decline and perhaps even the cessation of the behavior. Thus, although certain reinforcing events and relationships between environmental conditions and behavior may maximize learning and performance, an educational program must be sensitive to the essential requirements needed for the continuation of this behavior under different conditions. Many programs fail because inadequate attention is provided this problem. Factors relating to schedules of reinforcement, self-reinforcement, and discriminative influence must be considered.

REINFORCEMENT CHARACTERISTICS OF CHILDREN WITH DIFFICULTIES

In evaluating the responsiveness to reinforcing events of children with severe learning and behavior difficulties, various characteristics distinguish them in a relative sense from other children who progress normally in development and adaptation. These are described along with program suggestions for reducing these differences.

1. *As a result of excessive failure experiences and, in some instances, various cognitive behavior limitations, there are likely to be fewer reinforcing events available in the educational environment.* The typical incentive conditions of passing grades, teacher approval, task accomplishment, and so on may not be effective due to the excessive failure which has been experienced by the child. His own efforts have not produced these school-related consequences with sufficient frequency for them to serve as incentives.

Program Implications. A systematic structured program must be provided for developing new reinforcing events and for increasing the effectiveness of existing ones.

2. *The child is likely to require more immediate and frequent reinforcement for effective learning and for consistent use of behaviors presently in his repertoire.* He is less able to maintain effort and persistence over lengthy periods of time without externally presented reinforcing

events. In popular terms he is less able to "delay gratification." Thus, the more immediate the reinforcing event and, when generalized events are used, the more physically durable these events are which bridge the time gap between behavior and the subsequent final reinforcing consequence, the more effective they are.

Program Implications.   The school program must provide for a range of tangible and other immediately available events. A structured program of teaching delay of reinforcement is necessary.

3. *Social reinforcement in its various forms, especially that provided by school personnel, is less likely to be as effective in influencing behavior as are more concrete tangible events.* Those social events associated with school personnel that do have reinforcement qualities are frequently relatively weak and quickly lose their effectiveness if used excessively. Reynolds and Risley* and Bereiter and Engelmann* all suggest that material reinforcers are disproportionately strong and that social reinforcement (attention, praise, approval) from adults is a weak reinforcer among children from culturally disadvantaged homes. Adults appear to be important chiefly as dispensers of material reinforcers. Rosen* and Staats and Butterfield* emphasize that children and adolescents from "culturally deprived" lower-class homes do not acquire the "reinforcer system" to insure successful involvement and learning in the traditional classrooms which rely upon achievement and social reinforcement. Quay et al.,* Patterson,* and Wahler* find social reinforcement from adults to be relatively ineffectual in modifying problem behavior areas of children with negativistic and aggressive behavior patterns.

Reynolds and Risley 1968; Bereiter and Engelmann 1966

Rosen 1956 Staats and Butterfield 1965

Quay et al. 1966; Patterson 1971; Wahler 1972

Shy and isolated children frequently will require strong, tangible reinforcers for the development of social interaction skills. Many of these children not only have a deficit repertoire of social skills but may also find that social attention produces uncomfortable emotional reactions.

Program Implications.   Frequent primary and secondary tangible reinforcers for appropriate behavior must be paired consistently with a range of social events to increase the value of these social events as positive reinforcers.

4. *In some instances, children may be quite responsive to social reinforcement, but only when provided by highly specific individuals.* These "selective responders" are likely to demonstrate anxiety or related negative emotional reactions when not in the presence of the socially reinforcing person or group.* Social attention, praise, or approval, when provided by persons other than, for example, the mother or father or by gang members, will have little reinforcing effect. This type of characteristic frequently is observed in children who exhibit phobic behavior associated

Patterson and Brodsky 1966

with separation anxiety or by the adolescent delinquent who relates only to members of his gang.

> **Program Implications.** The education program must insure consistent association of a variety of other persons with those individuals and events which are reinforcing.

5. *The child will have had less successful exposure to a wide range of activities which for most children hold exciting reinforcement value.* His experiences have been more restrictive and more negative. He is less likely to become curious about or enthusiastic over novel events as newness in his previous experiences has too frequently resulted in unpleasant consequences.

> **Program Implications.** The program should use reinforcer exposure and reinforcer sampling to increase the range of available events which may serve as reinforcing events.

6. *The school environment does not provide on a programmatic basis the types of reinforcing events that are of most value to many adolescents.* The difficult adolescent, for example, may be overly responsive to such events and activities as drugs, alcohol, money, clothes, and the like, excessive free and unsupervised time, and sexual stimulation from members of the opposite or same sex.

> **Program Implications.** A systematic program should be provided for improving the reinforcement value of a variety of more acceptable (and personally enhancing) reinforcing events. Considerable flexibility is required in the educational environment as the potential value of other types of reinforcing events are demonstrated.

7. *The child will be less skillful in using self-reinforcement procedures to initiate, strengthen, and maintain appropriate behaviors.* He will be more under the influence of externally provided events. He will demonstrate less confidence in his ability to meet the requirements of various tasks or interpersonal situations and will be less able, by self-management skills, to offset the resulting apprehension. Children with chronic learning and behavior difficulties have not learned to set realistic learning and performance standards for themselves—those standards which they can attain and which are typically reinforced by the environment—and thus have had less opportunity to develop skills of administering satisfying feedback to themselves. These self-administered events, which for most children are powerful activation and reinforcement events, are relatively weak or nonexistent. Thus the child is excessively dependent upon the

external world to give him direction, to maintain his behavior, and to reinforce him.

> **Program Implications.** A systematic program should be provided for developing self-management skills. (See Chapter 12.)

8. *Fewer achievement-related activities have acquired "intrinsic" reinforcement qualities.* Such events as having correct answers, task accomplishment, creative endeavors, initiating new ventures, competition, and the challenge of difficulties frequently hold limited reinforcement qualities. In fact, many of these, due to previous failure, may hold aversive qualities for the child.

> **Program Implications.** The education program should provide carefully structured experiences using each of these types of activities to insure frequent association with other positive events.

9. *There is considerable variation in the reinforcement effectiveness of specific events as well as in the types of consequences which will stimulate and reinforce the child.* He may fluctuate between requiring rather basic consequences—primary and tangible secondary events—to being susceptible to consequences much higher on a developmental hierarchy of effective reinforcing events—task completion, approval. Teacher approval or opportunity to engage in recreational activities may be most effective on one occasion but be of little or no reinforcing value on another. Additionally, satiation occurs quickly. This seems to fluctuate with the frequent inconsistent emotional-attitudinal behaviors of the child.

> **Program Implications.** A program which insures availability of a wide range and magnitude of potential reinforcing events should be coupled with efforts to influence more consistent positive emotional-attitudinal behavior patterns.

10. *A disproportionate number of events in the child's educational environment have aversive qualities which will influence behavior through negative reinforcement.* Much of the child's lack of interest, noninvolvement, or "poor motivation" may represent active avoidance reactions.

> **Program Implications.** Aversive aspects of the educational environment must be identified and systematically eliminated or reduced by gradual exposure and positive reinforcement given for approach behavior.

11. *A sudden removal or reduction in the availability of reinforcing events may result in excessive depression or rejection.* Morale drops suddenly. Behavior rate and magnitude reduce abruptly. Such change in the reinforcement schedule is apparently a significant secondary aversive event developed through frequent previous experiences of unpredictable or prolonged withdrawal of reinforcement.

Program Implications.   The educational program must avoid sudden changes in availability of reinforcing events.

In summary, these motivational characteristics of children with severe learning and behavior difficulties emphasize the critical need to identify those reinforcing events which do work with each child or adolescent, to use these in teaching him new competency skills, and to initiate a systematic program of creating new sources of positive reinforcement, especially those of a social, "intrinsic," and self-managed nature because these will result in greater personal flexibility and independence.

REFERENCES

Addison, R. M., and Homme, L. E. The reinforcing event (RE) menu. *National Society for Programmed Instruction Journal*, 1966, 5, 8–9.

Allen, K. E., Hart, B. M., Buell, J. S., Harris, F. R., and Wolf, M. M. Effects of social reinforcement on isolate behavior of a nursery school child. *Child Development*, 1964, 35, 511–518.

Ayllon, T., Layman, D., and Kandel, H. A behavioral-educational alternative to drug control of hyperactive children. *Journal of Applied Behavior Analysis*, 1975, 8, 137–146.

Bailey, J. S., Timbers, G. D., Phillips, E. L., and Wolf, M. M. Modification of articulation errors of predelinquents by their peers. *Journal of Applied Behavior Analysis*, 1971, 4, 265–281.

Baker, J. G., Stanish, B., and Fraser, B. Comparative effects of a token economy in nursery school. *Mental Retardation*, 1972, 10, 16–19.

Bandura, A. *Principles of Behavior Modification*. New York: Holt, Rinehart & Winston, 1969.

Becker, W. C. *Parents Are Teachers*. Champaign, Ill.: Research, 1971.

Becker, W. C., Engelmann, S., and Thomas, D. R. *Teaching: A Course in Applied Psychology*. Chicago: Science Research Associates, 1971.

Becker, W. C., Madsen, C. H., Arnold, C. T., and Thomas, D. R. The contingent use of teacher attention and praise in reducing classroom behavior problems. *Journal of Special Education*, 1967, 1, 287–307.

Bereiter, C., and Engelmann, S. *Teaching Disadvantaged Children in the Preschool*. Englewood Cliffs, N.J.: Prentice-Hall, 1966.

Bettelheim, B. *Love Is Not Enough*. New York: Free Press, 1950.

Bijou, S. W. What psychology has to offer education—now. *Journal of Applied Behavior Analysis*, 1970, 3, 65–71.

Bijou, S. W., and Baer, D. M. *Child Development*. Vol. I. *A Systematic and Empirical Theory*. New York: Appleton-Century-Crofts, 1961.

Bijou, S. W., and Sturges, P. T. Positive reinforcers for experimental studies with children: consumables and manipulatables. *Child Development*, 1959, 30, 151–170.

Birnbrauer, J. S., and Lawler, J. Token reinforcement for learning. *Mental Retardation*, 1964, 2, 275–279.

Blackham, G. J., and Silberman, A. *Modification of Child Behavior*. Belmont, Calif.: Wadsworth, 1971.

Blackham, G. J., and Silberman, A. *Modification of Child and Adolescent Behavior*. (2nd Ed.) Belmont, Calif.: Wadsworth, 1975.

Breyer, N. L., and Allen, G. J. Effects of implementing a token economy on teacher attending behavior. *Journal of Applied Behavior Analysis*, 1975, 8, 373–380.

Brigham, T. A., Graubard, P. S., and Stans, A. Analysis of the effects of sequential reinforcement contingencies on aspects of composition. *Journal of Applied Behavior Analysis*, 1972, 5, 421–429.

Broden, M., Hall, R., Dunlap, A., and Clark, R. Effects of teacher attention and a token reinforcement system in a junior high school special education class. *Exceptional Children*, 1970, 36, 341–349.

Buehler, R. E., Patterson, G. R., and Furniss, J. M. The reinforcement of behavior in institutional settings. *Behavior Research and Therapy*, 1966, 4, 157–167.

Bushell, D., Wrobel, P. A., and Michaelis, M. L. Applying "group" contingencies to the classroom study behavior of preschool children. *Journal of Applied Behavior Analysis*, 1968, 1, 55–61.

Chadwick, B. A., and Day, R. C. Systematic reinforcement: Academic performance of underachieving students. *Journal of Applied Behavior Analysis*, 1971, 4, 311–319.

Christopherson, E. R., Arnold, C. M., Hill, D. W., and Quilitch, H. R. The home point system: Token reinforcement procedures for application by parents of children with behavior problems. *Journal of Applied Behavior Analysis*, 1972, 5, 485–497.

Christy, P. R. Does use of tangible rewards with individual children affect peer observers? *Journal of Applied Behavior Analysis*, 1975, 8, 187–196.

Clarizio, H. F. *Toward Positive Classroom Discipline*. New York: John Wiley, 1971.

Clark, H. B., Boyd, S. B., and Macrae, J. W. A classroom program teaching disadvantaged youths to write biographic information. *Journal of Applied Behavior Analysis*, 1975, 8, 67–75.

Cowen, E. L., and Lorion, R. P. Which kids are helped? *Journal of Special Education*, 1974, 8, 187–192.

Daley, M. F. The "reinforcement menu": Finding effective reinforcers. In J. D. Krumboltz and C. E. Thoresen (Eds.) *Behavioral Counseling*. New York: Holt, Rinehart & Winston, 1969. Pp. 43–45.

Drabman, R. S., and Lahey, B. B. Feedback in classroom behavior modification: Effects on the target and her classmates. *Journal of Applied Behavior Analysis*, 1974, 7, 591–598.

Evans, G. W., and Oswalt, G. L. Acceleration of academic progress through the manipulation of peer influence. *Behavior Research and Therapy*, 1968, 6, 189–195.

Festinger, L. *A Theory of Cognitive Dissonance*. Evanston, Ill.: Row, Peterson, 1957.

Fink, W. T., and Carnine, D. W. Control of arithmetic errors using informational feedback and graphing. *Journal of Applied Behavior Analysis*, 1975, 8, 461.

Gardner, W. I. Effects of failure on intellectually retarded and normal boys. *American Journal of Mental Deficiency*, 1966, 70, 899–902.

Garris, R. P. Developmental reinforcement and education. Paper presented at the Second Scientific Conference on Learning Disabilities, Brussels, Belgium, 1975.

Grieger, R. N., Mordock, J. B., and Breyer, N. General guidelines for conducting behavior modification programs in public school settings. *Journal of School Psychology*, 1970, 8, 259–266.

Hall, R. V., Lund, D., and Jackson, D. Effects of teacher attention on study behavior. *Journal of Applied Behavior Analysis*, 1968, 1, 1–12.

Hamblin, R. L., Buckholdt, D., Ferritor, D., Kozloff, M., and Blackwell, L. *The Humanization Processes: A Social, Behavioral Analysis of Children's Problems*. New York: John Wiley, 1971.

Hart, B. M., Reynolds, N. J., Baer, D. M., Brawley, E. K., and Harris, F. R. Effects of contingent and non-contingent social reinforcement of the cooperative play of a preschool child. *Journal of Applied Behavior Analysis*, 1968, 1, 73–76.

Hart, B. M., and Risley, T. R. Establishing use of descriptive adjectives in the spontaneous speech of disadvantaged preschool children. *Journal of Applied Behavior Analysis*, 1968, 1, 109–120.

Heitzman, A. J. Effects of a token reinforcement system on the reading and arithmetic skills learning of migrant primary school pupils. *Journal of Educational Research*, 1970, 63, 455–458.

Hewett, F. M. and Forness, S. R. *Education of Exceptional Learners*. Boston: Allyn and Bacon, 1974.

Homme, L. *How to Use Contingency Contracting in the Classroom*. Champaign, Ill.: Research, 1970.

Homme, L. E., deBaca, P. C., Devine, J. V., Steinhorst, R., and Rickert, E. J. Use of the Premack principle in controlling the behavior of nursery school children. *Journal of Experimental Analysis of Behavior*, 1963, 6, 544.

Jensen, A. R. Social class and verbal learning. In M. Duetsch, I. Katz, and A. R. Jensen (Eds.) *Social Class, Race, and Psychological Development*. New York: Holt, Rinehart & Winston, 1968.

Kanfer, F. H., and Phillips, J. S. *Learning Foundations of Behavior Therapy*. New York: John Wiley, 1970.

Kazdin, A. E. *Behavior Modification in Applied Settings*. Homewood, Ill.: Dorsey, 1975.

Kazdin, A. E., and Boatzin, R. R. The token economy: An evaluative review. *Journal of Applied Behavior Analysis*, 1972, 5, 343–372.

Kirby, F. D., and Toler, H. C. Modification of preschool isolate behavior: A case study. *Journal of Applied Behavior Analysis*, 1970, 3, 309–314.

Koegel, R. L., and Rincover, A. Treatment of psychotic children in a classroom environment: 1. Learning in a large group. *Journal of Applied Behavior Analysis*, 1974, 7, 45–59.

Koppitz, E. M. *Children with Learning Disabilities: A Five Year Follow-Up Study*. New York: Grune and Stratton, 1971.

Kozloff, M. A. *Reaching the Autistic Child: A Parent Training Program*. Champaign, Ill.: Research, 1973.

Lattal, K. A. Contingency management of tooth-brushing behavior in a summer camp for children. *Journal of Applied Behavior Analysis*, 1969, 2, 195–198.

Levin, G. R., and Simmons, J. J. Response to food and praise by emotionally disturbed boys. *Psychological Reports*, 1962, 11, 539–546.

Liberman, R. P., Ferris, C., Salgado, P., and Salgado, J. Replication of the achievement place model in California. *Journal of Applied Behavior Analysis*, 1975, 8, 287–299.

Lovaas, O. I. A behavior therapy approach to the treatment of childhood schizophrenia. *Symposium on Child Development*. (Vol. 1.) Minneapolis: University of Minnesota Press, 1967. Pp. 108–159.

Lovaas, O. I., Freitag, G., Gold., V.J., and Kassorla, I. C. Experimental studies in childhood schizophrenia: Analysis of self-destructive behavior. *Journal of Experimental Child Psychology*, 1965, 2, 67–84.

Lovitt, T. C., and Curtiss, K. A. Effects of manipulating an antecedent event on mathematics response rate. *Journal of Applied Behavior Analysis*, 1968, 1, 329–333.

Lovitt, T. C., Lovitt, A. O., Eaton, M. D., and Kirkwood, M. The deceleration of inappropriate comments by a natural consequence. *Journal of School Psychology*, 1973, 11, 149–157.

Luria, A. R. *The Role of Speech in the Regulation of Normal and Abnormal Behavior*. New York: Liveright, 1961.

MacMillan, D. L. *Behavior Modification in Education*. New York: MacMillan, 1973.

MacMillan, D. L., and Forness, S. R. Behavior modification: Limitations and liabilities. *Exceptional Children*, 1970, 37, 291–297.

Madsen, C. H., Becker, W. C., and Thomas, D. R. Rules, praise, and ignoring: Elements of elementary classroom control. *Journal of Applied Behavior Analysis*, 1968, 1, 139–150.

Maehr, M. L. Learning theory, some limitations of the application of reinforcement theory to education. *School and Society*, 1968, 96, 108–110.

Marx, M. H. (Ed.) *Learning: Theories*. New York: MacMillan, 1970.

McKenzie, H. S., Clark, M., Wolf, M. M., Kothera,

R., and Benson, C. Behavior modification of children with learning disabilities using grades as tokens and allowances as backup reinforcers. *Exceptional Children*, 1968, 34, 745–752.

Metz, J. R. Conditioning generalized imitation in autistic children. *Journal of Experimental Child Psychology*, 1965, 2, 389–399.

Mordock, J. B. *The Other Child: An Introduction to Exceptionality*. New York: Harper, 1975.

O'Leary, K. D., and Becker, W. C. Behavior modification of an adjustment class: A token reinforcement program. *Exceptional Children*, 1967, 33, 637–642.

O'Leary, K. D., and Drabman, R. Token reinforcement in the classroom: A review. *Psychology Bulletin*, 1971, 75, 379–398.

O'Leary, K. D., Kaufman, K. F., Kass, R. E., and Drabman, R. S. The effects of loud and soft reprimands on the behavior of disruptive students. *Exceptional Children*, 1970, 37, 145–155.

Osborne, J. G. Free-time as a reinforcer in the management of classroom behavior. *Journal of Applied Behavior Analysis*, 1969, 2, 113–118.

Patterson, G. R. *Families*. Champaign, Ill.: Research, 1971.

Patterson, G. R., and Brodsky, G. A behavior modification programme for a child with multiple problem behaviors. *Journal of Child Psychology and Psychiatry*, 1966, 7, 277–295.

Peterson, R. F., and Peterson, L. R. The use of positive reinforcement in the control of self-destructive behavior in a retarded boy. *Journal of Experimental Child Psychology*, 1968, 6, 351–360.

Phillips, E. L. Achievement Place: Token reinforcement procedures in a home-style rehabilitation setting for "predelinquent" boys. *Journal of Applied Behavior Analysis*, 1968, 1, 213–223.

Phillips, E. L., Phillips, E. A., Fixsen, D. L., and Wolf, M. M. Achievement Place: Modification of the behaviors of pre-delinquent boys within a token economy. *Journal of Applied Behavior Analysis*, 1971, 4, 45–59.

Premack, D. Toward empirical behavior laws: I. Positive reinforcement. *Psychological Review*, 1959, 66, 219–233.

Quay, H. C., Werry, J. S., McQueen, M., and Sprague, R. L. Remediation of the conduct problem child in the special class setting. *Exceptional Children*, 1966, 32, 509–515.

Reynolds, N. J., and Risley, J. R. The role of social and material reinforcers in increasing talking of a disadvantaged preschool child. *Journal of Applied Behavior Analysis*, 1968, 1, 253–262.

Risley, T. R., and Wolf, M. Establishing functional speech in echolalic children. *Behavior Research and Therapy*, 1967, 5, 73–88.

Rosen, R. C. The achievement syndrome: A psychocultural dimension of social stratification. *American Sociological Review*, 1956, 21, 203–211.

Rosenberg, H. Contingency management for the educable retarded. *Journal for Special Educators of the Mentally Retarded*, 1971, 8, 46–50.

Ross, J. A., and O'Driscoll, J. Long-term retention after use of a free-time contingency to increase spelling accuracy. *Behavior Research and Therapy*, 1972, 10, 1975.

Sailor, W., Guess, D., Rutherford, G., and Baer, D. Control of tantrum behavior by operant techniques during experimental verbal training. *Journal of Applied Behavior Analysis*, 1968, 1, 237–243.

Skinner, B. F. *Science and Human Behavior*. New York: Macmillan, 1953.

Skinner, B. F. *Contingencies of Reinforcement: A Theoretical Analysis*. New York: Appleton-Century-Crofts, 1969.

Smeets, P. M., and Striefel, S. The effects of different reinforcement conditions on the test performance of multihandicapped deaf children. *Journal of Applied Behavior Analysis*, 1975, 8, 83–89.

Spradlin, J. E., and Girardeau, F. L. The behavior of moderately and severely retarded persons. In N. R. Ellis (Ed.) *International Review of Research in Mental Retardation*. (Vol. 1.) New York: Academic, 1966. Pp. 257–298.

Staats, A. W. *Child Learning, Intelligence, and Personality*. New York: Harper, 1971.

Staats, A. W. *Social Behaviorism*. Homewood, Ill.: Dorsey, 1975.

Staats, A., and Butterfield, W. Treatment of non-reading in a culturally deprived juvenile delinquent: An application of learning principles. *Child Development*, 1965, 36, 925–942.

Staats, A., Minke, K., Goodwin, W., and Landeen,

J. Cognitive behavior modification: "Motivated learning" reading treatment with subprofessional therapy-technicians. *Behavior Research and Therapy*, 1967, 5, 283–299.

Stuart, R. B. Behavioral contracting with the families of delinquents. *Journal of Behavior Therapy and Experimental Psychiatry*, 1971, 2, 1–11.

Sulzer, B., and Mayer, G. R. *Behavior Modification Procedures for School Personnel*. Hinsdale, Ill.: Dryden, 1972.

Surratt, P. R., Ulrich, R. E., and Hawkins, R. P. An elementary student as a behavioral engineer. *Journal of Applied Behavior Analysis*, 1969, 2, 213–223.

Truax, C. B., and Carkhuff, R. R. *Toward Effective Counseling and Psychotherapy: Training and Practice*. Chicago: Aldine, 1967.

Twardosz, S., and Sajwaj, T. Multiple effects of a procedure to increase sitting in a hyperactive retarded boy. *Journal of Applied Behavior Analysis*, 1972, 5, 73–78.

Van Houten, R., Hill, S., and Parsons, M. An analysis of a performance feedback system: The effects of timing and feedback, public posting, and praise upon academic performance and peer interaction. *Journal of Applied Behavior Analysis*, 1975, 8, 449–457.

Wahler, R. G. Some ecological problems in child behavior modification. In S. W. Bijou and E. Ribes-Inesta (Eds.) *Behavior Modification: Issues and Extensions*. New York: Academic, 1972. Pp. 7–18.

Walker, H. M., and Buckley, N. K. *Token Reinforcement Techniques*. Eugene, Oregon: E-B Press, 1974.

Watson, L. S. *How to Use Behavior Modification with Mentally Retarded and Autistic Children*. Columbus, Ohio: Behavior Modification Technology, 1972.

Weathers, L., and Liberman, R. P. Contingency contracting with families and delinquent adolescents. *Behavior Therapy*, 1975, 6, 356–366.

White, R. W. Motivation reconsidered: The concept of competence. In I. J. Gordon (Ed.) *Human Development: Readings in Research*. Glenview, Ill.: Scott, Foresman, 1965.

Wiesen, A. E., and Watson, E. Elimination of attention seeking behavior in a retarded child. *Ameri-*

can *Journal of Mental Deficiency*, 1967, 72, 50–52.

Wolf, M., Giles, D., and Hall, R. Experiments with token reinforcement in a remedial classroom. *Behavior Research and Therapy*, 1968, 6, 51–64.

Wolf, M., Risley, T., Johnston, M., Harris, F., and Allen, E. Application of operant conditioning procedure to the behavior problems of an autistic child: A follow-up and extension. *Behavior Research and Therapy*, 1967, 5, 103–111.

Wolf, M., Risley, T., and Mees, H. Application of operant conditioning procedures to the behavior problems of an autistic child. *Behavior Research and Therapy*, 1964, 1, 305–312.

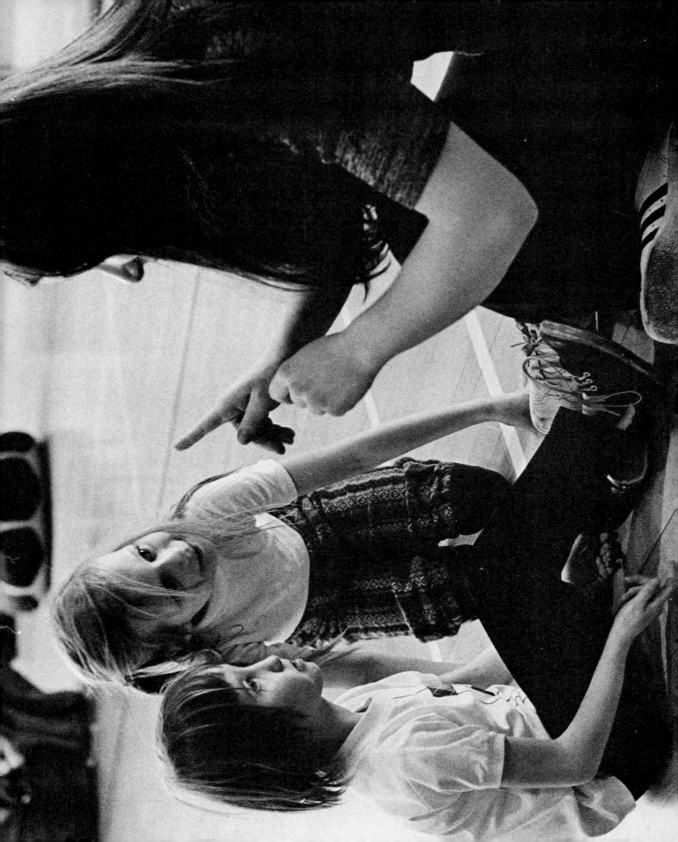

9

Influencing the Development and Persistence of Behavior Characteristics

The use of reinforcement procedures to strengthen behavior obviously depends upon the initial occurrence of the desired behavior. Before a child can be reinforced for correctly labeling a picture, solving addition and subtraction problems, or for correctly matching colors, certain behaviors must occur. Before a child can learn to verbally label a blue color as "blue" when presented with the request, "What color is this?" he must be able to say "blue." If the child can verbalize the concept, the teaching task is to get the behavior to occur consistently under the right conditions, i.e., whenever a blue light or object is presented and he is asked to identify the color or to describe the object. But if the child is unable to say "blue," the most powerful reinforcing event would be of no value to teaching the child to verbally label a blue crayon.

Before an adolescent can become independent in fulfilling his assignments or in making and retaining friends, he first must have the numerous separate component behaviors involved in these rather complex skills. Most academic and social behaviors are comprised of several smaller response units which together serve a specific function for the child. Learning psychologists refer to this integrated sequence as a *chain* of separate responses that become linked together due to their functional qualities. That is, particular combinations of behaviors become linked

277

together in sequence when such combinations are followed by positive or negative reinforcement. Other combinations, such as those serving no consistent reinforcement purpose, do not get linked together in any reliable manner.

TEACHING A NEW BEHAVIOR

If the component behaviors which comprise most prosocial behavior patterns are not in the child's repertoire in the desired form, a procedure called *behavior shaping* may be used to encourage their development. In this procedure successive approximations of the desired behavior are reinforced. Behaviors which the child *does* demonstrate and which have *some* similarity to the behavior to be developed are reinforced in the presence of specific cues. The desired behavior is shaped gradually by successively reinforcing closer and closer approximations of this desired goal. The disruptive and hyperactive adolescent is reinforced initially for any effort to be attentive to a task. Gradually, the child is required to be more precise in his attending behavior prior to reinforcement. The successive changes may be slight in some cases. Keen observation is required by the teacher to insure that any changes, however small, are provided reinforcement.

The initial approximations of the desired behaviors which are being reinforced may be quite different from the final educational objective. But they must be reinforced since the attempts form the basis for strengthening similar behaviors which may follow and are improvements or closer approximations of the desired goal behavior. As the stages in the shaping procedure progress, the behaviors for which reinforcement is provided are increasingly similar to the goal behavior. The approximation sequence which is reinforced is not left to chance. The child may require various prods, physical guidance, prompts, prosthetic devices, or highly redundant cues to insure continuous movement toward the goal behavior. Behaviors which are not increasingly similar are not reinforced; those which reflect improvements are. The child with learning and behavior difficulties frequently fails to learn when the educational program requires too much behavioral change at a given time. The child or adolescent is unable to make the transition from what he does presently to what the program is requiring. The child might be quite capable of learning new patterns of behavior or more complex combinations of present behavior *if the learning tasks were presented in a sequential order in small steps.* The shaping procedure provides the teacher with a means of turning failure into success.

Inappropriate as well as appropriate behavior may be shaped inadvertently by the process of reinforcement of successive approximations. For example, aggressive destructive behavior is not acquired suddenly. Rather, such behavior is acquired gradually through a complex series of steps extending over a long period of time. If reinforcement in the form of attention or removal of aversive conditions is provided on numerous occasions following loud aggressive behavior, such reinforcement sustains the behavior.

Procedure of Behavior Shaping

Behavior shaping as a teaching procedure consists of the following steps:

1. *Setting precise behavioral objectives, including acceptable criterion levels.* Examples would include: "Cathy will look at me on every occasion when requested to do so." "Donna will speak loudly enough on every occasion for the teacher to understand her request." "Dan will say the word 'ball' on every occasion when shown a ball and asked to name it." "On every occasion Helen will dress herself when asked to do so." It is desirable to inform the child of the behavioral objectives, including both what she will do and the level of desired performance. Whenever appropriate, the child should participate with the teacher in deciding upon the new behavioral skills to be developed.

2. *Identifying present-related behaviors.* These are the skills or behaviors which the child presently engages in and which will provide the *initial starting point* from which to teach—shape—the goal behavior. "Sue sits at the work table for a short period when the teacher stands or sits beside her." Sitting for longer periods of time and maintaining this behavior with less and less teacher prompting will be shaped gradually by successively reinforcing larger and larger segments of this behavior pattern. "Don occasionally verbalizes the sound *be* when shown a ball and asked, 'What is this?' " This will form the basis for gradual shaping of the sounds comprising the word "ball."

3. *Specifying the elements of the teaching program.* The precise activities of the teacher are described. What will the teacher do to get the child's attention and to insure that he will engage in the desired behavior?

4. *Specifying the reinforcing events to be used and the manner in which these will be provided.* What will be done following the desired behavior to insure that it will be strengthened in the presence of the appropriate cues? Examples would include: "Al will be given animated praise immediately following every occasion of the desired behavior." "Training in dressing will be held just prior to meals in order to optimize the value of food items which will be used to reinforce dressing behavior." "Barbara will be given recognition by the male teacher whenever she makes any effort to speak out in class."

5. *Developing a tentative outline of the steps in the program.* Complex skills are described as a series of smaller intermediate steps. The behavioral objective may represent a rather circumscribed behavior such as saying the word "ball" when shown a ball and asked, "What is this?" In this case the program may move through a series of steps, each of which represents closer verbal approximations of the desired pronunciation. The steps should be small enough to insure continuous success and at the same time large enough to insure efficient learning.

The initial listing of steps of a shaping program is viewed as only tentative, as a specific child may be unable to move from one designated step to another in the manner outlined by the teacher. In some instances the steps may be too difficult, and then the task will be analyzed and restructured into small steps. In other instances, the child may be able to skip a number of steps as he begins to experience success.

After the teaching program has begun, it is important that the child experience frequent success and that he is reinforced promptly and consistently for acceptable approximations. If the child is achieving success, movement to the next step representing more complex behavior should follow. As soon as the approximation occurs and is reinforced, a more complex approximation should be required. If the behavioral criterion (approximation) is set too high and the child is unsuccessful, the educator should return to a preceding easier step and reinforce this behavior a few more times. In some instances, it will be necessary to add new steps which represent less complex transitions. In any case, the child should be moved continuously from the starting behavior toward an increasingly similar approximation of the final behavioral objective goal.

Johnston et al. 1966   Johnston et al.* provide illustration of a shaping procedure to strengthen vigorous play activity on a piece of climbing equipment in a young child who was physically inactive:

Initially the child almost never used the climbing frame. The teachers began providing social reinforcement for successive approximations of the desired play activity. Whenever the child approached or walked by the climbing frame, a teacher would smile and speak to him. She terminated her attention when he moved away. The criterion for reinforcement was gradually changed to required closer and closer proximity. The child eventually touched the frame and was soon climbing on it. Following this activity, reinforcement was provided only for climbing and remaining for longer periods on the frame. Within a short period of time the child was engaging in typical vigorous play activity on the climbing frame. By skillful use of the shaping procedure, the teacher attained her desired goal without having to resort to other procedures involving persuading, convincing, pushing, or requiring him to engage in an activity that apparently was of little initial interest to him.

DEVELOPMENT OF COMPLEX BEHAVIOR PATTERNS

Most behavioral objectives of an education program will represent more complex behavior patterns. The desired behavior pattern may be comprised of a number of independent or discrete behaviors, some or all of which may be in the child's repertoire. The procedure of task analysis may be used by which a final complex behavior is broken down into its component parts. (The process of task analysis of academic tasks is discussed in some detail in Chapter 16.) These individual behavior units may have been taught the child through a shaping procedure. In this case the educational program seeks to integrate or chain the simpler segments together into a more complex pattern of behavior. The program is described in a series of steps or segments which increasingly approximate the final behavioral objective. These programs may be concerned with such objectives as following classroom routine, being assertive, successfully engaging in language lessons requiring a variety of separate skills, developing independence in lunchtime activities (sitting, eating, cleaning table, remaining at table until teacher dismisses), demonstrating skill in complex mathematical solution, approaching and talking to strangers, and following directions involving use of various separate skills. These examples emphasize that any desired behavior pattern can be translated into behavior shaping and chaining (teaching) programs.

A child may know how to sit in a chair, to work on a puzzle, to sit and begin work when requested to do so, to put his completed tasks away, and to remain at his work desk until requested to dress for outdoor play. However, considerable teacher monitoring is required to get each of these behaviors to occur and to insure smooth progression from beginning to end. As the child has all the behavior components in his repertoire, the program objective becomes that of chaining these into an independent integrated pattern.

Gagné* has emphasized the conditions within the learner and the conditions in the environment which are essential for effective learning of complex sequences of individual behavior components. These include:

Gagné 1970

1. The individual behavior components must be in the child's repertoire.
2. These individual behavior components must occur sequentially in the correct order.
3. The individual behavior components must be performed in close time succession.
4. The sequence of responses must be repeated to insure that the rough spots are eliminated and that forgetting is prevented.
5. The sequence of behaviors must be followed immediately by reinforcing consequences. (If reinforcement is not forthcoming, the final component is not acquired and the functional qualities of previous components are lost.)

Beginning with the Final Link in the Chain

In integrating behavior components into more complex patterns, the goal is to bring more behavior segments under the influence of a final reinforcing consequence. Learning is frequently facilitated by beginning with the behavior that immediately precedes the final reinforcing consequence. This process is called *backward chaining*. As this final behavior segment is strengthened, longer and more complex sequences of behaviors are gradually added prior to the final behavior segment which results in the desired consequence. In a picture puzzle with six parts, the puzzle is presented to the child with the final piece removed. As the child is able to place this piece successfully and receive reinforcement on a few occasions, two pieces are removed. Following successful completion of these two pieces, the puzzle is presented to the child with three, then four, then five, and finally six pieces removed. The reinforcing consequence, which is presented following correct placement of the final piece, serves to strengthen the entire sequence from beginning to end.

In a similar fashion, the last bead in a string pattern, the last part of a picture to be colored, the last segment of a figure to be drawn, or the last toy to be put onto the toy shelf may be the behavior segment initially presented to the child. As he is able to complete these final steps of a more complex behavior pattern, he is provided an increasingly larger number of steps to complete prior to receiving reinforcement. Each step serves as a signal for the next steps which eventually result in the reinforcer.

In teaching a "mentally retarded" child to dress himself, Larsen and Bricker* suggested:

Larsen and Bricker 1968

> We would not give him his pants and tell him to put them on. Instead we would start by putting them on his legs and pulling them almost all the way up, teaching him to just pull them up the last inch or so to start with. Gradually we would teach him to pull them up further and further, until he could pull them up from the floor. Then we would start teaching him to put on one leg of the pants, after we had already put the other one on for him. Finally, we would teach him to put on both legs and pull them up by himself. [p. 24]

Forward Chaining

Of course, it may not be possible or feasible to begin with the final behavior component. The teacher would begin with the first behavior segment and add others from beginning to end by promoting the proper order. Reinforcement is provided for larger and larger component sequences until the entire behavior pattern is maintained by the final reinforcing event. In other behavior patterns, the teacher may use a combination of backward and forward chaining.

The following is an illustration of a more complex behavior pattern developed by initial reinforcement of less complex segments and gradual integration into the desired goal:

BEHAVIORAL OBJECTIVE: The child will sit at his desk when work time is announced, will attend to instructions provided the group, will complete the ten perceptual-motor tasks presented, and will bring his completed work to the teacher.

REINFORCEMENT PROCEDURE: The child will be provided a "smiling face" sticker to put on his completed work and social reinforcement or praise from the teacher. Five "smiling faces" may be exchanged at the end of the class period for a variety of activities such as listening to music, looking at a slide viewer, taking a Polaroid picture, or finger painting.

STEP 1. The child is given one task and as the teacher stands watching he completes it correctly. He is praised immediately and given a "smiling face" sticker. He is given a second and then a third, fourth, and fifth task while the teacher is standing near by. She reinforces each as it is finished. As the child receives the fifth sticker and thus fills his sticker card, the teacher takes him to the reinforcement area and permits him to select a desired activity in exchange for the filled card. She verbalizes the relationship between the good work, the "smiling faces," and the desired consequences.

STEP 2. The child completes two problems prior to receiving a sticker. He now raises his hand when finished and the teacher comes to his desk. The number of problems required for each "smiling face" is shifted to three, four, and then five.

STEP 3. The child completes five problems and then brings them to the teacher's desk prior to reinforcement.

STEP 4. The child sits at his desk at work time and attends to group instruction. He completes the five problems, brings these to the teacher's desk, and receives a "smiling face" consequence.

STEP 5. The number of problems required prior to reinforcement is gradually shifted to ten.

STEP 6. The child now sits at his desk when work time is announced, attends to group instructions, completes his task, and takes it to the teacher's desk upon completion.

The entire sequence of behavior is being maintained by the final reinforcing consequences provided by the teacher. Gradually increasing the requirements results in the final reinforcing event influencing and maintaining *more and more* behavior. Once the behavioral objective has been reached, teacher-provided reinforcement should be continued for a sufficient period of time to insure that the behavior will be maintained. Eventually, this behavior pattern will become a component of more and more complex and extensive "independent behavior" patterns.

If difficulty is experienced in using these procedures, the educator should ask the following:

1. *Am I moving from one step to another too rapidly?* If so, the preceding behavior has not been reinforced sufficiently to develop adequate strength. The child soon forgets or becomes involved in other competing behaviors.
2. *Am I requiring too great a behavioral improvement as I move from one step to another?* If so, the child will make little progress and will become highly frustrated over his lack of success.
3. *Are my steps too simple?* If so, the program is inefficient and the child may become bored and refuse to participate.

PROMPTING PROCEDURES

A desired behavior or pattern of behavior, or approximations of these, may be in the child's repertoire but may occur only infrequently at the right time or place. In these instances the child or adolescent may be able to behave appropriately if shown or told what to do. There is no necessity in such cases for shaping by reinforcing successive approximations of the desired behavior. The tactic in these cases is to arrange the prompting and reinforcing components of the environment to insure that the behavior will occur and will be reinforced—strengthened—under appropriate conditions.

In these cases, as well as in the previously discussed instances in which some initial approximation of the desired behavior is needed, various techniques are available to encourage the child to engage in the behavior which then can be reinforced under the right cue conditions. These prompting procedures include:

Visual modeling and other types of visual cueing.
Verbal instruction, verbal modeling, and other types of auditory cueing.
Physical guidance.
Precise environmental arrangements.

Those initial prompting stimulus events, in isolation or in combination, needed to insure occurrence of the desired behavior are used in addition to the usual or natural discriminative events which eventually will come to influence the behavior. In using any one or combination of the prompting procedures, the objective is to insure the occurrence of the desired response so that its relationship to specific discriminative conditions may be strengthened. As the behavior gains strength, the prompts become redundant and unnecessary and are gradually removed. The child, for example, may be shown what to do—visual modeling—as the teacher describes what is expected—verbal instruction. The teacher may then assist the child in engaging in the desired behavior—physical guidance. These prompts are all phased out as the child becomes able to behave under appropriate external and internal cue influence.

Becker et al.* describe two kinds of prompts that may be used to insure discriminated responding. First are those prompts which aid in the discrimination of the relevant cues, these cues serving as signals for the occurrence of the behavior being taught. These "S-prompts" are used to make the discrimination easier. In teaching reading, for example, silent letters may be made smaller than the other letters to prompt their silentness, or an arrow may be placed under the letters of a word to direct the child to read sounds from left to right as is done in the Distar Reading Program.* The second type of prompt is the "R-prompt" which facilitates the occurrence of the desired response in the presence of the appropriate cue. The child's hand may be guided as he traces the letters in "boy."

Becker et al. 1971

Engelmann and Bruner 1971

Visual Prompting

Children can learn a behavior pattern more quickly if guided in a manner that insures few errors. Practice does not make for effective or efficient learning if excessive errors are being made. Prompts can be used to facilitate desired behavior and then gradually removed as the child is able to behave appropriately in the presence of more natural cues. For example, while teaching a child to write letters or to draw geometric forms, considerable visual and mechanical prompts may be provided initially and then gradually removed as the skills develop. In teaching a child to color within the lines of a drawing, heavy thread may be used as an outline of the picture. The size of the thread can be progressively reduced as the child learns to color within the lines.

Auditory Prompting

For any particular child, those prompting procedures are selected which hold greatest promise of facilitating the occurrence of the desired behavior under desired cue conditions. Some children are able to follow verbal directions and can produce the desired behavior patterns after these are described to them. "John, when the bell rings, bring your paper to me." The teacher then taps the bell and reinforces John as he hands the paper to her. After a few trials, the prompting verbal instruction is no longer needed because John has learned that when the bell rings he is to hand his paper to the teacher. As another example, Tammy is asked to label a red ball but is unable to do so. The teacher then provides the prompt, "Tammy say 'red ball,'" as she places a red ball on the table. As the child says "red ball" when the red ball is presented, the teacher smiles warmly and exclaims "That's great, Tammy." The teacher gradually fades her R-prompts as Tammy is able to respond correctly to the question, "What is this?"

Herman and Tramontana 1971   Herman and Tramontana* used precise verbal instructions to get children with high rates of disruptive behavior to engage in appropriate behavior during a rest period. The verbal instructions and the reinforcement provided following the occurrence of the instructed behavior resulted in a rapid increase in the rate of the desired behavior. To emphasize the necessity for reinforcement once the behavior does occur, these teachers provided instruction without reinforcement. The disruptive behavior quickly reappeared.

Physical Guidance

In other instances various forms of physical guidance may prove valuable. The teacher may take the child's hand and move him through a cutting, coloring, or drawing task as the appropriate stimulus is provided. The physical guidance is gradually removed as the child's behavior begins to occur in the presence of the verbal request to engage in these behaviors.

A teacher may request, "Sue, look at me." The child may continue in her stereotyped self-stimulation and give no indication that the verbal request had any influence on her. If the teacher deems it valuable to teach Sue to look at her when requested to do so, the accompanying procedures may be attempted:

Appropriate Cue Condition	Prompt	Behavior	Consequence
(1) Cue: "Sue, look at me."		Sue continues play and does not look at teacher.	No teacher-provided consequences.
(2) Cue: "Sue, look at me" is accompanied by the prompt.	Teacher gently places her hand under Sue's chin and moves her toward eye contact with teacher.	Child momentarily looks at teacher under these prompting conditions.	Teacher immediately places candy in child's mouth, smiles at her, and exclaims, "Good girl, Sue."

(3) This sequence is repeated a few times. With each succeeding request the amount of physical guidance is reduced.

(4) In order to increase the likelihood of eye contact during the physical guidance prompt, the

teacher begins to hold the candy close to and directly in front of her own eyes. As the child looks toward the candy, eye contact is made and the child is reinforced immediately.

(5) This visual prompt is gradually removed as the child begins to look at the teacher's face, including eye contact, when requested to do so.

(6) The final behavioral objective of Sue looking at teacher when requested to do so is maintained by frequent social reinforcement.

Visual and Auditory Modeling

It is frequently valuable for the teacher or peer to *demonstrate or model* the desired behavior as the child observes. This exposure to the desired behavior should also include a demonstration of the consequences of the desired behavior as it occurs. Immediately following observation, the child should be prompted to engage in the desired behavior and be reinforced immediately. The modeling procedure may be supplemented by other prompting tactics such as verbal or gestural instructions and physical guidance.

Many social and sex-type behaviors are acquired through observation of such behaviors in other people. The teacher may demonstrate through role playing the components of behavior patterns such as walking gracefully, eating correctly, applying makeup, correct posture, approaching a stranger, and being polite. These prompts are removed as the behavior patterns begin to be cued by more natural events.

Lahey* and Lahey and Lawrence* modeled the use of descriptive adjectives for preschool through fourth-grade children from low- and middle-income families, as other examples, and found a marked increase in the frequency of this aspect of speech. The immediate increase in the use of descriptive adjectives other than the specific ones used by the teacher suggested that the children already knew the words but did not frequently use them. To modify various articulation difficulties of young adolescents, Bailey et al.* successfully used "predelinquent" peers to provide desired speech models. *Lahey 1971; Lahey and Lawrence 1974*

Bailey et al. 1971

Precise Environmental Arrangement

A related procedure for increasing the likelihood of occurrence of desired behavior is to restrict the likelihood of occurrence of behaviors which may compete with the desired one. The development of skills of attending to and persisting at a task may be facilitated by placing the child in a highly restricted environment in which distracting auditory and visual stimulation are minimal. The child may be placed in a small training booth with a teacher, or a small screen may be placed around the child's desk during times when he is working on table tasks.

Shores and Haubrich,* in illustration, placed hyperactive and dis- *Shores and Haubrich 1969* tractible "emotionally disturbed" children in cubicles for periods of time and measured academic performance (reading and arithmetic rates) and attending behavior. While in the cubicles, the children's attending behavior increased significantly. Gorton* found that for brain-injured and non-brain-injured "mentally retarded" children, reduced extraneous (auditory and visual) stimulation resulted in increases in performance of arithmetic tasks.

Gorton 1972

Prompting procedures for producing the desired behavior thus may become effective due to reduced stimulation and related inappropriate response possibilities. As the desired behavior gains some strength and as the prompts are gradually removed, the child may move slowly through a series of environments which increasingly represent closer similarity to the natural classroom one.

Gradual Removal of Prompts: Fading

As the desired behavior gains in strength in the presence of the desired stimulus conditions, prompting should be removed. The goal is for behavior to occur spontaneously under natural cue conditions without supportive or additional prompts. The child should hang his coat on the coatrack when he comes into the classroom without an additional prompt from the teacher. The adolescent should complete his independent study project without teacher prodding.

Excessive verbal prompting (the teacher saying *blue* and later *bl* and then *b* as prompts for the child to label the blue color), gestural cueing (the teacher drawing an imaginary circle as a prompt following the assignment to "draw a circle"), physical guidance (the teacher holding the child's hand as he colors inside the boundary of the picture), or whatever combinations are being used, should become less conclusive and less frequent as the behavior becomes stronger. During this *fading* phase, other stimulus components more natural to the behavior and to the environment in which it is to occur will assume the cuing function. The picture, the desk, the blue color, the verbal request, or entering the classroom with a coat on will begin to cue or control the desired behavior. The teacher's request to "keep working," "watch those lines," "put your coat up," "do it this way," thus will become excessive or redundant. The natural components of the environment will be sufficient.

Figure 9.1 illustrates the gradual fading of redundant cues in teaching a child to write the word *cat*, and writing the word *cat* from dictation would represent the final objective.

Bricker and Bricker 1970

Bricker and Bricker* provide an excellent description of a shaping program used in teaching generalized motor imitation skills in the young, severely language-handicapped child. The use of various combinations of prompts and their gradual removal are described:

Teacher Instruction	Stimulus

Trace the word _cat._

cat

Write the word _cat._

cat

Write the word _cat._

ca

Write the word _cat._

c

Copy the word _cat._
(Teacher writes _cat_ on child's tablet.)

Copy the word _cat._
(Teacher writes _cat_ on board.)

Write the word _cat._
(Teacher dictates.)

FIGURE 9.1.   _Example of a Gradual Fading Procedure_

A consistent stimulus such as, "Do this," should be used with the motor imitation training so that it becomes a discriminative signal for an imitative response from the child. Following the command of "Do this," the trainer
should execute the behavior to be imitated, such as placing his hands on his

head and leaving them there, while an assistant standing behind the child physically prompts the child to imitate the response. The assistant prompts the behavior by taking the child's hands and placing them on the child's head and then slowly removes his own hands from the child's. When the child keeps his hands in the correct position without the prompt, the assistant quickly reinforces the child. The procedure is recycled but with the assistant using fewer prompts on each trial. The child's behavior is closely observed and when it is apparent that the child is ready to spontaneously imitate a part of the response, the prompt for that part is withheld. . . . Prompting and fading are continued until the child imitates the response spontaneously and does so in the presence of the discriminative signal "Do this," followed by the modeled movement. [p. 107]

Care should be taken to insure that prompts are not maintained for an excessive length of time as the child may come to depend excessively upon them. The general rule is to remove the prompts as quickly as possible. At the same time, care must be taken not to remove the prompts too suddenly because the behavior may abruptly stop.

Finally, the teacher must be sensitive to individual differences. Children will acquire new behaviors at different rates, will need different types of prompts for optimal learning, will require prompts for varying lengths of time, and, as emphasized, will respond differently to reinforcing events. Improvement, even though minor, must be reinforced. The teacher must be senstitive to minor changes in behavior in the direction of a previously set behavior goal. The education program must constantly encourage new behavior patterns representing more complex forms and combinations of behavior patterns than the child presently exhibits.

INFLUENCING CONSISTENCY OF BEHAVIOR

The goal of an educational program for children and adolescents with learning and behavior difficulties is concerned both with influencing more complex and varied behavior patterns and with insuring that these behaviors occur consistently under appropriate conditions. Certain environmental events provide the child with information about the appropriateness and inappropriateness of various behaviors.

Most behaviors occur only under certain conditions. The child routinely makes appropriate social responses when he meets his teacher. He routinely enters the classroom when the 8:15 bell rings. He only infrequently enters the classroom prior to this time. He promptly discontinues his disruptive behavior upon seeing the principal enter the classroom. He opens his lunch box only during the noon recess period. In each of these examples, the behavior described has a high probability of occurrence in the presence of certain environmental conditions. When the conditions are not present, the behavior is unlikely to occur. These are illustrations of a most significant aspect of learning, that of *discrimination* and the resulting influence which environmental events gain over behavior. In each of these instances that behavior occurred which was likely to result either in positive reinforcement or in the avoidance of aversive consequences. Cues or stimulus events were present which marked the occasion for a given behavior or a range of functionally equivalent behaviors that would result in reinforcement. Any other behaviors in these situations would likely have resulted in neutral or negative reactions from the environment.

These *cues* or *discriminative stimuli* mark the time, place, and other conditions under which various behaviors are appropriate. Cues, both internal and external, present at any specific time and situation inform the child which of the numerous behaviors in his repertoires will result in positive or negative consequences in specific situations. These cues, which precede behavior, account for the consistency in a child's behavior. Once a child learns new behavior patterns, these begin to appear only under certain cue conditions. The behavior occurs under conditions similar to past conditions in which the behavior has resulted in reinforcement. Examples would include:

Sing in the music room, not during class discussions.
Daydream during rest period, not during class period.
Color on paper; do not color on desk.
Cry when hurt; do not cry following minor bumps or bruises.
Yell on the athletic field, not in the school hallway.
Make decisions when calm, not when angry.

These discriminations are acquired by differential reinforcement as follows:

Cue	Child Behavior	Consequence
a. Classroom	Sitting attentively	Positive reinforcement: teacher praise
b. Classroom	Talking loudly	Punishment: scolding from teacher
a. "Show me the red ball."	Pointing to the *red* ball	Positive reinforcement: token
b. "Show me the red ball."	Pointing to the *blue* ball	No reinforcement: Teacher says, "That is *not* red. This is the red ball" as she points to the red ball.

After the sequence of cue   →   behavior   →   consequences is repeated on numerous occasions, the child begins to behave more selectively in the classroom environment. This discrimination is facilitated by informational feedback concerning the correctness of the child's behavior. If an error is made, the child is informed of the correct behavior and the distinguishing aspects of the discriminative cues.

To continue a previous example, as the bell rang, Jim entered the classroom, sat in his chair at the work table, and opened his book. This response sequence following the 8:15 bell had previously been reinforced by a variety of events including those of greetings from teachers and peers, the attention provided as he answered the roll call, and the like. Additionally, such behavior may have gained strength if it resulted in the removal of certain aversive conditions including criticism and threats from the teacher and principal. To repeat, a particular cue, signal, or stimulus gains discriminative control over the behavior as a result of its consistent association with subsequent positive or negative reinforcement.

When the relationship between a behavior and the related reinforcing conditions is disrupted, the discriminative stimuli will lose the influence function, and the behavior will no longer occur at a high or consistent rate whenever the discriminative stimuli are presented. Other behaviors, reinforced more reliably in the presence of these stimulus conditions, will come to the fore.

As another example, consider the act of opening a lunch box at times other than during the noon lunch period. If the act had not been followed in the past by the student's being able to eat his sandwich, he will have developed a discrimination. He will have learned that only during the lunch period do behaviors *preparatory* to his eating his lunch result in his being able to eat lunch. Such preparatory behaviors thus are controlled by those cues that mark the appropriate time and place for these behaviors to result in reinforcement.

Relationship between "Knowing" and "Doing"

Children frequently know what to do and, further, may intend to behave in a desired manner but end up misbehaving. "I know he does not intentionally disregard my requests but he just will not do what he knows is expected" is a frequently heard comment. The hyperactive and distractible child or adolescent, for example, "knows" that he should sit and work but the sound of laughter across the room or the sounds associated with an athletic contest encourage him to leave his work unfinished and join in the competing activity. The impulsive child may know that he should be more reflective. The "emotionally disturbed" adolescent knows that he should control his temper when frustrated or confronted, but discriminative events other than this "knowledge" influence his excessive outburst. Too many competing cues are present. Too many other events contrary to those required control behaviors. This problem could be avoided in many instances by more careful arrangement of cues and subsequent consequences for the appropriate behavior. A child should not be "tempted" by cues for competing behaviors until the appropriate behavior has acquired sufficient strength to overcome the temptation. As the appropriate behavior becomes attached to the desired discriminative cues through consistent reinforcement, these cues will become more effective in controlling the behavior. Other cues, for behaviors which are inappropriate, will become less influential and less likely to produce competing behaviors.

Correction of Errors

As suggested, in arranging learning experiences for the development of adequate discriminations, the educator should plan to correct inappropriate behaviors which occur in the presence of the desired cue. If the child makes the wrong response, the teacher should immediately encourage the child in the appropriate behavior in the presence of the desired cue and the subsequent reinforcer. The discriminative events should be labeled by the teacher and repeated by the child as he makes the appropriate response. For example, if the child forgets to hang his coat as he enters the room, the teacher should have him put his coat on again, go out of the room, and reenter. As he enters the room he should hang his coat and be reinforced promptly. After a number of experiences of this nature, the cues associated with entering the room will come to remind the child to hang his coat.

If the impulsive child reacts too quickly, instruct him specifically to slow down and to think before acting. So that the child, during this delay, does not focus on irrelevant cues, his attention should be directed to the relevant stimulus features. In teaching discriminations to children who experience reversal difficulties, for instance, the teacher should use visual and verbal cues to emphasize the distinctive features of the discriminative cues. Immediate feedback and guided practice of the appropriate discrimination should follow any errors. Stromer* demonstrated such procedures in remedying letter and number reversals under naming, dictation, and copying conditions in children from regular and special education classes. Examples of discrimination difficulties included saying p for q, writing 9 with the circle on right side of the stem, and reversing letters on both sides of the "body midline." Remediation procedures included modeling of correct and incorrect symbol formation, teacher feedback following both the correct and incorrect child responses, praise for correct responses, charting of correct responses, and temporal delays imposed between dictated letters and child responses. Reversal was eliminated, with only occasional errors. Follow-up demonstrated enduring training effects.

Stromer 1975

Discrimination and Memory Difficulties

Children with exceptional learning and behavior characteristics frequently display various attentional, perceptual, and cognitive difficulties which interfere with the development of adequate discriminations and associated specific cue influence. The child may tend to become confused because he does not recognize the appropriate cues. He does not know what behavior is being requested since the cues are too indistinct or too complex for him. Werry and Sprague* and Sprague and Toppe* provide evidence that children with learning difficulties who display hyperactive behavior patterns are less efficient in various learning tasks, including simple discrimination ones, when compared to other children of comparable cognitive and chronological-age characteristics. Apparently, the excessive motor movements interfere with the child's attending to relevant aspects of the stimulus conditions for sufficient periods of time for discriminations to be acquired. Zeaman and House* emphasize that discrimination difficulties in children with general cognitive deficits may be related to poor attentional skills. After the child is taught to attend to relevant stimulus dimensions in a discrimination task, his learning is noticeably improved. Epstein et al.,* Hallahan and Cruickshank,* and Keogh* describe the attentional and discrimination difficulties in hyperactive, impulsive children who may be labeled "learning disabled," "brain-injured," or "mentally retarded." Harcum and Harcum* demonstrated that training in a reflective tempo could result in improvement in visual discriminations of "educable mentally retarded" children. Lowry and Ross* likewise demonstrated significant improvement in the visual discrimination performance of impulsive, "severely retarded" children following an imposed delay between stimulation and responding. Finally, Duckworth et al.* used extended teacher praise: "Mary, I like the way you looked at all the answers before marking your paper." "Bobby, you took your time and did very well on this one." Performance of impulsive "educable mentally retarded" children on visual discrimination tasks requiring visual and auditory information processing did improve.

In some cases, auditory or visual memory difficulties interfere with adequate performance in discrimination situations. The child may begin an activity appropriately but then forget what she is to do. The teacher may request, "Julie, put this book on my desk and bring me the box of crayons." She starts toward the desk but soon forgets; the auditory cues provided by the teacher have not been sufficient to keep her behavior going to completion. In the case of this particular child, more frequent cuing is needed. The teacher may repeat the cues in various phases of the activity. The child may repeat the directions aloud as she engages in the activity. She may be given visual cues such as a figure drawing, depicting different steps in the activity, which she can check off as they are completed. These redundant prompts can be reduced gradually as the child gains proficiency in responding to the more natural cues associated with the activity.

Werry and Sprague 1970; Sprague and Toppe 1966

Zeaman and House 1963

Epstein et al. 1975; Hallahan and Cruickshank 1973; Keogh 1971 Harcum and Harcum 1973 Lowry and Ross 1975

Duckworth et al. 1974

There are varying theoretical notions relative to historical and contemporary factors which contribute to the learning and retention difficulties of children. Zigler* has emphasized atypical motivational and related variables evolving out of a history of social deprivation and excessive failure experiences. Butterfield and Belmont* and Butterfield et al.* have focused on deficits in mediational verbal (rehearsal) skills as underlying various acquisition and retention difficulties in children with general cognitive limitations. These positions, and those associated with discrimination difficulties of children with "autistic" behavior patterns,* are described in greater detail in Chapter 13.

Zigler 1969, 1973

Butterfield and Belmont 1972; Butterfield et al. 1973

Lovaas and Schreibman 1971; Lovaas et al. 1971

Provision of Distinctive Cues

In arranging an educational program, it is essential that cues be arranged to provide the child with precise information about the appropriateness or inappropriateness of various alternative behaviors. In teaching discriminations to the child, the teacher may initially provide distinctive and perhaps even redundant cues. As the desired behavior becomes more consistent, the redundant cues are gradually removed. The use of distinctive cues is essential in complex and difficult behavior patterns. The longer the time required to complete an activity the more the need for distinct and frequent cueing. Training prompts, i.e., prompts that will be faded out as an entire behavior pattern becomes stronger, should be provided at those times when the child's behavior is likely to "break down."

Children described as having short attention spans, as being distractible, or as being unable to persist at a specific activity require especially consistent, distinct, and frequent cueing for appropriate behavior. In these cases, and especially in the early stages of learning new behaviors, it is also highly important to reduce to a minimum those cues which control competing behaviors. Additionally, it should be remembered, cues become effective in influencing desired behaviors only if these are followed consistently and frequently with reinforcing consequences.

A child with difficulty in acquiring adequate discriminations may be requested to label differentiating aspects of the situation, to rehearse correct cue-response relationship, and to describe what he is to do in specific future situations. Or the teacher may anticipate difficult situations by reviewing with children the desired behavior: "Remember, as soon as the bell rings, we will put the books on the shelf. What will we do when the bell rings? When will we put the books away?" Such a procedure serves to emphasize the relationship between cues and associated behaviors.

The teacher should heed a word of caution: Neither nagging nor criticizing is effective cueing. The adult who, as a result of his own anger or frustration, punishes the child in one way or another after he fails to behave in a discriminating manner does not assist the child. If the child is not responding appropriately to the cues being presented, the educational program is at fault, not the child. The cue → behavior → consequences sequence should be examined and modified to insure more appropriate learning and behaving.

Negative Effects of Discrimination Difficulties

Behaviors frequently do not acquire the specificity desired in terms of the stimulus events under which the behavior occurs. Generalization occurs across similar stimulus conditions. When the differences across situations are quite minimal, they may be difficult for the child or adolescent to discern. Then the child responds in the same manner in situations which require different modes of behavior. The child may label all circular objects—eggs, grapefruits, and apples—with the verbal response "ball." Or he may not understand why he cannot play with the teacher and peers in the classroom when he can play with them on the playground. If the discriminations required are beyond the child's present discrimination capacity or skill level, disruptive emotionality is likely to result. A conflict may be created. The child may be aware that he is expected to behave differentially but may be unable to discern the cue differences required for the discrimination behavior. Under such conditions the child may become highly upset, either being angry at himself for his "dumbness" or at the environment for creating the conflict. Hyperactivity, distractibility, loss of previous discriminations, and behavioral rigidity or perseveration are other reactions which may result.

A more specific differentiation of behaviors will appear as discrimination training is provided. As an approach to the discrimination difficulty with circular objects, the child is reinforced for labeling a ball correctly and not reinforced for labeling as "ball" any other object. Behavior occurring in the presence of certain specific cues is provided reinforcement. That same behavior occurring in the presence of other cues, even though similar, is not reinforced. In this manner highly similar situations can come to mark the occasion for highly different behavior.

INFLUENCING BEHAVIOR BY PROVIDING MODELS

As noted, modeling or demonstration may be helpful in (1) promoting new response patterns, (2) increasing the likelihood that desired behavior already learned by the child will occur, and (3) strengthening or weakening the observer's inhibitions or established response patterns. As an example of the last named, an adolescent may be tempted to slip out of the boring economics class but inhibits the impulse on seeing the teacher catch and reprimand another student as he attempts to leave the room. Or an adolescent who typically inhibits his impulses to skip class may not attend economics class after observing others skipping. Experience with the use of modeling has demonstrated that a wide range of deficit and excessive behavior patterns may be influenced.* Aggression, study behavior, a reflective cognitive tempo, avoidance behavior, social withdrawal, and fear reactions (to mention a few) have all been influenced as a result of a child's observation of these behaviors in others.

Bandura 1969; Staats 1975

In teaching new behaviors, the adult shows the child or adolescent how to complete certain tasks, how to pronounce a word, how to draw a circle, how to tie a bow, how to swing a golf club or kick a football, and how to engage in literally hundreds of other behavior patterns. Speech, for example, could not be acquired without imitation of models. Children soon learn to imitate what they hear and see others do. In fact, a child without imitation skills has an extremely difficult time acquiring any but the most basic of behaviors. As children with extreme developmental difficulties have poorly developed skills of imitation, it becomes essential that these skills be taught in a highly structured systematic manner.

Teaching and Using Generalized Imitative Skills

There is evidence that even the more severely disabled not only will imitate the behavior of others when this imitated behavior is reinforced but also will acquire generalized imitation skills.* In an appropriate training program, children will gradually begin to imitate even new behaviors which, being new to them, have never had previous reinforcement. In the absence of a generalized imitative repertoire, the teacher is left with a slow process of arduously shaping new behaviors. The teacher of children with developmental difficulties must evaluate the generalized imitative skills of each child and provide a remediation training program when the child demonstrates limited imitative behaviors.

Baer et al. 1967; Martin 1971; Metz 1965

In teaching imitation skills:

1. *Select a group of behaviors to be imitated.* These should begin with relatively simple movements early in the training program and move progressively to more complex behaviors. Behaviors which the children will use in social situations and which may be used in shaping speech should be selected.

Bricker and Bricker* used the following movement in a program designed to train a motor imitation repertoire. These are ordered according to increasing difficulty:

Bricker and Bricker 1970

Step on board	Swing feet
Token in box	Walk in place
Sit on box	Hands on mouth

Cups in cups	Bow up and down
Pat box with hand	Raise foot
Blow cotton	Finger on feet
Pat knees	Turn around
Open mouth	Move head up and down
Hands on head	Wave arms
Touch ear	Wave arms extended

Baer et al. 1967

Baer et al.* used 130 motor responses in training generalized imitation skills in severely retarded children who initially showed no imitation whatsoever. These behaviors ranged from simple ones such as "raise left arm," "nod yes," and "tap chair seat" to more complex ones such as "walk and hold book on head," "put hands on door knob," and "place box inside

Metz 1965

ring of beads." Examples of the motor behaviors used by Metz* in his successful program of teaching generalized imitation to children with severe autistic behavior patterns include:

Throw softball	Slide block across floor
Clap hands	Run across room
Squat	Throw bean bag
Squeeze horn	Arrange configuration of blocks
Mark with chalk on slate	Place cloth over blocks

2. *Identify reinforcers.* Initially, food may be necessary. It is desirable, however, to establish tokens and social events such as praise as effective reinforcers as quickly as possible because they provide more efficient and flexible training possibilities.

3. *Initiate training.* After the behaviors to be imitated have been selected and the reinforcing events and procedure of delivery have been established, training begins. Training should occur in an environmental setting with minimal sources of distraction. At the start, it is desirable to use both a trainer and an assistant. The trainer calls the child by name and says, "Do this." He then demonstrates the desired behavior. If the child imitates the behavior within a specified period (ten to twenty seconds), he is promptly reinforced with "Good" and a token or food reinforcer. If the child does not imitate the behavior, the trainer again repeats the sequence. The assistant then physically guides the child through the behavior and promptly provides a reinforcer. As this sequence is repeated, the external guidance is gradually faded until the child spontaneously imitates the demonstrated behavior following the trainer's discriminative cue, "Do this."

When the child imitates the initial behavior with high consistency, a second behavior is presented. If the child imitates this one spontaneously, he is provided practice in imitating both responses. This procedure is continued until he is able to imitate a number of demonstrated behaviors.

The frequency of reinforcement is reduced to whatever level is possible to maintain a high level of correct response. The behaviors to be imitated should be demonstrated in a random fashion to avoid the development of specific chains of behavior.

4. *Intersperse new behaviors, which have not been presented previously and which have never been reinforced, among ones previously reinforced.* The new behaviors are not provided reinforcement. If the child imitates them with consistency, a generalized imitative pattern is demonstrated. The training should be continued until the child, without hesitation or error, is able to imitate both previously reinforced and new behaviors.

5. *Use different trainers at this stage to enhance generalization of this imitative repertoire.* Additionally, the training should occur in various settings which become increasingly similar to the child's natural environments.

As the child becomes skillful in imitating the demonstrated behaviors, inappropriate motor and emotional behaviors frequently decline. The experience becomes a fun activity for many children. As the child begins to imitate some responses, it becomes progressively easier for him to acquire new imitative behaviors.

After the generalized imitative repertoire of motor behaviors has been established, the educator will be able to use the specific behaviors and the generalized repertoire to teach other behaviors.

Teaching Social Behaviors.   Paloutzian et al.,* after initially training nonimitative children to imitate twenty-four motor responses, used these newly acquired imitation skills to teach social interaction with peers. The children were taught to imitate the following social interaction behaviors: passing a bean bag, walking to a peer and gently stroking his face, pulling a peer in a wagon, pushing another child in a swing, and rocking another child in a rocking chair or hobby horse. The children required fewer training sessions to learn to imitate these more complex behaviors than required initially to learn the relatively simple motor responses. The trainers also reported that the children began to demonstrate positive emotional reactions of delight during training sessions.

Paloutzian 1971

Prior to and following the training, the social interaction behaviors of these children were rated during daily scheduled free-play periods. The children demonstrated considerably more and a high level of social interaction behaviors in free-play settings following the imitation training experiences than was evident prior to training. Thus, the social interactions skills acquired in the training sessions generalized to other settings.

Teaching Speech.   One of the most central deficits of children with "autistic" behavior patterns relates to functional speech. In light of results of studies which suggest a significant relationship between the early development of speech (by the age of five) and later social adjustment (see Eisenberg*), it is essential that the initial focus of a developmental education program is that of teaching functional speech. The following program components, described by Garcia and DeHaven,* Hartung,* Lovaas,* and Risley and Wolf* have produced favorable results:

*Eisenberg 1956
Garcia and DeHaven
1974; Hartung 1970;
Lovaas 1968; Risley
and Wolf 1967*

1. Attention and eye contact must be shaped initially. The child cannot learn to imitate the motor and verbal behaviors of the teacher until he is able to attend to her. Attention and eye contact may be maintained initially by holding a food reinforcer directly in front of the teacher's face. Later, attention may be attracted by the use of loud noises such as shouting the child's name, "Betty, look!" or a sharp slap on the table top. Additionally, the child's head may be held or turned so that she faces the teacher.
2. After some attentional skills have been shaped, the next step is to teach the child to imitate motor behaviors demonstrated by the teacher. Consistent motor-imitative behaviors enhance speech training.
3. The motor behavior is used as a basis for shaping verbal behaviors. The child is requested to initiate a series of motor responses such as opening his mouth, moving his tongue, and shaking his head and then is presented a verbal model to imitate. The progression may start with gross motor imitation, continue with fine motor imitation, go on to motor imitation involving facial movements, and may finally involve verbalizations.
4. The child is reinforced initially for all vocal sounds and for visually fixating on the teacher's mouth and eyes.
5. In teaching specific vocal sounds to nonverbal children, those sounds, such as the letter *b*, that can be prompted by manually assisting the child should be the sounds selected. The teacher makes the sound *b* and prompts the child to make the sound by holding the child's lips closed with her fingers and quickly removing them when the child exhales (see Lovaas* for a more detailed description).

Lovaas 1968

6. Those sounds are selected that have concomitant visual components which can be exaggerated when the teacher pronounces them, such as the labial *m* and the front or open-mouthed vowel *a*. The exaggeration emphasizes the lip and mouth placements.
7. For the child who does have some verbal skills, the teacher selects words or sounds which the child already uses and builds on these.
8. The teacher initially avoids sounds that have only auditory components such as the *k*, *g*, *s*, and *l*.
9. After the child is making vocal sounds, the teacher begins to reinforce the child for making the sounds within a designated period of time— five to ten seconds—following the teacher's sounds.
10. Next, sounds are reinforced that resemble those of the teacher's modeled sound. It is helpful to prompt the child by holding and guiding the child's lips. This assistance is gradually faded as the child begins to imitate correctly.

11. New sounds and words are added as the child correctly and consistently imitates a single word. New and old themes are alternated to insure frequent success.
12. After the child has successfully imitated a few words, it is not unusual to find the emergence of echolalia. The child begins to imitate numerous words and even short phrases.
13. After imitative responses occur with consistency, the child is taught to name objects. This is accompanied by presenting an object, labeling it, and having the child imitate the name. The labeling prompt is gradually removed as the child is able to spontaneously name the object. Following naming, the child is taught to answer questions, use phrases, and finally to use functional speech.

Facilitating Observational Learning

Most effective learning occurs whenever the child imitates immediately what he sees or hears others do. At the same time, there is evidence that a child may be influenced by what he observes even though he may not engage in the behavior until a later time. In either event, the child is more likely to imitate an observed behavior if he also observes the model receiving reinforcing consequences. Further, it is likely that maximum effects of exposure to a model will be realized if the consequences provided the model's behavior are events which are highly reinforcing to the observing child. Of course, for the imitated behavior to become an established and reliable aspect of the child's repertoire, it must be reinforced as he engages in it.

The educator may also find film presentation of models engaging in desired behavior to be effective in influencing the occurrence of this behavior in a child. An experience of O'Connor* illustrates the potential usefulness of this mode of presentation. Children with relatively severe deficits in social behavior attending nursery school classes were shown films projected through a large TV console. The sound-color film lasting some twenty-three minutes portrayed a sequence of scenes in which children interacted. Initially a child was shown observing others and then joining in the social activities. As he became involved, play materials were offered him, and peers talked and generally showed pleasure over his advances into the activity. The scenes progressed toward a more spontaneous uninhibited gleeful play activity. Children who had observed the filmed presentation showed a significant increase in social responsiveness. Other socially withdrawn children who did not see the filmed presentation of peer interaction remained socially withdrawn.

O'Connor 1969

Characteristics of Models

Children and adolescents are more likely to imitate the behavior of those teachers, parents, siblings, peers, and others whom they like—those

Ross 1970

who are or have been major sources of reinforcement for them.* The child may imitate inappropriate behavior just as he may imitate desirable ways of behaving. Behaviors of a teacher other than those intended may be imitated. Stevenson,* after reviewing incidental learning studies, noted that children are quite likely to imitate the behavior of adults who are viewed by them as nurturant and as having charge of desired reinforcing events.

Stevenson 1972

Peers, especially those of the same sex, frequently become the most influential models. Peers who are leaders or otherwise enjoy some status in the observer's eyes, close friends, someone with characteristics similar to those of the observer, or peers whose behavior frequently does result in reinforcers are most likely to be attended to and imitated. The model may even be a stranger who has characteristics which the child likes. Cartoon figures, TV figures, or puppets frequently can be used to model various behaviors which the child will imitate. On the other hand, behavior that is modeled by a teacher or peer who is of neutral or negative value to a child will be imitated less frequently.

It is also likely that children generally will be more influenced by observation of multiple models engaging in the behavior to be imitated than would be found if observation is made of a single model. If modeling is used to increase the social interaction of a child who is socially withdrawn, it would be best to have him observe a number of different peers approaching other children and engaging in various types of social interaction in various situations. Csapo* suggests that an implusive child may be grouped with peers who are more reflective so that imitation of the successful models may occur and reflective behavior be strengthened through direct and vicarious reinforcement. The imitation of this reflective orientation could be enhanced by the teacher's description of the specific behaviors, e.g., slower response time, scanning, and attending, of the reflective peers.

Csapo 1972

Imitation of Inappropriate Behavior

If placed in an environment with peers who exhibit an excessive number of inappropriate behavior patterns, it is highly likely that a child or adolescent will imitate many of these behaviors. This is especially true if the inappropriate behavior is reinforced. He will more likely imitate behavior observed to result in desired reinforcers than behavior that does not. Peer attention is highly reinforcing to many children or adolescents. An adolescent may imitate another peer who engages in excessive swearing, loud disruptive talk, or clowning behaviors because these actions gain prompt attention from peers and adults. The educator may attempt to ignore these behaviors, but peer attention may maintain them at high strength. This emphasizes the need to place children with various difficulties in environments with peers who can provide good behavior models.

Cognitive, emotional, and social behaviors are subject to imitation learning. If possible, the teacher should at least attempt to remove any obvious reinforcement for inappropriate peer behaviors in order to reduce modeling effects.

Imitation of Complex Behavior

It is probably true that many of the more desirable and complex behavior patterns which children should acquire depend to a large extent on literally hundreds of observations of the patterns being modeled by significant others. Patterns of behavior labeled as patience, social skills, calmness, or kindness, as examples, would most likely develop only in those social environments in which significant people consistently demonstrated these behaviors. Children frequently behave precisely as the educator or parent behaves, especially if nurturant and otherwise reinforcing. If the adult model is loud and punitive or impulsive, the child may well learn this orientation. If calm and pleasant, the child is more likely to develop these behavior patterns. Epstein et al.* suggested that it may be valuable to place extremely impulsive children with experienced, reflective teachers. Thus, through the process of modeling and social reinforcement the child may become more reflective. *Epstein et al. 1975*

In addition to the usefulness of observational learning in the acquisition and use of various social and interpersonal behaviors, various cognitive skills may be acquired whenever a child is exposed to an appropriate model. In illustration, Ross et al.* demonstrated that children with generalized cognitive deficits could learn to use mediational links in verbal learning tasks as effectively under observational learning conditions as under intentional training conditions. *Ross et al. 1973*

Insured Observation

In providing a model for the child to imitate, it should be insured that the child is in fact attending to the various components of the demonstrated behavior. This may necessitate such cues as, "Look how I hold this" or "Look, I put the big red one in first and then the little blue one in last." For best results, the child should be encouraged to rehearse the behavior immediately: "Now you try it," with appropriate correction and reinforcement provided. The classroom peers may be used to model desired behavior. "Watch Nancy find the *red square*. Good, Nancy, you found it." "Jackie, show your classmates how you shape the clay." In using a peer model, best results will be obtained if highly preferred peers are used. Under this condition, the child is more likely to attend to critical discriminative cues, the precise form of the behavior, and to the related consequences of the behavior.

Use Procedure of Successive Approximation

In facilitating the acquisition of new behaviors in children with exceptional learning and behavior characteristics, it frequently becomes necessary to use a procedure of modeling, and reinforcing, successive approximations of the desired behavior. Complex patterns of behavior may be reduced to smaller subunits which are strengthened through modeling and reinforcement and later put together in more complex combinations or patterns.

The modeling of new behaviors has an additional effect for many children with exceptional learning and behavior characteristics. Most such children have experienced difficulty and frequent failure with new tasks. As a result many children actively avoid becoming involved in learning new behavior due to the unpleasantness associated with previous involvement. Demonstration of new behaviors by a person with whom the child does have some positive relationship removes some of the uncertainty and uncomfortableness associated with attempting new behaviors.

Additional Effects of Observation

As suggested, exposure to the behavior of a model may have other effects than facilitating the acquisition of new behavior. First, there is evidence to suggest that a child may be less likely to engage in observed behaviors which result in punishment to the model. Observation may thus serve to *inhibit* some behaviors. Second, the child may be more likely to engage in undesired behavior which typically occurs infrequently if he observes this behavior in others—*a disinhibition effect.* This effect is even more likely if the observed undesired behavior is rewarded or produces no aversive consequences. Third, the observation of desired behavior of others may serve as a cue for occurrence of behaviors presently in the child's repertoire but which occur infrequently. For example, a child may know how to work quietly but does so less frequently than desired. Exposure to a child who is working quietly may serve to increase the likelihood of the *Kazdin 1973*   same behavior on the part of the observing child. Kazdin* and Broden et *Broden et al. 1970*   al.* demonstrated that social reinforcement given to children for attentive behavior in a classroom setting also increased the attentive behavior of physically adjacent peers even though these peers received no direct reinforcing attention.

The teacher may make use of the rules of observational learning in the manner in which she deals with inappropriate behavior. If a child is overly aggressive toward peers, the teacher may ignore the aggressive child and provide special attention to the peers. This will demonstrate to the child that his aggressive behavior produces nothing for him from the teacher and also that the teacher attends to other types of behaviors. *Allen et al. 1970*   Allen et al.* used this tactic in successfully eliminating a boy's behaviors which included hitting and kicking children, spitting, and running off with other children's toys. The teachers provided undivided attention to the child being assaulted and ignored the aggressor. Consistent use of this tactic resulted in a gradual disappearance of the aggressive and disruptive behaviors.

As another example, if a child who has the required skills refuses to cooperate or to participate in an activity, the teacher may publicly reinforce participating children with high-preference reinforcers while the noncooperative child is observing. In so doing the teacher may remark loudly enough for the noncooperative child to hear, "Jill, I am pleased with the way you are working with Sue," or whatever comment is appropriate to the behaviors being reinforced. Such tactics may well be rather ineffective with children characterized by generalized isolated-behavior patterns or with limited social-participation skills. In these instances modeling should be combined with a more structured behavior-shaping program.

BEHAVIOR REHEARSAL

New patterns of behavior may be influenced by having the child rehearse these behaviors under simulated or highly structured conditions. A highly aggressive adolescent may not know how to be polite or cooperative. Prompting the adolescent to rehearse more appropriate ways of interacting with peers in a play-acting or role-playing setting may provide him with these behavioral skills. As these behaviors gain in strength, the similarity to the natural situations in which aggressive behavior previously occurred can be increased gradually.

Behavior rehearsal is also quite valuable in preparing for new situations or for situations in which inappropriate behavior has a high likelihood of occurring. Under highly structured conditions, children can "walk through" the appropriate behavior patterns and can be provided cues and reinforcers which increase the likelihood of occurrence of the behaviors under future conditions. A child who is most likely to misbehave may be asked to demonstrate the appropriate behavior to the peer group. With sufficient prompting from the teacher, the child will be able to model the desired behavior and receive the social approval of teacher and peers.

Gittelman* demonstrated the value of behavior rehearsal in his work with a group of children characterized by aggressive outbursts. Initially, the children listed, in an intensity hierarchy from mild to severe, those situations in which aggressive behavior resulted in negative consequences. Each member of the group acted out these situations, ending with those which provoked the most intense anger. In each situation, the child rehearsed more appropriate ways of responding to anger, with the result that inappropriate aggressive outbursts decreased.

Gittelman 1965

USE OF REINFORCEMENT PROCEDURES IN GROUPS

A natural concern expressed by educators inexperienced in the use of positive reinforcement procedures is, "Will the children who are not being reinforced become upset or suffer other negative effects?" Also, "Is it possible to use reinforcement procedures such as tokens with all children in the class? I don't see how I would ever have time for such activities." The obvious reply to these concerns is that every child in the classroom should be provided positive reinforcement frequently and consistently. *The type of reinforcing events and the time and frequency of providing them will obviously differ from child to child and from class to class.* Some children will require frequent social reinforcement; others will require much less attention. Some will require frequent tangible reinforcers; others may learn and perform satisfactorily with only infrequent tangible consequences. Some children with severe learning difficulties or problem behaviors may require close reinforcement attention; other children may function more independently of teacher-provided reinforcement. A token system of reinforcement may be used with all children for some activities but not for others. In a successful program described earlier, Bushell et al.* used *Bushell et al. 1968* tokens with all members of a class. The tokens were awarded each child contingent upon his own appropriate behavior.

On some occasions the reinforcing events may be placed on a group contingency basis. In this type of arrangement, the class as a whole will be reinforced on the basis of some designated behaviors expected of all members of the class. Any deviation from these expected behaviors by any member of the class will result in possible loss of reinforcement by the entire class. Packard* used this group contingency procedure in a program *Packard 1970* designed to increase the classroom attention of an entire class of children.

> *The teacher defined the types of attending behaviors which she desired during a preacademic language class—position of body and eyes, no inappropriate noise, following instructions. A red light, connected to a timer, was turned off when all class members were engaged in appropriate attending behavior. At the end of the class period, the entire class was provided access to a play activity (recess, gym, or a group game in the room) if attending behavior had been present for a designated percentage of the class period. If this criterion had not been met, the reinforcing activity was not provided. If this criterion had been exceeded by a certain percentage, the class was provided a bonus of additional time for play activity. The amount of time spent in attentive behavior under this group reinforcement procedure was gradually increased until a high level of attending behavior became evident.*

Packard 1970　　　Packard,* in emphasizing the possible effect of peer influence in a group contingency program, noted:

A program of reinforcing attention would be proportionately enhanced by making peer approval or disapproval contingent on a student's attention to task . . . . Subjective observation and other anecdotal evidence . . . indicated considerable peer interaction of this type. Though such pressure never reached the "back-alley trouncing" stage, there were frequent instances, both during and after classes, of students not hesitating to remind or even scold a classmate for "keeping the light on," and to congratulate an improved student. [p. 26]

Lovitt et al.* used a variation of the group contingency procedure in increasing spelling accuracy with fourth graders. Free time served as the reinforcing event for all members of the class who obtained high achievement.

Lovitt et al. 1969

In another variation of the group procedure, Patterson* arranged a classroom program for a hyperactive boy so that the boy could earn reinforcing events for the entire class for each ten seconds he remained at his desk and worked at a task. This represents an individual contingency with associated group reward. Peers assisted the boy by not attending to him when he was working. Peers also provided considerable social praise between classes and encouraged him to continue in his appropriate attending behavior. Barrish et al.* used a contingency arranged for the inappropriate behavior—out-of-seat, talking out—of specific children while the consequence—possible loss of privileges—of the specific children's behavior was shared by all members of the group. The individual contingencies for the group consequences were successfully applied during math and reading periods.

Patterson 1965

Barrish et al. 1969

Ward and Baker,* in response to another concern which teachers have over the use of reinforcement procedures in the classroom, evaluated the effects on other class members when teachers provided selective social reinforcement to individual children who presented specific patterns of problem behaviors. Children who either presented a high frequency of disruptive classroom behaviors or who were withdrawn and nonattentive were provided frequent social attention for appropriate classroom behavior. Other class members were responded to as they had been prior to the initiation of the specific behavior management programs for these problem children. Children receiving the selective social attention for appropriate behaviors showed a significant decrease in undesired behaviors. Ward and Baker concluded that there was no support for the argument that providing selective attention to some children in the classroom results in negative effects on the other children.

Ward and Baker 1968

Rosenbaum et al.* evaluated the relative effectiveness of individual and group reward programs in influencing hyperactivity in children in a classroom setting. In the individual reward program, children in different classrooms (one to a class) were provided private contingency programs in which each participating child was reinforced for behaviors which competed with hyperactivity. In the group reward program, the entire class was

Rosenbaum et al. 1975

rewarded contingent on appropriate behavior of the single child. Both individual and group reward programs were effective in decreasing hyperactivity. Of interest were the results of a questionnaire designed to assess teacher satisfaction with the two reinforcement approaches. The group reward program was significantly more popular than the individual reward program.

Drabman et al. 1974

In summary, behavior management programs using positive reinforcement and mild punishment procedures (loss of reinforcers) may be designed for the entire class or for individual members of the class. Drabman et al.* report that variations of group contingency programs may be as effective as individual reinforcement, as determined by individual performance in influencing appropriate classroom behaviors of elementary-age children. Optimal flexibility must be maintained to insure that individual differences among children will be attended to. If the educator is hesitant about using group contingency procedures, he should begin on a small scale. Perhaps one child should be selected initially. After some successful experience, the teacher may gradually add other children to whom positive reinforcement is provided in a specific response-contingent manner.

HOW IS BEHAVIOR MAINTAINED?

A child's behavior requires reinforcement not only as it is learned initially but also for it to be *maintained* over time. Behavior, regardless of its strength at any specific time following an educational program, requires reinforcement on occasion for the behavior to become a stable aspect of the child's repertoire. An important consideration is to insure that behavior will continue to occur in those future situations in which *reinforcement may be of a different kind and be less frequent and consistent than was present when the behavior was initially acquired.* The educator is concerned both that behaviors are maintained in the original learning environment and that the behavior, if it relates to situations other than the instructional one, is maintained in these other settings. The procedures for facilitating generalization of behavior change from the instructional situation to other settings will be discussed in the following section. The present discussion is concerned with procedures for insuring maintenance of the behavior in any setting once it begins to occur with some regularity.

Baer et al. 1968

As Baer et al.* have emphasized, although response maintenance may occur automatically, it can only be assured if systematically programmed.

Even in a highly structured educational program, it is not feasible to provide reinforcement indefinitely every time a behavior occurs. Also, when a contrived reinforcement system is used, such as a token program, it is not feasible nor desirable that the token program remain in operation indefinitely. It is obvious that reinforcement in the natural environment is not contrived nor continuous. Typically the more complex and social the behavior, the less likely it is that reinforcement will be provided continuously once the child or adolescent is removed from an individualized reinforcement program.

Problems can be created as a child moves from one environment to a new one in which reinforcement for specific behaviors is provided less frequently. A sudden change in the frequency or type of reinforcement can produce disruptive emotional reactions along with a disappearance of the previously reinforced behavior.

> *Kit, a five-year-old child with severe learning problems, was reinforced quite frequently by a mother who attempted to make him as happy as possible by immediate compliance to his request. Upon entering an educational program, Kit discovered that many of his requests were not fulfilled. He engaged in frequent emotional outbursts and quickly isolated himself from the other children. He did not know how to function in an environment that failed to respond to his every request.*

Patterns or Schedules of Reinforcement

While it is true that behavior is strengthened initially most effectively by continuous reinforcement, it is also found that following a history of continuous reinforcement, behavior is likely to disappear or become less likely to occur when reinforcement is discontinued or significantly reduced. Patterns of *intermittent* or *partial reinforcement,* which are most practical to implement and which represent the pattern of reinforcement provided in the everyday social environment, also result in behavior which is more durable, resistant to extinction, or which is maintained in strength over periods of time where reduction or elimination of reinforcement will take place. Under these schedules, reinforcement is provided some of the time following the desired behavior but not on every occasion. Some of an adolescent's activities are reinforced on one occasion but not on another. Social responses are not always provided suitable reciprocal social courtesy. Verbal requests are refused at times. A child's study behavior does not always result in desirable consequences. Further, the natural environment is so structured that a certain amount of behavior or number of responses is required prior to reinforcement. In other instances, reinforcement is available only after certain intervals of time have elapsed. Figures 9.2 and 9.3 provide illustration of various schedules.

In addition to resistance to extinction, these various patterns of reinforcement have a significant influence on (1) the rate of responding and (2) the particular pattern of responding. For example, in teaching new academic behaviors, the educator is concerned with the child engaging in

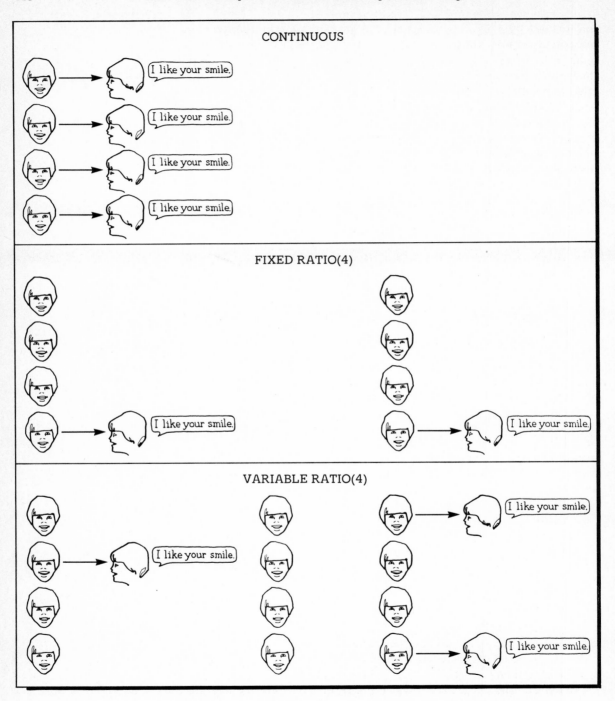

Figure 9.2 Depicting Continuous and Ratio Schedules of Reinforcement

the desired reading or arithmetic behaviors as well as related questions concerning the rate of reading or the time spent in solving difficult problems.

Reinforcement may be provided in the natural environment only after a certain performance level or number of responses has been made. This pattern of reinforcement is known as a *ratio reinforcement schedule.* There is a ratio of a give number of responses to one reinforcement. On other occasions behavior is reinforced after a certain passage of time. This procedure defines an *interval schedule.* Reinforcement is provided the first response occurring after the interval elapse.

Reinforcement under each of these may be either fixed or variable in nature. Under a *fixed schedule* the child is reinforced only after specified behaviors have occurred a designated number of times or after passage of specific periods of time. Reinforcement requires the same number of re-

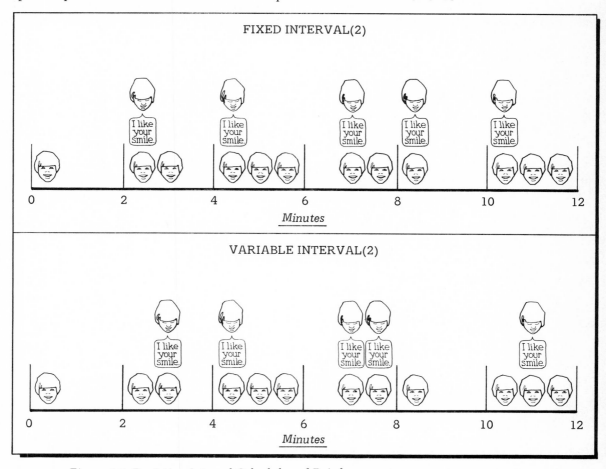

Figure 9.3 *Depicting Interval Schedules of Reinforcement*

sponses or periods of time. Providing a token for each ten math problems solved illustrates a *fixed-ratio schedule*. Providing free time for every thirty minutes of study behavior illustrates the *fixed-interval schedule*.

In the *variable-reinforcement arrangement,* behavior is reinforced randomly around a given time or ratio value. Reinforcement depends upon elapsed interval or number but the specific values vary. Under these conditions there are no particular cues which forecast that reinforcement is imminent. Under a *variable-ratio schedule* a response is reinforced on the average, for example, one time for every twenty-five correct spelling words, while the actual number of responses separating reinforcement may range, for example, from five to forty. Jones and Kazdin* used a *variable interval* of seven minutes in providing reinforcement to "mentally retarded" children in a token reinforcement program. At unpredictable times, but on the average of every seven minutes during the morning class session, the teacher would provide reinforcement for every child who was engaged in appropriate behavior.

Jones and Kazdin 1975

Effects of Specific Patterns of Reinforcement

Fixed Interval.   Under a fixed-interval reinforcement schedule, it is typical to observe that behavior increases in rate prior to reinforcement and suddenly drops off for a time after reinforcement is received. The number of responses may vary widely from one reinforcement to the next. Thus, rather variable behavior is present. As the number of responses is irrelevant to reinforcement, the child may learn to "tell time" and not respond immediately after reinforcement delivery. If the interval between reinforcement is too long, behavior is difficult to maintain. Paychecks on a biweekly basis for the adolescent in a work-study program are frequently quite inadequate to maintain high-rate behavior. It is not surprising under such conditions that work behavior is erratic and of low rate and that absenteeism is frequent. Thus, a fixed-interval schedule frequently fails to maintain a consistent level of behavior over a period of time and is a relatively poor schedule to follow.

Variable Interval.   A variable-interval schedule of providing reinforcement influences the reduction in performance following reinforcement which was noted under the fixed interval. A stable and uniform overall response rate typically results. Further, it is difficult to extinguish behavior after development under this schedule. Much social behavior is the result of this type of influence.

Fixed Ratio.   The ratio schedule represents the pattern of reinforcement which influences most human behavior. Many children and adolescents with exceptional learning and behavior characteristics will function best under a ratio schedule that provides frequent reinforcers.

Under high fixed-ratio schedules, for example, the rate of behaving is relatively low after reinforcement because a large number of behaviors must be produced before the next reinforcer is provided. Thus, it may be best to reinforce the child with low-magnitude reinforcers on five different occasions following a small designated number of behaviors than to reinforce him one time after a larger number of required behaviors even though the total amount of reinforcement may be the same. This is especially true in cases where adequate self-managed secondary reinforcers have not been established to span the time lag between the performances and later delivery of reinforcement.

Variable Ratio.   Another means of dealing with the inefficiency involved in a high fixed-ratio schedule is that of shifting from a fixed to a variable schedule. As reinforcement is provided in a variable manner, a smooth high rate of behavior can be obtained as long as the reinforcers are of sufficient magnitude and do not occur too infrequently.

Facilitating Resistance to Extinction

Resistance to extinction is a function not only of the previous schedule of reinforcement but also of the number and size or amount of previous reinforcement. Additionally, extinction is a smoother process following a pattern of intermittent reinforcement than when following continuous reinforcement. It can be said that the child has more frustration or stress tolerance after a history of intermittent reinforcement. He is less prone to exhibit aggressive or emotional outbursts as is observed in extinction following continuous reinforcement. Such relationships between certain classes of behavior and schedules of reinforcement would suggest that the low frustration tolerance and low disposition to perform in the face of failure characteristic of many children and adolescents could be viewed as a result both of insufficient reinforcement and of insufficient experience on intermittent schedules of reinforcement.

Typically, intermittent reinforcement, regardless of the nature of the schedule or pattern followed, produces a greater rate of behavior than does continuous reinforcement. Although rate of performance does fall as the frequency of reinforcement is reduced, optimum rates are found under conditions where reinforcement is provided intermittently. Also, in general, decreasing the probability of reinforcement serves to increase the resistance to extinction. Such a schedule teaches perseverance. The child learns that following a period of nonreinforcement, reinforcement will occur once again if performance is maintained.

Of course, there is a limit to the amount of behavior that the teacher may require prior to reinforcing a child. As the amount of behavior required is increased beyond a certain point, the child waits longer and longer after each reinforcement prior to reinitiating the desired behavior.

Requiring the child to complete fifty math problems prior to reinforcement, for example, may result in a complete loss of the desired behavior. Too much is required for each reinforcer. If the teacher begins to reinforce after completion of only forty problems, the child may again complete the assignments. He may, however, stall excessively after each reinforcement prior to beginning his new set of forty problems. In general, a low disposition to perform is partially the result of limited or infrequent reinforcement.

When Jill complies—with teacher requests—with a behavior that has been acquired recently, the teacher begins to reinforce her socially sometimes but not at other times. After experience with this time-to-time schedule of receiving reinforcement, the behavior continues to occur for increasingly longer periods of time in which reinforcement is not provided. This does not imply, of course, that the behavior will continue indefinitely under periods of nonreinforcement. Regardless of its reinforcement history, behavior must still be reinforced on occasion, that is, must result in some positive feedback if it is to continue in a reliable fashion. Ideally this feedback, as has been emphasized, should come from the activity itself (intrinsic reinforcement) or be self-delivered by the child through his own verbal behaviors.

Johnston et al. 1966 The procedure of gradual reduction of the frequency of reinforcement after a behavioral pattern has been acquired was followed in the previously mentioned program of Johnston et al.* After using continuous social reinforcement to strengthen vigorous physical activity in a child, the teacher gradually reduced both the number of times that she attended to the child's climbing behavior as well as the amount of attention she would provide on any one occasion.

It is also true that after experience with partial reinforcement, a given number of reinforcers will become more efficient. The child is less likely to become satiated with any specific reinforcing event if he receives fewer reinforcers. Fewer reinforcers will be required to keep the behavior occurring in a reliable manner at appropriate times. The child or adolescent will complete more puzzles, make more polite responses, persist longer at a task, complete more math minipacs, and play for longer periods prior to seeking adult attention as he gains experience with a schedule of less frequent reinforcement.

How to Reduce Reinforcement

These relationships between patterns or schedules of reinforcement and persistence of behavior over periods of infrequent reinforcement are easily translated into classroom procedures. As new behaviors are being acquired, reinforcing consequences should be provided frequently. After the behavior begins to occur with some consistency, the behavior should be reinforced externally less and less frequently. The reinforcement should be provided in an irregular fashion if optimal persistence of a behavior pattern is desired. If an attempt is being made to increase the number of simple tasks completed by a child prior to his becoming disruptive, reinforcement may be provided after two completed tasks, then after three, then after one, after four, after two, after five, after one, after three, after six, and after two.

This random or variable ratio pattern of reinforcement, as noted, results in durable behavior. In this manner, the child does not know when reinforcement is forthcoming and is more likely to work steadily and to persist for longer periods without looking for the reinforcing consequence. Reinforcing on a predictable schedule of every five minutes or after ten correct responses creates conditions which may produce problem behaviors. The child may behave appropriately (attending, studying, completing tasks, as examples) only when reinforcement is likely to occur. Also, the child learns to expect reinforcement at a given time and if it is not provided, frustration behavior is likely to result.

The Rate of Reinforcement Reduction

As suggested, there is no hard and fast rule relating to the absolute amount of reduction in reinforcement. It may be reduced from 100 percent to 90, then to 80, to 74, to 70, to 50, and finally to 30 percent or even less of the time the behavior occurs. This reduction should be gradual. If reinforcement is changed from continuous to less frequent, and the child begins to make too many errors, takes too long in responding, or behaves infrequently, it is evident that the change in schedule of reinforcement has been too severe. In these cases, the frequency of reinforcement should be increased again for a while and, after consistency is regained and practiced, a second attempt at gradual reduction in reinforcement frequency should be initiated.

Patterns of Reinforcement and Persistence of Problem Behavior

In view of the relationship between pattern of reinforcement and persistence of behavior, educators should be attentive to their own inadvertant and occasional reinforcement of a child's undesired behaviors. This occasional reinforcement can produce patterns that are quite persistent. If a teacher who does not feel well or is in a hurry "gives in" on occasion to a child's misbehavior (because the surrender terminates the whining or demanding), she may well be creating a condition in which the undesired behavior is most resistant to elimination. The child learns that whining and demanding occasionally and eventually pays off.

Bothersome patterns such as "lying," "cheating," or "stealing" may become rather strong as a result of reinforcing consequences which, albeit infrequent, nevertheless occur. Such behaviors produce an occasional reinforcing consequence. Lying and cheating behavior, for example, may remove the child from a highly unpleasant situation, even though punishment on occasion may be given for such behavior at a later time. Recall, however, the rule that behavior is influenced by immediate consequences. If the child lacks sufficiently strong self-management skills and if the cheating or lying behavior results on occasion in immediate removal of unpleasant conditions, it is likely to reoccur under similar conditions in the future. In fact, behaviors acquired and maintained by negative reinforcement are highly resistant to extinction, especially if the aversive event removed or avoided is intense.

Delay of Reinforcement

As most reinforcing events in the everyday social environment are seldom provided immediately following a desired behavior, response maintenance may be facilitated by providing children with experience in delay of reinforcement. After behavior is well established, the delay between behavior and reinforcement should be increased. Or if a token program is being used, the time between providing the token and its exchange for a backup reinforcer can be extended. This delay is independent of the particular pattern by which reinforcement is provided. Initially, tokens and their frequent exchange or verbal statements on when reinforcement will be given may be needed to insure behavior at high strength. Gradually, however, effort should be directed toward teaching the child to maintain his own behavior without the necessity of external social support. Following completion of a task, for example, the child can remind himself of the social reinforcement that will be provided later in the day when he shares his accomplishments with his parents.

Summary

Although frequent and immediate reinforcement may be required initially to teach new behaviors or strengthen existing ones, well-established behavior is maintained by less frequent reinforcement. Also, the type and/or magnitude of the reinforcer used initially to strengthen the behavior may or may not be necessary to maintain it. A child may require primary reinforcers when first learning a new behavior pattern, but secondary tangible and social events which the teacher provides may gradually replace the primary reinforcement. In most instances, naturally provided consequences should gradually replace the teacher-provided ones. At first, a child may require teacher-provided primary and secondary reinforcers to interact appropriately with other children. After the child has had experience with the new behavior, the attention of other children along with other aspects of the new activity become quite reinforcing in themselves and are sufficient to maintain the behavior. The teacher-provided reinforcers should be withdrawn. Thus the educator will constantly be shifting the types and frequency of reinforcing events provided. As one behavior is acquired, contrived reinforcers can be faded as the behavior becomes self-maintaining either by naturally occurring consequences (i.e., completion of activity, feedback from peers) or by self-control procedures such as self-reinforcement, self-reprimand, and goal setting. The teaching program can shift to other educational goals requiring more precise contingency management.

A recent study by Jones and Kazdin* illustrates the use of several procedures to enhance maintenance of behavior after changing the rein-forcement conditions for the behavior. Four "educably mentally retarded" children demonstrating inappropriate behaviors which interfered with task performance in the classroom were provided token reinforcement for desired alternative behaviors. After the initiation of the reinforcement contingency, there was an immediate reduction in the inappropriate behavior. After fifteen days under this contingency, peer praise was provided children who earned tokens, and a delay in providing backup reinforcers was begun. Following five days under these conditions, tokens were no longer provided; teacher and peer praise were substituted for "good" behavior. Additionally, the four students could earn a treat for the entire group. Finally, the entire program—token, teacher, and peer reinforcement and the group reward—was withdrawn. During a twelve-week follow-up, the inappropriate behaviors remained at a low rate of occurrence. Thus response maintenance was demonstrated.

Jones and Kazdin 1975

GENERALIZATION OF BEHAVIOR CHANGE

The major goal of an educational program is to teach behaviors which will occur and be maintained in numerous other settings. It is true, however, that once behaviors are acquired by a child or adolescent, whether these be appropriate or inappropriate for the time and situation, they do not always spontaneously or automatically occur at other times or in other situations. Patterson and Cobb* have demonstrated that behavior frequently is situation-specific and quite influenced by the conditions (setting events, reinforcement contingencies, and discriminative events) present in specific situations. Educational intervention in a special setting such as a resource room or self-contained special classroom, or of a structured and systematic nature as with a contingency contract or a token economy program, reflects setting, discriminative, and reinforcing conditions which differ from those present in the typical school environment. Thus, fortuitous generalization to these typical settings which contain different conditions cannot be expected as a consistent occurrence. The everyday environment is not as consistent or persistent as an individualized educational environment in prompting or in reinforcing behavior.

A child may learn to be highly negativistic when required to be

Patterson and Cobb 1971

cooperative with peers in group projects, during difficult perceptual-motor activities, or under such conditions as "when a female adult" is present. At other times or under other conditions, the same child may be quite coopera- tive and successful. Likewise, a child may learn new behaviors under one set of conditions (at school) but not demonstrate these newly acquired behaviors in other settings (at home). Or a class of adolescents with learn- ing and behavior difficulties may show greatly improved academic per- formance in a resource room with a token economy program but revert to old patterns of behaving when returned to the regular class. It is rather commonplace for teachers to report: "He attends to his tasks in the therapy room with Ms. Schroeter but I have trouble holding his attention in the classroom." "His self-care and grooming skills are quite good at school but his mother reports that he seldom shows them at home." "He uses words quite freely with the speech therapists but I don't hear them in class." "He is most cooperative in art class and in athletic activites but not in English and math classes." The behaviors acquired under the discriminative and reinforcement conditions present in one situation may not generalize to other settings if these differ greatly in critical aspects. However, such generalization or transfer may be facilitated.

As suggested, it is not unusual to find that discriminative cues and reinforcing conditions influencing newly acquired behaviors can be highly specific to those which were present in the initial learning setting. The specific teacher, the time of day, the physical characteristics of the room such as lighting and furniture, the nature of the peer group, and other simi- lar types of events may come to exert strong influence over the behavior. As the child moves to other dissimilar settings, the behavior disappears or be- comes rather erratic. This observation emphasizes the value of modifying the problem behavior in the environmental setting in which the desired behavior is expected to occur. If the child is removed from the classroom and provided "special therapy" elsewhere, a problem of generalization of any newly acquired behavior to the classroom may be created. If the child is removed, specific attention must be given to the problem of generalization.

It is not being suggested that behaviors acquired in one setting never generalize to other settings; on the contrary, many academic, social, emo- tional, attitudinal, and other behavior repertoires do generalize spontane- *Hanley 1970*   ously. However, as emphasized by Hanley* in his thorough review of research on applied behavior analysis in the classroom, sufficient problems of generalization of behavior from the specific training setting to other settings are encountered in work with children and adolescents with learn- ing and behavior difficulties to justify the teacher's careful attention to procedures of facilitating generalization.

As illustrations of the lack of transfer of desired behavior change *Herman and*   from the program setting to other situations, Herman and Tramontana* *Tramontana 1971*   were able to get appropriate rest-time behavior to occur in four boys with high rates of disruptive behavior under token reinforcement conditions in a special therapy room. However, this appropriate rest behavior did not occur in the regular classroom. Wahler* described the absence of spontaneous generalization of behavior change from a child's home to the school setting. A behavior management program was initiated in the home of a five-year-old boy who displayed a general pattern of stubborn and disruptive behavior in both home and school settings. Although this behavior reduced significantly as new behaviors of cooperation were reinforced by the parents at home, the more appropriate mode of interaction did not generalize to the school setting. At school he remained a stubborn and disruptive child. This behavior did change in the school, however, when the teachers initiated a similar behavior change program in that setting. Another child described as having low motivation for schoolwork in both school and home setting was provided a behavior management program in the home. Under the new reinforcement conditions followed by the parents, the child soon showed appropriate interest in schoolwork at home. But this new behavior did not demonstrate itself in the school setting until the teachers began a similar reinforcement program.

Wahler 1969

The problem of transfer becomes especially pertinent when new social or academic behaviors are learned or new performance or achievement levels are attained under highly organized reinforcement conditions such as those found in token economy programs. As implied earlier, the efficacy of token programs has been firmly establised in the education and management of children and adolescents with a wide variety of exceptional learning and behavior characteristics. A major issue, however, is that of achieving long-term maintenance of behavioral characteristics in a child following reduction or termination of the contributed token systems and the subsequent transfer of the child to other settings. For example, O'Leary et al.* described a successful use of a token program in reducing disruptive behavior in children during afternoon classes but found no generalization of appropriate behavior to morning classes in which the token reinforcement program was not in effect. Similarly, Glavin et al.* and Glavin* reported that improved social behavior of "extremely disruptive or overly withdrawn" children, which was obtained in a behaviorally oriented resource room, did not generalize to the regular classroom. Neither of these programs, it should be noted, included procedures to enhance transfer from the token reinforcement system to the contingency conditions which were present in other settings.

O'Leary et al. 1969

Glavin et al. 1971; Glavin 1974

FACILITATING GENERALIZATION OF BEHAVIOR CHANGE

In avoiding or reducing some of these difficulties of generalization or transfer of behavior across different settings and conditions, there are four approaches the educator should try.

Increase Similarity between Training and Other Situations

The educator should attempt to arrange the training setting to be as similar as possible to other settings to which the behavior is expected to generalize. This similarity should include both the discriminative events which signal the occurrence of the behavior as well as the reinforcement conditions (events and schedules) which serve to maintain it. If the environments of the school classroom, therapy room, or special training room are distinctly different from other settings, a specific transfer or generalization program should be devised to facilitate the transition from one setting to the other. After the desired behavior acquired in the training settings has gained some initial strength, discriminative cues and reinforcement conditions from other settings should be introduced gradually. As they gain consistent influence over the behavior, the specific redundant training-setting cues should be faded and eventually removed. The following is an example of transfer training.

> Ms. Steele was able to teach seven-year-old Josh to respond verbally to many pictures, questions, and other cues in the language-therapy room. However, none of this verbal responsiveness generalized to the classroom setting. In this setting, Josh would attend to his teacher and peers, would comply with various requests, would communicate with them in terms of physical gestures, but would not do so verbally. To facilitate generalization to the classroom setting, the teacher-assistant in the regular classroom began to attend the individual language sessions with Ms. Steele and Josh. Gradually, the teacher-assistant began to present various components of the language lesson to Josh. After he began to respond consistently to her, the classroom teacher herself sat in on some of the lessons. Ms. Steele would initiate the lesson but then would assume an inactive role. She began to leave the room for longer periods of time as the teacher-assistant and teacher taught the lesson. The next step consisted of bringing first one, then two, and finally three of Josh's peers into the language lesson. After Josh was able to communicate verbally under these cue conditions, the final step was taken to move the lesson into the classroom setting. Effective generalization had been accomplished.

Koegel and Rincover 1974

Koegel and Rincover* reported a similar initial difficulty of generalization from one-to-one training conditions to classroom conditions with children with extreme "autistic" behavior patterns. Generalization effects were obtained, however, as the program gradually "faded in" the classroom stimulus situation, thus greatly increasing the similarity between the training and classroom environment. Rincover and Koegel* noted that some autistic children do not transfer newly acquired behaviors across situations due to their extreme overselectivity of stimulus cues which serve as discriminative events. In their experience, children frequently responded to incidental cues present in the training environment,

Rincover and Koegel 1975

such as physical characteristics of the training materials or of the teacher. When the environment was changed and the incidental cue was no longer present, the children were unable to respond correctly.

These examples illustrate the occasional necessity to plan for the gradual and systematic transfer of behaviors from one set of cues to others present in different environments. If effective generalization of behavior does not occur, the teacher must gradually introduce a set of experiences into the training setting which contain "outside" discriminative and reinforcement influence. The influence of the new experiences will then transfer from the training setting to other appropriate ones.

In many instances it will be necessary to match the reinforcement conditions of the educational setting to those present in other settings. A child may acquire new skills only when provided frequent immediate token reinforcers exchanged at frequent intervals for high-preference activities and objects. The new behaviors may drop out quickly, however, if the child is placed in a classroom in which only infrequent social reinforcement is provided. The training environment in this instance would gradually diminish the frequent token reinforcers and provide naturally occurring reinforcers on an infrequent basis. Systematic experience with delay, and inconsistency of external reinforcement, may be required for generalization and maintenance.

Chadwick and Day* provided a token reinforcement program for an entire class of twenty-five seriously underachieving eight- to twelve-year-old children. During the six-week token program in which children were provided social reinforcement and points for academic work (accuracy and rate) and appropriate personal and social classroom behavior related to academic behavior, a significant increase in academic achievement and appropriate classroom behavior was obtained. The children worked longer, faster, and more accurately under these reinforcement conditions. At the end of this period the token program was terminated while the rate of social reinforcement was continued. The childrens' improved academic performance continued under this more natural reinforcement condition. *Chadwick and Day 1971*

Phillips et al.,* in using a token reinforcement program to influence various behaviors of "predelinquent" youth, demonstrated that once behavior was established under a continuous reinforcement schedule the contingency could be faded gradually without loss of behavior. Medland and Stachnik* demonstrated that classroom conditions previously paired with tangible reinforcers became effective in maintaining the behavioral gains obtained under the token reinforcement contingency. Walker and Buckley,* after successfully using a token program in an experimental education classroom to influence the academic and behavior problems of eight- to twelve-year-old children, reprogrammed the regular classroom to which the children returned after two months. The social and token reinforcement and the academic materials were highly similar to those used in the experimental classroom. During this two-month maintenance period, approximately 75 percent of the positive gains were maintained. *Phillips et al. 1971*

Medland and Stachnik 1972

Walker and Buckley 1972

Practice New Behavior in Numerous Settings

Risley and Wolf 1967

Risley and Wolf,* in shaping appropriate speech in children who mechanically repeat what they hear others say, emphasize that generalization of speech from the training setting to natural settings is enhanced by having the children practice the speech with adequate reinforceing consequences in a wide range of places and under various conditions. Different people (family members, peers, teachers, neighbors) should cue and reinforce speech in a variety of locations—school, store, bus, church, home. This rule is applicable to any newly acquired behavior which is expected to occur in numerous situations outside the training setting in which behavior was acquired and practiced.

Train People in the Natural Environment

People in the natural environments of the child should be trained to use discriminative and reinforcing events in a manner similar to those used in the educational program.

Walker and Buckley 1972

If the contrived reinforcers and schedule of reinforcement required in the training program cannot be removed entirely due to the ineffectiveness of natural reinforcers and schedules, it may be necessary for teachers and parents to use procedures similar to those used in the training setting. In the previously described Walker and Buckley* program, a procedure of "peer reprogramming" was used successfully with some children to maintain gains in academic and behavioral areas. After return from the experimental classroom to the regular class, the problem children could earn points for appropriate social and academic behavior. After a certain number of points were earned, these could be exchanged for group reinforcement (special activities) for the entire class. Peers were most effective in influencing desired behavior. In a later study, Walker et al.* demonstrated that by training teachers in behavior maintenance techniques desired effects could be maintained after return to the regular classroom.

Walker et al. 1975

Hislop et al. 1973

Hislop et al.* made effective use of a combination of procedures to enhance long-term generalization of behavior gains obtained in a special class token economy program for functionally retarded children. Parallel programming—half-time in special class and half-time in regular class—active school consultation between special and regular staffs concomitant with remedial programming, parent involvement, and gradual phasing of children from the special to regular classrooms on a full-time basis were effective in insuring long-term transfer and maintenance of gains observed in the token program.

Wahler 1969

In the previously described Wahler* program, teachers were trained to use the same procedures in the classroom which parents had used in the home to increase the cooperative and study behaviors of their children. Patterson and Brodsky* used various behavior management procedures in a clinic setting to produce desired behavior change in a boy who exhib-

Patterson and Brodsky 1966

ited numerous problem behaviors. Temper tantrums, which showed a pronounced reduction in frequency and duration in a clinic training setting, quickly disappeared in the kindergarten class setting following the initiation by adults in this school setting of appropriate training procedures.

In most programs designed to change "autistic" behavior patterns, parents and others are trained to utilize those events and schedules found effective in the training program.* Lovaas et al.,* in following autistic children from one to four years after removal from treatment, reported that those children whose parents had been trained to carry out the behavior therapy maintained their initial gains and continued to improve. Other children who were institutionalized, and thus were not provided continued behavioral programming, showed regression.

For example, Kozloff 1973; Risley and Wolf 1967; Lovaas et al. 1973

Teach the Child to Manage His Own Behavior

Behavior may generalize from one setting to another if the child or adolescent is taught to self-instruct and to reinforce himself. This is accomplished by teaching him adequate verbal labels which he uses as discriminative cues to control certain of his behaviors in choice situations. He also may be taught to reinforce himself by labeling his appropriate behavior with such comments as "good job," "that's great," or "you finished that hard one," or to provide himself with extrinsic reinforcers available to him. (Detailed procedures for enhancing self-management is discussed in Chapter 12.)

Summary

It is evident that maintenance of behavior over time and generalization or transfer from the learning to other settings are interrelated. Both must be provided careful consideration in educational programs for children with exceptional learning and behavior characteristics. Even though in many instances both maintenance and generalization will occur spontaneously as a result of various reinforcement and cue conditions inherent in situations other than those present during learning, such cannot be depended upon. The greater the number and severity of learning and behavior difficulties present in a child, the greater the necessity for systematic programming for maintenance and generalization.

CONCURRENT BEHAVIOR CHANGE

Although behavior management programs are designed to influence specific problem behavior areas, it is not uncommon to find desirable changes in other behaviors which were provided no apparent attention. Several examples of behavioral education programs are described briefly to illustrate this finding. Buell et al.* worked with one child.

Buell et al. 1968

> The child showed no cooperative play with peers, never used their names, seldom spoke to them or touched them, and showed only a low rate of parallel play as her major form of social interaction. She rarely used the outdoor play equipment. Although she interacted frequently with the teacher, this behavior was of a dependent and immature baby-like nature.
>
> One focus of the developmental education program was on increasing the child's use of outdoor play equipment. It was reasoned that if her rate of using the play equipment was increased and maintained, she would have considerable opportunity for a variety of interactions with peers. These new experiences should contribute to her social development.
>
> A behavior-shaping program was implemented using physical guidance as a prompt and social reinforcement of successive approximations of appropriate and prolonged play behavior. Consistent, continuous social reinforcement was provided for all forms of equipment play.
>
> Use of outdoor play equipment during times when it was available to the child rose from approximately 2 percent prior to the program to a near 70 percent rate within two months. Other primarily child-oriented behaviors showed a collateral change. The child began to touch other children, to use their names, and to play cooperatively with them. At the same time the baby behavior disappeared.

Nordquist 1971

Nordquist* gives us a second illustration of concurrent behavior change.

> A five-year-old boy was provided a behavior management program designed to change his oppositional behavior. The boy was disruptive, often refusing to comply with adult requests and had an average of one tantrum per day. A long history of bed wetting was reported. The program consisted of socially reinforcing the boy for appropriate compliance and other social behaviors and of isolating him in his room if he exhibited oppositional behavior. The boy's parents ignored his bed wetting.
>
> Cooperative behavior improved greatly and oppositional behavior reduced to a minimum following initiation of the program. The bed wetting also was eliminated completely even though it was not provided any direct attention. These behavior changes remained stable over a continuous eighteen-month period.

Wahler et al. 1970

In a highly similar program Wahler et al.* used social reinforcement and brief isolation periods to control oppositional behavior in a young boy who stuttered frequently. It was found that the rate of stuttering lowered as the child began to develop improved skills of cooperation, although no direct program attention had been given to the stuttering.

From Twardosz and Sajwaj* comes a third illustration.

Twardosz and Sajwaj 1972

> *Sitting behavior was reinforced in a hyperactive four-year-old boy who attended an early education program with seven other children with learning and behavior difficulties. He had poorly developed social skills, did not spontaneously talk to anyone, responded echolalically to questions, rarely played with toys, and spent most of his time either lying on the floor in unusual squirming postures or in walking around the room. After being reinforced with tokens and praise for sitting at a table during playtime in which table toys were provided, the boy showed a dramatic increase in time spent in sitting at the table. This new behavior resulted in an equally significant reduction in his inappropriate posturing behavior and a most desirable increase in the amount of time playing with toys and in being in close proximity to other children.*

The results of these behavior management programs lend support to the observation that no single or group of a child's behaviors exist in isolation. Changes in any behavior will potentially result in changes in the likelihood of occurrence of other behaviors. This change may be related to a number of possible influences.

Increased Opportunity to Behave Appropriately

If the child engages frequently in inappropriate behavior he has less opportunity to learn or demonstrate more desired ways of behaving. A reduction in or elimination of the inappropriate behavior will give the child more time to attend to and interact with learning programs provided in the educational setting. Risley* was successful in increasing the amount of eye contact and the imitation behavior of a child after successful elimination of various stereotyped behaviors which previously occurred at a very high rate. Prior to the elimination of the inappropriate behavior, Risley was unable to encourage the child to engage in the socially desirable behaviors. Koegel et al.* found that spontaneous play behavior increased in young "autistic" children following the suppression of high occurrences of self-stimulatory behavior. Thus, one possible beneficial side effect of eliminating strongly disruptive behavior is that the child is more available for involvement in a program designed to teach appropriate ways of behaving.

Risley 1968

Koegel et al. 1974

Increased Likelihood of Behaving Appropriately

Every child has a large number of responses in his repertoire at any time. If some of these are occurring at a frequent rate, others cannot be occurring. If a child engages in frequent temper tantrums, he cannot be smiling and playing with other children even though these skills are in his repertoire. Thus, a second beneficial side effect of reduction in, or elimination of, inappropriate behaviors is the increased likelihood that appropriate behaviors will occur. Carlson et al.* observed that after reduction of excessive temper tantrum behavior in a child she began to play and take part in group activities with her peers on the playground and to look noticeably happier.

Carlson et al. 1968

Increased Positive Influence of Social Environment

Changes in appropriate behavior will potentially result in changes in the child's social environment which may have a beneficial effect on other behaviors. A child with highly aggressive behaviors may well frighten other children away. Elimination of these aggressive behaviors will open new modes of social interaction and reinforcement.

Increased Likelihood of Generalized Behavior Patterns

Increase in the strength of any particular response, whether appropriate or inappropriate, may result in an increase in the strength of other similar behaviors. Behavior management programs concerned with the development of imitation skills in young children illustrate this beneficial side effect.* After reinforcing the child for imitating various motor responses, it was noted that the child began to imitate new behaviors which previously had never been reinforced. He acquired a generalized pattern of imitation. In a similar manner, a child who has been reinforced for approaching and interacting with peers in his class will play new games with children even though he has never been reinforced specifically for playing these games. Thus, reinforcement of any new behavior potentially facilitates the development of more general behavior patterns.

Garcia et al. 1971

HOW CHILDREN INFLUENCE ADULT BEHAVIOR

Children and adolescents obviously influence the behavior of parents and teachers in the same manner that they are influenced by the adults. If the teacher is successful in influencing the acquisition and appropriate occurrence of desired behavior patterns, these teacher behaviors will be strengthened. The specific behaviors are reinforced by the positive feedback. Under similar circumstances in the future, the teacher will be more likely to use these or similar approaches.

On the other hand, a teacher can also develop inappropriate teaching habits in terms of the effects which these produce. A harsh threat may indeed result in a temporary reduction in an adolescent's bothersome behavior. Such teacher behavior is thus strengthened as it produces an immediate (albeit temporary) removal of an unpleasant condition. This was illustrated in a recent observation.

> A group of four- and five-year-old children with cognitive behavior deficits were seated in a semicircle around a teacher and were asked to sit quietly as she presented each of them with individually prepared table tasks. Sue, sitting at one end of the table, began making a clucking sound as the teacher was presenting materials to children at the opposite end of the table. The teacher turned suddenly, shook her finger at Sue and said, "No." Sue immediately broke out in a big smile and replied, "Hi." The teacher turned again to the other children. The sequence was repeated on two additional occasions. After each reprimand, Sue sat quietly for a few seconds prior to beginning her disruptive clucking. After the teacher turned away following the third reprimand, Sue next stood up and reached for the work materials on the table in front of the teacher. This brought an immediate "No" from the teacher followed by the teacher grasping Sue's hand and firmly returning the child to her chair. This procedure was followed two additional times before the teacher gave Sue her table work. Following this, Sue became quite absorbed in her coloring task and created no more difficulty for the teacher during the period.

In analyzing this interaction pattern between Sue and the teacher, it becomes clear that Sue's disruptive behavior was being strengthened and maintained by the rather immediate and consistent teacher attention which it produced. At the same time, the teacher's behaviors of finger shaking, frowning at the child, and verbalizing "No" were also being maintained as these produced an immediate though temporary termination of the disturbing activity. In this interactional pattern the teacher was maintaining the child's disruptive behavior just as the child was maintaining the teacher's ineffective reprimanding behavior. The suppressive effects of the reprimand were so temporary that the teacher's tactics were ineffective in influencing the child's behavior. The example does illustrate, nonetheless, how behavior can be influenced by consequences which may not be detected by the educator.

REFERENCES

Allen, K. E., Turner, K. D., and Everett, P. M. A behavior modification classroom for Head Start children with problem behaviors. *Exceptional Children*, 1970, 37, 119–127.

Baer, D. M., Peterson, R. F., and Sherman, J. A. The development of imitation by reinforcing behavioral similarity to a model. *Journal of Experimental Analysis of Behavior*, 1967, 10, 405–416.

Baer, D. M., Wolf, M. M., and Risley, T. R. Some current dimensions of applied behavior analysis. *Journal of Applied Behavior Analysis*, 1968, 1, 91–97.

Bailey, J. S., Timbers, G. D., Phillips, E. L., and Wolf, M. M. Modification of articulation errors of pre-delinquents by their peers. *Journal of Applied Behavior Analysis*, 1971, 4, 265–281.

Bandura, A. *Principles of Behavior Modification*. New York: Holt, Rinehart & Winston, 1969.

Barrish, H., Saunders, M., and Wolf, M. Good behavior game: Effects of individual contingencies for group consequences on disruptive behavior in a classroom. *Journal of Applied Behavior Analysis*, 1969, 2, 119–124.

Becker, W. C., Engelmann, S., and Thomas, D. R. *Teaching: A Course in Applied Psychology*. Chicago: Science Research Associates, 1971.

Bricker, W. A., and Bricker, D. D. A program of language training for the severely language-handicapped child. *Exceptional Children*, 1970, 37, 101–111.

Broden, M., Bruce, C., Mitchell, M., Carter, V., and Hall, R. Effects of teacher attention on attending behavior of two boys at adjacent desks. *Journal of Applied Behavior Analysis*, 1970, 3, 199–203.

Buell, J., Stoddard, P., Harris, F. R., and Baer, D. M. Collateral social development accompanying reinforcement of outdoor play in a preschool child. *Journal of Applied Behavior Analysis*, 1968, 1, 167–173.

Bushell, D., Wrobel, P., and Michaelis, M. Applying "group" contingencies to the classroom study behavior of preschool children. *Journal of Applied Behavior Analysis*, 1968, 1, 55–61.

Butterfield, E. C., and Belmont, J. M. The role of verbal processes in short-term memory. In R. L. Schiefelbusch (Ed.) *Language Research with the Mentally Retarded*. Baltimore: University Park Press, 1972. Pp. 231–248.

Butterfield, E. C., Wambold, C., and Belmont, J. M. On the theory and practice of improving short-term memory. *American Journal of Mental Deficiency*, 1973, 77, 644–669.

Carlson, C. S., Arnold, C. R., Becker, W. C., and Madsen, C. H. The elimination of tantrum behavior of a child in an elementary classroom. *Behavior Research and Therapy*, 1968, 6, 117–119.

Chadwick, B. A., and Day, R. C. Systematic reinforcement: Academic performance of underachieving students. *Journal of Applied Behavior Analysis*, 1971, 4, 311–319.

Csapo, M. Peer models reverse the "one bad apple spoils the barrel" theory. *Teaching Exceptional Children*, 1972, 5, 20–24.

Drabman, R., Spitalnik, R., and Spitalnik, K. Sociometric and disruptive behavior as a function of four types of token reinforcement programs. *Journal of Applied Behavior Analysis*, 1974, 7, 93–101.

Duckworth, S. V., Ragland, G. G., Sommerfeld, R. E., and Wyne, M. D. Modification of conceptual impulsivity in retarded children. *American Journal of Mental Deficiency*, 1974, 79, 59–63.

Eisenberg, L. The autistic child in adolescence. *American Journal of Psychiatry*, 1956, 112, 607–612.

Engelmann, S., and Bruner, E. *Participant's Manual, DISTAR Orientation* (Rev. Ed.) Chicago: Science Research Associates, 1971.

Epstein, M. H., Hallahan, D. P., and Kauffman, J. M. Implications of the reflectivity-impulsivity dimension for special education. *Journal of Special Education*, 1975, 9, 11–25.

Gagné, R. M. *The Conditions of Learning*. (2nd Ed.) New York: Holt, Rinehart & Winston, 1970.

Garcia, E., Baer, D. M., and Firestone, I. The development of generalized imitation within topographically determined boundaries. *Journal of Applied Behavior Analysis*, 1971, 4, 101–112.

Garcia, E., and DeHaven, E. Use of operant techniques in the establishment and generalization of language: A review and analysis. *American Journal of Mental Deficiency*, 1974, 79, 169–178.

Gittelman, M. Behavioral rehearsal as a technique in child treatment. *Journal of Child Psychology and Psychiatry*, 1965, 6, 251–255.

Glavin, J. P. Behaviorally oriented resource rooms: A follow-up. *Journal of Special Education*, 1974, 8, 337–347.

Glavin, J. P., Quay, H. C., Annesley, R. F., and Werry, J. S. An experimental resource room program for classroom behavior problem children. *Exceptional Children*, 1971, 38, 131–137.

Gorton, C. E. The effects of various classroom environments on performance of a mental task by mentally retarded and normal children. *Education and Training of the Mentally Retarded*, 1972, 7, 32–38.

Hallahan, D. P., and Cruickshank, W. M. *Psychoeducational Foundations of Learning Disabilties*. Englewood Cliffs, N. J.: Prentice-Hall, 1973.

Hanley, E. M. Review of research involving applied behavior analysis in the classroom. *Review of Educational Research*, 1970, 40, 597–625.

Harcum, P. M., and Harcum, E. R. Tempo modification in visual perception of EMR children. *Perceptual and Motor Skills*, 1973, 37, 179–188.

Hartung, J. R. A review of procedures to increase verbal imitation skills and functional speech in autistic children. *Journal of Speech and Hearing Disorders*, 1970, 35, 203–217.

Herman, S. H., and Tramontana, J. Instructions and group versus individual reinforcement in modifying disruptive group behavior. *Journal of Applied Behavior Analysis*, 1971, 4, 113–119.

Hislop, M. W., Moore, S., and Stanish, B. Remedial classroom programming: Long-term transfer effects from a token economy system. *Mental Retardation*, 1973, 11, 18–21.

Johnston, M. K., Kelley, C. S., Harris, F. R., and Wolf, M. M. An application of reinforcement principles to development of motor skills of a young child. *Child Development*, 1966, 37, 379–387.

Jones, R. T., and Kazdin, A. E. Programming response maintenance after withdrawing token reinforcement. *Behavior Therapy*, 1975, 6, 153–164.

Kazdin, A. E. The effect of vicarious reinforcement of attentive behavior in the classroom. *Journal of Applied Behavior Analysis*, 1973, 6, 71–78.

Keogh, B. K. Hyperactivity and learning disorders: Review and speculation. *Exceptional Children*, 1971, 38, 101–109.

Koegel, R. L., Firestone, P. B., Kramme, K. W., and Dunlap, G. Increasing spontaneous play by suppressing self-stimulation in autistic children. *Journal of Applied Behavior Analysis*, 1974, 7, 521–528.

Koegel, R. L., and Rincover, A. Treatment of psychotic children in a classroom environment: 1. Learning in a large group. *Journal of Applied Behavior Analysis*, 1974, 7, 45–59.

Kozloff, M. A. *Reaching the Autistic Child: A Parent Training Program*. Champaign, Ill.: Research, 1973.

Lahey, B. B. Modification of the frequency of descriptive adjectives in the speech of Head Start children through modeling without reinforcement. *Journal of Applied Behavior Analysis*, 1971, 4, 19–22.

Lahey, B. B., and Lawrence, J. H. An analysis of the effects of modeling on morphemic and syntactic features as a function of family income and age. *Journal of Applied Behavior Analysis*, 1974, 7, 482.

Larsen, L. A., and Bricker, W. A. A manual for parents and teachers of severely and moderately retarded children. *IMRID Papers and Reports*, Vol. V., No. 22. Nashville: George Peabody College, 1968.

Lovaas, O. I. A program for the establishment of speech in psychotic children. In H. Sloane and B. MacAulay (Eds.) *Operant Procedures in Remedial Speech and Language Training*. Boston: Houghton Mifflin, 1968. Pp. 125–154.

Lovaas, O. I., Koegel, R., Simmons, J. Q., and Long, J. S. Some generalization and follow-up measures on autistic children in behavior therapy. *Journal of Applied Behavior Analysis*, 1973, 6, 131–166.

Lovaas, O. I., and Schreibman, L. Stimulus overselectivity of autistic children in a two-stimulus situation. *Behavior Research and Therapy*, 1971, 9, 305–310.

Lovaas, O. I., Schreibman, L., Koegel, R., and Rehm, R. Selective responding by autistic children to multiple sensory input. *Journal of Abnormal Psychology*, 1971, 77, 211–222.

Lovitt, T. C., Guppy, T. E., and Blattner, J. E. The use of free-time contingency with fourth graders to increase spelling accuracy. *Behavior Research and Therapy*, 1969, 7, 151–156.

Lowry, P., and Ross, L. Severely retarded children as impulsive responders: Improved performance with response delay. *American Journal of Mental Deficiency*, 1975, 80, 133–138.

Martin, J. A. The control of imitative and non-imitative behaviors in severely retarded children through "generalized instuction-following." *Journal of Experimental Child Psychology*, 1971, 11, 390–400.

Medland, M. B., and Stachnik, T. J. Good-behavior game: A replication and systematic analysis. *Journal of Applied Behavior Analysis*, 1972, 5, 45–51.

Metz, J. R. Conditioning generalized imitation in autistic children. *Journal of Experimental Child Psychology*, 1965, 2, 389–399.

Nordquist, V. M. The modification of a child's enuresis: Some response-response relationships. *Journal of Applied Behavior Analysis*, 1971, 4, 241–247.

O'Connor, R. D. Modification of social withdrawal through symbolic modeling. *Journal of Applied Behavior Analysis*, 1969, 2, 15–22.

O'Leary, K. D., Becker, W. C., Evans, M. B., and Saudargas, R. A. A token reinforcement program in a public school: A replication and systematic analysis. *Journal of Applied Behavior Analysis*, 1969, 2, 3–13.

Packard, R. G. The control of "classroom attention": A group contingency for complex behavior. *Journal of Applied Behavior Analysis*, 1970, 3, 13–28.

Paloutzian, R. F., Hasazi, J., Streifel, J., and Edgar, C. L. Promotion of positive social interaction in severely retarded young children. *American Journal of Mental Deficiency*, 1971, 75, 519–524.

Patterson, G. R. An application of conditioning techniques to the control of a hyperactive child. In L. P. Ullman and L. Krasner (Eds.) *Case Studies in Behavior Modification*. New York: Holt, Rinehart & Winston, 1965. Pp. 370–375.

Patterson, G. R. and Brodsky, G. A behavior modification programme for a child with multiple problem behaviors. *Journal of Child Psychology and Psychiatry*, 1966, 7, 277–295.

Patterson, G. R., and Cobb, J. Dyadic analysis of aggressive behaviors. In J. P. Hill (Ed.) *Minnesota Symposium on Child Psychology*, Vol. 5. Minneapolis: University of Minnesota Press, 1971. Pp. 72–129.

Phillips, E. L., Phillips, E. A., Fixsen, D. L., and Wolf, M. M. Achievement Place: Modification of the behaviors of pre-delinquent boys within a token economy. *Journal of Applied Behavior Analysis*, 1971, 4, 45–59.

Rincover, A., and Koegel, R. L. Setting generality and stimulus control in autistic children. *Journal of Applied Behavior Analysis*, 1975, 8, 235–246.

Risley, T. R. The effects and side effects of punishing the autistic behavior of a deviant child. *Journal of Applied Behavior Analysis*, 1968, 1, 21–34.

Risley, T. R., and Wolf, M. M. Establishing functional speech in echolalic children. *Behavior Research and Therapy*, 1967, 5, 73–88.

Rosenbaum, A., O'Leary, K. D., and Jacob, R. G. Behavioral intervention with hyperactive children: Group consequences as a supplement to individual contingencies. *Behavior Therapy*, 1975, 6, 315–323.

Ross, D. M. Effect on learning of psychological attachment to a film model. *American Journal of Mental Deficiency*, 1970, 74, 701–707.

Ross, D. M., Ross, S. A., and Downing, M. L. Intentional training vs. observational learning of mediational strategies in EMR children. *American Journal of Mental Deficiency*, 1973, 78, 292–299.

Shores, R. E., and Haubrich, P. A. Effect of cubicles in educating emotionally disturbed children. *Exceptional Children*, 1969, 36, 21–26.

Sprague, R. L., and Toppe, L. K. Relationship between activity level and delay of reinforcement in the retarded. *Journal of Experimental Child Psychology*, 1966, 3, 390–397

Staats, A. W. *Social Behaviorism*. Homewood, Ill.: Dorsey, 1975.

Stevenson, H. W. *Children's Learning*. New York: Appleton-Century-Crofts, 1972.

Stromer, R. Modifying letter and number reversals in elementary school children. *Journal of Applied Behavior Analysis*, 1975, 8, 211.

Twardosz, S., and Sajwaj, T. Multiple effects of a procedure to increase sitting in a hyperactive retarded boy. *Journal of Applied Behavior Analysis*, 1972, 5, 73–78.

Wahler, R. G. Setting generality: Some specific and general effects of child behavior therapy. *Journal of Applied Behavior Analysis*, 1969, 2, 239–246.

Wahler, R. G., Sperling, K. A., Thomas, M. R.,

Tetter, N. C., and Luper, H. T. The modification of childhood stuttering: Some response-response relationships. *Journal of Experimental Child Psychology*, 1970, 9, 411–428.

Walker, H. M., and Buckley, N. K. Programming generalization and maintenance of treatment effects across time and settings. *Journal of Applied Behavior Analysis*, 1972, 5, 209–224.

Walker, H. M., Hops, H., and Johnson, S. M. Generalization and maintenance of classroom treatment effects. *Behavior Therapy*, 1975, 6, 188–200.

Ward, M. H., and Baker, B. L. Reinforcement therapy in the classroom. *Journal of Applied Behavior Analysis*, 1968, 1, 323–328.

Werry, J. S., and Sprague, R. L. Hyperactivity. In C. G. Costello (Ed.) *Symptoms of Psychopathology: A Handbook*. New York: John Wiley, 1970. Pp. 397–417.

Zeaman, D., and House, B. J. The role of attention in retardate discrimination learning. In N. R. Ellis (Ed.) *Handbook of Mental Deficiency*. New York: McGraw-Hill, 1963. Pp. 159–223.

Zigler, E. Developmental versus difference theories of mental retardation and the problem of motivation. *American Journal of Mental Deficiency*, 1969, 73, 536–556.

Zigler, E. The retarded child as a whole person. In D. K. Routh (Ed.) *The Experimental Psychology of Mental Retardation*. Chicago: Aldine, 1973. Pp. 231–322.

10

Reducing or Eliminating Behavior Characteristics

Children and adolescents acquire a range of inappropriate learning and behavior characteristics which can be highly disturbing both to the person and his environment. Tom's constant interruptions when the teacher is talking with other children and his tendency to refuse to fulfill classroom assignments are disturbing behaviors that require attention. Other patterns may be acceptable under certain conditions but not under others. Sue's whining behavior when her older sister does not give in to her may be quite acceptable to her parents "because Sue is so handicapped." This same behavior at school would be viewed as unacceptable by teachers and peers.

Some children become hyperactive, noncooperative, poor learners, disruptive, noncompliant, nonattentive, or dependent. In numerous instances, these inappropriate learning and behavior characteristics have been strengthened by consequences which these behaviors have produced. The child who is aggressive and noncompliant is not intentionally naughty. He does not find various learning tasks unpleasant and anxiety producing as a result of any deliberate desire on his part. He does not behave in these ways because he is mentally retarded, emotionally disturbed, learning disabled, or physically handicapped. He engages in these behaviors due to thousands of educational experiences gained in his social environments. In most instances these environments have not intended to create inappropriate learning and behavior characteristics. In fact, those in the environment who interact with children and adolescents are seldom even aware of the role which various experiences may assume in influencing the development of undesirable learning and behavior characteristics. Regardless of the intent or awareness of parents, siblings, teachers, or other social agents, however, the manner in which those in the educational/social environments react as the child behaves does produce an immediate effect which does influence the manner in which the child will behave in the future.

As emphasized, inappropriate as well as appropriate behaviors may be strengthened by consequences which follow the behavior. If whining behavior results in the child "having his way," the behavior of whining under the same and similar situations is more likely to reoccur. If the adolescent's sullen attitude produces peer attention, it may well be strengthened. If the child's cooperative behavior results in teacher's approval, the child is more likely to be cooperative in the future.

Just as there are procedures which, when followed, will contribute to the strength of learning and behavior characteristics, there are also procedures which may be used to inhibit, decrease in strength, or eliminate a child's behavior patterns. The procedures available for this task include: (1) *reinforcing alternative behaviors*, (2) *extinction*, (3) *satiation*, (4) *stimulus change*, (5) *overcorrection*, and (6) *punishment*, which may involve either the *presentation* following behavior of some aversive consequence or the *removal* of various positive consequences as a result of specific behaviors engaged in by a child. The reader should note that the strength of appropriate as well as inappropriate behaviors may be reduced by these procedures. Desired behavior may be eliminated from a child's repertoire, for example, if reinforcing consequences no longer follow the behavior. Or a child who is taken advantage of by other children when he attempts to be cooperative soon ceases to be cooperative. These procedures, some of which were introduced in Table 8.1, are summarized in Table 10.1.

REINFORCING ALTERNATIVE BEHAVIORS

Reinforcing Physically Incompatible Behaviors

The major focus of educational program efforts designed to deal with problem behaviors should be on strengthening those desirable learning and behavior characteristics which will compete with and eventually replace undesirable patterns. Whenever possible, it is helpful to reinforce those characteristics which are actually physically incompatible with undesired ones. In this instance, if the child is engaging in desired behavior, he cannot at the same time be engaging in the undesired one. If he is attending, he is not distractible. If he is subvocally rehearsing information presented by the teacher, he cannot be daydreaming. Rude behavior could be ignored by the teacher and polite behavior reinforced in a systematic manner. A child who is out of his chair excessively could be reinforced for

TABLE 10.1. *Procedures for Decreasing the Strength of Behavior*

Learning Principle	*Educational Procedure*	*Example of Procedure*
Reinforcing Alternative Behavior	Positive reinforcement is provided those behaviors which will replace the inappropriate behaviors.	Susan, who is hyperactive and distractible, is reinforced positively for remaining at her desk and attending to her math assignment.
Extinction of: Behavior maintained by positive reinforcement	Behavior is not followed by the positive event associated with previous occurrence.	The teacher ignores Jeffrey following his disruptive comments.
Behavior maintained by negative reinforcement	Behavior is not followed by the removal of the aversive event associated with previous occurrence.	Helen is not permitted to leave the classroom following her temper tantrum.
Satiation	Behavior to be extinguished is engaged in a repetitive and excessive manner.	Ms. Mize requires Jennie to make derogatory comments for fifteen minutes while the classmates stop their work and listen.
Stimulus Change	Discriminative events which control behavior are removed, or events which inhibit behavior or which influence competing behavior are presented.	Jim is moved to the front row to control his excessive talking.
Overcorrection Restitution	Following inappropriate behavior, the child is required to restore the environment to an improved state.	Cleo, who marked on the wall next to her desk, washed the entire wall until all marks were removed.
Positive Practice	Following inappropriate behavior, the child is provided an opportunity to practice the appropriate behavior repeatedly.	Kathy, who forgot to ask permission prior to leaving the classroom, is required to practice asking permission for ten consecutive trials.

TABLE 10.1.   Continued

Learning Principle	Educational Procedure	Example of Procedure
Punishment Presentation of Aversive Events	Behavior is followed by an aversive consequence.	John, who had just arrived twenty minutes late, was reprimanded by the coach.
Time-out	Behavior results in the removal of possible reinforcing events for a designated period of time.	Mr. Jeffrey turns away from Alan and does not attend to him for three minutes following his outburst.
Response-cost	Behavior results in the loss of reinforcing events.	Richard loses his weekend dating privileges following his refusal to complete his homework assignments.

remaining seated and for engaging in an assigned task. Such planned reinforcement of remaining-at-desk and other task-related behaviors would strengthen these behaviors and thus render unnecessary other less-desired procedures which attempt to suppress or inhibit inappropriate behavior. Ayllon et al.,* in illustration, strengthened math and reading behaviors in hyperactive "learning disabled" children and found that incompatible hyperactivity decreased significantly.

Ayllon et al. 1975

Reinforcing Other Positive Behaviors

On other occasions, although physically incompatible behavior cannot be strengthened through positive reinforcement, it would be possible to teach a more appropriate alternative behavior which gradually would replace the undesired one. Positive reinforcement of competing behaviors which will replace the undesired one informs the child precisely what he can do to obtain positive reinforcement and to avoid or terminate unpleasant consequences. Ayllon and Roberts* eliminated high rates of disruptive classroom behavior in five boys attending a fifth-grade class of thirty-eight students by providing token reinforcement for academic performance. Prior to the program the boys' average level of disruption was 34 percent while their reading accuracy performance was below 50 percent; after

Ayllon and Roberts 1974

systematic token reinforcement was applied to reading performance only, reading performance increased to 85 percent and disruptive behavior dropped to about 5 percent.

Providing positive reinforcement for desired behaviors which replaced inappropriate ones was used successfully in a program described by Hamblin et al.* The children were described as "five extraordinarily aggressive four-year-old boys" who had been diagnosed by psychiatrists as hyperactive and who had not responded to drug therapy. Hamblin noted that the classroom teacher

Hamblin et al. 1971

> was, variously, strict disciplinarian, wise counselor, clever arbitrator and sweet peacemaker. In each role, however, she failed miserably. After the eighth day, the average of the children was 150 sequences of aggression per day! . . . Wild? Very. These were barbarous little boys who enjoyed battle. Miss Sally did her best but they were just more clever than she, and they *always* won. Whether she wanted to or not, they could always drag her into the fray, and just go at it harder and harder until she capitulated. She was finally drawn to their level, trading a kick for a kick and spit for a spit in the face. [Pp. 101–102]

The teacher initiated a procedure of providing token reinforcement for cooperative behavior (compliance with another's request or spontaneously helping the teacher or another boy) and turning her back on an aggressor. After a few weeks of this new procedure, the frequency of aggression went down to a near-normal level and cooperation increased to a level which exceeded that found in the typical preschool classroom.

Both Positive and Negative Reinforcement Useful

Desired behaviors which compete with and eventually replace inappropriate behaviors may be strengthened by procedures involving negative as well as positive reinforcement. A child who engages in rude behavior may be required to sit in isolation following rude behavior. He may be permitted to shorten his confinement by being polite to his peers. Polite behavior may also be reinforced positively by peers and teacher at a later time as he is polite to them in appropriate circumstances. Thus, a general behavioral pattern of being polite to others is strengthened because it results in the removal of unpleasant conditions associated with isolation (negative reinforcement) and also produces, at other times, pleasant consequences (positive reinforcement).

Selecting Desired Alternative Behaviors

It is easy to criticize or otherwise punish inappropriate behavior as it occurs; it is more difficult to identify and to provide systematic reinforcement for appropriate alternative modes of responding. The major question should be: "What should the child be doing at the time he is behaving inappropriately?'' Once this is established and demonstrated to the child, such behaviors or reasonable alternatives can more easily be strengthened through reinforcement. It may be helpful to encourage the child to rehearse the alternative behaviors and then to provide whatever guidance is necessary to insure that these behaviors will occur at the appropriate time and place.

In preparation for initiating a procedure of reinforcing alternative behaviors, it is useful to list acceptable alternatives to undesired behaviors.

Undesired Behavior	*Alternative Desired Behaviors*
Crying.	Smiling.
Wandering around room.	Sitting at table, completing table tasks.
Hitting and pushing peers; teasing, annoying, threatening, and disparaging peers.	Interacting cooperatively with peers; providing complimentary comments.
Sitting passively in bored inactivity.	Initiating solitary activities of an academic or leisure nature.
Engaging in stereotyped hand-waving.	Using hands in appropriate motor activity such as throwing a ball, drawing, or cutting.
Active refusal to cooperate with teacher.	Cooperative attitude in school activities.

In considering which alternative behaviors to reinforce, select those most beneficial for the individual child. A child who is aggressive toward younger peers could be taught to stay away from these peers. However, this alternative behavior pattern would not reflect constructive social skills. A more acceptable alternative behavior pattern to replace the aggressive one would consist of such skills as providing assistance to, playing, and working cooperatively with younger peers. These competing behavior patterns should be rehearsed by the child and reinforced by the teacher in situations in which the undesired behavior occurs. Such rehearsal usually increases the likelihood that such alternative behaviors will occur in the future. Whenever possible, all reinforcement following undesired behavior should be terminated, and reinforcement provided only as a consequence of the alternative behaviors.

Differentially Reinforcing Other Behaviors

In reinforcing behaviors as acceptable alternatives to undesired ones, various procedures are available to the educator. First, a procedure involving *differential reinforcement of other behaviors* (DRO) may be used. Reinforcement is provided any and all other appropriate behaviors which occur under the conditions in which the inappropriate behavior occurs. Hyperactive and distractible Judy may be reinforced for any behaviors which compete with these modes of responding. Reinforcement may be provided for such behaviors as task persistence, attention to verbal instruction, remaining at desk, watching a slide presentation, responding appropriately under distracting stimulation, and staying on her cot for a designated period of time during rest period. If possible, attention would not be provided undesired behaviors. Thus, undesired behaviors are ignored and a range of other, appropriate, competing behaviors is provided positive reinforcement.

A study by Becker et al.* demonstrates the value of differential positive reinforcement of a range of desired behaviors that replaced a variety of disruptive ones.

Becker et al. 1967

A group of culturally deprived children attending elementary-school classes were identified as exhibiting a high rate of disruptive behaviors judged to be incompatible with learning. These included such activities as getting out of one's seat, walking around, rocking in one's chair, tapping a pencil or other objects, grabbing objects or work, destroying another's property, hitting, slapping, kicking, pulling hair, crying, answering teacher without being called on, ignoring teacher's request, and making comments when no question is asked. Through a set of explicit rules the classroom teacher initially reminded the children of the expected behaviors. Then, whenever possible, she began ignoring the inappropriate behavior and praising any behavior which facilitated learning. Statements of praise and recognition were used: "Good job; you're doing fine." "I like the way you're working quietly." "I see Johnny is ready to work." After a few weeks of providing this social reinforcement for appropriate behaviors (many of which directly competed with the child's unruly behavior), a significant reduction was noted in those behaviors incompatible with effective classroom learning. Seven-year-old Albert had been described as a noisy child who fought with others, would not stay in his seat, blurted out, did little required work, sulked, and responded negatively to everything. These behaviors showed a dramatic reduction following the initiation and consistent use of the "ignore and praise" technique. After a few weeks the teacher described him as a "delightful child and an enthusiastic member of class."

As another example of differential reinforcement of incompatible behaviors, Brown and Elliott* describe their experience with a group of children attending a nursery school program. Behaviors of physical and verbal aggression were ignored and cooperative and nonaggressive behaviors were provided immediate and frequent teacher attention. Within a

Brown and Elliott 1965

few days a significant reduction was noted in both physical and verbal aggressive behaviors.

As a second tactic for reinforcing competing behaviors, reinforcement may be provided a single specific behavior. A child who is rude may be reinforced specifically for being polite. A child who is out of her seat excessively may be reinforced specifically for remaining in her chair.

Differentially Reinforcing Low-rate Responding

Finally, the teacher may reinforce the child for engaging less frequently in the undesired behavior. This procedure, called *differential reinforcement of low-rate responding*, would be used typically in combination with the previous procedures. The child would be reinforced both for alternative behaviors and for decreasing occurrence of the undesired behaviors. This procedure was used effectively to eliminate a child's excessive scratching behavior:*

Allen and Harris 1966

> In this behavior management program, a five-year-old child was provided with both tangible and social reinforcement following periods of time in which the scratching behavior did not occur. Whenever the scratching did occur, it was ignored. At the initiation of the program, the child would scratch herself until she bled. The scratching over the past year had resulted in large sores and scabs on her forehead, nose, cheeks, chin, and one arm and leg. Pediatric and psychiatric consultation had failed to eliminate the behavior or to identify a medical basis for it. Within a few weeks of reinforcing the child for increasingly longer periods in which no scratching had occurred, the excessive scratching behavior was eliminated.

When using a procedure of reinforcing alternative behaviors, the possibility of reoccurrence of the inappropriate behavior remains. Even though the undesired behavior may occur with less frequency and may eventually disappear as other behaviors become relatively stronger, this inappropriate behavior may reappear if the alternative behaviors are not maintained through positive reinforcement. Many behavior change programs using a procedure of reinforcing alternative behaviors fail because the social environments do not continue to reinforce the desired behaviors for a sufficient period of time.

EXTINCTION

It is possible to decrease the strength of both appropriate and inappropriate behavior patterns by removing the reinforcing consequences which serve to maintain these behaviors. Under these revised conditions, a particular behavior is no longer followed by reinforcing consequences. If a social behavior occurs frequently when it is followed by praise from the teacher or attention from peers, the frequency of occurrence of the behavior could be reduced and perhaps eliminated if the praise or attention were no longer produced by the behavior. As described in Chapter 8, many of a child's behaviors are acquired and maintained because they help the child to escape from or avoid aversive consequences. If Susan's complaining behaviors failed to remove unpleasant class assignments, this behavior would reduce in frequency. An adolescent crams prior to an examination in order to avoid a failing grade. If such a study routine resulted in failing grades, i.e., did not remove the aversive consequence of failure, such behavior would decrease. Thus, behaviors maintained by negative reinforcement as well as those influenced by positive reinforcement can be extinguished if the sources of reinforcement can be removed. Behavior, then, that no longer results in positive consequences or the removal of aversive conditions will begin to occur with less frequency.

> *John, a five-year-old nonverbal child with Down's Syndrome, had learned to forcefully take toys and books away from his younger brother. This aggressive behavior pattern had been learned and continued to occur because it produced reinforcing consequences (obtaining the toys and books). Mother, although inconsistent in her response to this behavior, generally thought that John's behavior was acceptable because, "John can't talk and has no other means of making his wishes known." She rationalized, "His younger brother doesn't mind, though, because he knows John is retarded and can't help himself," even though the sibling frequently cried when John took things from him. When John entered a developmental education program, he attempted the same behavior on numerous occasions. He soon discovered that such behavior did not work; the other children would not give in to his aggressiveness. The behavior gradually disappeared in this new setting, though John was quite upset in the beginning. The behavior served no purpose in the school setting; the other children would not permit him to take their possessions. Extinction occurred; the behavior disappeared in the school setting because it was not reinforced as it had been previously. John continued his aggressive behavior at home, nonetheless, as it still worked. If this extinction procedure were followed in the home environment, the previously reinforced aggressive behavior would eventually disappear in this setting also, especially if the parents gradually shaped desired alternative means of obtaining objects from others.*

In a similar case, Terry engaged in frequent disruptive whining and shouting in the home.* Both parents, after determining that these episodes occurred on an average of ten times daily, immediately turned away from the boy when he whined or shouted. They engaged in other activities and

Hall et al. 1972

later attended to him when he was behaving appropriately. Following consistent use of this extinction procedure for about a month, the obnoxious whining and shouting behavior decreased to a daily level of two or so occurrences.

Since extinction can be most useful in an educational program designed to reduce or virtually eliminate the occurrence of problem behaviors, consideration of the following characteristic will maximize its usefulness.

Reinforcing Events May Be Difficult to Identify and Remove

An extinction procedure will be useful only if the reinforcing events maintaining the behavior can be identified and removed. This is sometimes difficult, especially for behavior which has been present for a long period of time. It is not unusual for a specific behavior pattern to be maintained by multiple sources of reinforcement. A disruptive behavior pattern, for example, may be reinforced positively by peer attention and by occasional teacher attention. Additionally, the behavior may be reinforced negatively if it results in the child's removal from an unpleasant situation. It is not unusual for the behavior itself to have secondary reinforcing characteristics, as it has been associated frequently with other sources of reinforcement. The behavior would be maintained for a period of time independent of other sources of reinforcement. Eliminating the disruptive behavior by following an extinction procedure would require removal of the positive reinforcement associated with peer and teacher attention as well as the negative reinforcement associated with the contingent termination of unpleasant conditions. To be effective, reinforcing conditions must be withheld for a sufficient length of time to insure that the reinforcement associated with the behavior itself is eliminated.

In attempting to eliminate various disruptive comments among members of her class, a teacher may begin to ignore such behaviors and to attend to more appropriate ones. She may be relatively unsuccessful, however, as reinforcement may be provided by peers. If hers is a class of disruptive, acting-out boys who frequently talk in a loud voice, interrupt others, repeat nonsense statements, and engage in similar inappropriate behaviors, it will become evident that peer reactions are most influential in maintaining these. Even though the teacher ignores the disruptive behaviors (withhold her reactions to them), it is unlikely that extinction would occur. In many such group settings where social reinforcement for inappropriate behavior is provided by peers, it is difficult—if not impossible—to utilize an extinction procedure effectively.

In some instances, the teacher may enlist the assistance of her students in cooperatively removing social consequences of disruptive behavior. Pierce* reported considerable improvement in various of a child's disruptive behaviors (stereotyped movement, excessive running around,

Pierce 1971

talking about imaginary events, and generally "acting crazy") after the child's teacher and classmates worked together in ignoring these behaviors and in attending to appropriate actions.

Behavior May Show Temporary Increase

In following an extinction procedure, there may be an initial increase in the frequency or intensity of the behavior which no longer is being reinforced. Such increased strength is usually accompanied by emotional behavior as seen, for instance, in the aggressive temper tantrum outburst of a child following withdrawal of some expected reinforcer. To illustrate, if Jane had previously received the teacher's attention whenever she yelled at her peers, her yelling may well become more frequent and louder for a short period of time after the teacher initiates the extinction procedure of ignoring her yelling.

Hawkins et al.* and Allen et al.* report similar experiences when using extinction to eliminate temper tantrums in children. In one instance a child, whose tantrums averaged five minutes prior to extinction, continued in tantrum behavior for twenty-seven minutes on the first occasion of nonreinforcement. *Thus the problem behavior put on extinction may intensify or get worse before it gets better.* This period of intensified behavior may last for hours or even for days, depending upon the behavior and the type and pattern of previous reinforcement. Behaviors associated with highly valued reinforcing events may well become more frequent and intense following initiation of an extinction procedure than if relatively unimportant reinforcing events had been provided on a less frequent basis.

Hawkins et al. 1966; Allen et al. 1970

The educator must exercise care and avoid reinforcing this more intense behavior as it occurs. If the withheld reinforcing consequence is provided as the behavior becomes worse, this more aggravating behavior may be strengthened and thus be difficult to eliminate. In these instances a more difficult problem will develop. In summary, a temporary increase in the difficulty of the behavior is a predictable result of extinction. The resurgent behavior will subside if consistent nonreinforcement is implemented.

Aggressive and Emotional Behaviors May Occur

As noted, it is not unusual for children and adolescents to display a range of more disruptive emotional behaviors under extinction conditions in which valuable positive consequences are no longer forthcoming. They may whine, cry, scream, become violent, become destructive of property, attack others, or engage in self-abusive behavior. Such children may be described as having a low-frustration tolerance. They have not developed skills of pursuing alternative ways of attaining the same or equally desirable reinforcers. As an example:

Ann had learned that Mother would let her continue playing if she whined loudly when asked to stop playing and get ready for bed. Her whining had been reinforced by the longer play period which it produced. Mother decided to ignore Ann's whining and she began to persist in her request for the child to stop playing. Under the new conditions, the whining no longer produced the positive consequence of an extended play period. The child initially engaged in more intense and vigorous emotional outbursts involving crying, screaming, and shouting, "Let me play, I don't want to go to bed." Mother remained calm and required, and then praised, cooperative behavior. The emotional outbursts, including the initial whining behavior, gradually became less frequent and intense and eventually disappeared.

The appearance and intensity of frustration reactions are related to the schedule of previous reinforcement and to the value to the child of the lost reinforcing events as well as to other of the child's characteristics. If the behavior has been reinforced frequently and consistently, the child is likely to become upset when reinforcement is terminated. In contrast, the more intermittent the previous reinforcement, the less the likelihood that the child will become disruptive. A child who has been taught to "self-control" his reactions to disappointment may demonstrate no observable frustration reactions.

Slow Reduction in Behavior Strength May Result

An extinction procedure typically results in a slow but steady decline in the nonreinforced behavior. It may take one or two weeks or longer before any decline is noted. On other occasions, however, behavior may disappear quickly following removal of reinforcing consequences. The number of times given behavior pattern will occur after reinforcing consequences have been withdrawn is related to the following:

1. The number of times the behavior has been reinforced prior to the beginning of extinction.
2. The type and magnitude of previous reinforcing experiences.
3. The pattern of reinforcement previously provided.
4. The availability of alternative means of behaving which will produce the same or equally appealing reinforcers.
5. The relative value of the reinforcer to the child at the time extinction is initiated.
6. The difficulty level of the behavior.
7. The level of assurance held by the child or adolescent that reinforcement is no longer forthcoming following the behavior.

If a child is informed that previously available consequences will no longer follow specific behavior, and if his previous experiences suggest that such information is highly reliable, the child may quickly refrain from further use of the behavior and seek other ways of producing the reinforcing consequences. If the child has had inconsistent experiences with such information, however, there may be litttle effect. That is, the greater the previous experience with extinction, the more rapid extinction will be. The child thus may learn to discriminate between situations in which reinforcement will occur and those where it may not.

The child with exceptional learning and behavior characteristics may terminate efforts at problem solution or social interaction with specific peers, for example, if numerous previous learning and extinction sequences have taught him that whenever behavior does not *immediately* result in an expected reinforcing consequence, the likelihood is minimal that further attempts will produce the desired result. Thus, behavior stops suddenly upon occurrence of nonreinforcement. Such discriminative behavior may be highly adaptive on numerous occasions, but it may become maladaptive if adopted as a general mode of reaction. It may be necessary for the teacher to provide structured systematic experiences in discriminating between situations in which "one-trial extinction" is adaptive and those in which persistence or increased effort in the face or some nonreinforcement will subsequently result in goal attainment.

Behavior that is more demanding, complex, or difficult will disappear more quickly when no longer reinforced than will a behavior requiring less effort. As noted in the previous chapter, if behavior is initially reinforced frequently, and then only in an intermittent manner, it is more likely to persist longer and occur more frequently after reinforcement has been terminated than will those behavior patterns which have been acquired and maintained through continuous reinforcement. If the behavior is being maintained by a very infrequent pattern of reinforcement, it will be most resistant to extinction, especially if the reinforcing event is quite valuable to the child. If the teacher is inconsistent in nonreinforcement during an extinction procedure, i. e., at times inadvertently *reinforcing* the behavior, the teacher may produce a behavior that becomes even more difficult to eliminate. The adolescent whose somatic complaints have resulted irregularly but rather frequently in his being excused from an unpleasant class assignment or activity is likely to persist in the complaining long after such behavior no longer results in his being excused. However, as MacMillan* has noted, the individual characteristics of each child *MacMillan 1973* interact with the schedule of reinforcement to determine the effects which an occasional reinforcement during extinction may have. Depending on the child's experience with extinction, he may have developed his own "rule" which directs his behavior under extinction conditions. An occasional inadvertent reinforcement may have little effect, if this occurrence is in conflict with the rule which the child has made.

To summarize, a behavior with a limited history of reinforcement will disappear sooner than one with a more extensive history of reinforcement. The more times the behavior has previously resulted in positive consequences, the more it will persist following the termination of reinforcing consequences. Also, the more continuously the behavior has been reinforced in the past, the more likely it is that disruptive emotional reactions will occur when reinforcement is no longer provided. A behavior which has been strengthened and maintained by highly valuable reinforcers will be more difficult to eliminate than one which has resulted in less valuable consequences. The educator should keep in mind that specific reinforcing events may vary considerably in value from child to child. Teacher attention or approval may be highly valuable to one adolescent and relatively insignificant to another. Thus the former adolescent may respond quite differently to the removal of teacher approval following specific behaviors than would be true of the latter. He may persist in the previously reinforced behavior for a much longer period of time in the hopes of obtaining the highly prized teacher approval.

Avoid Occasional Reinforcement

The relationship between persistence of behavior over periods of no reinforcement and the previous patterns by which this behavior was strengthened and maintained suggests that the educator must be prepared to withstand an indefinite period of withholding reinforcement following inappropriate behavior. Too often the educator is prone to give up after a few occassions of not reinforcing the undesired behavior, especially when the behavior pattern and related emotional reactions increase in intensity. As suggested, this increase is predictable and will usually disappear if the teacher persists in the procedure. It is most important that reinforcement of the undesired behavior *not* be provided during the extinction period. Even a single contingent reinforcement prior to complete elimination of the behavior may result in its reappearance at renewed strength. However, as noted earlier, the specific effects of reinforcement during extinction are dependent upon the value of the reinforcing event to the child, to his previous experiences with extinction, and the manner in which he conceptualizes—the "rule" he makes concerning—the renewed reinforcement.

Use the Removed Reinforcer

Hart et al. 1964

Whenever possible, when removing a reinforcing event in an effort to extinguish some undesired behavior, this event should be used to strengthen new alternative behavior patterns. An experience reported by Hart et al.* illustrates this strategy:

A four-year-old boy attending a nursery program frequently burst into crying episodes whenever confronted with the least amount of frustration. An average of eight crying outbursts was observed during the morning session. During a ten-day period, the teachers virtually eliminated this high rate by ignoring the crying episodes but attending to the boy whenever he showed any appropriate response to frustration. Social attention, which the teachers had initially provided whenever crying occurred, was apparently maintaining the crying behavior. This same consequence—social attention—was used by the teachers to strengthen competing appropriate behavior.

Other Undesired Behaviors May Appear

It is not unusual, after elimination of a problem behavior by extinction, to find that other problem behaviors occur in the same situation. This may happen because a number of behaviors may be under the influence of a single or a group of similar reinforcing consequences. If one behavior (in a group of related behaviors comprising a response class) no longer results in the desired consequence, other behaviors may be tried by the child. Some of these other behaviors may be socially appropriate and others may be as undesirable as the initial behavior which was extinguished.

Ullman and Krasner* report an interesting experience with a child who exhibited a long succession of maladaptive behaviors following initiation of an extinction procedure. The child's camp counselor ceased attending to him when he engaged in various self-punishment behaviors such as hitting, slapping, or biting himself. Following extinction of these inappropriate behaviors, the child engaged in rather intense temper tantrums. After these brought no social attention, he began to remove his clothes in public. Next, he stole food from other children's plates. Following the appearance, and extinction, of these other inappropriate behaviors, the child finally behaved appropriately. This behavior brought immediate social attention from the counselor.

Ullman and Krasner 1965

The example emphasizes the interrelationship among behaviors. The educator should neither be surprised nor discouraged when a child demonstrates a sequence of inappropriate behaviors. These apparently had been selectively reinforced more frequently than had more appropriate patterns of behavior.

Other Undesired Behaviors Should Not Be Strengthened

The educator must be careful during an extinction period not to strengthen other undesired behaviors. If teacher attention has inadvertently been reinforcing the behavior patterns which are to be extinguished, this form of social reinforcement should thereafter only be provided following appropriate behaviors.

A child had learned that his arm-waving during class could attract teacher attention. When this behavior began to occur excessively, the teacher decided to eliminate it through nonattention. After a few experiences of arm-waving without attracting the teacher's attention, the child began to stand in his chair and wave his arm rapidly. The teacher, aggravated at this new display of unwanted behavior, reprimanded him on occasion and at other infrequent times would instruct the child to come to her desk. As the teacher's attention was quite pleasing to the child, he was taught to engage in a more disturbing pattern than was initially present.

Desirable Behavior May Be Eliminated

It should be emphasized again that desirable as well as undesirable behavior may decrease in strength or be eliminated by extinction conditions. Once acquired, any behavior must be reinforced on occasion to be maintained. Newly acquired skills—being assertive toward imposing authority or interacting with peers, as examples—must be reinforced occasionally or the behaviors will become less frequent. Even well-established behaviors will become less stable and eventually disappear if reinforcement in one form or another is not provided on occasion. Recently acquired behavior of less than maximum strength must continue to be reinforced if extinction is to be avoided.

Use in Combination with Reinforcing Alternative Behavior

As emphasized, an extinction procedure should seldom be used in isolation. Such a procedure does not strengthen desired behaviors to replace those extinguished. In fact, when extinction is terminated, the behavior may reappear unless some competing behavior has been reinforced. In some cases, the child's social environment could not tolerate the temporary increase in behavior strength associated with the initiation of extinction in the absence of a plan to strengthen acceptable replacement behaviors. Reinforcement of appropriate alternative behavior becomes an integral component of an educational program using an extinction *Madsen et al. 1968* procedure. Madsen et al.* found disruptive behavior of children in elementary classes to remain unchanged following initiation of a procedure of ignoring the misbehavior. After initiation of an added feature involving social reinforcement of appropriate behavior, however, a *Hall et al. 1971* significant reduction in disruptive behavior followed. Hall et al.* used an extinction combined with a variety of positive reinforcement procedures in eliminating disruptive classroom behavior in a number of children presenting various exceptional learning and behavior characteristics.

Behavior May Reappear

In using an extinction procedure to eliminate undesired behavior patterns, the educator should not assume that once the behavior no longer occurs it is literally eliminated completely from the child's repertoire. An extinction procedure merely influences the behavior by changing the events which control its occurrence. A behavior pattern, virtually eliminated under specific conditions, may reappear as conditions change. For example, behavior eliminated through nonreinforcement during a time when the reinforcer is of limited value to a child may reappear later when the child values the reinforcer more. Also, behavior may be eliminated by extinction in one classroom but not in others in which extinction conditions are not in effect. Thus, the behavior itself is not eliminated from the child's repertoire, but consistent nonreinforcement results in its abatement.

It is a common observation that a behavior can reappear at some later time following its initial disappearance under extinction conditions. Almost every teacher has had this experience and has commented, "I thought we got rid of that immature behavior last week." This phenomenon is called *spontaneous recovery*, or temporary reappearance of previously extinguished behavior. If reinforcement is provided as the behavior reoccurs, it may quickly regain its original strength, especially if other appropriate behaviors do not result in desired reinforcing events. To emphasize, continued persistence in using the extinction procedure, in *combination* with reinforcing desired behavior, will result in a more reliable disappearance of the target behavior. This underscores the necessity of reinforcing alternative behaviors for use by the child in producing positive consequences.

Extinguish Avoidance Behavior

The reduction or extinction of avoidance behaviors becomes a most critical aspect of a program designed to promote positive behavior development. As noted, children and adolescents with exceptional learning and behavior characteristics have acquired through negative reinforcement a wide array of avoidance behaviors. Academic situations, situations involving competition, new situations, social interaction with strangers, situations which require a change in routine, and contact with authority figures—to identify a few—become aversive situations and are avoided frequently. As a consequence, the child or adolescent selectively and effectively removes himself from a wide range of situations which hold promise of considerable positive reinforcement. Such behaviors may be maintained for long periods of time due to the difficulty involved in the extinction of such avoidance reactions. If an avoidance behavior, once begun, is quite successful in avoiding an aversive situation, the child may not be again confronted with the aversive conditions. He is thus in no position to discover whether or not there has been any reduction in the aversiveness previously associated with the event or situation.

In such situations, the educator must insure that the child does approach the originally aversive situation so that he may discover that reinforcing characteristics are now a part of the environment. In illustration, the aversiveness of a classroom may be reduced drastically by reducing the requirements needed for goal attainment. Requirements which included the completion of thirty minutes of reading, twenty-five correct spelling words, or forty items produced in fifteen minutes may have been quite difficult and thus aversive. If found to be so, the child or adolescent may have engaged in a range of disruptive and/or competing emotional behaviors and thus successfully avoided the requirements altogether. Reduction of the requirements by 20 percent, for example, may reduce the aversiveness of the requirements to the point where successful completion, and thus reinforcer attainment, would be possible. In this case a combination of describing the changed contingencies to the child and providing positive reinforcement of approximations of the desired behavior may prove successful in reducing and gradually eliminating the avoidance behavior. (Further discussion of procedures for eliminating avoidance behavior and associated negative emotionality is provided in Chapter 11.)

A Final Comment on Extinction

In using extinction, the educator should avoid a sudden overall reduction in the total positive reinforcement provided a child. With many problem children, it is not unusual to find that most social attention is provided for inappropriate behaviors. Appropriate behavior not infrequently is typically ignored or reinforced much less than undesired behavior. Sudden implementation of a procedure or removal of social attention for inappropriate behaviors may leave the child with little social reinforcement. In such cases, a limited number of problems should be selected for extinction. At the same time, the withdrawn social attention should be provided contingently for more desired activities.

In conclusion, although extinction may be valuable, especially when dealing with relatively circumscribed behaviors and when used in conjunction with other procedures, practical problems are encountered. Analyzing and managing the reinforcement contingencies, especially of complex behavior and behavior of long standing, become difficult undertakings. It is difficult to identify the reinforcing events and, once identified, to remove them. Some behaviors are maintained by several different events. Also, highly influential reinforcing components are attached to or are aspects of the problem behaviors. Thus, the behavior may maintain itself for a time independent of external consequences through its own secondary reinforcement qualities.

SATIATION

In selected cases, a procedure which encourages the child to engage in a bothersome behavior over and over again until he tires of it himself may prove valuable. The purpose is not to ridicule the child but rather to call his attention to the undesirable features of his bothersome actions.

> Tim may hum or talk to himself when requested to work quietly. This behavior is distracting to others and appears to be maintained by occasional attention from his peers. Mrs. Kinlock might interrupt the class activity and state, "Tim likes to hum and talk to himself. Let's all stop our work and listen while Tim does this. Now, Tim, continue with your humming and talking." If Tim stops, the teacher would encourage him to continue until he appears to be quite tired of the behavior.

The effects of a satiation procedure (also called *negative practice*) may be somewhat temporary, especially if the behavior has been in the child's repertoire for an extended period of time. The teacher can increase the value of a satiation procedure by insuring, in the interim period in which the behavior is absent or of low strength, that more positive reinforcement is provided for appropriate replacement behaviors.

CHANGING THE STIMULUS ENVIRONMENT

Problem behaviors may be controlled on a temporary basis by changing the stimulus conditions which influence these behaviors:

> A classroom with a water fountain was a convenient excuse for Laurie's frequent trips to drink water. Under these conditions she seldom completed her work. The teacher announced that the fountain would be turned off during desk work and, further, that those who completed their work could have free access to the fountain during the afternoon arts and crafts period. The problem was solved by removing the cues which controlled the excessive behavior.

In other instances, the teacher may identify stimulus situations in which inappropriate behavior has a high likelihood of occurring. For example, Susan is likely to become overly emotional and hyperactive when she is unable to complete tasks assigned to her. The teacher could remove difficult tasks when it appears that Susan will experience difficulty and provide her with alternative easier ones.

Instead of removing stimulus conditions which may result in inappropriate behaviors, the educator may find it useful to present cues which inhibit the problem behavior. The teacher-aide may be seated next to a hyperactive child to reduce the likelihood that the child will roam around the room.

Finally, the teacher may prompt desired behavior so it need not compete with problem behavior. She may ask Percy to help pass out toys or puzzles to his classmates at a time when he is usually taking possessions away from them.

These procedures—removing discriminative events which result in problem behaviors, presenting cues which inhibit problem behaviors, and presenting cues for competing desired behaviors—all produce temporary results. These procedures are used to increase the likelihood that desired behaviors may occur. The goal becomes that of strengthening desired behaviors to replace problem ones.

OVERCORRECTION

Foxx and Azrin 1972

Overcorrection is a procedure developed by Foxx and Azrin* and is an alternative to procedures which involve the presentation of aversive consequences and other less effective procedures used to modify self-stimulation activities, such as hand waving and body rocking, and such socially disruptive behaviors as aggression and enuresis. The general objective of the overcorrection procedure is to educate the individual to assume full responsibility for the disruption caused by his misbehavior. This is done by (1) requiring the child after a disruptive activity to acceptably restore the environmental effects to an improved state and (2) to practice correct forms of relevant appropriate behavior.

Foxx and Azrin 1973

The restoration of the environmental effects is known as *restitutional overcorrection*. For example, if a child excessively places unacceptable objects in his mouth, a two-minute oral hygiene procedure may be used.* The rationale for this restitutional overcorrection procedure is to suggest to the child that putting undesirable objects in his mouth results in exposure to potentially harmful microorganisms and that this possibility of self-infection must be eliminated. The oral hygiene procedure requires the child to brush his teeth with toothbrush and wipe his mouth with a washcloth that have been immersed in an oral antiseptic. This eliminates any potentially harmful germs that may have been obtained from mouthing objects.

Azrin and Powers 1975

Azrin and Powers* illustrate the *positive practice overcorrection* approach—when an error or disruptive action occurs, the individual is required to practice the correct manner of behaving—in reducing the classroom disruptive behaviors of a group of seven- to eleven-year-old "emotionally disturbed" boys. The boys initially were informed of classroom rules of conduct. If a rule was broken, the child was required to (1) recite the classroom rule describing the appropriate behavior, (2) practice the desired behavior, (3) repeat the desired behavior for several trials, and (4) engage in further positive practice during the recess period. The effectiveness of this procedure was compared to procedures involving a reminder and disapproval, and a loss-of-recess penalty. There was a 95 to 98 percent reduction in disruptive behavior as a result of the positive practice contingency. The reminder and disapproval procedure produced minimal results and the loss-of-recess contingency reduced the inappropriate behavior by only 60 percent. Azrin and Powers conclude: "The re-educative, nonpunitive spirit of the Positive Practice procedure may be its major advantage . . . The spirit of the new procedure is re-educative in that the child is told in effect, you forgot to follow the rule, so let's practice how you should have done it so you will be able to remember more easily next time" (p. 532).

PUNISHMENT

Punishment, as a rule of influencing behavior, indicates that those behaviors resulting in unpleasant consequences will be less likely to be repeated. Such consequences inhibit the preceding behavior. Under similar circumstances in the future, the behavior is less likely to occur again. On the first day of school, if Tim approaches Simon and greets him with a friendly "Hello" and Simon reacts with a nasty reply or pokes him in the stomach, he is less likely to engage in this social behavior. The punishment rule refers both to (1) *the presentation of aversive (unpleasant) consequences following behavior,* for example, behavior results in physical pain, being yelled at, ridiculed, frowned at, or threatened; and (2) *the removal or withdrawal following behavior of positive consequences which the child has or which are available to him,* for example, sitting the child in a corner and thus removing him from his peer group, reducing his play time, taking away his weekend privileges, losing a friend. The latter may involve *time-out* or *response cost* procedures. The relative effects of punishment in suppressing behavior are related to the intensity and frequency of punishment, the timing of the punishment, and what opportunity the child may have to make alternative responses. The effects also depend upon the strength of the behavior being punished and on the frequency and value of the positively reinforcing events which may be maintaining the behavior. *Under varying conditions punishment may result merely in emotional arousal or in temporary suppression, partial suppression, or, for all practical purposes, permanent suppression of the punished behavior.* Each of the procedures and the factors involved in its use are described in the following sections.

Ullman and Krasner 1969

Punishing consequences may represent (1) naturally occurring unpleasant results of various behaviors or (2) unpleasant events arranged by others. As examples of the former, the child eats too much candy and gets sick, the child takes his gloves off in the snow and his fingers hurt, the adolescent touches a hot pot of coffee and is burned, the adolescent over-exerts himself and becomes excessively fatigued. The behaviors resulting in each of these unpleasant consequences will be less likely to be repeated. The rule of punishment in a sense is a rule of self-protection.

Unpleasant consequences following specific behaviors may also be arranged by the teacher or delivered by others to discourage the reoccurrence of these behaviors. Just as there are rules of nature which suggest that certain behaviors should be avoided, there are also rules of social living which discourage various behaviors. The child hits a peer and gets hit in return. Another child is rude to his peers and they no longer include him in their group. An adolescent is dishonest and is rejected by his peers.

While teaching these rules of social living, adults may sometimes find it necessary to arrange for unpleasant consequences whenever the child or adolescent ignores the rules. For best results these rules, and the resulting unpleasant consequences for breaking them, should not be arbitrary nor presented in a harsh, punitive, ridiculing, or derogatory fashion. The rules of social living and the resulting consequences should be logical and understandable. In every case, the child should have a choice. Adherence to the rules of social living result in positive consequences or the avoidance of negative ones; if the rules are not followed there will be specified logical unpleasant consequences.

Punishment may or may not involve physical pain. In fact, aversive consequences used by school personnel to influence behavior seldom, if ever, involve physical pain. *However, poor grades, dismissal from a peer group, disapproval, reprimand, and the multitude of other aversive events inherent in the educational and social setting typically may have more "aversiveness" qualities than does physical punishment.* The educator should be sensitive to the individual meaning which a child or adolescent attaches to various aversive consequences. An adolescent, reprimanded by a teacher in the presence of his peers, may experience considerably more "psychological pain" than he would experience if punished physically.

Each of the punishment procedures mentioned above should be viewed as a limited and infrequently used aspect of an educational program. The excessive use of punishment procedures can only result in aggressive outbursts and in excessively inhibited and overly emotional children. The educator using punishment in a harsh, punitive, demeaning, hostile, or aggressive manner when angry or aggravated provides an aggressive model to imitate, both to the child being punished and for others who observe. Children and adolescents are more apt to use these same modes of behavior when angry or when they have control over someone else, such as a younger or less effective peer or sibling. When used in skillful combination with procedures based on positive practice and positive reinforcement, however, the selective use of punishment procedures may contribute to desired behavior development in children and adolescents. The potential usefulness as well as the potential dangers and limitations of punishment procedures are discussed.

Presentation of Aversive Consequences (PAC)

The presentation of unpleasant consequences following undesired behaviors may result in temporary suppression or relatively permanent control of these behaviors, depending upon the intensity of the punishment. Temporary reduction of specific behavior may be most beneficial, because the educator is able to use this period of time to teach and strengthen more appropriate means of behaving. In some instances, a child's disruptive behavior may occur with such frequency that he is unlikely to engage in more appropriate behavior. Koegel et al.[*] demonstrated that with the suppression of high-rate self-stimulatory behavior in "autistic" children there was an increase in unreinforced spontaneous appropriate play with toys. Risley,[*] also, found that suppression of disruptive behaviors in a brain-damaged "autistic" child facilitated the acquisition of new desirable behaviors. Such findings suggest that some behaviors may be functionally incompatible with the occurrence or acquisition of more desired activities.

Koegel et al. 1974

Risley 1968

A PAC procedure also provides information to observing peers about the consequences of specific types of behaviors. This observation may assist the children in inhibiting such behavior and in selecting more desired modes of responding. Finally, mild punishment may assist a child in making a discrimination between correct-incorrect or appropriate-inappropriate behavior. There are, however, other effects to be considered.

Does Not Teach Desired Behavior.   As noted, a PAC procedure does not teach the child what he should do. It suppresses or inhibits behavior, but when used in isolation the procedure does not provide a more appropriate mode of behavior as a replacement. It merely serves to reduce (typically on a rather temporary basis) the likelihood that the punished behavior will occur.

The limitations of a punishment approach used in isolation are illustrated by the following experience with Kit, a five-year-old socially isolated boy.

Kit was creating considerable problems with his female peers in a child development center by frequently pulling their hair. The teacher, under the supposition that if Kit could experience the pain associated with hair pulling he would realize what he was doing and thus refrain from pulling the hair of the girls, initiated a procedure of pulling Kit's hair immediately whenever he engaged in this behavior. The procedure was indeed effective in reducing his hair-pulling behavior. But as Kit had only poorly developed skills of interacting with other children, he became rather isolated from them. Now he just sat and engaged in no peer interactions. The teacher was pleased with her rather short-sighted strategy because it worked in terminating the

> *bothersome behavior. The punishment, however, did not teach Kit other more appropriate ways of interacting.*

A PAC procedure thus represents only one aspect of an appropriate behavior change program. The program also must provide for alternative desirable behaviors resulting in positive consequences. As punishment is used to reduce or eliminate inappropriate behavior, positive consequences should be used to increase the strength of alternative appropriate behaviors. In this manner desired competing behaviors will replace inappropriate behavior.

Effects of Mild PAC Highly Specific and Temporary.   When PAC is used in isolation and when the aversive event is not too intense, it is not unusual for the effects of punishment to be restricted to highly specific conditions. Further, the suppressive effect is likely to disappear quickly. Punishment will have a carry-over influence on undesired behavior only if there is some likelihood of a repeat of behavior resulting in some unpleasant consequences. In some instances, the child may adapt to the punishment and behave inappropriately even though punishment follows. Threats, for example, may lose their effectiveness after some use.

A teacher may influence certain disruptive behaviors with a rule that unpleasant consequences will follow such behaviors, and other more acceptable behaviors will then become more attractive. However, unless the educator provides consistent positive consequences for these other behaviors, *they may occur only as long as punishment is likely to follow disruptive behavior.* As noted, the most desirable procedure is to provide positive reinforcement for these more desirable behaviors as inappropriate behavior is suppressed. As these gain strength, the punishment contingency can be removed as it becomes nonfunctional. Under conditions in which behavior is under punishment control, a reduced likelihood of punishment may result in a sudden reappearance of the disruptive behavior. A substitute teacher who does not represent the punishment control may find a class to be highly disruptive even though the regular teacher has "well-behaved" children. A child may learn not to hit another child in Mrs. Gill's classroom because of previous punishment in this setting. He may continue, however, hitting children on the playground when Mrs. Gill is absent.

In summary, the PAC procedure not only fails to teach the child what he should do, it may serve to suppress inappropriate behaviors only under highly specific conditions. As these conditions are removed or changed, the suppressed behavior may reoccur.

Relative Effects of Mild and Intense Aversive Consequences.   Inhibiting effects of a mild aversive consequence are frequently temporary. The behavior is not eliminated; it is merely inhibited for a period of time. The punished behavior may not occur for a short period of time following the aversive consequence, but unless alternative behaviors are strengthened the behavior may reappear.

In contrast, extremely intense aversive consequences may suppress punished behavior for long periods of time. The possible negative effects, however, frequently are too great to justify use of such consequences. The child may become highly emotional, engage in explosive aggressive outbursts, or become generally inhibited and withdrawn. He may become fearful and nonresponsive to aspects of his environment other than those associated directly with the intense punishment.

The educator should be sensitive to the behavioral effects of intense and frequent punishment because some children may exhibit symptoms of such an experiential history. In such cases, use of even a mild form of punishment should be avoided since any punishment may provoke intense emotional reactions and related avoidance behaviors.

Negative Side Effects of Frequent Mild Punishment.   The negative effects of using intense aversive consequences also may be observed when mildly aversive consequences are used excessively. A child or adolescent who frequently experiences unpleasant consequences may reduce his general interaction with his environment. The obese adolescent, who is ridiculed for his fatness, may find any social contact with peers to be aversive and thus avoid contact whenever possible. Thus, behaviors other than those punished may be inhibited, resulting in a shy and nonresponsive child. A child criticized frequently by peers for clumsy motor behavior when playing group games soon begins to avoid the playground or group activities. These become unpleasant places and activities. This may occur even though the aversive events may be so mild that they are relatively ineffective in suppressing undesirable behavior.

Further, a child may develop a distinct dislike for the teacher who punishes too frequently, and will tend to avoid him. The teacher, becoming a cue for unpleasant emotional reactions, alienates himself. The child does not seek to please him, to attend to him, or imitate his behavior—except through fear of noncompliance—because the teacher does not represent a positive social reinforcing agent. The child, when in the presence of the teacher, may attempt to escape from the classroom. Later, the child may develop excuses to avoid the class altogether.

A child punished too frequently by parents and teachers may begin to feel uncomfortable around all adults, or around those adults who resemble in one way or another those providing aversive consequences. In a similar manner, such cues as time, place, or activity may become associated with the unpleasant emotional reactions accompanying punishment. Situations in which punishment is a likelihood will be avoided.

Further, frequent mild punishment may produce aggressive behavioral reactions, excessive negative emotionality, anger, and temper tantrums. These obviously will temporarily be disruptive to the child and decrease his competency in dealing with academic and interpersonal situations. His learning is disrupted. Not infrequently the child becomes temporarily unresponsive to his social environment. These behaviors may be directed toward the person associated with the punishment or displaced toward an innocent person or object. It is not unusual for excessively punished adolescents to engage in such behaviors as destruction of school property, excessive fighting, and intense emotional outbursts at minimal provocation. Under these circumstances the educator may feel that he must increase his punishment because "I cannot let him get away with such bad behavior." The teacher runs the risk of increasing the likelihood of inappropriate behavioral reactions. He also places himself in a position of greatly decreasing his effectiveness as a person concerned with influencing appropriate behavior patterns. Thus, when punishment is used, the possibility exists that the child or adolescent will behave aggressively toward the person providing the punishment. This aggressiveness may, on a temporary basis, remove the source of punishment. In this manner, aggressive behavior may be strengthened by negative reinforcement.

A teacher using the rule of punishment too frequently, or providing infrequent but highly unpleasant consequences, will most likely invite fear, anxiety, and dislike. The teacher who is harsh or who threatens or punishes too frequently is likely to produce a variety of disruptive and other undesirable behavior patterns. The shy, uninvolved child, for example, avoids becoming involved in those situations associated with frequent previous punishment.

Another child may be harsh and aggressive to other children by imitating the aggressive behavior patterns modeled by the adult. If parents and teachers use punishment too frequently, children and adolescents are likely to use similar tactics in interacting with peers over whom they have some control. Additionally, children are apt to self-punish or self-criticize more frequently; they are more apt to develop more derogatory or demeaning concepts of themselves.

In view of these possible negative effects, a PAC procedure arranged by the teacher should be used sparingly and, even in these instances, only after careful planning. To be most effective with children with learning and behavior difficulties, procedures involving positive reinforcement must far outnumber those having unpleasant consequences. Through frequent association with the delivery of positive consequences, aspects of the educational environment will acquire some of the desirable reinforcing characteristics of these events. The child will like the teacher and will acquire new behaviors in order to obtain his approval, attention, affection, or praise.

PAC May Not Be Effective.   It is not unusual to observe persistence of behavior which results in consequences that, to the teacher, appear to be unpleasant. Parents or teachers may report, "He seems to enjoy being punished because he will insist on doing those things that he knows will lead to unpleasant consequences." A child may behave in a certain manner "to see if he can get away with it." On occasion he does "get away with it" (he is reinforced), and at other times he is punished. This unique combination of reinforcement, punishment, and extinction has taught the child, "Sometimes I get reinforced for the behavior. At other times I don't. On occasion, I get punished." The child does not persist in inappropriate behavior because he is devilish or naughty. He behaves in this manner because his experiences with those directing his environment have taught him these behaviors. The occasional positive reinforcement following the behavior apparently is sufficiently influential to override the possible unpleasant consequences of punishment.

In some instances aversive consequences may signal the occurrence of reinforcing events. The adult may be considerably more attentive, more positive, and more available immediately after punishing the child than at other times. Those behaviors which produce the unpleasant consequences are strengthened by the subsequent positive reinforcement; the social attention in the guise of punishment may be more reinforcing than the unpleasant consequence is aversive. Under these conditions, contrary to expectations, the preceding behavior would be strengthened or maintained, not inhibited.

PAC Procedure Is Unpleasant to Teachers.   When a PAC procedure is used excessively, it becomes highly difficult to manage. Excessive use is quite inefficient because it must be provided immediately and consistently or else the punished behavior will reappear. It is also true that most teachers do not enjoy using a PAC procedure. Presenting aversive consequences is emotionally disquieting to the teacher. Additionally, an emotional climate is created that disrupts children other than the child being punished. Children in such an environment are more likely to be passive and fearful or negativistic and noncooperative. However, it should be recognized, as noted earlier, that to the extent punishment is effective in reducing the child's inappropriate behavior, the use of such procedures by teachers is likely to be perpetuated. Such teacher behavior is strengthened through negative reinforcement.

Removal of Pleasant Consequences

Even though the child's behaviors may on occasion produce physical pain from peers or from natural events, for example, fast running on occasion results in falling and pain, staying outside in subfreezing weather results in ears, nose, and fingers hurting, yelling at a peer results in being yelled at in return, punishment procedures involving inflicting physical pain or other derogatory consequences such as being harsh or threatening should be avoided whenever possible. Procedures of *time-out* and *response-cost* remain as means of discouraging undesired behavior patterns.

Time-out from Positive Reinforcement (TO)

Time-out is a procedure of temporarily removing the child from a reinforcing situation, following inappropriate behavior, to a location in which reinforcement is minimal or unlikely to occur. In the school setting, the child who persists in disruptive behavior may be removed from the presence of teacher and peers and placed in an isolated or quiet room or location containing a minimal number of objects, little or no social stimulation, and minimal opportunity for interesting activities. In this setting the child has little opportunity to receive positive reinforcement. Following a designated period of time (usually less than ten minutes), the child is given the choice to return to the classroom.

In other instances the source of positive reinforcement is removed following inappropriate behavior. Following John's rude behavior, the teacher may turn away from him and ignore him for a period of time. Such a procedure of withdrawal of attention may be a discriminative stimulus for "rejection" or some other unpleasant affective response. Another child who begins to be messy in his self-feeding may lose his lunch tray for a short period of time. A child who becomes distractible or acts silly during individual language therapy may be ignored by the teacher until he once again pays attention. Watson* terminated all training activities at the moment a young "autistic" child began to cry or whine. After the child terminated this negativistic behavior, the teacher resumed interaction with the child. This negativistic behavior was virtually eliminated within a few training sessions following initiation of the TO procedure. Thus, a time-out may be effective due to (1) the removal of the possibility of positive reinforcement for the undesired behavior, (2) the reduction in the likelihood that the child will receive any externally provided positive reinforcement for any behavior for a period of time, and/or (3) the possible suppressing effects of the occurrence of conditioned aversive events.

Watson 1972

The use of a TO procedure involving the removal of the child from a reinforcing environment is illustrated in the writer's experience with Lisa, a four-year-old child attending nursery school:*

Briskin and Gardner 1968

> This child was described as hyperactive, disruptive, and difficult to control in the school setting. Specific inappropriate behaviors included screaming and throwing things in fits of anger, crying or whining when not getting her way, not waiting her turn to engage in art projects and physical activities, hitting, biting, grabbing, rough pushing, not responding to verbal instructions, and leaving the room, group, or activity without reason or permission. After an observational period revealed the average frequency of these behaviors in structured and unstructured activity periods throughout the school day, a TO procedure was initiated. Whenever any of these behaviors occurred during the three structured periods, Lisa was immediately removed from the classroom and seated outside for a two-minute

period. The only verbal interaction during the TO consisted of a short statement informing Lisa why she was taken from the classroom: "You pushed Jill, you must sit in the chair." "You are whining; sit in the chair." Following the two-minute period, she was returned to the classroom.

As a means of strengthening desired behaviors to replace the inappropriate ones, an additional procedure was used of providing prompt teacher praise and other forms of social interaction following occurrence of appropriate behaviors. Although initially Lisa voiced her objections when placed in TO, she soon accepted the action as an unpleasant consequence which she produced by her own disruptive behaviors. Within a few days inappropriate behavior was reduced from an average of 31 percent to 2 percent of the time spent at school. There was a concurrent increase in appropriate behavior which was maintained over a follow-up period. It is interesting to note that improvement in Lisa's behavior had pronounced positive effect on the teacher, aides, other children, and on Lisa's mother. All interacted more readily with Lisa and provided her with the social attention which apparently was quite valuable to her.

This experience emphasizes both the importance of social attention to children and the highly critical significance of providing social attention for appropriate behaviors and not primarily as a reaction to disruptive behaviors. Observation of Lisa prior to initiation of the program revealed that adults in the school environment were giving Lisa almost constant attention for her disruptive behaviors. She was seldom provided attention when she did behave appropriately. Attention which appeared necessary as a means of controlling her inappropriate behavior patterns was apparently having the opposite effect of strengthening and maintaining it. The initiation of a TO procedure for unacceptable behavior and an enriched amount of social reinforcement following desired behavior resulted in a happier, more enjoyable, and accepted child.

A TO procedure may be effective in eliminating bothersome behavior even in children with severe developmental difficulties who appear to be relatively unresponsive to social reinforcement. Watson* describes *Watson 1972* the successful use of a combined TO and extinction procedure in modifying the temper tantrums in "a profoundly retarded psychotic child." Following the beginning of a temper tantrum, the child was completely ignored by everyone in his environment for five minutes. The weekly frequency dropped from a high of fifty to a level of infrequent occurrence within approximately three weeks.

In using a TO procedure the teacher should:

Administer It in a Matter-of-fact Nonemotional Manner.   Scolding, reprimanding, or otherwise rejecting the child are to be avoided. In implementing a TO, the teacher is merely being instrumental in removing the child on a temporary basis from sources of positive reinforcement.

Insure That Removal from a Situation or Location Is in Fact Unpleasant to the Child.   The situation from which the child is removed must contain sources of reinforcement of value to the child. With Lisa, even though in frequent conflict with teachers and peers, she remained physically close to them. Their presence apparently was reinforcing, since Lisa could easily have avoided them by isolating herself. It was speculated that temporary removal from teachers and peers would be unpleasant and thus serve to inhibit inappropriate behavior. If the situation from which the child is removed is actually aversive to the child, the preceding behaviors may be strengthened (negative reinforcement) rather than being inhibited. The shy child may find that removal from the peer group reduces her apprehension. Thus, whatever behaviors resulted in her removal would be strengthened through negative reinforcement. In such instances, the TO procedure would strengthen rather than reduce the problem behaviors. Additionally, a time-out procedure may be inappropriate for an isolated child because it removes her from the social situation in which she potentially can learn appropriate social interaction skills.

Steeves et al. 1970   Steeves et al.* present results which indicated that an "autistic" child would voluntarily impose a time-out for himself during an educational task in which positive reinforcement was provided for correct responding. This child apparently found time-out periods to be reinforcing instead of aversive.

Be Consistent in the TO Procedure.   The procedure should be continued until sufficient time has elapsed to evaluate its effectiveness. If the child's misbehavior is reinforced on occasion, this reinforcement may well offset the suppressive effects of more frequent TO's.

The Physical Location of the TO Period Must Be Carefully Evaluated to Insure That the TO Area Is Rather Void of Sources of Positive Reinforcement.   Placing the child in a hallway, sending him to the nurse's office, or sitting him in a supply closet may be quite reinforcing due to the opportunity for new sources of attention or activities. Under these conditions, the contingent behavior pattern may be strengthened rather than weakened.

Keep the TO Period Relatively Short.   Periods from one to ten minutes have been found to be effective with many children. Longer periods may be reinforcing to the teacher, since the child spends less time in the classroom, but a longer time-out period seldom contributes to eliminating the child's problematic behavior. Lengthy time-out periods also are undesirable because the child is removed from the natural environment in which he can learn more prosocial behaviors. He has no opportunity for being positively reinforced while isolated from the group. In view of this consideration, the TO procedure should not be used if the child is constantly being removed from the teaching environment.

The earlier mentioned Briskin and Gardner* program found a two-minute TO period effective. Sibley and her associates* used a five-minute period in a successful program designed to decrease the aggressive, negative attention-getting and resisting behaviors of a five-year-old boy in a kindergarten setting. White and his colleagues* found even a one-minute TO period effective in suppressing aggressive, tantrum, and self-destructive behaviors in moderately and severely "retarded" children.

Briskin and Gardner 1968; Sibley et al. 1969

White et al. 1972

In many instances a child may display disruptive behaviors when TO is initiated. In illustration, assume that a teacher uses a five-minute TO period following some inappropriate behavior. On imposing the TO consequence, the child may scream, cry, kick, attack the physical environment, and display similar frustration behaviors. The teacher should begin timing the TO period following the cessation of these behaviors. If the TO period is terminated during the child's disruptive actions, these behaviors may be strengthened. Thus, the TO period should follow the cessation of disruptive behaviors. The child is returned to his previous activity or environment when he is behaving appropriately. This behavior is likely to be strengthened since it precedes the removal of the unpleasant TO period.

Reinforce Alternative Behaviors.   A TO procedure is used to stop and eliminate undesired behaviors; *it does not teach appropriate behaviors.* Once the TO procedure is no longer used, the punished behavior is likely to reappear unless competing behaviors have been reinforced. This was evident in a program by Pendergrass.* A two-minute TO procedure was used to suppress persistent, high-rate misbehavior in two severely withdrawn children. Positive reinforcement for appropriate behaviors was not provided. The misbehavior reappeared after the TO procedure was no longer used. Abbott* describes the successful combined use of TO for inappropriate disruptive, resistant, and aggressive behaviors and positive social reinforcement for alternative desirable behaviors. Following consistent reinforcement, the appropriate behaviors soon began to replace the inappropriate behaviors which were being discouraged by the TO experiences. Kubany et al.* successfully reduced the highly disruptive classroom behavior of a boy by combining token reinforcement and TO. Accumulated time on a "Good Behavior Clock" for appropriate classroom behavior earned token reinforcers for the child and backup reinforcers which were shared with peers. Following occurrence of disruptive behavior, the clock was stopped and remained off until appropriate behavior was evident. Thus TO was used to discourage disruptive behavior and positive reinforcement was used to strengthen desired behavior.

Pendergrass 1972

Abbott 1969

Kubany et al. 1971

Inform the Child of the Behaviors Which Result in TO.   As TO is implemented, the specific behaviors which resulted in this consequence should be described in a matter-of-fact manner. This precisely identifies the unacceptable behaviors and focuses on the relationship between these behaviors and the contingent unpleasant consequences.

Response Cost (RC)

Inappropriate behavior patterns may be discouraged by requiring the child or adolescent to forfeit some positive event which he has in his possession or which would be provided for him. His inappropriate behaviors cost him; a certain number or amount of reinforcing events are removed from him. Following inappropriate behavior, for example, the child or adolescent may lose recess privileges, may not have use of the photo lab for two days, may lose his role as teacher assistant for a day, or may not practice with the team for a week. A child who takes an excessive amount of time in cleaning up his mess after play may lose some of the time available for watching cartoons. If watching cartoons is a highly desired activity, the child may be provided a set amount of time for cleaning up after play. Any time in excess of the allotted time will be subtracted from his cartoon-watching period. The purpose is not to be punitive. It is to suggest to him that he has responsibilities, that relationships are comprised of "being respectful of" as well as "being respected."

Response Cost Differs from Extinction.   The removal of positive reinforcers after inappropriate behavior is quite different from an extinction procedure. In an extinction procedure, behavior previously followed by reinforcers no longer produces those reinforcers. A response cost, in contrast, involves the removal of reinforcing events or privileges in the possession of or available to the child.

Response Cost May Result in Immediate Effects.   Wise use of an RC procedure frequently results in rapid reduction of undesired behavior. However, there is considerable variation among children and adolescents in the nature and degree of behavioral effects associated with this procedure. To be effective, the teacher must initially identify, and then be in a position to remove, reinforcing events available to the child. This requires that the child or adolescent does have events in his possession which can be removed, such as use of the family automobile, money or tokens, snack time, free playtime, and other privileges or objects. Schmidt and Ulrich* used an RC procedure to maintain an acceptable level of classroom noise and to encourage children to remain at their desks during lesson periods. Classes of elementary-level children were reinforced with additional free time when they maintained an acceptable noise level and remained at their desks and were penalized by loss of free time for violation of these requirements. An immediate positive effect was noted under these contingencies.

Schmidt and Ulrich 1969

An RC procedure is easy to manage whenever a token system is in operation. This was illustrated in a program of Perline and Levinsky* who used an RC procedure in combination with a tactic of providing token reinforcers for positive behaviors incompatible with a number of disruptive aggressive and hyperactive behaviors. Tokens were awarded four

Perline and Levinsky 1968

"severely retarded" children whenever they engaged in desired behaviors. After maladaptive behavior, a token was removed from the child. An immediate drop in maladaptive behavior was obtained under these conditions.

Phillips* also illustrated the effectiveness of a response cost procedure when used in a token program which provided reinforcement for specified desired behavior. With predelinquent adolescent boys, a variety of behaviors, including aggressive verbal behavior, bathroom untidiness, lack of punctuality, and poor grammar showed obvious improvement under the RC condition.   *Phillips 1968*

As with any punishment procedure, the RC approach is more effective if used infrequently. Also, the magnitude of fines should be within reasonable limits. If the fine is frequent and/or excessive, discouragement and frustration behaviors are likely to result.

Provide an Opportunity to Obtain Lost Reinforcers.   A strategy of providing an opportunity to regain reinforcing events following appropriate behavior effectively combines a positive reinforcement procedure with the RC one. This combined approach results in the strengthening of appropriate competing behaviors. This is critical, because the RC procedure only discourages specific behaviors from reoccurring. As bothersome behavior is reduced in strength, desired behavior is more likely to occur and, if reinforced, to be strengthened. The role of an RC procedure is to inhibit inappropriate behavior so that alternative appropriate behavior may occur and be reinforced and thus strengthened.

The educator using an RC procedure must insure that the rules involved in removing reinforcing events are understood by the child. Also, he must insure that the child has alternative appropriate behaviors for use in avoiding the RC. The RC procedure under these conditions can be presented to the child in a matter-of-fact manner. A choice is available. A specified number or amount of reinforcing events will be removed from the child following inappropriate behavior. Following appropriate behavior, positive events will be provided.

A behavior management program of Sulzbacher and Houser* provides an illustration of the effective use of the RC procedure with a group of children. "Mildly retarded" children attending a primary level class were causing considerable disruption in the classroom procedure by frequently using the "naughty finger" (raised fist with middle finger extended). The teacher awarded the class a special ten-minute recess at the end of the day. However, if any member of the class made the naughty finger gesture, or if other children made reference to it, one minute of the ten was lost by the entire class. The RC procedure resulted in an immediate reduction in the undesirable behaviors from an average of sixteen occurrences prior to the RC procedure to an average of two occurrences after the RC was used.   *Schulzbacher and Houser 1968*

Kazdin* emphasizes the usefulness of the RC procedure in suppres-   *Kazdin 1972* sing behavior. A number of studies reviewed by Kazdin report only minimal reappearance of suppressed behavior after termination of the negative contingency. Further, undesirable side effects occasionally associated with the PAC procedure such as increased aggression, social disruption, or increased escape behavior typically are not found in using RC.

Response Cost Varies in Effectiveness.   Some experience has suggested that a response cost procedure may be as effective as positive reinforcement for controlling inappropriate classroom behavior and for insuring the occurrence of desired social and academic activities. Kaufman and O'Leary,* with a group of highly disruptive "emotionally disturbed" adolescents, found that disruptive classroom behavior was effectively reduced and reading skills were increased equally well under either a reward or a response cost contingency. This same result was obtained by Iwata and Bailey* with "mentally retarded" students attending special education classes. Both reward and response cost procedures were equally effective in reducing classroom rule violations. Daily arithmetic performance doubled under both conditions. When students were permitted to choose either contingency, no preference was observed.

Kaufman and O'Leary 1972

Iwata and Bailey 1974

In both of these studies, students under the response cost contingency were given "free" tokens at the beginning of the class period. These were later removed when inappropriate behavior occurred. Under the reward contingency, tokens were provided following desired behavior.

McLaughlin and Malaby 1972

In contrast, McLaughlin and Malaby* found that contingent tokens provided for quiet behavior produced lower rates of inappropriate verbalizations during class than did contingent token loss for inappropriate verbalizations in fifth and sixth grade "culturally disadvantaged" children. However, the tokens removed had previously been earned contingent on the occurrence of appropriate behavior. Apparently, the response cost procedure was rather aversive and thus produced disruptive side effects.

Kaufman and O'Leary 1972

Thus the relative effectiveness of reward or response cost procedures may be related to whether the tokens removed under the response cost contingency have been provided on a "free" basis or if these had previously been earned. Kaufman and O'Leary* also mentioned other factors which may influence (1) the effectiveness of an RC procedure in suppressing inappropriate behavior and in encouraging desired activities and (2) the likelihood of occurrence of negative side effects. These include:

1. The latency between the occurrence of the inappropriate behavior and the time the fine is provided. If there is a delay between the misbehavior and the loss of tokens, the student is less likely to become disruptive in the form of arguing or acting aggressively toward the person imposing the fine.
2. The value of the backup reinforcer. The greater the loss, the greater the likelihood of negative side effects.
3. The student's dislike of the teacher.

4. The student's perceived worth of the behavior that the teacher is attempting to strengthen.

THE TIMING OF PUNISHMENT

To achieve maximum effects in inhibiting inappropriate behavior, unpleasant consequences should immediately follow the behavior. There is evidence to suggest that effects are greater when punishment is provided at the time the child initiates an inappropriate behavioral sequence than would be evident if punishment is provided sometime after the misbehavior.* An inappropriate behavior typically represents a chain of behaviors which ends in an undesirable activity. If the teacher wishes to punish a child for removing materials from the supply cabinet, she should attempt to reprimand or otherwise punish the child as he reaches for the materials rather than doing so later after he has the materials and has used them. Or, if punishment is provided a child who forcefully takes possessions from his smaller peers, it is best to administer the punishment as he reaches and begins to pull a book away from his peer. If punished only after gaining possession and using the book, the behavior already has been reinforced. Punishment at that time is less likely to have a suppressive effect on the undesired behavior.

Walters et al. 1965

Additionally, delay in presenting unpleasant consequences may result in suppression of the wrong behavior. A threat such as, "Mother will hear about your misbehavior when she comes to take you home. I'm sure she will be upset," may create a state of emotionality because the child will dread mother's arrival. If the mother does punish the child for earlier misbehavior, she is inadvertently punishing responses which immediately precede the unpleasant consequences. Also, mother's appearance may acquire aversive properties and her son may hesitate to approach her. If this sequence is repeated frequently, the son may actively avoid mother when she does appear.

Cromwell et al.* suggest possible additional negative consequences associated with delay of punishment. Children for whom punishment for misdeeds was promised, then delayed, and afterward was inconsistently carried out by parents were characterized by a deterioration in attention and socially responsive behavior. After misbehavior, the child frequently experienced periods of not knowing when and if he would get punished. In contrast, no long-term effects on overall adjustment were noted in children who were punished immediately following misbehavior and the punishment was clearly associated with the misbehavior. These authors suggested: "Thus, the uncertain anticipation of punishment, rather than punishment itself, clearly appears to be the crucial factor associated with behavior deterioration" (p. 12).

Cromwell et al. 1975

Finally, the punishment obviously should be contingent upon the

occurrence of an undesired behavior. Noncontingent punishment, especially if intense, can produce some widespread adverse effects.* The child,
under such conditions, is in a constant state of apprehension over when an
unpredictable aversive event may occur. If he is unable to totally avoid the
situations in which such may occur, he is in conflict on what to do to avoid
the punishment. The specific effects of such conditions produce a range of
undesirable behavioral consequences and are described in Chapter 13.
Again, punishment, if it is used, should obviously be used in a contingent
manner to suppress undesirable behaviors.

Martin 1971

HOW UNPLEASANT CONSEQUENCES SHOULD BE ARRANGED

The manner in which the rule of punishment is used becomes
critical. The child and adolescent must learn to choose between those
behaviors which result in pleasant consequences and others resulting in
unpleasant consequences. To protect the child from all natually occurring
unpleasant consequences would be unjust to a child. As noted earlier, a
child learns that touching a hot stove produces unpleasant consequences
or that violating expectations of peers results in rejection. The rule of
punishment indicates that, following the unpleasant consequences, such
behavior would be less likely to be repeated.

A child or adolescent learns that he cannot take possessions from
peers as such behavior may result in such unpleasant consequences as
losing their friendship. Thus, an educational program teaches a child to
choose between behaviors which produce pleasant consequences and
those which produce unpleasant ones. This is accomplished by providing
certain rules of social living which guide behavior. On many occasions the
child can learn to understand or appreciate the rules only by experiencing
the unpleasant consequences which follow his violation of the rules. At the
same time, *it is essential that the child or adolescent experience far more
positive consequences than negative ones.* The school experiences must be
arranged to insure that the child is protected from excessive aversive
consequences. A procedure of punishing a child for nonattendance and
poor academic achievement should be replaced with one which provides
encouragement and positive consequences for school attendance and
achievement. Choices involving negative consequences should be introduced gradually in the child's experiences and not suddenly imposed on
him.

Vicarious Experiences with Consequences

The child may be provided background experience in making
choices between appropriate and inappropriate behaviors and their related

consequences through various activities and games which demonstrate these relationships. Puppet play, animated stories, cartoons, and role-playing activities may be used to good advantage to demonstrate that certain behaviors result in desired consequences and other behaviors produce unpleasant results.

Emphasis on Choice

In the arrangement of the learning environment, both pleasant and unpleasant consequences should be as naturally and logically related as possible to the behaviors which produce them. The child must have a choice between acceptable behavior which will be reinforced positively and the unacceptable behavior which will be punished. Providing reinforcement for alternative desired behavior increases the efficacy of punishment. These behaviors can replace the suppressed punished ones. As the effects of punishment dissipate, the child will have acquired other behaviors which will result in positive consequences. This emphasis on providing the child a choice between punished and positively reinforced behavior serves to reduce the possible negative side effects sometimes associated with punishment. For example, the teacher may have a rule that a child must remain seated at the table throughout snack and lunchtime. The positive consequences of this behavior are eating food and enjoying the company of his peers. The unpleasant consequence of leaving the table prior to completion of the meal—an application of the punishment rule—is a logical one: Once the child leaves the table without teacher permission, he may not return to finish his meal. In this instance, the child has a choice. The aversive consequence—not being able to eat the rest of the meal—is not a harsh, punitive result delivered by an angry adult. It is the logical consequence of not following the rule demonstrated previously to the child. The child makes a choice and experiences the related consequence.

The rule of punishment, when used in this manner, provides the child with opportunities to make decisions about his own behavior. The adult is not angry, rejecting, or otherwise negative. She responds to his choice in a matter-of-fact fashion. "I see, John, you decided not to eat your food today." The child's behavior produced the unpleasant consequence.

WHEN PUNISHMENT SHOULD BE USED

As described earlier, undesirable behaviors may be eliminated by extinction or suppressed temporarily by negative practice and by changing the stimulus environment. These procedures, used in combination with positive practice and providing positive reinforcement for competing acceptable behaviors, will be valuable in handling most of the problem behaviors presented by children with exceptional learning and behavior characteristics. If these are not effective, or if progress is quite slow, it may be helpful to use mild punishment to assist the child in making a discrimination between acceptable and unacceptable behavior. Again, other more positive procedures should be used initially. If these fail, a punishment procedure may be added to complement other behavior change tactics. The selective use of punishment as a means of influencing prosocial behavior does not introduce artificial or unnatural experiences in the lives of children and adolescents. Quite the contrary, as Johnston* suggests: "Throughout our daily activities we are constantly barraged by a variety of stimuli which have punishing effects, whether it be someone's frown or bumping into a chair we did not see. In other words, unconditioned and conditioned punishing stimuli as consequences to behavior delivered by our social and physical environment are as much a natural part of our lives as are positively reinforcing consequences" (p. 1051). Aronfreed* and Parke* emphasize its extensive use in child rearing.

Johnston 1972

Aronfreed 1968
Parke 1970

The educator can show and inform a child what to do but on occasion will find that inappropriate behaviors have been strengthened by previous reinforcement. Permitting the child to experience unpleasant consequences in a contingent fashion, and at the same time insuring that he experiences frequent pleasant consequences for alternative appropriate behavior, may serve to facilitate positive behavior development. Punishment may be used on occasion to hasten the elimination of inappropriate behavior and to increase the likely appearance of other alternative acceptable behavior.

In other cases, disruptive behavior may be too frequent or intense to be ignored and the educator may be unable to encourage the child to behave in a more acceptable manner. The teacher may be unable to control all sources of reinforcement associated with disruptive behavior. Peers frequently influence inappropriate behaviors by social attention. As frequently occurring inappropriate behavior is likely to be imitated by observing peers, punishment may be needed to terminate the spread of this behavior. Punishment of one child may serve to inhibit the behavior both in the punished child and in other children who observe the punishment. Children who observe others being punished for a certain behavior are less likely for a time to engage in that behavior themselves.* Punishment of one child thus may be useful in inhibiting bothersome behavior in a number of observers, and this in turn provides opportunity for occurrence and reinforcement of acceptable behaviors.

Walters et al. 1965

In a few cases, inappropriate behavior may be of such strength that alternative appropriate behavior is unlikely to occur. At times a crisis is reached between teacher and child which can be resolved only by a rather immediate reduction in inappropriate behavior. The teacher may feel that highly disruptive behaviors may no longer be tolerated. Temporary management of the disruptive behavior by punishment procedures may result in the child's remaining in the class and thus having an opportunity for learning competing appropriate behavior.

Carlson et al.* describe such a situation.

Carlson et al. 1968

> *A child in an elementary classroom was creating considerable difficulty by frequent and intense tantrum behaviors of profane screaming, running wildly from place to place, picking up chairs, throwing them, and attacking other children. She was described as having obvious learning difficulties and poor peer relationships. Sending the child to the school office at the initiation of a tantrum had no beneficial effect due to the excessive social attention associated with this tactic. As no suitable time-out facility was available, a procedure was initiated of holding the child in her chair during her tantrums. The chair was placed in the back of the classroom. Such a tactic was aversive as she resented being touched or held. Reinforcement was given to those peers who refrained from looking at the child at the time of use of this tantrum control procedure. Reinforcement was provided for time periods in which tantrum behavior did not occur. This skillful combination of punishment for tantrum behavior and positive reinforcement for appropriate competing behaviors resulted in a rapid reduction of disruption. After the tantrum behavior disappeared, the child began to engage in a range of academic and social behaviors which resulted in positive attention from teacher and peers.*

Finally, in some selected instances, a child may reside in a family setting in which aversive control through punishment and threat is the major mode of behavior influence. If the child is placed suddenly in a school environment which attempts only to reinforce appropriate behavior and to ignore inappropriate modes of responding, he initially may be excessively disruptive and uncontrolled. In these unusual instances, it may be necessary to remove the threat of punishment gradually while effects of positive reinforcement begin to gain influence over appropriate behavior. MacMillan et al.* elaborate upon these and similar concerns and should be consulted by the interested reader.

MacMillan et al. 1973

GUIDELINES FOR USE OF PUNISHMENT PROCEDURES

In using the rules of punishment, attention should be paid to the following guidelines so as to produce the most desirable behavioral effects and the smallest number of negative side effects.

1. *Use punishment infrequently and only in combination with positive procedures.* As suggested, punishment is a temporary procedure for

use with positive reinforcement. It should not be used as a major technique of behavior control. The teacher, teacher-assistant, or whoever administers punishment should provide a large number of positive reinforcers at frequent times for varied behaviors in different situations. In this manner the adult will be associated predominantly with positive experiences and thus serve as a cue to the child for positive emotional reactions. As has been noted, punishment, if used too frequently, will either lose its value as the child adapts to it or will result in generalized avoidance behavior. The inappropriate behavior may no longer occur, but the child may begin to interact less with all aspects of situations in which excessive punishment has been used.

2. *Prior to punishment, define precisely the inappropriate behavior, the conditions under which it occurs, and its strength.* To insure consistency and fairness, the educator should identify precisely the behavior, and its form and strength, which will result in aversive consequences and define the situations in which the behavior will be punished.

3. *Define precisely the punishment procedure to be used before initiating it.* It is easy to decide on the spur of the moment to reprimand a child in front of his peers, or to penalize him with loss of recess privileges because he disrupted your well-planned class lecture. However well such impulsive reactions may satisfy the emotional needs of the teacher, such procedures hardly contribute to the child's emotional or social development. If a punishment procedure is to be used by the teacher, the exact form—RC, TO, PAC—and magnitude—three-minute TO, loss of ten minutes recess, disapproving comments—should be decided upon prior to its implementation.

4. *Define explicitly the circumstances in which punishment will be used.* After defining the behaviors which will result in punishment, and the form and magnitude of the punishment, the teacher should further delineate the circumstances of administering punishment. If disapproval is selected, should it be provided in the presence of peers or other teachers or should it be a private matter? If an adolescent is required to repeat an assignment, should this requirement be announced to the class or only to the person being punished?

5. *Specify alternative behaviors which will replace the punished ones along with the reinforcement procedures for strengthening these.* In many instances, discernable negative side effects may be avoided when frequent valuable reinforcers are provided for alternative behaviors. If they are, the setting and the people associated with the punishment may acquire positive reinforcing features instead of negative ones. In this manner, mild punishment may actually facilitate the development of a variety of more desirable behavioral characteristics.

6. *Time-out or response cost are favored over procedures involving the presentation of aversive events.* There is less likelihood of negative side effects in using TO or RC procedures. Further, these types of punishment contingencies are more representative of those present in most social environments.

7. *Inform the child in a clear and precise manner about those behaviors resulting in positive consequences and those producing negative consequences, as well as the specifics of the punishment procedures.* The child has a right to know beforehand what to expect and when to expect it. If necessary, demonstration of the relationships between behavior and consequences may be provided. The child may observe others or he may be "walked through" the sequence. A rule of punishment should not be presented unless implemented. Empty threats only serve to teach the child to ignore rules. When punishment is used, the child must understand why he is being punished and what he can do to avoid it in the future.

8. *Implement rules regarding punishment consistently and immediately.* Punishment should be initiated immediately following the misbehavior and be provided on a continuous schedule until suppression is accomplished. The child cannot be allowed to avoid the consequences.

If the child's behavior produces unpleasant consequences after he chooses to ignore a rule of social living, he should not receive sympathy or relief. The teacher must aim to be objective and controlled. It is desirable to label for the child the specific behaviors which have produced the unpleasant consequences and to encourage him to describe alternative acceptable behaviors. Excessive emotionality should be avoided when implementing various punishment procedures. Extra attention, affection, or other positive reinforcers should not be provided at the time punishment occurs. As emphasized, the child should be provided these positive consequences at frequent other times in his daily life following appropriate behaviors. If positive consequences closely follow punishment, the child may learn to misbehave in order to receive, after the punishment, the subsequent positive reinforcement.

9. *Provide alternative behavioral possibilities.* There must be a choice between desired behavior and positive consequences and inappropriate behavior and unpleasant consequences. Whenever possible, events which are reinforcing and were previously associated with inappropriate behavior should become contingent on desired alternative behaviors.

In fulfilling this requirement, the child must have appropriate alternative behaviors in his repertoire, and the environmental control over inappropriate behavior must not be excessively strong. *The sole purpose of punishment is to facilitate the strengthening of appropriate behavior patterns by reducing the likelihood of competing inappropriate behavior*

Walters and Parke 1967

patterns. This was emphasized by Walters and Parke* after critically reviewing the research relating to the influence of punishment on children's behavior. These writers stated: "In real life situations the suppressive effect of punishment is usually only of value if alternative prosocial responses are elicited and strengthened while the undesirable behavior is held in check" (p. 217). The value of teaching alternative behavior was also emphasized in their conclusion that there is "considerable evidence that the suppressive effects of punishment may be sufficiently powerful to permit ample time for the initiation of a program of strengthening alternative prosocial patterns of behavior. The initiation of such a program may well forestall the occurrence of undesirable side effects" (p. 218).

10. *Present maximum intensity of the aversive event from the beginning.* If the intensity of the punishment is gradually increased, the child may learn to adapt to each succeeding increment. Further, a mild aversive event such as a threat may be effective initially in suppressing behavior but, not infrequently, the child may soon adapt to this level of aversiveness and the behavior will reappear.* Thus, the more frequently a mild aversive consequence is used, the greater the possibility that it will become ineffective. Intensity, however, is an individual matter, and other characteristics of the child will interact with the aversive event to determine its suppressive effects. Short time-out periods and minor response cost penalties may have rather dramatic effects for some children, quickly suppressing high-strength behavior. For others, more intense forms of aversive consequences will be needed for suppressive effects.

Kazdin 1971; Phillips 1968

The intensity of the negative consequence should match the strength of the misbehavior. A well-established behavior will require aversive consequences of greater intensity or amount for inhibition than would behavior of lower strength.

11. *When using a punishment procedure, exercise care to insure that consequences are in fact unpleasant to the child.* Consequences viewed by teacher or parent as punishing may not be so to the child. A verbal reprimand or threat may actually serve a reinforcing function and thus strengthen behavior producing it. Sending the child out of the classroom may actually be reinforcing if aspects of the room environment (teacher, activities, groups) are unpleasant to the child. He finds that being out of the room is more pleasant than being in the room. Of course, being out of the room may be the lesser of two evils; it may be unpleasant, but not as much as being in the room.

12. *Insure that the unpleasantness of aversive consequences is stronger than the positive consequences associated with undesired behavior.* It is not infrequent for a teacher or parent to exclaim, "I can't understand it. He keeps on fighting with Joe even though he is punished every time." Apparently the reinforcing consequences associated with

fighting behavior have a maintaining effect greater than the suppressive effects of punishment. In such cases, it would be foolish to continue punishing the child unless the reinforcing effects could be removed. Other tactics of reduction or removal of these reinforcing events, along with strengthening alternative behaviors, would best serve the child's needs. Thus, whenever possible, remove the reinforcing events associated with the punished behavior. Punishment will then be more effective in suppressing the inappropriate behavior.

13. *After the child is informed of the punishment rule, routine use of a threat or warning about further undesired behavior producing unpleasant consequences is to be discouraged.* When the teacher is emotionally upset, nagging and punishment are likely to result in harsh or inappropriate punishment. Such behaviors as, "Stop that or I'll send you out of the room," "John, sit down this instant or you can't listen to the music" are inappropriate. These demands, intended to inhibit these behaviors, may actually facilitate them. Also, if the child is warned or threatened, he may learn that continuation of his misbehavior will result in punishment only after a warning and not at times when no warning is provided. On the other hand, it may be helpful on occasions in which misbehavior is likely to occur for the teacher to remind the child of the appropriate behavior before he responds inappropriately: "Sue, remember to finish your work." "John, you have almost finished your project. After you finish we'll take a break." "Tim, remember to remain in your chair until we've finished."

14. *When reprimand is used as a punishment procedure, present it so that it does not attract the attention of other children.* Studies by O'Leary and Becker* and by O'Leary et al.* suggest that a loud reprimand directed toward a single child, which could be heard by other children in the group, will have less effect on reducing the strength of disruptive behavior than when the reprimand is presented in a soft manner heard only by the child being punished. It is possible that the loud reprimand provides the disruptive child with peer attention, which may serve to further strengthen the disruptive behavior. A loud reprimand would also serve to distract other children from their schoolwork activities.

O'Leary and Becker 1968; O'Leary et al. 1970

A soft, rather than a loud, procedure of reprimanding children in selected instances could also be justified from the position that punishment should be a private matter between the teacher and a specific child. Presenting a reprimand which is heard only by the child whose behavior is inappropriate informs him of the undesired behavior and of the disappointment of the teacher in relation to this specific behavior. It avoids placing the child in an embarrassing or demeaning position in the eyes of his peers as is possible when the teacher's reprimand is heard by his peers in the class.

15. *If punishment effects are not evident rather immediately, it is probably best to discontinue the procedure.* If punishment procedures which are used reflect the guidelines discussed, punishment will exert a rather immediate effect. If no such effect is evident, continued punishment is likely to result in negative side effects. Thus, punishment procedures should be terminated if suppression effects are not noted soon after the initiation of the punishment procedure.

16. *In using mild punishment to suppress behavior which occurs in numerous settings, it will typically be necessary to implement the punishment contingency in each setting.* In this manner, events in each setting will "remind" the child of the punishment contingency and thus will serve to suppress the behavior. Additionally, positive reinforcement procedures used in each setting to strenghten appropriate competing behaviors will provide cues for desired behavior.

17. *Punishment procedures should be phased out of an educational program as quickly as possible.* Under no circumstances should behavior remain under predominately aversive control. The child should enjoy behaving appropriately rather than refraining from behaving inappropriately due to fear of aversive consequences. In addition to ethical consideration, a program should emphasize positive reinforcement because behavior suppressed through punishment is likely to reappear following termination of the punishment contingency.

18. *To reemphasize, when punishment is used, label the contingencies for the child.* Whenever punishment is used, inform the child which of his behaviors produced the aversive consequence. Remind him of alternative acceptable behaviors. Inform the child in a matter-of-fact manner that the responsibility is his in deciding on more acceptable modes of behaving. In this manner the child is more likely to develop cognitive self-management skills in dealing with the contingencies present in various situations. Aronfreed,* Parke,* and Sears et al.* emphasize the role of mediational "reasoning" in enhancing the effectiveness of punishment.

Aronfreed 1968; Parke 1970; Sears et al. 1957

REFERENCES

Abbott, M. S. Modification of the classroom behavior of a "disadvantaged" kindergarten boy by social reinforcement and isolation. *Journal of Education*, 1969, 151, 31–45.

Allen, K. E., and Harris, F. R. Elimination of a child's excessive scratching by training the mother in reinforcement procedures. *Behavior Research and Therapy*, 1966, 4, 79–84.

Allen, K. E., Turner, K. D., and Everett, P. M. A behavior modification classroom for Head Start children with problem behaviors. *Exceptional Children*, 1970, 37, 119–127.

Aronfreed, J. Aversive control of socialization. In W. J. Arnold (Ed.) *Nebraska Symposium on Motivation, 1968*. Lincoln: University of Nebraska Press, 1968.

Ayllon, T., Layman, D., and Kandel H. A behavioral-educational alternative to drug control of hyperactive children. *Journal of Applied Behavior Analysis*, 1975, 8, 137–146.

Allyon, T., and Roberts, M.D. Eliminating discipline problems by strengthening academic performance. *Journal of Applied Behavior Analysis*, 1974, 7, 71–76.

Azrin, N. H., and Powers, M.A. Eliminating classroom disturbances of emotionally disturbed children by positive practice. *Behavior Therapy*, 1975, 6, 525–534.

Becker, W. C., Madsen, C. H., Arnold, C.T., and Thomas, D.R. The contingent use of teacher attention and praise in reducing classroom behavior problems. *Journal of Special Education*, 1967, 1, 287–307.

Briskin, A. S., and Gardner, W. I. Social reinforcement in reducing inappropriate behavior. *Young Children*, 1968, 24, 84–89.

Brown, P., and Elliott, R. Control of aggression in a nursery school class. *Journal of Experimental Child Psychology*, 1965, 2, 103–107.

Carlson, C. S., Arnold, C. R., Becker, W. C., and Madsen, C. H. The elimination of tantrum behavior of a child in an elementary classroom. *Behavior Research and Therapy*, 1968, 6, 117–119.

Cromwell, R. L., Blashfield, R. K., and Strauss, J. S. Criteria for classification systems. In N. Hobbs (Ed.) *Issues in the Classification of Children*. Vol. 1. San Francisco: Jossey-Bass, 1975. Pp. 4–25.

Foxx, R. M., and Azrin, N. H. Restitution: A method of eliminating aggressive-disruptive behavior of retarded and brain-damaged patients. *Behavior Research and Therapy*, 1972, 10, 15–27.

Foxx, R. M., and Azrin, N. H. The elimination of autistic self-stimulatory behavior by overcorrection. *Journal of Applied Behavior Analysis*, 1973, 6, 1–14.

Hall, R. V., Fox, R., Willard, D., Goldsmith, L., Emerson, M., Owen, M., Davis, F., and Porcia, E. The teacher as observer and experimenter in the modification of disputing and talking-out behaviors. *Journal of Applied Behavior Analysis*, 1971, 4, 141–149.

Hall, R. V., Axelrod, S., Tyler, L., Grief, E., Jones, F. C., and Robertson, R. Modification of behavior problems in the home with a parent as observer and experimenter. *Journal of Applied Behavior Analysis*, 1972, 5, 53–64.

Hamblin, R. L., Buckholdt, D., Ferritor, D., Kozloff, M., and Blackwell, L. *The Humanization Processes: A Social Behavioral Analysis of Children's Problems*. New York: Wiley-Interscience, 1971.

Hart, B. M., Allen, K. E., Buell, J. S., Harris, F. R., and Wolf, M. M. Effects of social reinforcement on operant crying. *Journal of Experimental Child Psychology*, 1964, 1, 145–153.

Hawkins, R. P., Peterson, R. F., Schweid, E., and Bijou, S. W. Behavior therapy in the home: Amelioration of problem parent-child relations with the parent in a therapeutic role. *Journal of Experimental Child Psychology*, 1966, 4, 99–107.

Iwata, B. A., and Bailey, J. S. Reward versus cost token systems: An analysis of the effects on students and teacher. *Journal of Applied Behavior Analysis*, 1974, 7, 567–576.

Johnston, J. M. Punishment of human behavior. *American Psychologist*, 1972, 27, 1033–1054.

Kaufman, K. F., and O'Leary, K. D. Reward, cost, and self-evaluation procedures for disruptive adolescents in a psychiatric hospital school. *Journal of Applied Behavior Analysis*, 1972, 5, 293–309.

Kazdin, A. E. The effect of response cost in suppressing behavior in a pre-psychotic retardate. *Journal of Behavior Therapy and Experimental Psychiatry*, 1971, 2, 137–140.

Kazdin, A. E. Response cost: The removal of conditioned reinforcers for therapeutic change. *Behavior Therapy*, 1972, 3, 533–546.

Koegel, R. L., Firestone, P. B., Kramme, K. W., and Dunlap, G. Increasing spontaneous play by suppressing self-stimulation in autistic children. *Journal of Applied Behavior Analysis*, 1974, 7, 521–528.

Kubany, E. S., Weiss, L. E., and Sloggett, B. B. The good behavior clock: A reinforcement/time-out procedure for reducing disruptive classroom behavior. *Journal of Behavior Therapy and Experimental Psychiatry*, 1971, 2, 173–179.

McLaughlin, T., and Malaby, J. Reducing and measuring inappropriate verbalizations in a token classroom. *Journal of Applied Behavior Analysis*, 1972, 5, 329–333.

MacMillan, D. L. *Behavior Modification in Education*. New York: Macmillan, 1973.

MacMillan, D. L., Forness, S. R., and Trumbull, B. M. The role of punishment in the classroom. *Exceptional Children*, 1973, 40, 85–96.

Madsen, C. H., Becker, W. C., Thomas, D. R., Koser, L., and Plager, E. An analysis of the reinforcing function of "sit down" commands. In R. K. Parker (Ed.) *Readings in Educational Psychology*. Boston: Allyn and Bacon, 1968. Pp. 265–278.

Martin, B. *Anxiety and Neurotic Disorders*. New York: John Wiley, 1971.

O'Leary, K. D., and Becker, W. C. The effects of the intensity of a teacher's reprimands on children's behavior. *Journal of School Psychology*, 1968, 7, 8–11.

O'Leary, K. D., Kaufman, K. F., Kass, R. E., and Drabman, R. S. The effects of loud and soft reprimands on the behavior of disruptive students. *Exceptional Children*, 1970, 37, 145–155.

Parke, R. D. The role of punishment in the socialization process. In R. A. Hoppe, G. A. Milton, and E. Simmel (Eds.) *Early Experiences in the Processes of Socialization*. New York: Academic, 1970.

Pendergrass, V. E. Timeout from positive reinforcement following persistent, high-rate behavior in retardates. *Journal of Applied Behavior Analysis*, 1972, 85–91.

Perline, I. H., and Levinsky, D. Controlling maladaptive classroom behavior in the severely retarded. *American Journal of Mental Deficiency*, 1968, 73, 74–78.

Phillips, E. L. Achievement Place: Token reinforcement procedures in a home-style rehabilitation setting for "predelinquent" boys. *Journal of Applied Behavior Analysis*, 1968, 1, 213–223.

Pierce, M. L. A behavior modification approach to facilitating a disturbed child's school re-entry by teaching time-out procedures to the child's classmates. *School Applications of Learning Theory*, 1971, 3, 1–6.

Risley, T. R. The effects and side effects of punishing the autistic behaviors of deviant child. *Journal of Applied Behavior Analysis*, 1968, 1, 21–34.

Schmidt, G. W., and Ullrich, R. E. Effects of group contingent events upon classroom noise. *Journal of Applied Behavior Analysis*, 1969, 2, 171–179.

Sears, R. R., Maccoby, E. E., and Levin, H. *Patterns of Child Rearing*. Evanston, Ill.: Row, Peterson, 1957.

Sibley, S. A., Abbott, M. S., and Cooper, B. P. Modification of the classroom behavior of a disadvantaged kindergarten boy by social reinforcement and isolation. *Journal of Experimental Child Psychology*, 1969, 7, 203–219.

Steeves, J. M., Martin, G. L., and Pear, J. J. Self-imposed time-out by autistic children during an operant training program. *Behavior Therapy*, 1970, 1, 371–381.

Sulzbacher, S. I., and Houser, J. E. A tactic to eliminate disruptive behaviors in the classroom: Group contingent consequences. *American Journal of Mental Deficiency*, 1968, 73, 88–90.

Ullman, L. P., and Krasner, L. (Eds.) *Case Studies in Behavior Modification*, New York: Holt, Rinehart & Winston, 1965.

Ullman, L. P., and Krasner, L. *A Psychological Approach to Abnormal Behavior*. Englewood Cliffs, N. J.: Prentice-Hall, 1969.

Walters, R. H., and Parke, R. D. The influence of punishment and related disciplinary techniques on the social behavior of children: Theory and empirical findings. In B. A. Maher (Ed.) *Progress in Experimental Personality Research.* Vol. IV. New York: Academic, 1967, Pp. 179–228.

Walters, R. H., Parke, R. D., and Cane, V. A. Timing of punishment and the observation of consequences to others as determinants of response inhibition. *Journal of Experimental Child Psychology,* 1965, 2, 10–30.

Watson, L. S. *How to Use Behavior Modification with Mentally Retarded and Autistic Children.* Columbus, Ohio: Behavior Modification Technology, 1972.

White, G. D., Nielsen, G., and Johnson, S. M. Time-out duration and the suppression of deviant behavior in children. *Journal of Applied Behavior Analysis,* 1972, 5, 111–120.

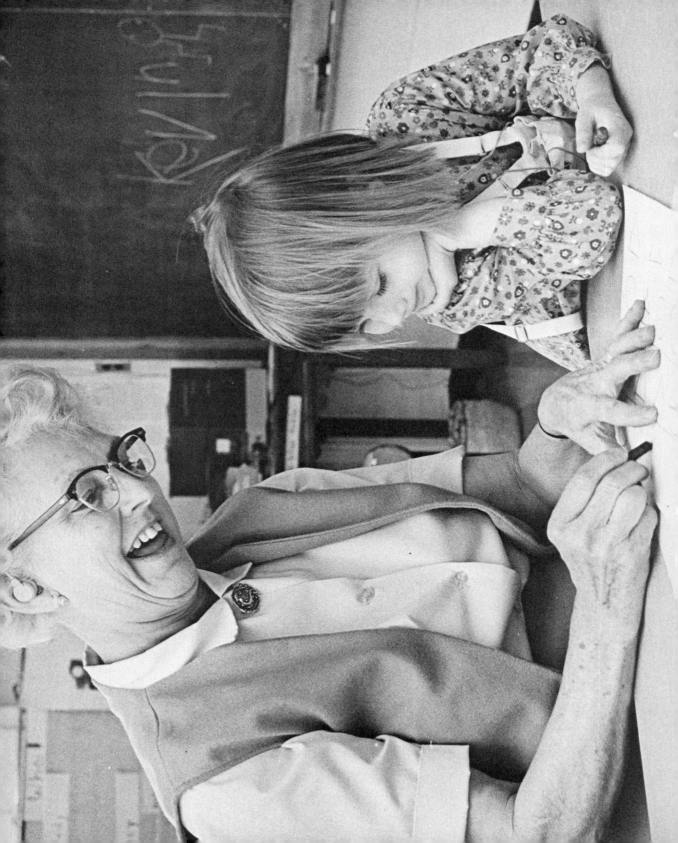

11

Influencing Emotional and Attitudinal Characteristics

As described in the introductory chapter, children with "emotional disturbances" and "behavior disorders" are estimated to comprise some 2 percent of the total school population. Well over 170,000 children and youth are presently enrolled in special services for the "emotionally disturbed" provided by local public school systems in the United States. Difficulties in emotional learning and expression and the disruptive role which exceptional emotional characteristics assume in producing a range of learning, social, and interpersonal difficulties are high-lighted in current views of "emotional disturbance" in children and youth.* Additionally, careful evaluation of the exceptional learning and behavior characteristics of other "categories of exceptional children" reveals that in each category emotional difficulties are outstanding features which require specialized educational attention. The "mentally retarded," "learning-disabled," "brain-injured," "socially maladjusted," "speech-impaired," and those with chronic sensory and physical disabilities have all been described as having exceptional emotional characteristics.*

Graubard 1973; Hallahane and Kauffman 1976; Knoblock 1971; Ross 1974

The educator involved in services to "exceptional" children thus should be knowledgeable about emotional learning concepts and skilled in programming for both the development of desired emotional characteristics and the reduction in the child's disruptive emotionality. Traditionally, the special educator has left serious program concern for the emotional aspects of a child's problems to other experts—the psychologist, the counselor, the psychiatrist, the social worker. This fragmented treatment

Bryan and Bryan 1975; Cruickshank 1971; Dunn 1973; Haring 1974

approach has not proved successful. Therefore, the present chapter (1) introduces the special educator to the basic behavioral approach concepts of emotional learning and expression and (2) enumerates general and specific procedures of educational programming for dealing directly and systematically with difficulties of emotional development and expression.

INFLUENCING EXCEPTIONAL EMOTIONAL CHARACTERISTICS

Children and adolescents *learn* to be anxious, fearful, happy, or sad, and to engage in a variety of other specific and general emotional and attitudinal behavior patterns. The emotional and attitudinal characteristics of children with learning and behavior difficulties are influenced by the educator and others in the school environment even though such adults may be quite unaware of *what* specifically is being influenced or even *how* such behavioral characteristics are influenced.

A child's learning and behavioral difficulties can be reduced in many instances by careful attention to the manner in which competing disruptive emotional and attitudinal behaviors may be controlled or eliminated. Children with exceptional learning characteristics frequently have considerable difficulty with appropriate emotional expression and control. Attitudinal characteristics inconsistent with effective learning are frequently present. Some children respond with emotions which are too intense at too frequent times to too many aspects of their school environment. Other children are apt to be emotionally bland and to show an insufficient amount and variety of emotional responsiveness. Negative attitudes toward school and teacher as well as toward goals of competency and achievement characterize too many children and adolescents with exceptional learning and behavior characteristics. These emotional and attitudinal characteristics interfere with the acquisition of critical cognitive and social behaviors. The child or adolescent, as a result, is even more likely to encounter experiences which contribute to additional undesirable emotional and attitudinal behaviors.

But children and adolescents can acquire more appropriate and enhancing patterns of emotional and attitudinal responsiveness. They can do so by being exposed to emotionally stable and expressive teachers who provide carefully designed program experiences and plentiful sources of meaningful positive reinforcement. Social experiences in a structured environment, which insure successful school and interpersonal contacts and systematically offset the negative emotional impact of previous frightening and unpleasant consequences, will reduce the general adjustment difficulties of children with learning and behavior problems. Children and youth who are able to approach and interact with their school environments in a relaxed and trusting manner are children who are free to learn and free to be

enthusiastic about learning.* These general response patterns result from   *Rogers 1969*
numerous experiences which provide consistent and predictable positive
consequences for competency behavior.

As emotionality, both positive and negative, represents a central
feature of patterns of attitudinal behavior, the topic of emotional learning
will be considered initially. Following this, the manner in which attitudinal behavior is developed, maintained, and modified will be considered.

UNLEARNED EMOTIONAL RESPONSES

At a basic level certain stimulus events automatically produce certain emotional reactions. These reactions are unlearned or reflexive. These
occur naturally, without the benefit of previous learning experiences,
whenever certain stimulus events are presented. A diaper pin sticking the
child, wet diapers, hunger, thirst, extremes in temperature, and intense
light or noise produce certain reflexive motor and other muscular and
glandular *respondent* or *emotional* behaviors. Whenever these stimulus
conditions are present, the child is described as feeling uncomfortable,
being unhappy, or as being distressed or in pain. These are events which
the child dislikes and which he avoids if possible. The infant has only a few
reflexive behaviors which serve to remove these painful events. Yet the
child soon learns many new behaviors which remove or avoid events
resulting in unpleasant emotional or feeling states.

Other events produce emotional conditions of relaxation or pleasure. Providing food to the hungry child, liquid to the thirsty child, warmth
to the child who is cold, physical stroking (cuddling), removing physical
irritants (for example, wet diapers)—these events produce feelings of pleasure, delight, or satisfaction. The child likes these events and behaves in
whatever manner will produce them.

Thus there are primary events which, when presented or removed,
will produce or coincide with various primitive or basic emotional states.
These states may be described as variations of feelings of pleasure or
delight and of pain or distress.

BASIC RULE OF EMOTIONAL OR RESPONDENT LEARNING

As the child gains new experiences by interacting with his physical
and social environments, two important changes occur in his emotional
responsiveness. First, the rather undifferentiated emotional reactions of
distress and delight elaborate into a range of other reactions such as joy,
anxiety, affection, glee, disgust, guilt, happiness, jealousy, anger, and
sadness.

Second, a number of events other than the initial primary ones come to influence the occurrence of these emotional reactions. A mother's smile can result in positive feelings for the child. The sight of a dog can cause a child to be fearful. The child can become anxious when left by his mother. He may become gleefully excited when he is promised a new toy. He may experience considerable satisfaction over his accomplishments. As he gets older, he may experience stomachaches when anticipating a test in school, or anger when reprimanded by an adult. These new associations between events or activities and emotional behaviors are developed through a process of emotional (respondent) learning. The basic rule of emotional learning is as follows:

When a neutral event is paired frequently with any other event which produces an emotional reaction, this neutral event presented alone will begin to produce the emotional response.

The procedure to follow in applying this rule would be:

step 1 | Identify an event that produces an emotional response.

step 2 | Identify a neutral event which you would like to have produce this emotional response.

step 3 | Arrange for the simultaneous occurrence—pairing—of these two events on a number of occasions. As a result of these pairings, the neutral stimulus when presented alone will begin to produce the emotional response.

An event is viewed as neutral if, prior to learning, it does not produce a specified emotional reaction. This neutral event, for the older child, may be any aspect of the child's experience: words, sounds, a classroom setting, a person, tone of a person's voice, or an activity such as listening to music, reading a book, solving a difficult problem, or coloring with water colors.

A mother's smile and her soothing tone of voice, when presented while the child is enjoying his food or his warm bath water, will soon independently begin to result in comforting emotional feelings of pleasure, relaxation, or delight for the child. In this instance, the food or warm water is an unlearned or *unconditioned stimulus event*. The emotional state of relaxation or delight is the unlearned or *unconditioned response*. After a number of temporal associations of unconditioned and neutral events, learning occurs, and the neutral events of mother's smile and tone of voice will begin to produce the positive feelings; the smile and soothing voice thus become *conditioned or learned stimulus events*. These conditioned events when presented alone now produce emotional responses, called *conditioned responses* which are similar to the original *unconditioned responses*. In this manner various emotional responses may become attached to a wide range of preceding stimulus events, including the child's own overt and covert verbal behaviors.

A mother who frowns at her child, yells "No" and "Bad boy" as she slaps his hand will soon find that the frown alone, or the frown and "No" or "Bad" will produce the uncomfortable and disruptive emotional reactions produced initially only by the hand slap. In this instance of learning, the slap represents the unconditioned stimulus which produced the unconditioned emotional reaction of distress. The frown, "No," and "Bad," all neutral stimuli initially, after a number of pairings with the slap, become conditioned events which produce the conditioned emotional reaction of distress in the absence of the slap. Again, the critical factor in the learning is the temporal pairing of the unconditioned stimulus and the previously neutral events. After a few such pairings the neutral events become conditioned stimulus events. Any neutral cue present at the time the child engages in an emotional response may come to produce an emotional reaction highly similar to the initial unconditioned one.

Generality of the Basic Rule of Emotional Learning

The basic rule of emotional learning underlies the development of the specific and generalized emotional patterns of children and adolescents. A teacher who shows disappointment with, reprimands, or otherwise frequently punishes the students in her class will become a conditioned cue for apprehension and related negative emotional reactions in her pupils. In fact, many of the specific cues present as she punishes the children may later serve to produce the disruptive emotional reactions. These may be such events as the teacher's voice quality and tone, the type of clothes that she wears, the classroom activities occurring as punishment is provided, and the time of day.

If a visually impaired adolescent consistently has difficulty with specific types of assignments, for example, such tasks can become conditioned cues for negative emotional reactions. He begins to dislike the tasks. Behaviors which will either help him to avoid these or to remove them once presented to him will be strengthened through negative reinforcement. In extreme cases, the entire physical characteristics of the classroom or school environment can become cues for conditioned emotional responses such as apprehension, anxiety, and distress. The adolescent will become uncomfortable whenever in the classroom and will strive to get away from it whenever possible. The speech-impaired child may find that social situations requiring him to talk may become conditioned cues for negative emotionality. The child's speech may be inhibited as a result. Speech behavior itself, if paired frequently with aversive consequences, may serve to provoke negative emotionality which increases the speech production difficulties of the child. Brutten and Shoemaker,* Johnson,* and Sheehan* present descriptions of the role of negative emotionality in

Brutten and Shoemaker 1968; Johnson 1959; Sheehan 1953

the development and perpetuation of stuttering. Basically, anxiety becomes attached to various disfluencies of a child's speech due to the negative reaction of parents and others when such disfluencies occur. Over hundreds of such experiences, increasingly higher levels of negative emotionality become attached to many aspects of the speech process and thus serve to intensify and maintain fluency difficulties.

On the other hand, the teacher who is calm and relaxed and who reinforces children with positive events will come to produce desirable emotional reactions in children. They will feel good about being with the teacher, about being in school, and about engaging in the variety of activities which the teacher presents to them. Those events occurring simultaneously on the numerous occasions when the child is provided positive reinforcers, while initially neutral, will become conditioned events which independently will produce positive emotional reactions.

Summary

Cues associated a number of times with events which produce a type of emotional reaction will themselves gradually begin to produce it. A child can come to like or dislike, enjoy or be fearful of, become involved in or avoid numerous aspects of his physical and social environments. In like manner, he will come to like or dislike numerous aspects of his own physical, learning, and behavioral characteristics. The specific combination of feelings and associated approach or avoidance behavior patterns developed by a specific child or adolescent depends upon the nature of the emotional experiences which become associated with various people, places, things, and activities.

CONDITIONED EVENTS AS SECONDARY REINFORCING AND AVERSIVE EVENTS

Secondary Reinforcing Events

The basic rule of emotional learning can be recognized as the rule described in Chapter 8 for developing secondary reinforcing events: *Conditioned events for positive emotional responses also function as secondary reinforcing events.* As such these events when present act both to produce positive emotional reactions and to reinforce or strengthen any immediately preceding operant behavior. Every time a primary or secondary reinforcer is presented to a child, it not only strengthens the preceding behavior but also produces a positive emotional reaction. Additionally, emotional learning occurs, since any new event which is present at the time of the positive emotional response may become a new conditioned stimulus for this reaction. Thus, the child reports that he feels good about or likes those of his activities which produce or provide positive reinforcers. The child may be described as demonstrating positive attitudes in relation to specific activities or toward a wide range of related activities. This is a reflection of his experiences with these activities, the resulting positive reinforcers provided, and the related positive emotional reactions which are produced by these positive reinforcing events. The mere anticipation of activities and events can produce positive emotional reactions of enthusiasm and delight which facilitate the child's approach and involvement in these experiences.

Secondary Aversive Events

The basic rule of emotional learning is the same as that described in Chapter 8 as involved in the development of secondary aversive events: *Those events which acquire aversive qualities through learning are conditioned events for negative emotional responses.* As such these events act both to produce negative emotional reactions and to influence operant behavior through negative reinforcement and punishment. The child reports a dislike for these events and engages in whatever behavior will reduce, terminate, or avoid them. A child may become upset even before he is directly confronted with an unpleasant activity, place, person, or event by thinking about, hearing about, or otherwise experiencing cues which remind him of or signal the probable occurrence of the aversive event. The child with severe articulation difficulties, in illustration, may be highly anxious when reminded that he is to describe his class project to his peers. The symbolic representation of the future experience is a conditioned event for negative emotional reactions.

MAINTENANCE OF SECONDARY EVENTS

These conditioned stimulus and secondary reinforcing and aversive events which influence emotional behaviors and strengthen contingent operant behaviors will gradually lose their effectiveness unless occasionally reinforced. That is, these events must be paired temporally on occasion with other effective unconditioned or secondary events. Otherwise, extinction will occur and the events will regain their neutral qualities. However, as described shortly, rate of extinction is related to a number of factors.

HIGHER ORDER CONDITIONING

As implied in the preceding discussion of the basic rule of emotional learning, neutral events paired with well-established conditioned events may also gain influence over emotional reactions. Emotional responses can begin to be influenced by neutral events associated previously with conditioned stimulus events. This represents the rule of *higher order conditioning* of emotional responses. A child may receive attention and praise from the teacher when he correctly identifies the primary colors. Assuming that praise is a conditioned cue which produces positive emotional reactions, the activity of successful color identification can become a conditioned event for a positive emotional response. After a number of associations the child may appear to be pleased or satisfied with his successful color identification, even when the teacher is not present or when praise is not provided. Attending to the presentation of a language lesson may be a pleasurable activity for a child if this attending behavior has been previously associated with other events which produce positive emotional reactions.

Development of Generalized Emotional Characteristics

The same rule of higher order conditioning is involved in the development of more general emotional and attitudinal behavior patterns. A child reinforced positively on numerous occasions for a range of different activities may acquire a general pattern of being pleased or satisfied with being involved in or with successfully completing activities or tasks. He may be described as having a positive attitude toward work and may develop what has been called *achievement motivation*. Aspects of initiating activities, persisting at activities, solving difficult tasks, and task completion may become conditioned events for positive emotional reactions. These events have acquired secondary reinforcing qualities through numerous previous associations with other positive consequences. These activities are self-perpetuating to the extent that on occasion they are associated temporally with other reinforcing events.

Just as numerous aspects of the child's environment may become conditioned events for *positive* emotional reactions, through higher order conditioning, other events may come to control *negative* emotionality. Due to her cerebral palsy, visual-perceptual, and related eye-hand coordination difficulties, Sue Ellen may experience considerable difficulty with such relatively simple tasks as stringing beads, coloring, and cutting. The teacher, believing that the child can learn if she would exert sufficient effort and patience, requires Sue Ellen to remain with these tasks even after she becomes extremely frustrated. The child often becomes highly disorganized and on occasion even begins to cry. The teacher becomes a conditioned event for negative emotionality. The child begins to show a dislike for other activities with which the teacher is associated. Through higher order conditioning, these activities may become conditioned events for negative emotional reactions. If the child is unsuccessful in most of her school activities, many cues in the school environment can become conditioned events for negative emotionality. The child will become generally unhappy or perhaps even fearful over many of her contacts with school-related events.

What Influences the Intensity and Strength of Learned Emotionality?

Intense emotional responses can become conditioned to new stimulus events in a single or small number of associations. The more intense the initial stimulus event is, the more intense the emotional reaction. A minor frightening experience will produce a mild emotional reaction. A traumatic frightening experience will produce a strong and intense emotional reaction. Conditioned stimuli associated with these will influence similar reactions. This rule may be stated as follows:

The more intense the emotional reaction, the fewer the number of pairings required for the development of a new conditioned cue which will produce the emotional reaction.

A dog may attack a child and produce intense fearfulness in the child. In the future, the sight of the dog and sound of his bark serve as conditioned events which will provide intense emotionality. A teacher with a biting, sarcastic remark may be highly embarrassing to a learning-impaired adolescent who experiences difficulty in reading aloud to his classmates. A few such experiences may result in intense negative emotional reactions becoming associated with the presence of the teacher or even with future class attendance. In the same manner, a conditioned event previously associated with events which produce highly intense positive and satisfying emotional reactions will come to influence similar highly positive emotional reactions after a few associations.

The frequency of temporal pairing of neutral and conditioned or unconditioned events also influences the strength, or reliability of the occurrence, of new conditioned events. A teacher who becomes associated with events which produce only mild positive emotional reactions will become, after a larger number of associations, a conditioned event for similar mild emotional responses. This rule is as follows:

The larger the number of associations between an emotionally provoking event and an initial neutral event, the stronger the relationship becomes between the new conditioned event and the emotional response.

A teacher who reinforces a child on numerous occasions will become a strong conditioned cue for positive emotional reactions. The teacher who only infrequently provides reinforcing events will become a less reliable conditioned cue for positive emotional reactions. The *number of associations* interacts with the *intensity of the emotional reaction* to determine the actual influence or strength of a conditioned stimulus at any given time. This suggests that a conditioned stimulus associated with a large number of events producing intense emotional reactions will have a more persistent influence over emotional behavior than will a conditioned event which has been paired less frequently with events producing emotional reactions of equal intensity.

GENERALIZATION OF CONTROLLING EVENTS

Emotional reactions can be controlled by new cues which have never been associated directly with the occurrence of these reactions.

In this rule of *stimulus generalization*, cues most similar to events which do influence emotional responses are more likely to become conditioned events than are less similar events. The child on the first day of school may be fearful of the teacher simply because she is a strange adult. Numerous previous experiences with strange adults have been unpleasant for the child. The teacher as a strange adult is a conditioned cue for a fearful emotional reaction.

Vernon 1972   Vernon* reports an example of stimulus generalization.

> *A girl would not talk in the presence of her teachers even though she talked freely with peers and family members. A careful exploration of the child's school experiences failed to identify any negative emotional incidents which might account for this highly selective mutism. It was speculated, after examination of the child's previous home experiences, that generalization had occurred from an authoritative and dominating father to the teachers. The child had experienced considerable negative emotionality as a result of the father's rather harsh reprimanding tactics in relation to the child's speech. The teachers, with their rules, admonitions, and directions, behaved in a "father-type" manner. Thus the teacher, through stimulus generalization, produced negative emotionality in the child. The child was able to avoid being reprimanded by not talking to teachers.*

Awareness Not Essential to Emotional Learning or Generalization

This case illustrates an important feature of emotional learning. The child or adolescent may be quite unaware that previously neutral events are influencing his emotional behaviors. The temporal pairing of events and the related stimulus generalization may occur without the child labeling—being aware of—these occurrences. On later occasions, the child may experience an emotional reaction and be unable to understand why he is responding in such a manner.

In a similar manner, involvement in a new task at school may produce negative emotionality because involvement with other new tasks at home and at school has frequently resulted in unpleasant consequences. The cues associated with initiating the new task, due to similarity to previous tasks, cause negative emotional reactions. The child may eventually develop a general attitude of disinterest or apathy. He refrains from entering into new tasks. Or, if forced to become involved, he may react in a most active and emotionally disruptive manner. Again, these behavior patterns may occur in a new situation in which the child has had no previous experience. In many instances multiple and rather subtle aspects of situations, activities, and relationships may influence negative emotionality. The child or adolescent is usually not able to identify those components which produce uncomfortable emotional states.

This rule concerning generalization of stimulus events which influence emotionality may explain many baffling and apparently inexplicable emotional reactions: "I don't know why he doesn't like me. I've never been harsh to him," or "His intense temper tantrums after I reprimanded him is a mystery to me. I think this is the first time I've even criticized him."

There also may be generalization across stimulus events which influence positive emotionality. A child may be enjoying a positive emotional relationship with his parents at the time of entrance into a new neighborhood and school program. The new teachers whom the child has never met may be strong conditioned events for positive emotional reactions. In like manner, a child who enjoys play and other school activities as a result of consistent pleasant consequences is more likely to enjoy other similar situations or activities. The wider the range of positive experiences which result in the development of more conditioned events for positive emotionality, the greater the possibility of generalization to new situations.

It is true also that the reduction in negative emotionality associated with a person, situation, or event frequently results in a discernable reduction in negative emotionality previously produced by other similar events. A child may dislike and be wary of adults because of experiences with a harsh parent. A reduction in the negative emotionality associated with father as a result of a series of consistent positive experiences with him may in turn result in a reduction in fearfulness toward other adults.

Semantic Generalization

In addition to generalization of emotional influence to stimulus events physically similar to those directly involved in emotional learning, there may be *semantic generalization*. Staats and Staats* have   *Staats and Staats 1963* demonstrated that words can become conditioned stimuli for positive or negative emotional responses through repeated temporal pairing with other events which produce the emotional responses. Other words with similar meaning will then begin to elicit the emotional reactions without the benefit of any learning experience.

Once a word has become a learned cue which reliably elicits an emotional response, other words, activities, or events which are temporally paired repeatedly with this word will begin to control similar emotional responses. Thus a child may learn to dislike or develop a bias for a variety of people, situations, or activities, not through direct experience with these, but rather by the emotional learning that occurs when these are repeatedly labeled by words that do produce negative emotional responses.

These rules concerning the generalization across events which influence emotional behavior emphasize that no emotional experience can be viewed as an *isolated incident*. Any experience provided a child or adolescent has a potentially broader effect on his behavior development and functioning.

REDUCING UNDESIRED EMOTIONAL BEHAVIOR

It has been suggested that a child may learn to be apprehensive, fearful, unhappy, anxious, discontented, or sad in many situations due to previous associations of these or similar situations with unpleasant experiences. The more intense and frequent the associations with unpleasant experiences, the greater the likelihood that the child will engage in excessive emotional behavior which disrupts and interferes with appropriate learning and with enjoyable social interactions. The basic rule which underlies the elimination of the influence which conditioned events have over these negative emotional responses is as follows:

> **Repeated presentation of the conditioned stimulus which controls emotionality without pairing it with the unconditioned stimulus, or with the conditioned event in higher-order conditioning, will result in the gradual reduction and eventual elimination of the effectiveness of the conditioned stimulus in producing the emotional behavior.**

The conditioned stimulus thus gradually loses its influence over the emotional behavior. This procedure is called *extinction*. The particular stimulus events, of course, can regain control over the emotional behavior through future additional pairings with the unconditioned stimulus or with one which serves as such in higher-order conditioning.

Rate of Extinction

The number of experiences required for extinction generally depends upon the level of previous learning. The more frequent and intense the previous pairings of unconditioned and conditioned events, the slower the rate of extinction. A teacher who has punished a child in a mild manner only a limited number of times will soon cease to create negative emotionality once she no longer punishes the child as she interacts with him. On the other hand, a teacher or other aspects of the school environment that represent strong conditioned cues for apprehension and anxiety will continue to produce these emotional reactions for an extended period of time even though no new negative consequences are forthcoming.

The mere passage of time does not result in a reduction of the influence which conditioned events have over emotional reactions. An adolescent, for example, may bring a dislike for competition, or a more general reaction of depression, into the school setting even though these were learned some weeks or months prior to his enrollment in the new school. At an earlier time the dislike may have been a realistic one attached to a potentially punishing situation. The likelihood of punishment, however, may no longer exist. Aspects of the school environment nonetheless may maintain influence over the negative emotional reaction for extended periods of time unless new learning occurs. The teacher cannot assume, "Oh, he'll get over it. Just give him time." The adolescent must receive new experiences in the presence of the conditioned or similar events in which aversive consequences are no longer provided. If left to chance, extinction of negative emotional reactions can be lengthy and frequently unpredictable. This emphasizes the need for an active and systematic educational approach to influencing negative as well as more appropriate positive emotional behavior.

FACILITATING REDUCTION OF UNDESIRED EMOTIONALITY

In view of the difficulty in using an extinction procedure to eliminate or reduce excessive undesired emotionality, the educator may facilitate the process by exposing the child to situations likely to produce contrasting and incompatible emotional reactions. This procedure of *counterconditioning* or *desensitization* may be used to speed up the elimination of conditioned stimulus control of undesirable emotional behavior. This procedure involves both (1) the presentation of the conditioned stimulus for negative emotionality in the absence of further pairing with other aversive events (an extinction procedure) and (2) the added feature of presenting other stimulus events which produce more favorable emotional reactions. It emphasizes the presentation of events which produce uncomfortable emotional responses on those occasions in which the child or adolescent is likely to be relaxed, comfortable, or otherwise experiencing positive feelings. These positive emotional reactions compete with the negative ones. A child cannot be relaxed and anxious or happy and sad at the same time. As Staats* has emphasized, in using this procedure it is critical that the positive emotional response is stronger than the negative emotionality associated with the feared object. Otherwise the procedure may backfire, with the result that the negative emotionality will become attached to the positive event.

Staats 1975

Use of Progressive Relaxation

Initially, in some instances it may be necessary to create appropriate emotional responses which will compete with the undesired ones. Wolpe* has pioneered in the use of a progressive relaxation procedure in insuring emotional states which are incompatible with excessive anxiety reactions. The child, while in a state of relaxation, is gradually exposed to descriptions of situations, objects, or persons which are anxiety provoking. After a number of such exposures, during which the descriptions of the anxiety-provoking events gradually but progressively become increasingly similar to the actual events, the child learns to respond in a more relaxed manner. Word and Rozynko* described the use of this procedure in eliminating an eleven-year-old girl's fear of participating in a reading group. The fear, based on previous unpleasant experiences with an overly critical reading teacher, was eliminated following exposure of the child, while in a state of relaxation, to verbal descriptions of reading activities in situations which progressively approximated realistic classroom conditions.

Wolpe 1958, 1969

Word and Rozynko 1974

Use of Emotive Imagery

Lazarus and Abramovitz* used a variation of the desensitization procedure in eliminating children's phobias through the use of "emotive imagery." Instead of inducing muscular relaxation as the anxiety-inhibiting response, the educator attempted to arouse in each child such feelings as self-assertion, pride, affection, and mirth. This was accomplished by determining from each child who his favorite television, movie, and fiction hero images were. After determining the nature and magnitude of each child's fears and arranging these in a hierarchy from least to most feared, the child was asked to close his eyes and to imagine some event which involved his favorite hero. The clinician gradually introduced into the story phobic items low on the hierarchy. If any discomfort was experienced as phobic items were introduced, the child was instructed to raise his finger. Other less anxiety-arousing items were intro-

Lazarus and Abramovitz 1962

duced. This procedure was continued until the most feared situation was introduced without provoking apprehension.

Lazarus and Abramovitz* illustrated the procedure of arousing emotive imagery in reducing an intense fear of dogs in a fourteen-year-old boy:

Lazarus and Abramovitz 1962

> The adolescent had an intense desire for a certain Alfa Romeo sports car and to race it at the Indianapolis 500 event. Emotive imagery was induced as follows: "Close your eyes. I want you to imagine, clearly and vividly, that your wish has come true. The Alfa Romeo is now in your possession. It is your car. It is standing in the street outside your block. You are looking at it now. Notice the beautiful sleek lines. You decide to go for a drive with some friends of yours. You sit down at the wheel, and you feel a thrill of pride as you realize that you own this magnificent machine. You start up and listen to the wonderful roar of the exhaust. You let the clutch in and the car streaks off. You are out in the clear open road now; the car is performing like a pedigree; the speedometer is climbing into the nineties; you have a wonderful feeling of being in perfect control; you look at the trees whizzing by and you see a little dog standing next to one of them—if you feel any anxiety, just raise your finger." [Pp. 110–111]

Lazarus and Abramovitz* also used this emotive-imagery approach with nine phobic children whose ages ranged from seven to fourteen years. Seven children were reported to lose their phobias in a mean of 3.3 sessions, and follow-up evaluation up to twelve months later revealed no relapses or symptom substitution.

Lazarus and Abramovitz 1962

Other Examples of Desensitization

A teacher who produces negative emotionality in a child may refrain in her everyday interactions from punishing the child and at the same time may provide him with numerous positive reinforcers (smile, praise, privileges) which produce pleasant emotional reactions. She may interact with him when he is eating, playing, watching an athletic contest, enjoying music, resting, or otherwise having fun. After a number of such pairings, the teacher may lose her fear-provoking qualities and eventually will come to influence positive emotional responses. Under these new conditions, the child may begin to like the teacher as she becomes a positive conditioned reinforcer.

If a child is afraid of pets due to previous negative experiences with dogs and cats, a rabbit may be introduced in the classroom during times when the child is relaxed and happy. This exposure should be quite gradual and every effort made to insure that the child is relaxed during the introduction of the pet. After a number of such exposures, the fear response to the rabbit will be reduced.

The rule associated with counterconditioning in the reduction of undesired emotional reactions is:

Excessive fear reactions may be reduced by exposing the child to the fear object, event, or activity at times when he is experiencing positive emotionality. Other negative emotional reactions such as disgust, anxiety, discomfort, guilt, and apprehension may be reduced or eliminated as reactions to specific situations by following the same rule.

INFLUENCING EMOTIONAL BEHAVIOR THROUGH OBSERVATION OF OTHERS

Acquiring New Emotional Responses

"Scott is just like his mother. He's afraid of many things. I don't know why he gets so emotional. He's never had bad experiences that I know of." "We have trouble getting Jackie to ride the bus. She is just as afraid of riding the bus as her mother is. I don't know why she's afraid. Jackie had never been in a bus until she enrolled in school, and she hasn't had any bad experiences on the bus."

These and similar comments suggest that emotional reactions may be acquired without direct, emotionally arousing experiences. This learning may result from the child's emotional arousal as he observes others engaging in emotional behaviors. A parent who expresses a fear of darkness, strangers, bugs, or thunderstorms, or who demonstrates obvious distaste for certain foods, people, clothing, or music is likely to instill similar fears and dislikes in her child who on numerous occasions observes these emotional reactions.

Children and youth may learn a wide range of positive and negative emotional behaviors if exposed to other people engaging in these behaviors in the presence of specific events. The basic rule of emotional learning accounts for this learning. The person being observed by the child engages in an emotional response, which in turn arouses a similar emotional reaction in the child. Any neutral stimulus events temporally associated with this arousal become conditioned events which, after a few associations, will begin to produce the emotional reaction. This learning occurs in the following pattern:

step 1 | Child observes someone (peer, sibling, teacher, parent) engage in some emotional behavior—peer becomes upset when math teacher criticizes her.

step 2 | The child becomes emotionally aroused as a result of this observation.

step 3 | Neutral cues—the math teacher, the math class—are temporally associated with the child's emotional arousal.

| step 4 | These neutral cues, after a few pairings, become conditioned events which produce the emotional arousal—child becomes upset when math teacher approaches her or calls her name. |

In such observational learning of emotional reactions, faster learning occurs in an observer who is intensely aroused. In addition, the larger the number of observations and subsequent emotional arousals the greater the strength of the conditioned emotional reaction.

Reduction of Emotional Behaviors

It is true also that emotional reactions to specific events can be reduced or eliminated through observational learning. Fears or other negative emotions may be extinguished by having a child observe others demonstrating positive emotional reactions in the presence of events which produce negative emotions.

The steps involved in using this rule to influence the reduction or elimination of emotional behavior are:

| step 1 | Identify conditioned events which produce negative emotionality in the child who is the observer. |

| step 2 | Identify a model for which these events do not produce negative emotionality and toward which the model could behave in a positive manner. |

| step 3 | Arrange for the model to approach and remain in the presence of the conditioned events. |

| step 4 | Arrange for the child to observe the model interacting in a positive manner with the fear-provoking event. |

| step 5 | Repeat this observation on a number of occasions. The conditioned event will gradually lose its influence in producing the negative emotional reaction. |

In using this procedure, the instructional program must be arranged to insure that the child actually observes the model approaching and remaining in the presence of the feared object. If the observation is too unpleasant, the child may quickly turn his attention to other aspects of his environment. Also, if the fear object produces an intense emotional reaction, the child may become highly aroused as he observes a model actually interacting with the fear object. Under these circumstances, the fear response would not be reduced. In this case, the model should gradually approach the feared object. Each successive exposure will progressively approximate a natural presentation of the feared event. In each step, the model should display positive affect and related approach behavior in his interaction with the feared cues. If any apprehension is displayed by the model, even so mild, this will interfere with the extinction process.

The extinction process can be enhanced by using a model that the child views as a friend, someone he likes, has confidence in, and is likely to imitate. If the model is a stranger or differs greatly from the child in other ways, the child is less likely to be influenced by what he sees.

Bandura et al. 1967, 1968

Bandura et al.* provide examples of the use of modeling procedures in successfully reducing the fear of dogs in a group of children:

> These children observed a fearless peer model exhibit progressively more fear-provoking interactions with a dog. The physical restraint of the dog, the closeness and amount of contact with the dog, and the duration of interaction between the model and dog were varied. All of the model's experience with the dog was pleasant and fun-like in nature. Some children observed several different girls and boys of varying ages interacting positively with many dogs. The size and fearsomeness of the dogs increased with each successive observation experience. Exposure to either types of modeled experiences resulted in a significant reduction of the initial fear of dogs exhibited by the observer. Children, after observing peers approaching and playing with dogs, were able to engage in this behavior themselves.

GENERALIZED EMOTIONAL CONDITIONS

Various patterns of emotional reactions, which may be called *emotional states or moods,* are of interest because these reactions serve as discriminative events and, as such, they make more likely the occurrence of certain subsequent behaviors. A child who is angry or excessively anxious is less likely to engage in cooperative and productive behaviors than would be true at other times when he was not so aroused. In contrast, a child who is smiling, relaxed, or otherwise in a positive emotional state is more likely to engage in behaviors of cooperation, concentration, or even persistence in the face of difficulty. The effective educator attempts to influence the occurrence of these positive emotional states as well as takes advantage of such states when they occur spontaneously.

It is not unusual, as noted earlier, for children with learning and behavior problems to be described as "being in a bad mood," "being grouchy," or "down in the dumps." These descriptions imply that the child's emotional state influences his responsiveness to a variety of aspects of his environment. The educator will find it necessary to attempt to identify and control aspects of the child's world which produce unhappy states. At the same time, he will attempt to counterbalance these by presenting other events which produce a more appropriate emotional state. To restate, verbal instructions, encouragement, charm, "turning on his personality," and reminding the children of future positive consequences may all be used to create a more pleasant emotional mood in children and adolescents. "Let's settle down now and finish so that we can listen to our favorite record." "Let's all listen carefully and I shall tell a funny story before we begin our work today." "Remember that game of who can laugh the loudest? Let's see who can smile and laugh like Santa Claus. John, you go first." "Let's practice our self-control and show the visiting school board members that adolescents are quite responsible." These tactics may set the stage for a relaxed emotional state and subsequent periods of concentrated productivity.

RELATIONSHIP BETWEEN NEGATIVE EMOTIONALITY AND AVOIDANCE BEHAVIOR

As noted, a child learns to escape or avoid unpleasant events. If a situation, activity, or person is one which the educator wishes the child to avoid, this should be paired with stimulus events which produce negative emotionality. After sufficient temporal pairings, this event will become a conditioned aversive event which will result in negative emotionality. Recall also that this same conditioned aversive event will become a discriminative event for avoidance behavior. By escaping and staying away from these aversive events the child is able to remove the unpleasant emotionality. The avoidance behavior is reinforced negatively through this removal.

In this manner, as described earlier, words and other symbols can acquire aversive characteristics and control certain behaviors. Words such as "No," "Danger," "Hot," or thoughts such as "They will call me stupid," become aversive events through an emotional conditioning procedure and result in those behaviors that will remove these from the child's immediate experience.

The teacher of children and youth with exceptional learning and behavior characteristics must deal with many patterns of avoidance behavior which need to be eliminated. As there are many conditioned aversive events associated with school activities, an excessive amount of the child's behavior is of an avoidance nature. The educational program must focus on the reduction of this nonadaptive avoidance behavior.

The following example demonstrates the relationship between negative emotionality and avoidance behavior and describes possible procedures for dealing with these undesired modes of responding.

Kim, a "moderately retarded" child with severe visual difficulties, has begun to avoid other children in the classroom and prefers to play alone. When encouraged by the teacher to join her classmates in any type of activity, Kim displays an obvious negative emotional reaction. At times, when the teacher pressures her too much, she begins to cry and will run into the corner and hide her face in her lap.

Although the teacher was unable to provide any background information on the types of negative experiences that resulted in this fear and related avoidance behavior pattern, observation of Kim in the classroom does suggest that close physical proximity and the possibility of interaction with her peers have become aversive events which control negative emotionality. Being close to other children is a discriminative cue for avoidance behavior. This avoidance behavior apparently had been strengthened as it resulted in the removal of the aversive cues and related negative emotionality.

As the aversiveness associated with the presence of other children controls the avoidance behavior, the behavior change approach used with Kim would consist of: (1) a counterconditioning procedure to eliminate the aversive components of peers, and (2) a positive reinforcement procedure to strengthen appropriate peer interaction. Peers would be associated with the presentation of numerous events producing positive emotional responses in Kim. Additionally, Kim would be guided through a graduated and increasingly complex series of contacts with peers and provided high-preference reinforcing events for any improvement in social interaction behaviors.

School Phobia as Avoidance Reaction

School phobias and related generalized withdrawal patterns may be viewed as avoidance reactions. Aspects of a general setting acquire aversive qualities (conditioned cues for negative emotionality), which in turn produce escape and avoidance behavior. Patterson and Brodsky* describe a successful behavior change program.

Patterson and Brodsky 1966

The program was designed to eliminate the intense fear reaction and related tantrum behavior exhibited by a five-year-old boy when his mother attempted to leave him at school. Various modeling and counterconditioning procedures were used to decrease the negative emotionality associated with being separated from mother. Additionally, tangible and social reinforcers were provided for approaching and interacting with the school environment. The extensive avoidance behavior pattern diminished as the fear associated with separation from mother was eliminated and as aspects of the school environment (teacher, peers, activities) became stronger conditioned stimuli for positive emotionality.

A final example of a behavior management program designed to deal with negative emotionality and a related general avoidance pattern of behavior is described in greater detail because it provides an illustration of the combined use of a number of different procedures. The program was developed by Ross et al.* for a six-year-old boy enrolled in a preschool program whose entry into public school had been delayed because he exhibited extreme social withdrawal from peers. He avoided looking at other children, withdrew from any possible physical proximity or tactual contact, ducked his head or turned away when a peer initiated verbal contact, abruptly left a solitary activity upon arrival of a peer, would run away when an adult advocated social interaction with peers, and would hide during large-group social interaction. When forced by peers into close physical proximity, he exhibited intense fearfulness.

Ross et al. 1971

The therapeutic education program provided consisted of the following:

Initially, a male teacher whom the boy had not met established himself as a conditioned event for positive emotional responses. He rewarded the child with a variety of tangible and social reinforcers for imitating many of his behaviors. This was done to insure that the child would become emotionally attached to the teacher. The teacher became an important source of secondary reinforcement and produced considerable positive emotionality in the child. The teacher could then require various behaviors from the child and could reinforce these with his approval and praise. A female adult was introduced and the child began to interact with this adult.

After the male teacher had established a good relationship with the child, a series of experiences were designed to eliminate the child's fear and avoidance behavior and to teach him social interaction and motor and general game skills. Initially, the child was exposed to interactions between the teacher and other children. This was designed to permit the child to observe approach and interaction behaviors which produced no negative consequences. The child hid his face in his hands and even cried on several occasions. When this happened, the adult would describe the interaction to the child.

The child was given short presentations of pictures, stories, and movies. This allowed the teacher and the female adult to discuss aspects of the presentations while the child was present and to emphasize the reward value of interaction with other children.

The teacher, while the child was present, showed extreme reluctance about peer interactions and would ask the female adult specific and somewhat fearful questions. This allowed her to provide reassurance to the teacher about approach and interaction behavior. The boy was not drawn into these discussions. The purpose of this experience was to expose him to specific reassurances in the absence of his own fearful reactions.

The adults demonstrated appropriate social behavior within the context of prearranged arguments about humorous social interactions. The boy was drawn into these arguments to assist the teacher to win the argument with the other adult.

The teacher engaged in social interaction with other children with the boy accompanying him. The boy initially assisted the teacher by carrying materials. Gradually, he entered into more direct and active interactions. The teacher remained close by to insure success for the boy.

The adults provided the boy with practice in general game skills, tricks, rituals, slang, and other behaviors which would facilitate the boy's effective interaction in a peer group.

Finally, the boy was taken to a park area separate from the school and sent into a group of children (strangers) while one of the adults remained at a distance. He was gradually encouraged to engage in longer and closer social interactions. These experiences formed the basis for other role-playing and modeling sessions to give the child additional reinforced practice at social interaction.

The results of these modeling procedures with guided participation were highly positive. The boy was able to interact with his peer group without undue fear or avoidance. These newly acquired behaviors were maintained and generalized to other settings. In a two-month follow-up:

> In playground settings that differed markedly from the protected preschool setting, the boy was able to join ongoing play groups, initiate verbal contacts, and sustain effective social interactions, all with children who were complete strangers to him. Furthermore, the boy accomplished these tasks competently, unhesitatingly, with obvious pleasure, and with no adult intervention whatsoever. (p. 277)

Summary

Programs designed to reduce the strength of or eliminate avoidance behavior patterns should include: (1) Procedures for reducing the aversiveness of the events, activities, situations, or people which the child is avoiding. This emotional relearning may be accomplished in vivo, through the use of imagery, or through modeling procedures. (2) Procedures for increasing the positive reinforcement value of those aspects of the child's life which he is avoiding. (3) Procedures for teaching competency skills which will result in the child obtaining positive reinforcers in the previously avoided environment.

DEVELOPMENT AND MODIFICATION OF ATTITUDINAL CHARACTERISTICS

McGinnies 1970 As the child gains experience in a variety of situations, various of his behaviors become interrelated into general patterns of behaviors called attitudes. McGinnies* has suggested: When a certain class of performances either increases or decreases in frequency as a result of having been selectively reinforced or punished, and when these performances have verbal and emotional components indicative of acceptance or rejection of some social object, we say that the individual has acquired an attitude. [p. 330]

In this view, attitudes represent classes of behaviors that have become interrelated as a result of numerous positive or negative consequences which these behaviors have produced. As a child interacts with situations or types of situations with some common stimulus aspects, either directly or vicariously through observation of others, these situations begin to influence related emotional, verbal, and other overt behavioral reactions. The verbal responses to certain types of stimulus events may be covert (subvocal) or may be overt. In a sense, attitudes, or interrelated patterns of behaviors, represent a disposition to behave in a given manner in certain situations. A child with a strong negative attitude toward education, for example, has a high likelihood of displaying a variety of negative reactions toward education-related situations and activities. In contrast, a child described as displaying a strong positive attitude toward education is likely to engage in a wide range of appropriate verbal, emotional, and achievement-related behaviors.

Positive Attitudinal Behaviors

In illustration, a child attending an educational program gradually acquires an interrelated pattern of emotional, verbal, and other behavioral reactions to various aspects of the school environment. If the child's experiences are predominately positive, he develops a positive attitude toward school activities. That is, he eagerly attends school, participates in classroom activities, makes positive statements about the teacher, himself as a student, and the classroom and his school activities, completes school assignments, cooperates with the teacher, and interacts appropriately with his peers. These emotional, cognitive, and overt behavioral patterns are acquired gradually by the contingent positive reinforcement that has been associated with literally hundreds of different school experiences. In this manner, the child acquires a general disposition to respond to specific environment settings in a given manner as a result of his history of experiences. These environmental events come to control or influence the occurrence of the behaviors which comprise the attitude. These interrelated behavioral patterns are acquired and maintained by the effects which they produce.

Negative Attitudinal Behaviors

If the child's experiences with school have been predominately of a negative nature, as may be the case of the multihandicapped youngster, he gradually acquires an interrelated group of negative emotional, cognitive, and overt behavioral reactions, that is, a negative attitude. Typically, negative attitudes appear to have a greater or more intense emotionality component than do positive attitudes.

The child with a negative attitude toward school may make negative verbal statements about school activities, become negatively emotionally aroused when discussing or when engaging in school activities, and may engage in a variety of behaviors that actively and consistently compete with desired school activities.

In educational programs designed to develop, facilitate, or modify attitudes in children and adolescents, the multidimensional nature of such behavior patterns must be recognized. Efforts to change one component, e.g., verbal, without concomitant efforts directed toward changing other components are not likely to produce satisfactory changes in the child's attitudinal patterns. Ideally, simultaneous efforts should be initiated to influence cognitive, emotional, and related overt behaviors. If it is deemed desirable to influence a child's negative attitude toward authority, for instance, educational experiences should be planned to modify the child's verbal behaviors toward authority and his emotional reactions toward authority, as well as his overt approach and avoidance responses to persons with authority characteristics. Attempts at change in the cognitive sphere, as is typical in counseling and insight therapy, may facilitate some positive change but will be relatively ineffective in comparison with efforts at modifying all three aspects of the attitudes.

SELF-CONCEPT BEHAVIORS

Attitudinal patterns directed toward aspects of oneself are defined as self-concept behaviors. These self-directed attitudes refer to the verbal labels used by a child to describe aspects of himself, i.e., his physical characteristics, his behavioral repertoires, and his learning characteristics, and to the positive and negative emotionality influenced by these labels. The self-concept features of the child and adolescent with exceptional learning and behavior characteristics are not unusually of a predominately negative nature. The child is described as "not liking himself," "doesn't believe that he could do it even if he tried," or "not thinking much of her capabilities." These verbal-emotional behavior patterns serve as conditioned and discriminative events to influence other of a child's behavior in numerous situations. If a child labels himself in relation to a task or social situation as "I'm dumb," or "I can't do that because I'm too slow," he is likely to avoid appropriate interaction with the situation.

EMOTIONAL CHARACTERISTICS OF CHILDREN WITH LEARNING AND BEHAVIOR PROBLEMS

In planning educational experiences for children and youth with learning and behavior difficulties, the following should be considered. Due to having experienced numerous failures in a wide range of academic and interpersonal situations, the child has limitations in the number of competency behavioral characteristics producing positive consequences which he can use. Additionally, numerous inappropriate behavioral characteristics have developed that create an excessive number of negative consequences. As a result, when comparing these children and youth with "normal" peers without a history of excessive failure, the following points should be kept in mind:

There are fewer aspects of the child's environment which produce positive emotional reactions. The child has had fewer experiences of being successful and reinforced with a range of tangible and social reinforcers. As a result less emotional learning involving positive feelings has occurred. There are fewer people, places, activities, and events that he likes, has fun with, approaches, or that make him feel good.

There are more aspects of the child's environment which produce negative emotionality. Many of these events are associated with the typical school routine. Being asked to participate in certain activities may be a cue for considerable emotional discomfort. He is more likely to be in a bad mood and to object to advances made by others to get him involved. He is more likely to experience generalized emotional states of anxiety and apprehension.

There is greater likelihood that the child will engage in intense and disorganizing episodes of negative emotionality. There is also increased likelihood that the child will engage in episodes of aggressive behaviors. This may reflect a natural frustration reaction to being placed in situations which produce extremely unpleasant emotions, and not being able to escape from it. The child may strike out verbally or physically in a blind or disorganized fashion. These behavioral reactions are more likely to occur among children and adolescents with learning and behavior difficulties since more aspects of their environment produce unpleasant emotionality from which the child is unable to escape or avoid.

The usual events which produce positive emotional responses in most children, or which are neutral, may in fact become cues for negative emotional reactions. The teacher's smile or a display of affection would be a positive reinforcer for most children and would result in positive feelings on the part of the child. Some studies of children with learning and behavior difficulties suggest, however, that such social stimulation may have a negative effect on some children. Thus, the teacher who smiles at a child in expectation that such would be pleasing may be disappointed. For some children, such social behavior may be an aversive event which produces a negative emotional response of anxiety or apprehension. The smile, in this case, would produce avoidance behavior. The child would engage in those behaviors that would terminate and, if possible, avoid the teacher's smile. For other children, being in the presence of people may be a cue for apprehension; engaging in solitary activity may be more enjoyable. Being left at school by mother, a neutral event for most children, may produce intense anxiety and related panic behavior.

Minor sources of irritation or frustration may produce unusually strong emotional reactions. When confronted with a task which is difficult, the child may engage in a temper outburst or may become excessively negativistic. When confronted with conflict or other sources of frustration or dissappointment, he is more likely to overrespond. The child may be described as having a low frustration tolerance. Minor signs of rejection may produce a general inhibition of social interaction.

There are fewer positive self-referents depicting emotional reactions. The child is less likely to report such feelings as: "I like myself." "I feel good." "I'm happy." "I can do this." "I'm excited." "I'm pleased." Labels depicting adequacy and positive emotional states are seldom used by others to refer to children with developmental difficulties. Labels such as pretty, sweet, good, great, fast, strong, skillful, smart, and quick, which become conditioned events for positive emotional reactions for most children, fail to gain this influence with children who experience excessive failure in learning and social interaction situations. Positive self-referents which produce healthy emotional responses are typically absent.

There are more negative self-referents depicting emotional reactions. The child is likely to report such feelings as: "I don't like myself." "I hate myself." "I can't learn because I'm dumb." "I don't feel good." Labels which reflect inadequacy have been used excessively by others in their interaction with him. Such terms as slow, ugly, bad, stupid, poor, crippled, damaged, handicapped, dumb, and weak become part of the child's self-referents. These typically become conditioned cues for negative emotional reactions. The child may be described as having excessive "feelings of inadequacy," "feelings of inferiority," "poor attitude toward himself," or as reflecting poor self-concept behaviors. These negative self-referents and related negative emotional reactions arise out of literally hundreds of previous failure experiences. As suggested, these create difficulty since they serve as discriminative stimuli for avoidance behavior. If the child reports, "I can't do that," "I don't want to," "I'm ugly," "I'm dumb," in relation to many aspects of the school environment, he is highly unlikely to attempt interaction with the school environment.

There are more negative and fewer positive referents depicting emotional reactions toward others and things. The child is likely to report such feelings as: "I don't like that." "I hate you." "I'm afraid of that." These arise out of the multitude of aversive consequences which have become associated with academic and social activities.

The child may have a more limited range of emotional reactions or he may demonstrate difficulty in discriminating the appropriateness of various emotional reactions. He may laugh or cry at the wrong time, he may become sad or happy in response to inappropriate events, or he may express fear of events which represent no real danger to him. In other cases, a child may not have developed the usual emotional caution over potentially harmful events and therefore does not develop adaptive defensive behavior. He does not seem to be able to anticipate danger or aversive situations. These events are not conditioned events for negative emotional reactions.

IMPLICATIONS FOR EDUCATIONAL PROGRAMS

In view of the above described unusual emotional characteristics of many children and adolescents with exceptional learning and behavior difficulties, the educational experiences, whether in the regular classroom or in other special instructional environments, must be designed to influence these. If an "emotionally disturbed" child balks at engaging in an academic task, the teacher must not assume that the child is being willfully negativistic or stubborn. Aspects of the task situation may well control negative emotional reactions which underlie the avoidance behavior. If the "learning disabled" adolescent becomes excessively emotional when instructional demands are placed on him, *the educator must view both the academic deficits arising from the learning difficulties and the excessive emotionality as interrelated instructional problems.* Active program efforts directed toward improvement in academic skills and toward the development of more appropriate emotional behaviors will contribute to the child's competency.

Increase the Influence over Positive Emotional Behavior

Providing planned and systematic experiences in increasing the number, type, and strength of internal and external events resulting in positive emotionality and related positive self-referents should be a central focus of the educational program of all children with exceptional characteristics. Individualized program approaches will produce the best results because each child and adolescent differs in emotional and attitudinal characteristics.

It should be remembered that every successful experience results in positive emotional learning. Thus, effective instructional programming which results in continuous academic growth will also influence positive emotional growth.

Additionally, successful attainment by the child should be labeled positively by the teacher, and the child should be encouraged to use these labels to refer to himself. These self-referent or self-concept labels are best taught as the child or adolescent is successfully engaging in various activities. Emphasis should be given to both the *end product* ("You did well on these math problems.") and the *process* ("You checked your work as you completed each problem and kept at it until you finished. You're really using your head now!") Both process and end product behaviors should be labeled and reinforced so that each component will acquire influence over positive emotional behaviors. After numerous successful experiences with activities requiring persistence, careful attention to detail, mediational problem solving and the like, these activities will become conditioned events for positive emotional and related verbal behaviors. The child will begin to be "pleased with himself," "feel adequate," and "have confidence in his capabilities." As an illustration of a specific learning experience in which positive self-concept behaviors may be strengthened, consider the following reading activity provided a hyperactive, distractible child in a "learning disabilities" class:

Cue	*Behavior*	*Consequence*
"John, read your story to the class."	John reads the story, correcting his mistakes by using his newly acquired sound-blending skills.	Mr. Craig praises him and labels both the end product and process behaviors: "You did an excellent job at reading. I like the way you put your sounds together."

Teacher praise as a secondary event for positive emotionality becomes associated with the reading activity. While the child is "being pleased" with his skillful reading, Mr. Craig may label the behavior again with such comments as "You're getting better," or "Your hard work is paying off." These labels become associated with positive feelings after a number of pairings and become conditioned events for positive emotionality. Such labels and associated positive emotionality increase the likelihood that John will become involved in reading activities in the future. After similar experiences of this nature are repeated on 10, 100, 1,000, 3,000 occasions, the child gradually develops a more positive self-concept and positive emotionality behaviors.

Decrease the Influence over Negative Emotional Behavior

Children and youth who overrespond to minor sources of frustration, and other children who demonstrate intense negative emotional reactions to events or people which represent no actual danger, should be provided with extinction and counterconditioning experiences. As these crippling reactions are reduced or eliminated, the child is better able to explore and learn about his environment.

Structure Program Experiences

Generally, a child with exceptional learning and behavior characteristics can become emotionally comfortable and less likely to engage in disruptive emotional responsiveness in a program that is structured and predictable. A program with routine and well-defined limits provides the consistency which results in security—freedom from excessive fear or apprehension—and enjoyment. The child in this environment is able to be successful. He can develop generalized positive emotional patterns. He can learn to tolerate increasing amounts of frustration and social conflict without resorting to intense and disruptive emotional outbursts. As the child acquires a wider range of positive emotional reactions through the success which a highly structured program brings, he can then be exposed gradually to less and less structure. He can be taught to make decisions and to accept the consequences of these decisions. This can be done through demonstration by the teacher, by guided practice of the observed behaviors, and by joint participation with the teacher and peers in successful completion of numerous social and nonsocial problems.

Model Appropriate Emotional Characteristics

In providing a program for influencing the positive emotional and attitudinal behaviors of children, the teacher and other significant adults in the school environment must consistently demonstrate those behaviors which they wish the child to acquire. If the child is to learn to be relaxed, enthusiastic, cheerful, and realistically positive about himself or herself, the teacher must consistently model these reactions. Children should be provided with many opportunities to practice various emotional behaviors and to label or describe them. This can be done through role-playing experiences or as the child reacts to various social interactions and other situations throughout the school day.

To employ a role-playing procedure with younger children, the teacher may introduce a game to the children which requires them to show how a child would feel in various situations. A puppet may be used to enhance the attention and participation of the children. The puppet would be described as being in situations which would result in his being sad, happy, apprehensive, pleasantly surprised, pleased, contented, angry, and the like. The children would be guided into acting out the various feelings depicted and encouraged to describe their feelings. With older children and adolescents, experiences which occur during the school day may be used as a basis for role playing and behavior rehearsal of various emotional-social reactions.

The teacher should utilize any of the day's experiences to teach the child or adolescent to engage in and describe various feelings. A teacher may express satisfaction to a child for the task that the child has just completed. "I feel good because you finished the task. It's fun to do things. I'm glad you did it. I'm going to do one of those puzzles and you tell me how you feel." She then finishes the puzzle and guides the child into expressing satisfaction. The teacher next gives the child another puzzle and then guides him into expressing pleasure over his own accomplishment. In a similar manner, the teacher can assist the child in talking about his feelings when he is angry, sad, unhappy, or disappointed. The child can be assisted in identifying the relationship between the emotional reaction and environmental events which produce them.

Summary

Children with exceptional learning and behavior characteristics are quite likely to exhibit a variety of difficulties in emotional responsiveness. The educational program must analyze the emotional characteristics of each child and provide him with specific and systematic experiences to offset the difficulties and to teach him alternative positive emotional behaviors. Every experience in the school environment will potentially result in emotional learning. The sensitive teacher will utilize these events to contribute positively to the child's emotional competency.

REFERENCES

Bandura, A., Grusec, J. E., and Menlove, F. L. Vicarious extinction of avoidance behavior. *Journal of Personality and Social Psychology*, 1967, 5, 16–23.

Bandura, A., and Menlove, F. L. Factors determining vicarious extinction of avoidance behavior through symbolic modeling. *Journal of Personality and Social Psychology*, 1968, 8, 99–108.

Brutten, E. J., and Shoemaker, D. J. *The Modification of Stuttering.* Englewood Cliffs, N. J.: Prentice-Hall, 1968.

Bryan, T. H., and Bryan, J. H. *Understanding Learning Disabilities.* Port Washington, N. Y.: Alfred, 1975.

Cruickshank, W. M. (Ed.) *Psychology of Exceptional Children and Youth.* (3rd Ed.) Englewood Cliffs, N. J.: Prentice-Hall, 1971.

Dunn, L. M. *Exceptional Children in the Schools: Special Education in Transition.* (2nd Ed.) New York: Holt, Rinehart & Winston, 1973.

Graubard, P. S. Children with behavior disabilities. In L. M. Dunn (Ed.) *Exceptional Children in the Schools: Special Education in Transition.* (2nd Ed.) New York: Holt, Rinehart & Winston, 1973. Pp. 245–298.

Hallahan, D. P., and Kauffman, J. M. *Introduction to Learning Disabilities: A Psycho-Behavioral Approach.* Englewood Cliffs, N. J.: Prentice-Hall, 1976.

Haring, N. G. (Ed.) *Behavior of Exceptional Children.* Columbus, Ohio: Charles E. Merrill, 1974.

Johnson, W. (Ed.) *The Onset of Stuttering.* Minneapolis: University of Minnesota Press, 1959.

Knoblock, P. Psychological considerations of emotionally disturbed children. In W. M. Cruickshank, (Ed.) *Psychology of Exceptional Children and Youth.* (3rd Ed.) Englewood Cliffs, N. J.: Prentice-Hall, 1971. Pp. 565–599.

Lazarus, A. A., and Abramovitz, A. The use of "emotive imagery" in the treatment of children's phobias. *Journal of Mental Science*, 1962, 108, 191–195.

McGinnies, E. *Social Behavior: A Functional Analysis.* Boston: Houghton Mifflin, 1970.

Patterson, G. R., and Brodsky, G. A behavior modification programme for a child with multiple problem behaviors. *Journal of Child Psychology and Psychiatry*, 1966, 7, 277–295.

Rogers, C. R. *Freedom to Learn.* Columbus, Ohio: Charles E. Merrill, 1969.

Ross, A. O. *Psychological Disorders of Children.* New York: McGraw-Hill, 1974.

Ross, D. M., Ross, S. A., and Evans, T. A. The modification of extreme social withdrawal by modeling with guided participation. *Journal of Behavior Therapy and Experimental Psychiatry*, 1971, 2, 273–279.

Sheehan, J. G. Theory and treatment of stuttering as an approach-avoidance conflict. *Journal of Psychology*, 1953, 36, 27–49.

Staats, A. W. *Social Behaviorism.* Homewood, Ill.: Dorsey, 1975.

Staats, A. W., and Staats, C. K. *Complex Human Behavior.* New York: Holt, Rinehart & Winston, 1963.

Vernon, W. M. *Motivating Children.* New York: Holt, Rinehart & Winston, 1972.

Wolpe, J. *Psychotherapy by Reciprocal Inhibition.* Stanford, Calif.: Stanford University Press, 1958.

Wolpe, J. *The Practice of Behavior Therapy.* Oxford: Pergamon, 1969.

Word, P., and Rozynko, V. Behavior therapy of an eleven-year-old girl with reading problems. *Journal of Learning Disabilities*, 1974, 7, 27–30.

12

Development and Use of Self-Management Skills

A variety of procedures have been described previously which demonstrate that aspects of the social, academic, and personal behaviors of the child and adolescent may be influenced by many external environmental events. The influence of events which precede and those which follow specific behaviors has been illustrated. The present chapter describes the development and role of internal behavioral events, e.g., thoughts, self-instruction, images, self-evaluation, standard setting, self-reinforcement, self-criticism, and the manner in which these (1) influence the occurrence or nonoccurrence of other of the child's behaviors and (2) interact with external stimulus events to determine the specific influence which those events will have on the child.

One of the central themes of the humanistic behavioral approach, as emphasized in Chapter 6, and indeed perhaps the ultimate goal of education, is to insure that a child learn increasingly varied and complex skills of self-management.[1] With these skills the child or adolescent is in a position to self-influence those behaviors which will be most enhancing to him. As the child develops skills of self-direction, he will become less and less dependent upon external events, including the behavior of others, to provide the direction and incentive for his own behavior. Although it may be necessary to provide children with highly structured instructional and interpersonal contingency-managed experiences as they are developing skills of self-management, this extensive external influence can be sys-

1. Various terms are used to refer to the same set of skills. The following are used as comparable terms in this chapter: self-control, self-regulation, self-direction, and self-management.

*Kurtz and Neisworth
1976; Mahoney and
Mahoney 1976*

tematically reduced as the child gains a variety of skills for influencing his own behavior.*

Children with exceptional learning and behavior characteristics, depending upon the type, intensity, and pervasiveness of their problems, have unusual difficulty in acquiring and effectively using a full range of self-management skills. In fact, one of the central features of many children with learning and behavior difficulties is the absence or poorly developed repertoire of self-directing skills. The child has difficulty in intentionally directing, controlling, managing, inhibiting, cueing, or maintaining much of his own behavior which would be adaptive in various learning and interpersonal situations. Due to such factors as (1) excessive failure experiences and resulting negative emotional learning, (2) the relative paucity of consistent positive reinforcement in various of his environments, and (3) the resulting difficulties of developing patterns of competency behaviors, the child's internal reactions may have little systematic *positive* influence over other of his behaviors. On the contrary, for children with exceptional learning and behavior characteristics, many of their internal behaviors may have a disruptive negative influence on other of their behaviors. The child may have strong patterns of thinking negatively about himself and his competencies, may respond with disruptive emotionality to too many external events—academic or interpersonal—and internal events—his own thoughts—and may have too many fear-provoking or anxiety-arousing thoughts and images such as "I hate that teacher." "They will criticize me if I talk." Such self-statements as "I am dumb, stupid, weak, inadequate" represent behaviors that may have pervasive disruptive and inhibiting effects. Such negative self-concept behaviors serve as conditioned events for negative emotionality and as discriminative events for avoidance reactions. Such reactions may become critical in influencing the child's reasoning, planning, and decision-making activities.

Not only may a child's private events be of a negative or disruptive fashion, but too many of his behaviors may be controlled by external events. In illustration, a child may spend excessive time in daydreaming activities in order to avoid attempts at meeting what are to him, in terms of his present competencies or his self-labeling of his competencies, unreasonable performance expectations of teachers and parents. He may be quite unsuccessful at using thoughts about alternative acceptable behaviors to direct himself into more productive activity. Such cognitive self-controlling behaviors, even if attempted previously, have little strength due to lack of subsequent reinforcement.

Finally, the child and adolescent with exceptional learning and behavior characteristics, due to excessive aversive experiences, not unusually has too many disruptive behavior patterns which he engages in "blindly." The overly emotional child who engages in immediate and frequent temper tantrums when placed in various confrontation situations, the child who quickly withdraws into passive inactivity when faced with conflict, and the hyperactive child who reacts impulsively in every situation requiring planning and forethought represent examples. There is little or no intervening internal verbal behavior which would mediate or monitor, and thus influence, these "blind" or impulsive reactions.

These characteristics will be highlighted on appropriate occasions in the remainder of the chapter. Along with a discussion of aspects and strategies of self-management, attention will be focused on studies which describe the usefulness of various self-management procedures with children and adolescents. The chapter concludes with suggested procedures for insuring that children with exceptional learning and behavior characteristics will acquire more effective skills of self-management.

WHAT IS SELF-REGULATION?

In a general sense, self-regulation will refer to those behaviors engaged in by a child with an intent to influence certain alternative behaviors available in his or her repertoire. The "intent" aspect of self-regulation implies the occurrence of cognitive-symbolic processes, or behavioral chains, and the use of these to influence other of the child's behaviors. Skinner* suggested that whenever a person "controls himself, chooses a course of action, thinks out the solution to a problem, or strives toward an increase in self-knowledge, he is *behaving*. He controls himself precisely as he would control the behavior of anyone else—through the manipulation of variables of which behavior is a function" (p. 228). *Skinner 1953*

Cognitive behaviors (thoughts, images) used in an intentional fashion may influence other thoughts and images as well as overt behaviors. Due to the unobservability of such covert processes (stimulus and response relationships), the proof of the presence and effects of self-regulation resides in changes in observable behavior patterns. For example, following self-regulation there is an increase or decrease in something that the child does—he works longer, produces more, complains less, responds less impulsively, is away from his work less, fights less, smiles more, makes better grades, and so forth. In illustration, an adolescent girl who is obese may "talk to herself" and thus influence the type and quantity of food consumption. Or the adolescent who is failing a course due to excessive class absences may "imagine the displeasure of parents" and "talk herself into class attendance" when tempted by peers to skip class. In these instances, covert behaviors (thoughts, images) influenced the likelihood of occurrence of other of the adolescent's overt behaviors. It is not being suggested that the mere occurrence of covert cognitive activities will in fact have the intended influence. An obese adolescent may say to herself on numerous occasions that she will not eat excessively but still does so. To become effective, self-regulating events must result in alternative behaviors which are strengthened by subsequent reinforcement just as is true of any overt behavior. The mediating thoughts, in the presence of cues for excessive eating, then will become effective discriminative events for these alternative behaviors.

Thus, in viewing the development and influence of self-regulation behaviors, the assumption is made that these are the results (i.e., are learned, maintained, eliminated, and generalized in influence) of the same principles which influence observable behaviors. A child's self-observation, self-cueing, self-reinforcement, or self-punishment behaviors must be reinforced if these are to become aspects of the child's self-regulation repertoire.*

Bandura 1969; Skinner 1953; Thoresen and Mahoney 1974

NATURE OF EVENTS INFLUENCING BEHAVIOR

It is evident that most of the behavior of children and adolescents is under the influence of a complex array of events. Certain combinations of these stimulus events—called a stimulus complex—may be composed entirely or predominately of external stimuli. Under this condition the child's behavior is said to be under the control or influence of external sources. Whenever various discriminative events occur, the child engages in specific behaviors. Although a relative matter, the child may in extreme instances have little choice or freedom in the manner in which he responds to or is influenced by these external events. Other behaviors may be predominately under the influence of an internal stimulus complex. These internal events may include thoughts, images, and/or emotional cue conditions. As suggested earlier, these internal events may represent reactions which are under strong external influence. An "emotionally disturbed" child may rather automatically engage in disruptive emotionality and related self-derogatory thoughts when criticized by the teacher for certain of his social behaviors. These internal reactions will then serve as a stimulus complex for other covert and overt behavioral reactions.

In other instances, internal events may function in a more deliberated manner to influence one out of a series of other responses available in the child's repertoire. When faced with a self-generated or an externally generated behavioral demand situation, the child may cognitively consider various alternatives and select a specific plan of action. He may then direct his behavior in the face of cues which have influence over contrary modes of reacting. The child, in this instance, is self-controlling in that he engages in certain behaviors to regulate the occurrence of certain other of his behaviors.

RELATIVE NATURE OF LOCUS OF CONTROL

It is evident that the locus of control of behavior is a matter of degree. Seldom is any behavior at any specific time under total external or total internal influence. In the vast majority of instances, behavior is influenced by a continuously changing continuum of external and internal events (see Figure 12.1). Also, seldom does behavior have a 100 percent likelihood of occurrence. As components of a stimulus complex change, the likelihood of occurrence of specific behavior changes. In illustration, an adolescent may be polite on most occasions in social situations when he is in a "good mood." However, the likelihood of his being polite in the same or similar social situations when he is in a "bad mood" may change dramatically. Certain critical components of the controlling stimulus complex have changed. But the adolescent may learn "self-controlling" behaviors that would significantly increase the likelihood of his being able to act politely though in a "bad mood." He may through self-observation covertly label his "bad mood" and further covertly say to himself, "I'm in a bad mood today and am likely to be impolite. I must watch myself and cue myself to behave politely." Such behavior, if self-reinforced (covertly and/or overtly) or reinforced by social consequences, could be strengthened and thus serve as a major controlling component of a stimulus complex which includes being in a "bad mood."

This example emphasizes again that no one controls, manages, or regulates his behavior in any absolute sense. A child influences other of his behaviors by what he does. These behaviors may be highly related to external influences or to internal influences. These internal influences (the "bad mood," for instance) may rather automatically influence other of a child's covert or overt behaviors or may influence cognitive-symbolic reactions which intervene as self-regulation to increase or decrease the likelihood of further alternative behaviors. These alternative "self-controlled" behaviors eventually result in feedback from external sources which in turn influences them in a positive or negative manner. Thus, as emphasized by Skinner* and Staats,* a child's self-controlling behaviors have *Skinner 1953; Staats* developed under and are maintained, at least partially, by external conse- *1971* quences. The child may "control" his temper in a provoking situation through engaging in mediating thinking behaviors (e.g., "I must not get mad") and behave appropriately. The child may not only feel proud of his maturity—he may covertly verbalize this to himself and feel good about it—but he typically would be praised by his social environment for such maturity. Thus, basic self-regulation skills are initially developed and maintained in children by external influences. As most self-control efforts have delayed external consequences, the child's mediational skills serve to bridge the time delay. Thus, the child who has a wide array of influential

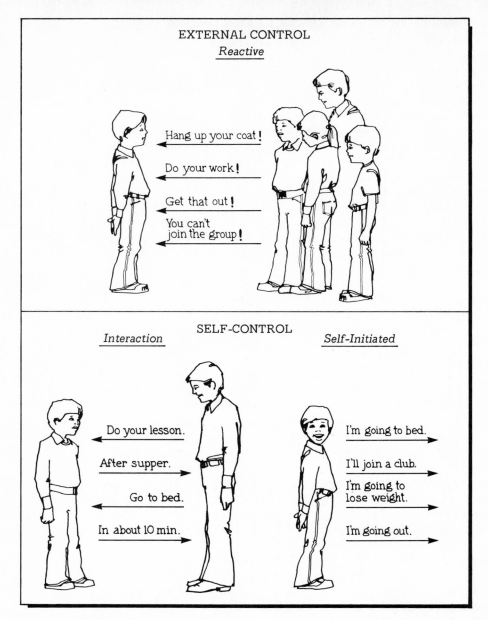

FIGURE 12.1   *Depicting External and Internal Sources of Behavior Control*

self-controlling skills including self-observation, self-cueing, self-encouragement, self-reinforcement, and self-punishment not only has more freedom from external influences but also is more effective in day-by-day problem solving.

It is important to recognize that behavioral patterns which initially are influenced by self-regulatory events may become rather routine and no longer necessitate mediational intervention. The adolescent may eventually behave in a polite manner regardless of his mood state without the necessity for such self-controlling covert statements as "I must be careful and be polite." The self-regulation involving labeling, monitoring, and mediationally influencing polite behavior may gradually be eliminated as the adolescent is reinforced for being polite under a variety of conditions. Cues other than the self-regulatory ones gain influence over the politeness. Only under future changes in the stimulus complex influencing polite behavior may it be necessary for active or deliberate covert involvement in the chain of events which results in polite behavior. Under these new conditions, where once again the likelihood of impolite behavior is increased, there may be a need for the mediating behaviors controlling the alternative polite behavior.

ROLE OF LANGUAGE

Self-regulation requires the presence of a language repertoire. Whenever a child labels (responds verbally to) any aspect of himself or his external world, he is potentially influencing the nature and relative likelihood of further reactions. A child may implicitly state, "I can do that," when faced with a task imposed by teacher or peer. He is thus more likely to engage in various behaviors such as cooperation, maximum effort, and enthusiasm than would be the case if his self-evaluative stance was "That's too hard. I will fail if I try that."

In viewing the development of self-regulation in children, Luria* *Luria 1961, 1966* has suggested that the child progresses through three stages: (1) The speech of others initially controls and directs a child's behavior. (2) The child's own overt speech begins to regulate other of his behaviors. (3) The child's covert speech (thoughts) come to self-regulate.

Staats* suggests that the child's self-direction skill "ordinarily does *Staats 1971* not begin to emerge until after four years of age. Some observations of various kinds place the child's ability to direct his own behavior through his language between the ages of five to seven" (p. 255).

Early in the development of speech, a child learns to label certain contingencies. He then begins to use this information to influence other of his behaviors. By stating implicitly, "If I do that, I will please Mother," "Mother will be angry if I do that," "If I finish, I will get to play some more," he begins to influence those behaviors which are to his advantage. He also learns that it is best to do what he says he will do. He learns to label that which will please others and to "talk himself through" the behavioral sequence, even in the presence of conflicting cues for alternative behaviors. After numerous experiences, the activities of planning and following through with plans acquire secondary reinforcement properties. He is thus reinforced for his own mediating speech and for the influence which this behavior has in directing other behaviors. Through considerable trial-and-error experiences, the child gradually acquires those self-directing behavioral sequences which result in positive consequences from external sources. Thus, certain of a child's behaviors become the causes of other of his behaviors. He learns what he can or cannot do and the effects which certain of his behaviors produce. The child thus acquires certain patterns of behavior which become interrelated in a *controlling* and *controlled* manner.

It should be noted that the degree of self-regulation that can be attained obviously is related to the type and variety of behavioral alternatives available in the child's total repertoire. If he is rather restricted in what he is able to do, he thus is restricted in the amount of self-regulation possible. The child is free to self-regulate, then, only to the extent that he has alternative behaviors in his repertoire.

Thoresen 1973   In addition, the degree to which the child is aware of possible controlling events contributes to his freedom of self-regulation. Thoresen* suggested:

> In many ways the difference between individual freedom and control by others lies in who is manipulating what stimuli or who is using and controlling information that influences human action. Awareness is the basis of freedom and self-control because it provides the individual with the information he needs to change his own sources of stimulation, both internal and external. The freedom to act depends on the person's being aware of, or knowing what kinds of information (stimuli) influence his own behavior. This awareness must include internal or covert stimuli as well as external data for both internal and external behavior. [p. 400]

As noted in Chapter 11, the acquisition of certain "value" labels—acceptable, good, bad, competent, weak, excellent, strong—by a child has behavior influence implications far beyond what might appear on the surface. A child whose behavior is labeled as "good" or "adequate" or "competent" by others may be strengthened by these positive consequences. The label may then be used by the child to describe his own behavior. He behaves and may self-label some task as an "adequate" or "good job." These labels can serve as conditioned events for positive emotional responses and may thus be involved in classical conditioning of the behavior itself. The behavior acquires the funtion of producing a positive emotional response. Secondly, the label "good" following behavior serves as a reinforcer for that behavior which produced it. This reinforcing function is maintained as it produces on occasion reinforcing feedback from other sources. The child, if he acquires a number of such positive verbal responses, is more likely to engage in behavior similar to that which produced the labels from others—and eventually which he self-reinforces. An "I can do" label increases the likelihood that the child will engage in a wide range of behaviors which will result in both social and self-reinforcement. These behaviors will thus acquire secondary positive reinforcing value themselves and are more likely to reoccur and to be rewarding or enhancing. Such form the basis, in a hierarchial sense, for more complex and varied behaviors to be acquired.

EFFECTS OF INAPPROPRIATE SELF-KNOWLEDGE

Children with exceptional learning and behavior characteristics typically demonstrate difficulty in the acquisition and effective use of self-directing behaviors. If a child is delayed or restricted in his language skills, he is obviously hampered in the development of self-management skills. He may learn that many of his characteristics are not those that are pleasing to others. He does not have the general skills which others expect of him. His environment does not provide him with appropriate educative experiences of labeling contingencies and of using implicit speech to self-direct. As noted, too many of his self-reactions are of a self-defeating rather than of a self-enhancing nature. His planning, his decision making, and his abortive attempts at self-direction are too frequently punished instead of reinforced. Additionally, many of his behaviors may actively compete with self-regulation and thus render covert cognitive control difficult or impossible.

Many of the labels and implied contingencies which are learned are incorrect or else represent overgeneralizations. His failure experiences resulting in non-reward and other more direct aversive consequences (being yelled at, criticized, or otherwise punished) may result in self-labeling that further complicates the development of effective self-regulation. The child with a history of experiences that could be labeled "dumb," "stupid," "weak," or "inadequate" which occur along with other forms of social rejection begins to label his own behaviors as stupid, dumb, poor, and the like. He begins to avoid those situations, via negative reinforcement, which have high probability of provoking such self-delivered consequences. These "self-concept" behaviors serve as conditioned stimuli and discriminative events for extensive avoidance behavior. Such verbal behaviors become central in the child's reasoning, planning, and decision-making activities. Thus, regardless of the correctness or incorrectness of a child's knowledge of what he can do, of his worth to others, of what others think of various of his abilities and capabilities, or of the contingencies that exist between his behavior and various consequences, this knowledge still may influence other of his behaviors. He may set standards far below his potential, or far above it. These implicit behaviors—"Well, I can't possibly do that"—may influence other of his behaviors and have significant negative motivational effect. Other thoughts and images may result in disruptive emotionality which distorts what a child may be able to do under more facilitative emotional and motivational conditions. Thus, inappropriate self-knowledge, and the disruptive effects it may have, reduces the child's facility at planning and consequently the nature of his involvement in problem-solving and interpersonal activities.

SELF-MANAGEMENT PROCEDURES

As illustrated, there are a variety of self-control procedures which serve various functions in regulating a child's behavior. Certain of a child's covert behaviors may serve a discriminative function and exert stimulus control over other internal behaviors—thoughts, images, emotional responses—and overt behaviors of any class. He may arouse himself to activity by anticipating future consequences and may prod himself to continue his activity until the goal and resulting consequences are attained. Or he may, in covertly considering possible negative consequences, avoid selecting certain courses of action. Thus, his own behavior may be of value in both initiating and suppressing other of his behaviors. Further, he may influence the future likelihood of specific of his behaviors through (1) self-administered punishment (self presentation of external and/or internal unpleasant consequences or self-removal of external or internal pleasant consequences) and/or (2) self-administered positive or negative reinforcement (self-delivery of external or internal positive reinforcers or self-removal of external or internal aversive conditions). As noted by Bandura,* *Bandura 1974* self-reinforcing or self-punishing activities may entail several subsidiary processes including (1) a self-prescribed standard of behavior, (2) which frequently involves comparisons with other individuals or groups, (3) reinforcers under the child's own control, and (4) the child himself serving as his own reinforcing agent. Ineffective self-management may be due to difficulties or insufficient learning experiences in any one or all of these areas.

Thoresen and Mahoney 1974 Through *environmental planning,** the child or adolescent may plan and implement changes in relevant environmental factors prior to the time in which he engages in a specific behavior which he wishes to influence. For example, an adolescent may ask his peers to criticize him if he skips class or to call his parents if he is observed smoking. Or he may engage in *behavioral programming* by using self-administered consequences following the occurrence of a behavior which he wishes to influence. Figure 12.2 illustrates these procedures.

ENVIRONMENTAL PLANNING   BEHAVIORAL PROGRAMMING

FIGURE 12.2.   *Depicting Self-management Procedures of Environmental Planning and Behavioral Programming*

As an initial step in developing effective skills of self-management, the child must learn to observe his own behavior, to identify events which influence him, and to describe the consequences of his behavior. This may include *self-recording* which involves the child's keeping an objective record of the frequency of a specific behavior or class of behaviors.

Kunzelmann* introduced a method of self-observation and recording involving a "countoon." Figure 12.3 presents an example of a countoon for a child who makes frequent disruptive comments in class. Note that the countoon depicts in picture sequence what the child did before and after the disruptive behavior occurred. The child draws a circle around the number indicating the frequency of the behavior within a specified period of time. The countoons can be used to depict either appropriate or inappropriate behavior.

Kunzelmann 1970

Self-assessment may be involved during which the child examines his own behavior and decides if he has or has not performed a specific behavior or class of behaviors, or if his level or quality of performance meets self-imposed or externally determined standards. He is then in a position to self-regulate events in one manner or another and thereby to

WHAT I DO		WHAT HAPPENS	WHAT I DO	MY COUNT

FIGURE 12.3.   *Depicting a Countoon Procedure of Self-Recording*

influence other of his behaviors. Thus, to become an effective self-manager the child must acquire skills of self-observation and self-evaluation so he can realistically assess his own competencies and learning facility, can set his own behavioral objectives, and can work out a contingency system for attainment of these objectives. As Lovitt and Curtiss* note: "Translated to a school situation, this would be an individual who knew his academic capabilities in terms of skill levels and rate of performance, could arrange a series of activities or steps to achieve a variety of self-imposed objectives, and could grant himself reinforcers on a prearranged schedule to accomplish certain behavioral sequences" (p. 49). Such a self-manager in the school setting would be involved both in the *self-determination of reinforcement* and the *self-administration of reinforcement* in relation to behavioral standards that had been predetermined either solely by the self-manager or in negotiation with the teacher.

Lovitt and Curtiss 1969

There are obvious practical advantages associated with teaching children to better manage their own behavior toward goal attainment. In terms of teacher time and effort, child-managed behavior change programs are more practical and less expensive. As a child gains experience with an externally managed educational program, the responsibility of monitoring his own behavior can be turned over to him.

Additionally, self-managed educational programs should lead to (1) greater generalization both across situations and across behaviors which are influenced and (2) greater resistance to extinction than would be present if the behavior changes were externally managed.* As suggested in Chapter 9, behavior learned in one setting is more likely to occur and be maintained in other future settings if the child has self-management skills of verbal cueing and self-reinforcement. The learner "carries around with him" both aspects of the discriminative cues to insure occurrence of the behavior in appropriate situations and also components of those reinforcing events which insure that the behavior will be maintained.

Johnson 1970; Johnson and Martin 1973

EFFECTS OF SELF-OBSERVATION AND SELF-RECORDING

A child's success in regulating his own behavior is dependent on his knowledge of and control over current overt and covert events. That is, he must have skills of identifying the antecedent cueing, the subsequent reinforcing, or punishing events that influence certain of his behaviors. As Thoresen and Mahoney* have suggested, the child must come to "know thy controlling variables." An initial step in gaining self-knowledge is that of the self-recording of specific problematic or prosocial behaviors.

Thoresen and Mahoney 1974

It is not unusual to discover that the act of self-observation may result in changes in the observed behavior. Broden et al.* describe this reactive effect in their work with two adolescents. The first case involved an eighth-grade student who was failing a history course. This student had expressed to a school counselor an interest in improving her study skills but had been unsuccessful even after counseling sessions involving discussion of her problems. The student agreed to self-record the amount of time spent in attentive study behavior during the history class period. This involved her recording on a printed form her attentive or nonattentive behavior whenever she thought about it during the class. An independent observer, about whom the student was unaware, noted an increase of 30 to 80 percent of the class period spent in study behavior. The student's grade also improved. In a second case, self-recording of disruptive talking-out behavior was decreased following initiation of a self-recording procedure. These educators suggested that self-observation and recording should be most effective as a procedure for initiating desirable levels of appropriate behavior to a point where the teacher can more easily provide natural reinforcers in the form of praise, attention, grades, and so on.

Broden et al. 1971

McKenzie and Rushall* found that desired behavior could be increased in frequency by having children and adolescent publicly display their self-recordings. Members of competitive swimming teams—

McKenzie and Rushall 1974

chronically absent, late, and poor participants in training activities—were requested to self-record on a bulletin board for all to see their attendance and level of accomplishment of training objectives. There was a significant, stable, and long-lasting improvement in the target behaviors.

Thomas et al. 1971

Thomas et al.* report the successful use of self-monitoring in eliminating a high-rate vocal tic in an eighteen-year-old male with multiple tics. Following the initiation of a procedure to count the number of occurrences of the vocal tic on a hand counter throughout the day, there was a rapid reduction and eventual elimination of this bothersome be-

Hutzell et al. 1974

havior. Hutzell et al.* report similar success with an eleven-year-old boy who had developed a skipping motion while walking, a severe head-jerk, and an intermittent utterance of a particular noise which closely resembled a "bark"—reactions which are called Gilles de la Tourette's Syndrome. This child, sensitive to the social embarrassment resulting from such involuntary reactions, was highly motivated to change. During thirty-minute sessions twice weekly, the boy initially was instructed to count the number of times he jerked his head. To insure that he could discriminate the beginning of this behavior, the teacher demonstrated the head jerking and then required the boy to role play for two minutes by actively jerking his head and counting each response. Following this, the boy was given the responsibility of counting his head jerking throughout the thirty-minute periods. Within seven sessions, the head jerking had reduced to a low rate. Self-recording was then required of the barking behavior, which reduced to a near zero level within ten sessions. The behavior changes were maintained during follow-up observation over the next year.

EFFECTS OF TEACHING SELF-INSTRUCTION SKILLS

Studies have indicated that children labeled as "hyperactive" and "impulsive" exert less verbal influence over other of their behaviors and use covert speech in a less regulatory fashion than do other "reflective"

Meichenbaum and Cameron 1974

children.* The "impulsive" children thus do not have skills of influencing their behavior in a regulating manner. The children respond without thinking and frequently do quite poorly in tasks which require a more planful, deliberated approach for correct solution. The child thus functions below his potential due to his excessive impulsive reactions and to the lack of effective mediational skills of influencing more appropriate problem-

Epstein et al. 1975

solving skills.*

Palkes et al. 1968; Palkes et al. 1971

Palkes et al.* and Palkes et. al.* postulated that hyperactive impulsive children may not internalize speech adequately and therefore are deficient in verbal control of voluntary motor behavior. These educators instructed hyperactive boys ranging in age from seven to thirteen years to look and think prior to initiating a task and to verbalize directions to themselves at appropriate times in task solution. Such training resulted in improved performance on tasks requiring maze solution.

Lovitt and Curtiss* report a significant improvement in the academic performance of an eleven-year-old boy attending a class for children with behavior "disorders." The boy was described as exhibiting extreme variability in responding to mathematics materials. When working on math problems, he would typically respond impulsively, with the result that his error rate was much higher than his correct rate of response. After the teacher instructed him to verbalize the problem prior to attempting written solution, his error rate dropped considerably, usually near zero. Concurrently, his rate of correct responding increased. It was also noted that the child's variability reduced considerably after the self-cueing verbal behavior was initiated. Finally, after some experience with this overt verbalization tactic, this procedure was terminated with the result that his rate of correct responding continued to increase, with little increase in error rate noted. Apparently the child had learned, through his own verbal self-cueing, to be more deliberate in using his competencies in mathematics. *Lovitt and Curtiss 1968*

Meichenbaum and Goodman* taught such impulsive children a more comprehensive set of self-instruction skills as a means of developing self-management. These children were attending special education classes as a result of such exceptional characteristics as marked hyperactivity, impulsivity, and distractibility. In this program a variety of motor and cognitive tasks was used and the following training experiences provided: *Meichenbaum and Goodman 1971*

1. Initially, the teacher acted as a model in performing a task while the child watched.
2. The child then performed the same task as the teacher provided verbal instructions.
3. Following this, the child was requested to repeat the task while verbalizing instructions aloud.
4. Next, the child completed the task while whispering the instructions.
5. Finally, while self-instructing covertly, the child performed the task.

In the training program, the teacher verbalized, as the task was being completed, such self-directing content as follows:

> Okay, what is it I have to do? You want me to copy the picture with the different lines. I have to go slowly and carefully. Okay, draw the line down, down, good; then to the right; that's it; now down some more and to the left. Good, I'm doing fine so far. Remember, go slowly. Now back up again. No, I was supposed to go down. That's okay. Just erase the line carefully. . . . Good. Even if I make an error I can go slowly and carefully. Okay, I have to go down now. Finished. I did it! [p. 118]

The training program thus included a number of self-regulation components: initial questions about what was to be done and answers to the questions in the form of planning and rehearsal, self-guidance through verbal cueing, and self-reinforcement. After exposure to such a program, the child learns to evaluate the requirements of a task prior to beginning it, to cognitively rehearse solutions, to guide his performance through self-instructions, and to reinforce himself upon successful completion. The training program also included tactics to follow after making an error in performance since previous research* had suggested that "impulsive" children typically display a marked deterioration in their performance after errors were made.

Meichenbaum and Goodman 1969

The tasks in the training program, initially requiring rather simple sensorimotor abilities such as copying line patterns, coloring figures within certain boundaries, and reproducing designs, were made progressively more difficult until they included those requiring complex problem-solving abilities such as following sequential instructions, completing pictorial series from the Primary Mental Abilities Test, and solving conceptual tasks as on the Ravens Matrices Test. In each, the teacher initially modeled appropriate self-verbalizations and then guided the child through a fading procedure which terminated in covert self-regulation. Following training, children showed significant improvement in performance on a variety of tasks requiring cognitive self-direction and reflectivity, as indicated by scores on the Porteus Maze Test, Wechsler Intelligence Scale for Children, and Kagans Matching Familiar Figures Test.

Robin et al. 1975

Robin et al.* demonstrated the value of self-instructional procedures in teaching printing skills to young children with writing deficiencies. Children provided a self-instructional program patterned after the Meichenbaum and Goodman* procedure described above were more successful in remediating their writing deficiencies than were children who were provided direct training alone.

Meichenbaum and Goodman 1971

In training for self-regulation, Meichenbaum and Cameron* recommend that such training begin on tasks at which the child is already successful. As verbal self-direction is practiced with these tasks, the difficulty level of the tasks is progressively increased. Additionally, an older "impulsive" child may act as an instructor in teaching a young child how to talk himself through a task. The older child will thus be exposed to appropriate self-regulation tactics through modeling these for other children.

Meichenbaum and Cameron 1974

Other studies have demonstrated the usefulness of self-instruction in controlling various inappropriate behaviors. Following self-direction training, O'Leary* reported more "honest" behavior in settings conducive to transgressions, Monohan and O'Leary* reported a reduction in rule-breaking behavior, and Hartig and Kanfer* emphasized the role of self-instruction in children's resistance to temptation. Goodwin and Mahoney* taught hyperactive, impulsive six- to eleven-year-old boys to cope with verbal aggression from peers by exposing the boys, through a series of self-

O'Leary 1968
Monohan and O'Leary 1971; Hartig and Kanfer 1973; Goodwin and Mahoney 1975

instructions, to models portrayed as coping with verbal assaults. The coping statements (e.g., "I'm not going to let them bug me." "I won't get mad.") were repeated by a teacher, and the model's overt actions were pointed out, discussed, and verbally emphasized. Each coping self-statement was repeated and labeled as an effective way to handle verbal aggression. The child was then asked to verbalize as many of these coping responses as he could recall. The child's coping behavior showed a dramatic improvement after training.

Weil and Goldfried* report an interesting variation of the self-instructive procedure in teaching a child self-relaxation. This eleven-year-old girl initially presented two problems of long standing: insomnia and her fear of remaining at home at night, even with a babysitter, when her parents went out. These problems resulted in a chronic fatigue state and were affecting the child's performance at school. While lying in bed in the evening, the child was initially given instructions for relaxation. Next, a tape recording of relaxation instructions was used. Finally, the child was instructed that, as soon as she was in bed and ready to go to sleep, she should concentrate only on self-relaxation. After some experience with self-relaxation, the child was able to fall asleep without difficulty. Concurrently, without any specific treatment attention, the child's fear of being alone at night disappeared.

Weil and Goldfried 1973

EFFECTS OF SELF-EVALUATION AND SELF-REINFORCEMENT

There is considerable criticism of educational practices in which major sources of control reside in the external environment. Silberman,* Holt,* and other critics of education practices suggest that children allowed to participate in the design and maintenance of their learning environment would be happier and more productive. Gagné (1965) has emphasized that "the student must be progressively weaned from dependence on the teacher or other agent external to himself" (p. 213). As Glynn* has noted, however, there is need to make a clear distinction between *extrinsic reinforcers,* on the one hand, and *external control of a child's behavior* on the other. Glynn writes, "Clearly, educators do not object to extrinsic reinforcers per se, since grades, promotions, degrees, diplomas, and medals appear to enjoy the same widespread usage that Skinner noted in 1953. Moreover, it is difficult to imagine a classroom where teacher praise and reprimand are not used in an attempt to control child behavior" (p. 123). The basic objection, then, appears to reside in the degree to which external agents, not being used specifically as extrinsic reinforcers, control the child's behavior. If children and adolescents were able to self-admin-

Silberman 1970
Holt 1972

Glynn 1970

ister external reinforcers, they would have more freedom over the effects which these events would have on their behavior. Self-administration of contingent reinforcement systems could have a facilitative effect by functioning (1) to enhance the discrimination of reinforced behavior and (2) to condition self-evaluative statements as secondary reinforcers.

Johnson 1970

Johnson* evaluated the relative effectiveness of self-reinforcement procedures and external reinforcement procedures in maintaining attentive behavior in inattentive elementary-age children. He found that attention to a task was maintained just as well by children who reinforced themselves with tokens for task performance when compared to children who were provided token reinforcement by the teacher. A greater persistence of desired behavior was noted in the children who self-administered the reinforcement after tokens were no longer available. In a later report,

Johnson and Martin 1973

Johnson and Martin* more deliberately reinforced positive self-evaluative statements in an effort to enhance the secondary reinforcement qualities of such statements. Following correct responding to a discrimination task, children were instructed to state aloud (self-evaluation), "I was right." Such statements, when accurately representing a correct discrimination, were followed by a token which could be exchanged for a variety of backup reinforcers. When token reinforcement was terminated, children with experience in verbal self-evaluation demonstrated a greater resistance to extinction than did children who had only been reinforced by the teacher.

Glynn 1970

Lovitt and Curtiss 1969

Glynn* found that adolescent girls were able to improve their academic performance in history and geography lessons when given the choice to self-reinforce their performance with extrinsic events. Lovitt and Curtiss,* in a series of three studies involving a twelve-year-old child attending a school program for children with "behavioral disorders," discovered that self-imposed contingencies resulted in a higher academic response rate than when contingencies were teacher-imposed. The child's academic behavior consisted of reading, math, spelling, English, and writing. These educators also demonstrated that the critical variable accounting for this accelerated rate of academic behavior was a function of the self-management variable and not of any differences in magnitude of reinforcement provided for higher academic performance.

Glynn et al. 1973

Glynn et al.* provided elementary-age children an opportunity to use various self-control procedures—self-assessment of acceptable behavior, self-recording, and self-administration of reinforcement—and found that previously established high rates of classroom work behavior could be effectively maintained. It was also noted that productive behavior was more stable during the time in which students engaged in behavioral self-control activities. In a similar vein, Knapczyk and Livingston,* in a

Knapczyk and Livingston 1973

junior high school special education program for the "educable mentally retarded," found that students who self-regulated their academic performance level produced at a level commensurate with the level obtained when performance was evaluated by the teacher.

Felixbrod and O'Leary 1973

Felixbrod and O'Leary* provide additional support for the procedure of allowing children to self-determine their academic performance standards. Elementary-age children who determined the specific standard of performance in an arithemetic class and were reinforced externally by the teacher performed as well as they did when the teacher determined performance standards. These children, however, performed better under external reinforcement than under no externally provided reinforcement. It was interesting to note that children tended to become more lenient over time in their self-selected performance requirements. Thus, social surveillance, which externally reinforces stringent self-selected standards or which provides mild aversive consequences for excessively lenient standards, may be required for children to learn more functional skills of self-selection of performance standards.

Kaufman and O'Leary* reported that highly disruptive "emotionally disturbed" adolescents responded positively to a token reinforcement program initiated in a remedial reading classroom. During the time in which the token contingency was in effect, there was marked decrease in disruptive behavior and an increase in reading skills. Following experience in this teacher-controlled token program, the adolescents were provided the following instructions:

Kaufman and O'Leary 1972

> Beginning today I am going to ask you to give yourself your own ratings. You will decide how many tokens you deserve (or lose) based on how you behaved during the rating period. . . . You make your judgment based upon your own observation of how you followed the rules and tell me and the class how many tokens you deserve. [p. 299]

After initiation of this procedure, disruptive behavior remained at the low level obtained under previous condition of teacher evaluation.

A follow-up study of a similar group of "emotionally disturbed" adolescents displaying high levels of disruptive classroom behavior by Santogrossi et al.,* however, did not find a reduction of disruptive behavior during periods of self-evaluation. The adolescents soon discovered that regardless of the lack of accuracy of their self-evaluation, token reinforcement was still provided. These findings emphasize that any positive behavior influence features associated with self-evaluation and accompanying external reinforcement may be offset by other strong, incompatible behavioral characteristics. In such cases, a more intensive, systematic, and lengthy program of teaching self-management will be required.

Santogrossi et al. 1973

Boldstad and Johnson* described successful use of self-regulation procedures to reduce disruptive behaviors (talking out, aggression, and out-of-seat behaviors) of elementary-age children in the classroom. After demonstrating that disruptive behaviors could be reduced by a teacher-administered token reinforcement program for lower rates of inappropriate behavior, some children were permitted to self-evaluate and self-administer the reinforcers based on their evaluation in terms of previously

Boldstad and Johnson 1972

agreed-upon criterion of acceptable behavior. Results indicated that the self-regulation children averaged approximately 40 percent fewer disruptive behaviors than did the teacher-managed group. Considerable variability among the children was noted, suggesting that some were much more skillful at influencing their behavior through self-regulation than were others. With this group of children, contrary to the observations of Santogrossi et al.* in their work with highly disruptive adolescents, an acceptable degree of accuracy was noted in their self-observing and recording of the frequency of their disruptive behavior. Additionally, as is critical to the effectiveness of any self-reinforcement procedure, the children did demonstrate acceptable honesty in the magnitude of self-award of token reinforcers. That is, the self-awarded reinforcers were consistent in magnitude with the reward system that had previously been presented to the children, even though each had an opportunity to overestimate his behavior and thus to reward himself excessively.

Santogrossi et al. 1973

Drabman et al. 1973

In a similar experience, Drabman et al.* report success in teaching self-evaluation and self-reinforcement skills to nine- and ten-year-old "highly disruptive boys with academic and emotional problems." In a one-hour reading class divided into four fifteen-minute work sessions, disruptive behavior decreased noticeably and academic performance increased significantly after initiating a token reinforcement program in which points were provided for "good behavior" and for completion of assignments. Following this, children were exposed to a variety of experiences designed to facilitate the development of self-evaluation skills. Initially, children were reinforced with bonus points if they were able to match exactly in self-rating (on two five-point scales of "good" behavior and academic performance) the rating provided by the teacher, and to receive the points if within one point above or below the teacher's rating. Deviations of more than one point resulted in no points for that particular work session. Teachers lavishly praised perfect matches. During the next four weeks, various of the children were selected to be reinforced for matching the teachers' ratings. During this time children were highly praised for their accuracy in self-ratings, and the importance of honesty was stressed whenever a child misbehaved or did not complete his assignment. Children continued to receive the number of points they had awarded themselves.

During the final phase of the teacher program, all checking by the teacher was discontinued. The children gave themselves a rating at the end of the work sessions and received the amount of points which they had self-awarded. The success of the program was described as follows:

By the last phase of the study, the children would enter the class, work on their academic assignments, behave appropriately, and honestly evaluate their performance at the end of each reinforcement interval without any external monitoring. . . . Apparently the shaping procedures adopted in this program were effective in teaching relatively honest and accurate self-evaluation. [p. 15]

Disruptive behavior was virtually eliminated and an average of .72 year's gain was obtained on the California Achievement Reading Vocabulary Test during the two and one-half months of the program. Additionally, the improved behavior generalized and was maintained in periods of time when no external reinforcement system was in effect. Thus, the new skills of self-management appeared to facilitate the occurrence of appropriate behavior independent of externally related reinforcement.

Frederiksen and Frederiksen* demonstrated that "mildly retarded" children attending a junior high special education class were able to increase their on-task and to decrease their disruptive behaviors through self-assessment and self-reinforcement procedures. This occurred although they had been exposed to a teacher-determined token reinforcement program for fourteen weeks where no formal training or specific reinforcement of acuracy of self-assessment was provided. At the end of eleven weeks of self-reinforcement, a high rate of on-task behavior and a low rate of disruptive behavior were present. *Frederiksen and Frederiksen 1975*

As a final example illustrating the use of covert self-reinforcement, Krop et al.* suggested that a child's self-concept, or positive self-evaluative statements, could be improved as a consequence of covert reinforcement, a procedure described by Cautela* which employs reinforcing stimuli presented in imagination. After occurrence of behavior that is to be strengthened, the child imagines a pleasant scene involving an event, person, or activity. Following covert reinforcement training of "emotionally disturbed" children, Krop et al. then instructed them to self-reinforce with a pleasant imagery following a positive self-evaluation statement. Covert reinforcement proved superior to externally delivered tangible reinforcement in increasing the positive self-concept behaviors of these children. *Krop et al. 1971* *Cautela 1970*

In summary, there is some encouraging support for the conclusion that for many children with exceptional learning and behavior difficulties, self-regulation procedures can be effective in establishing and in maintaining desired changes in learning and behavior characteristics.

TEACHING SELF-MANAGEMENT

There is obviously a wide range of individual differences among children and adolescents in the type and effectiveness of their self-management skills. One outstanding characteristic of children with exceptional learning and behavior characteristics is the general deficiency in the presence of and effective use of skillful self-regulatory behaviors. Some children have little influence over their own behavior. They may not use self-instruction to arouse themselves to action, to initiate, to inhibit, or to guide other of the behaviors which would be adaptive and self-enhancing. In too many instances, even when self-controlling attempts are made, other external and internal events compete with and override these effects. Competing and contrary behaviors result which further weaken the self-management attempts. Following are some of the characteristics, all previously discussed, which comprise various exceptional behavior patterns and which are incompatible with deliberate and positive self-management:

1. Impulsivity and related faulty scanning and attentional difficulties.
2. Excessive disruptive emotionality.
3. Excessive disruptive behavior patterns which represent an "automatic" or nondeliberated or choice nature.
4. Hyperactivity which impedes accurate self-observation and self-analysis of events influencing various behavior patterns.
5. Excessive dependency on external social direction for standards of behavior, types of behaviors, and for direction as to when and where various behaviors should occur.
6. Excessive dependence on external sources of reinforcement in providing the incentives for performance of behavior already in the child's repertoire and for strengthening new behavior patterns.
7. Excessive dependence on external threats of negative consequences to inhibit or suppress inappropriate modes of behavior.
8. Excessive negative labels and related trains of thought producing strong negative emotionality that is personally distressing and behaviorally disruptive.
9. Excessive self-criticism due to nonattainment of performance standards which frequently are unrealistic.
10. Dysfunctions in self-reinforcement system. This coupled with unrealistic standards (either too high or too low) create problems of chronic discouragement, feelings of worthlessness, and lack of purposefulness.

Any individualized education program which provides more consistent and extensive success experiences in academic and social endeavors will reduce the impact of these and related characteristics which actively compete with appropriate self-regulatory skills. The child will thus be a more receptive learner in programs designed specifically to teach various self-management behaviors. The following types of procedures are representative of program efforts which may prove valuable in dealing with the characteristics enumerated.

Self-Regulation of Impulsive Behavior

The child who behaves impulsively in performance tasks and/or who is generally hyperactive may be taught to self-instruct and thus to mediate a more deliberate planned mode of problem solution. Modeling, direct training with considerable behavior rehearsal, and verbal instructions may be used to guide the child through the correct self-regulating patterns. In exposing a child to reflective peer and teacher models, attention should be drawn both to a slower response style and to scanning for and attending to pertinent aspects of a problem situation. The Meichenbaum and Goodman* instructional program described earlier provides a general format of what might be done. The instructional support should be faded gradually as the child becomes successful. The types of tasks and situations (social and academic) should be varied to insure practice and success with a variety of demand requirements. Rules of self-direction can be provided: "Think before you behave." "Use your head." "You can think this one through." These rules can then serve as general discriminative events for use in a variety of different tasks and situations.

Meichenbaum and Goodman 1971

Self-Regulation of Excessive Emotionality

The child with excessive disruptive emotionality can be taught to (1) anticipate and thus avoid situations which result in such disruptive emotional reactions and (2) to intervene cognitively when in heightened states of negative emotionality. He may learn self-induced relaxation responses or to use verbal cueing to engage in competing behaviors.

Self-Regulation of Disruptive Social Behavior

The child or adolescent who engages in frequent disruptive behaviors such as physical or verbal aggression, negativism, and the like may initially be guided through a behavior management program to engage in appropriate behaviors. As more appropriate adaptive behaviors are shaped by external guidance and reinforcement, the child will be taught to identify the internal and external situational cues for inappropriate behavior, to set standards of more appropriate behavior, to label this appropriate behavior as it occurs, to self-reinforce through positive self-statements the occurence of appropriate behavior, and to self-criticize the occurence of inappropriate behavior. These self-mangement behaviors will develop, however, only under conditions of frequent external cueing and positive reinforcement.

Self-Regulation of Independent Behavior

The child or adolescent who is excessively dependent on externally imposed standards of behavior, on cueing for behavior, and for sources of reinforcement and inhibition must be exposed to numerous experiences which shape contrary competency and independence skills. Once the child is able to demonstrate competency, he can be provided experiences in using these in a self-directing manner. Setting behavioral requirements that the child can attain insures that he will be successful and can realistically learn positive self-labels. The overly dependent child must be provided a multitude of educative experiences of labeling his own behaviors: "I can do." "I did that." "I am smart." "If I work hard, I can accomplish." These, when reinforced by socially significant adults and peers, will gradually acquire reinforcing qualities. The child, thus, will be in a position to direct and self-reinforce.

Self-Regulation of Realistic Performance Standards

In teaching children skills of setting performance standards and associated self-reinforcement for attainment of performance goals, they should be exposed initially to realistic performance standards set by the teacher. The performance objective, the behaviors required to attain the goal, and the consequences of goal attainment should be negotiated by teacher and child, emphasized by the teacher and rehearsed by the child. As standards are met, reinforcement should be provided and the goal attainment labeled. The child should be prompted to verbalize: "I did that." "I finished that." "I knew I could do what I said I could."

Following these kinds of experiences, children should be provided those involving self-evaluation of attainment of academic and social behavior standards, and reinforced for the degree of match with teacher-evaluated performance levels. As illustrated by Drabman et al.,* children get quite involved in such self-evaluation activities. After considerable experience with external monitoring and social praise for increased self-evaluation skills, the external monitoring can be removed gradually. Periodic and unannounced monitoring can be reintroduced to insure and strengthen realistic standards and self-evaluation. External reinforcers (self-selected and self-delivered) will be interspersed with covert self-reinforcement. Bandura* has emphasized the value of exposure to a variety of influential peer and adult models in setting differential standards and in subsequent self-reinforcement for goal attainment.

Drabman et al. 1973

Bandura 1974

CONCLUDING REMARKS

As emphasized repeatedly throughout the previous chapters, children can become competent and independent only to the extent that they are successful in acquiring a broad range of behaviors which can be used to attain consistent and frequent positive reinforcement. Although it may initially be necessary to provide highly structured educative experiences with externally provided reinforcers, the humanistic behavioral approach systematically shifts the control *from* the external environment *to* the child. The key to successful self-management lies in educational experiences which provide success for attainment of academic and social standards that continually become more varied and complex.

REFERENCES

Bandura, A. *Principles of Behavior Modification.* New York: Holt, Rinehart & Winston, 1969.

Bandura, A. Self-reinforcement processes. In M. J. Mahoney and C. E. Thoresen (Eds.). *Self-Control: Power to the Person.* Monterey, Calif.: Brooks/Cole, 1974. Pp. 86–110.

Boldstad, O. D., and Johnson, S. M. Self-regulation in the modification of disruptive classroom behavior. *Journal of Applied Behavior Analysis,* 1972, 5, 443–454.

Broden, M., Hall, R. V., and Mitts, B. The effect of self-recording on the classroom behavior of two eighth-grade students. *Journal of Applied Behavior Analysis,* 1971, 4, 191–199.

Cautela, J. R. Covert reinforcement. *Behavior Therapy,* 1970, 1, 33–50.

Drabman, R. S., Spitalnik, R., and O'Leary, K. D. Teaching self-control to disruptive children. *Journal of Abnormal Psychology,* 1973, 82, 10–16.

Epstein, M. H., Hallahan, D. P., and Kauffman, J. M. Implications of the reflectivity-impulsivity dimension for special education. *Journal of Special Education,* 1975, 9, 11–25.

Felixbrod, J. J., and O'Leary, K. D. Effects of reinforcement on children's academic behavior as a function of self-determined and externally imposed contingencies. *Journal of Applied Behavior Analysis,* 1973, 6, 241–250.

Frederiksen, L. W., and Frederiksen, C. B. Teacher-determined and self-determined token reinforcement in a special education classroom. *Behavior Therapy,* 1975, 6, 310–314.

Gagné, R. M. *The Conditions of Learning.* (2nd ed.) New York: Holt, Rinehart, & Winston, 1970.

Glynn, E. L. Classroom applications of self-determined reinforcement. *Journal of Applied Behavior Analysis,* 1970, 3, 123–132.

Glynn, E. L., Thomas, J. D., and Shee, S. M. Behavioral self-control of on-task behavior in an elementary classroom. *Journal of Applied Behavior Analysis,* 1973, 6, 105–113.

Goodwin, S. E., and Mahoney, M. J. Modification of aggression through modeling: An experimental probe. *Journal of Behavior Therapy and Experimental Psychiatry,* 1975, 6, 200–202.

Hartig, M., and Kanfer, F. H. The role of verbal self-instruction in children's resistance to temptation. *Journal of Personality and Social Psychology,* 1973, 25, 259–267.

Holt, J. *Freedom and Beyond.* New York: E. P. Dutton, 1972.

Hutzell, R. R., Platzek, D., and Logue, P. E. Control of symptoms of Gilles de la Tourette's Syndrome by self-monitoring. *Journal of Behavior Therapy and Experimental Psychiatry,* 1974, 5, 71–76.

Johnson, S. M. Self-reinforcement versus external reinforcement in behavior modification with children. *Developmental Psychology,* 1970, 3, 147–148.

Johnson, S. W., and Martin, S. Developing self-evaluation as a conditioned reinforcer. In B. Ashem and E. G. Poser (Eds.) *Behavior Modification with Children.* New York: Pergamon, 1973. Pp. 69–78.

Kaufman, K. F., and O'Leary, K. D. Reward, cost and self-evaluation procedures for disruptive adolescents in a psychiatric hospital school. *Journal of Applied Behavior Analysis,* 1972, 5, 293–309.

Knapczyk, D. R., and Livington, G. Self-recording and student teacher supervision: Variables within a token economy structure. *Journal of Applied Behavior Analysis,* 1973, 6, 481–486.

Krop, H., Calhoon, B., and Verrier, R. Modification of the "self-concept" of emotionally disturbed children by covert reinforcement. *Behavior Therapy,* 1971, 2, 201–204.

Kunzelmann, H. P. (Ed.) *Precision Teaching: An Initial Training Sequence.* Seattle, Wash.: Special Child Publications, 1970.

Kurtz, P. D., and Neisworth, J. T. Self control possibilities for exceptional children. *Exceptional Children,* 1976, 42, 213–217.

Lovitt, T. C., and Curtiss, K. A. Effects of manipulating an antecedent event on mathematics response rate. *Journal of Applied Behavior Analysis,* 1968, 1, 329–333.

Lovitt, T. C., and Curtiss, K. A. Academic response rate as a function of teacher- and self-imposed contingencies. *Journal of Applied Behavior Analysis,* 1969, 2, 49–53.

Luria, A. R. *The Role of Speech in the Regulation*

of Normal and Abnormal Behavior. New York: Liveright, 1961.

Luria, A. R. *Higher Cortical Functions in Man.* New York: Basic Books, 1966.

Mahoney, M. J., and Mahoney, K. Self-control techniques with the mentally retarded. *Exceptional Children,* 1976, 42, 338–339.

McKenzie, T. L., and Rushall, B. S. Effects of self-recording on attendance and performance in a competitive swimming training environment. *Journal of Applied Behavior Analysis,* 1974, 7, 199–206.

Meichenbaum, D., and Cameron, R. The clinical potential of modifying what clients say to themselves. In M. J. Mahoney and C. E. Thoresen (Eds.) *Self-Control: Power to the Person.* Monterey, Calif.: Brooks/Cole, 1974. Pp. 263–290.

Meichenbaum, D., and Goodman, J. The developmental control of operant motor responding by verbal operants. *Journal of Experimental Child Psychology,* 1969, 7, 553–565.

Meichenbaum, D., and Goodman, J. Training impulsive children to talk to themselves. A means of developing self-control. *Journal of Abnormal Psychology,* 1971, 77, 115–125.

Monohan, J., and O'Leary, K. D. Effects of self-instruction on rule-breaking behavior. *Psychological Reports,* 1971, 29, 1059–1066.

O'Leary, K. D. The effects of self-instruction on immoral behavior. *Journal of Experimental Child Psychology,* 1968, 6, 297–301.

Palkes, H., Stewart, M., and Freedman, J. Improvement in maze performance of hyperactive boys as a function of verbal training procedures. *Journal of Special Education,* 1971, 5, 337–342.

Palkes, H., Stewart, M., and Kahana, B. Porteus maze performance of hyperactive boys after training in self-directed verbal commands. *Child Development,* 1968, 39, 817–826.

Robin, A. L., Armel, S., and O'Leary, K. D. The effects of self-instruction on writing. *Behavior Therapy,* 1975, 6, 178–187.

Santogrossi, D. A., O'Leary, K. D., Romanczyk, R. G., and Kaufman, K. F. Self-evaluation by adolescents in a psychiatric hospital school token program. *Journal of Applied Behavior Analysis,* 1973, 6, 277–287.

Silberman, C. *Crisis in the Classroom.* New York: Random House, 1970.

Skinner, B. F. *Science and Human Behavior.* New York: Macmillan, 1953.

Staats, A. W. *Child Learning, Intelligence and Personality.* New York: Harper, 1971.

Thomas, E. J., Abrams, K. S., and Johnson, J. B. Self-monitoring and reciprocal inhibition in the modification of multiple tics of Gilles de la Tourette's Syndrome, *Journal of Behavior Therapy and Experimental Psychiatry,* 1971, 2, 159–171.

Thoresen, C. E. Behavioral Humanism. In C. E. Thoresen (Ed.) *Behavior Modification in Education.* Chicago: Univeristy of Chicago Press, 1973. Pp. 385–421.

Thoresen, C. E., and Mahoney, M. J. *Behavioral Self-Control.* New York: Holt, Rinehart & Winston, 1974.

Weil, G., and Goldfried, M. Treatment of insomnia in an eleven-year-old child through self-relaxation. *Behavior Therapy,* 1973, 4, 282–294.

13

Learning Foundations of Exceptional Characteristics

If exceptional learning and behavior characteristics of children and youth are a product, at least partially, of past learning experiences, it becomes meaningful to identify the kinds of learning conditions—deficits or distortions—which may account for these deficit and excessive characteristics. More specifically, what types of learning and related factors may account for such exceptional learning and behavior characteristics as poor study skills, excessive disruptive behavior, excessive avoidance behaviors, poor social skills, poor speech skills, excessive quarrelsome behavior, limited spontaneity, poor self-concept behaviors, limited achievement motivation, delayed language development, slow rate of acquiring and retaining new knowledge and skills, poor academic achievement, poor self-reflection skills, poor compliance to requests, and excessive anxiety?

The assumption that the absence or inconsistent occurrence of desired behavior is due at least partially to some distortions or deficiencies in the learning history and/or the present learning environment of children and adolescents implies that changes in the present learning environments may influence the development and use of more desired behavioral characteristics. The position also suggests that as every individual (1) is the product of a different environmental and learning history, (2) has a unique set of present behavioral repertoires, (3) has a unique set of present learning characteristics reflecting physical and psychological variables, and (4) lives in a unique present enviornment, differential educational programs will result from individual evaluation of each child.

As examples, a child may presently live in a rather depressing, anxiety-provoking home environment. He may know how to be happy, but presently is not exposed to any "happy-invoking" experiences. Another child exhibiting the same general sad or depressed behavior pattern may have little if any happy responses in his repertoire. In fact, he may have many negative emotional responses that actively compete with the occurrence of happy emotional reactions. Two adolescents with severe hearing loss may both be isolated from peer social groups due to communication difficulties. One adolescent may be highly defensive over his handicap while the other may be most eager and emotionally responsive to a program designed to insure more normal peer relations. Thus, quite different behavior change programs would be required in all cases.

THE VICIOUS DEFEAT CYCLE

Generally, the larger the number of exceptional learning and behavior characteristics a child has, the greater the likelihood that he will acquire additional problematic patterns. Figure 13.1 depicts this cycle. This cycle is a result of the following conditions:

1. *The mere presence of most exceptional learning and behavior characteristics renders it more difficult for the child to be successful, that is, to acquire those reinforcing consequences and the resulting positive emotional experiences available to most children.*[1] The child experiences more frustration, failure, and related negative emotionality, e.g., a child with excessive avoidance or withdrawal behavior patterns is not exposed to those learning experiences which would insure the development of age-appropriate social behaviors. The older he gets without having acquired these behaviors, the less appropriately he will be able to behave in a manner similar to his CA peers. Excessive withdrawal behavior produces deficit behavior areas. For example, a physically handicapped adolescent requiring crutches for mobility is greatly restricted in what he can do and in the time required to accomplish tasks requiring mobility. He is constantly reminded of his limitations as he trudges down the hallway on the way to class while his more agile peers rush by in exuberant social interchange. He is constantly reminded of his limitations and hates his physical characteristics. This attitude keeps him away from many situations which he potentially could enjoy.

The same is true when considering academic difficulties. A child who experiences difficulties in acquiring preacademic skills during kindergarten will experience even more difficulty in the first grade if the teacher expects him to perform at the "first-grade level." Not only must the child learn the skills prerequisite to first-grade performance, he also must learn the first-grade academic skills. Over the years, if the learning difficulties continue, the child will, of course, experience even more difficulties as

---

1. Obvious exceptions to this statement are those children with accelerated learning and creative characteristics.

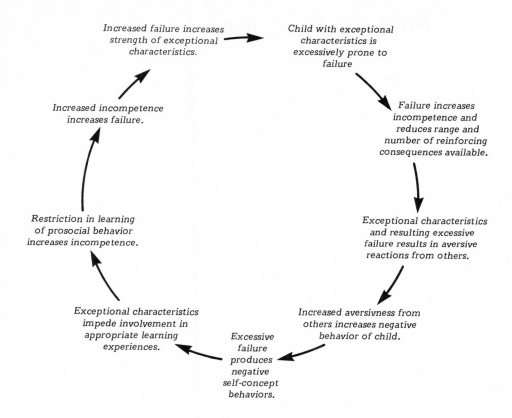

FIGURE 13.1.   *Depicting the Defeat Cycle of Children with Exceptional Characteristics*

each higher grade curriculum requires competencies presumed to have been acquired in earlier grades. Additionally, he will acquire many anti-learning behaviors which render it increasingly difficult to be successful, for instance, hyperactivity, poor attention span, anxiety, or negative attitudes. Koppitz* provides data which suggest that few children and youth with a lengthy history of severe learning difficulties are able to "catch up" even when provided specialized educational experiences.

Koppitz 1971

A child will become even more inadequate—that is, less "intelligent" and competent in cognitive and interpersonal areas—if he is exposed to age-relevant learning experiences but is unsuccessful due to (1) poorly developed or absent prerequisite characteristics, such as poor perceptual, memory, speech production, selective attention, or motor coordination skills, (2) disruptive competing behavioral characteristics, (3) inappropriate incentive-reinforcer components, (4) a poorly organized or sequenced educational exposure, or (5) physical limitations—auditory, visual, muscular, or neurological disabilities. As he grows older without these functions, skills, or knowledge, he will be even less able to adapt to the learning, performance, or social-interpersonal requirements of other situations. Also, due to his inadequacy, he will be more prone to avoid such learning and performance situations in the future due to their aversive characteristics.* Werry and Sprague* emphasize this interaction effect in their statement concerning children who display hyperactive behavior in the classroom: "It appears that the hyperactivity may be actively interfering with the learning process. If this is the case, then it is relatively easy to understand how a hyperactive child could fall behind his peers in the class. Furthermore, it is quite possible that, when the child falls behind his peer group, he may develop an aversion or an avoidance response to academic material that is proving difficult to him, and thus becomes even more hyperactive" (p. 400).

Ross 1976; Senf 1969; Werry and Sprague 1970

     2. *The restricted number of reinforcing events (e.g., peer attention or approval, unusual academic achievement) which the child can obtain become unusually strong in influencing the development and maintenance of behavioral characteristics.* Thus, peers with inadequate social, interpersonal, and academic characteristics influence these same characteristics in the child. The "socialized delinquent," as described by Quay,* represents an example. As a second example, the blind child, avoiding normal peer interaction and social situations, relies excessively on the enjoyment of staying alone and listening to the radio or a talking book. Even the intellectually accelerated child or adolescent may rely excessively on academic achievement as his major source of reinforcement to the detriment of his social and emotional development.

Quay 1972

     It is observed also that reinforcing events which most children obtain following *appropriate* behavior may become most frequently available only after some *inappropriate* behavior for many children with exceptional learning and behavior characteristics. For example, a child may not have the learning and/or behavioral characteristics which the significant social environment expects and thus is provided little social attention, approval, or praise. The child, valuing social attention from adults and peers, may discover that his disruptive behavior or his excessive dependency behavior may result in the desired social attention. The child is thus influenced by the contingencies in effect to develop and engage in obnoxious or inappropriate behaviors because these are successful in producing adult attention, even though this attention may be of a negative sort. Regardless of its negative flavor, it remains more influential than no attention at all.

These contingencies frequently render some inappropriate learning and/or behavioral characteristics unusually strong due to the child's limited number of acceptable alternative behavior patterns which produce more general social attention. A child thus may develop an unusually strong pattern of whining, loud complaining, hyperactivity, nonattending, and physical aggression. Other more desirable characteristics such as task attention, persistence, achievement motivation, or spontaneous self-rehearsal of new learning tasks do not become strong since these do not result in meaningful consequences.

3. *Problematic behavior patterns are quite likely to produce aversive reactions from many others in the child's family and school environments—rejection, ridicule, isolation, or active punishment—which in turn will produce additional negative behavior on the part of the child or adolescent.* The same is true of unacceptable physical (muscular, neurological, cosmetic) and sensory difficulties. The auditorily impaired, the visually impaired, the child with cleft palate or lip, the cerebral palsied, the child with epilepsy, and the child with other chronic health problems are all likely to produce excessive open or subtle negative reactions. Parents become overly solicitous or rejecting as do teachers and peers. The child is less able to develop those desirable social and emotional characteristics which result in positive reactions from others. This intensifies the inappropriateness of the reactions from others which in turn produces more negative emotionality and incompetency in the child.

A less obvious rejecting reaction, but one no less damaging to a child's development if continued or magnified, is illustrated in a study by Bryan.* Children diagnosed as "learning-disabled" were observed over a five-month period to evaluate classroom activity and interactions with peers and teachers. In evaluating the number of times the teacher responded to an initiation of contact by a child, it was noted that only 43 percent of initiated contact by the learning-disabled child was responded to. In comparison, the teacher responded to 76 percent of the contacts initiated by other children in the classroom. This lack of responsiveness by the teacher is likely to result in increasing alienation of the child. It was observed that the teacher responded to the problem children with more reproofs. Bryan also reported that peers, while interacting with the "learning-disabled" child as much as with other children, also were more likely to ignore him. Such failure experiences render the child increasingly inadequate in academic and social situations.

Bryan 1974

4. *The child is likely to develop verbal concepts of himself and related negative emotional reactions which interfere further with his involvement in and assimilation of numerous needed experiences.* The greater the number and pervasiveness of exceptional learning and behavior characteristics, the more likely it becomes that the child will view himself as inadequate, handicapped, or the like. As noted previously, the child's

self-concept behaviors and his entire motivational system become more defeating.

5. *Too many of the child's exceptional characteristics interfere with his becoming involved in appropriate learning endeavors.* In other instances, such as in performance situations requiring behaviors which are actually in the child's repertoire, his exceptional characteristics not infrequently are stronger. These decrease the possibility that the child will use his appropriate skills. In illustration, a child who is distractible, hyperactive, highly anxious, depressed, or who daydreams is engaging in behaviors incompatible with his attending to and interacting with appropriate aspects of a classroom environment even though these latter behaviors are in his repertoire. In other instances the prerequisite behaviors may be quite weak or absent. His persistence skills may be weak. His "interest" may be minimal. He does not find as reinforcing the task, the peer relationships, or the promised consequences. He may not have such self-management skills as self-cueing and self-reinforcement to maintain his behavior for the period of time required to solve a problem or to finish a performance task.

As a result of these and related factors, a child is deprived of the opportunity to acquire further appropriate behavior, and an unfortunate "defeat cycle" is initiated.

6. *The child cannot meet the behavioral criteria of tasks, interpersonal interactions, and so on, and this produces less reinforcement and more failure, which results in negative emotionality and related defensive behavior reactions, which further decrease the likelihood of his learning those prosocial behaviors that would produce positive consequences.*

Kagan 1966

Kagan* describes this maladaptive cycle in specific reference to the child who fails excessively due to his impulsive approach to cognitive tasks. Kagan suggests: "Gradually the child may withdraw from problem situations, and apathy and hostility may become characteristic reactions toward intellectual situations" (p. 521). Staats* emphasizes this in his description of "the downward spiral of cumulative-hierarchial learning." He notes that as a result of ineffective learning a child "will find himself in a less propitious social circumstance of reward for learning. Thus his attentional and working behaviors will be poor, and his learning will be at a less rapid rate than would be the case in better motivating conditions. . . . The less advanced the performance, the less the reward. The less the reward, the less the maintenance of learning behaviors." Further, "The social consequences of being a loser . . . can create conditions by which the child learns undesirable behaviors that are considered to be adnormal. These behaviors will frequently be such that they interfere with the further learning of the repertoires of skills demanded by society. When this occurs, the downward spiral of relative learning is accelerated" (p. 285). In a

Staats 1971, 1975

similar vein, Zigler* speaks of the reduced flexibility and inefficient performance on tasks of cognitive functioning of children with developmental retardation as relating at least partially to the depressing influence of excessive failure experiences.

Zigler 1969, 1973

HISTORICAL AND CONTEMPORARY LEARNING INFLUENCES

The following groups of psychological factors have been suggested by various writers* as underlying the exceptional learning and behavior characteristics of children and adolescents. The inadequate excessive and deficit behavioral characteristics of a particular child may be related in part to any one or to a combination of both historical and contemproary factors. The factors discussed are not mutually exclusive. A functional analysis may be helpful in identifying the specific contemporary factors operative for a given child. In most cases, the absolute and relative significance of certain factors may be estimated only after optimal behavior change experiences have been provided.

For example, Bijou 1966; Gardner 1971, 1974; Martin 1971; O'Leary and Wilson 1975; Quay and Werry 1972; Ross 1974; Staats 1971, 1975

As noted, factors described as accounting for behavioral deficits and for the development and maintenance of excessive behavioral patterns are comprised of both *historical* and *contemporary* ones. The discussion of historical factors emphasizes variables which have influenced the development of those learning and behavioral difficulties which presently characterize a child. Discussion of contemporary factors focuses on the types of conditions which, as a consequence of prior learning, influence the present development of inappropriate learning and behavior characteristics. Additionally, emphasis is given to the contemporary conditions which serve to maintain, perpetuate, and intensify a child's problems. This distinction between historical and contemporary factors serves to emphasize that even though historical factors may account for the development of present characteristics, these characteristics may be influenced, maintained, and modified only by dealing with present events. A child may exhibit learning difficulties as a result of a previous inappropriate teaching environment, but these learning difficulties can only be reduced or eliminated by skillful modification of present events which results in more appropriate learning and performance. Figure 13.2 depicts the multitude of historical and contemporary factors which may contribute to the child's exceptional characteristics. Any combination of these factors in prolonged interaction with the child's ever changing characteristics produces the defeat cycle as illustrated in Figure 13.1.

In evaluating the significance of these learning factors, the reader should recognize, as noted earlier, that deficit and excessive problems may well be a primary or secondary result of neurological, sensory, and other

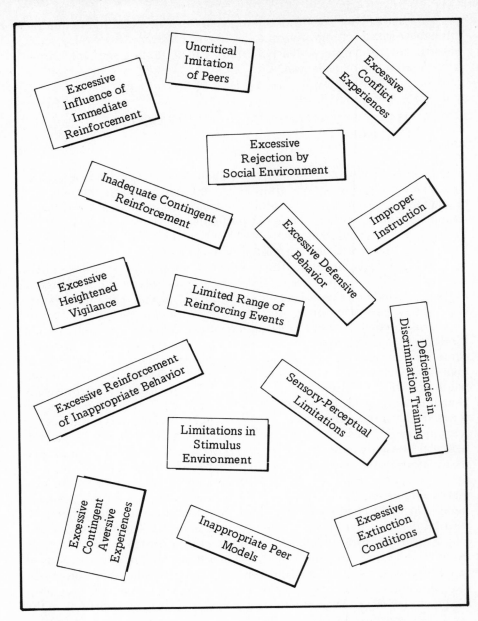

FIGURE 13.2   Depicting the Multitude of Learning Variables Influencing the Development and Perpetuation of Exceptional Characteristics

physical factors. No assumption is made that all exceptional learning and behavior characteristics are the result of distortions or deficits in the child's learning environments. A child with Down's Syndrome, for example, has an underdeveloped nervous system which impairs the effectiveness of even the most well-designed learning environments. Subtle central nervous system deviations in children popularly called "learning disabled" may well impede, under normal classroom instruction, the acquisition and maintenance (memory) of language, perceptual, and motor skills. A hard-of-hearing or deaf child or a blind or partially sighted child obviously experiences difficulty in learning except under instructional environments which accommodate to their sensory disability. In almost every instance, nevertheless, careful attention to the child's learning experiences will result either in prevention of or a reduction in his learning and behavior difficulties.

DEFICIENCIES IN REINFORCEMENT COMPONENTS

Many of the learning and behavioral inadequacies involving both deficit and excessive characteristics result from various deficiencies and distortions of reinforcement characteristics of the child's previous and present environments. The *types* and *amounts* of reinforcing events available in the environment, the types of reinforcing events actually experienced by the child, the *contingency* characteristics of the reinforcing events, as well as the *schedule* by which the child has and does experience reinforcement may all be involved. Recall that reinforcing events and the frequency of their availability in a learning situation interact with the motivational characteristics of any specific child. If a child or adolescent is highly dependent upon a limited number of external events, he obviously must be in an environment which will match these individual requirements if consistent learning and performance is to be influenced.

Inadequate Contingent Reinforcing Events

Learning and behavior problems may result from or be intensified by an improper reinforcement history which has been deficient in reinforcing events provided contingent upon desired behavior. The child may not develop behavior deemed desirable by home and school because the reinforcing consequences of approximations of this behavior have been too *small, infrequent,* or *inappropriate.* The child may avoid active involvement in learning activities due to inadequate incentive conditions which do not match his motivational characteristics. School activities, instead of being intrinsically interesting to a child with exceptional learning and behavior characteristics, frequently are difficult and unpleasant because the reinforcing events associated with such have been and are inadequate.

Even though the school may attempt to match reinforcing consequences to the difficulty level of a specific task, the events may be relatively ineffectual due to a child's high-strength competing behaviors which make it quite difficult for the child to engage in or persist at desired behavior. This is illustrated by Michael's high level of distractibility. He has been removed from a regular classroom program and placed in a special developmental education group program designed for children with exceptional learning characteristics. Michael does not remain at any one activity for more than a few minutes at a time. He frequently wanders around the room, attempts to intrude into the activities of others, goes to the toilet frequently, asks for drinks of water, and is generally impulsive and disruptive. All of these behaviors are incompatible with his attending to and becoming actively involved in the language and related academic activities during instructional periods. Teacher approval is of insufficient incentive value to strengthen those desired attending and related behaviors which would serve to replace the disruptive activities.

Programs all too frequently assume that a child should be influenced by incentive events which are quite abstract, as by being involved in group activity or by a feeling of achievement upon task completion, or which are too infrequent and too far removed from the behaviors being taught, such as grades or parental approval provided at end of a week, month, or semester. Not unusually, the reinforcing events available in home or school environments are woefully weak for the child or adolescent in comparison to the reinforcement value of competing activities or events such as drugs, sexual activities, daydreaming, peer attention of gang members, hyperactivity, and the like.

One frequent result of an environment with too small, infrequent, or inappropriate reinforcing components is disruptive behavior. Disruptive behavior may become quite strong when such behavior results in the child's removal from the activity and relationship requirements of a school program. To the extent that school activities acquire aversive components, any behavior that removes or reduces this aversiveness is strengthened. This was illustrated in the previously described case of Michael. Whenever prodded to persist in his academic behavior, Michael characteristically would become negativistic and occasionally would engage in rather noisy emotional outbursts. Whenever he behaved in this manner, class requirements were terminated and he was removed from this environment. This consequence of removal from an aversive requirement served to make more likely the occurrence of the disruptive behaviors whenever Michael was placed in similar circumstances. The disruptive behavior pattern did not occur because Michael willfully enjoyed upsetting his teachers and peers. In all likelihood, Michael was not even aware of the events which influenced his self-defeating behaviors. Rather, these exceptional behavior patterns occurred as the program inadvertently permitted the wrong aspects of the school environment to gain strong influence over this behavior pattern.

Another consequence of an inadequate reinforcement history is the development of a general attitude of disinterest and limited involvement. Behavior patterns which match environmental expectations are not developed, with the result that the child is described as being unmotivated. A more meaningful description would focus on the deficits in the reinforcing components of the environment and on the resulting improper motivational system of the child. Both impose limitations on the child in his development and use of a range of appropriate behaviors.

As noted previously, the educator should make a distinction between what a specific child is able to do but does not, and those behavior patterns required by the school program which a child does not have in his repertoire. In the latter case of deficit behaviors, a longer period of behavior development under appropriate reinforcement conditions may be required to offset these deficits. In the former case, rapid reduction in a child's difficulties may be realized once a more appropriate reinforcing environment is provided. For example, an adolescent may have all the skills necessary for acceptable performance in a prevocational training program. He may, however, due to limited reinforcing consequences associated with attendance and performance, present a general pattern of high absenteeism and of low quality and quantity achievement when he does attend. A dramatic change in performance may be noted merely by changes in the kind, magnitude, and schedule of incentive conditions provided for more appropriate behavior. Ayllon et al.* provide a second example of rapid *Ayllon et al. 1975* increase in appropriate learning and performance as a function of increased suitability of reinforcement conditions. Three children, ages eight to ten, attending a self-contained learning disabilities class, were under drug therapy for their hyperactivity and all displayed poor academic progress. After terminating the drug therapy and placing the children on a token reinforcement program which provided immediate token reinforcement for correct academic behavior, math and reading performance increased from an average of 12 percent correct to an average of 85 percent correct. Thus, a change in the nature of the reinforcement consequences contingent on correct academic behavior resulted in a dramatic positive change in reading and math performance.

Limited Range of Reinforcing Events

The limited behavioral repertoires of some children may result both from the infrequency or inconsistency with which reinforcing consequences are available as well as from the limited range of incentive conditions among all those available which do in fact have reinforcing properties for specific children. As was described earlier, there are a few primary stimulus events which, under certain conditions, fulfill a reinforcing function for everyone—food, water, warmth, and the like. Most events, however, gain their reinforcement qualities through consistent association with other reinforcing events. Children may fail to acquire appropriate behavior patterns due to a paucity of effective reinforcing events available in their environment. There may be a poor match between the motivational characteristics of specific children and the incentive conditions available in various learning and performance situations.

Ferster 1961   Ferster* has speculated that some children labeled as autistic exhibit broad behavioral limitations as a result of a general deficiency in acquired reinforcers, especially an absence of acquired rewarding as-
Lovaas and Koegel 1972   pects of social stimuli. Lovaas and Koegel* summarize this position quite succinctly:

> The presence or absence of an approving smile, while neutral to the newborn infant, gradually assumes reinforcing functions as the child interacts with his parents. . . . Normal children appear to acquire much of their behaviors on the basis of secondary reinforcers. If autistic children do not respond to praise, smiles, hugs, interpersonal closeness, correctness, novelty, and other secondary reinforcers which support so much behavior in normal children, it would be logical to argue that their behavioral development should be accordingly deficient. Thus, much of an autistic child's failure to develop appropriate behavior could be viewed as a function of the total or parital failure of his environment to be meaningful to him, that is, to have failed in the acquisition of secondary reinforcers. [p. 240]

Many events available to most children in our society may not exert a reinforcing effect on some children with chronic learning and behavior difficulties. These events either have not been available to a child in the past or else have not been associated sufficiently with other reinforcing events to acquire strong secondary reinforcing properties. Many events meaningful to most children such as listening to music, carrying on a conversation, playing with other children, watching cartoons, being successful, solving difficult problems, pleasing parents and other adults, and similar events may hold neutral or even aversive reinforcing value for some children with exceptional learning and behavior characteristics. These children may never have had the opportunity to participate successfully in these, or else have done so too infrequently. Such events as parental and teacher approval or approval from academically successful peers may have little incentive or reinforcement value since such events have not been associated consistently with other effective reinforcing events. The child in the school may be expected to initiate and maintain various academic and social activities by using self-control skills which he lacks. The school may expect that certain activities will have acquired intrinsic value for a child. This expectation of a higher social-emotional-motivational level than is characteristic of a child results in failure for him.

Educational personnel frequently represent a subculture different from that of many children with exceptional learning and behavior patterns. Outstanding differences exist between groups representing different subcultures both in the events which are reinforcing and in the pattern by which these events are provided. The teacher, in using such events as praise, approval, or feedback concerning correctness or incorrectness of behavior, and grades in an effort to strengthen desired behaviors frequently finds these events to be totally ineffective with many children. The educator, in a sense, is imposing his or her subcultural reinforcement system onto the students and is expecting them to be influenced by these events in the manner that he or she would be. For example, the teacher, by urging children to adhere to classroom requirements and by praising them occasionally for desired behavior, is depending upon abstract social reinforcers which may have been seldom present in the children's environments. Such events are likely to exert little systematic influence over many children and adolescents with exceptional learning and behavior characteristics. Such practices of overdependence on a limited range of relatively inappropriate incentive consequences add considerably to the difficulties of these children.

One additional result of a limitation in the amount and range of effective incentive events available is the possibility that the child will become excessively dependent upon and thus highly influenced by social attention of peers. The not uncommon practice of isolating a group of highly disruptive children into a self-contained special program is especially devastating. In such a group, the disruptive child is likely to receive social feedback for his disruptive and antilearning behavior from his disruptive peers. If he were to behave in a manner consistent with the educational program goals, little peer attention would be forthcoming.

Standards of behavior of the socially reinforcing peers—those behaviors reinforced by peers—are typically different from those acceptable to the educator. This is especially true of adolescents labeled as socialized delinquents. In the school program the child will be attended to by his peers if he behaves inappropriately. This excessive peer effect on disruptive behavior was forcefully illustrated by a group of adolescents attending a social adjustment program. The instructor spent most of his time attempting to control a wide range of disruptive behaviors of various members of the group. He had little success as the disruptive behavior was quickly reinforced by peer attention. A silly comment resulted in laughter from the peers which served not only to maintain the strength of this type of disruptive behavior but also served as a cue for other silly behavior from some other class member. Teacher attention for appropriate behavior was of little influence compared to the influence of the social feedback provided by peers.

Excessive Influence of Immediate Reinforcement

Closely related to the problem of a limited range of reinforcing events is the observation that many children with excessive learning and behavior difficulties may be overly dependent upon immediate reinforcement. If newly emerging behaviors are not reinforced frequently and immediately, the behaviors do not gain strength. Additionally, many children with exceptional learning and behavior characteristics, especially the young and the severely limited, find tangible events more reinforcing than abstract ones. The availability of delayed rewards serves little or no reinforcement function in influencing previous behavior for which it may be intended. Emerging behavior is extinguished under such circumstances and other behaviors, resulting in immediate reinforcement, are strengthened. These other behaviors frequently are inconsistent with the educational objectives set for children.

A factor influencing excessive reliance on immediate and tangible reinforcers is that of the poorly developed skill of self-reinforcement characteristic of many children with exceptional characteristics. Many children do not learn to "pat themselves on the back" for appropriate behavior and thereby are unable to maintain the behavior unless other immediate external sources of reinforcement are provided. They are influenced by "chance" incentive conditions more than are their more able peers who have self-reinforcing skills. Also, many such children have limited self-imposed standards, while most children become "self-reinforced" when the expected standard or goal is attained. All these reinforcement deficits render the child more under the influence of immediate and chance sources of reinforcement. Under circumstances in which immediate, effective, reinforcing events are not systematically provided following desired behavior, a range of excessive and deficit problem characteristics frequently result.

Noncontingent Reinforcement

In some environments, reinforcement is provided in an indiscriminate, unsystematic, or noncontingent fashion. That behavior which, by chance, is reinforced most frequently becomes the dominant response. In other environments a wide range of behaviors is provided reinforcement independent of any contingency requirements. These may represent aspects of a "therapeutic" program based on the belief that children should behave as they feel like behaving and that they should be provided unconditional positive regard. In other instances, the environment may view the child as "sick," or unable to learn, and thus not responsible for his behavior. In such a welfare-type environment, a variety of both adequate and inadequate characteristics are strengthened by this free and noncontingent availability of positive consequences. This was seen recently in a classroom in which an adolescent girl exhibited unpredictable emotional outbursts. For fear that unusual management difficulties might be created if program requirements were initated, the educator permitted the adolescent to do whatever she wished. She was free to participate, or not participate. Although she spent considerable time in a variety of nonproductive and frequently aimless activities, she still received the same postive consequences as did her productive peers. The program, by this noncontingent reinforcement procedure, i.e., reinforcement not systematically provided following specific target behaviors, was strengthening numerous behaviors incompatible with appropriate academic and social development. In such contingency-free environments, the adolescent is unable to acquire such characteristics as self-discipline, patterns of responsible behavior, attitudes of reciprocity, and the like.

Excessive Extinction Conditions

Behavior must be reinforced occassionally in order to be maintained. In the absence of such occasional reinforcement, behavior is weakened and eventually replaced by other behavior which is reinforced. Such extinction conditions are frequently observed when a child is removed from highly specialized and well-staffed programs in which reinforcement has been provided frequently and systematically. Placement in a less structured environment which does not provide the reinforcement procedures of the treatment program may result in rapid and extensive loss of the child's newly acquired behaviors.

As noted earlier, reinforcers used in a program designed to foster rapid and extensive *acquisition* of appropriate modes of behavior are frequently of an *arbitrary* nature.* These are events not readily available in the natural surroundings and relationships of the child as he moves from the highly structured program environment to more natural ones of school and home. These arbitrary reinforcers thus are usually inappropriate for insuring *maintenance* of behavior. (Recall the discussion in Chapter 9 concerning principles and procedures relating to behavior maintenance.)

Bijou 1970; MacMillan and Forness 1970

Likewise, the special education teacher may find that as she moves from one lesson to another, her student has forgotten what previously had been learned. Frequently, this is a result of assuming too early in the learning process that the behavior is well developed and thereby maintained by acquired intrinsic or irregularly provided extrinsic reinforcing events.

Well-meaning parents also create conditions of excessive extinction by their highly irregular manner of interacting with their children. For a variety of reasons, parents on occasion may spend considerable time with their children and strengthen various behavior patterns only to disappear or become unavailable for extended periods of time. This absenteeism of parents results in the nonmaintenance of much behavior learned by the child under more favorable interpersonal conditions.

EXCESSIVE REINFORCEMENT OF INAPPROPRIATE BEHAVIOR

Numerous patterns of inappropriate behavior are frequently reinforced, both positively and negatively, by unsuspected social agents insensitive to these rules of reinforcement learning. Various aggressive, socially disruptive, and dependency modes of behaving may be strengthened by the attention which such behaviors produce. The teacher or parent may give in to a child's demands in order to terminate such aversive behaviors as crying, temper tantrums, or hyperactivity. Such consequences may further increase the likelihood of these behaviors. Examples will illustrate the role of both positive and negative reinforcement. Jack, a sixteen-year-old with limited cognitive development, tends to "lose control" whenever confronted with tasks requiring concentrated activity. The teacher, fearful that this "emotionally disturbed" adolescent will become too upset, gives in to his demands and tries to comfort him. Joyce, a fifteen-year-old, has dizzy spells while in prevocational training. The teacher-counselor and co-workers are very sympathetic toward Joyce whenever she complains of the dizzy spells and provide her with considerable concern. In both instances inappropriate behaviors are reinforced by social consequences provided by peers and staff members.

Behaviors aversive to others may be rather weak, but these may be the dominant behaviors engaged in by a child or adolescent as other appropriate behaviors are less frequently reinforced by the environment. It is not unusual for the social environment to ignore appropriate behavior whenever it does occur because prosocial behavior is expected of everyone. On the other hand, inappropriate behaviors bring all kinds of reactions or results from the social environment, ranging from attention to removal of unpleasant task requirements. Such contingent consequences may thus strengthen and perpetuate these behaviors.

It is important to recall that inappropriate behavior may be quite strong or resistant to elimination as a result of a peculiar history of partial or intermittent reinforcement. An adolescent presently may be reinforced only infrequently for inadequate behavior, but the behavior may still remain at relatively high strength due to a history of intermittent reinforcement which renders it highly resistant to extinction.

In some cases inadequate behavior resulting in punishment may be maintained as a result of the positive reinforcement that follows. To illustrate, a child may behave disruptively in the classroom even though he is reprimanded by the teacher and rejected by his peers. However, these aversive consequences may be followed frequently by the child being sent to the school counselor's office for a "therapy session," an activity which may be highly reinforcing to the child. He thus may be reinforced inadvertently for behaving inappropriately.

It is evident that nonattainment of potentially positive reinforcers renders numerous situations rather aversive. Aversiveness becomes attached to environments in which failure has been routine rather than the exception, or in which the child has been required to expend more effort than is reasonable for the amount of reinforcement payoff available. In these environments inappropriate behaviors are strengthened by negative reinforcement as these either remove the child from the aversive environment or, at a minimum, reduce the time he must remain in it. This removal or reduction of aversive conditions strengthens the inappropriate behavior and may become the predominant reinforcing contingency.

As noted earlier, when a child has only a limited repertoire of behaviors appropriate to specific situations, this may overemphasize the few behaviors which the child or adolescent does have. The few available behaviors may be so overused, (and "misused") that they may be viewed as excessive, bizarre, and inappropriate. This may result in the child being removed from an uncomfortable classroom situation. Consequently, such negative reinforcement may result in the further strengthening of these behaviors. These same behaviors, if occurring as aspects of a more extensive array of appropriate behaviors, might be viewed as mildly odd or inappropriate but not nearly as bizarre or maladaptive as when they occur within a limited behavioral repertoire.

Prior to ending this discussion of reinforcement deficiencies in the experiential histories of children with exceptional learning and behavior characteristics, further mention should be made of the work of Zigler* and *Zigler et al. 1969, 1973* his colleagues. Zigler has emphasized that children from highly restricted environments, for example, institutionalized or culturally disadvantaged settings, and who are characterized by generalized cognitive deficits have motivational histories that have an adverse influence on their problem-solving strategies. These children, in comparison with those of normal or typical developmental histories, have experienced more failure, less social approval and other forms of positive social reinforcement from adults, and less satisfactory interactions with adults. Zigler suggests the following consequences:

1. Lower expectancy of achievement in the performance of tasks.
2. A sense of mistrust or wariness toward adults.
3. Heightened motivation, however, to interact with adults and to seek their approval.
4. Heightened sensitivity to tangible events as reinforcers and reduced expectation that knowledge of correctness of problem-solving behavior will be reinforcing.
5. Tendency to be outer-directed and to focus on extraneous cues in a problem situation. Likely to attend to irrelevant aspects of a task or to the reactions of the adult for information to direct their behavior. Less likely to depend upon own resources to seek solutions to problems.

Any of these characteristics decreases the likelihood that the child will be successful in social and academic pursuits.

DEFICIENCIES IN DISCRIMINATION TRAINING

It is not unusual to note that a child's inadequacies reflect the fact that other more appropriate behaviors, even though in the child's repertoire, are not likely to occur at the appropriate time or place. Those environmental events which designate the time and place in which certain behaviors would be most appropriate do not have sufficient influence to insure their reliable and discriminating occurrence. The child has not experienced consistent differential reinforcement for certain desired behavior in the presence of distinctive cues.

Social Discrimination Difficulties

One prominent feature of many children and adolescents with exceptional learning and behavior characteristics is their difficulty in making fine discriminations. Much inappropriate behavior is not unusual or bizarre in any *absolute* sense. It is nonadaptive as it occurs at the *wrong* time and/or place. The child has difficulty knowing just what to do even though he has the appropriate behaviors in his repertoires. Or, even more aggravating or damaging in developing appropriate interpersonal relationships, many do not know when to stop responding. Specific behaviors may be appropriate. The frequency or magnitude of the behavior, however, may be most inappropriate in varying situations.

This discrimination deficit is illustrated by a sixteen-year-old referred by the classroom teacher to the school counselor with the statement, "She can't make friends because she doesn't know when to stop talking." This adolescent girl attending special classes for the "mentally retarded" was apparently not influenced by her unappreciative audience though they presented such cues as changes in facial expression, negative verbal comments, and other attempts at ignoring her lengthy verbal episodes. Inquiry into the reinforcement history of this adolescent revealed a mother and an aunt who would listen patiently to her for extended periods of time, reinforcing her socially for her nondiscriminating verbal barrages as a result of their pleasure that their "dull" child was so verbal. Behavior resulting in social reinforcement from an appreciative audience in one setting was not appropriate in others. The behavior had not acquired the specificity needed to meet the requirements of adequate peer interaction. In popular terms, the girl had no tact or had poor social sensitivity. This failure to respond differently under different social cue conditions resulted in behavior which was aversive to peers and which decreased the possibility that desired social relationships could develop.

Uncritical Imitation of Peer Behavior

Another discrimination deficit characteristic of many children and adolescents described as socially inadequate or delinquent is that the behavior of peers is imitated without discretion. The adolescent is easily influenced by dominant peers. He attends to too few stimulus components of a complex situation and thus engages in behavior that results in numerous negative consequences. The adolescent, as a result of peer attention and approval, may follow gang members into socially deviant behavior. Socially sanctioned behavior does not produce valuable immediate reinforcers and thus is not under appropriate discriminative cue influence.

Overly Restrictive Range of Discriminative Events

Other children may be excessively influenced by an overly restrictive range of cues. Too much of their behavior is influenced by the social cues provided by a few specific people. These overly dependent children will respond in socially significant situations only after excessive prompting, urging, and prodding by specific others. Decisions cannot be made, behavior cannot be initiated except in direct imitation of similar action of others. The behaviors of specific others become the discriminative events influencing their behavior. Such a restricted range of controlling stimulus events reflects a dependency which impeded adequate social development.

Sensory Perceptual Difficulties

As noted, auditory, tactual, and kinesthetic perceptual discrimination difficulties are quite prevalent among some children with exceptional learning and behavior characteristics. Problems are created and intensified by indiscriminate instructional programs which make no allowances for differences among children in the relative efficacy with which they handle stimulation across sensory modalities. Some children learn best under auditory stimulation, others when provided multisensory stimulation. Other children are overselective in reaction to multisensory stimulation and display obvious discrimination learning difficulties. Johnson and Myklebust* have noted, "The number of sensory modalities to be activated for input can be determined solely on the basis of the child's total capacities and tolerance levels. If both auditory and visual stimulations are given . . . one may obliterate incoming signals from the other. Moreover, some children can tolerate information from just one modality at a time, or from only certain modality combinations such as auditory-tactile" (p. 60).

Johnson and Myklebust 1967

Lovaas and Schreibman* and Lovaas et al.* present data which indicate that children labeled as autistic are overselective in their response to multisensory stimulation. When presented with a complex stimulus array involving auditory, visual, and tactile cues, the children responded to only one component of the complex cue. No one sense modality was preferred over the other. The children apparently ignored cues other than those initially selected. These writers speculated that such a stimulus overselectivity may be involved in the extreme learning difficulties seen in

Lovaas and Schreibman 1971; Lovaas et al. 1971

Lovaas and Schreibman
1971

such children. Lovaas and Schreibman* state, "Since a necessary condition for much learning involves the contiguous or near-contiguous presentation of stimuli, it is reasonable to assume that if the child cannot adequately use simultaneous stimuli, learning may not occur. This deficit could be responsible for the failure of autistic children to develop certain complex behavior, such as meaningful speech, or certain stimulus functions, such as secondary reinforcers (symbolic rewards). Such a deficit might also interfere with the performance of behavior the child has already acquired" (p. 305).

Schreibman 1975

In a related study, Schreibman* evaluated the effectiveness of various types of prompts in facilitating visual and auditory discrimination learning in a group of eight-and-one-half- to fourteen-year-old autistic children. The children usually failed to learn the required discriminations without a prompt. Additionally, the children always failed to learn a previously unlearned discrimination when an extra-stimulus prompt was employed; they usually did learn when a within-stimulus prompt was employed. These findings were independent of the modality (visual or auditory) required for the discrimination. Again, support was provided for the supposition that autistic children will learn discriminations which do not require them to respond to multiple cues.

Summary

Children with learning and behavior difficulties are frequently confronted with situations requiring them to behave differentially to subtle and somewhat complex cues. These discrimination requirements are too difficult for many children to handle due to inadequate or improper discrimination training. The type of instructional procedures used in effectively teaching most children simple and complex discriminations obviously are not appropriate for some children with various perceptual and stimulus overselectivity difficulties. Being required to respond in a discriminating manner without adequate discrimination skills may produce a variety of behaviors such as hyperactivity, distractibility, and a loss of previously demonstrated discriminations. In other instances, behavioral rigidity or perserveration may result.

LIMITATIONS IN THE STIMULUS ENVIRONMENT

Behavioral deficits and excesses frequently may be correlated with a restricted or inappropriate stimulating environment. Either the *range and type* of stimulation or the *lack of consistency or distinctiveness* of the learning environment may have resulted in limited behavior development or in the development of excessive behavioral characteristics which impede successful learning. The child with visual and auditory difficulties requires modification in the usual instructional environment if adequate learning is to occur. Many children with sensory difficulties are not provided the discriminating education experiences required for desired development of academic and social skills. Thus, problems are intensified by an inadequate stimulus environment. Children with other severe physical difficulties such as the cerebral palsied, the child with epilepsy, or the child with chronic health problems may suffer the deleterious effects of a restricted stimulus environment. Such children seldom are provided the "normal educational experiences" provided the typical child. Even if provided adequate instructional stimulation, many learning and behavior difficulties may result from the social rejection and isolation that occurs. Peer relationships are not as frequent, spontaneous, natural, or carefree. Adults too frequently respond with overconcern and pity or with subtle or more obvious rejection.

The child with limited cognitive skills, by definition, has difficulty in acquiring the complex range of adaptive behaviors necessary for general social adaptation. Adequate behavior development requires prolonged systematic exposure to a set of conditions designed both to initiate, strengthen, and maintain desired behaviors, and to discourage and eliminate undesired behaviors. It becomes readily apparent to even the casual observer of the American education scene that too few children with obvious learning and behavior difficulties have such an environment available throughout their developmental years. Secondary-level educational programs are frequently confronted with the task of offsetting the effects of highly inappropriate conditions which many adolescents have experienced throughout earlier critical years. Yet, as noted earlier, a report by Heber et al.* provides encouraging support for the position that general *Heber et al. 1972* learning and behavior deficits associated with limitations in stimulation provided some children in "disadvantaged" homes can be avoided by enriching the environmental experiences early in the child's life.

Thus, one major class of factors related to the child's present exceptional characteristics, whether these be general or specific, is that of *improper experience or instruction, or lack of appropriate experience or instruction.* The effects of such accumulate over time in producing various behavioral deficits and excessive characteristics which further impede acquisition and retention of new behavior characteristics.

Improper Instruction

Improper instruction refers to poor educational programming as judged in relation to standard teaching methods and materials. Improper instruction has reference both to the child who has been highly restricted in the general types of experiences seemingly crucial to the development of linguistic, cognitive, and perceptual skills (defined as culturally deprived or underpriviledged) and also to the child who has had highly individual and idiosyncratic combinations of learning requirements but who has not been provided the specific types of educational stimulations required for him to learn. What might be proper instruction or experiences for most may well be improper for specific children. The behavioral approach assumes the position that "if a child hasn't yet learned, he hasn't yet been successfully taught."

Obviously there are limitations to what any child can learn, but until a highly individualized, well-designed instructional program has been provided, one does not know what these limitations are. Thus it is recognized that even if a child has attended an educational program judged to be adequate for most children, but has not learned at an expected level, that particular educational program was improper for him, just as a highly restricted degree of language stimulation may be improper for children who grow up in poverty conditions. Again, certain environments may result in exceptional learning and behavior characteristics due to *restrictions in the amount* of stimulation or to the *inappropriateness* of the stimulation relative to the unique characteristics of specific children. Some environments may be judged to be quite rich in the type, range, and frequency of stimulation. However, such educational programs may represent a limited stimulus environment for a specific child. The program may simply be geared to a level of behavior development which is too complex for the child involved. The environment may require auditory and visual perceptual skills, memory skills, language skills, mediational skills, and the like which the child does not have. The child thus is unable to behave and learn successfully in this environment.

Poorly Developed Prerequisite Skills

To emphasize, absence of or inadequately developed prerequisite or essential concomitant skills such as attentional skills, mediational skills, memory skills, rehearsal strategies, self-management skills, and so on may contribute to learning difficulties. Some education programs utilize instructional procedures which assume prerequisites which the child does not have or set educational objectives which children are unable to fulfill. The manner and rate of instruction may not be matched to unique learner requirements. The required behavior represents too large an increment from what the child presently is able to accomplish or perhaps assumes prerequisite or facilitative skills which he does not have. Hallahan and Cruickshank,* Hewett,* Koegel and Schreibman,* and Zeaman and House* have all described the attentional difficulties associated with children labeled mentally retarded, autistic, learning disabled, and emotionally disturbed. Butterfield and Belmont* emphasize the role of poor rehearsal skills in the learning and memory difficulties of children with generalized cognitive deficits.

Hallahan and Cruickshank 1973; Hewett 1974; Koegel and Schreibman 1974; Zeaman and House 1963; Butterfield and Belmont 1972

The child may not know what to do or how to do it. The symbolic verbal models, i. e., instructions, which are frequently used by a teacher may not provide sufficient direction for the child. Or, the child may simply be unable to accomplish the objective because he does not have the prerequisite behaviors. Hewett* has emphasized the necessity of teaching the child to attend to and participate in instructional activities prior to his developing high-level competencies.

Hewett 1974

Antilearning Characteristics

The child may have high-rate competing behavior patterns such as hyperactivity, distractibility, self-stimulation, excessive daydreaming, and heightened generalized anxiety which actively interfere with his responding to the instructional program.* As a result, reinforcement, even if available, is not obtained because the child does not meet the instructional or behavioral expectations of the teacher. Excessive failure may be experienced and, as noted, a passive, low-motivated, and limited interaction with various elements of the environment may result. The situation may become quite aversive due to excessive failure and, thus, actively avoided.

Cruickshank, 1971; Keogh 1971

In other instances the stimulus environment may be inappropriate to more specific types of characteristics of a child. A child with various perceptual and central processing difficulties may be unable to learn satisfactorily if the teaching environment is not designed to compensate for these difficulties. A child, for example, may have extreme difficulty in visual or in auditory discriminations and be unable to learn various preacademic and academic skills. Or a child from a disadvantaged home may be provided an educational experience which predominately requires the auditory channel of information reception and processing, although many such children may be better visual learners.

Inappropriate Peer Models

As suggested earlier, inappropriate learning conditions are created by the prevalent practice of placing children and adolescents with difficult academic and behavior problems together in the same physical setting and program. Such a practice insures that the social models for behavior will be provided by those who are least discriminating in behaviors which would be socially appropriate. In the example described earlier, inappropriate behavior in a group of highly disruptive adolescents was almost constantly facilitated by the social stimulation and reinforcement of other equally disruptive peers. The teacher, who was the only person in the environment who could represent appropriate social and cognitive models of behavior, was of little influence as he spent most of his efforts in attempts at managing the disruptive environment. These high-rate disruptive behaviors were being maintained by sources of reinforcement that were beyond the influence of the teacher. A wide variety of self-defeating characteristics can be acquired in such an inadequate stimulus environment—excessive anxiety, antilearning attitudes, derogatory notions of school and school personnel, and a general pessimism concerning one's own adequacy and worth.

Even speech difficulties can be acquired by imitation of inappropriate speech behavior in others. Eisenson* suggests that articulation, phonation, and fluency may all be influenced by exposure to inappropriate speech models.

Eisenson 1971

Summary

The presence of various factors associated with limitations in the stimulus environment, *in isolation or in interaction,* may result in a high likelihood that a child will experience mild to profound learning and behavior difficulties. The result may be a highly specific idiosyncratic pattern—"specific learning disability"—or a more generalized one—"mental retardation," "severe emotional disturbance." *In most instances, learning difficulties represent interactive effects.* The behavioral position assumes a rather empirical attitude concerning the specific combination of variables which may be operative in any child at any one time. As there is no sound evidence of any common experiential, neurophysiological, or psychological defect or disability in children with behavior or learning difficulties, the educator must search for relationships between learning proficiency, behavioral adequacy, and objectively measurable physical and environmental conditions.

EXCESSIVE CONTINGENT OR NONCONTINGENT AVERSIVE EXPERIENCES

A significant factor in the development and perpetuation of exceptional learning and behavior characteristics is that of excessive contingent and noncontingent aversive experiences. The greater the child's difficulties, the more likely he is to obtain further aversive experiences which in turn adds to his ineptness.

When a child is unable to meet a performance criterion (teacher, parent, or peer expectation) due to his behavioral deficits, or if he engages in behavior or has physical features which produce uncomfortable reactions in others, he becomes a target of a wide range of aversive stimulation. He is not reinforced in situations which require the deficit behavior. In addition, he is apt to receive considerable general social punishment; adults and his more able peers may criticize him, make fun of him, require him to become involved in situations in which he cannot perform, increase their demands upon him, reject him, and the like. Thus, an excessive amount of his behavior and/or his physical features produce negative social attention from the normal social environment. Except in a highly controlled, therapeutic, and therefore somewhat unnatural or artificial environment, the child's behavior or his general social stimulus features may obtain few consistent positive social reinforcements. He has low social prestige; his behavior may have few reinforcing properties for general social relationships and interactions. Few of those in his social environment find his behavior rewarding to them and consequently will not attend to or seek his company or interactions. This subtle rejection has been noted when the "mentally retarded" child is mainstreamed. As Gottlieb and Davis* report, when he has little to offer his more competent peers, they may treat him as a nonentity.

Gottieb and Davis 1973

In most cases, the social environment will not even encourage his physical presence. Only limited social reinforcement is forthcoming to support appropriate behaviors which could serve to facilitate the development of more social prestige. Consequently, much of his general social experience merely serves to extinguish attempts at appropriate social behaviors, or, through suppression and aversive control, to limit the total behaviors which are expressed. As he has no adequate group or gang with which to interact, appropriate social reinforcement is greatly reduced. As Ferster* has suggested, under these circumstances the probability is greatly decreased that the individual will be able to make a successful social adjustment in view of the fact that a major, most readily available source of reinforcement—social in nature—is not provided.

Ferster 1958

Numerous studies support the supposition that various speech difficulties such as defects of articulation, phonation, fluency, and more general language dysfunctions, result from excessive aversive learning experiences.* Parental rejection in the form of disapproval and criticism of speech may result in avoidance of or reduction in speech activities.

Eisenson 1971

Types of Aversive Events

As noted earlier, some events are naturally unpleasant to a child, for example, extreme states of deprivation of food, water, or air, painful stimulation such as a slap on the hand, loud noises, and extremes in temperature. These are *primary* aversive events in the sense that the child, without benefit of prior learning, naturally seeks to escape from or terminate the unpleasant conditions.

Additionally, when a child is placed in a situation that requires discriminations that are too difficult, a psychological state is created which is aversive. Maher* has commented that such a situation "is aversive quite apart from any history of punishment which may be associated with any of the stimuli present" (p. 138). Difficult discrimination, in essence, describes a conflict situation in which a child is concurrently stimulated to engage in

Maher 1966

incompatible or competing responses which have comparable strength. The child does not know what to do. Under conflict conditions, negative consequences result regardless of the alternative chosen by the child.

The most aversive types of conflict situations are those of an *Lundin 1969* *approach-avoidance* or of an *avoidance-avoidance* nature.* In an approach-avoidance conflict, a child is stimulated to engage in some activity which will result in both positive and negative consequences. The adolescent with epilepsy only partially controlled by medication may enjoy going to parties with his peers but fear the embarrassment of having a seizure when with them. Thus, social interaction with peers outside the home has both positive and negative features. In an avoidance-avoidance conflict situation, a child's behavior produces negative consequences regardless of what he does. An adolescent, in illustration, may be required by his parents to attend a remedial reading class in which he experiences considerable failure. If he does not engage in this highly unpleasant activity, his parents will punish him. The child is thus punished regardless of what he does. If unable to escape from such avoidance-avoidance conditions, the child may exhibit a variety of maladaptive behaviors ranging from an inflexible approach to conflict resolution to indirect aggression manifested in such actions as destruction of school property, physical attacks on innocent peers, and disorganizing temper outbursts. Conflict situations of this nature, as noted by Maher, are "inherently aversive and will elicit avoidance behavior if this is possible under the prevailing conditions. Where it is not possible, the pattern of response which emerges will resemble those elicited by direct noxious stimulation" (p. 139).

Conflict Results in Negative Emotional Learning

Under conflict conditions a wide range of neutral events may acquire some of the aversiveness of the conflict situation. These neutral events such as a frown, social interaction, gesture, presence of an authority figure, competitive activities, or an arithmetic workbook may have little or no unpleasantness associated with them initially. However, these events may acquire unpleasant qualities if associated frequently with the occurrence of conflict conditions which are already aversive to the child.

Reduction in Positive Reinforcement Is Aversive

Also recall that events become aversive as these signal reduction in frequency or amount of positive reinforcers. Others become aversive as these coincide with or precede and signal the occurrence of other unpleasant events. Scolding, yelling, criticizing, and reprimanding by the teacher may become aversive events as they mark the occasion for a reduction in positive reinforcement. The teacher is much less likely, after reprimanding a child, to provide positive social comments or to grant privileges such as free play or telling a favorite story. A threat by the teacher may become aversive; it has been associated with various aversive consequences such as physical punishment or of being denied access to a TV show or to the music room. A peer's scream and angry facial expression may become quite aversive; in the past these have coincided with painful physical attacks.

Effects of Contingent Aversive Events

The presentation of aversive stimulation following behavior—punishment—results in the suppression of this behavior, a process described earlier. The more intense the aversive consequences the greater the suppressive effects, not only on the specific behavior punished but also across a broad range of behaviors.

There is frequently seen a broad generalization of suppressive effects. Not only do punished behaviors decrease in frequency of occurrence, but also there is frequently a reduction or temporary elimination of other behavior patterns quite unrelated to the punished behavior. A generalized pattern of stubbornness or withdrawal represents one example of this effect. A generalized reaction of hopelessness represents another.

Emotional Aspects of Aversive Conditions

Excessive aversive stimulation may result in inappropriate affective or emotional behaviors which frequently serve to compete with those more desirable aspects of a child's behavioral repertoires. As described earlier, events present when aversive conditions and the resulting negative emotionality are experienced soon become conditioned events for disruptive emotionality. If a child is exposed to numerous aversive experiences (punishment, conflicts), a pattern of pervasive anxiety may develop. There is some evidence that higher levels of arousal for anxiety result in an increased facility in acquiring further anxiety reactions to new cues. Thus more events—people, activities, situations—are likely to become conditioned events for negative emotionality. The child who is generally fearful is more prone to form new conditioned stimuli for fear responses.*   *Martin 1971*
The child is also likely to show greater physiological arousal to stress, has more difficulty adjusting to repeated stress, and shows a slower recovery to stress. Thus, a perpetual cycle of failure and unhappiness is facilitated.

DEVELOPMENT OF DEFENSIVE BEHAVIOR

Patterns of avoidance (defensive) behavior develop whenever there is excessive aversive stimulation.* Whenever a child finds himself in the   *Lundin 1969; Martin 1971*
presence of aversive conditions, he attempts to reduce or remove the unpleasantness. That behavior which results in his escape from the un-

pleasantness will be strengthened through negative reinforcement. Other present events begin to serve as warning signals or preaversive events for avoidance behavior. The mere thought of the possibility of someone initiating a conversation after the school play was a sufficiently aversive signal for John, a twelve-year-old with a severe stuttering problem, to avoid the school function completely. He decided to remain at home in the safety of his room and listen to records. The child may thus learn to stay away from both situations *previously* associated with aversiveness as well as persons or situations which represent *possible* occurrence of aversive conditions.

As noted, in conflict situations the child may attempt to escape from the unpleasant conditions. If this is not possible, he will behave in whatever manner partially reduces the conflict. One aspect of the response pattern will be those unconditioned and conditioned emotional responses elicited by any aversive or noxious event. Conflict, then, may result in disorganization and reduced competency.

Observation of the child with exceptional learning and behavior characteristics reveals excessive hesitancy about entering into various activities, especially those that involve competition with peers or against a standard performance requiring cognitive or other skills. This hesitancy may be a reflection of a previous history of insufficient positive reinforcement, of excessive aversive stimulation, or, as is more likely, of a combination of the two factors. Such "becoming involved" behavior is of low magnitude due to its association with a low likelihood of being successful. Additionally, as has been suggested, the hesitancy may represent active avoidance behavior which indicates that previous attempts at participation have resulted in aversive consequences. Nonparticipation in such activities avoids the possibility of repetition of these aversive events.

Passivity Results

In those situations where the child or adolescent is forced by parents or other authority figures to be physically present in a situation that has greater aversive than positive features, a pattern of passive, disinterested behavior may occur. The child may just not become involved. He may sulk or pout; he may spend excessive periods of time in preparation for initiating a task or may even sit idly for extended periods. Much of the low motivation or lack of interest which characterize many children with chronic learning and behavior problems is a manifestation of excessive aversive stimulation. The negative components for "not doing" are less intense than those associated with attempts at becoming involved.

Low Expectancy of Success

In experiences by the writer with a group of learning-problem children and adolescents, the following types of comments were frequently heard whenever they were provided opportunities to obtain desired incentives in an unfamiliar activity: "Oh, no! I can't do that." "I'd never earn that even if I did OK." "Oh, you're kidding me—I couldn't do good enough to get that." Such terms as "low, generalized expectancy of success,"* "failure avoiders,"* and "negative reaction tendency"* have been used to describe such behavioral characteristics. These writers generally agree that the avoidance behavior has resulted from a history of excessive failure or nonreinforcement in a wide range of settings. By avoiding situations and by demonstrating "low-effort behavior" when confronted with situations which present the possibility of receiving desired incentives only for appropriate responses, success is highly improbable. Consequently, the possibility of developing new appropriate behaviors is quite low.

Gardner 1966

Cromwell 1963; Zigler 1966

Excessive Heightened Vigilance

When threat of occurrence of aversive events is present (real or imagined), but there is no specific warning signal, the child may spend considerable effort and time in engaging in excessive avoidance behavior. He is in a state of vigilance which further interferes with the occurrence of more adaptive behaviors. Sidman* has emphasized that such avoidance behavior becomes highly persistent and resistant to extinction, especially if such behavior previously had successfully resulted in the avoidance of strong aversive events. This unusual persistence of responses which are successful in reducing or avoiding intense negative emotionality is a central factor in a range of defensive or "neurotic" behavior patterns seen in the "emotionally disturbed" student. As noted earlier, intense negative emotionality does not extinguish rapidly even when avoidance behavior is not permitted. When the child acquires anticipatory avoidance behaviors which prevent intense levels of negative emotionality from being aroused, the emotional responses and the avoidance behaviors both become extremely persistent.

Sidman 1955

REFERENCES

Ayllon, T., Layman, D., and Kandel, H. A behavioral-educational alternative to drug control of hyperactive children. *Journal of Applied Behavior Analysis*, 1975, 8, 137–146.

Bijou, S. W. A functional analysis of retarded development. In N. R. Ellis (Ed.) *International Review of Research in Mental Retardation.* (Vol. 1.) New York: Academic, 1966, Pp. 1–20.

Bijou, S. W. What psychology has to offer education—now. *Journal of Applied Behavior Analysis*, 1970, 3, 65–71.

Bryan, T. An observational analysis of classroom behaviors of children with learning disabilities. *Journal of Learning Disabilities*, 1974, 7, 26–34.

Butterfield, E. C., and Belmont, J. M. The role of verbal processes in short-term memory. In R. L. Schiefelbusch (Ed.) *Language Research with the Mentally Retarded.* Baltimore: University Park Press, 1972. Pp. 231–248.

Cruiskshank, W. W. (Ed.) *Psychology of Exceptional Children and Youth.* (3rd Ed.) Englewood Cliffs, N. J.: Prentice-Hall, 1971.

Cromwell, R. L. A social learning approach to mental retardation. In N. R. Ellis (Ed.) *Handbook of Mental Deficiency.* New York: McGraw-Hill, 1963. Pp. 41–91.

Eisenson, J. Speech defects: Nature, causes, and psychological concomitants. In W. M. Cruickshank (Ed.) *Psychology of Exceptional Children and Youth.* (3rd Ed.) Englewood Cliffs, N. J.: Prentice-Hall, 1971. Pp. 175–210.

Ferster, C. B. Reinforcement and punishment in the control of human behavior by social agencies. *Psychiatric Research Reports*, 1958, 101–118.

Ferster, C. B. Positive reinforcement and behavioral deficits of autistic children. *Child Development*, 1961, 32, 437–456.

Gardner, W. I. Effects of failure on intellectually retarded and normal boys. *American Journal of Mental Deficiency*, 1966, 70, 899–902.

Gardner, W. I. *Behavior Modification in Mental Retardation.* Chicago: Aldine-Atherton, 1971.

Gottlieb, J., and Davis, J. E. Social acceptance of EMR children during overt behavioral interactions.

American Journal of Mental Deficiency, 1973, 78, 141–143.

Hallahan, D. P., and Cruickshank, W. M. *Psychoeducational Foundations of Learning Disabilities.* Englewood Cliffs, N. J.: Prentice-Hall, 1973.

Heber, R., Garber, H., Harrington, S., Hoffman, C., and Falender, C. *Rehabilitation of Families at Risk for Mental Retardation.* Madison, Wisc.: Rehabilitation Research and Training Center in Mental Retardation Progress Report, 1972.

Hewett, F. M. and Forness, S. R. *Education of Exceptional Learners.* Boston: Allyn and Bacon, 1974.

Johnson, D. J., and Myklebust, H. R. *Learning Disabilities: Educational Principles and Practices.* New York: Grune and Stratton, 1967.

Kagan, J. Developmental studies in reflection and analysis. In A. Kidd and J. Rivoire (Eds.) *Perceptual Development in Children.* New York: International Universities Press, 1966.

Keogh, B. K. Hyperactivity and learning disorders: Review and speculation. *Exceptional Children*, 1971, 38, 101–109.

Koegel, R. L., and Schreibman, L. The role of stimulus variables in teaching autistic children. In O. I. Lovaas and B. D. Bucher (Eds.) *Perspectives in Behavior Modification with Deviant Children.* Englewood Cliffs, N. J.: Prentice-Hall, 1974. Pp. 537–546.

Koppitz, E. M. *Children with Learning Disabilities: A Five-Year* Follow-up Study. New York: Grune and Stratton, 1971.

Lovaas, O. I., and Koegel, R. L. Behavior therapy with autistic children. In C. E. Thoresen (Ed.) *Behavior Modification in Education.* Chicago: University of Chicago Press, 1972. Pp. 230–258.

Lovaas, O. I., and Schreibman, L. Stimulus overselectivity of autistic children in a two-stimulus situation. *Behavior Research and Therapy*, 1971, 9, 305–310.

Lovaas, O. I., Schreibman, L., Koegel, R., and Rehm, R. Selective responding by autistic children to multiple sensory input. *Journal of Abnormal Psychology*, 1971, 77, 211–222.

Lundin, R. W. *Personality: A Behavioral Analysis.* New York: Macmillan, 1969.

MacMillan, D. L., and Forness, S. R. Behavior modification: Limitations and liabilities. *Exceptional Children,* 1970, 37, 291–297.

Maher, B. A. *Principles of Psychopathology: An Experimental Approach.* New York: McGraw-Hill, 1966.

Martin, B. *Anxiety and Neurotic Disorders.* New York: John Wiley, 1971.

O'Leary, K. D., and Wilson, G. T. *Behavior Therapy: Applications and Outcome.* Englewood Cliffs, N. J.: Prentice-Hall, 1975.

Quay, H. C. Patterns of aggression, withdrawal, and immaturity. In H. C. Quay and J. S. Werry (Eds.) *Psychopathological Disorders of Childhood.* New York: John Wiley, 1972. Pp. 1–29.

Quay, H. C., and Werry, J. S. (Eds.) *Psychopathological Disorders of Childhood.* New York: Wiley, 1972.

Ross, A. O. *Psychological Aspects of Learning Disabilities and Reading Disorders.* New York: McGraw-Hill, 1976.

Ross, A. O. *Psychological Disorders of Children.* New York: McGraw-Hill, 1974.

Schreibman, L. Effects of within-stimulus and extra-stimulus prompting on discrimination learning in autistic children. *Journal of Applied Behavior Analysis,* 1975, 8, 91–112.

Senf, G. M. An information-integration theory and its application to normal reading acquisition and reading disability. In N. D. Bryant and C. E. Kass (Eds.) *Leadership Training Institute in Learning Disabilities: Final Report.* (Vol. 2.) Tucson, Ariz.: University of Arizona, 1972. Pp. 305–391.

Sidman, M. On the persistence of avoidance behavior. *Journal of Abnormal and Social Psychology,* 1955, 50, 217–220.

Staats, A. W. *Child Learning, Intelligence, and Personality.* New York: Harper, 1971.

Staats, A. W. *Social Behaviorism.* Homewood, Ill.: Dorsey, 1975.

Werry, J. S., and Sprague, R. L. Hyperactivity. In C. G. Costello (Ed.) *Symptoms of Psychopathology: A Handbook.* New York: John Wiley, 1970. Pp. 397–417.

Zeaman, D., and House, B. J. The role of attention in retardate discrimination learning. In N. R. Ellis (Ed.) *Handbook of Mental Deficiency.* New York: McGraw-Hill, 1963. Pp. 159–223.

Zigler, E. Research on personality structure in the retardate. In N. R. Ellis (Ed.) *International Review of Research in Mental Retardation* (Vol. I.) New York: Academic, 1966. Pp. 77–108.

Zigler, E. Developmental versus difference theories of mental retardation and the problem of motivation. *American Journal of Mental Deficiency,* 1969, 73, 536–556.

Zigler, E. The retarded child as a whole person. In D. K. Routh (Ed.) *The Experimental Psychology of Mental Retardation.* Chicago: Aldine, 1973. Pp. 231–322.

PART IV

Behavioral Assessment and Program Development for Children with Exceptional Characteristics

14

Behavioral Assessment

The three chapters of this final section provide a description of the rationale and procedures of the behavioral approach of assessment and detail its relationship to the (1) development of individualized learning programs for individual children and (2) evaluation of the effectiveness of these learning programs in influencing a child's exceptional characteristics and in increasing his competency. Assessment refers to the identification and measurement of a broad range of factors relevant to the most effective alteration of a child's difficulties. Whenever instructive, brief comparisons are made with traditional assessment procedures, the assumptions underlying their use, and the uses and limitations of such traditional assessment data in making various administrative and learning program decisions about children and adolescents with exceptional learning and behavior characteristics.

PURPOSE OF BEHAVIORAL ASSESSMENT

The primary feature of behavioral assessment is to provide data which give direction to devising individual programs for behavioral change. Assessment information is required (1) in delineating the specific and relevant environmental and behavior target areas where change should occur and (2) in providing information about the specific behavior change procedures best suited to insure change for a particular child.* *Goldfried and Pomeranz 1968*
These behavior change programs may be concerned with influencing exceptional deficit or excessive characteristics of any nature—academic, social, emotional, cognitive, attitudinal, interpersonal, language, or motor, as examples.

475

The target areas selected for change efforts may include any combination or all of the following: (1) antecedent situational events, (2) mediational responses and the associated effect which these may have on other internal behaviors, (3) the observable problem behaviors, and (4) the environmental consequences which, if changed, would hold promise of influencing the exceptional deficit or excessive characteristics. Thus, the assessment results may, for example, suggest that a child's physical, instructional, and/or social environments be changed, that internal behavioral skills be strengthened, that performance requirements be reduced, or that the responses of significant others be changed as tactics to reduce a child's excessive anxiety reaction. Or, a systematic desensitization procedure may be used to reduce the negative emotionality reaction to unalterable aspects of the child's natural environment. As a specific example, consider ten-year-old Paul who is highly disruptive in math class. One goal of the general intervention program would be a decrease in his disruptive behavior since it both interferes with the class instructional program and is highly incompatible with Paul's academic, social, and emotional development. The specific targets of Paul's intervention program could be:

1. *The disruptive behavior itself.* The teacher could initiate a procedure of punishing the disruptive behavior through a combined response cost and time-out approach. The disruptive behavior under this new contingency may thus be controlled.
2. *The antecedents which cue the disruptive behavior.* The math class may be quite aversive to Paul due to the rigid performance standards set by an impersonal and demanding teacher and to some obvious deficits in Paul's math skills. The disruptive behavior is assumed to be maintained by negative reinforcement and/or represents frustration reactions to an avoidance-avoidance conflict—if he refuses to attend class he is punished; if he attends class he is punished. It could be reduced or eliminated by a more appropriate match between Paul's academic and motivational characteristics and the performance standards required of him. Success experiences under this new contingency could effectively reduce the aversiveness of the classroom and thus render the disruptive behavior nonfunctional.
3. *Mediational behaviors which cue the disruptive behavior.* The child may spend excessive time in thinking about various fantasies. The overt disruptive behavior may occur when the teacher intrudes upon this pleasant covert activity.
4. *Changes in environmental consequences.* The teacher may choose to ignore the disruptive behavior and differentially reinforce any other acceptable behavior.

Obviously all of the factors are interrelated at one level or another. However, the more crucial targets for change, and the associated behavior change procedures, should evolve as assessment is completed.

This *program focus* of the behavioral assessment approach distinguishes it from the diagnostic emphasis of traditional assessment approaches. The behavioral focus, in fact, views as nonfunctional the traditional distinction between diagnosis first and then treatment or intervention. Assessment from the behavioral focus is undertaken solely as a basis for devising general and specific intervention program elements. Learner and environment characteristics, and not diagnostic categories, are of interest, as these are the events which can be influenced by the educational program. Once behavioral assessment is initiated, it continues until program objectives have been met.

ASSESSMENT PROCEDURES

The procedures used in behavioral assessment are selected to provide the types of information deemed most pertinent to devising effective individualized educational programs for behavior change. The behavioral approach is concerned with "narrow-band" (specific child-related) rather than with "broad-band" (group-related) assessment.* Although it is frequently of value to know how a child compares to other children (interindividual) on some behavioral dimensions, e.g., reading achievement, general cognitive skills, or expressive language skills, the most pertinent assessment concerns are focused on more specific delineation of the child's behavioral characteristics (intra-individual) as this more specific information forms the basis for initiation of an effective individualized educative experience. Two children attending a special education class for the "mentally retarded" may obtain comparable mental ages and intelligence quotients on a norm-referenced intelligence test but have entirely different combinations of more specific characteristics of value to the educator in developing an instructional program. Thus, separate profiles of intra-individual differences would be needed for individualization of educational experiences.

Adelman 1971

Focus on Observable Behaviors

As exceptional learning and behavioral characteristics represent the focus of concern, assessment procedures are selected to provide information about what the child or adolescent "does" in various situations. It attempts to identify relationships or to provide meaningful hunches about possible relationships, between exceptional characteristics on the one hand and those covert and overt environmental conditions on the other hand which serve (1) to impede or to support effective learning and resulting behavior development and (2) to impede or to facilitate the occurrence and maintenance of behavioral skills once acquired. Whenever possible, direct observation is made of the child in situations and conditions in which the exceptional learning and behavior characteristics occur. Observation in situ is assumed to provide more functionally useful information than observation of the child as he responds to test materials or other stimulation in an office or playroom. The concern in behavioral assessment is on *what* the child does, *how* he does it, *where* he does it, and *when* he does it. This differs from the traditional psychodynamic, trait, and psychometric approaches to assessment of academic, ability, and personality characteristics. In these traditional approaches, assessment procedures

Goldfried and Kent 1972; O'Leary 1972

are selected which presumably identify what the individual "has"* or how he or she compares to others in some rank order,* e.g., Susan *has* a psycholinguistic disability or Jeffrey earned a perceptual score which is at the thirteenth percentile of children his own age.

Sample versus Sign Approach to Interpretation of Assessment Data

In making observations of behavior in specific situations, an attempt is made to obtain reliable samples to enhance predictability. The observations made of the manner in which the child behaves in defined situations must also adequately represent the behavior and its strength during periods and across situations in which observations are not made. Except in highly unusual instances, behavior does fluctuate over time periods and situations within a given day and across days. The multihandicapped adolescent may be quite positive in his attitude concerning his studies on most occasions but has bad days in which he is most negativistic. As a result, repeated observations (samples) should be made over time and across situations to insure representativeness. Confidence can thus be placed in the assumption that the obtained samples do constitute a subset of the actual behaviors of interest.

The traditional approach to assessment, in contrast, views test behaviors as *signs* or indirect manifestations of some underlying personality construct, trait, ability, or intellect. The behaviors obtained during assessment, depending upon the theoretical orientation, are then translated into reflections of motives, defenses, psychological functions, traits, aptitudes, psycholinguistic abilities, or the like. Intelligence tests such as the Stanford-Binet "in providing an I.Q. number, leaves unanalyzed what the child does or does not have. Such a test, therefore, can provide little in the

Staats 1975

way of directives for treatment" (p. 428).*

Kirk et al. 1968
Frostig et al. 1964

Many psychometric tests, including the newer diagnostic ones such as the Illinois Test of Psycholinguistic Abilities (ITPA)* and the Frostig Developmental Test of Visual Perception (DTVP)* are *norm-referenced*. A child's score on such tests is compared to some standard or group norm and provides some indication of where he stands in respect to some hypothetical average.*

Glaser 1963

For children with exceptional characteristics, these tests are administered to determine the degree of deviancy, handicap, or disability.

As noted by Drew et al.,* "Such information, viewed singularly, tells little   *Drew et al., 1972*
concerning the actual skills a student possesses or the operations he can
actually perform but, instead, focuses on relative abilities" (p. 3).

Product versus Process Program Focus

In fact, on norm-referenced tests the actual performances of a child
are frequently of minimal interest. Rather, as suggested, these are viewed as
signs of internal central features, e.g., intellect, ability, aptitude, trait. In
some instances, individual programs are designed on the basis of a profile
analysis of some test performance. For example, the ITPA* and the Frostig   *Kirk and Kirk 1971*
DTVP* are used to devise programs *designed to influence the presumed*   *Frostig and Horne 1964*
internal psycholinguistic and perceptual abilities or disabilities which the
child's test performance represents. Thus, programs based on traditional
"sign" assessment procedures are frequently used in an attempt to
influence internal *processes* instead of focusing on influencing what the
child does, i.e., the product. As an example, Bateman* suggests: "A child   *Bateman 1967*
who has been unable to learn might be found to score very poorly on
measure of auditory closure or visual memory. The auditory closure or
visual memory deficit would be seen as a correlated disability, and initial
remedial efforts would be directed toward the disability" (p. 216).

This program focus thus is in contrast to the behavioral assessment
and program approach of focusing on what the child actually does do in
various stimulus environments and of providing program experiences to
directly increase his competency in significant behavioral areas. Cohen*   *Cohen 1969*
and Lovitt,* as examples, emphasize that if children experience reading   *Lovitt 1975*
difficulties, the assessment procedure and the resulting educational program should focus on letters and words and not on presumed laterality,
dominance, and spatial orientation process difficulties.

Mann,* in reflecting his concern over the appearance of diagnostic   *Mann 1971*
"ability" tests and their use in devising programs to train the internal
abilities, noted:

> A *volte-face*, however, is past due in the education of the handicapped. This
> can be accomplished by focusing our attention upon educational progress
> rather than "organismic processes" (*sic* abilities) and by systematically train-
> ing those hierarchies of skills that children need to acquire in order to reach
> educationally *relevant* goals with appropriate modifications of the instruc-
> tional situations they find themselves in. Let us free ourselves from the
> specious belief that tests directly measure organismic processes, and avoid
> the dangers of developing prematurely narrowed programs committed to the
> training of reifications. [p. 12]

And later: "But if we consider ability assessment and training programs
conceptually valid, then we are on the trail of the snark, and a snark, as
everyone knows, is a boojum" (p. 12).

Possible Usefulness of Norm-referenced Information

Hammill 1971; Blooms et al. 1971; Drew et al. 1972

It is not being suggested that behavioral assessment should disregard norm-referenced information. Hammill,* Blooms et al.,* and Drew et al.* all plead for total assessment which provides both intra- and interindividual information. It may be important as an initial step in more specific individualized behavioral assessment to know if a child does not have the basic cognitive behavior repertoires, as measured by norm-referenced intelligence tests, which are assumed to be present by and are prerequisites for the teaching environment in which a child may be placed. If a child is failing his academic subjects, it is important to know if the academic tasks required are beyond the child's present skills of acquisition and retention. Assuming reliable evaluation, it may thus be noted that there is a mismatch between general task requirements of the instructional program placement and the child's present cognitive skills. As there is a reasonably high predictive relationship between intelligence test scores and academic achievement, it would be safe to predict that in such a case the child would continue to fail unless a more individualized instructional program was provided. An administrative decision may be made that the child remain in his present class setting or that he be placed in another instructional program environment which represents a closer match with his cognitive skills. *In either case* more specific assessment would be needed to design a specific instructional program for the child. This example provides illustration of the possible use of traditional norm-referenced assessment procedures in combination with more individual-directed behavioral data.

Additional Types of Assessment Procedures

In addition to direct observation of the child as he interacts in real-life situations, assessment procedures useful in providing the types of individual data deemed valuable for effective educational program development and implementation would include the following.

Self-Reports.   A valuable source of information about a child and the possible factors involved in his behavior is the child himself. An open interview relative to the problem areas and the child's view of these frequently provide pertinent information. Inquiry about the child's mediational behaviors obviously depends upon self-report.

Exposure to Structured or Contrived Situations.   The child may be requested to role play how he would behave if he were actually in defined situations. In other instances, the child's physical and social environments may be structured in a specific manner to determine how the child would react. The child, in this case, would not be aware of the intent of the contrived situation until after his experiences with it had been observed.

Information from Others.   Significant adults and peers are valuable sources of information about a child. It may not be possible to observe the child directly while he engages in behavior in some aspects of his natural environment. Thus, program procedures may depend to a great extent on information provided by others.

Performance on Criterion-referenced Tasks.   The term *criterion-referenced* was suggested by Glaser* to distinguish between tests which were norm-referenced and those observational procedures designed to measure an individual child's performance relative to some specified behavioral objectives. These may be informal teacher-made tests or may be commercially prepared assessment procedures.

Glaser 1963

In evaluation of academic skills, criterion-referenced measures provide very specific information concerning the performance level on various instructional objectives. Instead of providing, as is done by most achievement tests, norm-referenced information that a child, for example, is at grade level 4.3 in reading skills, criterion-referenced tests provide specific information about what the child actually does, i. e., his word-attack skills, speed of reading, use of context cues, or the types of errors made such as substitutions, reversals, or omissions. As noted by Gorth and Hambleton,* Proger and Mann,* and Westerman,* criterion-referenced measures are valuable in educational programming for children with exceptional characteristics in answering the following specific questions about objectively defined instructional (behavioral) objectives: (1) Does the child already know what is to be taught? (2) Has he learned what has been taught? (3) Has he remembered what has been taught?

Gorth and Hambleton 1972; Proger and Mann 1973; Westerman 1971

Thus, criterion-referenced measures, developed by the teacher and based on the content to be taught a specific child or group, indicate (1) what the child can do and those skills which need to be taught and (2) the progress that the child makes in relation to the instructional goal criteria. Answers to each of the questions provide direction to structuring, or restructuring, the specific educational experiences provided the child. As Drew et al.* noted:

Drew et al. 1972

> Because of the nature of criterion-referenced evaluation . . . the instructional progress may be easily monitored. Operational criteria are specified and serve as instructional objectives. As the student progresses to the point where performance of these criterion behaviors becomes possible, the educational plan may be modified and the procedures and content recycled to stay in phase with student growth. [p. 4]

In addition to using criterion-referenced measures to evaluate specific academic and related skills, the child's present behaviors in relation to a variety of other behavioral criteria may be assessed. Although the topic of developing criterion behavioral objectives is discussed in Chapter 15, it should prove instructive to illustrate the manner in which such objectives are used to assess a child's present behavior. One of the objectives which Ms. Chen has for children enrolled in her early education class is that each will become independent in fulfilling naptime requirements. She developed the following behavioral criteria: *Following lunch and when requested by teacher to do so, the child will follow in an independent manner naptime routine from start to finish.*

The components of the naptime routine and the definition of "independent manner" are as follows:

_____ 1. When naptime is announced the child without delay will obtain mat and spread it on the floor in a designated place on every occasion.

_____ 2. The child will lie on mat without reminder from teacher.

_____ 3. The child will remain in position on mat without disturbance throughout the nap period.

_____ 4. At completion of nap period, the child will fold mat without assistance and return it to storage shelf.

_____ 5. After placing mat neatly in correct location, the child will move to the worktable and sit in the chair without reminder from teacher.

The child would be evaluated on each of the behavioral components. By observing the child in the classroom situation during naptime, the educator can determine which of the specific criterion behaviors the child has met and which ones are not demonstrated satisfactorily. This assessment data on the unmet behavioral components can form the basis for a behavior change program.

STEPS IN PROGRAM DEVELOPMENT AND EVALUATION

A brief account is provided below of the step-by-step process of devising, implementing, and evaluating programs of behavior change, with an emphasis on the role assumed by behavioral assessment. Following this description, detailed consideration of some of the steps in the process will be provided.

Initial Impression That Problem Exists

The initial step in devising a program for influencing a child's learning and behavioral characteristics is that of finding that a problem exists. In taking this step the educator recognizes that the child does not learn or behave as desired or expected in some area or areas.[1] At this initial stage, impressions about what the child does, as well as what is expected, are usually subjective and rather nonspecific. "He seems to be uninterested in his studies." "He is nonattentive and hyperactive most of the time when I am around." "He seems aloof and unhappy around his peers." "He is just not keeping up with the class in any of his studies."

The problem areas may reflect learning and behavior deficits, excessive behavior patterns, or a combination of these exceptional areas. Any of the areas reflected in the behavioral classification system described in Chapter 5 may be of concern. Deficit problem areas usually represent concern with how best to teach new behaviors—oral and written spelling of new words, public speaking skills to an adolescent—or how these can be improved, strengthened, or maintained. A focus on excessive behavior characteristics will reflect concern about some *disruptive* behavior: "He gets too emotional when he fails." "He's constantly alienating his friends with his complaining."

Setting General Program Objectives

The next step, that of enumerating general program objectives, emphasizes the theme of behavioral assessment, that of devising individualized programs of behavior change. As an example, ten-year-old Jill is failing math and language arts, quarrels with her peers frequently, and is disruptive to the class by her frequent demands on the teacher. Initially, the educator may set the following general program objectives: "I would be satisfied if she would attain at least minimal pass in academics, get along with her peers, and relate to me in a courteous manner." These are all stated in positive terms and serve to direct the teacher and the behavioral assessment toward identifying program procedures which might be effective in influencing the development of these positive behavior characteristics. Such an early focus on *positive program objectives* also directs the behavioral assessment away from searching for "emotional disturbance," "perceptual disabilities," or other internal pathology, such as "repressed hostility" or "poor ego strength," as explanation for the exceptional learning and/or behavior characteristics.

Objective Definitions of Exceptional Characteristics

After gaining a general impression that problems exist and stating some general positive program objectives, the next step is to define what the child or adolescent *does do* in situations which expect or require a level

---

1. The child or adolescent himself may recognize that a problem exists. Ideally, the steps involved in self-assessment and development of programs of behavior change would follow the same sequence.

or type of behavior—acquisition, maintenance, or reliable discriminated occurrence—which is not demonstrated. Thus, the general impressions are translated into defined and more specific *does do* behaviors which are observed under specific conditions. These conditions may be of an instructional nature—for example, Sue, an eight-year-old attending remedial reading class, recognizes only five of the thirty words used in the basic reader—or may represent nonacademic requirements of a general or specific nature—for instance, Tony, a fourteen-year-old hard-of-hearing adolescent, refuses to attend dramatics class.

The behaviors of the child are described in clear terms which will permit objective measurements of these behaviors: "Kathryn, attending a special education resource room for the 'mentally retarded,' attempts oral spelling but seldom gets a word correct." "Theo was in four fights this week." Following this, a specific description is made of what the child or adolescent is *expected to do* and the *basis for the expectation*. The descriptions should also be of a nature that permits objective measurement. As described earlier in Chapter 5, *the discrepancy between what is expected and what the child does do defines the exceptional characteristics*. It is obvious that the nature and magnitude of exceptional learning and behavior characteristics are quite related to the relative nature of the behavioral expectations. One teacher may expect attentive, compliant, and polite students while another instructor may encourage independent, assertive, and questioning children. Thus, the same general behaviors occurring in these different environments may be viewed as exceptional in one and as relatively typical in another. These objective descriptions of *should do* and *does do* behaviors serve as a basis for assessment planning.

Developing Assessment Questions

The next step is planning for objective measurement of the *does do* behaviors and of developing general impressions about factors which may contribute to the exceptional behavior characteristics. What are possible factors contributing to the exceptional learning and behavior characteristics? In illustration, an adolescent may be experiencing difficulty in learning the subject matter in most of his academic courses. Hypotheses may be developed regarding restrictions in general cognitive skills, poor sound-blending skills, absence of prerequisite knowledge required in the academic courses, difficulties in remembering visually presented stimuli, high-rate competing emotionality, specific motivational difficulties, and specific sensory discrimination difficulties. For another child who is excessively "unhappy," hunches may be developed relative to poor social skills, poor self-concept behaviors, insufficient success experiences, and excessive preoccupation with behavioral standards that are unrealistic.

These impressions appear when initial information is obtained in the process of defining the exceptional behavior characteristics as these occur in various situations comprising the child's experiences. As behavior is a function of a unique child as he interacts with his unique environ-ments, *assessment of both the child and his environment or life situation is needed.* That is, what does the child do under specific stimulus condi-tions? Lovitt* has emphasized the value of assessment of rather discrete *Lovitt 1967* aspects of the environment of children with exceptional learning and behavior characteristics. (The reader will recall, as an example, the stimulus preference peculiarities of various children described in earlier chapters.) Again, impressions of what might be producing or contributing to exceptional characteristics are translated into assessment questions.

Selecting Appropriate Assessment Procedures

Assessment procedures are next selected which provide informa-tion pertinent to these assessment questions. In illustration, if a child is alienating his friends, those assessment procedures would be selected which would provide information on specifically how the child is behav-ing toward his friends, the environmental correlates of this behavior, and the immediate consequences of this behavior—the *conditions, behaviors,* and *consequences.* If the child is failing his spelling or arithmetic course, standardized and informal procedures would be used which would show the specific spelling or arithmetic skills he does have—norm- and/or criterion-referenced procedures—and how he does behave when exposed to specific spelling or arithmetic tasks. Assessment procedures focus on both his specific spelling or arithmetic responses and on other behaviors which either facilitate or detract from his learning and performance of academic skills. Ideally, the assessment would include observation of the child during the instructional program in the classroom. This provides opportunity to observe what the teacher does as he or she relates to the child and what other types of behaviors are present, including emotional and broader attitudinal ones, which may interfere with effective learning, retention, and performance of spelling or arithmetic skills.

As exceptional characteristics are aspects of, and thus interact with, other competency components as well as exceptional components of the child's total repertoires, assessment questions and procedures are de-veloped in the following additional areas.

The Child's Related Characteristics.   Related behavior characteris-tics are assessed which may (1) contribute directly or indirectly to the exceptional characteristics or (2) be used as supportive behavioral re-sources in an intervention program. As examples, if the child is experienc-ing learning difficulties, assessment of his cognitive skills may prove useful as an initial step in understanding the failure; it may be found that the child does not have the general prerequisite repertoires needed either to acquire the academic skills nor to keep pace with the rate at which the instructional program is presented. Or the child may not have the pre-requisite attending skills needed for effective acquisition of visual learning tasks. It would also be valuable to evaluate the nature of the child's self-management skills, either to use as resources or, if these are weak in relation to the requirements of his environment, to identify as targets for intervention programming. What other things does the child do well which may be used as a basis for developing more appropriate behaviors in his problem areas? To what extent can the child or adolescent become involved in his own program of behavior change? Will knowledge of the program objectives and the reinforcement contingencies influence his self-cueing and self-reinforcing behaviors? How much verbal control does the child have over other classes of his behavior? Is there a reliable relationship between what the adolescent will verbally agree to do and what he actually will accomplish under appropriate incentive conditions?

Finally, positive behavioral characteristics which may be useful in an intervention program should be noted. A child with reading difficulties may nevertheless have basic requisite skills for learning to read, that is, auditory discrimination and memory, visual discrimination and memory, vocabulary, and comprehension of materials heard.

The Child's Reinforcement Hierarchy.   As emphasized throughout the book, in most instances of exceptional characteristics, there is a mismatch between the child's reinforcement characteristics and those required in his environments. Thus, basic to any behavioral intervention procedure is information about the types of events that are reinforcing, the satiation level of these, and the schedules of reinforcement which are effective. As emphasized, many performance deficits reflect motivational deficits, not capacity deficits; a child may have response capability *Wallace 1966, 1967* (defined by Wallace* as the child's behavioral repertoire or potential) but does not perform in a given way as a result of inappropriate incentive conditions available to the child in his current environments.

As emphasized, an analysis of the child and his environments will provide both a range of potential reinforcing events and a tentative hierarchy of these events on the basis of relative strength. Specificity is needed in the case of children with exceptional characteristics. It would be useful, for instance, to identify the types of potential social reinforcement—praise, attention, affection, approval, control of others—as well as the types of influential social agents—peers, male authority figures, females. An adolescent may be influenced by social reinforcement of attention and approval, but only if provided by peers. The same consequences may have neutral or even negative effect if provided by adult authority figures.

The Frequency, Intensity, and Sources of Aversive Aspects of the Child's Experiences.   As most severe patterns of exceptional behavior either result from or produce aversive experiences, it is essential that the source, frequency, and intensity of these experiences be assessed. Whenever a child fails excessively, a variety of defensive or avoidance behaviors develop as attempts to reduce or remove sources of aversiveness. Conflict situations produce aversiveness which further intensifies the child's adaptation efforts. Thus, not only must assessment be made of the obvious punishing consequences of specific behaviors, but also attention should focus on identifying the nature and intensities of the child's conflict experiences. As noted earlier, reduction in the intensity of these antecedent events may significantly reduce the occurrence of exceptional avoidance behaviors.

The Availability of Intervention Program Resources in the Child's Naturalistic Environment.   How available and adequate are people in the child's life—parents, teachers, peers, counselors—who may be used in a program of behavior change?

Developing General and Specific Program Implications

Consistent with the diagnostic-prescriptive feature of behavioral assessment, each assessment question and assessment procedure has associated general and specific program implications. As an example, consider eleven-year-old Yvonne who is being considered for placement in a "learning disabilities" program due to chronic insufficient progress in her academic progam. The following assessment questions, assessment procedures, and program implications may be generated:

Assessment Questions	*Assessment Procedures*	*Possible Program Implications*
Are general cognitive skills commensurate with the level and rate of class instruction?	Norm-referenced intelligence tests (e.g., Stanford-Binet Intelligence Scale; Wechsler Intelligence Scale for Children)	Placement in more appropriate group instructional program
Are specific sensory, perceptual, and cognitive skills commensurate with the type, level, and rate of class instruction?	Norm-referenced and criterion-referenced tests (e.g., Illinois Test of Psycholinguistic Abilities; Wepman Auditory Discrimination Test)	Match instructional method, including type, level, and rate, to specific strengths and weaknesses of student
Are specific prerequisite academic skills present?	Norm-referenced and criterion-referenced tests (e.g., Metropolitan Achievement Tests; Gates-Russell Spelling Diagnostic Test)	Match specific instructional program to skill level of student
Is there an appropriate match between the motivational characteristics of the child and the incentive conditions of the instructional program?	Motivational analysis of student and of instructional program	Design of appropriate incentive system for the specific performance requirements
Are disruptive competing behaviors present?	Direct observation of student in instructional program	Specific program for reducing competing behaviors

If no logical program implications are directly associated with specific evaluation questions, these should be discarded. For example, the internal deviancy model may raise the differential evaluation question: "Is the child learning disabled or emotionally disturbed?" The behavioral approach rejects this type of assessment question because there are no associated functional program implications. Behavior change programs are not designed to deal with diagnostic categories but rather with learner characteristics.

McIntosh and Dunn
1973

McIntosh and Dunn* noted that no matter which differential diagnostic label is attached to a child, "the educational intervention will probably be to detect specific troublesome behaviors and remediate them. Etiologies and categories have little influence on this process" (p. 553). Examples of these specific troublesome behaviors would include: "spends 50 percent of his time pacing the floor," "initiates social interactions on the avarage of two times daily in a group of peers who initiate peer interaction on an average of twenty-five times daily," "has only 10 percent of the prerequisite skills required for successful learning of the language arts module," "remembers only 15 percent of the factual information included in materials read."

Impressions Gained of Severity of Exceptional Behavior Characteristics

Some impression should be gained of the severity of the exceptional characteristics. What are the short- and long-term consequences of the characteristics if these were to remain unchanged? Will the child be retained in second grade, dismissed from school, be rejected by his peer group, develop more intense patterns of withdrawal?

Impressions about the severity of specific exceptional characteristics, if continued in present forms and strengths or in less desired form or strength, provide the basis for deciding upon the priorities of assessment and of related behavior change programs. As it is not possible in most instances to deal with all deficit and excessive behaviors patterns, which ones should be given initial consideration?

Initiation of Assessment

The more formal aspects of assessment are initiated at this point. In observing the exceptional characteristics as these occur under real-life conditions, the behavioral assessment may represent a *static or clinical behavior analysis** or a *functional behavior analysis*. In the former,

Ferster 1967; Gardner
1971

hunches concerning factors which may contribute to the exceptional characteristics are developed during the observation of what the child does and how he is responded to in defined settings, i.e., standardized, contrived, or naturalistic. In a functional analysis, these hunches serve as a basis for initiating changes in suspected contributing events in some systematic manner. Observation is made of the target behaviors to determine if these are influenced if antecedent or consequent events are changed. If behavior systematically changes when external or internal events are changed, a functional relationship is suggested. That is, the behavior can be said to be a function of the identified events. More specific procedures for establishing functionality and the degree of confidence that can be placed in such observed covariation are discussed in the following chapter.

As assessment is undertaken, there is frequently need for modification of the initial assessment plan. As noted in earlier chapters, assessment activities not unusually result in positive changes in the problem behaviors. This has been reported by a number of different people.* Such improvement in problem characteristics during assessment appears to be related to changes in the manner in which the educator or others interact with the child being assessed. The adult may begin to focus more on the interpersonal and/or instructional experiences provided and the possible effects of these on the child. This new awareness may in turn result in changes in the manner in which the child is treated. Also, as noted in Chapter 12, a child or adolescent who becomes involved in assessing his own behavior, e.g., in self-recording specific responses, may demonstrate spontaneous change in problem behaviors. The self-awareness creates new internal or mediational conditions which may serve to cue competing behaviors or to inhibit the problem characteristics.

For example, Ackerman 1972; Patterson 1971; Tharp and Wetzel, 1969

Formulation of Intervention Program

After assessment data are obtained, plans for changing the child's experiences are formulated. The intervention program consists of (1) *objectively defined behavioral objectives* and (2) *educative procedures designed to facilitate attainment of the program goals.* As suggested earlier, the intervention plans may focus primarily on (1) changing the child's covert and overt repertoires in order to produce more positive feedback from aspects of his social environments, and (2) changing the child's physical and social environments (antecedents and consequences) to insure more appropriate behavior development and/or performance. For example, the performance requirements may be reduced to coincide with the child's rate and level of learning facility. This change may result in a dramatic increase in successful experiences, thus reducing the aversiveness which may maintain disruptive behavior. New prerequisite behaviors may be acquired which result in more successful attainment of instructional objectives. Or mediational events, for example, the negative attitude of an adolescent, may be influenced significantly by a more personalized approach by an adult who had been excessively impersonal and demanding.

Possible Effects of Intervention Procedures

Impressions about the effects that behavioral changes would have on related behavior patterns become important both in lending direction to the intervention program and in establishing program priorities. In illustration, assume that disruptive behavior is being maintained by peer social attention. Prior to implementing a procedure for removing the source of reinforcement, it should be determined if the adolescent has other means of obtaining peer acceptance. If he has no other skills of insuring peer attention, reduction or elimination of the disruptive behavior may isolate him from peer interaction.

Additionally, the positive effects of various behavior changes should be considered. For instance, a socially isolated "emotionally disturbed" visually impaired child with deficits in recreational and social skills may, following development of these skills, be accepted into various peer groups from which he may receive a wide array of new reinforcing consequences. Or a "learning-disabled" adolescent may decrease his truancy following acquisition of functional reading skills. He may no longer feel like a "dummy" and may begin to enjoy his classes.

Thus, impressions about the possible effects of remediation of deficit and excessive learning and behavior characteristics will be most valuable in selecting specific behavior change procedures and in assigning intervention priorities. These considerations emphasize the critical and frequently complex interrelationships among the multiple variables involved in the development, implementation, and evaluation of programs and their effectiveness.

Evaluation of Intervention Program

Initiation of the intervention program should coincide with an evaluation procedure which provides quantitative data concerning its effectiveness. The continuing nature of the specific procedures used in the intervention program are determined by the effects which these produce on the exceptional characteristics. Continued criterion-referenced evaluation provides this program information.

The remainder of this chapter will focus on problems and procedures of defining and obtaining measurement of behavior. The discussion will relate primarily to behaviors of a nonacademic nature. Data-based assessment and programming for academic behaviors are discussed in

Chapter 16. Chapter 15 illustrates the translation of assessment data into intervention programs.

DESCRIBING WHAT THE CHILD DOES DO

After recognizing that a problem exists, the next step is to describe what a child actually does in a situation or situations which require a different rate of development, level, or type of behavior. The educator may expect a child to conform to classroom management standards, to attend class regularly, to initiate social interaction with peers, to complete a series of assignments without assistance, to express a positive attitude toward school, or to demonstrate positive self-concept behaviors and feelings of competency. The child or adolescent may be only partially successful and not be able to demonstrate the level of behavior required. The teacher or parent may expect a certain type of behavior—compliance to verbal requests, for example. The child may engage in other types of behaviors such as actively refusing, ignoring, or whining.

Focus on What the Child Does

It is easy to focus on what a child or adolescent *does not do:* "Jim is *not* interested." "He has *not* finished his assignments in weeks!" "He *cannot* pass this math course." However, an intervention program can only be based on what the child *does do* in various specific situations requiring behavior of a level or kind other than those engaged in by the child. Describing an adolescent as "not cooperating with any of his teachers" does not indicate what he does do in those situations requiring cooperation. What does the adolescent actually do in a situation that requires cooperation? Does he state openly that he will not cooperate? Does he provide logical justification for "noncooperative" behavior? What is the frequency and setting of "noncooperative" behavior?

What does the child do when provided a book and requested to read aloud to his classmates? Does he attempt to fulfill the request? Does he miss most of his attempted pronounciations? Does he become embarrassed and actively refuse to read?

Stating that an adolescent does not get along with his peers, does not make satisfactory progress in language arts, does not behave in a courteous manner, and does not have adequate study skills are equally as inadequate as descriptions of the child's behavioral characteristics. What does he do with his peers, what skills does he demonstrate in the language arts program, what does he do in situations that require courtesy, and what are his study skills?

These *does do* behaviors are the ones with which the educator must begin in a program to teach more desirable and complex forms and levels of discriminated behavior.

Behavior Described in Specific Terms

The description of what the child or adolescent does that differs from an expectation of what should be done or accomplished should be presented in specific objective terms. Consider the following:

"Mack has a poor self-concept."
"June is disruptive in class."
"Eugene is always talking."
"She is much too aggressive."
"Randy has limited expressive language skills."
"Barbara is hyperactive."

Each description is too general for development of specific behavior change programs. Words like poor, disruptive, always, too, limited, and aggressive mean different things to different people and represent indirect interpretations of what the child actually does. Two adolescents described as "disruptive" or "shy" may engage in quite different "disruptive" or "shy" behaviors under different conditions. Shirley may be disruptive in classes taught by young teachers but cooperative in classes taught with older male teachers. Kass, by contrast, may be disruptive in every class in an unpredictable fashion. These general descriptions, thus, should be translated into specific behaviors which comprise the general class descriptions. These behavioral descriptions should be sufficiently precise to insure a high degree of agreement among observers who independently assessed how the child behaved.

Behavior Described in Specific Situations

As described previously, the behavioral approach views both prosocial and problematic behavioral characteristics to be a function of a stimulus complex. Behavioral characteristics are not assumed to reflect internal traits, complexes, or abilities which occur independently of internal and external stimulus conditions. Thus, in describing behavioral characteristics, these must be lodged in specific situations. Goldfried and Kent,* Mischel,* and Staats,* for example, emphasize the dependence of behavioral characteristics on specific stimulus conditions. Behavioral variations are highly related to situational variations. To effectively "understand" behavior and to influence its change, descriptions of situations in which behavior occurs become an integral aspect of describing what the

Goldfried and Kent 1972; Mischel 1968; Staats 1975

child does do. As emphasized, internal stimulus conditions are viewed as of significance and should be included whenever some reliable account of their presence can be obtained.

Some behaviors occur only under highly specific situations and others may occur across seemingly different externally defined circumstances. John does not refuse to comply with standards of conduct on all occasions. He is friendly and cooperative with some adults. Susan is more likely to meet academic standards whenever her father is away from home than she is when father is in the home. Hyperactive children with severe academic achievement deficits may be attentive and productive when provided appropriate incentives.* These examples emphasize the need to lodge behaviors in specific situations or conditions in order to provide meaningful descriptions of the behavior. In so doing, those events which influence behavioral occurrence may become apparent.

For example, Ayllon et al. 1975

DESCRIPTION OF WHAT A CHILD SHOULD DO

As exceptional characteristics are defined in terms of discrepancies between what a child does and what is expected, it becomes necessary to describe in comparable specific behavioral-situational terms what the child *should do.* Obviously, the educator has an impression about what the child should learn, the rate of his learning, or how he should behave in various academic, social group, and interpersonal situations. If not, the child would not be viewed as representing a problem. Many of the expected behaviors are based on vaguely defined criterion-referenced concepts. The educator has an expectation that a child should be attentive, cooperative, relate to his peers, be happy, be productive, be self-controlled, and the like. However, in most instances, when pressed to define precisely and quantitatively the criterion reference he uses when describing a child as having difficulties in these behavioral areas, the educator quickly discovers that his impressions are quite qualitative and relative. As described in the following chapter, these vaguely defined criteria of exceptionality must be translated into more specific quantitative descriptions, i. e., objectives, as a basis both for devising specific instructional or intervention programs and for evaluating the effectiveness of educational experiences designed to influence these characteristics.

Many other of the child's expected characteristics are based on norm-referenced concepts. That is, the educator has an impression, for example, of what is expected in general of fifteen-year-old adolescents, fifth-grade students, or children with average or above average cognitive skills. A child is viewed as presenting a problem if he or she deviates significantly from these norm-based expectations. In reference to an age, grade, or aptitude group, the child is viewed as ranking below the average to a certain degree. A twelve-year-old girl may be viewed as demonstrating exceptional characteristics, if, on the norm-referenced test of cognitive skills, she earns a score comparable to that earned by a typical nine-year-old child. More specifically, she may be viewed as exhibiting general cognitive skill deficits because she deviates three years from the "norm" cognitive behaviors of twelve-year-olds. Or another twelve-year-old child may be viewed as exhibiting exceptional characteristics if he does not obtain an average fourth-grade level on a norm-referenced academic achievement test as would be expected of a twelve-year-old child attending sixth grade. He may thus be viewed as exhibiting a behavioral deficit in academic skills because he ranks two grades below that obtained by the typical, or norm-defined, twelve-year-old child attending sixth grade.

Using Norm- and Criterion-referenced Procedures

As emphasized earlier in a discussion of the types of assessment data needed for designing individualized intervention programs, such norm-referenced information must be supplemented with more specific criterion-referenced data. If the problem area is that of reading, it may initially be discovered, with norm-referenced achievement tests, that a child's reading comprehension and reading vocabulary are considerably below both his general cognitive skills and his academic skills in math. It would be necessary to define quite precisely the child's reading and related skills prior to setting realistic behavioral expectations and designing a meaningful individualized intervention program. The child, under more precise assessment, may exhibit deficits in letter sounds, vowels, and sound blending. The behavioral objectives of an instructional program could then become more individualized and detailed wih these more specific data.

Behavioral Objectives Based on Complex of Child Characteristics

The expected learning and behavioral characteristics thus serve to identify the degree of discrepancy between these and what the child does do, and also serve as a starting point in setting general program goals and associated objectively defined *behavioral objectives*. The behavioral objectives set for a particular child may differ from the expectations used in identifying the kind and degree of discrepancy which define the exceptional behavioral characteristics. In illustration, the previously mentioned twelve-year-old girl may earn a "mental age" of nine years on standardized measures of cognitive skills and a beginning grade placement on achievement tests of 4.0. Her expected performance on the basis of her chronological age would be "mental age" twelve and a sixth-grade achievement level. Thus, on the basis of CA expectation, she exhibits exceptional behavior characteristics (deficits) in general cognitive skills and in academic skills. Program goals, however, would not necessarily coincide with the criteria used in defining the expected behaviors. Even though parents may typically expect a twelve-year-old child to perform academically at a sixth-grade level, reliable information that describes the child's general cognitive repertoire as "mental age" nine would influence the setting of more realistic educational program objectives. A sixth-grade academic performance level would not be a realistic program goal at the present time for the child due to the broad deficits in prerequisite cognitive behaviors. Thus, behavioral objectives set as a realistic outcome of an individualized educational program would be based on a variety of behavioral and related data.

OBSERVATION AND MEASUREMENT OF BEHAVIOR

What the child presently does do and/or what he can do can be answered precisely only by observation of him in relevant situations. It is valuable to make a distinction between *does do* and *can do* behaviors, as there is frequently a gap between the learning and behavioral characteristics observed under his typical environmental conditions and those which are in his repertoire but which seldom occur due to environmental limitations.

As noted earlier, a wide variety of procedures of assessment are available for the measurement of a child's learning and behavioral characteristics. These include standardized tests, behavioral checklists and other parental or teacher ratings, developmental and personality inventories, child self-report, and other similar guides to reporting what the child does under specific or general conditions. Many of these are norm-referenced standardized tests and are used to observe a child's behavior under standard testing conditions. A child is shown a series of four pictures and told to "show me the animal." His response is evaluated in terms of a predetermined criterion. The standard educational psychology and testing books* provide ample description of these observational procedures. Hammill and Bartel,* Hallahan and Kauffman,* and Smith* provide detailed description of numerous norm-referenced and criterion-referenced procedures used successfully with children and adolescents with a broad range of learning and behavior difficulties and should be consulted in planning an assessment program for academic and related skills.

For example, Anastasi 1968; Cronback 1970; Thorndike and Hagen 1969

Hammill and Bartel 1975; Hallahan and Kauffman 1976; Smith 1968

The present discussion will focus on direct behavioral observation of a child's behavior as it occurs in natural settings. The concern is with what the child does do in the presence of various types of stimulating conditions. Jones et al.* emphasize the importance of direct naturalistic observation and provide research data which indicate that even parent

Jones et al. 1975

ratings, structured inventories, and child self-report scales do not yield the kind of specific behavioral information necessary for devising individualized intervention programs. To be most valuable, this description thus must denote *what* the child does under specified conditions—what are the provoking antecedents and what are the consequences?—as well as provide an indication of the strength of the behavior. Does he engage in a designated behavior such as temper tantrum, refusal to complete assignment, stuttering, absence from class, difficulty in remembering visually presented instructions, or self-derogatory comments on every possible occasion, on most occasions, or only infrequently under defined conditions? Once begun, how long does a specific behavior continue, e.g., when he "gets his feelings hurt" how long does he isolate himself from social contact? How intense is an episode of crying?

BEHAVIOR STRENGTH

Behavior may vary in terms of (1) *frequency* of occurrence, (2) *magnitude* or intensity, (3) *duration* of occurrence once begun, and (4) *latency* of time which elapses between being stimulated and responding. The specific measure of behavior strength used will depend on the particular type of behavior being observed. Measurement of behavior strength is needed as a means of objectively describing what the child does do prior to and after initiation of an intervention program.

Prior to the initiation of a specific program, some objective measure is needed of the strength of the behavior which the program is designed to influence. This initial measure of behavior strength is known as *baseline* recording and represents the *preprogram status* of the behavior. This is a measure of what the child's exceptional behavior characteristics are under present real-life (or contrived in some instances) conditions before a new set of conditions is initiated in an effort to influence—increase or decrease—its strength. As examples, Evelyn completed only 15 percent (averaged over ten assignments) of the assigned math problems, Timothy spent only ten minutes daily (averaged over a two-week period) in study activities, Catrina engaged in five disruptive behaviors (averaged over an eight-day period) during the language arts class. Such a baseline measure provides an objective account of the behavior and serves to provide a check on the adequacy of the definition of the "exceptional characteristic." If reliable measures can be obtained, the behavior has been defined appropriately. If not, the characteristic must be redefined until reliable measurement can be realized.

Without such baseline information, it is frequently difficult to determine if a specific educational program designed to influence the behavior has in fact been successful. Additionally, measures of initial behavior strength permit comparison of different children or adolescents. An adolescent who has an average of ten disruptive comments during English class has a higher strength of disruptive behavior under "English class" conditions than does one of his peers who engages in such behavior only five times per class. Such comparison data provide an objective basis for the assignment of program priorities within a class or group.

In obtaining measures of behavior strength, it should be emphasized again that focus is on what the child does actually do. Defined behavior with a zero level of occurrence in specific situations does not exist as a program variable. "Zero" behavior does not exist. Thus, stating that a child makes no correct discriminations when presented a criterion-referenced, visual perceptual-motor task provides no basis for developing an intervention program for improving his discrimination of various visual stimuli. Description must be made of the strength of behaviors which he actually demonstrated under the visual tasks stimuli. These form a basis for an educational program. Perfect performance on the task may be set as a long-term behavioral (program) objective. The actual program designed to teach this desired performance, however, must be based on what he does do.

RATE OF BEHAVIOR

Event Recording

The measure of behavior strength most useful with a wide variety of behaviors and which is typically the most easily obtained in natural settings is the *frequency* with which defined behavior occurs in defined settings. How many times does a designated behavior occur within a specified period of time? The frequency measure is illustrated in Figure 14.1. Frequency measures are valuable when dealing with behaviors that are discrete, i.e., those with a clearly definable beginning and end. Behavior frequency is simple to record and is usually sensitive to environmental changes.*

Kazdin 1973; Skinner 1966

Frequency may be translated into a *behavior rate* by expressing the frequency as the average number of times the behavior occurred in a specific period of time. This is necessary if observation periods vary in length or if an average minute, hour, day, or week is desired. In academic programming it is frequently desirable to know the rate of progress, for example, in reading or math. The number of words read, the number of math problems completed, or the number of words written in language arts class all represent examples. The number of responses made within a specified time period can be translated into a response rate. If Susanne completed twenty-five arithmetic problems in a fifty-minute period, her response rate per minute is .5. If Richard wrote 120 words in a ten-minute

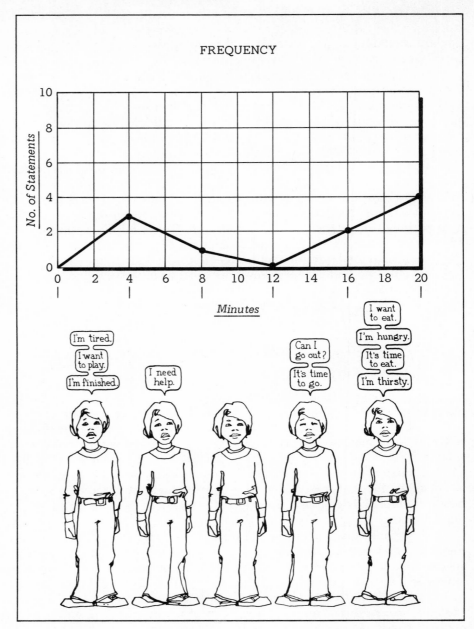

FIGURE 14.1. *Depicting Frequency of Statements Initiated within Four-Minute Periods*

creative writing period, his rate per minute is 12. Academic response rates represent useful data when the effectiveness of various instructional tactics such as student-controlled versus teacher-controlled contingencies is being evaluated.

Jonathan, a fourteen-year-old attending a public school class for the "emotionally disturbed," is frequently physically aggressive toward less assertive peers. To obtain a measure of the aggressive behavior, the number of times Jonathan hits, bites, pinches, pushes, or scratches his peers during the daily three-hour academic program is selected for baseline recording. The baseline data presented in Figure 14.2 indicate that Jonathan engaged in the defined behavior thirty-five times during the five-day observation period.

The total frequency of thirty-five could be divided by the number of observation periods—in this case five daily periods—and thus provide an average daily behavior rate of 7:

Name: _Jonathan Jones_   Observer: _M. Kepper_

Behavior: _hitting, biting, pushing, punching, scratching peers_

Physical/social situation: _Classroom during academic program_

Time unit: ___3 hours daily___

Date	Frequency	Number
10/21	⊬⊬⊬ /	6
10/22	⊬⊬⊬ ///	8
10/23	///	3
10/24	⊬⊬⊬ ⊬⊬⊬ /	11
10/25	⊬⊬⊬ //	7

Total   35

FIGURE 14.2.   *Event Recording of Behavior Frequency*

$$\text{Rate} = \frac{\text{no. of occurrences}}{\text{observation period}} = \frac{35}{5} = 7$$

During the five-day observation period, Jonathan engaged in the defined aggressive behaviors an average of seven times daily. This type of behavior measurement is known as *event recording*. Figure 14.3 provides illustration of daily frequency data translated into daily rates due to unequal observation periods. In this example, Ms. Holstein recorded the number of disruptive comments of six "problem" adolescents during English class group instruction. As the amount of time spent in group instruction varied from day to day, the total frequency was converted into a per-five-minute rate to reflect the unequal observation periods.

Branch and Sulzbacher 1968; Fargo and Behrns 1969

The educator will find various calculation aids useful in rapid translation of frequency data into response rates. Branch and Sulzbacher* and Fargo and Behrns* describe two such easy-to-use devices for obtaining a rapid approximation of response rate. The Rapid Wheel, described by Fargo and Behrns, is a circular slide rule with responses graduated on an outer axis and a frequency dimension in minutes on an inner axis. The wheel is rotated to align the responses on the outer circle and minutes on the inner circle for computation. The rate per minute is read on the outer circle opposite an arrow printed on the inner circle. These writers suggest that the Rapid Wheel is easily used by students to self-record their own response rates.

Continuous versus Time Sampling of Events.   In the example presented above, continuous recording of the occurrence of a defined behavioral event was followed. The total number of aggressive behaviors

Date	Frequency	Total	Data Collection Time		Total Time	Rate per 5 min.
			Start	Stop		
1/14	ＨＨＴ ＨＨＴ ＨＨＴ Ｉ	16	8:30	8:50	20 min.	4
1/15	ＨＨＴ ＨＨＴ ＩＩ	12	9:00	9:15	15 min.	4
1/16	ＨＨＴ Ｉ	6	8:30	9:00	30 min	1
1/17	ＨＨＴ ＨＨＴ ＨＨＴ ＨＨＴ ＩＩＩＩ	24	8:30	9:30	60 min	2
1/18	ＨＨＴ ＨＨＴ ＨＨＴ	15	9:30	9:45	15 min	5

FIGURE 14.3.   *Recording Sheet for Unequal Observation Periods*

which occurred throughout the entire three-hour academic period was recorded. Such continuous recording may not be feasible or necessary in many instances. All that is needed is a sample of behavioral occurrences that satisfactorily represents the total occurrence. The frequency may be high and relatively stable over periods of time. A sample of the behavior frequency may be representative of a more time-consuming continuous recording of each occurrence. In such instances a *time-sampling* procedure would be used.* The initial ten minutes of each thirty-minute period during the three-hour daily program, for example, may be selected for recording. Every occurrence of the defined behavior observed during each ten-minute period is recorded. The frequency data obtained during these smaller time samples are used to represent the overall strength of the defined behavior.

Arrington, 1943

Thus, the daily time period during which observation is made may refer to the entire school day, the lunch period, play period, the initial thirty minutes of each day in class, or any other period during which a behavior of concern may occur. The length of each observation period, as well as the time within the daily schedules during which behavior is measured, would obviously depend upon the type of behavior being observed as well as its general frequency. If the behavior occurred quite frequently and did not appear to occur any more or less frequently across different time periods in the daily schedule or in different situations, measurement of frequency may occur for short periods of time each day.

If, on the other hand, the defined behavior has a rather infrequent and erratic rate of occurrence, continuous recording of each event throughout a designated period may be most appropriate. For example, the child may engage in temper tantrums, crying episodes, refusals to comply, and aggressive behaviors at a bothersome but infrequent rate. Thus, relatively low-rate behaviors are best recorded by continuous event recording as these have a high likelihood of escaping less frequent observation.

Methods of recording events.   In event recording, every occurrence of a certain behavior during a specified time period is tallied. This may be done on a recording sheet as illustrated in Figure 14.2, on a note pad, on masking tape wrapped around the teacher's wrist, on the chalkboard, or by any other mechanical means. Such recordings provide a cumulative frequency within the designated time period. The method of recording would depend upon the behavior being observed and the circumstances of observation.

Some teachers have found a hand or wrist counter useful in recording behavior frequency. Lindsley* has described an inexpensive but reliable golf counter which has been used successfully. This method is especially useful when measurement is taken of behaviors which have a high rate of occurrence. As it is worn on the wrist, it is available when needed without eliminating the use of one hand as would be the case with a

Lindsley 1968

hand counter. Also, such a simple procedure of recording frequency leaves the teacher relatively free to engage in her normal activities, especially if the behavior rate is low.

An alternative to the wrist counter is a hand counter which can be purchased in many styles. A simple grocery counter usually provides up to four digits and can be held easily. Manual counters found in school supply stores usually have a ring for secure holding and vary in the number of *Mattos 1968* digits available. A harmonica-shaped manual counter,* has five separate three-digit display panels so that the observer, using the fingers of one hand, can record up to five behavior categories of a single child or a single behavior category for up to five children. These tend to be cumbersome and difficult to manipulate if one needs the use of both hands for some other activity. Masking tape and pen, paper and pencil, or chalkboard, as well as any of the event-recording methods described above, can be used for recording any behavior for which the teacher wishes a frequency count in a given period of time.

Appropriateness of Rate Measure.   The rate measure of behavior strength is valuable when observing such patterns as aggressive behavior, disruptive behavior, number of words or pages read, number of times a child cries during play period, number of spontaneous verbalizations, number of modules completed, number of mistakes made in a daily twenty-word spelling test, or number of times a child initiates social interaction.

Rate as a Percentage of Total Events.   In some instances it will be meaningful to express frequency data as a *percentage of times* that the defined behavior occurred out of the total number of possible occasions. In obtaining a measure of the strength of cooperativeness in an adolescent who is "quite negativistic to teacher requests," it would be useful to divide the total number of times the adolescent fulfilled the teacher's requests by the total number of requests made. If the teacher presented twenty-five different requests of Samuel during the day and he fulfilled ten of them, his rate of cooperativeness would be forty percent.

Such a percentage rate would be useful in describing behavior strength of the following kinds of behavior: the percentage of homework assignments completed, percentage of total verbal statements reflecting specific content, percentage of total words pronounced correctly, percentage of the total class passing the math test, percentage of items correctly finished, and the percentage of the total number of social interactions which were aggressive in nature.

Rate as a Percentage of Total Time.   A final rate measure of behavior strength refers to the percentage of a given period of time spent in a *Bryan 1974* designated behavior. Bryan* reported that children labeled as "learning disabled" spent less of their total academic study time in attending to a variety of school subjects when compared to the percentage of time spent in attending behavior of other children in the classroom. In a study reported by Briskin and Gardner,* a child attending a preschool program spent 54 percent of her time during structured activity periods in disruptive behaviors. This percentage figure provided a baseline measure as a basis of comparison of changes which coincided with an individualized intervention program designed to decrease her disruptive behaviors.

Briskin and Gardner 1968

Interval Recording

The Briskin and Gardner study mentioned above illustrates other observational procedures. In this study, instead of a frequency recording of every occurrence of various behaviors during a designated time period, the teacher used an interval procedure. Ongoing behaviors such as talking, fighting, sitting, playing, working, attending, or standing are difficult to count (frequency) because each occurrence may vary in duration, i.e., fifteen seconds, five minutes, three minutes. In *interval recording* the total observation session, for example, thirty, sixty, ninety minutes, is divided into a number of short and equal time periods such as ten, fifteen, or sixty seconds. The observer records *only* whether the designated behavior did or did not occur during the shorter interval instead of recording the number of different times a specific behavior may have occurred. The observer may combine an interval with a *time sampling* procedure in which he may, for example, observe only during the last thirty seconds of a designated interval and spend the remaining time in recording or in other activities. The observer only samples the behavior at specific times during a defined time interval and then records its occurrence or nonoccurrence.

In obtaining a measure of the child's disruptive behaviors in the Briskin and Gardner study, an observer recorded the occurrence of such behaviors during the initial five minutes of each of seven activity periods thoughout the day. Within each five-minute sample the observer would glance at the child for three seconds and then record for twelve seconds, look again for three seconds and record. If the behaviors were occurring during the three-second glance period, a plus sign was recorded; if not, a zero was recorded. In this manner, the observer was able to make 140 observations during a single school day. This procedure required only thirty-five minutes of observer time. The strength of the child's disruptive behavior was expressed as a percentage of the total time in which the child was observed to engage in disruptive behavior. Daily observation over six days provided an average rate of behavior strength during the pretreatment or baseline period.

Figure 14.4 depicts another example of the use of interval recording. The observation represents the presence or absence during five-minute

Name: _Alan Keine_									Observer: _Mr Lennie_			

Behavior: _Stereotyped rocking_

Physical/social situation: _Classroom during a 60 min play period._

Time interval: _5 min_

Interval Number

1	2	3	4	5	6	7	8	9	10	11	12	%	Date
+	+	O	+	+	+	+	O	O	+	+	O	66	4/5
+	+	o	O	+	+	+	+	+	+	O	O	66	4/6
O	+	+	+	O	O	+	O	O	+	+	O	50	4/7
+	+	o	+	+	O	+	+	+	+	+	O	75	4/8
+	+	+	O	O	O	O	+	+	O	+	O	50	4/9

+ = behavior did occur   0 = behavior did not occur

FIGURE 14.4.   *Interval Recording of Behavior*

segments of stereotyped behavior—defined as rocking back and forth—of a five-year-old boy. The plus sign designates the occurrence of the behavior during some part of the five-minute interval; the zero indicates no such behavior occurred during the five-minute period.

Zeilberger et al. 1968   Zeilberger et al.* used this procedure of interval recording in obtaining a measure of the strength of aggressive behavior of a child. The occurrence or nonoccurrence of aggressive behavior (defined as hitting, pushing, kicking, throwing, biting, scratching) was recorded in successive twenty-second intervals during a one-hour play period. The behavior strength was expressed as a percentage of total intervals during which aggressive behavior was recorded. During the baseline period, aggressive behavior occurred in 5 percent to 13 percent of the scored intervals. After initiation of a behavior management program, the aggressive behavior occurred only rarely.

An interval recording procedure is useful in that it can be used with almost any behavior, and observations can easily be converted to percentages.*

Bijou et al. 1968

It may be helpful to emphasize again that a time sampling procedure can be used in combination with continuous event recording as well as with an interval recording procedure. The total occurrence of a behavior within designated time samples can be recorded. Or, in interval recording, only the presence or absence of the behavior during designated subunits of time will be recorded.

INTENSITY OF BEHAVIOR

In addition to being concerned about influencing the percentage of times that defined behaviors occur or the rate of behavior within specified periods of time, the teacher may be concerned with the intensity or magnitude characteristics of a behavior pattern. Figure 14.5 illustrates this measure of behavior strength. As depicted, loudness of crying is measured over a sixty-second period. The maximum level of loudness during each segment is used as the measure of behavior strength.

Although more difficult to measure, especially in complex child behavior, the intensity or magnitude components of behavior, including loudness, vigor, or enthusiasm, are of importance at times. The rate of temper tantrum behavior may initially show little change after the teacher begins a specific program for controlling such behavior. However, there may be a steady decrease in the intensity of the temper outbursts. The child may not cry as loudly, thrash about as vigorously, or pound on his legs as rapidly as was characteristic prior to program initiation. A shy child may speak with such low volume that the teacher is unable to understand him when not standing close by. The behavior may be measured in terms of the approximate distance (number of feet) between the child and the teacher for her to understand the child. A program may be designed to shape increasingly louder speech. The effects of the program will be measured by an increase in distance between the child and teacher for understandable verbal communication. These and similar magnitude components of a complex behavior pattern should be defined and measured in one way or another in order to obtain adequate measures of behavior strength and change.

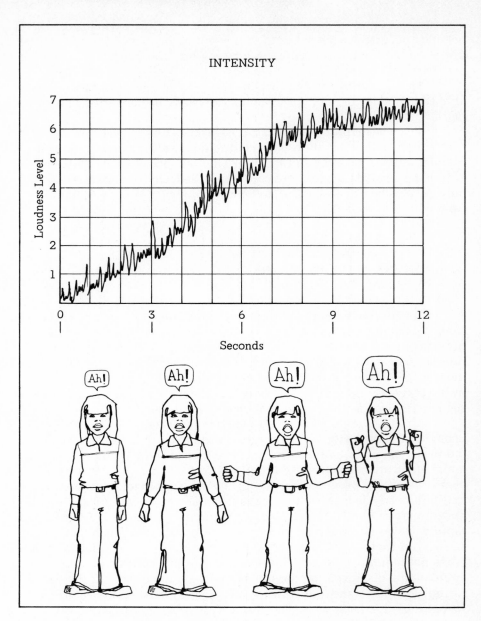

Figure 14.5.   Depicting an Intensity Measure of Behavior Strength

DURATION OF BEHAVIOR

Duration of behavior is another measure of strength useful in some instances. The use of a duration measure requires that (1) an observer can discern the beginning and end of a behavior, (2) continuous observation can be made, and (3) a timing device such as a stop watch is available. To be meaningful as a measure of behavior strength, precise definition of the characteristics of the behavior must be made. The length of time a child engages in crying behavior once begun, as illustrated in Figure 14.6, provides a measure of the strength of that behavior.

This measure of behavior strength was used in an experience reported by Williams* with a preschool child who would scream and fuss if   *Williams 1959* his parents left his room at night before he went to sleep. After the parents decided to attempt to eliminate the crying behavior, the child was place in bed and left. Recording of the duration of crying was initiated when the behavior management program was begun. Crying occurred for forty-five minutes the first time. On subsequent nights the length of time the child spent in crying gradually decreased—the strength declined. By the tenth

DURATION

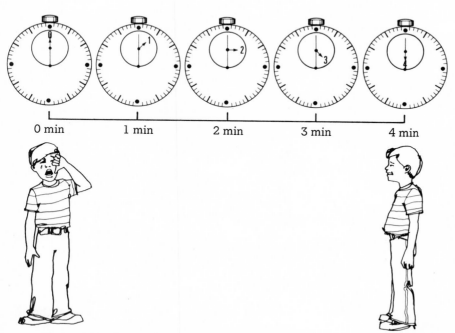

| 0 min | 1 min | 2 min | 3 min | 4 min |

Figure 14.6   *Depicting a Duration Measure of Behavior Strength*

occasion the crying behavior no longer occurred. Crying had not been eliminated completely; rather, the behavior showed no strength under the specific condition of being placed in bed and left alone. The child cried under other conditions at other times. This illustrates the concept presented in a previous chapter that behavior is never completely eliminated. It may just no longer occur in certain situations as new experiences are gained.

Whitman et al. 1970

Phillips 1968

As additional examples of the use of a duration measure of behavior strength, Whitman et al.* timed the number of minutes that withdrawn children spent in social interaction prior to, during, and following a program designed to increase social interaction behaviors. Phillips* used a duration measure to evaluate the effectiveness of a program designed to increase punctuality in predelinquent boys. Behavior strength was defined as the number of minutes early or late in returning home from school, going to bed, and returning home from errands before and after application of a positive reinforcement contingency.

Duration recording may be useful for such concerns as the amount of time a child spends out of seat on each occasion of leaving the chair, time spent in isolated activities following each occasion of becoming upset, amount of time sitting quietly after reprimand prior to another outburst, amount of time spent in cooperative endeavors, and amount of time spent in studying. Such recording would produce rate data by adding the duration time of each observation period and dividing that sum by the number of observation periods. "During the observation period he got out of his chair on fifteen different occasions. He remained out of his chair on an average of five minutes." "He remained in isolated activity following the thirteen crying episodes for an average of twenty minutes." "He sat quietly for an average of seventeen minutes after being reprimanded prior to becoming disruptive again. This represents twenty observations of behavior following reprimand." If the length of the observation periods varies from day to day, the data should be converted to percentage of duration of the designated behavior of the total time observed.

RESPONSE LATENCY

A final measure of behavior strength of importance in some instances is response latency. A behavior that occurs with promptness upon being requested may be described as representing a stronger pattern of compliance than that of a child, as illustrated in Figure 14.7, who stalls and ignores the request for a time prior to complying. The objective of a behavior change program in this instance would be to reduce the time delay or latency between request and compliance. A distractible child may have difficulty beginning work once it is presented to him. A measure of the amount of time which elapses between work assignment and the time

LATENCY

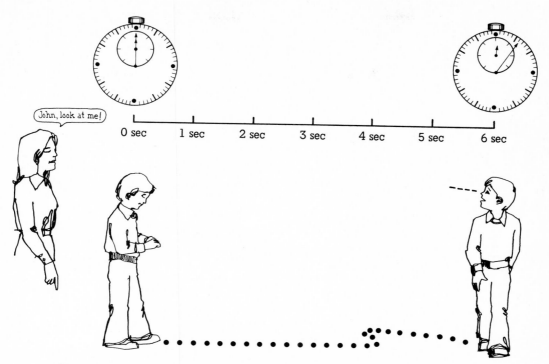

Figure 14.7   *Depicting a Latency Measure of Behavior Strength*

the child initiates the work would serve as a valuable baseline measure for a program designed to decrease the time delay between assignment and work. Or an impulsive child may respond too quickly once he is confronted with a problem. A measure of response delay may serve as a baseline measure for a program designed to teach a more careful and deliberate approach to problem solution.

LENGTH OF BASELINE PERIOD

The purpose of measurement during pretreatment or baseline period is to provide an initial reference point for evaluating the effects of any subsequent behavior change which may result from initiation of a behavior management program. The goal is to obtain a reliable indication of behavior strength. The number of different observation periods needed to obtain a reliable measure of strength would depend upon the fluctuation and the frequency of occurrence of the focal behavior. Typically, daily recordings over a week or two would be sufficient to denote a reliable trend within the fluctuation. For example, measures of academic performance rate, number of errors made, frequency of disruptive outbursts, or time spent in study activities may all provide reliable baseline features within a week or so. However, behavior which fluctuated considerably might require a longer period of baseline recording for obtaining a reliable index of typical behavior strength.

In some cases it would not be desirable to obtain an adequate baseline recording of behavior strength due to the nature of the behavior such as if a child begins biting her peers. A behavior change program should be initiated immediately. However, at a minimum, some procedure for measuring the strength of the behavior should be initiated as the behavior management program is begun. In this manner it is possible to get some impression about the effects of the program. If the initial program is unsuccessful, a baseline recording will thus be available for evaluating the effects of a modified program.

OBSERVER RELIABILITY

In the earlier discussion of behavior recording, the importance was noted of having assurance that the sample of behavior observed is representative of the same behavior during similar periods of time when no measurement is taken. "Would repeated observed samples of the behavior provide similar measures of strength?" is a pertinent question.

A basic methodological concern is that of *observer reliability*. If an observer reports that Katherine's rate of initiating social interaction with peers represents 60 percent of all social interactions initiated, there must be assurance that this 60 percent represents what Katherine actually did. An observer may consistently report a 60 percent rate but be consistently wrong. Without reliable measures of behavior strength, no confidence can be placed in presumed changes which appear to coincide with the initiation of a behavior change program. Thus, high observer reliability must be demonstrated prior to assuming that a high relationship exists between recorded behavior and actual behavior. That is, if two observers independently record behavior strength, they should show high agreement in their recording. If a high degree of agreement is lacking, no conclusions can be drawn about any reported changes in the observed behavior since these may be due to observer error and not to changes in a child's behavior following initiation of intervention procedures.

The factors resulting in poor observer agreement are usually related to (1) an inadequate definition of the behavior being recorded and (2) observer bias related to expectancies that various behaviors should or should not occur.

It would be best to use observers who had no knowledge of the types of intervention procedures being used or of when various phases of a behavior management program were ended or initiated. As emphasized earlier, behaviors to be measured must be defined in such a manner that an observer would consistently be able to designate the beginning and ending of the behavior. If not, the observer would be unable to show consistency in noting the frequency or in obtaining duration or latency data.

How Observer Reliability Is Determined

The usual procedure of determining reliability of behavior measures is by means of simultaneous recording by at least two independent observers. These independent recordings are compared and a reliability coefficient or score is calculated. In obtaining percentage of agreement in recording of frequency data, the smaller frequency is divided by the larger frequency. For example, if one observer reports twenty-five occurrences of a specific behavior and a second observer reports a count of twenty, the percentage of agreement would equal 80 per cent:

$$\frac{\text{smaller frequency}}{\text{larger frequency}} = \frac{20}{25} = 80 \text{ percent agreement}$$

It should be noted, however, that the percentage of agreement defined in this manner may not reflect the actual degree of agreement. The observers may not have both agreed on the presence of any specific occurrence. Unless permanent records of the child's behavior such as videotape are available for reliability checks, there is no way of determining if the specific behaviors represented in the twenty recordings of the second observer are also reflected in the twenty-five recordings of the first observer.

In duration recording, the percentage of agreement is computed as follows:

$$\frac{\text{shorter recorded duration}}{\text{larger recorded duration}} = \frac{100 \text{ sec}}{150 \text{ sec}} = 66 \text{ percent agreement}$$

In interval recording the interjudge reliability is computed as follows:

$$\frac{\text{number of agreements}}{\text{number of agreements plus disagreements}} = \frac{50}{50 + 25} = 66 \text{ percent}$$

An agreement is defined as the recording of an occurrence by both observers for the same interval. A disagreement is defined as one observer recording in an interval in which the second observer does not. Bijou et al.*   *Bijou et al. 1969* note that in this reliability calculation only those intervals are used in which one or both observers recorded an occurrence. When neither observer records an interval, this interval is discarded in the computation.

Wright 1960   Generally, interjudge agreement of at least 90 percent represents a reasonable standard.* Reliability indexes much below this level would create difficulty in the interpretation of reported changes, changes which may coincide with different phases of an educational program.

When Reliability Checks Should Be Made

Observers should make independent observations prior to the initiation of formal data collection as a check to insure that each observer agrees on the operational definition of the target behavior and on practices of recording. Following assurance that agreement level is suitable, reliability checks should be made during each of the phases of the program, especially if reliability is marginal.

GRAPHING BEHAVIORAL DATA

It is frequently valuable to convert data to some visual form so that an impression of behavior strength and changes in strength can be gained in a quick glance. A most useful method is to display the data in a line graph using equal-interval graph paper. Figure 14.8 illustrates the total frequency of occurrence of disruptive responses of an adolescent during language arts class and the frequency of occurrence of disruptive verbal comments. Note that *time* is represented on the graph by the horizontal axis, with the vertical axis used to indicate the frequency of the behavior. A program was initiated on the sixth day which entailed the child's recording his own disruptive verbal comments and which provided a positive reinforcement contingency for a self-controlled reduction in the number of such comments. Even though other disruptive behaviors were not included in the contingency, the adolescent did decrease both in the bothersome verbal behaviors and in his overall rate of disruptiveness.

As additional examples of the variety of data which may meaningfully be depicted in graphic form, the frequency, rate and interval data described previously in Figures 14.2, 14.3, and 14.4 are shown in Figures 14.9, 14.10, and 14.11

Use of Six-Cycle Log Paper in Charting

Lindsley 1972   An additional procedure for graphing behavioral data devised by Dr. O. R. Lindsley and his associates* makes use of six-cycle semilogarithmic chart paper.[2] The paper (1) includes on the vertical axis six exponential increments representing 0 to 1000 responses per minute broken down into six cycles (.001–.01, .01–.10, .10–1.0, 1.0–10, 10–100, and 100–1000), and (2) provides for twenty weeks of graphing on the horizontal axis. Thus a child's response data can be depicted for 140 days on a single chart. Positive features of the six-cycle log paper in displaying data include: (1) converts absolute data into a relative comparison without computing, (2) reveals whether or not the data follow a consistent relative change program, (3) retains the actual units of measurement of the absolute data, and (4) shows the relative change from any point to any succeeding point across time. By plotting behavior data over periods of time, the educator can readily see if the rate of behavior occurrence is accelerating, decelerating, or maintaining at the same level.

2. The paper may be obtained from Behavior Research Co., Box 3351, Kansas City, Kansas 66103.

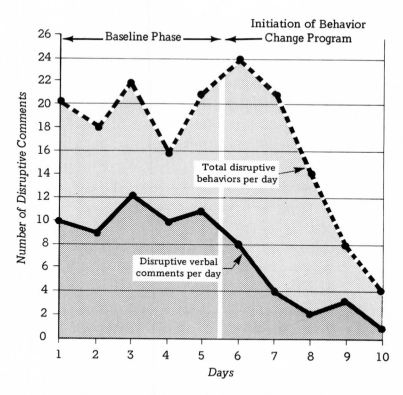

Figure 14.8   Number of Disruptive Responses

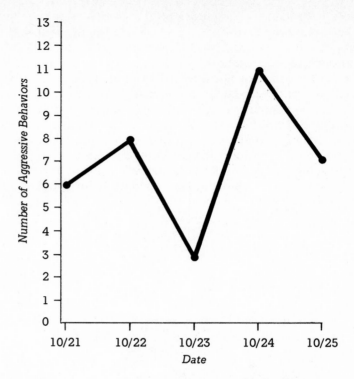

Figure 14.9 Number of Aggressive Responses

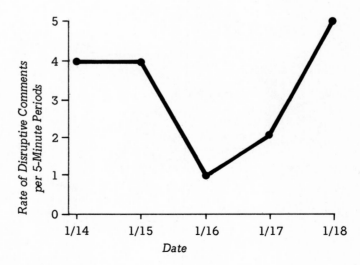

Figure 14.10. Rate of Disruptive Comments per Five Minutes in English Class

Bates and Bates,* Jordan and Robbins,* and Kunzelmann* provide detailed description of how the six-cycle log paper may be used and the central role such a charting procedure assumes in the system of educational management called *precision teaching*. In this system, the child's behavior rate is used to influence educational program decisions about what is taught and the manner in which it is taught.

Bates and Bates 1971; Jordan and Robbins 1972; Kunzelmann 1970

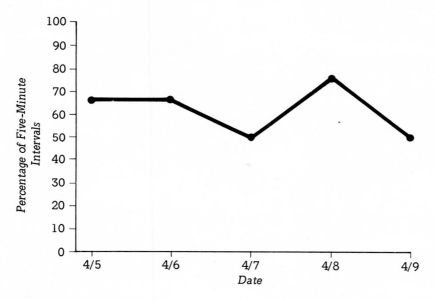

FIGURE 14.11 *Percentage of Intervals in Which Stereotyped Rocking Occurred*

REFERENCES

Ackerman, J. M. *Operant Conditioning Techniques for the Classroom Teacher.* Glenview, Ill.: Scott, Foresman, 1972.

Adelman, H. S. Remedial classroom instruction revisited. *Journal of Special Education,* 1971, 5, 311–322.

Anastasi, A. *Psychological Testing.* (3rd Ed.) New York: Macmillan, 1968.

Arrington, R. E. Time sampling in studies of social behavior. *Psychological Bulletin,* 1943, 40, 81–124.

Ayllon, T., Layman, D., and Kandel, H. H. A behavioral-educational alternative to drug contol of hyperactive children. *Journal of Applied Behavior Analysis,* 1975, 8, 137–146.

Bateman, B. Three approaches to diagnosis and educational planning for children with learning disabilities. *Academic Therapy Quarterly,* 1967, 3:1, 11–16.

Bates, S., and Bates, D. F. ". . . and a child shall lead them": Stephanie's chart story. *Teaching Exceptional Children,* 1971, 3:3, 111–113.

Bijou, S. W., Peterson, R. F., and Ault, M. H. A method to integrate descriptive and experimental field studies at the level of data and empirical concepts. *Journal of Applied Behavior Analysis,* 1968, 1, 175–191.

Bijou, S. W., Peterson, R. F., Harris, F. R., Allen, K. E., and Johnston, M. S. Methodology for experimental studies of young children in natural settings. *Psychological Record,* 1969, 19, 177–210.

Bloom, B. S., Hastings, J. T., and Madaus, G. F. *Handbook on Formative and Summative Evaluation of Student Learning.* New York: McGraw-Hill, 1971.

Branch, R., and Sulzbacher, S. Rapid computation of rates with a simple nomogram. *Journal of Applied Behavior Analysis,* 1968, 1, 251–252.

Briskin, A., and Gardner, W. I. Social Reinforcement in reducing inappropriate behavior. *Young Children,* 1968, 24, 84–89.

Bryan, T. S. An observational analysis of classroom behaviors of children with learning disabilities. *Journal of Learning Disabilities,* 1974, 7, 35–43.

Cohen, S. A. Studies in visual perception and reading in disadvantaged children. *Journal of Learning Disabilities,* 1969, 2, 6–14.

Cronback, L. J. *Essentials of Psychological Testing.* (3rd Ed.) New York: Harper, 1970.

Drew, C. J., Freston, C. W., and Logan, D. R. Criteria and reference on evaluation. *Focus on Exceptional Children,* 1972, 4:1, 1–10.

Fargo, G. A., and Behrns, C. Rapid computation and pupil self-recording of performance data. *Journal of Applied Behavior Analysis,* 1969, 2, 264.

Ferster, C. B. Classification of behavioral pathology. In L. Krasner and L. Ullman. (Eds.) *Research in Behavior Modification.* New York: Holt, Rinehart & Winston, 1967. Pp. 6–26.

Frostig, M., and Horne, D. *The Frostig Program for the Development of Visual Perception: Teacher's Guide.* Chicago: Follett, 1964.

Frostig, M., Lefever, D. W., and Whittlesey, J. R. B. *The Marianne Frostig Developmental Test of Visual Perception.* Palo Alto, Calif.: Consulting Psychologist Press, 1964.

Gardner, W. I. *Behavior Modification in Mental Retardation.* Chicago: Aldine, 1971.

Glaser, R. Instructional technology and the measurement of learning outcomes: Some Questions. *American Psychologist,* 1963, 18, 519–521.

Goldfried, M. R., and Kent, R. N. Traditional versus behavioral personality assessment: A comparison of methodological and theoretical assumptions. *Psychological Bulletin,* 1972, 77, 409–420.

Goldfried, M. R., and Pomeranz, D. M. Role of assessment in behavior modification. *Psychology Reports,* 1968, 23, 75–87.

Gorth, W. P., and Hambleton, R. K. Measurement considerations for criterion-referenced testing and special education. *Journal of Special Education,* 1972, 6, 303–314.

Hallahan, D. P., and Kauffman, J. M. *Introduction to Learning Disabilities: A Psycho-behavioral Approach.* Englewood Cliffs, N. J.: Prentice-Hall, 1976.

Hammill, D. D. Evaluating children for instructional purposes. *Academic Therapy,* 1971, 6, 341–353.

Hammill, D. D., and Bartel, N. R. *Teaching Children with Learning and Behavior Problems*. Boston: Allyn and Bacon, 1975.

Jones, R. R., Reid, J. B., and Patterson, G. R. Naturalistic observation in clinical assessment. In P. McReynolds (Ed.) *Advances in Psychological Assessment*. (Vol. 3.) San Francisco: Jossey-Bass, 1975. Pp. 42–95.

Jordan, J. B., and Robbins, L. S. (Ed.) *Let's Try Doing Something Else Kind of Thing: Behavioral Principles and the Exceptional Child*. Arlington, Va.: Council for Exceptional Children, 1972.

Kazdin, A. Methodological and assessment considerations in evaluating reinforcement programs in applied settings. *Journal of Applied Behavior Analysis*, 1973, 6, 517–531.

Kirk, S. A., and Kirk, W. D. *Psycholinguistic Learning Disabilities: Diagnosis and Remediation*. Chicago: University of Illinois Press, 1971.

Kirk, S. A., McCarthy, J. J., and Kirk, W. D. *The Illinois Test of Psycholinguistic Abilities*. (Rev. Ed.) Urbana: University of Illinois Press, 1968.

Kunzelmann, H. P. (Ed.) *Precision Teaching*. Seattle: Special Child Publications, 1970.

Lindsley, O. R. Technical note: A reliable wrist counter for recording behavior rates. *Journal of Applied Behavior Analysis*, 1968, 1, 77–78.

Lindsley, O. R. From Skinner to precision teaching: The child knows best. In J. B. Jordan and L. S. Robbins (Eds.) *Let's Try Doing Something Else Kind of Thing: Behavioral Principles and the Exceptional Child*. Arlington, Va.: Council for Exceptional Children, 1972. Pp. 2–11.

Lovitt, T. C. Assessment of Children with learning disabilities. *Exceptional Children*, 1967, 34, 233–239.

Lovitt, T. C. Applied behavior analysis and learning disabilities. Part 1: Characteristics of ABA, general recommendations and methodological limitations. *Journal of Learning Disabilities*, 1975, 8, 432–443.

Mann, L Psychometric phrenology and the new faculty psychology: The case against ability assessment and training. *Journal of Special Education*, 1971, 5, 3–14.

Mattos, R. L. A manual counter for recording mul-

tiple behavior. *Journal of Applied Behavior Analysis*, 1968, 1, 130.

McIntosh, D. K., and Dunn, L. M. Children with major specific learning disabilities. In L. M. Dunn (Ed.) *Exceptional Children in the Schools: Education in Transition*. (2nd Ed.) New York: Holt, Rinehart & Winston, 1973.

Mischel, W. *Personality and Assessment*. New York: John Wiley, 1968.

O'Leary, K. D. The assessment of psychopathology in children. In H. C. Quay and J. S. Werry (Eds.) *Psycho-pathological Disorders of Childhood*. New York: John Wiley, 1972. Pp. 234–272.

Patterson, G. R. *Families*. Champaign, Ill.: Research Press, 1971.

Phillips, E. L. Achievement Place: Token reinforcement procedures in a home-style rehabilitation setting for pre-delinquent boys. *Journal of Applied Behavior Analysis*, 1968, 1, 213–223.

Proger, B. B., and Mann, L. Criterion-referenced measurement: The world of gray versus black and white. *Journal of Learning Disabilities*, 1973, 6, 19–30.

Skinner, B. F. What is the experimental analysis of behavior? *Journal of Experimental Analysis of Behavior*, 1966, 9, 213–218.

Smith, R. M. *Clinical Teaching: Methods of Instruction for the Retarded*. New York: McGraw-Hill, 1968.

Staats, A. W. *Social Behaviorism*. Homewood, Ill.: Dorsey Press, 1975.

Tharp, R. G., and Wetzel, R. J. *Behavior Modification in the Natural Environment*. New York: Academic Press, 1969.

Thorndike, R. L., and Hagen, E. *Measurement and Evaluation in Psychology and Education*. New York: John Wiley, 1969.

Wallace, J. An abilities conception of personality: Some implications for personality measurement. *American Psychologist*, 1966, 21, 132–138.

Wallace, J. What units shall we employ? Allport's question revisited. *Journal of Consulting Psychology*, 1967, 31, 56–64.

Westerman, G. *Spelling and Writing*. San Rafael, Calif.: Dimensions, 1971.

Whitman, T. L., Mercurio, J. R., and Caponigri, V.

Development of social responses in two severely retarded children. *Journal of Applied Behavior Analysis,* 1970, 3, 133–138.

Williams, C. D. The elimination of tantrum behavior by extinction procedures. *Journal of Abnormal and Social Psychology,* 1959, 59, 269.

Wright, H. F. Observational Child Study. In P. H. Mussen (Ed.) *Handbook of Research Methods in Child Development.* New York: John Wiley, 1960. Pp. 71–139.

Zeilberger, J., Sampsen, S. E., and Slone, H. N. Modification of a child's problem behaviors in the home with the mother as therapist. *Journal of Applied Behavior Analysis,* 1968, 1, 47–53.

15

Design and Evaluation of Intervention Programs

In designing and providing educational services to children with exceptional characteristics, the educator must make decisions about (1) the competency behaviors to be developed (that is, the academic curricular and other program content), (2) the instructional materials used, and (3) the specific teaching or behavior influence methods used. These types of decisions must be made by the educator regardless of educational setting or the organizational structure of the instructional program—open classroom, resource room, self-contained special class, diagnostic-prescriptive center, or regular class—although the setting or structure may restrict or otherwise influence the nature of decisions made. In illustration, if a child with multiple exceptional characteristics attends a large regular class and is provided special services by an itinerant resource teacher, the types of procedures used may well be restricted by practical consideration of what can be managed in the classroom by the regular teacher.

The behavioral assessment procedures outlined in the previous chapter result in a description of the child's exceptional characteristics which, for general classification purposes, may be expressed in terms of the excessive and deficit categories of the behavioral classification system described in Chapter 5. Behavioral assessment of a specific child may reveal:

General and specific knowledge, ability, and skill deficits
Task-related behavior deficits
Interpersonal (social) behavior deficits
Excessive disruptive and nonfunctional competing behaviors
Excessive affective reactions
Excessive avoidance behaviors

Individualized program development requires that specific learner characteristics must be described in quantitative (norm- and criterion-referenced) detail, along with a delineation of hunches about general and specific correlated conditions (those which may have produced, account for the occurrence, and serve to maintain the behavioral characteristics). These hypotheses could potentially relate to environmental conditions or subject characteristics which may: (1) render likely the presence of deficit behaviors, such as poor instruction, inappropriate educational materials, or poor physical conditions, (2) render likely the occurrence of excessive behaviors, for example, low frustration tolerance, poor self-monitoring skills, or excessive aversive conditions, and (3) maintain present excessive behavior, for instance, high probability peer approval for disruptive "anti-adult" behavior.

In clinically integrating the results of the behavioral assessment with that of information concerning the child's physical characteristics and after consideration of the personal and environmental resources available for use in a behavior intervention program, the next steps involve:

1. The development of realistic program objectives, depicting in quantitative terms the types of behavioral changes expected.
2. The selection of target areas toward which present efforts will be directed. Recall from Chapter 14 that the program may emphasize antecedent situational events, mediational or other covert characteristics, the observable exceptional characteristics, or environmental contingencies or consequences. The target area(s) selected for program focus would be those which offer greatest promise of fulfilling the program objectives.
3. The selection of instructional or behavior change procedures best suited for effective and efficient attainment of the program goals.

In this process of program design and implementation, the educator utilizing the humanistic behavioral approach follows a diagnostic/prescriptive teaching model which focuses on the development of competency skills. The program is monitored frequently and modified as needed to insure continuous child progress. If the program is ineffective, program components (methods, materials, consequences, specific objectives) are modified. If the program is effective and the child acquires new skills, program components are changed to accommodate and make best use of these new skills.

Each aspect of program design and implementation is discussed. The chapter concludes with a description of procedures of evaluating the effectiveness of intervention programs.

SETTING BEHAVIORAL OBJECTIVES

As noted in the previous chapter, an early step in behavioral assessment is that of formulating general program objectives. Such objectives denote in general what a specific child or adolescent should do or what is expected of him. After assessment data are gathered relative to exceptional behavioral characteristics, program goals are refined into quantitatively defined *behavioral objectives*. It is perhaps true that many education and therapy programs for children and youth with exceptional characteristics have been relatively unsuccessful or inefficient because no clear delineation had been initially made of the specific outcome objectives of such programs. Thus, it is critical that precise and objectively defined behavioral objectives be set prior to the development and initiation of behavior change endeavors. The educator will know what the precise purpose is of the program content and tactics and when program goals have been reached. Additionally, if the objectives are not attained, the educator will know that a programming mistake has been made and thus will modify the program.

As the behavioral objectives designed for a specific child provide direction to the program and set the criteria for its success, it is essential that the objectives decided upon are *realistic*. Not only should these be possible for the child to attain, but the objectives should also be attainable within a reasonable period of time. Setting realistic behavioral objectives relative to a child's exceptional characteristics does require a detailed knowledge of learner characteristics.

Target and Terminal Behavioral Objectives

In setting program goals, it is useful for the educator to distinguish between *target* and *terminal* objectives. *Terminal* objectives refer to those behaviors within a curriculum or behavioral dimension or subdimension which represent reasonable progress or change from the child's present behavioral characteristics. The terminal objectives may also represent expected behavior in relation to an excessive behavior area such as non-compliance, stereotyped behavior, negative emotionality, or negative attitudes. The terminal goals at any one time are arbitrarily defined and obviously will differ in specificity from child to child. These objectives may represent components of an academic curriculum or may be behavioral goals associated with any repertoires and devised uniquely for an individual child.

The objectives set should be *reasonable* to insure that attainment will be realized. If too difficult, both child and educator will experience excessive failure. Reasonableness, obviously, is arbitrarily defined, especially in considering children with exceptional characteristics. As noted, children and adolescents with unusual learning and behavior difficulties may not acquire new behavioral skills in terms of a predictable (normative) progression and rate. Goals which can reasonably be expected within a short period of time are most effective in insuring continuous or frequent program monitoring. As these behavioral objectives are reached, other higher level or more complex terminal goals are set.

Once the terminal criterion behaviors are set, the *target, transitional, or short-term* behavioral objectives are described as a series of hierarchical sequentially ordered steps representing closer and closer progression toward attainment of the terminal behaviors. The targets, which represent immediate sequential steps along the various terminal behavior dimensions, become the focus of the program at any moment in time. Some targets become more critical than others and may receive major attention. In fact, it is not unusual after a program is implemented that an initially set target objective turns out to be too difficult. This requires the development of a series of less complex transitional objectives. The process of task analysis of academic program content is described in Chapter 16.

Again, in setting transitional objectives, each successive step should be relatively easy for the child to accomplish. If the initial set of immediate objectives is too difficult, the set must be further subdivided into easier steps to insure successful participation. This emphasizes that the initial target behaviors, selected for a particular child and representing step progression toward reaching a broader terminal objective, are viewed as tentative and subject to further elaboration as the child is exposed to the program.

Many behavior patterns are difficult to define and measure in an objective manner. Such characteristics as "to be happy," "to relate freely with others," "to be curious," or "to be socially sensitive" are examples of these goals. But if these behavioral characteristics are to be influenced in a systematic manner, they must be defined in terms of observable behavioral units. As an example, a teacher may have the impression that Hieta does not "relate to other children." She would describe a series of behaviors which, if present, would result in her concluding, "Ah, now Hieta is relating to her peers." These might include such behaviors as:

Hieta will look at others when they call her name.
Hieta will look at other children when they are the center of class attention.
Hieta will interact with other children when they initiate interaction with her.
Without prompting from teacher, Hieta will move close to other children.
Hieta will approach other children and initiate interaction with them.
Hieta will initiate and maintain cooperative play with her peers.
Hieta will smile and laugh appropriately when playing with other children.
Hieta will engage in affectionate behavior in response to affection provided by a peer.

With these more observable behavioral objectives, the teacher is in a position to assess Hieta's present behavior in each segment as a beginning point for the development of an educational program designed to teach these behaviors. As progress is made, the child would be described as having more desirable behaviors of "relating to others."

Characteristics of Behavioral Objectives

Behavioral objectives, both terminal and target, should be stated in a form which permits the educator to know if the objectives have been attained or not. Goals such as "increase his understanding," "improve his spelling skills," "teach him more independence," or "encourage more initiative" are acceptable as broad program goals but are all much too general to be acceptable as behavioral objectives. How much is implied by "increase" or "improve"? How would "understanding" be defined and measured? What is "independence" and "initiative" in terms of what the child will do in specific situations and how will these be measured?

Even statements of *should do* behavior in the form, "I want him to be courteous," are too general. What is implied by "being courteous"? What would the child do in certain situations or under what conditions that would lead the educator to conclude, "now he is courteous." How frequently should the child be "courteous" and under what conditions? Would an independent observer agree with the teacher that the child's behavior has changed from a position of "being rude" to a level of "acceptable courtesy"?

A statement concerning courtesy in fulfilling teacher requests of *should do* behaviors in the following form represents a distinct improvement: "When I make a request of Jim, he will comply with the request without excessive delay or negativism." However, even this statement requires further elaboration. What does "excessive" imply? What is "negativism"? Until these behavioral characteristics are objectively defined, it would not be possible to determine, in any satisfactory manner, if the behavioral goal had been reached or not.

Previous discussion focused on the necessity of behavior measurement. If behavioral objectives are not defined in terms that will be measurable in some reliable manner, the strength or nature of the initial behaviors cannot be measured nor can changes be evaluated.

In developing both terminal and target behavioral objectives, four conditions, as recommended by Mager* should be met:

Mager 1962

1. *The objective must be stated in performance terms.* What will the child do in order to demonstrate that he has reached the behavioral objective? The following statements illustrate this requirement:

The child:	names	goes	hangs up
	identifies	does	folds
	selects	says	draws

points to	places in	colors
repeats	picks up	writes
imitates	goes under	traces
puts on	ties	completes

Descriptive terms like knows, understands, feels, believes, or perceives, are inadequate due to the lack of specific behavioral referents. Different people are likely to define these in different ways.

2. *The objective will designate the important conditions under which the behavior is to occur:* in the classroom, during lunch period while sitting with his peers, when in a conflict situation, when given a unipac and requested to solve the problems.

3. *The objective will include a statement of the criterion of acceptable performance.* This will designate how well the behavior is to be performed. "The child, during lunchtime in the school cafeteria and eating with his peers and teacher, will eat his meal with the proper utensils without spilling. This objective will be demonstrated on five consecutive days." "The child, when shown pictures of a dog, cat, boy, ball, car, house, table, and chair, will label these with the correct name. He will do this daily for four days." "Given five particular vowel sounds in word contexts, each adolescent will spell them correctly, with 90 percent accuracy."

4. *The method of measuring the desired behavior must be described.* "The teacher will record the frequency of the *should do* behavioral objective during five-minute observation periods. A wrist counter will be used."

There are numerous reference materials available to the special educator which provide detailed illustration of precisely defined instructional objectives. Blake,* Hallahan and Kauffman,* and Meyen* provide illustration of behaviorally defined instructional objectives for categories of children labeled as mentally retarded and learning disabled. Additionally, there are a variety of commercially available academic programs which include well-sequenced and objectively defined curriculum and more specific behavioral objectives such as *The Sullivan Programmed Reading Series** and the *Distar* programs in arithmetic, reading, and language.* Following is an example of the behavioral objectives included in the Distar Arithmetic Program I:

Blake 1974; Hallahan and Kauffman 1976; Meyen 1972

Buchanan and Sullivan 1968; Englemann and Bruner 1971

Behavioral Objective 8: When presented with an oral addition problem such as "I have four and I plus three," the student should be able to (1) hold up four fingers, (2) count from four to seven touching a finger for each numeral as he counts, and (3) state the whole problem (four plus three equals seven).

FORMULATION OF INTERVENTION PROGRAM

What specifically will be done to influence the exceptional characteristics to attain the behavioral objectives developed for the child? As emphasized, program experiences must be systematic and individualized. The child may be a member of a larger group, but the specific experiences provided him in this group setting should be designed to deal with his unique combination of exceptional characteristics. The types of stimulation, the sensory channel(s) emphasized (e.g., visual versus auditory), the sequencing of stimulus presentation, the types and numbers of events which may be distracting or which may provoke competing emotionality, the prerequisite behaviors, supporting behavioral repertoires, the types of consequent events which are reinforcing, neutral, or aversive, and the schedules by which events must be provided if effective, all add to the uniqueness of each child and emphasize the necessity of individualizing program experiences to the fullest extent possible.

Program experiences should be provided in an environmental setting most conducive to the learning, occurrence, and maintenance of desired characteristics and in which the likelihood of inappropriate behaviors is minimized. In the school setting, the educator must have reasonable control over antecedent events as well as of influential consequences. If the educator is unable to monitor the noise level of a class, as an example, difficulty will be encountered in influencing auditory attending of a distractible child. If the educator has insufficient control over the events in the classroom setting which influence the child's distractible and hyperactive behaviors, it may be necessary to remove him from the classroom and into a "special environment" in which discriminative and reinforcing events may be presented in a more programmatic manner. After the desired attending and related behaviors are strengthened in this controlled setting, the child could be moved through a series of steps back into the original classroom environment. The noise level in the classroom may be unchanged, but it may no longer serve as a distracting event.

Components of Intervention Program

The intervention program is designed to eliminate the discrepancies between what the child presently does and the behavioral objectives set for him, that is, to develop increasing competency. The program includes the *instructional* and *consequence* components. The relationship between programming for target or transitional behavioral objectives and terminal behavioral objectives is illustrated in Figure 15.1. The initial program sequence continues until Target Objective$_1$ is reached. This new behavior becomes the entering behavior for the next target behavior objective, and so on. After the terminal behavioral objective is obtained, the teacher uses this behavior pattern as an entering behavior for a more complex behavioral

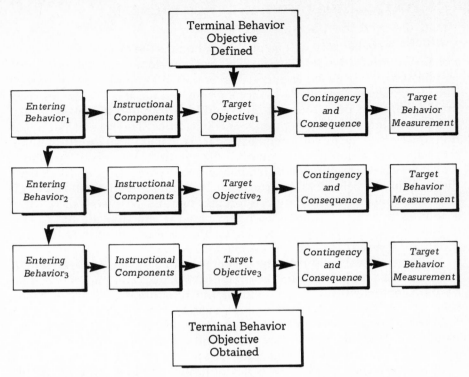

FIGURE 15.1   *Depicting the Relationship Between Target and Terminal Objectives*

objective. The educational program thus represents a never-ending cycle of specific intervention programs, each with a set of short- and long-term objectives and related program procedures for meeting these objectives.

Instructional Components

Instructional components refers, on the one hand, to those conditions arranged to facilitate the occurrence of deficit behaviors—or some initial acceptable approximation—under desired cue conditions: The child will identify the word correctly when the teacher points to it and requests that he read it; the adolescent will comply with teacher requests to assist his peers. Instructional components also refers to those conditions arranged to reduce the likelihood of occurrence of excessive inappropriate behavior: the adolescent will cue himself to engage in competing thoughts when he begins to dwell on thoughts of inadequacy; the child will self-manage his disruptive behavior and engage in competing appropriate social activities.

Description should be provided of (1) the prompting procedures used to facilitate the occurrence of the desired behavior or to inhibit inappropriate activities and (2) the discriminative cues that will eventually signal the time and place of desired behaviors. The manner in which instructional program elements will be faded and eventually removed as the behavioral objectives are met should be designated. Finally, procedures to facilitate generalization of the behavioral objectives obtained from the instructional environment (classroom, speech therapy room, counselor's office) to other appropriate environmental settings should be detailed. Thus, the instructional components will describe: *What will be done, in what setting, by whom, when, and with what.* As an example, the teacher will model the desired social behavior for John whenever he is rude to his peers in the classroom. John will be requested to role play the appropriate social response. To insure generalization, John will cue himself and covertly reinforce himself for the desired behavior.

Consequence Components

The consequence components of the intervention program refer to (1) the specific events (both externally delivered and controlled and self-delivered and controlled) which follow the occurrence of specified target behaviors, (2) the manner in which these will be provided, and (3) the contingency relationship between behavior and specified consequences. Brief examples will illustrate these aspects of the intervention program:

Upon completion of the academic task within the time allotted and at preselected performance standards, Tim will award himself fifteen points. These points can be exchanged later for a variety of leisure-time activities.

Whenever John makes a spontaneous comment during class discussion, the teacher will immediately attend to him in a natural and pleasant manner and interact with his comments.

When Susan engages in "crazy talk," she will be reminded in a calm but firm manner, "When you stop that nonsense, I shall be happy to talk to you." She will be ignored until she initiates appropriate conversation, at which time the teacher will provide pleasant social feedback and praise for her interesting conversation.

Contingent tokens for completion of assignments during Social Studies will be provided on a VR-5 schedule for another week.

Components of the intervention program are summarized in Table 15.1.

PROGRAMMING FOR EXCESSIVE EXCEPTIONAL CHARACTERISTICS

A behavior management program devised to deal with excessive behavior patterns will consist of two sets of closely interrelated proce-

TABLE 15.1. *Components of a Behavior Intervention Program*

Antecedent Events	Target Behavior	Consequences	Contingency
What will be done, by whom, with what, where, and when?	What behavior does the program wish to influence?	After the target behavior occurs what will happen?	What is the relationship between the target behavior and the consequence?

dures: (1) those concerned with decreasing the strength of the excessive behavior and (2) those directed toward increasing the strength of behavior to replace the excessive behavior pattern. The behavior objectives for an isolated child who unexpectedly bites other children may include reducing the biting behavior to a zero level and increasing the number of appropriate social responses by 30 percent. In assessment of the excessive behavior pattern as it occurs in various situations, the teacher should carefully observe the possible function which this behavior may serve for the child. The following example emphasizes the importance of this type of concern.

> Becky has a difficult time getting along with other children. She is isolated by other children and spends most of her time in solitary activity unless guided specifically by the teacher to become involved in structured interaction with peers. During these times she appears to enjoy this peer contact but will quickly withdraw whenever teacher is not present. Gradually, over the course of the first six weeks of the school term, Becky developed a variety of aggressive and other disruptive behaviors that involved her peers. The teacher attempted to ignore the behavior initially but finally decided that she had to do something to "get rid of that bothersome behavior. She is upsetting her peers too frequently. They really isolate her now. I have difficulty getting them to interact with her at all."
>
> During the baseline observation period, the teacher wondered about the consequences which were maintaining the behavior. She hypothesized that the peer attention, although of a seemingly negative nature, was the reinforcing event. It then occurred to her that this child, who had been quite shy, isolated, and without peer interaction skills, had at least developed some, although inappropriate, social behavior. If an intervention program were successful in eliminating these disruptive behaviors, the child would once again be without any means of interacting with her peers. A program was developed to teach more acceptable social interaction skills through modeling and guided participation. Peer and teacher attention paired with tangible events were used as reinforcers. The disruptive behavior was ignored whenever possible. As the child acquired skills interacting with her

*peers, first in highly structured situations and gradually under
increasingly unstructured conditions, the disruptive behaviors
disappeared.*

This example emphasizes that exceptional behavior characteristics
should neither be assessed nor dealt with in isolation. Any specific behavior must be viewed as one aspect of highly complex repertoires of
behavior which characterize a child. The events which function to maintain a behavior pattern, the interrelationships of various behavior patterns,
and behavior patterns viewed as acceptable alternatives of present behaviors must all be viewed from a point of "what is best for the child."

The following questions serve as a useful guide in devising an
intervention program for dealing with excessive exceptional characteristics:

1. What behavior (or behaviors) are creating difficulty?
2. Under what conditions does the behavior occur (place, time, conditions)?
3. Can the behavior be influenced by elimination or change in antecedent
   conditions?
4. What is the strength of the behavior (frequency, rate, duration, magnitude)?
5. What consequences does the behavior produce which may be maintaining the behavior? (Remember that reinforcement may occur only
   infrequently and still maintain the behavior—getting attention or
   avoiding unpleasant duties or situations, among others.)
6. Is the presumed reinforcement positive or negative?
7. Can the presumed reinforcing consequences (aversive and positive) be
   eliminated?
8. Can the presumed reinforcing events be used to strengthen acceptable
   competing behaviors?
9. Does the child have acceptable alternative behaviors in his repertoire
   which would be suitable in the situation?
10. Does the environment provide sufficient opportunity to obtain posi-
    tive consequences for acceptable behavior?
11. What behaviors should be taught to replace the excessive behaviors?

WHAT SPECIFIC PROCEDURES SHOULD BE USED

Numerous decisions are made prior to selecting the specific instructional and consequence strategies for use with a specific child. If an adolescent who seldom displays "happy" behavior engages consistently in some
excessive behaviors that interfere with his academic, social, and emotional
development, what specifically should be done? A number of different

approaches are possible, each requiring procedural decisions. The teacher may:

Provide aversive consequences following specific behaviors. If so, should a PAC, RC, or TO procedure be used? What are the specific features of the procedure selected? Who will manage the contingency?

Provide positive reinforcement for specific competing behavior patterns and ignore the excessive characteristics. What will be done to insure that the desired behavior will occur? Will physical guidance, modeling by peers, verbal prompting, or removal of distracting stimuli be used? What types of reinforcement—social, tangible, token, activity? What type of social reinforcement provided by whom in what manner? What schedule of reinforcement should be used?

Remove or modify the external discriminative events which cue the behavior.

Influence positive mediational and emotional responses to facilitate self-monitoring and management of the disruptive behavior and the negative mood.

Use an extinction procedure.

Insure a reduction in the number and level of class assignments under the supposition that the adolescent unable to complete her work is finding the school environment excessively aversive. A reduction in the level of aversiveness and an increase in the positive features of the classroom—now she can succeed—may effectively reduce or eliminate the inappropriate negativistic, disruptive, and "unhappy" behaviors, the precipitating conditions for these having been removed.

Use a systematic desensitization procedure to decrease the negative emotionality which appears to increase the likelihood of disruptive social behavior.

The specific procedures or combination of procedures will depend upon numerous factors. These include the characteristics of social settings and of the teacher and other persons who will administer the program. A program designed for a child may be ideal from a theoretical viewpoint, but may be difficult if not impossible to implement due to the characteristics of the physical and social environment in which the child resides. The room may be too noisy. The seating arrangement may not permit suitable reduction of visual distraction. The room may not permit a time-out location. There may be no area of the room which could be used for a reinforcement area. There may be too many children in the class for highly individualized programs. An adolescent may not have skills of self-management. Reinforcing events such as peer attention and removal of aversive conditions which maintain exceptional characteristics may be stronger than the incentive conditions which are available to the educator.

The educator may be unable to use various procedures even though these appear to be the best in terms of the behavioral assessment data. The adult may feel highly uncomfortable, for example, in using any type of punishment procedure. Or an extinction procedure with disruptive behavior may not be feasible because the educator will not tolerate the possible temporary increased level of disruption that is likely to occur. Another adult may be quite able to use social reinforcement but refuses to use token reinforcers due to her philosophic concepts.

It is evident that there are no "prepackaged" or "cookbook" programs that can be used effectively by everyone or with specific kinds of problems. Each educator will develop those programs that are most feasible in accomplishing the desired behavioral objectives in view of the particular combinations of child-environment-teacher characteristics.

As a final check prior to program initiation, the following listing of concerns may prove useful:

1. Have you identified the behaviors which you wish to influence today?
2. Are these target behaviors related to broader terminal behavior goals?
3. Have you specified the environmental setting in which you will present the procedures?
4. Are the instructional procedures appropriate for the behaviors which you wish to influence?
5. Are positive consequences available for the desired behavior and are these appropriate?
6. Have you specified the schedule for providing the consequences?
7. Have you specified the procedure for providing the consequences?
8. Have you specified the procedure to determine if the target behavior is being influenced?
9. Do you have alternative strategies if the program fails?

EVALUATING PROGRAM EFFECTIVENESS

As suggested by Kazdin,* a distinguishing feature of a behavioral approach is the careful evaluation of the education or training program. Assessment of behavior change, program implementation, and program evaluation are closely interrelated. There are various evaluative procedures for use in (1) assessing learner progress toward attainment of behavioral objectives and (2) providing some assurance that any observed behavior change was a result of the behavior intervention program.

Kazdin 1975

Baseline and Intervention Procedures

At a minimum, the educator is interested in knowing if the child's behavior is changing in the direction expected. As noted earlier, *baseline or preprogram* information should be available on the child's target behaviors. If measures of behavior strength continue to be obtained after the intervention program has been initiated, changes in behavior strength, such as rate measures, can be monitored. This change can be followed over time to determine its stability.

Any changes in behavior observed after initiation of the program cannot be assumed to be a function of the program elements. It is quite possible that behavior will change in strength quite independently of the specific components of an intervention program. Experiences provided at home, by peers, or by others unrelated to the intervention experiences may account for any observed changes. Parents may respond differently to children once they become aware of the severity of problems or the initiation of a "special" program. Thus, although continued measurement of behavior after the intervention program has begun is helpful in objective description of behavior change, it reveals no reliable information about the events responsible for the change.

Figure 15.2 provides illustration of various phases of program evaluation. In this case an adolescent's disruptive behaviors in four one-hour academic classes are recorded over a twenty-three-day period. The first five days represents the A or baseline phase during which the daily rate of disruptive behavior per sixty-minute class period is obtained under usual instructional procedures. Beginning on the sixth day, the adolescent was provided token reinforcement for rate of academic achievement. There was a noticeable reduction in disruptive behavior during this eight-day period. However, as noted, little assurance can be placed in identifying the particular events which resulted in or contributed to this reduction.

Return to Baseline Procedure

In addition to the *baseline* → *intervention* measurement procedure, the educator may go one step further in response to her concern: "Will the behavior change be maintained if I terminate the intervention program?" In this *baseline* → *intervention* → *baseline* procedure, measurement of behavior strength would be continued for a period of time after termination of intervention. If the desired behavior change noted after the initiation of the program continues after termination of the program, there would be no necessity to reinstate it. There would still be little assurance, however, that the observed changes in behavior were, in fact, related to the previous program experiences. If, however, as illustrated in Figure 15.2, there is a change in behavior in the direction of that which characterized the adolescent prior to intervention, there would be some support for the influence of the program on reducing disruptive behavior.

Complete Reversal

To gain additional assurance that the program experiences were functionally related to behavior change, the educator might take the additional step of reinstating the intervention program. If behavior once again showed a positive program effect, the educator has demonstrated a com-

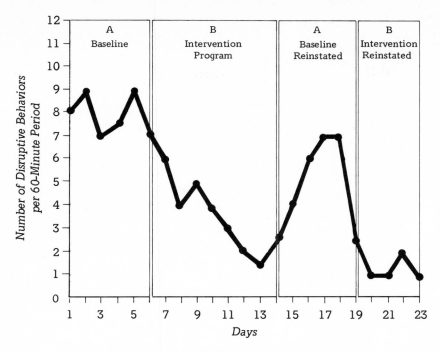

FIGURE 15.2   Depicting Phases of a Reversal Procedure

plete replication of initial baseline program effects. Even more confidence can be placed in the supposition that the behavior changes are functionally related to program changes. In taking this step of reinstatement of intervention program conditions, that is, *baseline → intervention → baseline → intervention*, the educator can feel reasonably assured that what he is doing does account for the observed positive changes. Figure 15.2 demonstrates the functionality of the intervention procedures in influencing the adolescent's disruptive behavior. This program evaluation procedure is called a *replication, reversal,* or *ABAB design.* Again, the purpose of the reversal procedure is to demonstrate a *functional relationship* between the target behavior and the program experiences.

Multiple-Baseline Design

An additional procedure that may be used to evaluate the effects of intervention programs is called a *multiple-baseline design.* Rather than removing and reinstating the intervention program once begun, the multiple-baseline procedure evaluates specific program effects by introducing the program at different points in time. There are three variations of this procedure: multiple-baseline across individuals, across behaviors, and across situations or times.

Hall et al.* demonstrated the use of a multiple-baseline across indi-   *Hall et al. 1970* viduals which illustrates the general format of the procedure. In working with high school students who were earning grades of D or F on class quizzes, Hall and his colleagues hypothesized that grades could be improved if after-school tutoring was made contingent on daily quiz grades of D or F. Initially, baseline data were obtained on daily grades for each of three students (see Figure 15.3). First, one student was informed that whenever a D or F grade was earned on a quiz, after-school tutoring would be required. Baseline data continued to be gathered on the remaining two students. After change was noted in the behavior of the first student, the after-school tutoring contingency was imposed on the second student for D or F grades. Finally, the third student was included in the contingency after the grades of the second student changed. As noted in Figure 15.3, as the contingency was introduced at different times for each of the three students, there was a related improvement in class grades. Thus, the use of the multiple-baseline procedure illustrated a clear relationship on three separate occasions between the introduction of the specific contingency of after-school tutoring and improvement in grades.

Changing-Criterion Design

Axelbrod et al. 1974

One additional program evaluation procedure introduced recently by Axelbrod et al.* is labeled the *changing-criterion design*. After a baseline period, the intervention program is introduced so that a specified level of responding is required prior to a specific reinforcement. For example, a child may be required to complete twenty math problems in a twenty-minute period prior to reinforcement. After this performance criterion is met consistently, the number of math problems required within the twenty-minute period is increased to twenty-five. The performance criterion is changed repeatedly until the program goal of thirty-five math problems is achieved. Attainment of the changing performance criterion contingent on reinforcement supports the functionality of the contingency.

Additional Procedures

Baer et al. 1968
Kazdin 1973; Sidman
1960

While a number of other procedures are available for assessment of program effectiveness, they entail technical features which are beyond the scope of this book. The interested reader should consult Baer et al.,* Kazdin,* and Sidman* for detailed discussion of the value and limitations of procedures used in evaluation of intervention programs.

Concluding Thoughts

The procedures for evaluating specific effects of intervention programs provide the special educator with relatively simple procedures for "keeping the program honest." Too many aspects of special education practices and related "psychological treatment" are accepted on faith and

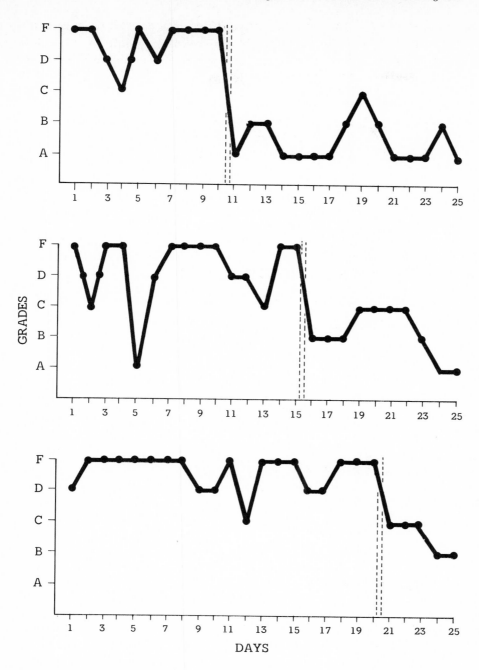

FIGURE 15.3   *Depicting Daily Grades of Three Adolescents before and after Requirement of After-school Tutoring (Adapted from R. V. Hall, C. Cristler, S. S. Cranston, and B. Tucker, "Teachers and parents as researchers using multiple baseline," Journal of Behavior Analysis 3 (1970), pp. 247–255. Copyright 1970 by the Society for the Experimental Analysis of Behavior, Inc. Used with permission.)*

are seldom exposed to a test of accountability. The behavioral approach, in contrast, insists on frequent measurement and evaluation of program effects. If programs, or any components of a program, are found to be ineffective in facilitating attainment of individualized behavioral objectives set for each child, these program components are discarded. With such an empirical attitude, everyone benefits—the child, the educator, and the broader society supporting educational services.

REFERENCES

Axelbrod, S., Hall, R. V., Weis, L., and Rohrer, S. Use of self-imposed contingencies to reduce the frequency of smoking behavior. In M. J. Mahoney and C. E. Thoresen (Eds.) *Self-Control: Power to the Person.* Monterey, Calif.: Brooks/Cole, 1974. Pp. 77–85.

Baer, D. M., Wolf, M. M., and Risley, T. R. Some current dimensions of applied behavior analysis. *Journal of Applied Behavior Analysis,* 1968, 1, 91–97.

Blake, K. A. *Teaching the Retarded.* Englewood Cliffs, N. J.: Prentice-Hall, 1974.

Buchanan, C. D., and Sullivan, M. W. *Teacher's Guide to Programmed Reading.* (Rev. ed.) New York: A Sullivan Associates Program from Webster Division, McGraw-Hill, 1968.

Bucher, B. E. Problems and prospects for psychotherapy research designs. In O. I. Lovaas and B. D. Bucher, *Perspectives in Behavior Modification with Deviant Children.* Englewood Cliffs, N. J.: Prentice-Hall, 1974. Pp. 48–64.

Englemann, S., and Bruner, E. *Participant's Manual, DISTAR Orientation.* (Rev. ed.) Chicago: Science Research Associates, 1971.

Hall, R. V., Cristler, C., Cranston, S. S., and Tucker, B. Teachers and parents as researchers using multiple baseline. *Journal of Behavior Analysis,* 1970, 3, 247–255.

Hallahan, D. P., and Kauffman, J. M. *Introduction to Learning Disabilities: A Psycho-Behavioral Approach.* Englewood Cliffs, N. J.: Prentice-Hall, 1976.

Kazdin, A. E. Methodological and assessment considerations in evaluating reinforcement programs in applied settings. *Journal of Applied Behavior Analysis,* 1973, 6, 517–531.

Kazdin, A. E. *Behavior Modification in Applied Settings.* Homewood, Ill.: Dorsey Press, 1975.

Mager, R. F. *Preparing Instructional Objectives.* Palo Alto, Calif.: Fearon, 1962.

Meyen, E. L. *Developing Units of Instruction: For the Mentally Retarded and Other Children with Learning Problems.* Dubuque, Iowa: William C. Brown, 1972.

Sidman, M. *Tactics of Scientific Research.* New York: Basic Books, 1960.

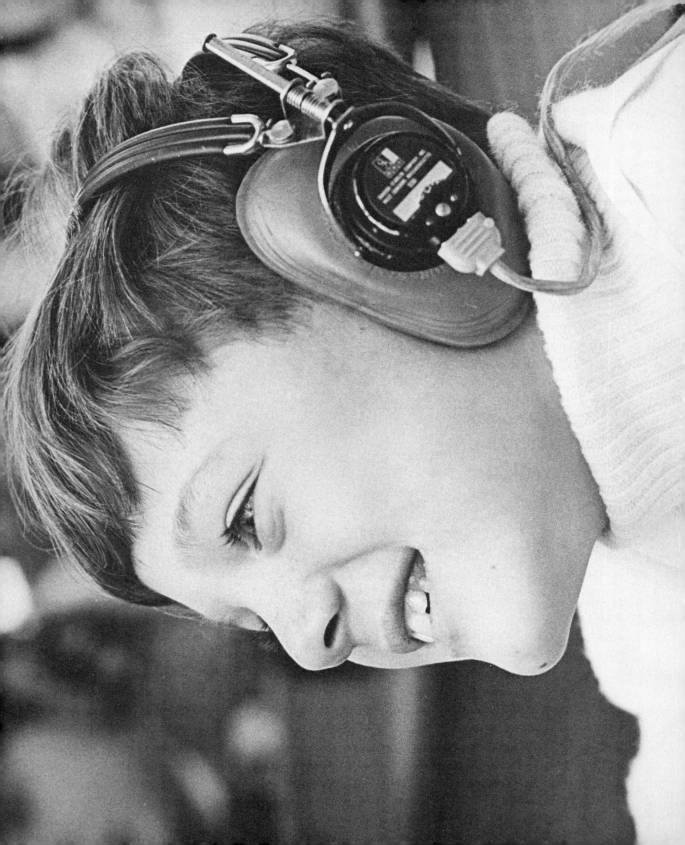

16 ———————————————————

Data-based Academic Programming[1]

Charles W. Norman

During the past decade there has been a steadily growing body of literature on the effectiveness of teaching programs based on behavioral learning principles. These programs have developed a range of academic skills in children including reading, math, and language. Children participating in these programs have included the "emotionally disturbed," "mentally retarded," "learning disabled," and children with other exceptional learning and behavior characteristics.*

Ulrich et al. 1974; Gardner 1974

Many of these programs, directed at specific learning problems, have used particular training procedures such as stimulus training, response shaping or chaining, response prompting, or contingency management. Taken as a whole, the programs demonstrate the application of many behavioral learning principles to a variety of academic learning problems of children with exceptional learning and behavior characteristics.*

Lovitt 1970, 1975

The logical conclusion of a review of these special education programs is that there is a need for a comprehensive and systematic approach to teaching academic skills. Data-based academic programming is an approach based on the integrated use of those principles and procedures found effective in teaching academic skills to exceptional children. It is a

---

1. This chapter was prepared by Dr. Charles W. Norman, Assistant Professor, Department of Studies in Behavioral Disabilities, University of Wisconsin at Madison.

set of procedures used to individualize the content and learning conditions of academic programs for children with exceptional learning and behavioral characteristics. *Task analysis, criterion-referenced assessment, functional analysis, direct teaching techniques,* and *daily performance evaluations* are among the procedures used in data-based academic programming. These procedures make it possible to design a learning environment that is unique for each child. This is accomplished by using the learner's characteristics to determine where to start instruction and the type of materials and programs to use. The child's responses to the instructional program are used as the primary data in evaluating learner progress and program effectiveness.

There are eight sections in this chapter, each designed to present the principles and procedures related to the various aspects of data-based academic programming. The first two sections present the basic characteristics and goals of a humanistic behavioral approach as these relate to the teaching of academic skills to exceptional learners. The third section presents an overview of the model of data-based academic programs. Included in the third section is the basic type of behavior present in most academic tasks and the steps involved in preparing individualized teaching programs. These steps (task analysis, assessment, programming, instruction, and evaluation) *involve* the use of a number of special procedures which are described and illustrated in each section.

CHARACTERISTICS OF DATA-BASED ACADEMIC PROGRAMS

There are a number of important aspects of a humanistic behavioral approach to academic programming for children with exceptional characteristics. It uses exceptional programs that are competency based and task oriented. Further, there is an emphasis on accountability based on the evaluation of learner progress. These characteristics make it possible to design and implement a learner-controlled program based on established functional relationships between the learner's academic behavior and the learning environment. The concept of *exceptional programs* means that the traditional categorical concepts of exceptionality such as mental retardation, emotional disturbance, or learning disability are defined in terms of the exceptional program needs of children and not as basic problems or limitations of the children.* An orientation towards exceptional programs accomplishes two basic purposes. First, it emphasizes the content and techniques of teaching required to provide an effective learning environment. Also, the educational program focus is shifted from assumed limitations of the learner to positive educational objectives and programs.

This shift is most clearly shown when dealing with children tradi-

Barrett and Lindsley 1962; Lindsley 1964; Kazdin and Craighead 1973; Schwartz 1968

tionally identified as learning disabled. The label has come to represent some inferred internal deviation assumed to interfere with the child's adaptation to usual educational programs. Although specialized education programs based on this internal-deviation concept are designed to compensate, or remediate, there still remains an assumption that there are limits to a child's growth.* This diagnostic label may ultimately become an explanation for the child's failure to progress.

Quay 1973

The program orientation of the humanistic behavioral approach views the child with exceptional characteristics in terms of specific academic behaviors to be developed through specialized teaching programs. Academic deficits or unique language repertoires define what needs to be taught, and they are not used as a basis for inference about internal limitations of the child and subsequent placement in general "disability" programs.* Progress by the child is seen as a result of the effectiveness of the learning environment.* In this orientation, failure to progress in an educational program reflects a "teaching disability," not a learning disability.

Reynolds and Balow 1972; Popham and Baker 1970, Engelmann 1970

Educator Accountability

The concept of exceptional educational programs not only shifts attention from a learner's assumed limitations, it also focuses on the *accountability of the teacher and the educational program.** When this happens it becomes readily apparent that the responsibility for learner progress is on the content and procedures used in the instructional program.* The objective of the educational program is to effect progress towards positive educational goals; therefore, the standard for program effectiveness is learner performance and progress.

Gallagher 1972a

Lovitt 1967; Kazdin 1973

It is not unusual for this standard to be ignored in many educational programs as learning environments are evaluated. All too often the presence of innovative materials, small classes, and curricula designated as specially selected for one exceptionality category or another is used to evaluate the educational program. Unfortunately, too little attention is given to actual progress of children in the programs. As a result, there is often little support for assumed appropriateness and effectiveness of the programs. Findings such as those by Dunn* and others* demonstrate the need for learner performance evaluations as the basis for program evaluations. These studies show that much of traditional special education has failed to promote actual academic growth in the children served. The humanistic behavioral approach to academic programming evaluates each particular program in terms of its effectiveness in promoting learner progress towards his or her individual educational goals. This means that the cost and time involved in a program, or its uniqueness, cannot be justified if it is not effective with the learner. Educators should be held accountable for providing educational programs that have demonstrated effectiveness.

Dunn 1968; Goldstein et al. 1965; Johnson 1962; Vacc 1972

Task-oriented Academic Programs

Academic programs based on humanistic behavioral principles are *task oriented*. This orientation designs learning environments to facilitate the learner's acquisition of concepts and skills required for academic tasks. The learning environment is designed to provide the necessary exposure to academic stimuli and sufficient opportunities to practice those behaviors required for mastery of these tasks.* The exceptional characteristics of the learner are used to plan further aspects of the learning experience. A child who experiences difficulty with visual and auditory discriminations required in a task would be provided with a modified learning environment that enhances the task stimuli to insure the necessary discriminations.* Physical or neurological problems may require special environmental modifications to assist the learner in responding. In either case, the focus is on the task to be learned, not the discrimination or response problems of the child.

Short 1974; Engelmann 1970

Tawny 1972; Haring and Hauck 1969

Competency-based Academic Programs

In addition to focusing on tasks, academic programs for children with exceptional characteristics are *competency based*. A competency orientation evaluates a learner's performance in relation to task performance criteria and not in relation to other children's performance.* This orientation is quite different from many approaches that identify the degree of difference between the performances of children with problems and some normal or average group of children. When such a norm-referenced approach is used, the individual with exceptional characteristics is evaluated in terms of his or her deviance and deficiencies in relation to others. This deficiency orientation then leads to programs to reduce the child's deviance. Such an orientation does not focus on the actual requirements of the task, only the differences between the levels of individual performance.

Popham and Husek 1969

A competency orientation, in contrast, is concerned with the level of performance required to master a task and to enable the learner to move successfully on to the next steps in an academic program. Learners are evaluated in terms of their mastery of the performance requirements of a task, not on the degree of difference between their performance and that attained by other children. Competency-based programs are designed to facilitate the development of the learner's skills in accomplishing tasks and not simply to reduce differences in performances between individuals.

Learner-controlled Academic Programs

The humanistic behavioral approach to education, in its emphasis on the uniqueness of the individual, uses educational programs that are *learner controlled.* This control is accomplished through systematic analysis and modification of educational programs to insure a maximum match between child and program. Thus, the progress and performances of the learner have a direct, functional control over the specifics of the educational program.

There are several critical implications of an approach that systematically utilizes the progress of the learner as the primary variable in determining the content, procedures, and direction of educational programs. As noted, this approach operationalizes the philosophy that the learner should control his or her program. It has further implications for decisions about the content, sequencing, and structure of the learning environment. Each component of the learning environment is subject to modification based on its effectiveness in promoting learner progress. Techniques or materials are chosen because of their effectiveness with the individual, not because of their common acceptance by educators. In this sense, no "traditional" practices are used for all children with exceptional characteristics. Commonly available methods, curricula, and materials are used as alternatives that are chosen only if demonstrated effective in a functional learning environment.* *Quay 1973*

In addition to selection of educational methods and materials on the basis of individual learning characteristics, teacher behaviors are also modified on the basis of their effects on the learner's progress. This critical aspect of an educational program is frequently ignored in analysis of learning environments. However, as the majority of the education program is conducted between teacher and child, the teacher's consistency and skill in providing the program are extremely significant sources of a child's success or failure. The behaviors of a teacher thus should be determined by their effects on the learner and not just reflect the personal or professional biases or tastes of the teacher.* *Striefel and Wetherby 1973*

Learner control of the environment requires that each component of the learning environment be available for modification based on its effect on the learner. When any component is exempted from possible modification, there is less likelihood that the learning environment will become fully individualized and effective.

GOALS AND DATA-BASED ACADEMIC PROGRAMS

The goals of data-based academic programs encompass the designing of individualized academic programs which are effective in promoting increases in a child's concepts, skills, and learning strategies. These goals are common to the various academic and preacademic programs provided for children with exceptional characteristics. Whether a child is learning the concepts of size, one-to-one correspondence, multiplication, or the skills of writing or verbal expression, the same basic goals underlie each program.

> **Goal 1** An academic program will enable the learner to demonstrate a concept or skill which previously was not evident or to increase his proficiency in a basic competency area.

This goal is basic to the concept of a humanistic behavioral approach to academic programming. It means that instead of emphasizing the errors and deficits of a child, the teacher programs for increased competency. Programs are designed to teach new skills or to improve initial approximations of desired behaviors. A focus on errors or other inappropriate performances of a child may reduce those behaviors but will not assure an equal growth in desired skills. This can occur for at least two reasons. First, a child with a deficit behavior repertoire consisting largely of incorrect or inappropriate concepts or skills may have no appropriate alternatives to replace the incorrect behaviors. Programs focused on the deceleration of errors make it necessary that the learner have alternative replacement behaviors.

Hasazi and Hasazi 1972

A second reason is related to the possible acceleration of errors due to positive reinforcement effects of attention provided when programs focus on errors. Hasazi and Hasazi* found that a child's reading errors were being maintained by teacher attention available in the procedures designed to correct the errors. Under these conditions, the learner's program experiences systematically support incorrect behaviors and fail to develop alternative correct behaviors.

A final justification for the skill development orientation of this goal is the common finding that the degree of difference between the competency of individuals with exceptional characteristics and the requirements of the general educational environment increases as children experience continued failure in those programs. It is necessary not only to discontinue adding to the child's academic retardation, it is also necessary to design programs to promote a maximum rate of competency development.

> **Goal 2** An academic program should begin instruction for a learner at a level appropriate to his entry skills.

This goal seems obvious enough. However, careful analysis of the skills required to participate in a learning experience, and assessment of a child's entry skill repertoire, is often missing in regular and special education. This is particularly the case when general subject characteristics such as chronological or mental age or categorical labels are used to place a child in an educational program. These general characteristics are seldom functionally related to the specific concepts or behaviors required on academic tasks.

Further, instructional programs require, in addition to the primary concepts or behaviors being taught, many concepts and skills related to subsequent instruction, to maintaining task behaviors, and to manipulating materials. As a result, the analysis of the entry skills required by a program should include the task concepts or skills, instructional procedures, materials in the learning environment, and the contingency programs to be used. When all these aspects are considered, the program can be initiated at a level appropriate to the learner's competency in each of the areas involved in the instructional program.

> **Goal 3** An academic program should provide the learner with a series of smoothly sequenced instructional steps.

A problem with many special educational programs is that a particular skill or concept is chosen as the target of the program rather than focusing on series of related concepts or skills. In the former, significant improvement in the target behaviors may occur, but the teacher is not prepared in any systematic manner to move on to higher levels. However, by planning a program based on a series of small steps, it becomes possible to reduce the number of concepts or skills to be acquired at each step. This in turn makes it possible to directly teach and maintain the desired concepts and skills.

> **Goal 4** An academic program should include instructional formats designed to effectively and efficiently teach the desired concept or skill.

This goal insures that instructional programs are designed to minimize the opportunity for errors and to maximize the learner's making the correct response. The goal is based on research demonstrating that many children with exceptional learning characteristics can learn efficiently when provided structured and carefully designed instructional programs.* However, when the learning environment presents many alternative or competing stimuli, and when there is opportunity for an excessive number of alternative responses, it becomes increasingly difficult for the child to discern the required concepts or skills required by the instructional program.

Bijou et al. 1966; Hewett et al. 1968; Bricker and Bricker 1970; Gallagher 1972b

This goal focuses accountability on the designers of the instructional program rather than placing responsibility on the child for determining what is to be learned.

> **Goal 5** An academic program should include precise procedures and criteria for evaluating the learner's progress and program effectiveness.

This goal emphasizes that evaluation and program modification decisions are based on learner performance. Such an empirical orientation requires (1) the use of frequent evaluations of learner performance and (2) the opportunity to implement and evaluate a variety of alternative learning programs. It is thus possible to monitor the rate of a child's competency development and to select those learning programs most effective in promoting that development.*

Bloom et al. 1971

These characteristics and goals of data-based academic programming provide the foundations for a model of programming that incorporates a variety of objective, competency-based procedures for systematically designing and implementing individualized learning environments. The remaining sections of this chapter will describe the model and procedures used to (1) analyze academic tasks, (2) assess learners' entry skills, (3) design instructional programs, and (4) to make objective program evaluation decisions.

MODEL OF DATA-BASED ACADEMIC PROGRAMMING

The general model includes the analysis of academic behaviors and the steps involved in preparing data-based academic programs. By reviewing the model, it is easier to understand what is learned and how individualized teaching programs are implemented. Data-based academic programming integrates a variety of special principles and procedures which have been demonstrated to be effective in establishing a wide range of academic behaviors. These principles and procedures have been used with children with a wide range of learning characteristics. Each principle and procedure has been selected for this model because it is consistent with the characteristics and goals of a humanistic behavioral approach to academic programming.

Nature of Academic Behavior

The model is based on the operant as the primary type of behavior developed in an academic program. Operant behavior is defined by a contingency which states the form of the behavior that will result in the delivery of a consequence.* This kind of definition of behavior is most appropriate to classroom programs which focus on tasks that require certain types of behavior in the presence of certain types of stimuli. These requirements may be very specific such as labeling colors or pictures or reading printed letters or numbers. In these instances, the curriculum clearly specifies the concepts and skills in objective terms. Consequences are then planned to accelerate correct, and reduce incorrect, behaviors.

Skinner 1968; Gagné 1970

Other tasks are less specific in terms of stimuli or behaviors. These still describe, however, broad, systematic relationships between events in the environment and the learner's behavior. In these instances, a child learns to discriminate general properties of stimuli such as size, order, or membership in a class of stimuli (i.e, plants, animals, and so on). Also the behaviors used to demonstrate that the child has made the discrimination may include a number of different but acceptable alternatives.* It may be acceptable for the child to label verbally objects, physically match objects, sort objects, or write statements that demonstrate the necessary discrimination. As with the specific stimulus and behavior tasks, there is a clear contingency for determining the learner's success.

Becker et al. 1971

These examples demonstrate the statement of academic concepts and skills in terms of operant behavior. Each example includes a clearly defined task composed of either a specific, systematic stimulus-behavior relationship or broad classes of stimuli and behaviors.

The use of an operant analysis of academic behavior is based on research demonstrating that learning of academic skills follows basic operant learning principles. Sidman and Stoddard,* for example, showed that stimulus programming was effective in teaching retarded individuals subtle discriminations. Bijou et al.* designed effective basic academic programs in math, based on task analysis and operant learning principles. Research by Lovitt with academic behaviors found that those behaviors are functionally related to consequation and different contingencies.*

Sidman and Stoddard 1966

Bijou et al. 1966

Lovitt and Smith 1972

Finally, an extensive instructional program (set of curriculum, methods, and materials) incorporating an operant analysis of academic concepts and skills has been found to be effective in teaching a wide range of academic tasks to children varying widely in learning characteristics.*

Becker et al. 1971

By using the operant analysis, academic tasks can be systematically analyzed and programmed in stimulus, behavior, and consequence components. Each component can then be directly developed by the use of basic procedures based on behavioral learning principles.

Steps in Data-based Academic Programming

The steps of *task analysis, assessment, programming, instruction,* and *evaluation* represent the major phases of data-based programming that lead to functional, individualized educational programs controlled by the learner's performance. Each of these steps has a special purpose in data-based academic programming, and each requires that the others be completed in order to produce an effective teaching program. A primary reason for breaking the approach to teaching into five steps is to make it easier to identify the different places in which the academic program can be individually modified for each learner. Also it facilitates integrating the various instructional activities into a carefully designed flow of events.

Task analysis involves developing a systematic sequence of learning conditions and responses which will lead to desired terminal objectives. This analysis is necessary to provide the content for assessment and the planning of subsequent objectives. The primary goal of *assessment*, the next step, is to identify the competencies the learner brings to the teaching situation and to set the immediate, short-range, and long-range curricular objectives for the learner. This phase involves identification of those discriminative stimuli, contingencies, and behaviors needed for successful learning. *Programming* is based on the assessment data and involves the systematic design of the sequences and methods of instruction for the immediate curriculum objectives. *Instruction* includes both the planning of (1) instructional routines used to teach specific tasks and (2) techniques for implementing and monitoring the instructional routines. In the final step—*evaluation,* the learner's performance is evaluated in terms of progress towards the performance criteria set in the objectives. This evaluation forms the basis for decisions about maintaining, changing, or terminating a learner's program. The steps preceding evaluation make it possible to isolate those learning conditions in the total educational program which could be modified to facilitate more desired learner performance.

In summary, the model of data-based programming describe the nature of academic behaviors and the steps to providing effective learning environments for the development of academic behaviors. The remaining sections discuss the concepts, principles, procedures and examples for each step in the data-based programming approach.

TASK ANALYSIS

Task analysis identifies the content and sequences of academic subject matter that is to be learned by the child. Often the analysis of curriculum tasks in the various content areas—reading, mathematics, writing, social studies, art—is done by the publishers of texts, instructional materials, or curriculum guides. The commercial producers use these analyses of academic subject areas to organize their presentation of material. Task analysis, therefore, is not a common process for most teachers to engage in during their teaching. However, children with exceptional learning characteristics many times require specially designed sequences or other modifications in the curriculum. Usually, the basic changes in curriculum involve developing a sequence of much smaller, easier tasks. This process—task analysis—is used to prepare detailed and carefully planned sequences of academic tasks. With a detailed set of tasks it is possible for the teacher to be more precise in determining the appropriate level and content for a learner's instructional program.

The term task analysis can be used to describe the process of analyzing academic tasks into small steps, or it can be used for the final list of steps. In either use the goal is to identify a series of simple learning steps that are ordered from least to most difficult. The difficulty may be in terms of the complexity of the discriminations or the complexity of the behaviors involved in the academic tasks.*

Bateman 1969

In its simplest form, a task analysis procedure starts with identifying a basic academic task such as oral reading of phonetically regular words, for example, cat, dog, or barn, printing the letters of the alphabet, or naming common animals. Next, the skills necessary to perform the task are identified. This may include visual discriminations, auditory discriminations, motor responses such as grasping pencil or pointing, moving eyes from left to right, or saying sounds. These skills are further analyzed to determine which skills are necessary for the performance of other skills, for instance, grasping a pencil precedes writing with a pencil. Finally, the steps leading up to the target task are ordered from least to most difficult. The order is usually also set up so that later steps require mastery of initial steps.*

Gagné 1970

The last phase of a task analysis involves determining performance criteria for each of the steps. One criterion in a task analysis might be the simple requirement that a target response occur. Performance criteria can also include the ratio of correct to error responses (i.e., ten out of twelve correct), the rate of correct and error responses (ten correct per minute and less than two errors per minute), or the rate of development of a competency (a required daily average increase in correct rates and decrease in errors). Regardless of their form, performance criteria are used to determine if a child has mastered a step.

The following is an example of a simple task analysis leading up to writing the letters of the alphabet.

Task	*Criteria*
5. Writes the letters of the alphabet in order when requested.	26 letters written in correct sequence.
4. Writes the letters of the alphabet when the letters are said by the teacher.	Writes each letter correctly.
3. Writes the letters of the alphabet when shown printed examples.	Writes each letter correctly.
2. Writes the letters of the alphabet when given a dotted outline to trace.	Writes each letter correctly.
1. Writes the letters of the alphabet when given stencils to trace within.	Writes each letter correctly.

This example would be broken into smaller steps if it were to be used for planning an actual teaching program. For example, there would be a number of substeps between steps 5 and 4 in which the child would be asked to write only parts of the alphabet.

Step 5. Writes the letters of the alphabet when requested.

Substep 5.3.	Writes the letters of the alphabet from R to Z when requested.
Substep 5.2.	Writes the letters of the alphabet from F to Q when requested.
Substep 5.1.	Writes the letters of the alphabet from A to E when requested.

This further breakdown exemplifies the concept of identifying a series of small steps that can be easily mastered and which, when put together, lead up to a terminal task.

The preceding example also demonstrates the basic stimulus-response nature of many academic tasks. Each step consisted of discriminative stimuli (teacher requests, verbal statement of letter to be written, dotted model, stenciled outline, or printed model) and a response to be made by the child (a written letter or sequence of written letters).

Task analyses can be designed to teach broader concepts based on the use of several discriminations which, when taken together, identify the concepts. This approach can be shown in a simple analysis of the concept "ball." Ball is a concept whose stimulus properties can be presented to the child in the form of many different actual balls, pictures of balls, drawings of balls. The task analysis then is based on establishing a task composed of a class of responses such as naming, pointing, or writing which demonstrates that the child can discriminate a class of stimuli that are balls or representations of balls.

S^D	R
big balls	says "ball"
little balls	points to balls
different colored balls	writes "ball"
pictures of balls	
drawings of balls	

The broad task of saying "ball," writing "ball," or pointing to ball when presented with any of the types of discriminative stimuli can be analyzed into a series of steps based on learning each of the component discriminations and each of the response forms.

When an instructional program is based on a task analysis of a task composed of classes of stimuli and responses, a child acquires the ability to discriminate the basic properties of a concept, not just a limited number of arbitrary instances. Also, as a child masters a variety of alternative behaviors in a task analysis, it becomes more likely that he or she will be able to meet the behavioral requirements of other learning situations.

Procedures of Task Analysis

The procedures for task analysis represented in the previous examples involve systematic steps in identifying stimulus conditions and response topographies. The following summarizes an operant learning approach to task analysis and programming:

Identify the basic discrimination(s) necessary for the terminal academic task.

Identify the basic response alternatives necessary for the terminal academic task.

Identify the response forms and/or sequence of responses which lead to the response alternatives for the terminal academic task.

Identify the discriminations which lead to the basic discriminations in the terminal academic task.

Arrange the discrimination and response tasks in a sequential order beginning with the simplest discriminations and responses.

Set performance criteria for each step.

Identify the materials required to present the discriminative stimuli and, if required, materials used by the learner to produce the required operations.

Content of Task Analysis

The content of a task analysis may be determined in several ways. When preparing a program for an individual exceptional child, the educational environment of the community classroom or special classroom can be analyzed. The purpose of this analysis would be to identify the set of concepts and skills required for initial success in the classroom. This analysis would probably lead to critical concepts and skills in areas such as reading, math, language, and writing. The task analysis completed for each area would not be likely to encompass all the skills necessary for total competency in any of the areas. Rather, the task analysis would focus on those concepts and skills necessary for the child to successfully enter the general curriculum sequence and instructional program. Common targets for such task analyses would be basic oral reading skills, counting, addition or subtraction skills, writing letters or numbers, and simple expressive language.

Another approach would consist of an initial systematic analysis of the classroom curriculum to identify the range of levels and content areas to be accomplished in the total academic program. This would be done independent of the particular students and would prepare a comprehensive set of curriculum goals for the academic instruction in the classroom. Each area and level in the academic program would be analyzed into goals and more specified tasks.

The specific content in either approach would consist of concepts or skills operationally defined by academic tasks. In the first approach, the focus is on immediate academic survival skills for an individual learner. The second approach results in an academic curriculum that would guide assessment and specific educational programming of children served.

The actual curriculum goals and objectives may also vary depending on the orientation of the academic programmer. These orientations may include traditional basic curriculum content: reading, math, language, writing, social studies, or science,* cognitively based curriculum sequences,* or behavioral repertoires.*

Bloom et al. 1971
Weikart et al. 1971,
Kamii 1971, Lavatelli
1973; Gagné 1970,
Hewett et al. 1968

To summarize, task analysis is principally an effort to identify the sequential behaviors which a child must master in attaining basic curriculum goals. These steps usually proceed from simple to complex behaviors and conditions. The orientation of the analyst will significantly effect the structure of the sequence and the nature of the targeted learner outcomes and lead to different content in the task analyses developed for a child. However, that content will be operationalized into task analyses that provide a comprehensive curriculum that consists of observable behaviors and learning conditions. Subsequent analysis of a child's exceptional learning characteristics during assessment will lead to design of an individualized program focused on tasks the learner is ready to master and the appropriate learning conditions to use in the academic program.

Task analysis can be a very time-consuming process. Yet it allows the educator to clearly specify the criterion behaviors conditions, and performance levels to be mastered by a child. It is done without preconceived notions about the learning characteristics of the children to be taught. In this way a task-oriented approach is initiated that is competency based.

ASSESSMENT

Assessment, and the later phase, evaluation, are the phases during which systematic data are collected on a child's performance. In both situations, the data are used to make decisions about the child's mastery of academic tasks. During assessment, the focus is on determining what tasks have been already mastered and which tasks are to be selected for programming. This focus is designed to identify the specific skills to be taught to the child. Evaluation utilizes many of the same procedures to determine the progress of the child on the behaviors selected for programming during assessment.

Also, during assessment a variety of stimulus presentations, consequences, schedules or other learning conditions may be systematically analyzed to determine those conditions which will initially be most effective in developing the target academic behaviors. In the evaluation phase, the purpose is to determine the effectiveness of later changes in the learning conditions. These phases share a focus on objective evaluation of the academic performance of the learner and the effects of various learning conditions. The difference is that assessment procedures are directed at determining the content and learning conditions to use in initiating instructional programs. Evaluation procedures, however, are directed at determining the extent of a child's progress and the effectiveness of the instructional programs.

Assessment in data-based academic programming is planned to lead to specific academic programs. There are several basic concepts related to program-oriented assessment of academic behaviors. As noted in previous chapters, these concepts represent critical differences between assessment focused on individualized programming and generalized comparisons of the ability or achievement levels of children.

Task Oriented

The first of these is the task orientation of assessment. It is focused on the specific concepts or skills the learner is capable of producing. This approach uses materials and situations that directly sample the learner's performance on academic tasks. Interpretation of the learner's performance is relatively straightforward; either the learner does or does not accomplish the task. Subsequent instruction is then planned to teach those specific tasks not accomplished. This is in contrast, as noted previously, to assessment procedures which use a variety of tasks assumed to require basic internal abilities such as memory, encoding, decoding, or intelligence. Those procedures use the assessment data to infer process disabilities and to plan programs to develop general abilities rather than more specific concepts or skills. As emphasized earlier, the research on this assessment and training approach has not supported the expected effectiveness of academic programs based on processes or abilities.* The application of behavioral principles to assessment and programming for exceptional children has shown the increased usefulness and effectiveness of task-oriented assessment for planning specific academic programs.*

Buckland and Balow 1973; Sabatino and Dorfman 1974; Ysseldyke and Salvia 1974; Salvia and Clark 1973; Bracht 1970

O'Leary 1972

Criterion Referenced

In addition to using objective task hierarchies for the content of assessment, this approach evaluates the learner's performance in relation to mastery criteria for the task. Criterion-referenced assessment assumes that it is more important to determine the learner's skills in accomplishing a task than to measure the learner's ability compared to many other per-

Bloom et al. 1971

sons. A criterion-referenced approach thus focuses on the individual's competency in relation to the skill level required to successfully master a series of academic tasks.* This approach is based on the adaptive growth of the individual, not his or her standing relative to other children.

Repeated Assessment

In addition to being task oriented and criterion referenced, the assessment procedures are designed to obtain a number of observations of the learner's performance on different academic tasks under standard conditions. There are several reasons for repeated observations. First is the variability of the behavior of children with learning and behavior difficulties. It is unlikely that a child's performance on a given day will be an accurate representation of what he or she will do on other days. Depending on what the child is experiencing throughout the home, school, play, and community settings, there may be significant changes each day in motivational variables. Secondly, an assessment procedure is itself a unique environment. As such, the child needs the opportunity to discern the discriminations and behaviors to be used in the assessment. A third reason for repeated assessment is to provide observations of other aspects of the child's repertoires.

Following a number of repeated assessment observations, it is possible to obtain data that represent stable and reliable estimates of the level and pattern of the child's performance on the academic assessment tasks. A particularly useful type of information is the trend of the child's performance over the assessment period. This is especially true when it is found that while a child does not reach criterion levels of performance during assessment, he consistently accelerates towards the criterion level. In such a situation a single assessment might have been assumed to indicate a need for direct instruction or proficiency building when, in fact, all that was needed was the opportunity to practice the concept or skill.

In summary, the primary goal of assessment in data-based academic programming is to facilitate the identification of the content, learning conditions, and sequence of educational experiences best suited to the individual child. The outcome of assessment is to identify the types of experiences a child will receive, based on his competence on various levels of the task analyses present in the educational program. The child's competency is assessed by a systematic sampling of learner performances on a number of task steps which then provides the data for estimates of performance for different levels of tasks. These estimates of performance are necessary to form a data base for decisions concerning the type of program for various content levels. The basic measures assess the accuracy, proficiency, and performance trends of the individual. For any given concept or behavior, any of the preceding properties may be the focus of educational programming.

Assessment Requirements and Programming Decisions

Data-based assessment requires:

1. Complete specification of task hierarchies including performance criterion.
2. Assessment materials and procedures to present the learner with examples of task conditions.
3. Procedures and materials for recording learner performances.
4. Analysis procedures for evaluating learner performances.
5. Decision rules to be used in specifying program goals based on the criterion-referenced educational assessment.

Criterion-referenced assessments based on these requirements allow the educator to make the various levels of program oriented decisions presented in Table 16.1.

The first three decisions lead to different types of programs for various levels of task content. The last decision identifies those skills which the learner is able to produce and maintain at *mastery level* under criterion conditions. Primary concern at decision level 1 is to specify the need for programs to develop stimulus control or response topographies. Such programs are known as *instructional programs*. The next decision level leads to *proficiency programs* designed to increase the learner's proficiency or rate of performance of discriminated responses. Proficiency programs emphasize programming procedures which will produce stable increases in response frequency. Decision level 3 leads to a third type of program—*maintenance*. These programs basically consist of repeated pre-

TABLE 16.1   *Assessment Decisions and Type of Program*

Decision	Type of Program	Focus of Program
Level 1	Instructional	Tasks to be taught.
Level 2	Proficiency	Tasks on which the learner requires proficiency development but on which the learner can produce correct discriminations and response topographies.
Level 3	Maintenance	Tasks on which it may be predicted that the learner will quickly attain criterion performance levels following a limited number of opportunities to practice the performances.
Level 4	Mastery	Tasks which the learner has mastered.

sentations of the criterion condition for performance over several days. The decision to present a maintenance program is based on the existence of an acceleration of performance towards the criterion performance level during the assessment period. In such a situation it is predicted that if the conditions are maintained, the learner will shortly attain stable criterion levels of performance.

Reasons for Programming Decisions

Programming-oriented decisions are divided into levels for two reasons. Each level can be reliably determined based on the child's performance data obtained during assessment. Also, the focus of each level (i.e., instruction, proficiency, maintenance) requires academic intervention procedures which use different principles and learning conditions. This approach does match programs to the child, but they are based on the specific functional learning characteristics of the child. Also, this approach is focused on task mastery rather than reducing the general relative difference between learners, irrespective of objective performance criteria for tasks.

Table 16.2 represents a portion of an assessment for a child in oral reading of phonetically regular words which demonstrates the various outcomes possible in a program-oriented assessment. This example is based on using a portion of a very simple task analysis of oral reading. The principle task requires that the learner correctly read words or letters (such as cat, barn, at) composed of long and short vowels or consonants. This task then has several steps based on the length and combinations of vowel and consonant sequences: consonants (C), vowels (V), consonant-vowel or vowel-consonant pairs (CV, VC), consonant-vowel-consonant (CVC), and consonant-vowel-consonant-consonant (CVCC) or consonant-consonant-vowel-consonant (CCVC). Words made up of these combinations (a, f, at, to, cat, barn, then) are the primary words used in pre-primer or primer reading materials used in the classroom.

The goal of the assessment is to determine the learner's pattern of performance on each level of the task analysis. Then the teacher can plan the type of program—instruction, proficiency, or maintenance—appropriate for the learner at each level of the task analysis. In order to make the program-oriented decision, the teacher provides the learner with daily opportunities to read words at each level. At the end of a five-day period the teacher can analyze the learner's performance charts and evaluate the data in relation to the performance criteria for each level. The graphs in Table 16.2 demonstrate four different performance patterns, each leading to a different program decision.

Further analysis of the particular errors at the CCVC, CVCC level would allow the educator to identify particular words which may be accounting for the errors. Finally, the assessment for the child in this example yields the following outline of the content and types of programs to be designed and implemented.

Type of Words		Type of Program
CVCC, CCVC	(barn, then)	Instructional
CVC	(cat, Dan)	Proficiency
VC, CV	(at, to)	Maintenance

While this example is obviously quite simple, it demonstrates the general assessment procedures for determining several types of programs to be developed for the learner at different levels of an academic task such as oral reading. Each program (instructional, proficiency, maintenance) can be focused on the different task levels based on the learner's performance. Finally, the learner's performance demonstrated that he or she had mastered the basic vowel and consonant sounds. With such a detailed assessment the teacher can focus his or her instructional planning on the level at which the learner is experiencing the most difficulty in establishing basic decoding (reading) skills.

Assessment Procedures

Data-based assessment procedures are in many respects an elaboration of the baseline phase of a functional analysis procedure. As described previously, baseline in functional analysis is obtained to provide data on pretreatment performance levels so that subsequent interventions may be evaluated for their effectiveness. Additionally, the baseline in a functional analysis assists the programmer in identifying the relevant performance variable (e.g., accuracy, rate, and so forth) on which to focus. This information is gathered by obtaining repeated, systematic observations of a particular behavior under controlled conditions. A data-based assessment procedure also serves this dual purpose: assessment and baseline for the evaluation of subsequent interventions. The procedure systematically includes a range of academic behaviors common to many children. Because educational tasks are commonly defined with a reasonable standardization, it is possible to have some standardization of the content and procedures for data-based academic assessment procedures.

A data-based assessment requires specification of content, performance, and criteria, and decision rules for evaluating assessment data, and procedures for administering the assessment. The remainder of this section discusses some suggestions for meeting these requirements.

Content Specification. The assessment process begins with the task analyses developed for the specification of curriculum content. Criterion-referenced assessment is designed to identify the task content the

TABLE 16.2. Decision Possibilities of Program-oriented Assessment

Task Level	Conditions/Criteria	Performance Data	Decision
CCVC, CVCC (then, barn)	Randomly sequenced CVCC, CVCC words or nonsense syllables. 60 words correct, 0–2 errors per minute		*Instructional* program for CCVC, CVCC words. Correct and error rates are both considerably lower than criterion.
CVC (cat, dog, Lem)	Randomly sequenced CVC words or nonsense syllables. 60 words correct, 0–2 errors per minute.		*Proficiency* program for CVC words. Correct rates are less than criterion and not accelerating. Error rates are below criterion levels.
CV, VC words or diagraphs (at, to, et, ma)	Randomly sequenced CV, VC diagraphs. 60 words correct, 0–2 errors per minute.		*Maintenance* program for VC, CV diagraphs. Correct rates accelerating steadily toward criterion. Error below criterion levels.
V, C vowel or consonant (a, e, v, f)	Randomly ordered sequences of V or C. 60 sounds correct, 0–2 errors per minute.		*Mastery.* The learner is at criterion level. **KEY** ●—●—● Correct words per min. ○—○—○ Errors per min.

child has mastered or those skills to be brought to criterion levels. The content of assessment is the set of specific behaviors to be produced under specific conditions. Task criteria are used to evaluate the child's performance. There is no inference of process abilities but, rather, an objective determination of specific operational competencies. The task analysis serves as the objective specification of competencies and conditions.

Criteria Specification.   Specification of performance criteria is usually a difficult task in preparing for the assessment. Traditionally, test construction approaches the development of criteria in such a way that tests and test items will result in maximum variability among those taking the test. This is done so that the tests may be used to predict subsequent performances, to rank or to select students, and to check the internal consistency of the test. A criterion-referenced test, however, employs criteria with a different purpose. Performance criteria are chosen with the basic purpose of assuring that mastery levels of performance on one step will enable the learner to move to the next step with minimal disruption of performance. In this case, the criteria are minimal standards required of all learners who are to master the task hierarchy. Attaining successful completion of task steps at criterion levels, rather than ranking students based on performance, is the goal. Evaluation of the performance criteria is based on learner progress through task levels, and not on the goal of selecting or differentiating students based on ability.

There are several ways of estimating mastery levels for performance criteria:*   *Gaasholt 1970*

1. *Use of response rates for immediately preceding steps.* This is most useful when a skill such as math facts is to be assessed. The same type of response is used for several task levels. Estimates of performance criteria can be based on rates of the required operation such as writing digits. Criterion for a task step such as simple addition $(1 + 2 = 3)$, where the student writes the digits in the sum, could be based on the rate of digit writing. One objection often raised to such a procedure is that solving problems involves more than simply writing digits. However, this appears to be the least subjective procedure for measuring performance. In any case, performance criteria should not significantly exceed the child's response rate on earlier tasks requiring the same topography of response.
2. *Use of response rates taken from children considered to have successfully mastered the task step under consideration as well as the next several related steps.* This procedure is somewhat subject to bias in the direction of using rates from the most able students. Rates should be chosen in terms of minimal mastery based on the performances of students able to perform at acceptable mastery level, not those who exceed the basic mastery criteria.
3. *Use of predicted rates based on the individual learner's projected level of performance obtained during the assessment.* This procedure requires that the assessor have a relatively precise estimate of the time to be allowed for subsequent interventions. If it is known that a two- or three-week block is all that is available for improving performance, then the learner's performance trend during assessment could be used to estimate the expected performance rate at the end of the allowed time for the intervention procedure. A limitation of this procedure is that the estimated performance level may not be adequate to assure smooth transition to subsequent steps.

4. *Use of empirically derived rates based on continuing evaluation of pupil progress through the curriculum task hierarchies.* In this procedure the educator analyzes the performance of many students over time to determine those rates that are associated with successful transitions through the task hierarchies.

A problem common to each of these procedures is that of estimation. Only the last procedure can ultimately assure the determination of criteria based on actual learner performances on the task rather than other, less directly related, learner characteristics. However, the empirical process requires time and, initially, criteria still need to be set. The first three procedures will assist the assessor in setting criteria. The criteria should be viewed as estimates and be left open to modification based on subsequent analyses of pupil progress during ongoing performance evaluations.

Assessment Materials.   Criterion-referenced educational assessment uses materials to present the learner with the stimulus conditions specified by the task hierarchy. This requires a variety of settings as well as materials. A task step that states, "When presented with three objects which differ only in size, the learner will point to the largest one when requested to 'point to the largest' each time the request is made," requires that assessment present three such objects and the command. Use of a picture and a pencil mark by the child on the largest one would not assess the objective. Similarly, asking a child to mark pictures whose names begin with a certain sound is not an appropriate assessment for a task that states the child will discriminate names of objects when they are verbally presented.

Some objectives involve sets of stimuli such as various classes of phonetically regular words. In these instances, the assessment must present a representative sample of the class of words. It would be difficult to present the child with all possible words, yet the sample presented must conform to the specifications set forth in the task. It is also important that assessment tasks accurately present the conditions set forth in the task. In the case of a task such as oral decoding of phonetically regular sets of letters (words), nonsense syllables may more accurately assess decoding skills. Use of actual words may result in the student's responding to letter configurations rather than engaging in decoding/blending behaviors.

Also, each set of assessment stimuli should include only stimulus and response requirements set forth in the objectives. Finally, the materials and procedures should minimize restrictions on the frequency of responding in the assessment situation. This is particularly necessary if accurate decisions concerning proficiency and performance trends are to be made.

Administration Procedures.   After a set of tasks have been identified and the materials assembled, the assessor will need to determine the specific instructions and time limits for the assessment of each step. At this point, each student is presented with the assessment tasks. The assessor records the actual performances and prepares summary data sheets for each task set for each student. The evaluation of the learner performance data obtained during the assessment may be evaluated by comparing the levels and trends of performance on the assessment tasks to the performance criteria stated in the task analysis.

Table 16.3 summarizes the relationships between assessment performance and task criteria to be used when evaluating assessment data and determining the type of program to be used.

The next section, programming, discusses the general principles and procedures for designing the types of tasks which were identified in the assessment phase.

PROGRAMMING

The child's exceptional learning characteristics and competency levels identified in the assessment make it possible to plan several learning environments to be presented to the child. Many of the studies of children

TABLE 16.3.   *Summary of Decisions Levels and Performance Patterns*

Decision	Type of Program	Pattern of Data
Level 1	Instructional	Correct rates below correct criterion, error rates above error criterion, and no trend towards desired criteria for either data.
Level 2	Proficiency	Correct rates below criterion for correct responses, error rates below criterion for error responses, and both rates appear stable.
Level 3	Maintenance	Correct rates near or approaching criterion for correct responses, error rates below criterion for error responses.
Level 4	Mastery	Both correct and error rates at criterion levels throughout the assessment period.

with exceptional learning characteristics have been conducted to analyze and demonstrate programming principles and instructional techniques. The principles and procedures in this and the next section draw from this background of empirically tested procedures.

The planning of academic programs usually starts with maintenance programs then proceeds to proficiency and instructional programs. This makes it possible to first start with those programs which require relatively less intervention (maintenance and proficiency) and then to develop instructional programs which will usually require the most planning and direct intervention.

Maintenance Programs

The first area of programming for which learning environments need to be designed is that of maintenance. Concepts or skills at this level are either mastered in some situations or can be predicted to be moving towards criterion level simply as a function of repeated opportunities for practice. The goal of maintenance programs is to facilitate attainment of criterion performance levels, maintenance of those levels of performance, and generalization to different settings.

Practice.   The simplest maintenance program is one in which the learner is allowed to continue practicing a concept or skill on which he or she has attained accuracy and is close to proficiency. In this situation, the learner is provided with a brief opportunity daily or several times a week to work on tasks requiring the concept or skill. Handwriting or reading assignments that are designed to allow the child to increase his fluency are good examples of common maintainance programs. These programs do not employ special reinforcement programs nor do they require teaching. The child is simply practicing something he can already do for the purpose of doing it with greater ease.

Generalization.   Each program designed for the initial teaching of a concept or skill (instructional) is planned with future generalization as a primary concern. However, a final aspect of maintenance programs is to provide the opportunity for the actual performance of the concept or skill under various conditions. This may include different teachers, alternative response forms, classroom settings, materials, peer groups, or varied consequence and contingency conditions.*

Schumaker and Sherman 1970; Sailor 1971; Frisch and Schumaker 1974; Koegel and Rincover 1974

Teachers generally have their own unique ways of giving the directions which call for basic concepts or skills taught in academic programs. "Put your name on the paper," "Name and date," "Don't forget what you're *always* to put on your paper" are all common stimuli for the child to write his or her name on a paper. Yet it is necessary that the name-writing behavior ultimately come under the control of each form of the direction.

Also, simply as a setting event, teachers vary sufficiently in a number of characteristics so that a child may discriminate only the one teacher directly involved in his program as the appropriate stimulus for the behaviors acquired in that teaching situation. Therefore, generalization programs designed to facilitate maintenance across situations should include systematic sampling of various teachers.

A similar case can be made for different peer groupings, classrooms, or materials. Each is slightly different even though the same behaviors may be appropriate in all settings. A behavioral approach accepts the responsibility of providing the learner with the opportunity to demonstrate concepts or skills in a wide variety of environments. Evaluation of the learner's performances in these settings will allow for a data-based decision that the learner can generalize.

Another critical aspect of maintenance is the persistence of a behavior under very extended reinforcement schedules with a wide range of reinforcing events. This is a special form of generalization that is quite separate from the stimulus and response topography issues discussed above. The principles and procedures in Chapter 9 are applicable to both academic and social behaviors. The problems of generalization create several areas of concern. First, most special education programs are designed for direct teaching of concepts or skills. Because of this the teacher plans to correct or reinforce each response. This is necessary to minimize errors and provide the learner with feedback to shape his behavior. Also, as there are usually smaller class sizes, the teacher has increased the opportunity for providing individualized consequences for her students. The learner is potentially provided with frequent, specific reinforcement. A regular classroom has larger class sizes, the children are expected to work independently for longer periods of time, and feedback or corrections may occur several hours, days, or even weeks later. Going from the first setting to the second obviously represents an abrupt and severe thinning of the reinforcement schedule.

Second, most classrooms utilize social reinforcers, grades, or simply the opportunity for more work. Programs for exceptional learners often employ tangible or token reinforcers not present in the regular classroom. Again, the issue is to program use of natural consequences as well as contingencies to facilitate generalization.

Proficiency Programs

Proficiency programs have a fairly simple purpose: to increase the rate of a child's behavior. Following the initial acquisition of a concept or skill, it is necessary to design an environment which will develop the learner's rate of performance. A focus on rate of performance is basically a practical issue. As a child masters more and more tasks in a task hierarchy, the units of behavior become more complex, requiring the performance of a number of subunits of behaviors. When any of the subunits is being developed and is the only target behavior, its rate of performance is less critical. When a number of subunits are combined to complete a task, each must be done relatively quickly in order to complete the total complex unit.

There are several approaches to building a learner's proficiency: *stimulus control, behavior shaping,* and *contingency programming.* Stimulus control involves the manipulation of antecedent events. These antecedent events may be program stimuli such as the directions used by the teacher.* A direction such as "work as quickly as you can" is more likely to set the occasion for increases in performance rates than simply assigning a task and saying, "Your work will be collected at the end of the hour." This does not mean that speed without quality is emphasized; rather, there should be direct encouragement of rapid, correct performance.

Lovitt and Smith 1972

Another antecedent variable is the extent to which the teacher or material paces the program through requiring the student to receive a separate stimulus for each response. This occurs most often in question-answer and direct tutoring programs in which the teacher controls when each individual response is to occur. While such teacher control is useful in the initial instructional phases of a program, there must be an eventual fading of individual response cues.

Another form of antecedent stimulus control is the use of certain learner behaviors to increase the rate of subsequent task performances. Lovitt and Curtiss* demonstrated that prior verbalization of the rules to be used in a math task increased subsequent task behavior. This type of procedure not only increases the rate of task performances, it also provides the learner with the opportunity to learn how to self-manage his or her own behaviors.

Lovitt and Curtiss 1968

Shaping programs can be used to refine the learner's behavior to more efficient forms. Handwriting and speech are examples of behaviors that become more easily produced as there is an increased refinement in the learner's production of the required behavior. There are a variety of techniques to improve behavioral efficiency. Also, it may be useful to teach alternative response forms to the learner. A child having extreme difficulty making writing or speech responses could be taught to use typewriters, communication boards, or other prosthetic devices that can be used more efficiently than natural response forms.

The primary approach to improving behavioral proficiency is through contingency programming. As pointed out in Chapter 9, schedules of reinforcement result in characteristic response patterns whose relative rates vary. Commonly, a continuous reinforcement schedule is employed during instruction. This kind of schedule is well suited to stimulus or response shaping and produces initial increases in response rates. However, variable ratio schedules or direct rate schedules which differentially reinforce high or low rates of responses are more effective in producing significant response rate changes. These rate-building schedules are necessary components of a proficiency program. Careful planning for systematic use of such schedules will also prevent an abrupt transition to the contingencies most common in educational environments: fixed or variable interval reinforcement. Interval schedules are very common as a result of academic programs being blocked into units based on the school's daily time schedule. Reinforcement is delivered on a time, not response rate, contingent basis. School work is assigned and at the end of an hour, half hour, or other time unit the work is collected and the learner is reinforced for appropriate work. This kind of schedule results in low rates compared to other schedules and is therefore in opposition to the goal of increased proficiency. The more appropriate alternative is to design ratio or rate schedules which are designed to improve behavioral proficiency.

The procedures for rate- or proficiency-building programs are common in the behavioral literature. However, it is an area of behavior often ignored. There are a number of arguments commonly presented against such a focus for academic programs. These arguments usually attempt to make a case for accuracy as a sufficient criterion for behavior. It is stated that children with exceptional learning characteristics have problems acquiring a concept or skill area and that accuracy is a major and sufficient goal. This orientation ignores a critical aspect of the exceptional learning characteristic of many children: They have very low rates of performance. As was discussed earlier, as a child acquires increasingly complex concepts and skills, there must be an increase in the child's performance of the subconcepts or skills. Otherwise there will be a steady decline in performance leading to an accurate but very inefficient learner. This inefficiency may ultimately lead to failure in meeting the criteria of most natural environments.

Instruction Programs

Instruction programs require complex and systematically designed learning environments. There are a number of task programming, teaching procedure, and materials design issues to be met. Each requires the application of a variety of principles and procedures. The ultimate goal is to develop the concepts or skills required by the instructional objectives identified for the learner in the assessment step.

Task programming may require additional concept and/or behavior analysis in which the discriminations and responses required by the initial task analysis are further broken down into smaller units. The purpose of the additional concept analysis is to identify concepts that require the least number of necessary discriminations. This will allow the teacher to design a program which will teach the learner to discriminate the stimuli relevant to the discrimination and those stimuli which are irrelevant. The first step in this process is to operationally define the concept in terms of observable stimuli. Next, the stimuli are divided into those stimuli which are relevant to the concept and those which are irrelevant. The relevant stimuli are then analyzed to determine which ones, when correctly discriminated, will allow the learner to rule out the greatest number of incorrect or irrelevant concepts. Following these steps, a program is designed to present the learner with a series of discrimination tasks beginning with very gross discriminations and proceeding to increasingly more difficult discriminations. Throughout the program, irrelevant stimuli are introduced in such a way as to provide the learner with opportunity to make discriminations in which the correct and incorrect stimuli are correlated with reinforcement *Becker et al. 1971* and the irrelevant stimuli do not lead to reinforcement.*

A similar analysis of the required response forms also needs to be done. This will allow the teacher to identify a series of increasingly more refined and/or complex responses to be developed in the instructional program. The response-building program may also include the systematic developmentof alternate responses that are appropriate for demonstrating the concept. The ultimate goal of the detailed stimulus- and response-training programs is to develop a series of tasks that meet the criteria of being clearly defined in simple units and which lead to the concept or skill identified in the immediate instructional objective.

Instructional Formats

It is also necessary to carefully program the form, complexity, and use of techniques to be used to teach the instructional tasks. This includes the directions, prompts, and correction procedures to be used by the teacher in presenting the task.

Becker et al. 1971 A task is itself a stimulus presentation that the child is expected to respond to in a certain way.* For example, a child is presented a picture of a house and is supposed to verbally label the object as "house." The particular stimulus and the response are not obvious without directions from the teacher. These directions serve two purposes: to indicate the stimulus properties to be discriminated—house—and the type of response—*"tell* me what this is."

A simple teaching format would consist of:

Stimulus item:	(picture)
Stimulus direction:	Point to house
Response direction:	*"Tell* me what this is."
Response:	"House"
Consequence:	"Great, you knew the name!"

This format could be used many times for a program to teach the concept of object names. Attention to the details of the directions given by the teacher will allow systematic programming of the teacher behaviors used to set the occasion for the correct discrimination and response. Events such as stimulus directions and response directions must already be functional before they're used in a teaching procedure. If pointing by the teacher does not lead the child to orient to the object pointed to, then pointing cannot be used as a prompt to teach a special type of discrimination.

Analysis of these teaching behaviors will lead to a hierarchy of teaching behaviors that the child must be capable of responding to correctly before they are used in instruction. Simpler forms, such as physical modeling or prompting, would be used before verbal behaviors in a hierarchy of teaching behaviors to be integrated into the instructional program. Systematic programming of the teaching behaviors will assure that at each step in an instructional program the learner has only task or teaching concepts to learn. In the earlier example, a child unable to follow the teacher's pointing cue and unable to decode the response direction would be unable to respond correctly to the instructional task because of the inability to respond correctly to teachers' behaviors.

The preceding discussion focused on programming antecedent stimuli. It is also important to program the subsequent stimuli to be used in an instructional program. These stimuli are all consequences of the learner's response and are designed to accelerate correct behaviors and decelerate incorrect responses. Acceleration procedures include the reinforcement and contingency control techniques discussed in Chapters 8 and 9. They also include techniques that increase the likelihood of correct responses through representing the directions and prompts for correct responses when the child emits an incorrect response. These techniques use directions, prompts, or modeling techniques established in the initial phases of an instructional program. They have to be established as stimuli which will reliably produce a correct response. When an error response is made, the established direction, prompt, or model can then be presented to the child. The correct response will be produced and the error replaced by the correct response. This procedure accelerates correct behavior through direct, specific stimulus control techniques rather than just relying on differential reinforcement.

Summary

Programming is used to design a sequence of task presentations, teaching behaviors, and reinforcement procedures which systematically teach an identified concept or skill through a series of discrete tasks. The program consists of a set of formats for tasks and teaching procedures that are used to complete the specification of the stimulus condition to be presented to the learner during instruction.

INSTRUCTION

This step includes the final design and presentation of the learning environment. In this step the details of the program (maintenance, proficiency, or instruction) are completed and presented to the learner. There are two major sets of procedures to be discussed in this step: specification of actual learning situation and monitoring of program implementation.

Specification of Complete Instructional Procedures

Gaasholt 1970

These procedures require the use of some standard format in which the teacher writes down the methods and materials used in presenting the instructional task in the formats designed in the programming phase. There are several formats commonly used in systematic instructional procedures.* Each of the formats share several common features: Antecedent stimuli are clearly stated, specific learner responses are identified, and the subsequent stimuli are also clearly stated. Table 16.4 illustrates the types of information included in an instructional plan.

By using a format that clearly lays out the procedures and materials to be used, the teacher can identify individual instructional components for future modifications, if necessary, based on evaluation of the learner's performance. The ability to analyze the several components of an instructional plan is critical if systematic individualization is to be accomplished.

TABLE 16.4. *Description of Instructional Plan Content*

Antecedent Stimuli	Acceleration Target		Deceleration Target	
	Behavior	Consequences	Behavior	Consequences
Task stimuli to be discriminated: pictures, words, objects, etc.	Clearly defined correct response.	Reinforcing stimuli such as tokens, praise, food, and stars; schedule for delivery, such as every time, or 1:5 ratio.	Clearly defined error responses or "no response."	Stimuli used to reduce errors (e.g., "No," ignore); re-present instructions for correct responses, i.e., repeat antecedent cues, model, or prompts.
Teacher behaviors: directions, prompts, model.				
Setting in which instruction is to occur: time of day, teacher, individual or group.				

Monitoring Program Implementation

A carefully detailed instructional plan is also necessary to allow the teacher to monitor the actual presentation of the program. The steps of task analysis, assessment, programming, and instruction are designed to produce a learning environment that is uniquely suited to the individual. The environment can be effective and the steps justified only if the program is implemented as designed. Failure to use the methods and materials chosen for task presentation is likely to severely reduce the likelihood of the learner making the correct response. Program monitoring can be accomplished several ways: selfmonitoring by the teacher, periodic supervision by other teachers, monitoring by parents in the classroom, or monitoring by the child. In any of these techniques, the person doing the monitoring would use the daily instructional plan and observe the teacher's presentation, looking for the procedures and materials described in the program.

EVALUATION

This step in data-based academic programming is designed to facilitate decision making about the learner's progress and the effectiveness of the academic programs. In general, the decisions to be made are focused on determining whether or not students have acquired new skills or improved their proficiencies on previously established skills. As precision in evaluation and decision making increases, it becomes possible to determine if the students have developed skills or proficiencies efficiently and have an ability to generalize those skills and proficiencies to new situations. Another area of decision making has to do with questions concerning the effectiveness of teaching methods or materials, the sequence of instruction, the effectiveness of assessment procedures in identifying behaviors to be taught, and the effectiveness of the behaviors of teachers, parents, or peers in facilitating the child's acquisition of concepts or skills and proficiency in those skills. Evaluation information of these questions makes it possible to make further decisions about the effectiveness of the resources and procedures which support the child's direct educational program.

Not all decisions related to the design and construction of a child's learning environment are based solely on child performance. Curriculum sequences, assessment techniques, instructional practices and materials, personnel staffing patterns, and administrative policies are often chosen independent of their effects on the actual performances of children in programs. Local fiscal resources, staff availability, legal requirements, and attitudes toward exceptional children all exert significant influence on the various program decision areas. While these considerations cannot be ignored, one of the purposes of data-based programming is to make decisions based primarily on the evaluation of the learner's performance.

The two primary areas to be evaluated are the individual learner's performance and the effectiveness of the components of the instructional program. The evaluation of the instructional program is used to facilitate ongoing refinement of the learning environment and to empirically verify which procedures were effective with the various exceptional learning characteristics of individuals. This latter purpose makes it possible to document for each learner the materials and procedures most effective in producing the best levels of performance. It also facilitates the collection of materials and procedures that have been proven to be effective with children with similar learning characteristics.

The following are common aspects of the child's behavior and the learning environment which may be evaluated.

Child Behavior	*Learning Environment*
Accuracy	Task sequences
Proficiency	Instructional materials
Rate of growth	Instructional methods
Breadth and generalization of concepts or skills	Consequence systems
	Teacher behaviors

The types of decisions which can be made about child behavior or the learning environment would include:

Child Behavior

Accuracy	Does the child discriminate critical differences in stimuli?
	What is the proportion of correct responses to error responses?
	Does the child's correct/error ratio meet the criteria of the instructional objective?
Proficiency	Does the child produce correct responses at the criterion rate?
	Does the fluency of the child's behavior satisfy the natural environment's criteria?
	Does the child produce behaviors at too high a rate?
Rate of growth	What is the rate of growth?
	Is the child progressing towards the terminal instructional objectives at a rate that will enable him to complete the required curriculum?
	Is there a decrease in the rate of growth?
Breadth and skills	Is the child capable of producing many alternative behaviors?

Is the child capable of producing a complex repertoire of required skills?

Generalization of skills	Is the child capable of producing alternative behaviors in novel situations?
	Are alternative consequences and contingencies effective in supporting the child's behavior?

Learning Environment

Sequence of tasks	Does the child complete the sequence of task steps with little disruption of performance?
	Is the task sequence in an appropriate order, or are some later steps actually necessary for earlier steps?
	Are all prerequisite or entry skills identified?
	What is the degree of performance change produced by the steps in the task sequence?
Instructional materials	Are the materials smoothly sequenced?
	Are the directions clear?
	Does the material limit the child's response rate?
Instructional methods	Are the teaching routines clear?
	Does the child possess the skills required to respond to the directions, prompts, or models?
Consequence systems	Are the designated reinforcers effective?
	Are the correction procedures effective?
Teacher behaviors	Does the teacher follow the instructional plan?

By using the learner's performance to evaluate, and change if necessary, the learning environment, a functional learner control of the academic program is put into effect.

Evaluation Procedures

Evaluation procedures to be used in the decision-making process are dependent on which aspects of child performance are to be evaluated, the type of evaluation to be conducted, and the decisions to be made. Another consideration is the relative importance of the decision to be made. Some decisions may be less critical than others, depending on the child's immediate needs and the concerns of the educational environments. A child who is producing severe aggressive behaviors is likely to evoke program-

TABLE 16.5. *Individual Child Performance Evaluation Decisions*

Level of Evaluation	Child Behavior	Evaluation Procedure	Data Requirements	Decisions
4	Rate of growth	Series of timed observation of specific skills	Regular, frequent timed observations	Changes or trends in acceleration or deceleration of correct and incorrect behaviors
3	Proficiency	Timed observation of specific skills	Consistent, precise timed samples of specific behavior under criterion conditions	Fluency of rate of performance of correct and incorrect behaviors
2	Accuracy	Observed frequency of occurrence of specific skills	Observation of repeated occurrences of behavior under criterion conditions	Accomplishment of criterion ratio of correct and incorrect behaviors
1	Breadth and generalization of skills	Checklist of demonstrated skills	Complete list of instructional and/or behavioral objectives; observation of the behavior under criterion conditions	Occurrence of behavior or variety of behaviors; occurrence of condition or conditions under which behavior or behaviors occur

ming for the development of alternative social behaviors. In such a case, precise evaluation procedures would be employed for the social behaviors and more generalized procedures would be used for the academic responses.

The evaluation procedures to be considered in this section refer to decisions about an individual child, his program, and what are the most effective learning environments for the development of that individual child's academic concepts or skills. This is in contrast to procedures which may be used to compare the child to other children in terms of standardized measures such as achievement tests. As was pointed out earlier, procedures which compare children are useful for selecting those likely to succeed, or those children who are relatively less successful than others, but they are not very helpful for individual evaluations or determining what to modify in a program.

Individual child evaluation procedures are directly related to specific progress evaluations and program modification decisions. Such evaluations operationalize the child performance control of the educational program. The result is a system that both modifies the child's behavior and is modified by the child. An interesting effect of the approach is that the teacher learns as much from the child as the child learns from the program. Specific program modification outcomes include refined task sequences, modified instructional procedures, individualized contingency systems, and refinement of task criteria.

Evaluation procedures may be broken into *formative* and *summative* evaluations, each having different functions.* Formative evaluations are used primarily to analyze the development of skills and to produce decisions about the modification of the ongoing program. Summative evaluations provide both documentation of the skills mastered by a child and a statement of program effectiveness. There are several levels of evaluation possible in each type of evaluation. The most general is the recording of the specific skills demonstrated by the child. Next, it is possible to document the frequency of occurrence of the specific skills. A third level is the recording of the proficiency of the child on specific skills. A fourth level is the recording of progress trends. This level of evaluation documents and analyzes increases or decreases in frequencies or proficiencies over time periods. The objective is to identify accelerating, decelerating, or unchanging levels of performance. Such trends can then be used to make predictive statements about a child's progress and the effects of an educational program on that progress trend.

Bloom et al. 1971

Each of these levels of evaluation require increasing precision in the data collection procedures and have different roles in a comprehensive formative and summative evaluation system. Table 16.5 summarizes the levels of evaluation, data requirements, and uses in decision making.

These evaluation procedures represent levels of increasing precision and detail. There is also an increasing precision to the decisions to be made. Initially the decisions of level 1 simply document whether or not a certain behavior occurs under designated conditions. Level 4 expands the decision to include the behavior, its conditions of occurrence, ratio of correct to incorrect behavior, fluency of correct behavior, and anticipated date of attainment of the criterion performance by the student. In exchange for the precision of level 4 decisions, there is an increase in the time and effort expended to obtain the necessary information to make the decision. Ultimately, the teacher must determine the priorities that are held for each level of evaluation for the various academic and social behaviors being developed in the program.

A brief discussion of each level may help clarify the procedures applicable at each level of evaluation.

LEVEL 1

Child behavior: Breadth and generalization of skills.

Evaluation procedure: Checklist of demonstrated skills.

How completed:

1. This level requires that there be a complete list of instructional and behavioral objectives that identify the variety of behaviors, conditions, and criteria for the learner.
2. The objectives should include:
   a. all conditions under which the behavior(s) is/are to occur.
   b. all behaviors to be produced under each of the identified conditions.
   c. criteria for the performance of the behavior.
3. The teacher then constructs a list of the primary conditions, behaviors, and criteria.
4. The learner is observed under each of the conditions and the occurrence or nonoccurrence of criteria levels of the behavior is observed.
5. The teacher records on the checklist a plus or minus for occurrence and the date the behavior was observed.
6. These observations may be made at the same time as in a pretest or posttest situation or over time, with the checklist serving as a record of the number of objectives met and the dates of mastery.

Decisions: Number of different behaviors produced by the child and various conditions under which behavior can be produced.

1. These decisions focus directly on the issues of the breadth of the child's behavioral repertoire and the various conditions to which the child may generalize those behaviors.
2. The decisions made at this level are primarily summative in that they document response repertoires and generalized discriminations.

LEVEL 2

Child behavior: Accuracy.

Evaluation procedure: Observed frequency of occurrence of specific skills under specific conditions.

How completed:

1. The teacher selects a particular behavior and identifies the specific conditions for occurrence.
2. The occurrence of correct and incorrect instances of the behavior is observed.
3. The teacher then records the number of correct and incorrect occurrences.

Decisions: Accomplishment of criterion ratios of correct and incorrect behaviors.

1. These decisions focus on the relative frequencies of correct and incorrect behaviors.

2. It can be determined what is the accuracy level of the child and the discrepancy between that level and the criterion level for the behavior.
3. This may be used for either formative or summative purposes. The number of such observations would depend on the use of the data. Formative evaluations would require more observations obtained over a period of time in order to obtain more stable estimates of accuracy levels prior to attainment of the criterion level.

LEVEL 3

Child behavior: Proficiency.

Evaluation procedure: Timed observation of specific skills.

How completed:

1. The teacher completes all of level 2 procedures.
2. In addition, a consistent time period is set aside for the child to produce the behavior and for the teacher to systematically observe and record the occurrence of correct and incorrect behaviors.

Decisions:

1. In addition to determining the accuracy of the child, the teacher may also determine the rate or fluency of performance of the behavior by the child.
2. This level will also facilitate future decisions concerning the criterion levels of accuracy and fluency to be required of the child to insure smooth progress to success levels of instructional or social behavior hierarchies.

LEVEL 4

Child behavior: Rate of growth.

Evaluation procedure: Series of timed observations of specific skills.

How completed:

1. The teacher repeats level 3 observations at consistent, frequent intervals.
2. A minimum of five to seven such observations will be made.

Decisions:

1. The principle decisions at this level are predictive. By analyzing the series of observed rates of performance obtained under controlled conditions, the teacher will be able to predict future levels of performance.
2. Using the analyses as a base, the teacher will be able to decide if a program should be modified, maintained, or terminated.
3. The first two decisions have to do with the trend of the child's performance towards the criterion level of the instructional or behavioral objectives.
   a. *Modify:*   A teacher would modify the program if it is predicted that the child will either reach the criterion level before a planned date or if it is predicted that the child will fail to reach the criteria on the planned date.
   b. *Maintain:*   A teacher would maintain the program if it is predicted that the child will reach the criterion level on the planned date.

c. *Terminate:*   A teacher would terminate a program if the evaluation demonstrates that the child has attained the criterion level and can maintain that level.

These evaluation procedures require various levels of specificity and precision in data collection and program documentation. As the teacher moves toward the higher levels of evaluation, there should be careful consideration of the benefits which can be obtained from the power in decision making. Level 4 evaluation is generally used for the primary behaviors that a child must produce precisely and frequently in an education program. These behaviors usually include letter writing, oral reading, basic discriminations, and functional social skills. Broader behaviors or less critical behaviors are better evaluated at level 1 or level 2. At these levels the teacher may monitor skill development while not being as concerned with detailed ongoing analyses of growth trends and predictive formative evaluations.

Resnick et al. 1973   Application of child performance evaluations to the several components of the data-based programming model allows for a continuing process of refinement and verification of the content and procedures of each component. An excellent example is the use of child performance to evaluate task analyses of curriculum areas reported by Resnick.* Task analyses are usually approximations of the structure and sequence of content areas in educational curriculums. Refined and comprehensive task analyses are often critical to the programming of instruction for exceptional children. The discriminations and response forms or alternatives many times must be extremely detailed and carefully sequenced in order to insure that stimulus- or response-shaping programs will be successful. Therefore, it is a critical concern to be able to analyze carefully the performance of a child as he or she proceeds from one level to another of a task ladder.

There are three basic areas of behavior change on which to focus in evaluating a task sequence: development of increasingly complex concepts or discriminations, development of more complex responses or patterns of responses, or increased proficiency on tasks. An ideal would be to observe concurrent development in all three areas: concepts, behaviors, and proficiencies. Usually, however, one of the areas at a time is emphasized. This is because children with exceptional learning characteristics require carefully planned programs which focus on each area separately.

The usual method of presenting a child with a curriculum sequence like oral reading is through printed materials such as books, booklets, or single sheets. These materials are usually divided in units or levels which are designed to present increasingly more difficult constructions and/or new vocabulary. The evenness of these sequences is generally evaluated on groups of children. A problem for the teacher of a child with a learning difficulty is that what is a fairly smooth sequence for a group of children may be extremely uneven for the particular child. What is needed then is a procedure to evaluate the smoothness of the curriculum and to pinpoint portions of the sequence and materials which produce a serious disruption of the child's performance. This could be accomplished by using the frequency of correct responses and error responses, as a child proceeds through an oral reading program, to evaluate the effects of each successive step in the task sequence on the child's performance. A common occurrence in any curriculum sequence is an initial reduction in correct responses and an increase in errors as a child proceeds from one step to another. By evaluating the extent of such changes, curriculum sequences can be modified to reduce the disruption in a child's progress.

This section has attempted to present the overriding purpose of evaluation: to use child performance to evaluate the components of an educational program. The assumption is that it is the performance problems of the child with exceptional needs which is the primary justification for the operation of the special education program. It is often easy to justify programs on the basis of cost, theoretical issues, administrative or political considerations, or similar input factors. While these factors must be considered, the goal should be to operationalize a child performance-controlled educational program. Use of an empirical, functional analysis approach to program evaluation will make this goal attainable. The requirements both in rigor of analysis and commitment to child control are considerable. However, the ultimate benefits in terms of effective educational programs should justify the effort.

SUMMARY

The primary goal of the procedures described in this chapter has been the development of individualized exceptional learning environments. This approach is based on an empirical approach to the analysis of learning environments in which the learner, through his behavior, controls the content and structure of academic programs.

The characteristics of a data-based academic programming model are that it is:

1. focused on *exceptional programs* and makes no assumptions about limitations in the child's ability to learn,
2. based on the concept of educator's *accountability* for the progress and growth of the learner,

3. *task oriented*, where the goal is to accomplish relevant and necessary tasks and not simply to make the exceptional child less "exceptional,"
4. *competency based*, where the child's mastery of concepts of skills is more important than the degree difference between the child's and other children's levels of performance,
5. *learner controlled* through the use of systematic evaluation procedures.

These characteristics operationalize the philosophy of a humanistic behavioral approach to the education of children with exceptional characteristics.

REFERENCES

Barrett, B. H., and Lindsley, O. R. Deficits in acquisition of operant discrimination and differentiation shown by institutionalized retarded children. *American Journal of Mental Deficiency*, 1962, 67, 424–436.

Bateman, B. *Essentials of Teaching*. Dimensions in Early Learning Series. San Rafael, Calif.: Dimensions, 1969.

Becker, W. C., Englemann, S., and Thomas, D. R. *Teaching: A Course in Applied Psychology*. Palo Alto, Calif.: Science Research Associates, 1971.

Bijou, S. W., Birnbrauer, J. S., Kidder, J. D., and Tague, C. E. Programmed instruction as an approach to teaching of reading, writing, and arithmetic to retarded children. *Psychological Record*, 1966, 16, 505–522.

Bloom, B. S., Hastings, J. T., and Madaus, G. F. *Handbook on Formative and Summative Evaluation of Student Learning*. New York: McGraw-Hill, 1971.

Bracht, G. H. Experimental factors related to aptitude-treatment interactions. *Review of Educational Research*, 1970, 49:5, 627–645.

Bricker, W. A., and Bricker, D. D. A program of language training for the severely language handicapped child. *Exceptional Children*, 1970, 37, 101–111.

Buckland, P., and Balow, B. Effect of visual perceptual training on reading achievement. *Exceptional Children*, 1973, 40, 299–304.

Dunn, L. M. Special education for the mildly retarded: Is much of it justified? *Exceptional Children*, 1968, 35, 5–22.

Engelmann, S. The effectiveness of direct verbal instruction in IQ performance and achievement in reading and arithmetic. In J. Hellmuth (Ed.), *Disadvantaged child. Vol. 3. Compensatory Education*. New York: Brunner/Mazel, 1970.

Frisch, S. A., and Schumaker, J. B. Training generalized receptive prepositions in retarded children. *Journal of Applied Behavior Analysis*, 1974, 7, 611–621.

Gaasholt, M. Precision techniques in the management of teacher and child behaviors. *Exceptional Children*, 1970, 37, 129–135.

Gagné, R. M. *The Conditions of Learning*. New York: Holt, Rinehart & Winston, 1970.

Gallagher, J. J. The special education contract for mildly handicapped children. *Exceptional Children*, 1972a, 38, 527–535.

Gallagher, P. A. Structuring academic tasks for emotionally disturbed boys. *Exceptional Children*, 1972b, 38, 711–720.

Gardner, W. I. *Children with Learning and Behavior Problems.* Boston: Allyn and Bacon, 1974.

Goldstein, H., Moss, J., and Jordon, L. A. A study of the effects of special class placement on educable mentally retarded children. U.S. Cooperative Research Project No. 619. University of Illinois, 1965.

Haring, N. G., and Hauck, M. A. Improved learning conditions in the establishment of reading skills with disabled readers. *Exceptional Children*, 1969, 35, 341–352.

Hasazi, J. E., and Hasazi, S. E. Effects of teacher attention of digit reversal behavior in an elementary school child. *Journal of Applied Behavior Analysis*, 1972, 5, 157–162.

Hewett, F. M., Taylor, F. D., and Artuso, A. A. The Santa Monica Project: Evaluation of an engineered classroom design with emotionally disturbed children. *Exceptional Children*, 1968, 35, 523–529.

Johnson, G. O. Special education for the mentally handicapped: A paradox. *Exceptional Children*, 1962, 29, 62–69.

Kamii, C. K. Evaluation of learning in pre-school education: Socio-emotional, perceptual-motor, cognitive development. In B. S. Bloom, J. T. Hastings and G. F. Madaus (Eds.), *Handbook of Formative and Summative Evaluation of Student Learning.* New York: McGraw-Hill, 1971. Pp. 281–344.

Kazdin, A. E. Methodological and assessment considerations in evaluating reinforcement program in applied settings. *Journal of Applied Behavior Analysis*, 1973, 6, 517–531.

Kazdin, A. E., and Craighead, W. E. Behavior modification in special education. In L. Mann and D. A. Sabatino (Eds.), *The First Review of Special Education.* Vol. 2 Philadelphia: Buttonwood Farms, 1973.

Koegel, R. L., and Rincover, A. Treatment of psychotic children in a classroom environment: Learning in a large group. *Journal of Applied Behavior Management*, 1974, 1, 45–49.

Lavatelli, C. S. *Piaget's Theory Applied to an Early Childhood Curriculum.* Boston: Center for Media Development, 1973.

Lindsley, O. R. Direct measurement and prosthesis of retarded behavior. *Journal of Education*, 1964, 147, 62–81.

Lovitt, T. Applied behavioral analysis and learning disabilities. Part 1: Characteristics of ABA, general recommendations and methodological limitations. *Journal of Learning Disabilities*, 1975, 8, 432–443.

Lovitt, T. Assessment of children with learning disabilities. *Exceptional Children*, 1967, 34:4, 233–239.

Lovitt, T. Behavior modification: The current scene. *Exceptional Children*, 1970, 37, 85–91.

Lovitt, T. C., and Curtiss, K. A. Effects of manipulating an antecedent event on mathematics response rate. *Journal of Applied Behavior Analysis*, 1968, 1, 329–333.

Lovitt, T. C., and Smith, J. O. Effects of instructions on individual's verbal behavior. *Exceptional Children*, 1972, 38, 685–693.

O'Leary, K. D. The assessment of psychopathology in children. In H. C. Quay and J. S. Werry (eds.), *Psychopathological Disorders in Childhood.* New York: John Wiley, 1972. Pp. 234–272.

Popham, W. J., and Baker, E. L. *Systematic Instruction.* Englewood Cliffs, N. J.: Prentice-Hall, 1970.

Popham, W. J., and Husek, T. R. Implications of criterion-referenced measurement. *Journal of Educational Measurement*, 1969, 6, 1–9.

Quay, H. C. Special education: Assumptions, techniques, and evaluative criteria. *Exceptional Children*, 1973, 41, 165–170.

Resnick, L. B., Wang, M. C., and Kaplan, J. Task analysis in curriculum design: A hierarchically sequenced introductory mathematic curriculum. *Journal of Applied Behavior Analysis*, 1973, 6, 679–710.

Reynolds, M. C., and Balow, B. Categories and variables in special education. *Exceptional Children*, 1972, 38, 357–366.

Sabatino, D. A., and Dorfman, N. Matching learner aptitude to two commerical reading programs. *Exceptional Children*, 1974, 41, 85–90.

Sailor, W. Reinforcement and generalization of productive plural allomorphs in two retarded children. *Journal of Applied Behavior Analysis*, 1971, 4, 305–310.

Salvia, J., and Clark, J. Use of deficits to identify the learning disabled. *Exceptional Children*, 1973, 39, 305–308.

Schumaker, J., and Sherman, J. A. Training generative verb usage by imitation and reinforcement procedures. *Journal of Applied Behavior Analysis,* 1970, 3, 273–287.

Schwartz, R. H. Toward a meaningful education for the retarded adolescent. *Mental Retardation,* 1968, 6:2, 34–35.

Short, J. Measurable objectives for educational programs. In R. Ulrich, T. Stachnik, and J. Mabry (Eds.), *Control of Human Behavior. Vol. III. Behavior modification in education.* Glenview, Ill.: Scott-Foresman, 1974. Pp. 255–265.

Sidman, M., and Stoddard, L. Programming perception and learning for retarded children. In N. Ellis (Ed.), *International Review of Research in Mental Retardation.* Vol. II. Academic Press, 1966.

Skinner, B. F. *Technology of Teaching.* New York: Appleton-Century-Crofts, 1968.

Striefel, S., and Wetherby, B. Instruction-following behavior of a retarded child and its controlling stimuli. *Journal of Applied Behavior Analysis,* 1973, 6, 663–610.

Tawny, J. W. Training letter discrimination in four-year-old children. *Journal of Applied Behavior Analysis,* 1972, 5, 455–465.

Ulrich, R., Stachnik, T., and Mabry, J. *Control of human behavior.* Glenview, Ill.: Scott, Foresman, 1974.

Vacc, N. A. Long-term effects of special class intervention for emotionally disturbed children. *Exceptional Children,* 1972, 39, 15–23.

Weikart, D. P., Rogers, L., Adcock, C., and McClelland, D. *The Cognitively Oriented Curriculum.* Washington, D.C.: National Association for the Education of Young Children, 1971.

Ysseldyke, J. E., and Salvia, J. Diagnostic-prescriptive teaching: Two models. *Exceptional Children,* 1974, 41, 181–185.

Author Index

Subject Index